DANIEL

Understanding the Dreams and Visions

Charlene Fortsch

Erica Dissler, Artist

Published By:

Prophecy Song

For information on how to obtain additional copies of this book,
or for marketing opportunities, contact the publisher at:

Prophecy Song
General Delivery
Anahim Lake, BC
Canada V0L 1C0
(250) 742-2388
Email: prophecysong@yahoo.ca

All Scripture quotations are from the King James Version unless otherwise indicated.

Cover Art Illustrated by: Erica Dissler

Cover Design Artists: David Berthiaume and Alex Arantes

Printed in Canada

Printed by

SASKATOON

Library of Congress Cataloging-in-Publication Data

Fortsch, Charlene R., 1951-
        Daniel understanding the dreams and visions / Charlene R. Fortsch;
        illustrated by Erica Dissler.

        ISBN: 0-9738632-0-X

        1. Bible. O.T. Daniel—Prophecies. I. Dissler, Erica
        II. Title.

BS1556.F67 2005   244'.5015   C2005-905912-5

DEDICATION

*This book
is dedicated
in loving memory of,
my youngest son,
Paul Oren Anthony.*

ACKNOWLEDGMENT

Words are inadequate to express my appreciation to all, who through the years, have played an important part in the preparation of this manuscript. Valuable suggestions have been made by many proof readers, free-lance editors, friends and family. Many have urgently requested that this work be published. On behalf of the encouragement, a completed work of endtime prophecy is now available. Because those to whom I owe a debt of gratitude are too many to name, I acknowledge them all in this general expression of warmest thanks. All of you know who you are! Thank you for everything.

Special thanks must be given to Richard, my husband, who lovingly and very patiently gave his time, finances, and consistent encouragement.

The editor, Butch Johnson, has spent endless patient hours giving guidance, proof reading, and confirming every single detail. Behind every author, there has to be a very special person who will accept this difficult task. All those involved with this work believe the Lord has provided the best editor there could be. On behalf of everyone, "Thank you Butch! We look forward to more of your assistance."

Our artist, Erica Dissler, has worked endless hours to create prophetic illustrations to match the Biblical texts. Most assuredly you will enjoy her creative talent. It has been a pleasure to work with her. Erica will also be illustrating the second book in this prophecy series.

Most importantly, I wish to express my deepest thanks to our Lord Jesus Christ, for His continued grace and faithfulness in guiding this work to its completion. He knows that for many readers, this book may be a new beginning in understanding the prophetic Book of Daniel.

May the Lord enlighten and broaden the understanding of every reader that opens these pages.

Charlene R. Fortsch

Foreword

Many years ago, a Pastor introduced me to the Bible. I was just a new Christian at the time and had virtually no understanding of the principles of Biblical interpretation. True, I had been raised in a home hearing some of the basic Bible stories like "Daniel in the Lion's Den," but I had no idea as to how to go about reading the Book that I had just been given. The instruction that I was given by this Pastor did not give me the necessary "tools" for good sound Bible study. As a result, I spent years bouncing from "pillar to post" looking at the various denominational perspectives that exist out there in the world of "Christianity." The necessary "tools" for sound Bible study were not taught there either.

What I found, was and still is, a religious world that is very confused as to what the Bible actually says. A religious world overrun with denominations all claiming to be "the way, the truth and the light." A religious world where the faith of many is so discordant and confused that many do not know what to believe. A religious world totally confused as to what the Bible actually does say. A religious world more interested in what their denomination says, (customs and traditions of man), than what the Bible has to offer.

Needless to say, this was a major dilemma for me as I was starting out on the "narrow path."

As I read and studied my Bible over the years, it became apparent that there are Principles of Study which, when adhered to, bring clarity and focused understanding. These Principles of Study brought Biblical patterns alive, as brush stroke was added to brush stroke, in my understanding of the overall Biblical picture. Experiencing Biblical truths fosters primitive Godliness — the same truths that in the past brought forth the faith of Abraham, Isaac, and Jacob.

As you, the Reader, become acquainted with these Principles of Bible Study, clearly outlined and explained in this book, and allow the Bible to be its own expositor, you will leave "denominational" confusion behind and enter into the world of "Biblical" Christianity.

Revelation 1:3

Blessed is he that readeth,
and they that hear the words
of this prophecy,
and keep those things
which are written therein:
for the time is at hand.

2 Timothy 3:16

And that from a child
thou hast known the holy scriptures,
which are able to make thee wise
unto salvation through faith
which is in Christ Jesus.

You are about to enter the world where the prophetic Book of Daniel speaks. Enjoy the adventure.

G. E. (Butch) Johnson, Editor
Whitehorse, Yukon

Table of Contents

PART I: UNDERSTANDING THE DREAMS AND VISIONS

Table of Contents

Table of Contents

Table of Contents

Table of Contents

How To Use This Book

Dear Reader:

Most of the pages in this manuscript have a left and right column. In the left column are the Scripture verses that are the focus of discussion. **Captions** are provided to summarize the thought(s) of a verse or verses. The right column provides an exposition of the verses. The following tools are used:

1. Supporting Scriptures and Bible Definitions;
2. Prophetic Keys explaining "Hermeneutic Rules and Principles;"
3. Definitions from Dictionaries and the *Strong's Exhaustive Concordance;*
4. Pictures and Illustrations;
5. Maps, Tables, and Charts;
6. Literary quotes and limited comments as required.

The manuscript follows the text of the Book of Daniel as found in the King James Version of the Bible. Chapter and verse context, continuity, sequencing, <u>and</u> "word picture" alignment in Scripture are the focal point and the foundation of the explanation. Anything that is underlined in the Scripture verse (of the left column) will have supporting documentation in the right column.

Patterns exist everywhere in Scripture for our benefit. These Scriptural patterns are "teaching tools" that lead the Bible student to a fuller understanding of Scriptural meanings. The Bible is **always** its own expositor. This eliminates the need of human opinion and speculation. A knowledge of secular history is helpful and necessary in understanding prophecy.

There are several "Introductory" pages before the text of Daniel Chapter 1. These pages give basic, foundational information for getting started. If some of the material on the introductory pages is difficult to understand, plan to revisit them later. At the appropriate time, the manuscript will give guidance as to how the "foundational information" and "Prophetic Keys" are to be applied. In the visions of Daniel, we will constantly review this information. As a result, you will gain a fuller understanding of how to apply the tools that are necessary to interpret all prophetic Books of the Bible. As much as possible, open spaces have been left on most pages for your own notes and comments. Many subject areas <u>cannot</u> be fully addressed in this manuscript. It is hoped that the information provided will encourage <u>each</u> reader to continue <u>his</u> own personal study of prophetic endtime events.

It is important to remember the following essential points:

1. Read <u>everything in order, from the beginning</u>. Prophecy is an exact science and must be studied in an orderly fashion. Don't be tempted to skip around, or to go to the end first. Reading and studying should be done decently and in order, otherwise one gets only part of the truth, and as a result, future study builds on a weak foundation. The end result is confusion. (Note: Pages 13-21 will give examples in pages throughout the manuscript. Become familiar with these examples as they introduce prophetic study tools. Then return to the original reading.)
2. The <u>use of repetition is intentional</u>. God, through Daniel the prophet, uses repetition to emphasize importance. Allow the repetition to cement concepts into your understanding.
3. <u>Use your own King James Bible</u> along with this manuscript/workbook. Don't take any outside written word for gospel truth. Search the Scripture for yourself, and allow the Bible to interpret itself. This will lend to a well developed understanding of prophecy.
4. <u>Use the tools provided</u>. Prophetic Keys, Glossary, Appendices, Charts, Maps, and Tables are provided for your ease of study. Use them, and review them often. Learn to become familiar with a *Strong's Exhaustive Concordance*. This concordance is a companion to <u>only</u> the King James Authorized Version of the Bible. Some words in our modern language have very different meanings from the original Hebrew or Greek words. Do not be afraid to use your concordance and consider the original meanings of Hebrew and Greek words.
5. The <u>chain link</u> is used where Scriptures <u>link</u> with other Scriptures throughout the Bible. A <u>Prophetic Key</u> will indicate that a Prophetic Rule is being applied to understand any part of Scripture, whether symbolic or literal.
6. Color has been used to help coordinate some of the structure. Any supporting Scripture that reflects the words of Jesus are printed in red. Supporting Scripture links, from either Daniel or Revelation are printed in blue.

Let's get started!

Prologue to Daniel's Book

**The Book of Daniel is One Facet of the Story
of the Great Controversy (Struggle)
Between Christ and Satan**

Lucifer Attempted to Rule Heaven —
to be Worshipped as God

This story begins in heaven. Before Lucifer fell, he was the most exalted being next to Christ. As "son of the morning" (ISA 14:12), he stood with Christ in the presence of God. Known as the covering Cherub, he was the lightbearer for God. Unfortunately, Lucifer thought of himself as equal in splendor and wisdom to God; one that deserved the worship of all created beings. This was the beginning of the controversy in Heaven. The covering Cherub, was determined to overthrow the worship of God. Lucifer did not reveal his plan and purpose all at once. Had he immediately exposed all of his plans to the universe, where sin and rebellion were not known, he would not have gained a following. This plot to overthrow the government of Heaven would take long and careful planning. Little by little, Lucifer began to find angels whose sympathy he could gain by criticizing how God managed the affairs of the Universe. He attempted to make the God of Love, and Lord of the Sabbath, appear as a selfish tyrant. He recruited many Heavenly Beings to his side, by assuming the guise of godliness, and at the same time portrayed God as the evil one. This point is an underpinning of the witchcraft/pagan, New Age System of today. This system reflects the character of self, which is the personification of the character of Satan.

Lucifer Instigated War In Heaven

Lucifer's rebellious seeds of murmuring, complaining, and strife germinated and caused divisions among the angels of Heaven. He felt that if he could weaken the unity in Heaven, it would negatively affect the power, seat, and authority of the Creator. The whole Universe had the choice of only two sides; there was no middle ground. One third of the Heavenly host chose the side of the god of rebellion and confusion. (REV 12:4) As a result, there was war in Heaven between Christ and Lucifer. REV 12:9 "And the great dragon was cast out, that old serpent, called the Devil, and Satan, which **deceiveth** the whole world: he was cast out into the earth, and his angels were cast out with him."

Lucifer Sought Ruling Power on Earth

Lucifer and his host were cast to this newly created Earth — the home of our first parents, Adam and Eve. God had given Adam power and dominion to be a caretaker over all the plants and animals of the earth. In the form of a serpent, Satan determined to destroy God's plan. Through deception, Eve disobeyed God's Word. At this

God Gave the
Scepter of Power
to Adam

Satan Usurps the Sceptre
of Ruling Power

point, Satan usurped the "dominion of power to rule," out of Adam's grasp. Opportunity was now open to him to bring created human beings under his domination, thereby receiving the worship he so desperately coveted.

As the descendants of man increased and populated the earth, Satan progressively enticed and deceived "nearly all" of man to turn from God. Approximately 1650 years later, "... God saw that the wickedness of man was great in the earth, and that <u>every</u> imagination of the thoughts of his heart was only <u>evil continually</u>." (GEN 6:5) There was no more good in man. Man reflected the character of Satan and his "cup of iniquity" was full! All of mankind, except eight individuals (Noah, his wife, three sons — Shem, Ham and Japheth, — and their wives) had given

**Satan
and his angels
cast out
of Heaven
to this Earth**

themselves over to Satan's plan. Noah and his family were preserved from the flood waters. Eventually, Ham's son, Cush, begat Nimrod.

The Reign of Nimrod — Lucifer's Representative

God's purpose for Noah and his sons was to replenish the earth by traveling abroad on the surface of the earth. This would have prevented the growth of large cities which historically had degenerated into wickedness. Once again, God's perfect plan was laid aside by man.

Nimrod caused the early descendants of Noah to rebel against God, just as Lucifer had led the angelic host to rebel. Nimrod was the first to teach the art of masonry in building the Tower of Babel. It was Nimrod who fulfilled Satan's plan and taught the people contempt for God. Being the grandson of Ham, (the son of Noah) he was a bold man of great strength. He persuaded the people not to credit God for their happiness, but to believe that it came about of their own efforts. They were the captain of their own ship!

Nimrod Built the Tower of Babel

Nimrod over time, changed the government into tyranny. Seeing no other way of turning men from the fear of God, he brought them into continual system dependency. It was likely that he blamed God for drowning their forefathers! To promote Satan's plan he would unite the world and build a tower too high for the next flood waters to reach regardless of God's promise to never flood the earth again! The multitude were ready to follow his determined leadership. Josephus writes: "They built a tower, neither sparing any pains, nor being in any degree negligent about the work. And by reason of the multitude of hands employed in it, it grew very high, sooner than any one could expect; but the thickness of it was so great, and it was so strongly built, that thereby its great height seemed, upon the view, to be less than it really was." *The Complete Works of Flavius Josephus,* Whiston, Kregel Publications, 1960, 1978, p. 30.

Satan now takes a step into the background and appears to pass the power of dominion over to Nimrod. He develops a system through which his evil devices produce a like minded people that will worship and serve him.

Lucifer Attempts to Establish a One World Government Passing the Sceptre of Power Through Nimrod

Nimrod's (Lucifer's) Attempt to Establish a One World Government

Nimrod's intention was to unite the whole known world into a One World Government that would be anti-God in nature. The Tower of Babel was to have two great purposes. 1) Babel would become the metropolis of the world and unite its inhabitants under fascist, dictatorial rule. 2) Its Tower was to be a monument to man and stand as a symbol of the wisdom of its builders. By building the city of Babel, Nimrod hoped to prevent the people from scattering abroad into colonies as the Lord intended. While in the midst of this building project, (when the Tower reached its full stature that it could today be called a *skyscraper*), the Lord came against it. (GEN 11:3-9)

Nimrod was worshipped by the early inhabitants of Babylon under his deified name, "Ninus." Nimrod, ("a mighty man before the Lord,") was the first to carry on war against his neighbors. He conquered all nations from Assyria to Lybia. The inhabitants of these lands were unacquainted with the art of war. Nimrod's reputation as a hunter, and a warrior, were later immortalized in the Assyrian, Babylonian, Egyptian, Greek, Roman, and American Indian Mysteries. His Egyptian name was Osiris. In Rome he was worshipped as Mars (which means "The Rebel"). His ancient Babel name was Merodach, (a Babylonian idol, JER 50:2) which means "To Be Bold," or "Rebel."

Sun worship has its roots in Nimrod's anti-God system. This was the birth of Paganism. Pagans believed their gods were angry, hateful, and unmerciful. These characteristics made the pagans to fearfully and reluctantly bow before them.

Their worship system centered upon winning the evil one's favor by pacifying him with sacrifice, appeasement, and worship.

Nimrod, (the first mason of this earth), was the founder of ancient Babylon, and the first to promote the forming of a One World Government. During life, _and_ after death, he was worshipped as a god. This was the beginning of the ancient religious culture of Babylon, eventually ruled by King Nebuchadnezzar, and spoken of in the Book of Daniel. (The visions of Daniel, one of the captives of Judah, are the subject of Daniel's prophetic Book.)

The accounts written in Daniel's Book show how each ruling king demanded worship. Pagan religious systems include the worship of the sun, moon, and stars. These customs of pagan worship were passed down to Babylon, Medo-Persia, Greece, and Pagan Imperial Rome.

God
Adam
Power to Rule Usurped by Satan
Nimrod at Babel
Babylon
Medo-Persia
Rome
Greece

The Call Out of
Sun Worship or "Spiritual Babylon"

All the while, God has been continually calling His people out of this system of pagan worship. Abraham was called out of Ur of the Chaldees (Babylon); Lot was called out of Sodom and Gomorrah; Moses was called out of Egypt, and Daniel with his three friends, chose not to be part of the false religious system of Babylon. Although Satan's systems are all pervasive, God has always had a remnant preserved on this earth — a remnant that would live and present the Truth of God and His righteousness, His unblemished plan of salvation and His constant and unconditional love for mankind.

Satan's Subtle Counterfeit

The very antichrist plans Lucifer tried to implement in Heaven, are now being used to condition the people of this world. Just as Lucifer did not expose his real plan, in heaven, so today, he has camouflaged the worship of himself, under a world-wide system of gods and goddesses, and man-defined "Christianity." (Note: Satan's plan, of false Pagan systems, did not end with the Fourth Kingdom of Pagan Imperial Rome.)

Sun worship has always been the rival religion to the worship of Jehovah. It was through sun worship that the worship of Lucifer was camouflaged throughout the Pagan world. Those who obeyed the Pagan precepts were actually bowing their knee before Lucifer.

Humans Will Choose Who They Will Serve
Till the Endtimes

As the angels of Heaven chose sides, so will the people of this world separate into two distinct groups (sheep and goats) before the end of this age. This line of distinction is given great attention in Revelation 13-14.

The Luciferian Plot (Conspiracy)

The Luciferian plot on planet Earth, to overthrow the worship of Jesus the Christ, has always worked in secrecy. It has not come upon the world suddenly, but in a progressive, manipulative, and coercive manner. The history of this great anti-God religion can be traced down through time, clearly demonstrating how primitive and modern man have been duped into the worship of Lucifer.

Satan Seeks Universal Control

Daniel was given four visions revealing four Pagan kingdoms which surrounded God's people, from 606 BC to the end of time. Satan has managed to work through these kingdoms to gain converts to his cause. As this world nears its end, Satan is doubling his efforts to reign supreme and be worshipped as the god of this world. He has always worked through political and religious systems in the past. His style has not changed. (Daniel's visions address seven systems within these four kingdoms.)

Daniel reveals some of these systems as being garbed in the cloak of "Christianity." The Lord's people are to be found in every religious system — Pagan or Christian. Daniel's visions are not condemning the individual members of these organizations, but the wicked antichrist sys-tem behind them.

Prologue to Daniel's Book

The Loud Cry Warning to "Come Out of Babylon"

Revelation 14 and 18 mention the Loud Call (or Loud Cry) for God's people to "come out of Babylon." Ancient Babylon is gone, but the cultural and religious system of ancient Babylon is found in every earthly political and religious system today. This system is known as "spiritual Babylon" (a symbolic term) and has all the characteristics of ancient Babylon.

God desires His people to sever all ties with Babylon in their everyday life; to seek, worship, and serve the true Creator God with all their heart, soul, and mind.

The Luciferian One World Order of the Future

For 6000 years, Satan's plan has been developing and unfolding. As time on this earth comes to an end, he will increase his efforts to set up a One World Government of Luciferian worship. Daniel's Fourth Vision exposes these evil plans and how Satan has manipulated the political and religious systems of the world.

Daniel's visions, along with secular history, assist the Bible student to grasp a full understanding of the great controversy this earth has been involved in. Daniel 12:10 contains a promise for the holy people: "… the wise shall understand."

Revelation 13:4 says: "And they worshipped the dragon [Lucifer/Satan] …" This verse carries a warning for all of mankind about how the world will be deceived into worshipping Satan before the end of the world, and the Second Coming of Jesus.

The Book of Daniel had its beginning in 606 BC when King Nebuchadnezzar, of Babylon, came down from the north to take Jerusalem and a host of God's people captive. What were the events that led up to this point in history? Why did God see it as being necessary to give insight to Daniel regarding the deliverance of His people down through the stream of time? Does Daniel reveal any information that exposes Satan and his plan? Is it shocking to know that:

- Lucifer's plan, right from the beginning, was to unite the entire world into a One World Government? One that would reject its Creator and all that He stands for?

- Luciferians have lived and died promoting the worship of Lucifer in many of the ancient and modern religious and political systems?
- The goal of Luciferianism is to exalt Lucifer as the only god of this world?

Today, the prophetic good news is: Lucifer's plan will fail!

Daniel's prophecies present the story of how the "scepter of power" has been passed from one system to another in an attempt to set up a Luciferian system of worship on this earth. The four visions found in Daniel introduce the overall prophecy. The Book of Revelation concludes the endtime prophecy, in full detail.

The Sceptre of Power
(or Dominion to Rule)
is Passed From
One System to Another
Until the
Full Circle
is Completed
and then
Jesus will Come!

"Doctrine" as Compared to "Prophecy"

PILLARS
represent immovable Biblical, doctrinal truths.

RACE HORSES
represent the forward, progressive movement of prophecy.

PROPHECY is unfulfilled history.

HISTORY is fulfilled prophecy.

The Bible contains many different literary styles from history, to poetry, to doctrine, and to prophecy. Occasionally there is confusion between the terms *doctrine* and *prophecy.*

DOCTRINE can be compared to *PILLARS* that do not move. Doctrines are eternal truths that stand firm in the Bible from Genesis to Revelation. They do not change!

PROPHECY is very different from *DOCTRINE.* Although prophecy often includes *doctrinal truths, prophecy is not doctrine. PROPHECY* can be compared to *RACE HORSES* that are constantly moving in a *forward, progressive manner.* One day, all prophecy will be fulfilled and stop the forward motion of prophetic time. *Doctrine,* however, will still stand firm forever.

Many prophetic expositors attempt to understand unfulfilled prophecy in a "best guess" manner. Prophecy is only fully understood at the time of fulfillment. Although we can discern much from past history to aid the understanding of unfulfilled prophecy, we must be aware that any interpretation of future prophecy <u>may</u> need to be adjusted.

Secular History Established as Prophecy Unfolds

At the time of the writing of the Prophetic Book of Daniel, the visions and dreams Daniel had, were just that. As time has moved mankind forward through the centuries, Daniel's visions and dreams have taken on new meaning. Most of Daniel's prophecies are now viewed as secular history. Small portions of unfulfilled prophetic Scripture, in Daniel, are in the process of unfolding right now.

As secular history is compared with Daniel's visions and dreams, it becomes evident that they are one in the same. Daniel reveals who the players are and the religious and political deception that is, and has been used, to transfer the scepter of power, seat, and authority from one kingdom to another.

Future prophecy has not entirely unfolded. We are not yet at the moment of Christ's return. Some future events have yet to take place. Therefore, it is important when viewing the prophecies of the near future that we keep an open mind as to the fulfillment of the final events leading up to the culmination of earth's history.

MATT 24:33 So likewise ye, when ye shall see all these things [prophecies fulfilled], know that it [Second Coming of Jesus] is near, even at the doors.

"Daniel" as Compared to a "Drama"

Classical literature has always stood the test of time and continues to be a best seller year after year. The prophetic Book of Daniel is a piece of classical literature and follows the same consistent patterns of a drama, a novel, or a play.

In a good book, each chapter introduces characters and actions into which the reader projects himself. As he reads, he begins to see that there are problems that are arising and he "can't put the book down" until he finds the solution. Chapter after chapter, the plot thickens as the crisis develops. The reader simply has to find out "who did what?" In a play or opera, the same kind of development takes place.

The Book of Daniel follows the same pattern. As the reader moves forward in the Book, he becomes aware of a question that is developing in his mind. "How will all this turn out?" In a good book or drama, each chapter adds more questions and, as they say, "the plot thickens." Not until the last act of the play or the last chapter of the book are all the questions answered. It is in the last chapter that the Villain is exposed, the Hero comes on the scene and rescues the Fair Maiden. That is called the "coup 'd theatre" or in the political world, a "coup 'd etat." A "coup 'd etat" is defined as a "blow" or "strike" in which everything is turned up-side down. It describes a "revolution" in governmental power. In a play on stage, the Villain is exposed, the Hero and Heroine are reunited and live happily ever after. All the questions are answered and the problems, solved. It is the last chapter or the last act in which this occurs.

All through the visions in Daniel's Book, the questions keep mounting. It is not until the last chapter that these questions are brought into focus. The problems are solved in the three timelines of Daniel 12:5-13. These last verses are "The Epilogue" and the focus of the entire Book of Daniel. It is the "last act or last chapter" of the whole play.

The First Vision in Daniel 2 would have no real meaning for God's people and would merely be a review of ancient history, IF it were not for the "Stone" that is brought into view. The real question in the reader's mind is "What will be the outcome of all this historical data?" King Nebuchadnezzar had a very similar question. The focus of this vision must be on the "Stone Kingdom" where the reader asks the question, "How long will this historical progression of wicked, earthly kingdoms continue to exist?" The answer that God gives to us is that the earthly kingdoms will last until the Stone Kingdom is established.

The Second Vision in Daniel 7 tells us that the True Hero appears on stage during the reign of the Fourth Kingdom. Here, He comes as "Prince Charming" and His Bride falls deeply in love with Him. But, He must go away to a far city to build a beautiful house for His Bride. While He is gone . . .

. . . the Villain also appears in the Second Vision of Daniel, seeking to steal away the Bride! He is known as the "Little Horn" of the Fifth Kingdom. The final verse of Daniel 7 describes his true character! He is mean to the Bride. We begin to wonder if he will capture the Bride and destroy her? "How long will he be on stage prowling about," is the question that is asked over and over. Sure enough, he is wounded in a street fight and it is expected that he will die! Daniel 7:25 tells us of this wound and its healing. Hope for the Bride rises!

In the Third Vision of Daniel 8, there is an explanation as to how this "Little Horn" and "king of fierce countenance" gain "power, seat, and great authority." By trickery and stealth, he moves politically within the church system. The question then arises, "How long until this rascal will be brought to judgment in the court?" Daniel 8:14 provides the answer in a 2300 year timeline.

Finally, in the last chapter of Daniel, (The Epilogue), the great drama of all the ages is solved. The question is, "How long shall it be to the end of these wonders?" The answer to that question is found in the three timelines that follow. It is evident that the prophetic periods of these three timelines extend to the "very eve of the great Second Coming" (represented by the "Stone Kingdom") and throw a flood of light on events then to transpire. It is these three timelines that are the "coup 'd etat" or the focus of the whole Book of Daniel. They are the endtime message for this hour in earth's history. These three timelines, consisting of 1260, 1290, and 1335 "literal days," are not fully explained in Daniel's Book. The full explanation is given in the Book of Revelation.

Daniel's four visions on the fate of earthly kingdoms, builds in each vision. In the last verses of Daniel 12, the reader is given a "peek" into what the future holds. The Hero presents "The Epilogue" — with the encouragement to study the Book of Revelation for the rest of the details of this prophetic story. The drama continues to unfold, until the reader knows the whole story of the Hero, His Bride, and the Villain. As far as possible, every question will be answered and every crisis solved. Enjoy one of the best pieces of classical literature ever written — God's final Word for the deliverance of His people.

An Introduction to the Book of Daniel

The Nature and Purpose of the Book of Daniel

The Book of Daniel is classified as *apocalyptic* or prophetic literature. In prophetic study of this literature, the Book of Daniel is the presentation of world history before it happens. Revelation is a fuller unfolding and explanation of it. The Bible student cannot understand the full picture until the two Books are brought together. Each Book is an integral part of the other. For this reason, Revelation must be studied with Daniel. Before Revelation can be fully appreciated, a thorough understanding of Daniel is essential.

The Four "Historic-Prophetic Outlines" in the Book of Daniel

Four times God permitted Daniel to see, in vision, the history of the world from his own day to the future restoration of the Kingdom of God. These four Historic-Prophetic Outlines trace the rise and fall of seven earthly kingdoms from 606 BC (about 600 years before Christ) to our own day, and are therefore prophetically *historic* in nature. These prophetic Outlines, as they build on each other and unfold in history, establish in the heart of the true Bible student, the divine authorship of the Word. Only the Creator, the Life-giving God of heaven, is able to foresee the future and make one hundred percent accurate revelations about future events. This He has done in Daniel 2:45b when Daniel states, "and the dream is certain, and the interpretation thereof sure." The proof of this promise is the unfolding of secular history.

"Recapping"

The four Historic-Prophetic Outlines are found in Daniel 2, Daniel 7, Daniel 8, and Daniel 11-12:4. After the first Outline, each new Historic-Prophetic Outline begins by repeating or *recapping* information (of earthly kingdoms) which was contained in the previous Outline. The Bible student can be sure he is on the right track as each Outline adds more detail and moves the events forward in time. This repetitive structure in the Book of Daniel insures an accurate, clearly focused interpretation of Scripture as it continues to line up with secular historical events. This enlarges and clarifies the prophetic picture one step at a time. At the beginning of each new vision, a chart will be given to demonstrate the structure of *recapping*. (See the first chart on page 28.)

The Rise and Fall of Seven Earthly Kingdoms in the Book of Daniel

The Book of Daniel is the story of the rise and fall of seven earthly kingdoms before the Heavenly Stone Kingdom is established on this earth. The short stories in the Book of Daniel, such as "The Three Hebrews in the Fiery Furnace," "Belshazzar's Feast with the Hand Writing on the Wall" and "Daniel in the Lion's Den," have delighted both children and adults for centuries. These stories picture the issues of "whom to worship," and "deliverance of God's people" down through time. As history continues to reveal itself, the same issues of whom to worship will bring about the fall of the final, or seventh earthly kingdom.

Historic-Prophetic Outlines **always** revolve around the people of God. Up until AD 34 the literal nation of Israel represented God's people. These Outlines broaden to be world-wide, encompassing no longer only "literal Israel," but God's people all over the world. His people are known as Spiritual Israel. (To understand the differences, see: (A) Literal Israel: ACTS 10:45 and ACTS 11:2; (B) Spiritual Israel: EPH 2:19; GAL 6:16; ROM 2:28-29). The Outlines in Daniel provide the foundational teaching for the Outlines in the Book of Revelation. Revelation focuses on events surrounding God's people at the very end of time.

An Introduction to the Book of Daniel

In Daniel 2, the Historic-Prophetic Outline begins with localized nations that surrounded Israel: Babylon, Medo-Persia, and Greece. Then the Outline expands to include Pagan Imperial Rome. The rest of the Book of Daniel, with its Historic-Prophetic Outlines, expands the picture to current events which affect the entire world. Revelation, in its prophetic office, expands the Outlines into current events that include "all of the world." (e.g. REV 13:3.)

Daniel 2 (along with secular history) traces the rise and fall of the first four earthly kingdoms — kingdoms, which progressively held dominion over all of the known world. Chapter 7 adds the rise of the Fifth Kingdom; Chapter 8 reveals information about the Sixth Kingdom. Daniel 11 gives information about the rise and fall of the Seventh Kingdom. Together these four visions give the history of seven earthly kingdoms that surround the people of God down through the stream of time. Knowledge of these seven earthly kingdoms, found in Daniel, identify the seven heads on the symbolic "composite beast" of Revelation 13:1-10. In this way, Daniel and Revelation join together and interpret each other. The Bible always provides the explanation.

Understanding "Outlines" in the Book of Daniel

An Outline is an organized framework which flows from item to item in order or sequence. Consequently, an Outline in the Bible is merely the sequential order of events of earthly kingdoms that ruled over God's people. In Daniel, these events revolve around seven earthly kingdoms. Secular history accurately provides dates for the kingdoms that have fallen and those that are in existence today. In the Book of Daniel there are four Historic-Prophetic Outlines (given in Daniel 2, 7, 8, 11-12:4). Each provide information on some or all of the seven earthly kingdoms. Each Outline in Daniel closes right at the brink of the coming of Jesus. (Revelation gives information on the future Heavenly Kingdom.) The Outlines are an essential component of **"The Structure of Daniel"** chart. This chart is used throughout each vision with a summary at the end of each vision chapter.

Understanding "Timelines" in the Book of Daniel

THERE IS ONLY **ONE** MAJOR LINE OF PROPHECY in the Book of Daniel that covers the span of time from 606 BC to the beginning of the establishment of Christ's Kingdom. There are seven **Timelines** within this Major Line of Prophecy. Each **Timeline** covers a specific span of time and has definite beginnings and endings. These timelines are appointed by "voices, decrees, or judicial legislative action." The "beginnings and endings" of the first four timelines can be dated according to historical events. At this point in time, it is not possible to know the "beginning and ending" dates of the last three timelines in Daniel 12 since these timelines have a future application and hang on events yet to happen. As the future becomes the "here and now," dates can be applied. Further information on timing and application of dates is investigated in the text. A summary table for each timeline will be provided in the specific chapter where the timeline is addressed by Scripture. (See page 61 for a sample of the first Prophetic Timeline Table given in Daniel 4.)

Note of Interest: The Book of Revelation addresses two Major Lines of Prophecy. 1) The First Line of Prophecy covers the span of time from AD 31 to the Second Coming of Jesus — approximately 2000 years. 2) The Second Line of Prophecy covers the span of time from "war in heaven before creation" to the "beginning of eternity" — approximately 7000 years. Both lines of prophecy in Revelation are attached to a distinct set of four visions given to John the Revelator.

An Introduction to the Book of Daniel

Definition: "Hermeneutic Principle"

For the writing of this manuscript on Daniel, the Hermeneutic Principles (listed on pages 16-21) are the rules needed for the *study of prophecy*. Hermeneutics, by definition, is the science of discovering and stating the rules which govern Bible study. To understand Scripture, consideration must be given to:

1. Biblical context;
2. Grammatical context and/or nuance of original text;
3. Sequence and continuity of Biblical verses;
4. Alignment of similar word pictures throughout Scripture;
5. Secular, historical evidence, and current events.

With a thorough study of the Scriptures, and an understanding of history along with a knowledge of current events, the reader will understand the future prophecies as they are fulfilled. The last generation (before Jesus comes) will have the broad panorama of <u>ALL</u> past history behind them, and an understanding of "God's Plan to Save His People." These prophecies are given to us to provide hope, joy, and confidence to those living at the time of the final fulfillment. Prophetic Keys (on pages 16-21), will be given throughout the manuscript to aid the Bible student in a clearer understanding of the Hermeneutic Principles.

Sequence and Continuity — An "Hermeneutic Principle"

As previously stated, an Outline is the orderly arrangement of items in sequence. As these items flow in perfect sequence, a moving picture or continuity of events is presented. In the four Outlines of Daniel, each item or verse is arranged within its Outline in sequential or chronological order. Time is always moving forward. (We cannot live yesterday over again, nor can we jump into tomorrow.) Therefore, the verses in an Outline must be kept in their <u>inspired</u> sequence and aligned with the unfolding of sequential, secular history. Keeping the sequence and continuity of verses within such an Outline in order, is an Hermeneutic Principle of prophetic interpretation. For example: each Outline addresses earthly kingdoms which have ruled or will rule over God's people. These kingdoms are <u>always</u> given in the same order (or sequence) as they appeared in history. Each verse in the Outline provides this information in a logical format, constantly moving the Prophetic Outline "forward in time." This logical method of Biblical application is known as "The Historicist 'School' of Biblical Exposition" [or Interpretation]. This logical interpretation of prophecy *must* be observed in the study of all Outlines given in Daniel. As mentioned earlier, the Hermeneutic Principles will be explained under the designated title of Prophetic Keys. They will be further explained in the manuscript with their corresponding application in Scripture.

Reading Level

Comments in this manuscript are written on a reading level and vocabulary similar to the Bible text. Unless otherwise indicated, all Bible texts are taken from the King James Authorized Version, a translation purportedly at a grade eight reading level. It may be necessary for the Bible student to use a dictionary if certain words are not understood. All definitions of Hebrew words (in the Old Testament) and Greek words (in the New Testament) are taken from the *Biblesoft's New Exhaustive Strong's Numbers and Concordance with Expanded Greek-Hebrew Dictionary;* Copyright © 1994, Biblesoft and International Bible Translators, Inc. Maps, pictures, illustrations, charts, and tables have been inserted to clarify the text and clearly identify where the prophecies are in the stream of time.

Prophetic Keys of "Hermeneutic Principles"

Prophetic
Key
Symbol

Note to Readers: These *principles* may seem difficult and obscure at first. As they are continually applied, their use becomes apparent! (Practice is so important!) Look for the "Prophetic Key" symbol in the manuscript that designates Scriptural *links* and *prophetic principles*. In this way, correct application will give added understanding of each new vision in Daniel.

Definition of Hermeneutics: The science of discovering and stating the rules which govern sound Bible study. These principles guide and direct us to a Biblical perspective of the knowledge God intends for us.

General Principles

1. God governs His universe by laws. His Word gives direction to assure the utmost happiness of His people. Prophetic exposition is an <u>*exact science*</u> and must strictly abide by the application of Hermeneutic Principles. Hermeneutic Principles must not be "used" to disturb either Biblically based doctrine or to violate prophetic constants. Integrity, logic, and common sense are essential in understanding prophecy.

2. All Scripture is inspired by God through the Holy Spirit. (2 TIM 3:16; 2 PETER 1:21) Inspired Scriptures are spiritually understood by Christians as a result of the power of the Holy Spirit (1 COR. 2:14) and not through the customs and traditions of man. Prophetic investigation is the right of ALL men — not the exclusive right of the clergy.

3. All Scripture is "Christ centered" forming a web of Truth, that continually points to the need of a Savior. (LUKE 24:27) Scripture <u>never</u> contradicts itself.

4. The Bible is <u>always</u> its own expositor or interpreter. Scripture unlocks Scripture as a result of <u>cross reference</u> Bible Study. (ISA 28:9-13) For a correct understanding of prophecy — conjecture, assumption, opinion, speculation, tradition, and guessing are all forbidden!

5. Scripture was written in ancient languages. An analytical concordance and dictionary are helpful to clarify meaning.

6. Identifying the literary *structure* of Scripture gives added interpretive insight. Note: Daniel wrote his Book with a specific, unique structure. John's Book of Revelation has a slightly <u>different structure</u>. As the individual structures are understood, the meaning of each prophetic Book unfolds. Both Books have an *overall prophetic structure*. This specific structure is given in two **Structural Charts**. (The Structure Chart for Daniel will be studied with each vision chapter. The chart for the Book of Revelation is found on pages 398-399.) Each individual vision in Daniel follows a specific *structural pattern*. Note: the following table shows how the arrangement of Revelation's structure is slightly different from Daniel's structure.

DANIEL'S Literary Structure	REVELATION'S Literary Structure
HEAVENLY SCENE	HEAVENLY SCENE
INTERLUDE QUESTION	PROPHETIC OUTLINE
HISTORIC-PROPHETIC OUTLINE	INTERLUDE
ANSWER TO QUESTION ENDTIME EVENT	ENDTIME EVENT

Prophetic Keys of "Hermeneutic Principles"

7. Prophecy is 'history written before it happens.' As time moves forward and history unfolds, prophecy is fulfilled and takes on a clear and focused meaning. Understanding secular history significantly assists in the unfolding and interpretation of prophecy. Prophecy is given to enable God's people to know where they are in the stream of time.

8. Prophecy may appear to have dual interpretations. The appropriate application of Hermeneutic Principles must be used to discern <u>endtime events</u>. This manuscript primarily addresses endtime events. Dual interpretations are not allowed to disturb the sequence and forward movement of any Historic-Prophetic Outline. When the "unfolding of history" moves the Outline forward in time to the current events of our day, incorrect interpretations from the past will fade away under the light of new truth.

9. **Daniel** is the presentation of world history before it happens, and **Revelation** is the '<u>unfolding</u>' of that prophecy. This 'unfolding' adds detail, clarity, and understanding. The Book of Daniel gives wisdom and understanding for the exposition of Revelation. Daniel's prophecies are built on **basic concepts** and, in turn, lay the foundation for fulfilling the prophecies of Revelation. These concepts are realized and understood by the consistent use of the Prophetic Keys; understanding context, continuity, verse sequencing, and alignment (see Prophetic Key #10); and the structure that unfolds in Daniel's Book. (The review charts on pages 44-45, 112-113, 172-173, and 344-345 will be very helpful to understand "structure" and its basic concepts.) The Bible student must understand the basic concepts in Daniel first, **then** the prophecies of Revelation will unfold. (e.g. It may be difficult to understand the seven heads on the composite beast of Revelation 13:1 if the seven earthly persecuting kingdoms of Daniel are not understood first.)

Principles on: "Time Moves Forward" in the "Historic-Prophetic Outlines"

10. Exposition of Historic-Prophetic Outlines requires that all verses in an Outline be kept in <u>context</u>, <u>continuity</u>, <u>verse sequencing</u>, and <u>alignment</u>. (For an explanation of these terms, see the Glossary.) The principle that "time moves forward" applies in the interpretation of Historic-Prophetic Outlines.

11. Historic-Prophetic Outlines **MUST** align with the chronological order of secular historical events and they **MUST** align with each other. Each succeeding vision recaps the kingdoms of the previous vision in a <u>forward progressive movement</u>.

12. "<u>Time</u>" in an Historic-Prophetic Outline, or a <u>timeline</u>, **always** moves forward — never backwards. Truth for today, is clearly seen, as prophecy unfolds and aligns itself with past and current events. Prophecy is usually understood at the time of fulfillment.

13. Each additional Historic-Prophetic Outline moves forward in time and **adds extra information to the previous Outline.** (e.g. The Historic-Prophetic Outline of Daniel 7 adds more information to the previous Historic-Prophetic Outline of Daniel 2.)

Prophetic Keys of "Hermeneutic Principles"

Principles on: "Symbolic Language" in Prophecy

14. The Bible is to be understood in its most obvious or literal sense, <u>UNLESS</u> a figure or symbol is employed. If a symbol is employed, the language is no longer only <u>literal</u>. (Note: Literal language is used to carry the terms of symbolic language. Otherwise none of the vision could be understood.)

15. The Historic-Prophetic Outlines in Daniel's first three visions of chapters 2, 7, and 8 are written using some symbolic language that introduces symbolic images, beasts, and horns.

16. In symbolic language, a symbol is a word picture of <u>something</u> which is not real. (e.g. Daniel 7:6 speaks of a leopard beast with four wings and four heads.)

17. Prophecy written in symbolic language is not of any private interpretation. (2 PETER 1:20) When a symbol is used, the Bible must be used to give the interpretation of <u>that</u> symbol. (2 PETER 1:19) Note the steps in the following example of Daniel 7:2-3:

    SYMBOL: "I saw in my vision … four great **beasts**."

    Step No. 1 — Interpretation

    DECODING: The Bible interprets the symbols as follows:
        "These great **beasts** … are **four kings**." (DAN 7:17)

    (Once the interpretation of the symbol is complete,
    then <u>application</u> can be made to the correct persons or circumstances.)

    Step No. 2 — Application

    APPLICATION: The **four kings,** representing kingdoms, are verified by secular history and
        applied to the kingdoms of **Babylon, Medo-Persia, Greece, and Rome.**
        (The First Kingdom was previously interpreted in Daniel 2. The Second and
        Third Kingdoms are directly interpreted in Daniel 8 by Angel Gabriel. Secular
        history interprets the remaining kingdom. The Bible always indicates where to
        begin.)

Prophetic Keys of "Hermeneutic Principles"

Principles on: "Literal Language" in Prophecy

18. The Bible is to be understood in its most obvious or literal sense, <u>UNLESS</u> a figure or symbol is employed. (e.g. There are <u>no</u> symbols in the fourth chapter of Daniel. Therefore, the text (and timeline) of Daniel 4 is to be taken literally.)

19. The Historic-Prophetic Outline in Daniel's Fourth Vision (chapters 10-12) is written in literal language. Therefore, it is to be interpreted literally. (Also see Prophetic Key #28 "Context is King.")

20. Prophecy written in literal language uses <u>application</u> to align historical events to Scripture. When prophecy is written without symbolism, then Step No. 1 (in Principle #17) is eliminated. Prophecy then needs no interpretation and only requires Step No. 2 — that of <u>application</u>. Note the following example in Daniel 11:3:

> **THE LITERAL VERSE:** "And a mighty king shall stand up, that shall rule with great dominion, and do according to his will.

> **APPLICATION OF VERSE:** "And a mighty king" [Alexander the Great who followed Xerxes I]
> "shall stand up" [come to the throne]
> "that shall rule with great dominion" [ruled all of the land to India]
> "and do according to his will" [was a great conqueror]
> Date of this verse: [331 BC]
> All <u>applications</u> align with secular history and former visions.

- The continuing prophecy of the "king of the north" and "king of the south" in the Historic-Prophetic Outline of Daniel 11 is completely written with literal language. To understand who the numerous "kings" represent, proper <u>application</u> is made aligning secular history with Scripture.

21. <u>Literal language</u> MAY use — <u>figures of speech and various devices such as similes, metaphors, titles, and types</u>, to develop and advance ideas. (In other places of Scripture, the Gospels deal with Parables and the Song of Solomon deals with an Allegory. A parable is a fictional story. An allegory is a figurative description of real facts. Both are used to illustrate an idea.)

a. <u>Similes</u>: are figures of speech in which <u>two essentially unlike things are compared</u>. Similes are tools of language which often employ the words, "like" or "as" using a story as an illustration. Revelation 9:7-10 has many similes. (e.g. "locusts were *like*;" "hair *as* the hair;" "tails *like* unto scorpions," etc.)

b. <u>Metaphors</u>: A metaphor is a word or phrase denoting an idea which represents something else. (e.g. For a "grumpy spouse" some may say "he was a *bear* this morning at the breakfast table." See Revelation 9:1 — "I saw a <u>star</u> fall from heaven." The star represents <u>Lucifer</u> the fallen being.)

c. <u>Titles</u>: are a claim or right to ownership and a just cause of possession or control. (e.g. In Daniel 11, the **titles** of "king of the north," and "king of the south" have claim or ownership over territory that has been conquered. Titles are <u>NOT</u> symbols.)

d. <u>Types</u>: are a group of things sharing common characteristics that distinguish them as an identifiable class such as a literal person, animal, or ritual representing a spiritual truth. (e.g. Characteristics of the Sanctuary Services in the Old Testament include: i) "type" [the lamb] in the Old Testament; ii) "antitype" [Jesus Christ the Lamb of God] in the New Testament.)

Prophetic Keys of "Hermeneutic Principles"

Principles on: "Time" and "Timelines" in Prophecy

22. The word *prophetic*, comes from the word *prophecy*. **NOTE:** **ALL** time in prophecy (whether literal or symbolic) is **prophetic time** and <u>occurs</u> **exactly** at the appointed time. Timelines are <u>never</u> severed.

23. Prophetic time, and timelines, contained in either a literal or symbolic context must be treated appropriately for the proper interpretation of that specific timeline. **NOTE:** It is <u>incorrect</u> to assume that ALL time and timelines in prophecy are symbolic time! a) When a timeline fits the requirements of Prophetic Keys #14-17, **then** (and only then) will the timeline be identified (according to the Bible) as <u>prophetic</u> symbolic time. b) When a timeline fits the requirements of Prophetic Keys #18-21, then the timeline is identified as <u>prophetic</u> literal time. Note point #22 again: symbolic time and literal time are <u>always</u> prophetic — beginning and ending on time! The word *prophetic* merely identifies any timeline as being predicted to occur. (Confusion results when the terms *symbolic* and *prophetic* are used as interchangeable terms. These terms are **never interchangeable**! Page 109 and the Glossary provide additional detailed information.)

24. *Prophetic time and timelines* will be **either** prophetic symbolic time **OR** prophetic literal time — never both! Timelines contained in a symbolic context must be decoded with the <u>Year-day Computation Principle</u> given in 24b. Prophetic terminology for decoding symbolic time is defined by Scripture. Examples:

a. Ezekiel 4:6 and Numbers 14:34 give the Bible interpretation for decoding one symbolic day as representing one literal year. This conversion is known as the Year-day Computation Principle. A "time" in Jewish prophecy represents 360 days in the Jewish Calendar. (See extra notes in point #25b.) Further explanation of this concept will be given in Daniel 7 and 8 to clarify how one symbolic day equals one literal year. This principle can also be applied in Revelation 12:6 ("… a thousand two hundred and threescore days ...") and Revelation 18 ("Therefore shall her plagues come in one day ..."). Following are <u>some</u> Year-day Computation calculations:

$$\text{One prophetic } symbolic\ day \text{ or one prophetic } time = 360 \text{ literal days or 1 literal year}$$
$$dividing\ of\ (symbolic)\ time\ \underline{or}\ half\ a\ (symbolic)\ time = 180 \text{ literal days } (360/2=180)$$
$$1/12^{th} \text{ of a prophetic } symbolic\ day = 30 \text{ literal days } (360/12 = 30)$$
$$1/24^{th} \text{ of a prophetic } symbolic\ day \text{ (or one hour)} = 15 \text{ literal days } (360/24 = 15)$$
$$\text{One } symbolic\ half\ hour = 7.5 \text{ literal days } (15/2 = 7.5)$$

b. **The Year-day Computation Principle** is used **only** to interpret a symbolic timeline that is contained within a symbolic Historic-Prophetic Outline. (e.g. Daniel 7:25 and Revelation 12:6 are calculated as 1260 literal years. Daniel 9 has similar examples.)

c. **The Rule of Adjustment** when timelines cross the *zero line*: When a date calculation is made from a BC date to an AD date, or vice versa, the addition or subtraction of <u>one year</u> is required to complete the calculation because — when crossing from BC to AD there is no zero year. First example: 457 BC + 483 years = AD 26 $\pm$ **1** (year for adjustment to AD) = **AD 27**. Second example: AD 1844 - 2300 years = 456 BC **- 1** (year for adjustment to BC) = **457 BC**.

d. Literal time **NEVER** applies the Year-day Computation Principle. A literal day always equals a 24 hour day. (e.g. In Daniel 4:16, 23, 25, 32 — the timeline of seven "times" equals seven "literal years." Daniel 12:7, 11, and 12 are literal day timelines of 1260, 1290, and 1335 days respectively.) In most cases <u>the use of symbols and context</u> determines how a literal or symbolic timeline is treated. See Prophetic Key #28.

Prophetic Keys of "Hermeneutic Principles"

25. *Prophetic time and timelines* can also be literal prophetic time. Timelines contained in a literal context are understood as literal time, meaning "a prophetic day is simply one literal day." Prophetic terminology for literal time is defined by Scripture. For example:

a. Genesis 1 gives the Bible interpretation for one literal day as a dark and light 24 hour period of time — as found in Daniel 4 ("seven times"); Daniel 12 ("a time, times, and an half"); and Revelation 12:14 ("a time, and times, and half a time").

b. Genesis 7 and 8 give the Biblical interpretation for *time* as 360 days according to the Jewish Calendar. This will be further explained in the literal text of Daniel 4 and applied in Daniel 12.

26. All timelines **begin and end** with voices or legislative decrees. A detailed explanation will be given in Daniel 4 with the same principle being applied in the time prophecies of Daniel 7-12.

27. In the prophecies of Daniel and Revelation, the <u>beginning</u> of timelines bring unpleasant news to <u>some</u> people. The ending of timelines will bring the good news of deliverance to God's people. (Deliverance of God's people is a key issue in the prophetic Books of Daniel and Revelation.)

Principles on: "Timelines When Context is King"

28. **Context is KING:** The grammatical language (whether literal or symbolic) determines the context of a passage of verses. This context determines how to interpret time or a timeline within that passage, even when there are symbols given. The verse or passage must be interpreted in the **context** in which it is written. The grammar (words which give the context) cannot be removed from that context <u>or</u> moved about at the whim of the reader. To do so is a direct violation of the interpretation of Scripture.

Principles on: "Second Coming of Jesus Christ"

29. Prophecy does <u>NOT</u> give the day and hour of the Second Coming of Jesus, but reveals when it is near, even at the door. (MATT 24:33, 36)

Principles on: "Vision Tidy-up Verses"

30. In Daniel, there are one or more <u>tidy-up verses</u> at the **END** of the each Historic-Prophetic Outline. These verses indicate that the Outline of persecuting kingdoms has come to an end.

- Daniel 2:46-49 are the tidy-up verses for the First Outline.
- Daniel 7:26 is the tidy-up verse for the Second Outline.
- Daniel 8:27 is the tidy-up verse for the Third Outline. However, this is NOT the end of the vision. There are several timelines in Daniel 9:24-27 that pertain to the first part of the vision in Daniel 8.
- Daniel 12:4 is the tidy-up verse for the Fourth Outline. Again, this is NOT the end of the vision. (This part of the structure has been introduced in Daniel's Third Vision.) <u>The following nine verses in Daniel 12:5-13 introduce three timelines that begin with the reign of the Seventh Kingdom in the Fourth Historic-Prophetic Outline.</u> These verses are an **Epilogue** (or summary of the last verses of Daniel 11) of how God finishes His work during the reign of the last earthly kingdom. This **Epilogue** is the most important focus of the Book of Daniel. The full interpretation for this **Epilogue** is the focus of the Book of Revelation.

DANIEL
The Story of the Rise and Fall of Earthly Kingdoms

CHAPTER 1

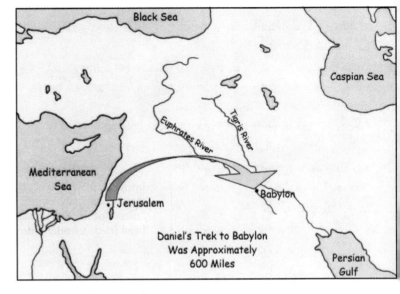

Daniel's Trek to Babylon
Was Approximately
600 Miles

Jerusalem Falls
(606 BC)

1 In the third year of the reign of Jehoiakim king of Judah came Nebuchadnezzar king of Babylon unto Jerusalem, <u>and besieged it</u>.

2 And the Lord gave Jehoiakim king of Judah into his hand, with part of <u>the vessels</u> of the house of God: which he carried into the land of Shinar to the house of his god; and he brought the vessels into the treasure house of his god.

Daniel and His Friends
Taken Captive

3 And the king spake unto Ashpenaz the master of his <u>eunuchs</u>, that he should bring certain of the children of Israel, and of the king's seed, and of the princes;

<u>Verses 1-3</u>

2 KINGS 24:10, 14 At that time the servants of Nebuchadnezzar king of Babylon came up against Jerusalem, and the <u>city was besieged</u>. 14 And he carried away all Jerusalem, and all the princes, and all the mighty men of valour, even ten thousand captives, and all the craftsmen and smiths: none remained, save the poorest sort of the people of the land.

JER 27:21-22 Yea, thus saith the LORD of hosts … concerning <u>the vessels</u> that remain in the house of the LORD … 22 They shall be carried to Babylon.

ISA 39:7 And of thy sons that shall issue from thee, which thou shalt beget, shall they take away; and they shall be <u>eunuchs</u> in the palace of the king of Babylon.

DAN 4:8 But at the last Daniel came in before me, whose name was Belteshazzar, according to the name of my god.

GEN 10:10 And the beginning of his [Nimrod's] kingdom was Babel … in the land of Shinar.

GEN 11:9 Therefore is the name of it called Babel; because the LORD did there confound the language of all the earth.

Note: The Babylonians had <u>many gods</u>. The chief deity was Bel, also known as Marduk. Daniel and his friends were named after these gods.

<u>*"eunuch"*</u> — A male of the human species castrated. *Noah Webster 1828.*

CHAPTER 1   The Story of the Rise and Fall of Earthly Kingdoms

4 Children in whom was no blemish, but well favoured, and skilful in all wisdom, and cunning in knowledge, and understanding science, and such as had ability in them to stand in the king's palace, and whom they might teach the learning and the tongue of the Chaldeans.

5 And the king appointed them a daily provision of the king's meat, and of the wine which he drank: so nourishing them three years, that at the end thereof they might stand before the king.

*King Nebuchadnezzar
Changes the Names of
Daniel and His Friends
to Reflect Heathen Worship*

6 Now among these were of the children of Judah, Daniel, Hananiah, Mishael, and Azariah:

7 Unto whom the prince of the eunuchs gave names: for he gave unto Daniel the name of Belteshazzar; and to Hananiah, of Shadrach; and to Mishael, of Meshach; and to Azariah, of Abed-nego.

Verses 4-7

"whom they might teach the learning" — King Nebuchadezzar planned to indoctrinate the captives from Jerusalem into Babylon's **cultural and religious system**. Cultural and religious assimilation was the goal. Changing their Hebrew names to Babylonian names was just the beginning. The "learning" of the Chaldeans and their culture included politics, education, arts, literature, and sports, to name a few. This cultural training was expected to have its influence on Daniel and his three friends. The influences that they would be exposed to were meant to shape their mind, character, personality, and eventually, their religious beliefs. When the time came, perhaps they too would bow down to the image raised by the King on the Plain of Dura. (DAN 3) What one thinks in his heart, and does with his hand, is who he is. If the Hebrews had not purposed in their heart that they would not deviate from their God, they would have accepted the "mark" of the Babylonian system in their forehead (to think), and in their hand (to do), leading them to bow down to the image on the plain of Dura. Satan's efforts are always trying to include God's people in his Babylonian/anti-Christ system. God says, "Come out of her my people that ye be not partakers of her sin." (REV 18:4) God has a new name for the people that heed His call. (See REV 14:1 and the following Scriptures.)

New Names for the Redeemed

ISA 62:2 and thou shalt be called by a new name, which the mouth of the LORD shall name.

REV 2:17 To him that overcometh will I give ... a new name.

> **Thought Question:** Does our current culture promote or discourage my relationship with my God? How are my children and I involved in a lifestyle similar to what Daniel and his three friends were experiencing as captives in Babylon?

"Chaldean" — from Chaldaia, Chaldea; region of ancient Babylonia. A member of an ancient Semitic people that became dominant in Babylonia. *Webster's Dictionary.*

Note: King Nebuchadnezzar's table displayed every food and drink in the most attractive manner to stimulate the appetite. Refined foods, pastries and sweets, unclean meats, seafood, and alcoholic drinks were served. Daniel and his friends adhered strictly to the unbending principle of self-control, which in every age, is a glory to God.

REV 14:7 Fear God, and give glory to him.

1 COR 10:31 Whether therefore ye eat, or drink, or whatsoever ye do, do all to the glory of God.

*Cultural Assimilation:
Jewish Names Changed to Babylonian Names*

- **Daniel** means "judge for God" and was changed to **Belteshazzar** meaning "prince of Bel."
- **Hananiah** means "gift of the Lord" and was changed to **Shadrach** meaning "servant of sin."
- **Mishael** means "who is what God is" and was changed to **Meshach**, the name of their moon god, meaning "who is what Aku is."
- **Azariah** means "whom Jehovah helps" and was changed to **Abed-nego,** meaning "servant of Nebo."

The King's Food Refused

8 But Daniel purposed in his heart that he would not defile himself with the portion of the king's meat, nor with the wine which he drank: therefore he requested of the prince of the eunuchs that he might not <u>defile</u> himself.

9 Now God had brought Daniel into favour and tender love with the prince of the eunuchs.

First Death Decree

10 And the prince of the eunuchs said unto Daniel, I fear my lord the king, who hath appointed your meat and your drink: for why should he see your faces worse liking than the children which are of your sort? then shall ye make me endanger my head to the king.

A Simple Diet Tested

11 Then said Daniel to Melzar, whom the prince of the eunuchs had set over Daniel, Hananiah, Mishael, and Azariah,

12 Prove thy servants, I beseech thee, ten days; and let them give us <u>pulse</u> to eat, and water to drink.

13 Then let our countenances be looked upon before thee, and the countenance of the children that eat of the portion of the king's meat: and as thou seest, deal with thy servants.

Verses 8-13

Note: Daniel and his three friends were designated by God to bring a knowledge of the Creator God to the Babylonians. Daniel was the leader of the group. None in the group ate unclean food. Neither was it their habit to use alcohol. Daniel and his friends made the decision not to defile their bodies with food and drink from the king's table. They were accustomed to using only "foods as grown" and water to drink. (See Leviticus 11 for a listing of unclean foods.)

"defile" — *Strong's* OT#1351 to soil or desecrate: KJV - defile, pollute, stain.

1 KINGS 8:50 give them [thy people] compassion before them who carried them captive, that they may have compassion on them.

Daniel Would Not Accept the Unclean Food — He Asked for Pulse

"pulse" — *Strong's* OT#2235 something sown, i.e. a vegetable (as food): KJV - pulse.

GEN 1:29 And God said, Behold, I have given you every herb bearing seed, which is upon the face of all the earth, and every tree, in the which is the fruit of a tree yielding seed; to you it shall be for meat.

GEN 3:18 and thou shalt eat the herb of the field.

CHAPTER 1   The Story of the Rise and Fall of Earthly Kingdoms

Daniel and His Friends
Are Proven for Ten Days

14 So he consented to them in this matter, and proved them ten days.

15 And at the end of ten days their <u>countenances</u> **appeared fairer and fatter in flesh than all the children which did eat the portion of the king's meat.**

16 Thus Melzar took away the portion of their meat, and the wine that they should drink; and gave them pulse.

Verses 14-16

Note: Daniel and his friends had been instructed since childhood not to defile their bodies with unclean food or drink. (PROV 22:6 "Train up a child in the way he should go: and when he is old, he will not depart from it.") A sanctified life requires a will and purpose to overcome the lusts of the flesh and to bring the appetite under the control of reason. Only in this way is God glorified. The Hebrew worthies guarded their bodies as the temples of the Holy Spirit in order to retain a clear mind and bring glory to their Creator.

ROM 12:1-2 I beseech you therefore, brethren, by the mercies of God, that ye present your bodies a living sacrifice, holy, acceptable unto God, which is your reasonable service. 2 And be not conformed to this world: but be ye transformed by the renewing of your mind, that ye may prove what is that good, and acceptable, and perfect, will of God.

1 COR 6:20 For ye are bought with a price: therefore glorify God in your body, and in your spirit, which are God's.

REV 14:7 Saying with a loud voice, Fear God, and give glory to him.

"countenance" — *Strong's* OT#4758 a view (the act of seeing); also an appearance (the thing seen), whether (real) a shape (especially if handsome, comeliness): KJV - apparently, appearance, fair, favoured, form, goodly, to look up to.

Healthy Countenances

Note: The striking contrast between these healthful countenances, and those who participated in the fare of Babylon, points toward that great contrast at the end of time. At that time the faces of the people of God who have lived to glorify Him, will shine in contrast to the darkened faces of the wicked.

As Jesus rides forth as a mighty conqueror "all faces [of the rejecters] are turned into paleness," (JER 30:6) and the terror of eternal despair causes "the faces of them to gather blackness." (NAH 2:10) However, the faces of the righteous will be lighted up as the countenances of Daniel and his friends.

EX 34:28-30 And he [Moses] was there with the LORD forty days and forty nights ... 29 when Moses came down from mount Sinai ... Moses wist not that the skin of his face shone. 30 And when Aaron and all the children of Israel saw Moses, behold, the skin of his face shone.

DANIEL

The Story of the Rise and Fall of Earthly Kingdoms

*Daniel and His Friends
Are Superior in
Knowledge and Wisdom*

17 As for these four children, God gave them knowledge and skill in all learning and wisdom: and <u>Daniel had understanding in all visions and dreams</u>.

18 Now at the end of the days that the king had said he should bring them in, then the prince of the eunuchs brought them in before Nebuchadnezzar.

19 And the king communed with them; and among them all was found none like Daniel, Hananiah, Mishael, and Azariah: therefore stood they before the king.

20 And in all matters of wisdom and understanding, that the king inquired of them, he found them <u>ten times better</u> than all the magicians and astrologers that were in all his realm.

21 And Daniel continued even unto the first year of king <u>Cyrus</u>.

Verses 17-21

NUM 12:6 Hear now my words: If there be a prophet among you, I the LORD will make myself known unto him in a vision, and will speak unto him in a dream.

1 KINGS 3:12 Behold, I have done according to thy words: lo, I have given thee <u>a wise and an understanding heart</u>; so that there was none like thee before thee, neither after thee shall any arise like unto thee.

Note: Daniel received three visions using symbolism (chapters 2, 7, and 8) from the reign of Nebuchadnezzar to Cyrus. Daniel 1:17 confirms that <u>Daniel had understanding in **ALL** visions</u> which also included the Historic-Prophetic Outline of the Fourth (literal) Vision in Daniel 10-12:4.

"ten times better" — in the short period of just ten days, the effects of "an indulged appetite" was obvious in the other captives, magicians, and astrologers.

DAN 6:28 So this Daniel prospered in the reign of Darius, and in the reign of <u>Cyrus</u> the Persian.

DAN 10:1 In the third year of <u>Cyrus</u> king of Persia a thing [vision] was revealed unto Daniel, whose name was called Belteshazzar.

Note: Daniel Chapter 1 is a testimony that one does not require flesh meat or rich food to have a strong body or a sound mind. The primary motive with Daniel was to glorify God. His life illustrates the response that came from a sanctified character. Fidelity to God's way in the Scriptures kept Daniel and his three friends faithful witnesses for the God of heaven; <u>and as they honored God, God honored them</u>. (Also see 1 SAM 2:30.) This chapter also indicates that the deep prophecies of Daniel will be better understood when care is observed in eating the best available foods.

A Brief History: The Babylonian Kingdom

The Babylonian Kingdom rose to power under a general who became King Nabopolassar.

Rulers Over the Kingdom

604 BC	Nabopolassar, father of Nebuchadnezzar
604 — 562 BC	Nebuchadnezzar
562 — 560 BC	Amel-Marduk
560 — 555 BC	Neriglissar, son-in-law of Amel-Marduk
555 — 555 BC	Labashi-Marduk, (for 9-months)
556 — 540 BC	Nabonidus (Belshazzar's father)
553 — 540 BC	Nabonidus with Belshazzar
540 — 538 BC	Belshazzar reigns alone to the end of the kingdom

Study Notes for Daniel 1

Daniel 1 Ruling Kingdom	Petition	Persons Involved	1st Death Decree	Deliverance
King Nebuchadnezzar of Babylon	ALL in the king's court were to eat the food and drink the wine from the king's table.	Melzar, chief of the eunuchs, was to serve the four Hebrews food from the king's table. The Hebrews refused this food.	Melzar felt he would receive the death decree by being beheaded if he did not follow the king's instructions.	At the end of ten days, the Hebrews were fairer and fatter than the rest that ate the king's food. Melzar continued to serve this simple diet.

RECAPPING STRUCTURE CHART

Four Historic-Prophetic Outlines of Earthly Kingdoms in the Book of Daniel

The "Symbols" of Daniel 2, 7, and 8 (Image, Beasts, and Horns) and the "Literal" Kings of Daniel 11
Consistently Refer to the Progression of Persecuting Kingdoms Surrounding God's People.

Daniel 2 Symbolic	**Daniel 7** Symbolic	**Daniel 8** Symbolic	**Daniel 11-12:4** Litera
Vision 1 - Prophetic Outline 1	**Vision 2** - Prophetic Outline 2	**Vision 3** - Prophetic Outline 3	**Vision 4** - Prophetic Outline

Kingdom #1 BABYLON 606 — 538 BC

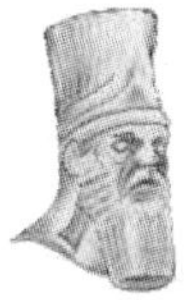

DAN 2:38

Gold Head

Kingdom #2 MEDO-PERSIA 538 — 331 BC

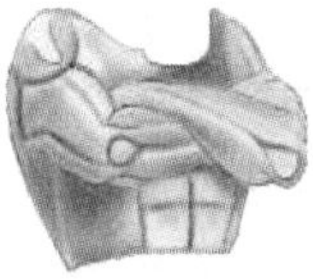

DAN 2:39

Silver Breast & Arms

Kingdom #3 GREECE 331 — 168 BC

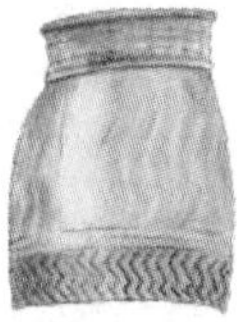

DAN 2:39

Brass Belly & Thighs

Kingdom #4 ROME (Pagan Imperial) 168 BC — AD 476

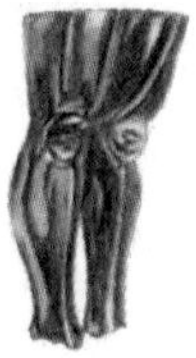

DAN 2:40

Iron Legs

Kingdom #5

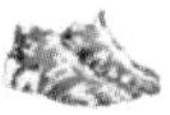

DAN 2:41

Feet Part of Iron

Kingdom #6

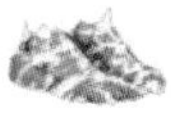

DAN 2:41

Feet Part of Clay

Kingdom #7

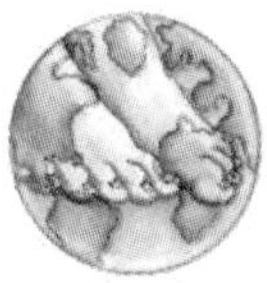

DAN 2:42-43

Toes of Iron & Clay

This chart shows the recapping of kingdoms in a "vertical" format. See page 13 for definition of recapping.

DANIEL
The Story of the Rise and Fall of Earthly Kingdoms

CHAPTER 2

**HEAVENLY SCENE
VISION ONE**
(Symbolic Image of
Metals and Clay)

*Nebuchadnezzar —
King of Babylon
Receives an Heavenly Vision
Through a Dream*

1 And in the second year of the reign of Nebuchadnezzar Nebuchadnezzar dreamed dreams, wherewith <u>his spirit was troubled,</u> and <u>his sleep brake from him.</u>

Introduction: See **The Structure of Daniel** Chart on page 47 for Vision One. The first **Heavenly Scene** in Daniel's Book is given to King Nebuchadnezzar in a dream, although he could not recall any of it. In Daniel 2:19 the same Heavenly Scene was given to Daniel during the night. *This Heavenly Scene is not revealed (to the reader) until verses 31-36,* where Daniel describes the vision to the king and then reveals that there are four earthly kingdoms in the **Historic-Prophetic Outline.** Beginning in verse 36, Daniel gives the interpretation of the dream that extends from 606 BC to the Stone Kingdom at the Second Coming of Christ. (In datable time, this Outline extends as far as AD 476.) The remaining three visions in Daniel's Book, recap and build upon this First Vision extending datable time forward in each vision. Note: The Recapping Structure Chart on page 28 will build with each additional vision.

**King Nebuchadnezzar is Given
an Heavenly Vision
in the Form of a Night Dream**

<u>Verse 1</u>

Note: Kings and Pharaohs of all ages had dreams (believed to be from their gods), for which they wanted interpretations. Also, their sleep was disturbed by these troubling dreams. Some examples from the Bible are:

"his spirit was troubled"

GEN 41:8 And it came to pass in the morning that <u>his</u> [Pharaoh of Egypt] <u>spirit was troubled</u>; and he sent and called for all the magicians of Egypt, and all the wise men thereof: and Pharaoh told them his dream; but there was none that could interpret them unto Pharaoh.

EX 7:11 Then Pharaoh also called the wise men and the sorcerers: now the magicians of Egypt, they also did in like manner with their enchantments.

"his sleep brake from him"

EST 6:1 On that night <u>could not the king</u> [Ahasuerus] <u>sleep</u>, and he commanded to bring the book of records of the chronicles; and they were read before the king.

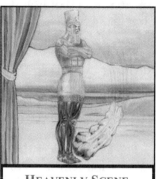

HEAVENLY SCENE
DAN 2:1, 19
GOLD HEAD
SILVER BREAST & ARMS
BRASS BELLY & THIGHS
IRON LEGS
CLAY & IRON —
FEET & TOES

Note: Only God pulls back the curtain of time to reveal future events. The thumbnail above will be used to build each step in the vision following the "Structure" guide given on page 47. Page 46 gives helpful information on how the Structure Chart is set up according to the way Daniel wrote his Book.

Prophetic Keys #15-16
The vision the king had in his dream was of a *symbolic* image — something that was not real. Later, in Daniel 4, the king had a dream that was *literal,* of which he could recall every detail, but the application to him was not known.

DANIEL

The Story of the Rise and Fall of Earthly Kingdoms

King Nebuchadnezzar
Asks the Chaldeans
to Interpret his Dream

2 Then the king commanded to call the <u>magicians</u>, and the <u>astrologers</u>, and the <u>sorcerers</u>, and the Chaldeans, for to shew the king his dreams. So they came and stood before the king.

3 And the king said unto them, I have dreamed a dream, and my spirit was <u>troubled</u> to know the dream.

4 Then spake the Chaldeans to the king in <u>Syriack</u>, O king, live for ever: tell thy servants the dream, and we will shew the interpretation.

5 The king answered and said to the Chaldeans, The <u>thing</u> [prophetic vision] is gone from me: if ye will not make known unto me the dream, with the interpretation thereof, ye shall be cut in pieces, and your houses shall be made a dunghill.

6 But if ye shew the dream, and the interpretation thereof, ye shall receive of me gifts and rewards and great honour: therefore shew me the dream, and the interpretation thereof.

7 They answered again and said, Let the king tell his servants the dream, and we will shew the interpretation of it.

King Nebuchadnezzar Decides to Call the Chaldeans to Show him the Dream

Verse 2

Strong's Concordance Definitions

"magicians" — OT#2748 <u>a horoscopist</u> (as drawing magical lines or circles): KJV - magician.

"astrologers" — OT#825 to lisp, i.e. <u>practice enchantment</u>; a conjurer: KJV - astrologer. (DEUT 18:10; JER 27:9)

"sorcerers" — OT#3784 to whisper a spell, i.e. to inchant or <u>practise magic</u>: KJV - sorcerer, use <u>witch craft</u>. (EX 7:ll; 22:18; MAL 3:5)

Thought Questions
- Who are the *magicians, astrologers, and sorcerers* of today?
- Has this system of societies traveled down through time from Ancient Babylon to modern Spiritual Babylon?
- Do world leaders of today investigate similar plans of strategy?
- Is this the source of true wisdom and knowledge?

Verses 3-5

Strong's Concordance Definitions

"troubled" — OT#6470 to tap, i.e. beat regularly; hence to impel or <u>agitate</u>: KJV - move, trouble.

"Syriack" — OT#762 KJV - in the Syrian language (tongue), in Syriac.

"thing" — OT#4406 a word, command, discourse, or <u>subject</u>: KJV - commandment, matter, thing. word. (In this case, the prophecy itself.)

The Chaldeans Ask the King to tell Them the Unknown Dream

DANIEL

The Story of the Rise and Fall of Earthly Kingdoms

The King Becomes
Frustrated
With the Chaldeans

8 The king answered and said, I know of certainty that ye would gain the time, because ye see the thing [subject matter of the prophetic vision] **is gone from me.**

9 But if ye will not make known unto me the dream, there is but one decree for you: for ye have prepared lying and corrupt words to speak before me, till the time be changed: therefore tell me the dream, and I shall know that ye can shew me the interpretation thereof.

The Chaldeans Could Not
Interpret the Dream

10 The Chaldeans answered before the king, and said, There is not a man upon the earth that can shew the king's matter: therefore there is no king, lord, nor ruler, that asked such things at any magician, or astrologer, or Chaldean.

11 And it is a rare thing that the king requireth, and there is none other that can shew it before the king, except the gods, whose dwelling is not with flesh.

A Death Decree
Goes Forth From the King

12 For this cause the king was angry and very furious, and commanded to destroy all the wise men of Babylon.

The Chaldeans Seek a
Way to Gain Some Time to
Prepare an Interpretation

GEN 18:14   Is any thing too hard for the LORD?

The Second Death Decree in Daniel's Book
was for ALL the Wise Men of Babylon

PROV 28:15   As a roaring lion, and a ranging bear; so is a wicked ruler over the poor people.

Daniel 2 Ruling Kingdom	Petition	Persons Involved	2nd Death Decree	Deliverance
King Nebuchadnezzar of Babylon	ALL wise men were commissioned to tell the king's dream and the interpretation thereof.	Wise men of Babylon, Daniel, and his three Hebrew friends.	Those that could not give the dream and the interpretation were to be slain.	God revealed the interpretation to Daniel and ALL the wise men were delivered from the death decree.

*Daniel and his Friends
Face a
Death Decree*

13 And <u>the decree went forth that the wise men should be slain</u>; and they sought Daniel and his fellows to be slain.

14 Then Daniel answered with counsel and wisdom to Arioch the captain of the king's guard, which was gone forth to slay the wise men of Babylon:

15 He answered and said to Arioch the king's captain, Why is the decree so hasty from the king? Then Arioch made the thing known to Daniel.

16 Then Daniel went in, and desired of the king that he would give him time, and that he would shew the king the interpretation.

17 Then Daniel went to his house, and made the thing known to Hananiah, Mishael, and Azariah, his companions:

*Daniel and his Friends
Ask God for Help*

18 That they would desire mercies of the God of heaven concerning this <u>secret</u>; that Daniel and his fellows should not perish with the rest of the wise men of Babylon.

Verses 13-17

Note: Daniel and his friends were classified as "wise men" of Babylon. Therefore, they were included in the death decree of King Nebuchadnezzar. Daniel, Hananiah, Mishael, and Azariah desired the mercies of the God of Heaven that they should not perish.

In the latter days, just before Jesus comes, God's righteous people will find themselves under accusations and death penalties and will face the final confrontation of a death decree. Prayer is the only resource at such a time. (Note the following Scriptures.)

*God's People Face
Death Decrees*

MATT 24:9 Then shall they deliver you up to be afflicted, <u>and shall kill you</u>.

DAN 3:20 And he commanded the most mighty men that were in his army to bind Shadrach, Meshach, and Abed-nego, and to cast them into the <u>burning fiery furnace</u>.

"Why is the decree so hasty?"

DAN 6:16 Then the king commanded, and they brought Daniel, and cast him into the <u>den of lions</u>.

EST 3:13 And the letters were sent by posts into all the king's provinces, <u>to destroy, to kill, and to cause to perish, all Jews</u>, both young and old, little children and women, in one day.

REV 13:15 And he had power to give life unto the image of the beast, that the image of the beast should both speak, and cause that as many as would not worship the image of the beast <u>should be killed</u>.

Verse 18

"secret" — *Strong's* OT#7328 meaning to attenuate, i.e. hide; <u>a mystery</u>: KJV - secret.

**Daniel and his Friends
Petition the Mercies of God**

DANIEL

The Story of the Rise and Fall of Earthly Kingdoms

Daniel Receives an Answer From God

19 Then was the secret revealed unto Daniel in a night vision. Then Daniel blessed the God of heaven.

Daniel Praises God

20 Daniel answered and said, Blessed be the name of God for ever and ever: for wisdom and might are his:

21 And he changeth the times and the seasons: he removeth kings, and setteth up kings: he giveth wisdom unto the wise, and knowledge to them that know understanding:

22 He revealeth the deep and secret things: he knoweth what is in the darkness, and the light dwelleth with him.

23 I thank thee, and praise thee, O thou God of my fathers, who hast given me wisdom and might, and hast made known unto me now what we desired of thee: for thou hast now made known unto us the king's matter.

Daniel Interprets Nebuchadnezzar's Dream

24 Therefore Daniel went in unto Arioch, whom the king had ordained to destroy the wise men of Babylon: he went and said thus unto him; Destroy not the wise men of Babylon: bring me in before the king, and I will shew unto the king the interpretation.

25 Then Arioch brought in Daniel before the king in haste and said thus unto him, I have found a man of the captives of Judah, that will make known unto the king the interpretation.

Verse 19

JOB 33:15-16 In a dream, in a vision of the night, when deep sleep falleth upon men, in slumberings upon the bed; 16 Then he openeth the ears of men, and sealeth their instruction.

NUM 12:6 And he said, Hear now my words: If there be a prophet among you, I the LORD will make myself known unto him in a vision, and will speak unto him in a dream.

Verse 20

PS 115:18 But we will bless the LORD from this time forth and for evermore. Praise the LORD.

Verse 21

JOB 12:18 He looseth the bond of kings, and girdeth their loins with a girdle.

PS 75:6-7 For promotion cometh neither from the east, nor from the west, nor from the south. 7 But God is the judge: he putteth down one, and setteth up another.

JER 27:5 I have made the earth, the man and the beast that are upon the ground, by my great power and by my outstretched arm, and have given it unto whom it seemed meet unto me.

JAMES 1:5 If any of you lack wisdom, let him ask of God, that giveth to all men liberally, and upbraideth not; and it shall be given him.

Verse 22

PS 25:14 The secret of the LORD is with them that fear him; and he will shew them his covenant.

JAMES 1:17 Every good gift and every perfect gift is from above, and cometh down from the Father.

Verse 23

AMOS 3:7 Surely the LORD GOD will do nothing, but he revealeth his secret unto his servants the prophets.

Daniel Gives Praise and Thanks to the God of Heaven

Note: Through a night vision, Daniel received the Heavenly Vision and the Interpretation from God.

Daniel is Brought Before the King

Reminder: See **The Structure of Daniel** Chart on page 47. Vision One is now moving from the **Heavenly Scene** to the **Interlude Question**. The **Interlude** is an interruption between the **Heavenly Scene** and the **Historic-Prophetic Outline**. This **Interlude Question** is addressed in Daniel 2:26 — "What is the secret of the dream?" The answer to this question will be given <u>after</u> the Historic-Prophetic Outline.

INTERLUDE QUESTION VISION ONE

"What is the Secret of the Dream?"

26 The king answered and said to Daniel, whose name was Belteshazzar, <u>Art thou able to make known unto me the dream which I have seen, and the</u> [secret] <u>interpretation thereof?</u>

Daniel Gives God the Credit

27 Daniel answered in the presence of the king, and said, The secret which the king hath demanded cannot the wise men, the astrologers, the magicians, the soothsayers, shew unto the king;

28 But <u>there is a God in heaven that revealeth secrets</u>, and maketh known to the king Nebuchadnezzar what shall be in the latter days. Thy dream, and the visions of thy head upon thy bed, are these;

29 As for thee, O king, thy thoughts came into thy mind upon thy bed, what should come to pass hereafter: and he that revealeth secrets maketh known to thee what shall come to pass.

30 But as for me, this secret is not revealed to me for any wisdom that I have more than any living, but for their sakes that shall make known the interpretation to the king, and that thou mightest know the thoughts of thy heart.

> **INTERLUDE QUESTION**
> **DAN 2:26**
> **WHAT IS THE SECRET OF THE DREAM?**

Note: The Interlude Question always breaks the Heavenly Scene from the interpretation presented in the Outline. King Nebuchadnezzar's question is answered at the end of the Outline. Review the information on page 46.

HEAVENLY SCENE
DAN 2:1, 19
GOLD HEAD
SILVER BREAST & ARMS
BRASS BELLY & THIGHS
IRON LEGS
CLAY & IRON —
FEET & TOES

INTERLUDE QUESTION
DAN 2:26
WHAT IS THE SECRET OF THE DREAM?

<u>Verse 28</u>

GEN 40:8   And they said unto him, We have dreamed a dream, and there is no interpreter of it. And Joseph said unto them, <u>Do not interpretations belong to God</u>? tell me them, I pray you.

AMOS 4:13   For, lo, he … declareth unto man what is his thought … The LORD, The God of hosts, is his name.

Daniel Informs the King that the Thoughts in his Head Came Through a Dream From the God in Heaven

DANIEL

The Story of the Rise and Fall of Earthly Kingdoms

Daniel Reveals the Heavenly Vision Given to Nebuchadnezzar in a Dream

31 Thou, O king, sawest, and behold a great image. This great image, whose brightness was excellent, stood before thee; and the form thereof was terrible.

32 This image's head was of fine gold, his breast and his arms of silver, his belly and his thighs of brass,

33 His legs of iron, his feet part of iron and part of clay.

34 Thou sawest till that a stone was cut out without hands, which smote the image upon his feet that were of iron and clay, and brake them to pieces.

35 Then was the iron, the clay, the brass, the silver, and the gold, broken to pieces together, and became like the chaff of the summer threshingfloors; and the wind carried them away, that no place was found for them: and the stone that smote the image became <u>a great mountain, and filled the whole earth</u>.

Verses 31-35

Prophetic Key #16 The description of this image is given in "symbolic language." This image was a symbol of a "word picture" that was NOT real.

Daniel Describes the Vision

Prophetic Key #14 Daniel explains the Heavenly Scene to the King. The image was symbolic, containing different metals and clay. The Bible established the interpretation for the first kingdom. Secular history will confirm the interpretation of the reamining components.

Prophetic Key #7 Prophecy is "history written in advance." As time moves forward, the different parts of the image are explained through an application to historical events.

Verse 35

ISA **2:2** And it shall come to pass in the last days, that <u>the mountain of the LORD'S house shall be established in the top of the mountains</u>, and shall be exalted above the hills; and all nations shall flow unto it.

ISA **57:13** When thou criest, let thy companies deliver thee; but the wind shall carry them all away; vanity shall take them: but he that putteth his trust in me shall possess the land, and shall inherit my holy mountain.

Reminder: See **The Structure of Daniel** Chart on page 47. Following the **Interlude Question**, Daniel 2:36 begins the **Historic-Prophetic Outline** of the First Vision. The interpretation of the **Heavenly Scene** is given in this **Historic-Prophetic Outline** which reveals the first four (historic) earthly kingdoms surrounding God's people. This Outline extends the time of earthly kingdoms from 606 BC to AD 476. The vision closes with the Second Coming of Jesus and His heavenly kingdom.

HISTORIC-PROPHETIC OUTLINE
VISION ONE

*The Dream Interpreted —
the First Historic-Prophetic
Outline Begins*

36 This is the dream; and we will tell the interpretation thereof before the king.

37 Thou, O king, art a king of kings: for the God of heaven hath given thee a kingdom, power, and strength, and glory.

38 And wheresoever the children of men dwell, the beasts of the field and the fowls of the heaven hath he given into thine hand, and hath made thee ruler over them all. <u>Thou art this head of gold</u>.

39 And after thee shall arise another kingdom inferior to thee, and another third kingdom of brass, which shall bear rule over all the earth.

40 And the fourth kingdom shall be strong as iron: forasmuch as iron breaketh in pieces and subdueth all things: and as iron that breaketh all these, shall it break in pieces and bruise.

Prophetic Key #10 Verses 38-40 are kept in order which establishes the order of the earthly kingdoms for the First Historic-Prophetic Outline.

HISTORIC-PROPHETIC OUTLINE
DAN 2:36-43
BABYLON
MEDO-PERSIA
GREECE
ROME (PAGAN IMPERIAL)
OUTLINE EXTENDS TO:
AD 476

<u>Verses 36-40</u>

Note: Daniel begins to give the Historic-Prophetic interpretation for the Heavenly Scene that was given to King Nebuchadnezzar in a dream. See the following page for the interpretation of the symbolic image.

<u>Verse 38</u>

Prophetic Key #17
SYMBOL: … image's head was of fine gold. (vs 32)
DECODING: <u>Thou</u> [King Nebuchadnezzar] <u>art this head of gold</u>. (vs 38)
APPLICATION: The **gold head** represents the First Kingdom of **Babylon**.

HEAVENLY SCENE
DAN 2:1, 19
GOLD HEAD
SILVER BREAST & ARMS
BRASS BELLY & THIGHS
IRON LEGS
CLAY & IRON — FEET & TOES

INTERLUDE QUESTION
DAN 2:26
WHAT IS THE SECRET OF THE DREAM?

HISTORIC-PROPHETIC OUTLINE
DAN 2:36-43
BABYLON
MEDO-PERSIA
GREECE
ROME (PAGAN IMPERIAL)
OUTLINE EXTENDS TO:
AD 476

Note:
- Through the Bible, <u>Vision One reveals only **the first** earthly kingdom</u> in the Book of Daniel. Secular history and the following visions will add the next kingdoms to this Prophetic Outline using Prophetic Key #13.
- Jesus lived and died during the reign of the fourth earthly kingdom — Pagan Imperial Rome.

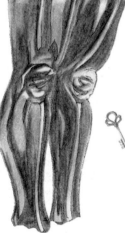

1ˢᵗ KINGDOM

Gold Head —
BABYLON

606-538 BC

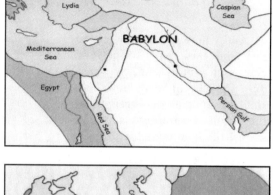

2ⁿᵈ KINGDOM

Silver Breast
& Arms —
MEDO-PERSIA

538-331 BC

3ʳᵈ KINGDOM

Brass Belly
& Thighs —
GREECE

331-168 BC

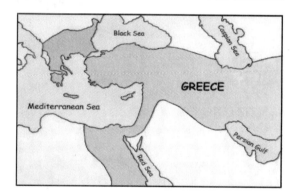

4ᵗʰ KINGDOM

Iron Legs —
ROME
(Pagan Imperial)

168 BC-AD **476**

Prophetic Key #11 Daniel reveals Babylon as the first earthly kingdom. Secular history reveals Medo-Persia, Greece, and Pagan Imperial Rome as the next three earthly kingdoms. These kingdoms align with the order of secular historical events following the decoding process through the use of **Prophetic Key #17**.

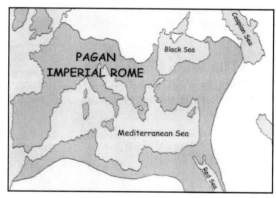

Prophetic Key #12 Each part of the Outline of earthly kingdoms has <u>moved forward in time</u>.

37

*Rome is Broken Up
by Ten Barbarous Tribes
(AD 476)*

41 And whereas thou sawest the feet and toes, part of potters' clay, and part of iron, <u>the kingdom shall be divided</u>; but there shall be in it of the strength of the iron, forasmuch as thou sawest the iron mixed with miry clay.

Verse 41

"the kingdom shall be divided" — By AD 476, the *iron kingdom* of Pagan Imperial Rome was broken up into ten divisions by the surrounding barbarous tribes as noted on the following map.

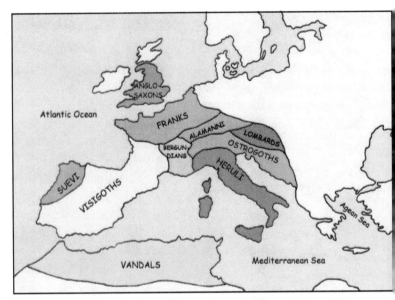

The Ten Divisions of Pagan Imperial Rome by AD 476
(The Outline of four earthly kingdoms stops at the above date.
The following visions extend prophecy beyond this date.)

Note: These ten divisions of Pagan Imperial Rome were the tools God used for the transition from the Fourth to the Fifth Kingdom in the Second Vision of Daniel 7. Just as the Fourth Kingdom was diverse (DAN 7:7), the fifth earthly kingdom is also diverse (DAN 7:24) from the preceding four kingdoms.

Feet — part of "iron."

Note: In the First Vision of Daniel 2, only the first four kingdoms are revealed and given specific mention.

Daniel 7 will introduce the fifth earthly kingdom which aligns with the *iron* in the feet.

Feet — part of "clay."

Daniel 8 will introduce the sixth earthly kingdom and explain how it attempts to align with the *clay* in the feet.

DANIEL

The Story of the Rise and Fall of Earthly Kingdoms

*The "Toes" Just Before
the Establishment of
the Stone Kingdom
of Jesus Christ*

42 And as the toes of the feet were part of iron, and part of clay, so the kingdom shall be partly strong, and partly broken.

43 And whereas thou sawest iron mixed with miry clay, (they shall mingle themselves with the seed of men: but they shall not cleave one to another, even as iron is not mixed with clay).

Verses 42-43

Note: These verses address the *toes* which are the last part of the image — designating the very "end of time" just before the Stone Kingdom of Jesus Christ is established.

Toes — part of "iron"
and part of "clay."

Note:

The "iron and clay" in the <u>toes</u> symbolize the very end of time. Daniel 11 and Revelation 17 will interpret the fuller significance for endtime events.

Interesting Notes About the Image

- The order of the metals in the image went from "most valuable" to "least valuable." Clay is of the "earth" as the metals are, but has <u>little</u> value and is very weak.
- Daniel 2:38 mentions that the following rising kingdoms after Babylon would be inferior.
- Each succeeding kingdom grew larger and extended further west in an effort to be a ruling "world kingdom."
- None of the kingdoms addressed in Daniel's Book are "world empires." They were only earthly kingdoms that ruled over God's people. Often God's people endured severe persecution from these earthly kingdoms.

Reminder: See **The Structure of Daniel** Chart on page 47. Following the **Historic-Prophetic Outline** of the First Vision is the **Answer** given in Daniel 2:44 to the **Interlude Question** of Daniel 2:26. The answer to the "secret of the dream" is that the "God of heaven will consume all the former kingdoms."

ANSWER TO QUESTION

("What is the Secret of the Dream?")

VISION ONE

"God of Heaven Consumes All These Kingdoms!"

44 And in the days of <u>these kings</u> shall the God of heaven set up a kingdom, which shall never be destroyed: and the kingdom shall not be left to other people, but it shall break in pieces and consume all these kingdoms, and it shall stand for ever.

> **ANSWER TO QUESTION**
> **DAN 2:44**
> **GOD OF HEAVEN CONSUMES ALL THESE KINGDOMS!**
>
> **ENDTIME EVENT**
> **DAN 2:45**
> **"STONE KINGDOM"**
> **SECOND COMING OF JESUS**

<u>Verse 44</u>

The iron kingdom in verse 40 extends the Historic-Prophetic Outline to AD 476. In this chapter, Daniel does not specifically mention any future kingdoms. Between verses 40 and 44 there is a large gap of time where no information is given for the time period from AD 476 to the Stone Kingdom of Jesus' Second Coming. The next three visions will add all the needed information that occurs during this gap of time.

"these kings" — information will be given in Daniel 11 and Revelation 17 regarding who "these kings" are and the proper timeframe.

🔑 **Prophetic Key #7** As time moves forward, prophecy unfolds and is clearly revealed.

Prophetic Key #13 The following prophetic visions in Daniel 7-12 will reveal information on future kingdoms. Dates will be established from secular historical data.

HEAVENLY SCENE
DAN 2:1, 19
GOLD HEAD
SILVER BREAST & ARMS
BRASS BELLY & THIGHS
IRON LEGS
CLAY & IRON —
FEET & TOES

INTERLUDE QUESTION
DAN 2:26
WHAT IS THE SECRET OF THE DREAM?

HISTORIC-PROPHETIC OUTLINE
DAN 2:36-43
BABYLON
MEDO-PERSIA
GREECE
ROME (PAGAN IMPERIAL)
OUTLINE EXTENDS TO:
AD 476

ANSWER TO QUESTION
DAN 2:44
GOD OF HEAVEN CONSUMES ALL THESE KINGDOMS!

ENDTIME EVENT
DAN 2:45
"STONE KINGDOM"
SECOND COMING OF JESUS

Reminder: (Continued) The **Endtime Event** is the establishment of the Heavenly Kingdom of Jesus through the arrival of the Stone Kingdom. This is when God's plan to save His people will be fully realized. (Each section in the thumbnail, as seen on page 40, has been completed in an orderly manner following the sequence of verses in Daniel 2.)

ENDTIME EVENT
VISION ONE

God Will Set Up
An Heavenly Kingdom
*Through **Jesus Christ***
That Lasts Forever

45 Forasmuch as thou sawest that the stone was cut out of the mountain without hands, and that it brake in pieces the iron, the brass, the clay, the silver, and the gold; the great God hath made known to the king what shall come to pass hereafter: and the dream is certain, and the interpretation thereof sure.

*The **End** of the First*
Historic-Prophetic Outline

<u>Verse 45</u>

<u>ALL the kings</u> of the earth (from verse 44) will be destroyed by the Stone Kingdom. Revelation 17 will provide further details. Consider the following Scriptures:

ISA 60:12 For the nation and kingdom that will not serve thee shall perish; yea, those nations shall be utterly wasted.

PS 2:9 Thou shalt break them with a rod of iron; thou shalt dash them in pieces like a potter's vessel.

ISA 2:2 And it shall come to pass in the last days, that the mountain of the LORD'S house shall be established in the top of the mountains.

Prophetic Key #29 The Historic-Prophetic Outline of earthly kingdoms ends with the establishment of Christ's kingdom. No indication as to the day and hour of this great event is given.

MATT 24:36 But of that day and hour knoweth no man, no, not the angels of heaven, but my Father only.

General Review and Theme of Vision One: "Christ our King"
- Daniel 2 reviewed the rise and fall of nations and reached its climax with the Second Coming of Jesus represented by the Stone Kingdom.

*"Tidy-Up" Verses for
Vision One*

46 Then the king Nebuchadnezzar fell upon his face, and worshipped Daniel, and commanded that they should offer an oblation and sweet odours unto him.

*King Nebuchadnezzar Praises
the God of Heaven*

47 The king answered unto Daniel, and said, Of a truth it is, that your God is a God of gods, and a Lord of kings, and a revealer of secrets, seeing thou couldest reveal this secret.

*King Nebuchadnezzar
Honors Daniel*

48 Then the king made Daniel a great man, and gave him many great gifts, and made him ruler over the whole province of Babylon, and chief of the governors over all the wise men of Babylon.

49 Then Daniel requested of the king, and he set Shadrach, Meshach, and Abed-nego, over the affairs of the province of Babylon: but Daniel sat in the gate of the king.

Verses 46-47

Prophetic Key #30 The last four verses of this chapter are noted as "tidy-up" verses. These verses indicate that the Historic-Prophetic Outline is completely finished and there is nothing more to be added.

The King Worships Daniel

Verses 48-49

GEN 41:40 Thou shalt be over my house, and according unto thy word shall all my people be ruled: only in the throne will I be greater than thou.

DAN 12:3 And they that be wise shall shine as the brightness of the firmament; and they that turn many to righteousness as the stars for ever and ever.

Prophetic Key #1 Prophetic interpretation is an exact science. "Hermeneutic" rules and principles must be used carefully and consistently for the correct interpretation of all prophecy.

**The King Honors Daniel
and his Friends**

"Hermeneutics" — The science of discovering and stating the rules which govern Bible study to determine the meaning that God intends for us to know.

A Biblical Hermeneutic Principle

Bible Prophecy Focuses Around the People of God

Until the time of Christ, Bible prophecy centered on Israel. Since the ascension of Christ, prophecy revolves around worldwide Christianity, and God's remnant people defined by Revelation 12:17.

Review: Babylon, Medo-Persia, Greece and Pagan Imperial Rome were not "World" or "Universal" kingdoms; but rather, were kingdoms dominating Israel's region of the old world affecting the work and well-being of God's people during their appointed time in history.

Helpful Points to Understand the Structure of Prophecy

(The following points on this page will be helpful for understanding the
general review of Outline One on the next two pages.)

1. Every vision will <u>reveal and describe kingdoms</u> that affect God's people.

2. Every vision <u>moves forward in time</u> within the context of verses.

3. Every vision (after Vision One) will give <u>additional information</u> either <u>about</u> "<u>persecutors</u>" of God's people, <u>or</u> "<u>timelines</u>" that affect God's people.

4. Every vision is given within <u>one major line of prophecy</u> from 606 BC to the establishment of Christ's Kingdom.

5. Every vision extends to <u>the establishment of Christ's kingdom OR to the very eve of Christ's Second Coming</u>.

6. After Vision One, the Historic-Prophetic Outline in the following three visions consistently <u>extends time further towards the establishment of Christ's kingdom</u>.

7. In every vision, the Historic-Prophetic Outline is written using either "<u>symbolic language</u>" or "<u>literal language</u>." **Prophetic Keys** (#22 to #27 on pages 20-21) give an understanding for interpreting any timelines that may be given within <u>the</u> Historic-Prophetic Outline. Timelines given within "<u>symbolic prophetic outlines</u>" must be interpreted from symbolic to literal time, using the Year-day Computation Principal provided in Numbers 14:34 and Ezekiel 4:6. Timelines within "<u>literal prophetic outlines</u>" do not need any conversion for a proper understanding of the timeline. These concepts will be explained in each individual vision.

Daniel 2 — Review of the Historic-Prophetic Outline in Vision 1

1. Vision 1 uses some symbolic language to introduce a Symbolic Image of Metals and Clay which are from the earth.
2. Vision 1 describes and reveals **Four earthly kingdoms** surrounding God's people.
3. Vision 1 extends from 606 BC to the Establishment of Christ's kingdom in One Major Line of Prophecy.
4. Vision 1 begins with a basic, simple Historic-Prophetic Outline. By the end of the Fourth Vision, content becomes more complex, focused, and established.
5. The symbols in Vision 1 must begin with a Biblical interpretation for at least the first symbol, because the "Bible is its own Interpreter." e.g. Daniel 2:38 "Thou art this head of gold" designates that Babylon was the First Kingdom. This principle establishes the interpretation for the other metals and clay of the statue.
6. The Outline of Vision 1 is decoded according to the same principles of Biblical interpretation and confirmed by secular history. With the aid of secular history, this vision begins the alignment of kingdoms for the following three visions.

   1st **Kingdom** = Gold Head = BABYLON (606 — 538 BC)
   2nd **Kingdom** = Silver Arms = MEDO-PERSIA (538 — 331 BC)
   3rd **Kingdom** = Brass Belly = GREECE (331 — 168 BC)
   4th **Kingdom** = Iron Legs = ROME (Pagan Imperial) (168 BC — AD 476)

   By AD 476 Rome had crumbled into ten Barbarous Divisions.
   (The ten Barbarous Divisions are identified and verified in Daniel 7 as ten Horns.)
   (Vision 1 does not contain any timelines within the Historic-Prophetic Outline.)

   Note: The "toes" will also link to the ten "kings" in Revelation 17:12.

7. **Datable Time:** Vision 1 only extends to AD 476 in **datable time**. Secular history confirms this information. **THEN** there is a <u>large gap</u> of time (from AD 476 to the Stone Kingdom) with no information given in this vision. The following visions will supply the missing information. **Note: Each kingdom has <u>moved forward in time</u> — a concept that cannot be violated in prophecy.**
8. **Emphasis in Vision 1** has been on ROME. This is represented by iron as the hardest metal in the Image. Rome is also the longest reigning and most severe persecuting kingdom that ever surrounded God's people.
9. **Vision 1 Tidy-up Verses:** The Daniel 2:46-49 verses tell us that the Historic-Prophetic Outline is complete.
10. **Endtime Event:** All visions end with something to do with the Second Coming. In Vision 1 the Stone Kingdom is set up.

Prophetic Key #6 The First Vision presents the **structure** that Daniel uses throughout each individual vision. The chart on page 45 provides the **structure** for the first Historic-Prophetic Outline in Daniel.

THE STRUCTURE OF DANIEL'S FIRST OUTLINE
The Rise and Fall of Earthly Kingdoms Surrounding God's People
One Major Line of Prophecy From 606 BC — to the Establishment of Christ's Kingdom

DANIEL 2 (Vision 1 uses some Symbolic language for the following Historic-Prophetic Outline.)
The Symbolic IMAGE with its Metal and Clay components represent the Literal Kingdoms in the Outline.

GOLD HEAD
DAN 2:38

#1 BABYLON
606 — 538 BC

SILVER ARMS
DAN 2:39

#2 MEDO-PERSIA
538 — 331 BC

BRASS BELLY
DAN 2:39

#3 GREECE
331 — 168 BC

IRON LEGS
DAN 2:40

#4 ROME
(Pagan Imperial)
168 BC — AD 476

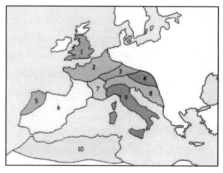

10 Divisions of Rome by AD 476

1.	Anglo-Saxons	6.	Visigoths
2.	Franks	7.	Burgundians
3.	Alamanni	8.	Heruli
4.	Lombards	9.	Ostrogoths
5.	Seuvi	10.	Vandals

Vision One
Time extends from
606 BC — AD 476

No Timelines
in this Vision.

IRON & CLAY
DAN 2:41-44

FEET & TOES
Future Kingdoms
and Kings

"Stone Kingdom"
of Jesus'
Second Coming
DAN 2:44-45

VISION #

1

45

Introduction

The first section of **"The Structure of Daniel" Chart** is found on page 47. In each vision, the Structure Chart will be the "roadmap" giving guidance and clarity while studying the four Heavenly Visions and their Outlines. Along with the **Prophetic Keys,** this chart is another important **KEY** to understanding the structure of the visions that Daniel was given. Each vision reveals God's plan to save His people from earthly persecuting rulers, and ultimately from this sinful earth at the end of time. All visions follow the Structure Chart in a systematic way, beginning first with the Heavenly Scene. Next, the Scriptures will address an Interlude Question. The Interlude is an "interruption" (or a "break") between the Heavenly Scene and the Historic-Prophetic Outline that follows. A Question is asked in the Interlude section, but the Answer is not given until the earthly kingdoms in the Outline are addressed. In the third box, the Historic-Prophetic Outline gives the order of literal earthly kingdoms that had dominion over God's people. The last box has two components: 1) The Answer to the Interlude Question and, 2) The Endtime Event that ushers in the Heavenly Kingdom. Each vision progressively adds more kingdoms and information to the Outline.

All four visions follow the exact same structure. Once this simple structure is understood, it will be easy to recognize the true interpretation of all the visions and the correct placement of all the timelines. Daniel's Structure also gives the foundational knowledge for understanding Revelation.

A large part of this structure is based on a very simple concept taught in the first years of elementary school — called "patterns and sequencing" or "recapping." This manuscript uses the word "recapping." (**Note:** The Book of Revelation has its own unique structure.)

VISION 1–DAN 2

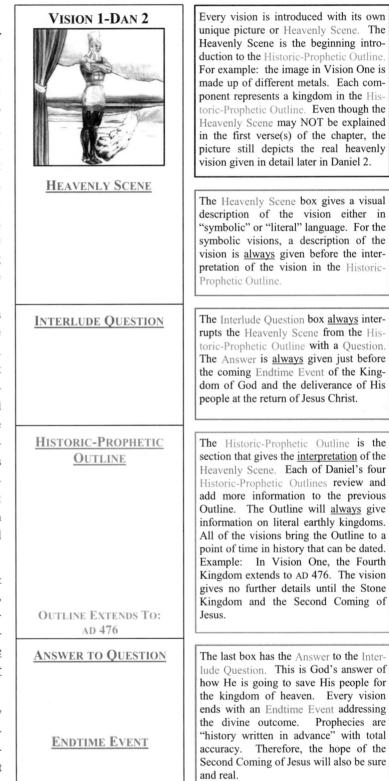

HEAVENLY SCENE

INTERLUDE QUESTION

HISTORIC-PROPHETIC OUTLINE

OUTLINE EXTENDS TO: AD 476

ANSWER TO QUESTION

ENDTIME EVENT

Every vision is introduced with its own unique picture or Heavenly Scene. The Heavenly Scene is the beginning introduction to the Historic-Prophetic Outline. For example: the image in Vision One is made up of different metals. Each component represents a kingdom in the Historic-Prophetic Outline. Even though the Heavenly Scene may NOT be explained in the first verse(s) of the chapter, the picture still depicts the real heavenly vision given in detail later in Daniel 2.

The Heavenly Scene box gives a visual description of the vision either in "symbolic" or "literal" language. For the symbolic visions, a description of the vision is <u>always</u> given before the interpretation of the vision in the Historic-Prophetic Outline.

The Interlude Question box <u>always</u> interrupts the Heavenly Scene from the Historic-Prophetic Outline with a Question. The Answer is <u>always</u> given just before the coming Endtime Event of the Kingdom of God and the deliverance of His people at the return of Jesus Christ.

The Historic-Prophetic Outline is the section that gives the <u>interpretation</u> of the Heavenly Scene. Each of Daniel's four Historic-Prophetic Outlines review and add more information to the previous Outline. The Outline will <u>always</u> give information on literal earthly kingdoms. All of the visions bring the Outline to a point of time in history that can be dated. Example: In Vision One, the Fourth Kingdom extends to AD 476. The vision gives no further details until the Stone Kingdom and the Second Coming of Jesus.

The last box has the Answer to the Interlude Question. This is God's answer of how He is going to save His people for the kingdom of heaven. Every vision ends with an Endtime Event addressing the divine outcome. Prophecies are "history written in advance" with total accuracy. Therefore, the hope of the Second Coming of Jesus will also be sure and real.

THE STRUCTURE OF DANIEL

FOUR VISIONS REVEAL GOD'S PLAN TO SAVE HIS PEOPLE

ne Major Line of Prophecy From 606 BC — to the Establishment of Christ's Kingdom

VISION 1 - DAN 2	VISION 2 - DAN 7	VISION 3 - DAN 8	VISION 4 - DAN 10-12
HEAVENLY SCENE **DAN 2:1, 19** **GOLD HEAD** **ILVER BREAST & ARMS** **BRASS BELLY & THIGHS** **IRON LEGS** **IRON & CLAY —** **FEET & TOES**			
NTERLUDE QUESTION **DAN 2:26** **WHAT IS THE SECRET OF THE DREAM?**			
HISTORIC-PROPHETIC OUTLINE **DAN 2:36-43** **BABYLON** **MEDO-PERSIA** **GREECE** **ROME (PAGAN IMPERIAL)** **OUTLINE EXTENDS TO:** **AD 476**			
NSWER TO QUESTION **DAN 2:44** **GOD OF HEAVEN CONSUMES ALL THESE KINGDOMS!** **ENDTIME EVENT** **DAN 2:45** **"STONE KINGDOM"** **ECOND COMING OF JESUS**			

Note: Only God pulls back the curtain of time in each vision to reveal future events.

CHAPTER 3

*King Nebuchadnezzar's
Counterfeit Image
(Approximate Date: 579 BC)*

1 **Nebuchadnezzar the king made an image of gold, whose height was <u>threescore</u> cubits, and the breadth thereof six cubits: he set it up in the plain of Dura, in the province of Babylon.**

*King Nebuchadnezzar
Demands Patriotism*

2 Then Nebuchadnezzar the king sent to gather together the princes, the governors, and the captains, the judges, the treasurers, the counsellers, the sheriffs, and all the rulers of the provinces, to come to the dedication of the image which Nebuchadnezzar the king had set up.

3 Then the princes, the governors, and captains, the judges, the treasurers, the counsellers, the sheriffs, and all the rulers of the provinces, were gathered together unto the dedication of the image that Nebuchadnezzar the king had set up; and they stood before the image that Nebuchadnezzar had set up.

Note: This chapter introduces a *death decree* for Daniel's three friends who refuse to bow down and worship an image that was set up by King Nebuchadnezzar (a man) in direct defiance of God's plan! Even though these Hebrew young men could not see their way through the "portals of the fiery furnace," their reaction to King Nebuchadnezzar introduced the true Deliverer to all the people on the Plain of Dura that day. At the end of time, God's people will also face a death decree over the issue of worship. Once again, the glory of the Deliverer will be revealed.

Verse 1

Note: King Nebuchadnezzar had a dream of an image that was composed of various metals. His construction of an image made of *gold* symbolized that the Babylonian kingdom would be glorious and stand forever. This was in direct defiance of the divine interpretation given by Daniel in the previous chapter.

"threescore" — meaning "60" — the number which the Babylonian religious system was founded on. Anu, the leading Babylonian god, was also assigned the number 60.

Ps 96:5 For all the gods of the nations are idols: but the LORD made the heavens.

Isa 46:6 They lavish gold out of the bag, and weigh silver in the balance, and hire a goldsmith; and he maketh it a god: they fall down, yea, they worship.

Hos 8:4 They have set up kings, but not by me: they have made princes, and I knew it not: of their silver and their gold have they made them idols, that they may be cut off.

1 Cor 8:4 we know that an idol is nothing in the world, and that there is none other God but one.

Verse 3

Matt 7:13-14 Enter ye in at the strait gate: for wide is the gate, and broad is the way, that leadeth to destruction, and many there be which go in thereat: 14 Because strait is the gate, and narrow is the way, which leadeth unto life, and few there be that find it.

Rev 13:3, 8 And I saw ... all the world wondered after the beast. 8 And all that dwell upon the earth shall worship him, whose names are not written in the book of life of the Lamb.

**The Golden Image
Was Set Up
on the Plain of Dura**

**ALL Were Gathered to
the Image Dedication
Fashioned in the
Likeness of Man**

DANIEL

The Story of the Rise and Fall of Earthly Kingdoms

*King Nebuchadnezzar
Demands Worship*

4 Then an herald cried aloud, To you it is commanded, O people, nations, and languages,

5 That at what time ye hear the sound of the cornet, flute, harp, sackbut, psaltery, dulcimer, and all kinds of musick, ye fall down and worship the golden image that Nebuchadnezzar the king hath set up:

6 And whoso falleth not down and worshippeth shall the same hour be cast into the midst of a burning fiery furnace.

7 Therefore at that time, when all the people heard the sound of the cornet, flute, harp, sackbut, psaltery, and all kinds of musick, all the people, the nations, and the languages, fell down and worshipped the golden image that Nebuchadnezzar the king had set up.

*Daniel's Friends Refuse
to Worship a False God*

8 Wherefore at that time certain Chaldeans came near, and accused the Jews.

*Daniel's Friends
Accused of Sedition*

9 They spake and said to the king Nebuchadnezzar, O king, live for ever.

10 Thou, O king, hast made a decree, that every man that shall hear the sound of the cornet, flute, harp, sackbut, psaltery, and dulcimer, and all kinds of musick, shall fall down and worship the golden image:

*God's People Never Obey
Man's Decrees
Over God's Laws*

DAN 6:7, 9-11 All the presidents of the kingdom … consulted together to establish a royal statute, and to make a firm decree, that whosoever shall ask a petition of any God or man for thirty days, save of thee, O king, he shall be cast into the den of lions. 9 Wherefore king Darius signed the writing and the decree. 10 Now when Daniel knew that the writing was signed … he kneeled upon his knees three times a day, and prayed. 11 Then these men assembled, and found Daniel praying and making supplication before his God.

Verse 8

**Daniel's Jewish Friends Refuse
to Bow Down in Worship**

EST 3:1-2 After these things did king Ahasuerus promote Haman ... 2 And all the king's servants … bowed, and reverenced Haman: for the king had so commanded concerning him. But Mordecai bowed not, nor did him reverence.

Verses 9-10

HOS 7:3 They make the king glad with their wickedness, and the princes with their lies.

**Instruments Orchestrated
the Command to Bow
Down and Worship
the Image**

Note: Daniel 3:1 mentions threescore cubits (60) and six cubits (6) for image dimensions. Verses 5, 10, and 15 list six instruments. Three "six's" can be found linked to literal Babylon that set up an "image for worship." This parallels characteristics of symbolic "Spiritual Babylon" in Revelation 13 that will also set up an "image for worship." Right now events are being orchestrated (in the world) for a "death decree" that will be enforced in the future on those who will not conform to the demands of a counterfeit religion with the number "666."

11 And whoso falleth not down and worshippeth, that he should be cast into the midst of a burning fiery furnace.

12 <u>There are certain Jews whom thou hast set over the affairs of the province of Babylon</u>, Shadrach, Meshach, and Abed-nego; these men, O king, <u>have not regarded thee: they serve not thy gods, nor worship the golden image which thou hast set up</u>.

King Nebuchadnezzar's Rage

13 Then Nebuchadnezzar in his rage and fury commanded to bring Shadrach, Meshach, and Abed-nego. Then they brought these men before the king.

*Nebuchadnezzar Offers
a Second Chance*

14 Nebuchadnezzar spake and said unto them, Is it true, O Shadrach, Meshach, and Abed-nego, do not ye serve my gods, nor worship the golden image which I have set up?

15 Now if ye be ready that at what time ye hear the sound of the cornet, flute, harp, sackbut, psaltery, and dulcimer, and all kinds of musick, ye fall down and worship the image which I have made; well: but if ye worship not, ye shall be cast the same hour into the midst of a burning fiery furnace; and <u>who is that God</u> that shall deliver you out of my hands?

Verse 12

DAN 2:49   and he [King Nebuchadnezzar] <u>set Shadrach, Meshach, and Abed-nego, over the affairs of the province of Babylon.</u>

"Come out of Babylon"

REV 18:4   And I heard another voice from heaven, saying, Come out of her [Babylon], my people, that ye be not partakers of her sins. (See Appendix 3A on page 54.)

"Certain Jews have not regarded thee."

Note: Out of the large multitude that were gathered to this event of dedication to the image, only a remnant of three would not bow down in worship to the image.

Verse 15

*Earthly Rulers Challenge
the Creator God*

EX 5:2   And Pharaoh said, <u>Who is the LORD</u>, that I should obey his voice to let Israel go? I know not the LORD, neither will I let Israel go.

*Daniel's Friends Prove They
Are Loyal to God Alone*

16 Shadrach, Meshach, and Abednego, answered and said to the king, O Nebuchadnezzar, we are not careful to answer thee in this matter,

17 If it be so, our God whom we serve is able to deliver us from the burning fiery furnace, and he will deliver us out of thine hand, O king,

18 But if not, be it known unto thee, O king, that we will not serve thy gods, nor worship the golden image which thou hast set up.

19 Then was Nebuchadnezzar full of fury, and the form of his visage was changed against Shadrach, Meshach, and Abednego: therefore he spake, and commanded that they should heat the furnace one seven times more than it was wont to be heated.

*Daniel's Friends Thrown
Into a Fiery Furnace*

20 And he commanded the most mighty men that were in his army to bind Shadrach, Meshach, and Abed-nego, and to cast them into the burning fiery furnace.

21 Then these men were bound in their coats, their hosen, and their hats, and their other garments, and were cast into the midst of the burning fiery furnace.

Verses 16-19

EX 20:3-5 Thou shalt have no other gods before me. 4 Thou shalt not make unto thee any graven image, or any likeness of any thing that is in heaven above, or that is in the earth beneath, or that is in the water under the earth: 5 Thou shalt not bow down thyself to them, nor serve them: for I the LORD thy God am a jealous God.

MATT 10:19 But when they deliver you up, take no thought how or what ye shall speak: for it shall be given you in that same hour what ye shall speak.

ACTS 20:24 But none of these things move me, neither count I my life dear unto myself, so that I might finish my course with joy, and the ministry, which I have received of the Lord Jesus, to testify the gospel of the grace of God.

*A Future Power Will Also
Speak a "Death Decree"*

REV 13:15 And he had power ... that as many as would not worship [the beast] ... should be killed.

REV 14:7 Fear God, and give glory to him ... and worship him that made heaven, and earth, and the sea, and the fountains of waters.

Verses 20-21

"Our God is able to deliver us."

**The Third Death Decree was for
Daniel's Friends —
Hands Bound for the Fiery Furnace**
(See table on page 52.)

22 Therefore because the king's commandment was urgent, and the furnace exceeding hot, the flame of the fire slew those men that took up Shadrach, Meshach, and Abed-nego.

23 And these three men, Shadrach, Meshach, and Abed-nego, fell down bound into the midst of the burning fiery furnace.

Jesus, "Son of God" was Also in the Furnace

24 Then Nebuchadnezzar the king was astonied, and rose up in haste, and spake, and said unto his counsellers, Did not we cast three men bound into the midst of the fire? They answered and said unto the king, True, O king.

25 He answered and said, Lo, I see four men loose, walking in the midst of the fire, and <u>they have no hurt</u>; and the form of the fourth is like the Son of God.

26 Then Nebuchadnezzar came near to the mouth of the burning fiery furnace, and spake, and said, Shadrach, Meshach, and Abed-nego, ye servants of the most high God, come forth, and come hither. Then Shadrach, Meshach, and Abed-nego, came forth of the midst of the fire.

Verse 23

Ps 33:18-19 Behold, the eye of the LORD is upon them that fear him, upon them that hope in his mercy; 19 To deliver their soul from death.

Ps 91:3-11 Surely he shall deliver thee from the snare of the fowler. 4 He shall cover thee with his feathers, and under his wings shalt thou trust: his truth shall be thy shield and buckler. 5 Thou shalt not be afraid. 6 Nor … for the destruction that wasteth at noonday. 7 … it shall not come nigh thee. 9 Because thou hast made the LORD, which is my refuge, even the most High, thy habitation; 10 There shall no evil befall thee. 11 For he shall give his angels charge over thee, to keep thee in all thy ways.

Verse 25

ISA 43:2 When thou passest … through the fire, <u>thou shalt not be burned</u>; neither shall the flame kindle upon thee.

The "Son of God" Joins Daniel's Friends in the Fiery Furnace

King Nebuchadnezzar Gives a Command to Come out of the Furnace

Daniel 3	Petition	Persons Involved	3rd Death Decree	Deliverance
Ruling Kingdom King Nebuchadnezzar of Babylon	ALL were commissioned to gather to bow down and worship the golden image, set up by a man who demanded worship.	The three Hebrews were confronted with worshipping the true Creator God or worshipping the golden image.	Being thrown into the fiery furnace was the death decree issued for anyone who would not bow down and worship the golden image.	The three Hebrews were delivered from the fiery furnace, without any trace of being in the flames.

*Daniel's Friends
Delivered*

27 And the princes, governors, and captains, and the king's counsellers, being gathered together, saw these men, upon whose bodies <u>the fire had no power</u>, nor was an hair of their head singed, neither were their coats changed, nor the smell of fire had passed on them.

*King Nebuchadnezzar
Honors God*

28 Then Nebuchadnezzar spake, and said, Blessed be the God of Shadrach, Meshach, and Abednego, who hath sent his angel, and delivered his servants that trusted in him, and have changed the king's word, and yielded their bodies, that they might not serve nor worship any god, except their own God.

*King Nebuchadnezzar
Worships the Living God*

29 Therefore I make a decree, That every people, nation, and language, which speak any thing amiss against the God of Shadrach, Meshach, and Abed-nego, shall be cut in pieces, and their houses shall be made a dunghill: because there is no other God that can deliver after this sort.

30 Then the king promoted Shadrach, Meshach, and Abednego, in the province of Babylon.

Verse 27

MARK 16:17-18   And these signs shall follow them that believe ... In my name. 18 They shall take up serpents; and if they drink any deadly thing, it shall not hurt them.

HEB 11:33-34   Who through faith subdued kingdoms, wrought righteousness, obtained promises, stopped the mouths of lions, 34 <u>Quenched the violence of fire</u>, escaped the edge of the sword, out of weakness were made strong.

Verse 28

PS 34:7-9   The angel of the LORD encampeth round about them that fear him, and delivereth them. 8 O taste and see that the LORD is good: blessed is the man that trusteth in him. 9 O fear the LORD, ye his saints: for there is no want to them that fear him.

JER 17:7   Blessed is the man that trusteth in the LORD, and whose hope the LORD is.

Verse 29

ROM 14:11-12   For it is written, As I live, saith the Lord, every knee shall bow to me, and every tongue shall confess to God. 12 So then every one of us shall give account of himself to God.

ISA 45:23   unto me every knee shall bow, every tongue shall swear.

PHIL 2:10-11   That at the name of Jesus every knee should bow, of things in heaven, and things in earth, and things under the earth; 11 And that every tongue should confess that Jesus Christ is Lord, to the glory of God the Father.

Verse 30

REV 5:10   And hast made us unto our God kings and priests: and we shall reign on the earth.

**King Nebuchadnezzar
Honors the True God**

Appendix 3A — "Coming Out" of Babylon

INTRODUCTION

"Entering Into" Babylonian Captivity

Long ago, in approximately 1437 BC, the Lord delivered His people (and a great multitude) out of Egyptian bondage. There in the wilderness, He began to patiently instruct them in the ways of relationship to the true Creator God.

- **EX 19:8** says: "And all the people answered together, and said, All that the LORD hath spoken we will do."

However, this promise did not last very long. Over the centuries, the apostasy of God's people mirrored the ways of the heathen nations around them. In falling back into idolatry, it was impossible for God's people to be a light to the surrounding nations. The Lord sought every means to bring the nation of Israel and Judah out of their state of rebellion. Many prophets predicted the dangers of disobedience to God's law and gave counsel of the soon coming judgment.

- One of these judgments is found in **JER 25:8-9, 11**: "Therefore thus saith the LORD of hosts; Because ye have not heard my words, 9 Behold, I will send and take all the families of the north, saith the LORD, and Nebuchadrezzar the king of Babylon, my servant, and will bring them against this land, and against the inhabitants thereof, and against all these nations round about, and will utterly destroy them, and make them an astonishment, and an hissing, and perpetual desolations. 11 And this whole land shall be a desolation, and an astonishment; and these nations shall serve the king of Babylon seventy years."

- Notice God's promise in **JER 29:10**: "For thus saith the LORD, That after seventy years be accomplished at Babylon I will visit you, and perform my good word toward you, in causing you to return to this place."

God's ultimate call was for His people to "come out of Babylon." This theme is found throughout the Bible and is emphasized in the prophecies of Daniel and Revelation.

There are many examples throughout Scripture where a person or group is called by God to "come out" of various cultures such as the pre-flood world, Ur, Sodom, Egypt, Babylon, etc. Sometimes man heeded God's instruction and was delivered, and other times he refused and reaped the consequences. As these examples in the Bible are examined, passages of Daniel and Revelation come into clear focus.

Daniel is the prophecy. Revelation is the revealing of that prophecy. In Daniel chapter 9, Daniel is looking forward to God's people "coming out" of Babylon. Revelation 18:1-4 presents the same theme for the future endtime scenario. It shoud be of interest to all Christians to know and understand the character of God and what He has planned for the endtime deliverance of His people. Each of the examples in Scripture are there for the express purpose of instructing mankind on how God has delivered His people in the past and how He will deliver them in the future.

- **ECCL 3:15** That which hath been is now; and that which is to be hath already been; and God requireth that which is past.

As the following word pictures develop throughout the Scriptures, it becomes very clear what God means when He says, "Come out of her, my people, that ye be not partakes of her sins." (REV 18:4)

Noah

When Noah, in Genesis 6 and 7, entered the ark and survived the flood, what was it that he left behind or "came out" of?

- Why was it that only Noah and his immediate family survived the water to a new land?
- Where were the rest of God's people?
- After all, weren't there more than just eight spiritually committed individuals?
- What happened to the godly culture?
- What can we learn from the cultural assimilation that had taken place?

The transformation towards evil began, when the sons of God (godly line of Seth), saw the daughters of men (godless line of Cain in GEN 6:2), and took them as their wives. The result of the union is explained in:

- **GEN 6:5**: And God saw that the wickedness of man was great in the earth, and that every imagination of the thoughts of his heart was only evil continually.

Slowly, the Godly line of Seth reflected the character of the daughters of men. Imperceptibly, Satan's character was being methodically developed in the mind, character, and personality of God's people. That which is Godly can never mix with evil and remain Godly. A cultural assimilation was taking place in these few verses that would lead to physical and spiritual death. The Godly are to be in the world but not of the world. (MATT 5:14-16)

Abram

When Abram and his family left Ur of the Chaldeans (GEN 12) to cross the waters of the Jordan River on their way to the Promised Land, what did they leave behind?

- What was Ur of the Chaldeans?
- Were there evil influences there that God wanted Abram and his family removed from?
- What were they?
- Was God concerned that Abram and his family might become like the society that they were surrounded by?

Appendix 3A — "Coming Out" of Babylon

- Was cultural assimilation one of God's concerns?
- Is that why God said, "Get thee out of thy country, and from thy kindred …" or, in the end time scenario of REV 18:4, "Come out of her my people …?"

Lot

When Lot separated himself from Abram and "… dwelt in the cities of the plain, and pitched his tent toward Sodom," (GEN 13:12) did he ever think of the impact of this exceedingly wicked culture on himself and his family? Eventually, Lot sat "in the gate" of Sodom. (GEN 10:1)

- With the upbringing and training that he had when he was with his Uncle Abram, from Ur to Haran and on to the Promised Land, did it not occur to him that good does not mix with evil?
- Did it surprise him when his daughters and sons-in-law chose not to "come out," but stay in the society of Sodom?
- Had Lot's daughters been trained up in the ways of God? Can the ways of God be trained out of us as we continue to associate with that which is evil?
- Had his daughters been slowly assimilated into the cultural wickedness of their surroundings where "… the men of Sodom were wicked and sinners before the Lord exceedingly." (GEN 13:13)
- Is it safe to say that the culture of Sodom, where wickedness reigned, reflected the character of Satan?
- What is the character of Satan?
- How does our association with this wickedness affect us?
- Is there a key personality trait in Satan's character that predominates and is at the root of his mind, character, and personality?

Hebrew People

When the Hebrews "came out" of Egypt, in the Book of Exodus, what did they "come out of?"

- Was the culture, defined by their politics, art, religion, education, economics/business/merchants, and general lifestyle, reflected in the statement made by Pharaoh in EX 5:2? "And Pharaoh said, Who is the LORD, that I should obey his voice to let Israel go? I know not the LORD, neither will I let Israel go."
- Did the character of the Pharaoh reflect the character of the general Egyptian population and hence the culture?
- Was it God's express purpose to deliver his people out of this situation and train them up in the way they should go to prepare them for their passage across the Jordan and into the Promised Land?
- Why was it that so many died in the wilderness?
- Why was it that they fought against the wilderness experience?

- After all, they had seen and participated firsthand in all the miracles of God. He provided everything for them. The miracles had been performed right before their eyes.
- Why could they not transition from Egypt dependency (Satan's counterfeit system) to God dependency?
- Did the cultural training of the past 400 years run so deep that dependency on God became impossible for them?
- Does cultural training today short-circuit dependency on God?

Are there miracles that surround my life and family that I can't see because of the culture which I have been raised up in?

Daniel

When Daniel and his three friends were taken captive, it was the express purpose of King Nebuchadnezzar that they be raised up in the "learning and the tongue of the Chaldeans" or the Babylonian culture. (DAN 1:4) The change of their names from Hebrew names, (which reflected their commitment to the true God), to Babylonian names, coupled with the "learning and the tongue of the Chaldeans" speaks volumes about cultural assimilation.

- If the learning of the Chaldeans had been accepted by these Hebrew youths, would they have bowed down to the image on the Plain of Dura (DAN 3); the image of the statue of a man that was **6**0 cubits high, **6** cubits wide, and introduced with **6** musical instruments?
- Was cultural assimilation at work there?
- What about all the rest of the Hebrew youths that had been taken from Jerusalem over the years? What happened to them?
- Were some of them on the Plain of Dura when it came time to bow down to the image of man?
- What is the significance of the image of man to the endtime, "Come out of her my people …?" (Is it possible that this image of man that has the number 666 has an endtime application as well?)

In Daniel 2:38, Daniel states that the gold head of the statue represented Nebuchadnezzar.

- What was the character of Nebuchadnezzar at this time?
- Does the king's character, demonstrated throughout Daniel 4, and specifically verse 30, reflect the "**I**" mentality of Satan in ISA 14:13-14? "For thou [Lucifer] hast said in thine heart, **I** will ascend into heaven, **I** will exalt my throne above the stars of God: **I** will sit also upon the mount of the congregation, in the sides of the north: 14 **I** will ascend above the heights of the clouds; **I will be like the most High**."

- Compare to **DAN 4:30**: "The king spake, and said, Is not this great Babylon, that **I** have built for the house of the kingdom by the might of **my** power, and for the honour of **my** majesty?"

Nebuchadnezzar was reflecting the character of Satan. Nebuchadnezzar, on the Plain of Dura, "demanded" worship just like Satan does. (MATT 4:9-10)

- After all, wasn't Nebuchadnezzar right in demanding worship since Satan had told mankind back in the Garden (GEN 3:5) that "… ye shall be as gods" — just like himself?
- Is this the culture in which we are being trained up?
- Does our modern culture of politics, economics, business, education, art, literature, and sports (to name a few), promote the exaltation of SELF and displace the worship of the one true God?

After 70 years of Babylonian captivity, the king of Medo-Persia released the Hebrews and encouraged them to return across the Jordan River to the Promised Land to re-build Jerusalem. Only a remnant returned. The rest of the Hebrews had accepted the surrounding culture; they had fit right into that which they had been introduced to 70 years earlier. Had they fit in spiritually as well? God's people are to "come out," not "fit in!" Mind, character, and personality, what one thinks and what one does, are being affected by what one chooses to be involved in. As we think (in the forehead/heart), and set our hand to do, so we are. (REV 14:9)

The character of a person at the end of time will be a perfect reflection of the character of the master he or she has chosen throughout life. In Matthew 25:32-33, Christ talks about the separation of the sheep and goats at the end of the age. Christ puts the sheep on His right (Christ's character), and the goats on His left (Satan's character). The separation (or sealing — HEB 8:10; 10:16-17) has taken place.

The Age of the Gentiles (LUKE 21:24) comes to fulfillment when, "Ye shall be as gods" is fully developed in the mind, character, and personality of the human race. The lie of Genesis 3:5, which the serpent presented to Eve in the garden, has been fully accepted by her unconverted, self-dependent offspring.

The character of Satan has NOT changed throughout time. It is the same today as it was 6000 years ago. He is working today in the same manner as he did back then. The patterns in Scripture are there to teach us. See:

2 TIM 3:1-5 This know also, that in the last days perilous times shall come. 2 For men shall be lovers of their own selves, covetous, boasters, proud, blasphemers, disobedient to parents, unthankful, unholy, 3 Without natural affection, trucebreakers, false accusers, incontinent, fierce, despisers of those that are good, 4 Traitors, heady, high-minded, lovers of pleasures more than lovers of God; 5

Having a form of godliness, but denying the power thereof: from such turn away.

REV 3:17 Because thou sayest, I am rich, and increased with goods, and have need of nothing; and knowest not that thou art wretched, and miserable, and poor, and blind, and naked.

2 THESS 2:10-11 And with all deceivableness of unrighteousness in them that perish; because they received not the love of the truth, that they might be saved. 11 And for this cause God shall send them strong delusion, that they should believe a lie.

Unconverted mankind has become self-dependent, not God dependent. (GEN 4) God's will for us is well stated in **EZE 36:26**: "I'll remove the stone heart from your body and replace it with a heart that's God-willed, not self-willed." (*The Message,* paraphrase by Eugene H. Peterson.)

"Coming Out" of Babylon

The message is again given in Daniel 3 to "come out" of literal Babylon. This is a representation of the Spiritual Babylon of Revelation 18. Both represent the same system that Noah, Abram, Lot, Daniel and his three friends, were instructed to "come out" of. It is a system founded on the character of Satan. It is a system that is Satan inspired and "self" driven. It is not *just* a religious system. It is a system where everything from religion to status, money, university degrees, cars, clothes, houses, etc., work together in a synergistic manner to train up people in the exaltation of a selfish, godless character — a character that totally reflects the mind, character, and personality of Satan.

Appendix 3B — The "Seal of God" or the "Mark of Man's System"

MATT 22:37-40 Jesus said unto him, Thou shalt love the Lord thy God with all thy heart, and with all thy soul, and with all thy mind. 38 This is the first and great commandment. 39 And the second is like unto it, Thou shalt love thy neighbour as thyself. 40 On these two commandments hang all the law and the prophets.

These two Commandments Jesus spoke of, are a summary of the Ten Commandments given to the Hebrews at Mount Sinai. The Ten Commandments likewise, are a summary of all God's Truths presented in His Word. These Truths were given by a loving Creator, to guide and direct His people as they move, both physically and spiritually, toward the Heavenly Promised Land. These Truths are the instrument used to convict the human heart of sin.

PS 19:7 The law of the LORD is perfect, converting the soul: the testimony of the LORD is sure, making wise the simple.

As each individual looks into the spirit of the Commandments, they have the opportunity to realize their desperate need for deliverance from the deceitfulness of the human heart and the hopelessness of the human plight.

JER 17:9 The heart is deceitful above all things, and desperately wicked: who can know it?

The Sacrificial Lamb (the type), in the Old Testament, pointing forward to the Messiah (the antitype) of the New Testament, is God's answer to the problem of sin. God was made available, a way to enter back into relationship with Him.

When we deny His Truth, as laid out in the Bible, and accept in the heart and mind the ways of the world, *we acknowledge the customs and traditions of man as having a higher priority in our lives than the ways of God.* We bow down to the ways of the world and turn our backs on the Truths of God. Our focus of worship becomes that which was manufactured in the image of man, rather than God Himself. What we choose to think in our heart, and what we choose to do with the hand, indicates who we worship. Some examples for consideration:

When God says that the world waxes old like a garment, and is going from a state of complexity to a state of simplicity, as demonstrated in nature (the Second Law of Thermodynamics), He means what He says.

Along comes man and says, just as Satan did in the Garden (GEN 3:5), "... did God say?" Man promotes his Theory of Evolution which states that things are moving from a state of simplicity to a state of complexity — a direct contradiction of Truth! Whom do we choose to believe?

2. When God says to parents, "... train up a child in the way he should go," He means what He says.

- Man comes along and says, "... did God say?" Because of our sinful, rebellious heart, we turn over our young children to man's school system, and man's day care system. Whom do we choose to believe?

3. When God says, eat whole foods as prescribed in Genesis 1:29 (fat content 7-12%), He means what He says.

- Along come the cooks of this world, with the Meat and Dairy industry, Refined Food and Fast Food industries, and say, "... did God say?" Now, man has a meat based, refined food diet, where 40% of our calories come from fat. Whom do we choose to believe?

4. When God says that it is natural for the female reproductive system to shut down between the ages of 45-55, He means what He says.

- Along comes man and says, like Satan did in the Garden, "... did God say?" and recommends Hormone Replacement Therapy. Whom do we choose to believe?

The above examples are all a denial of the First Commandment which deals with worship. What are the implications of the other nine Commandments? *All the ways of man are incorporated into the "Mark"* and are a direct challenge to the ways and authority of God. Bowing down to the literal image of man, raised on the Plain of Dura (Daniel 3:1), had to do with the acknowledgement of man's culture, over and above the Truths of God. In Daniel 3:1, the first "two "6's" pertain to the *physical* characteristics of the image. In verses 5, 10, and 15, the third "6" pertains to the *orchestration* of these physical characteristics of the image that brings about the "bowing down action." "666" describes what the system is and who it belongs to.

Daniel 3 is a excellent depiction of how events will transpire in the endtime, when the ways of man are accepted, and the ways of God are rejected. Those that accept the mark of man's system, — will bow down and follow man.

CHAPTER 4

**Nebuchadnezzar Authors
a Chapter of Scripture**
(Approximate Date: 569 BC)

*King Nebuchadnezzar's
Letter to the Nations*

1 Nebuchadnezzar the king, unto all people, nations, and languages, that dwell in all the earth; Peace be multiplied unto you.

2 I thought it good to shew the signs and wonders that <u>the high God</u> hath wrought toward me.

3 How great are his signs! and how mighty are his wonders! <u>his kingdom is an everlasting kingdom</u>, and his dominion is from generation to generation.

4 I Nebuchadnezzar was at rest in mine house, and flourishing in my palace:

5 I saw a dream which made me afraid, and the thoughts upon my bed and the <u>visions of my head troubled me</u>.

6 Therefore made I a <u>decree to bring in all the wise men of Babylon before me</u>, that they might make known unto me the interpretation of the dream.

7 Then came in the magicians, the astrologers, the Chaldeans, and the soothsayers: and I told the dream before them; <u>but they did not make known unto me the interpretation thereof.</u>

Note: This chapter was written by King Nebuchadnezzar about another dream given to him by God. Daniel was asked to give the interpretation.

 Prophetic Key #19 This vision was given as a *literal vision*. This may be why the king remembered the dream so well.

Prophetic Key #20 This <u>literal</u> vision did not need any outside interpretation from God, Gabriel, or the Bible itself.

Prophetic Key #21a/b This vision employs "types" and "similes" to illustrate the truth through a "parable" story. In several instances, two unlike things are compared. One example: the "tree" is equated to the "king."

Verse 2

Wonders from the Fiery Furnace

DAN 3:26 Then Nebuchadnezzar came near to the mouth of the burning fiery furnace, and spake, and said, Shadrach, Meshach, and Abed-nego, ye servants of <u>the most high God</u>, come forth, and come hither.

Verse 3

Reminder of an Everlasting Kingdom

DAN 2:44 And in the days of these kings shall <u>the God of heaven set up a kingdom, which shall never be destroyed</u>: and the kingdom shall not be left to other people, but it shall break in pieces and consume all these kingdoms, <u>and it shall stand for ever</u>.

Verse 5

Troubled Dreams From the Past

DAN 2:1 And in the second year of the reign of Nebuchadnezzar Nebuchadnezzar <u>dreamed dreams, wherewith his spirit was troubled,</u> and his sleep brake from him.

Verses 6-7

GEN 41:8 And it came to pass in the morning that his spirit was troubled; and <u>he sent and called for all the magicians</u> of Egypt, <u>and all the wise men</u> thereof: and Pharaoh told them his dream; <u>but there was none that could interpret them unto Pharaoh</u>.

ISA 44:24-25 Thus saith the LORD ... <u>I am the LORD</u> ... 25 that frustrateth the tokens of the liars, and maketh diviners mad; <u>that turneth wise men backward, and maketh their knowledge foolish</u>.

 Prophetic Key #12 Time **always** moves forward in all of Scripture and especially in prophecy. In this vision, the king explains the vision, Daniel gives the application of the vision, and then the vision is fulfilled. All of the events move forward in time.

**The King is Troubled
by a Dream**

8 But at the last Daniel came in before me, whose name was Belteshazzar, according to the name of my god, and <u>in whom is the spirit of the holy gods</u>: and before him I told the dream, saying,

9 O Belteshazzar, master of the magicians, because <u>I know that the spirit of the holy gods is in thee</u>, and no secret troubleth thee, tell me the visions of my dream that I have seen, and the interpretation thereof [meaning the application, since there are no symbols in this vision].

*King Nebuchadnezzar's
Dream [Vision] of a Tree*

10 Thus were the visions of mine head in my bed; I saw, and behold a tree in the midst of the earth, and the height thereof was great.

11 The tree grew, and was strong, and the height thereof reached unto heaven, and the sight thereof to the end of all the earth:

12 The leaves thereof were fair, and the fruit thereof much, and in it was meat for all: the beasts of the field had shadow under it, and the fowls of the heaven dwelt in the boughs thereof, and all flesh was fed of it.

13 I saw in the visions of my head upon my bed, and, behold, a <u>watcher</u> and an holy one came down from heaven;

Verses 8-9

Wizards Fail; Daniel is Called

ISA 8:19   And when they shall say unto you, Seek unto them that have familiar spirits, and unto wizards that peep, and that mutter: <u>should not a people seek unto their God</u>?

Daniel Called to Apply the Dream

Ps 25:14 <u>The secret of the LORD is with them that fear him</u>; and he will shew them his covenant.

Verses 10-12

Other Kings Were Compared to Trees

EZE 31:3, 5-6   Behold, the Assyrian was a cedar in Lebanon with fair branches ... and of an high stature; and his top was among the thick boughs. 5 Therefore his height was exalted above all the trees of the field, and his boughs were multiplied. 6 All the fowls of heaven made their nests in his boughs, and under his branches did all the beasts of the field bring forth their young, and under his shadow dwelt all great nations.

EZE 17:23   In the mountain of the height of Israel will I plant it: and it shall bring forth boughs, and bear fruit, and be a goodly cedar: and under it shall dwell all fowl of every wing; in the shadow of the branches thereof shall they dwell.

Verse 13

The "Watcher" is an Angel

PS 103:20   Bless the LORD, ye his angels, that excel in strength, that do his commandments, hearkening unto the voice of his word.

**The King's Dream
Was of a Great Tree**

 Prophetic Key #20 Proper *application* is made to a *watcher* [an holy one] to understand that this *being* is an *angel* from heaven.

*King Nebuchadnezzar's
Vision of the
Tree Being Cut Down*

14 He cried aloud, and said thus, Hew down the tree, and cut off his branches, shake off his leaves, and scatter his fruit: let the beasts get away from under it, and the fowls from his branches:

15 Nevertheless leave the stump of his roots in the earth, even with a band of iron and brass, in the tender grass of the field; and let it be wet with the dew of heaven, and let his portion be with the beasts in the grass of the earth:

*King Nebuchadnezzar's
Vision of the
Events During the
Seven Year Timeline*

16 Let his heart be changed from man's, and let a beast's heart be given unto him; and let seven times [seven literal years] **pass over him.**

Verses 14-15

*The Fate of Trees That Do Not
Bring Forth Good Fruit*

MATT 3:10 And now also the axe is laid unto the root of the trees: therefore every tree which bringeth not forth good fruit is hewn down, and cast into the fire.

JOB 14:7-9 For there is hope of a tree, if it be cut down, that it will sprout again, and that the tender branch thereof will not cease. 8 Though the root thereof wax old in the earth, and the stock thereof die in the ground; 9 Yet through the scent of water it will bud, and bring forth boughs like a plant.

Verse 16

"times" — *Strong's* OT#5732 **a set time**; technically, **a year**: KJV - time.

Note: This *seven times,* or seven years timeline, is the first of seven timelines in the Book of Daniel. All timelines begin with a ***decree.***

Prophetic Key #19 This chapter is written in full literal language. There are NO symbols employed.

Prophetic Key #25b All time in prophecy is *prophetic time.* Timelines contained within a literal setting are calculated as *prophetic literal time.* Therefore, the *seven times* is calculated as *seven literal years* of prophetic time in the verses of Daniel 4:16, 23, 25, and 32. (The word, *prophetic,* is derived from the word, *prophecy.* Therefore all prophecy, whether written in symbolic language or literal language is *prophetic time.* The term *prophetic time* is NOT interchangeable with the term *symbolic time.*)

Genesis 7 and 8 Give the Calculation of "days" in One Month

Note: Using the three texts from Genesis, the following information can be calculated: 5 months = 150 days.

GEN 7:11 In the six hundredth year of Noah's life, in the second month, the seventeenth day of the month, the same day were all the fountains of the great deep broken up, and the windows of heaven were opened.

GEN 7:24 And the waters prevailed upon the earth an hundred and fifty days.

GEN 8:4 And the ark rested in the seventh month, on the seventeenth day of the month, upon the mountains of Ararat.

Prophetic Key #24a The Jewish calendar was calculated on a 30 day month according to the creation solar year. Therefore, the Jewish calendar would have 360 days in one year or in a *time*.

Prophetic Key #24b The literal time of *seven years* in DAN 4:16 does NOT need the Year-day Principle applied.

DANIEL

The Story of the Rise and Fall of Earthly Kingdoms

King Nebuchadnezzar's
Vision of the
Seven Year Timeline
Beginning With a Decree

17 This matter is by the <u>decree</u> of the watchers, and the demand by the word of the holy ones ...

Verse 17

"<u>decree</u>" — In *theology,* predetermined purpose of God; the purpose or determination of an immutable Being, whose plan of operations is, like Himself, unchangeable. *Noah Webster 1828.*

Prophetic Key #26 All timelines in Daniel and Revelation begin and end with *decrees.* These decrees can be either through the legislation of an earthly judicial system, or through a divine heavenly voice. <u>Once a decree is given, the timeline begins and is NOT interrupted until the timeline is complete.</u> Timelines must also end with either the earthly judicial voice, or a voice from heaven.

Prophetic Key #27 This prophetic timeline begins with bad news. The king realized that bad news was associated with the tree being cut down by the holy one from heaven.

Prophetic Timeline #1: Details and Specifics

Timeline #1 (Length of Timeline)	Subject (of Timeline)	Prophetic Scripture For Timeline	Timeline Begins (with)	Speaking VOICE (Decree)	Timeline Ends (with)	Speaking VOICE (Decree)
7 "times" or 7 Literal Years	King Nebuchadnezzar and His Pride DAN 4:27	DAN 4:16, 23, 25, 32	King Driven to the Field as a Wild Beast DAN 4:31-33	Heavenly Voice Begins the king's Probation DAN 4:29, 31	Deliverance From Insanity After 7 Years DAN 4:34	The king's Voice of Praise DAN 4:34

17 ... to the intent that the living may know that the most High ruleth in the kingdom of men, and giveth it to whomsoever he will, and setteth up over it the basest of men.

Verse 17 (Concluded)

PS 9:16 The LORD is known by the judgment which he executeth: the wicked is snared in the work of his own hands.

PS 83:18 That men may know that thou, whose name alone is JEHOVAH, art the most high over all the earth.

DAN 2:21 And he changeth the times and the seasons: he removeth kings, and setteth up kings.

18 This dream I king Nebuchadnezzar have seen. Now thou, O Belteshazzar, declare the interpretation thereof, forasmuch as all the wise men of my kingdom are not able to make known unto me the interpretation: but thou art able; for the spirit of the holy gods is in thee.

*In a Courteous Reply
Daniel Interprets the
King's Dream of a Tree*

19 Then Daniel, whose name was Belteshazzar, was astonied for one hour, and his thoughts troubled him. The king spake, and said, Belteshazzar, let not the dream, or the interpretation thereof, trouble thee. Belteshazzar answered and said, My lord, <u>the dream be to them that hate thee, and the interpretation thereof to thine enemies.</u>

*Daniel's Application:
Description of the Tree*

20 <u>The tree that thou sawest,</u> **which grew, and was strong, whose height reached unto the heaven, and the sight thereof to all the earth;**

21 Whose leaves were fair, and the fruit thereof much, and in it was meat for all; under which the beasts of the field dwelt, and upon whose branches the fowls of the heaven had their habitation:

*Daniel's Application:
The Tree Represents
King Nebuchadnezzar*

22 <u>It is thou, O king,</u> **that art grown and become strong: for thy greatness is grown, and reacheth unto heaven, and thy dominion to the end of the earth.**

Verse 19

🔑 **Prophetic Key #21** The Daniel 4 prophecy is written in *literal language*. Daniel understood the dream and did not need a Biblical interpretation from God or the angel Gabriel. (Biblical interpretations are only needed for dreams and visions given in symbolic language.) However, Daniel hesitated one hour before giving the interpretation to the king. This was not because he didn't know the interpretation, but that he grieved about giving the king "the bad news." See the following Scripture.

A Courteous Reply Used in the Past

2 SAM 18:31-32 And, behold, Cushi came; and Cushi said, Tidings, my lord the king: for the LORD hath avenged thee this day of all them that rose up against thee. 32 And the king said unto Cushi, Is the young man Absalom safe? And Cushi answered, <u>The enemies of my lord the king, and all that rise against thee to do thee hurt, be as that young man is.</u>

Verses 20-22

🔑 **Prophetic Key #21a** Daniel used "similes" to give the king the application of this *literal* dream. He tells the king: "The tree that thou sawest … It is thou, O king." In "simile language" — "The king is <u>like</u> that great tree."

*King Nebuchadnezzar's Dominion
was Strong and Large*

JER 27:6-8 <u>And now have I given all these lands unto the hand of Nebuchadnezzar the king of Babylon,</u> my servant; and the beasts of the field have I given him also to serve him. 7 <u>And all nations shall serve him.</u> 8 And it shall come to pass, that the nation and kingdom which will not serve the same Nebuchadnezzar the king of Babylon, and that will not put their neck under the yoke of the king of Babylon, that nation will I punish, saith the LORD, with the sword, and with the famine, and with the pestilence, until I have consumed them by his hand.

Note: In the King James Version of the Bible, the word — "interpretation" refers both to interpretation of symbols and application of literal language.

**The "tree" Represented
King Nebuchadnezzar**

Daniel's Application:
Holy Beings Were to
Cut Down the Tree

23 And whereas the king saw a <u>watcher</u> and an holy one coming down from heaven, and saying, Hew the tree down, and destroy it; yet <u>leave the stump of the roots thereof in the earth, even with a band of iron and brass</u>, in the tender grass of the field; and let it be wet with the dew of heaven, and let his portion be with the beasts of the field, till <u>seven times</u> pass over him;

Daniel's Application:
The Seven Year Timeline
Will Begin with "a Decree"

24 This is the interpretation, O king, and this is the <u>decree</u> of the most High, which is come upon my lord the king:

Daniel's Application:
The King "likened" to a Beast
Represents the King's Insanity
(for Seven Years)

25 That they shall drive thee from men, and <u>thy dwelling shall be with the beasts of the field</u>, and they shall make thee to eat grass as oxen, and they shall wet thee with the dew of heaven, and <u>seven times</u> shall pass over thee, <u>till thou know that the most High ruleth in the kingdom of men, and giveth it to whomsoever he will</u>.

Daniel's Application:
The Living Stump Represents
King Nebuchadnezzar's Recovery

26 And whereas they commanded to leave the stump of the tree roots; <u>thy kingdom shall be sure unto thee</u>, after that thou shalt have known that the heavens do rule.

Verse 23

🔑 **Prophetic Key #22a** Daniel applies this part of the dream using "types." The *watcher* typifies a holy being with credentials from the God of heaven.

DAN 5:21 And he was driven from the sons of men; and his heart was made like the beasts, and his dwelling was with the wild asses: they fed him with grass like oxen, and his body was wet with the dew of heaven; till he knew that the most high God ruled in the kingdom of men, and that he appointeth over it whomsoever he will.

"Hew Down the Tree."

Verse 24

🔑 **Prophetic Keys #24d and #25** The term *seven times* is given <u>once</u> in the vision, <u>twice</u> in the application and <u>once</u> in the fulfilled prophecy. In **ALL** passages, the timeline refers to *seven literal years.*

Prophetic Key #26 Reminder — every timeline must begin with some kind of decree. Daniel 4:16, 23, 25, and 32 stated this decree would last seven times (or seven literal years). (See page 67 and Appendix 4A on pages 68-69.)

"decree" — *Strong's* OT#1504 **to cut down** or off; **(figuratively)** to destroy, divide, exclude, or decide: KJV - **cut down**, decree, divide, snatch.

Verse 25

Ps 107:40 He poureth contempt upon princes, and <u>causeth them to wander in the wilderness</u>, where there is no way.

Ps 9:16 The LORD is known by the judgment which he executeth: <u>the wicked is snared in the work of his own hands</u>.

Ps 83:18 That men may know that thou, <u>whose name alone is JEHOVAH</u>, art <u>the most high</u> over all the earth.

"Leave the stump of the tree roots; thy kingdom shall be sure unto thee."

Verse 26

🔑 **Prophetic Key #20a** The stump left in the earth with dew, would obviously sprout again which signified the restoration of King Nebuchadnezzar from his illness. This application aligns with historical events. (See JOB 14:7-9.)

Stern Warning:
Daniel Warns the
King To Repent

27 Wherefore, O king, let my counsel be acceptable unto thee, and break off thy sins by righteousness, and thine iniquities by <u>shewing mercy to the poor</u>; if it may be a lengthening of thy tranquillity.

King Nebuchadnezzar
Refuses to Repent —
Prophecy of the
Dream is Fulfilled
After Twelve Months

28 All this came upon the king Nebuchadnezzar.

29 <u>At the end of twelve months</u> he walked in the palace of the kingdom of Babylon.

King Nebuchadnezzar
Speaks of his Pride

30 The king spake, and said, Is not this great Babylon, that I have built for the house of the kingdom by the might of my power, and for the honour of my majesty?

Verse 27

Counsel for the King

ISA 58:7   Is it not to deal thy bread to the hungry, and that thou bring the poor that are cast out to thy house? when thou seest the naked, that thou cover him; and that thou hide not thyself from thine own flesh?

ACTS 8:22   <u>Repent therefore of this thy wickedness</u>, and pray God, if perhaps the thought of thine heart may be forgiven thee.

1 PETER 4:8   And above all things <u>have fervent charity</u> among yourselves: for charity shall cover the multitude of sins.

PS 41:1   <u>Blessed is he that considereth the poor</u>: the LORD will deliver him in time of trouble.

Verses 28-30

Note: <u>At the end of twelve months</u> (from the original warning) the heavenly decree was initiated by the prideful attitude of the king.

PROV 16:18   Pride goeth before destruction, and an haughty spirit before a fall.

ISA 26:11   Let favour be shewed to the wicked, yet will he not learn righteousness: in the land of uprightness will he deal unjustly, and will not behold the majesty of the LORD.

DAN 5:20   But when his heart was lifted up, and his mind hardened in pride, he was deposed from his kingly throne, and they took his glory from him.

"Is not this great Babylon, that I have built?"

🗝 **Prophetic Key #26** God gave the king twelve months to repent (vs 29). With no indication of repentance, the timeline began through the king's voice, [within the same hour, vs 33] followed by a heavenly voice [decree]. God's timelines are perfect and occur exactly on time.

Two Examples of God's Exact Prophetic Timelines

1)   120 Years to the Flood

GEN 6:3   yet his days shall be an <u>hundred and twenty years</u>.
GEN 7:13   <u>In the selfsame day</u> [they] entered ... into the ark (at the end of one hundred twenty years).

2)   400/430 Years to the Exodus

GEN 15:13   And he said ... thy seed shall be a stranger in a land ... <u>four hundred years</u>.
EX 12:41   And it came to pass at the end of the <u>four hundred and thirty years</u>, **even the selfsame day** it came to pass, that all the hosts of the LORD went out from the land of Egypt.   (See Appendix 4B, on pages 70-71, for explanation of the difference between the 400 and 430 years.)

Prophecy Fulfilled:
The Seven Year Timeline
Began with a
"Speaking Voice"

31 While the word was in the king's mouth, there fell a <u>voice</u> [decree] <u>from heaven, saying, O king Nebuchadnezzar, to thee it is spoken; The kingdom is departed from thee.</u>

Prophecy Fulfilled:
King Nebuchadnezzar
Struck Down
with <u>Lycanthropy</u> Disease

32 And they shall drive thee from men, and thy dwelling shall be with the beasts of the field: they shall make thee to eat grass as oxen, and <u>seven times</u> shall pass over thee, until thou know that the most High ruleth in the kingdom of men, and giveth it to whomsoever he will.

Prophecy Fulfilled:
The Seven year Timeline Begins

33 <u>The same hour was the thing</u> [the prophecy] <u>fulfilled</u> upon Nebuchadnezzar: and he was driven from men, and did eat grass as oxen, and his body was wet with the dew of heaven, till his hairs were grown like eagles' feathers, and his nails like birds' claws.

Verse 31

Prophetic Key #26   After twelve months of probation time, the seven year timeline began with a voice [decree] from heaven.

Prophetic Key #27   This timeline began with the bad news that the king would be as a beast in the field for seven years.

A Voice Fell From Heaven.

ACTS 12:23   <u>And immediately the angel of the Lord smote him,</u> because he gave not God the glory.

EZE 31:10, 12   Therefore thus saith the Lord GOD; Because thou hast lifted up thyself in height, and he hath shot up his top among the thick boughs, and his heart is lifted up in his height; 12 And strangers, the terrible of the nations, have cut him off, and have left him: upon the mountains and in all the valleys his branches are fallen, and his boughs are broken by all the rivers of the land; and all the people of the earth are gone down from his shadow, and have left him.

Verse 32

"lycanthropy" — a wolf, and man. *Noah Webster 1828.*

Dwelling Place With the Beasts

Verse 33

JOB 20:5   That the triumphing of the wicked is short, and the joy of the hypocrite but for a moment?

PS 37:35-36   I have seen the wicked in great power, and spreading himself like a green bay tree. 36 Yet he passed away, and, lo, he was not: yea, I sought him, but he could not be found.

DAN 5:21   And he was driven from the sons of men; and his heart was made like the beasts, and his dwelling was with the wild asses: they fed him with grass like oxen, and his body was wet with the dew of heaven; till he knew that the most high God ruled in the kingdom of men, and that he appointeth over it whomsoever he will.

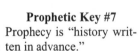 **Prophetic Key #7**
Prophecy is "history written in advance."

- Daniel gave the king the application of the prophecy.
- Within twelve months the prophecy began to be fulfilled.
- Within the next seven years, the fulfilled prophecy became history.

Prophecy Fulfilled:
King Nebuchadnezzar Healed
When he Praises God

34 And at the end of the days I Nebuchadnezzar lifted up mine eyes unto heaven, and mine understanding returned unto me, and I blessed the most High, and I praised and honoured him that liveth for ever, whose dominion is an everlasting dominion, and <u>his kingdom is from generation to generation:</u>

35 <u>And all the inhabitants of the earth are reputed as nothing:</u> and he doeth according to his will in the army of heaven, and among the inhabitants of the earth: and none can stay his hand, or say unto him, What doest thou?

36 At the same time my reason returned unto me; and for the glory of my kingdom, mine honour and brightness returned unto me; and my counsellers and my lords sought unto me; and I was established in my kingdom, and excellent majesty was added unto me.

37 Now I Nebuchadnezzar praise and extol and honour the King of heaven, all whose works are truth, and his ways judgment: and those that walk in pride he is able to abase.

 Prophetic Key #26 After seven years the *voice* of King Nebuchadnezzar declared praise and honour to the King of heaven.

Prophetic Key #27 This timeline ends with good news in verse 36. King Nebuchadnezzar is restored with full understanding, and royal dignity to rule over his kingdom.

Verse 34

PS 10:16 <u>The LORD is King for ever and ever</u>: the heathen are perished out of his land.

JER 10:10 But <u>the LORD is the true God, he is the living God, and an everlasting king</u>: at his wrath the earth shall tremble, and the nations shall not be able to abide his indignation.

Verse 35

PS 39:5 Behold, thou hast made my days as an handbreadth; and mine age is as nothing before thee: verily <u>every man at his best state is altogether vanity</u>.

ISA 40:15, 17 Behold, the nations are as a drop of a bucket, and are counted as the small dust of the balance: behold, he taketh up the isles as a very little thing. 17 <u>All nations before him are as nothing</u>; and they are counted to him less than nothing, and vanity.

PS 33:11 The counsel of the LORD standeth for ever, the thoughts of his heart to all generations.

PS 115:3 But our God is in the heavens: he hath done whatsoever he hath pleased.

JOB 9:12 Behold, he taketh away, who can hinder him? who will say unto him, What doest thou?

Verse 37

PROV 22:4 By humility and the fear of the LORD are riches, and honour, and life.

King Nebuchadnezzar Returns to his Kingdom

Nebuchadnezzar Honours the King of Heaven Again

Important Note: Daniel Chapter 4 sets the important precedent as to how all the timelines in Daniel and Revelation shall **begin and end**.

1. **DAN 4:17, 24** **A Decree** "This matter is by the decree of the watchers … this is the decree of the most High."
2. **DAN 4:31** **A Speaking Voice** "... there fell a voice from heaven, saying, O Nebuchadnezzar, to thee it is spoken."
3. **DAN 4:33** **A Fulfilled Prophecy** "The same hour was the thing [prophecy] fulfilled."

Additional Notes for Daniel 4

The Importance of Daniel 4

Daniel 4 is another *vision chapter*. This vision is related to the attitude of King Nebuchadnezzar and the hardness, or self-centeredness, of his heart. All other visions in Daniel's book are concerned with God's special (or peculiar) people, and how they would be delivered from their persecutors. The vision in chapter 4 is different and requires the application of some very important Prophetic Keys, essential to understanding the prophetic timelines of Daniel. (These identical Prophetic Keys are also applied in Revelation.)

It is interesting to note that the seven year timeline in this chapter is mentioned four times. The rest of the timelines in Daniel are mentioned only once. Repetition is present in this chapter to "grab" our attention. Something important is being taught here. Don't miss it!

This vision is given in literal language. No symbols are employed. Therefore, it is imperative that the vision be applied in a literal sense. To interpret it symbolically, when no symbolism is present, is error. This is the central lesson to be learned in Chapter 4.

Prophetic Keys #14-17 are NOT applicable to Daniel 4.

- Notice in verse 16 that Daniel "was astonied for one hour, and his thoughts troubled him." The reason for his astonishment was not because he did not understand the vision, but rather that he desired the application to refer to the king's enemies. Daniel knew exactly what the application was because this was a literal vision. No further explanation from God or the angel, Gabriel, was necessary.

Prophetic Key #24 is NOT applicable to Daniel 4. All four *seven year timelines* in Daniel 4 are encased within a literal context and do not need symbolic time conversion.

A problem presents itself when the vision of Daniel 4 is labeled as symbolic.

1. Daniel 4:16 describes the heavenly vision with the seven year timeline. IF the heavenly vision were written with symbolism, then the seven year timeline must be converted from prophetic symbolic time to prophetic literal time. Using Prophetic Key #24b the conversion would be:

- 7 (symbolic years or "times") x 360 (days per year) = 2520 prophetic symbolic days.

- Therefore: 2520 symbolic days = 2520 literal years. King Nebuchadnezzar did not live 2520 years!

2. In verse 25, Daniel gives the literal application of the vision along with the seven year timeline. In this verse the seven year timeline remains as seven literal years.

- Using **Prophetic Key #24d** 7 [literal] times = 7 literal years.

3. It is impossible for the same seven year timeline to have two totally different applications of 2520 years and 2520 days. The prophetic symbolic time of 2520 years is obviously incorrect. (The king would have lived a very long time as an animal before he received his kingdom back.)

4. This vision gives guidance on how to apply timelines correctly.

- Any timeline encased within symbolic language must be converted from symbolic time to literal time.

- Any timeline encased within a literal context, simply stays as literal time.

The following two pages are a discovery of what needs to be understood in order to correctly discern the upcoming timelines in Daniel 7-12.

Appendix 4A — How to Begin and End Prophetic Timelines

*Nebuchadnezzar's Heavenly Vision
(Given in Literal Language)*

16 Let his heart be changed from man's, and let a beast's heart be given unto him; and let seven times pass over him.

17 This matter is by the decree of the watchers, and the demand by the word of the holy ones: to the intent that the living may know that the most High ruleth in the kingdom of men, and giveth it to whomsoever he will, and setteth up over it the basest of men.

*Daniel's Literal Application:
Seven Times = Seven Literal Years*

23 And whereas the king saw a watcher and an holy one coming down from heaven, and saying, Hew the tree down, and destroy it; yet leave the stump of the roots thereof in the earth, even with a band of iron and brass, in the tender grass of the field; and let it be wet with the dew of heaven, and let his portion be with the beasts of the field, till seven times pass over him;

*Literal Application:
The Seven Year Timeline will
Begin with a Decree
[or a speaking voice]*

24 This is the interpretation, O king, and this is the decree of the most High, which is come upon my lord the king:

25 That they shall drive thee from men, and thy dwelling shall be with the beasts of the field, and they shall make thee to eat grass as oxen, and they shall wet thee with the dew of heaven, and seven times shall pass over thee, till thou know that the most High ruleth in the kingdom of men, and giveth it to whomsoever he will.

The King's Probationary Time Ends

29 At the end of twelve months he walked in the palace of the kingdom of Babylon.

King Nebuchadnezzar Speaks ...

30 The king spake, and said, Is not this great Babylon, that I have built for the house of the kingdom by the might of my power, and for the honour of my majesty?

31 While the word was in the king's mouth ...

The God of Heaven Speaks ...

... there fell a voice [decree of verse 24] from heaven, saying, O king Nebuchadnezzar, to thee it is spoken; The kingdom is departed from thee.

*A Fulfilled Prophecy Begins
the Seven Year Timeline*

32 And they shall drive thee from men, and thy dwelling shall be with the beasts of the field: they shall make thee to eat grass as oxen, and seven times shall pass over thee, until thou know that the most High ruleth in the kingdom of men, and giveth it to whomsoever he will.

Seven Year Timeline Begins Exactly on Time

33 The same hour [end of twelve months of verse 29] was the thing [prophetic vision] fulfilled upon Nebuchadnezzar: and he was driven from men, and did eat grass as oxen, and his body was wet with the dew of heaven, till his hairs were grown like eagles' feathers, and his nails like birds' claws.

*Nebuchadnezzar's Voice Ends the
Prophetic Timeline of Seven Years*

34 And at the end of the days [of the seven year timeline] I Nebuchadnezzar lifted up mine eyes unto heaven, and mine understanding returned unto me, and I blessed the most High, and I praised [with a speaking voice] and honoured him that liveth for ever, whose dominion is an everlasting dominion, and his kingdom is from generation to generation:

*Nebuchadnezzar is Restored to his Kingdom
at the End of the Seven Year Timeline*

36 At the same time my reason returned unto me; and for the glory of my kingdom, mine honour and brightness returned unto me; and my counsellers and my lords sought unto me; and I was established in my kingdom, and excellent majesty was added unto me.

Appendix 4A — How to Begin and End Prophetic Timelines

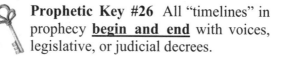 **Prophetic Key #26** All "timelines" in prophecy **begin and end** with voices, legislative, or judicial decrees.

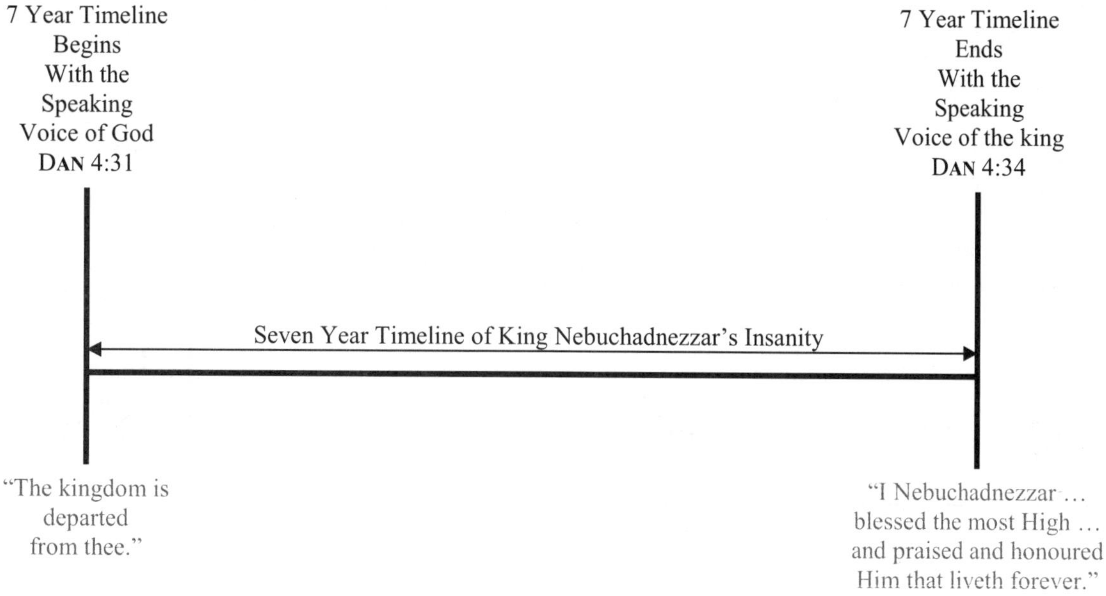

7 Year Timeline
Begins
With the
Speaking
Voice of God
DAN 4:31

7 Year Timeline
Ends
With the
Speaking
Voice of the king
DAN 4:34

Seven Year Timeline of King Nebuchadnezzar's Insanity

"The kingdom is
departed
from thee."

"I Nebuchadnezzar ...
blessed the most High ...
and praised and honoured
Him that liveth forever."

Note: All prophetic timelines in Daniel 7, 8, 9, and 12 will have speaking voices or decrees to begin and end the timelines. This principle also applies to the prophetic timelines in Revelation by:
1. A fulfilled prophecy;
2. A speaking voice, which is —
3. A decree.

LINE A

- **GEN 12:2** — Covenant given to Abraham.
- **GEN 12:4** — Abraham leaves Haran at age of 75.

LINE B

- **GEN 16:16** — Ishmael is born 11 years after Abraham left Haran. Abraham is 86 years old.

LINE C

- **GEN 17:21; 18:10, 14** — Promise of birth of Isaac in <u>one year</u>.
- Abraham is 99 years old.

LINE D

- **GEN 21:5** — Abraham is 100 years old when Isaac is born.
- **GEN 21:2** — Isaac is born at the **set time**.

LINE E

- **GEN 21:8** — I weaned at appr mately 5 years of a
- Ishmael is about years old.
- **GEN 21:9** — Ishr and Hagar mock Is (GAL 4:28-30)

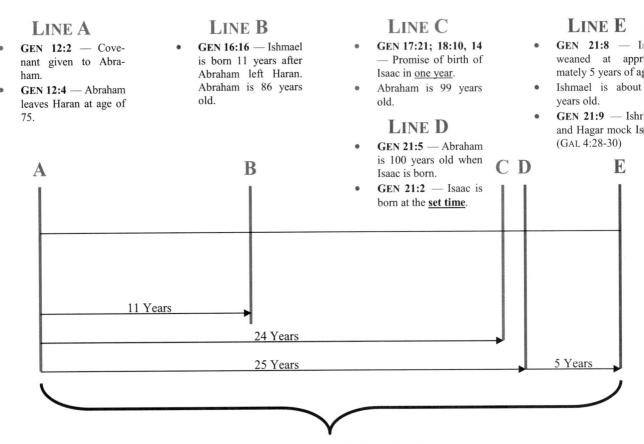

First 30 Years of the 430 Year Timeline

Four Hundred Years

GEN 15:13 And he said unto Abram, Know of a surety that thy seed shall be a stranger in a land that is not theirs, and shall serve them; and they shall afflict them **four hundred years**.

ACTS 7:6 And God spake on this wise, That his seed should sojourn in a strange land; and that they should bring them into bondage, and entreat them evil **four hundred years**.

Note: At this time the Egyptian kingdom extended northward including the land of Canaan.

The period of **four hundred years** found in the two Scriptures from **Genesis** and **Acts** can be harmonized with the **four hundred and thirty years** of the two Scriptures in Exodus and Galatians by acknowledging the different starting dates.

- The 430 years begins with Abraham's call to leave Haran.
- The 400 years begins 30 years later when Ishmael started to "afflict" Isaac.
- The 430 and 400 years both end with the Exodus from Egypt, and the giving of the Law at Mt. Sinai.

Four Hundred Thirty Years

EX 12:40 Now the sojourning of the children of Israel, who dwelt in Egypt, was **four hundred and thirty years**.

GAL 3:16-17 Now to Abraham and his seed were the promises made. He saith not, And to seeds, as of many; but as of one, And to thy seed, which is Christ. 17 And this I say, that the covenant, that was confirmed before of God in Christ, the law, which was **four hundred and thirty years** after, cannot disannul, that it should make the promise of none effect.

Line D
- **Gen 21:1-5** — Birth of Isaac.

Line F
- **Gen 25:26** — Birth of Jacob when Isaac is 60 years old.

Line G
- **Gen 47:9** — Jacob's entry into Egypt at 130 years of age.

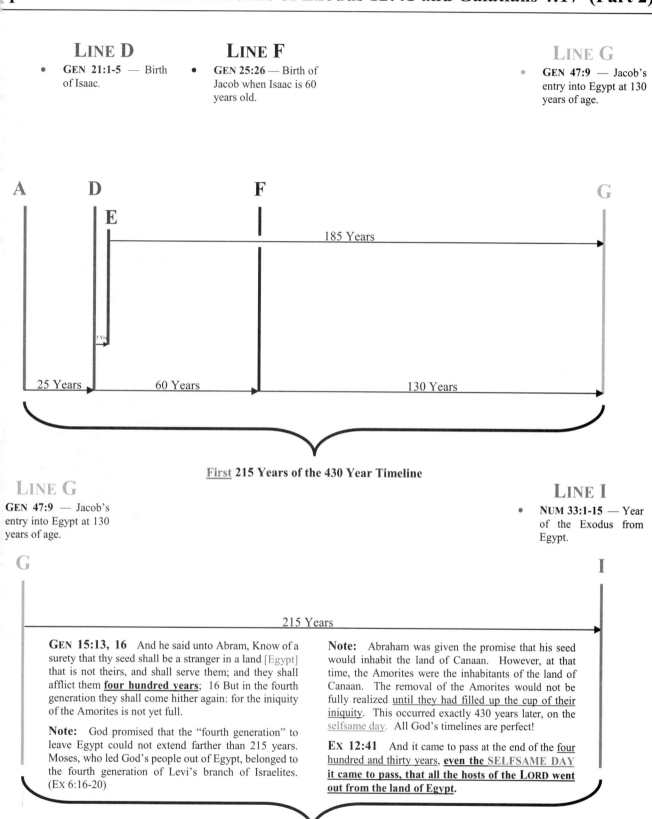

First 215 Years of the 430 Year Timeline

Line G
Gen 47:9 — Jacob's entry into Egypt at 130 years of age.

Line I
- **Num 33:1-15** — Year of the Exodus from Egypt.

Gen 15:13, 16 And he said unto Abram, Know of a surety that thy seed shall be a stranger in a land [Egypt] that is not theirs, and shall serve them; and they shall afflict them **four hundred years**; 16 But in the fourth generation they shall come hither again: for the iniquity of the Amorites is not yet full.

Note: God promised that the "fourth generation" to leave Egypt could not extend farther than 215 years. Moses, who led God's people out of Egypt, belonged to the fourth generation of Levi's branch of Israelites. (Ex 6:16-20)

Note: Abraham was given the promise that his seed would inhabit the land of Canaan. However, at that time, the Amorites were the inhabitants of the land of Canaan. The removal of the Amorites would not be fully realized until they had filled up the cup of their iniquity. This occurred exactly 430 years later, on the selfsame day. All God's timelines are perfect!

Ex 12:41 And it came to pass at the end of the four hundred and thirty years, **even the SELFSAME DAY it came to pass, that all the hosts of the LORD went out from the land of Egypt.**

Second 215 Years of the 430 Year Timeline

DANIEL
The Story of the Rise and Fall of Earthly Kingdoms

CHAPTER 5

Belshazzar —
(Nebuchadnezzar's Grandson)
Feasts on the Last Night
of Babylon's History
(538 BC)

1 Belshazzar the king made a great feast to a thousand of his lords, and drank wine before the thousand.

2 Belshazzar, whiles <u>he tasted the wine</u>, commanded to bring the golden and silver vessels which <u>his father</u> Nebuchadnezzar had taken out of the temple which was in Jerusalem; that the king, and his princes, his wives, and his concubines, might drink therein.

3 Then they brought the <u>golden vessels</u> that were taken out of the temple of the house of God which was at Jerusalem; and the king, and his princes, his wives, and his concubines, drank in them.

4 They drank wine, and praised the gods of gold, and of silver, of brass, of iron, of wood, and of stone.

Introduction: Daniel 5 describes the closing scenes of the Babylonian kingdom, and the transition of earthly power over God's people. This earthly power was transferred to Medo-Persia, represented by the silver breast and arms of the image in Daniel 2. (See page 37.) Daniel 5 also presents a picture of Babylon's indifference to the sacred trusts and obedience required in the worship of the true God. It also dramatically announces the message of doom and immediate judgment of Babylon. The fall of ancient Babylon also parallels the prophecies of the fall of Spiritual Babylon in Revelation.

Verse 1

Note: At this time in history, Nabonidus (father of Belshazzar) was away recuperating from an illness. During that time, Belshazzar was placed as co-ruler with his father over the affairs of Babylon. Therefore, Belshazzar was known as "king" of Babylon. (See page 26 for a review of the kings of Babylon.)

Verses 2-4

PROV 20:1 <u>Wine is a mocker</u>, strong drink is raging: and whosoever is deceived thereby is not wise.

"his father" — Belshazzar is actually the grandson of King Nebuchadnezzar. The word *father* is also understood to mean grandfather, or ancestor.

This banquet introduces Belshazzar's ultimate disregard for the sacred holy vessels, which had come from Jerusalem's temple. The entire immoral company performed its wickedness by drinking wine from these sacred vessels. The following Scriptures liken God's people to *holy vessels* of the Lord's temple.

ACTS 9:15 But the Lord said unto him, Go thy way: for <u>he is a chosen vessel unto me</u>.

ROM 9:22-23 What if God, willing to shew his wrath, and to make his power known, endured with much longsuffering the vessels of wrath fitted to destruction: 23 And that he might make known the riches of his glory on <u>the vessels of mercy</u>, which he had afore prepared unto glory.

1 THESS 4:4 That every one of you should <u>know how to possess his vessel</u> in sanctification and honour.

2 TIM 2:21 If a man therefore purge himself from these, <u>he shall be a vessel unto honour, sanctified, and meet for the master's use</u>, and prepared unto every good work.

**King Belshazzar Drinks
From the Holy Vessels
of God's Temple**

Note: Revelation 17 and 18 will describe the persecution of God's people (or the misuse of God's holy vessels) through the cruelty of Spiritual Babylon. Spiritual Babylon will be judged for the abuse of *these holy vessels.*

The Handwriting on the Wall

5 In the same hour came forth fingers of a man's hand, and wrote over against the candlestick upon the plaister of the wall of the king's palace: and the king saw the part of the hand that wrote.

Belshazzar's Terror

6 Then the king's countenance was changed, and his thoughts troubled him, so that the joints of his loins were loosed, and his knees smote one against another.

7 The king cried aloud to bring in the astrologers, the Chaldeans, and the soothsayers. And the king spake, and said to the wise men of Babylon, Whosoever shall read this writing, and shew me the interpretation thereof, shall be clothed with scarlet, and have a chain of gold about his neck, and shall be the third ruler in the kingdom.

The Wise Men Fail the Third Time in Giving a Correct Interpretation

8 Then came in all the king's wise men: but they could not read the writing, nor make known to the king the interpretation thereof.

9 Then was king Belshazzar greatly troubled, and his countenance was changed in him, and his lords were astonied.

Verse 5

DAN 4:31 While the word was in the king's mouth, there fell a voice from heaven, saying, O king Nebuchadnezzar, to thee it is spoken; The kingdom is departed from thee.

Verse 6

JOB 18:11-12 Terrors shall make him afraid on every side, and shall drive him to his feet. 12 His strength shall be hungerbitten, and destruction shall be ready at his side.

Verse 7

DAN 2:2 Then the king commanded to call the magicians, and the astrologers, and the sorcerers, and the Chaldeans, for to shew the king his dreams. So they came and stood before the king.

DAN 4:6 Therefore made I a decree to bring in all the wise men of Babylon before me, that they might make known unto me the interpretation of the dream.

ISA 47:13 Thou art wearied in the multitude of thy counsels. Let now the astrologers, the stargazers, the monthly prognosticators, stand up, and save thee from these things that shall come upon thee.

"third ruler" — Nabonidus was the first ruler; Belshazzar was the second ruler; therefore the person that provided the interpretation could not have a position higher than *third ruler*.

Verse 8

"they could not read the writing" — Verses 26-28 indicate that the words were written in Aramaic. However, the words were so few, and given in such a cryptic manner that their meanings and message was concealed.

DAN 2:10 The Chaldeans answered before the king, and said, There is not a man upon the earth that can shew the king's matter.

DAN 4:7 Then came in the magicians, the astrologers, the Chaldeans, and the soothsayers ... but they did not make known unto me the interpretation thereof.

*The Queen Mother
Recommends Daniel*

10 Now the queen, [Belshazzar's grandmother] **by reason of the words of the king and his lords, came into the banquet house: and the queen spake and said, <u>O king, live for ever</u>: let not thy thoughts trouble thee, nor let thy countenance be changed:**

11 There is a man in thy kingdom, <u>in whom is the spirit of the holy gods</u>; and in the days of thy father light and understanding and wisdom, like the wisdom of the gods, was found in him; whom the king Nebuchadnezzar thy father, the king, I say, thy father, made [Daniel] **master of the magicians, astrologers, Chaldeans, and soothsayers;**

12 Forasmuch as an excellent spirit, and knowledge, and understanding, interpreting of dreams, and shewing of hard sentences, and dissolving of doubts, were found in the same Daniel, whom the king named Belteshazzar: now let Daniel be called, and he will shew the interpretation.

Belshazzar Offers Daniel Riches

13 Then was Daniel brought in before the king. And the king spake and said unto Daniel, Art thou that Daniel, which art of the children of the captivity of Judah, whom the king my father brought out of Jewry?

14 I have even heard of thee, that the spirit of the gods is in thee, and that light and understanding and excellent wisdom is found in thee.

Verse 10

A Common Salutation

DAN 3:9 They spake and said to the king Nebuchadnezzar, <u>O king, live for ever</u>.

**Belshazzar Considers
the Advice of the
Queen Mother**

Verses 11-14

*The Queen Mother Recalls When
King Nebuchadnezzar
Requested an Interpretation
From Daniel*

DAN 2:26-28 The king answered and said to Daniel, whose name was Belteshazzar, Art thou able to make known unto me the dream which I have seen, and the interpretation thereof? 27 Daniel answered in the presence of the king, and said, The secret which the king hath demanded cannot the wise men, the astrologers, the magicians, the soothsayers, shew unto the king; 28 But there is a God in heaven that revealeth secrets, and maketh known to the king Nebuchadnezzar what shall be in the latter days.

DAN 4:9 O Belteshazzar, [Daniel] master of the magicians, because I know that <u>the spirit of the holy gods is in thee</u>, and no secret troubleth thee, tell me the visions of my dream that I have seen, and the interpretation thereof.

Note: The Queen Mother was the daughter of King Nebuchadnezzar. She remembered when her father requested Daniel's service in the past for the interpretation of his dreams. (Verse 22 indicates that Belshazzar was well acquainted with the historical facts of his grandfather and his friendship with Daniel.) In verse 13 Belshazzar confirms that Daniel is the "one" that the Queen Mother spoke about.

15 And now the wise men, the astrologers, have been brought in before me, that they should read this writing, and make known unto me the interpretation thereof: but they could not shew the interpretation of the thing:

16 And I have heard of thee, that thou canst make interpretations, and dissolve doubts: now if thou canst read the writing, and make known to me the interpretation thereof, thou shalt be clothed with scarlet, and have a chain of gold about thy neck, and shalt be the third ruler in the kingdom.

Daniel Refuses Rulership and Riches

17 Then Daniel answered and said before the king, Let thy gifts be to thyself, and give thy rewards to another; yet I will read the writing unto the king, and make known to him the interpretation.

Daniel Rebukes Belshazzar

18 O thou king, the most high God gave Nebuchadnezzar thy father a kingdom, and majesty, and glory, and honour:

Verse 18

Note: Before Daniel reads and interprets the handwriting on the wall, he takes a moment to remind Belshazzar what King Nebuchadnezzar had experienced because of his refusal to break off his sins and iniquities. (DAN 4:27) Daniel proceeded to show Belshazzar that his actions before God were just as wicked. Belshazzar had refused to learn anything from the experiences of King Nebuchadnezzar. Note the following verses:

DAN 2:37 Thou, O king, art a king of kings: for the God of heaven hath given thee a kingdom, power, and strength, and glory.

DAN 4:17, 22, 25 This matter is by the decree of the watchers … to the intent that the living may know that the most High ruleth in the kingdom of men, and giveth it to whomsoever he will. **22** It is thou, O king, that art grown and become strong: for thy greatness is grown, and reacheth unto heaven, and thy dominion to the end of the earth. **25** That they shall drive thee from men, and thy dwelling shall be with the beasts of the field, and they shall make thee to eat grass as oxen, and they shall wet thee with the dew of heaven, and seven times shall pass over thee, till thou know that the most High ruleth in the kingdom of men, and giveth it to whomsoever he will.

19 And for the majesty that he gave him, all people, nations, and languages, trembled and feared before him: whom he would he slew; and whom he would he kept alive; and whom he would he set up; and whom he would he put down.

Daniel Recalls the Fate of King Nebuchadnezzar

20 But when his heart was lifted up, and his mind hardened in pride, he was deposed from his kingly throne, and they took his glory from him:

21 And he was driven from the sons of men; and his heart was made like the beasts, and his dwelling was with the wild asses: they fed him with grass like oxen, and his body was wet with the dew of heaven; till he knew that the most high God ruled in the kingdom of men, and that he appointeth over it whomsoever he will.

Daniel Compares Belshazzar to King Nebuchadnezzar

22 And thou his son, O Belshazzar, <u>hast not humbled thine heart</u>, though thou knewest all this;

Verse 19

JER 27:6-7 And now have I given all these lands unto the hand of Nebuchadnezzar the king of Babylon, my servant; and the beasts of the field have I given him also to serve him. 7 And all nations shall serve him, and his son, and his son's son, until the very time of his land come: and then many nations and great kings shall serve themselves of him.

Verses 20-21

DAN 4:30-32 The king spake, and said, Is not this great Babylon, that I have built for the house of the kingdom by the might of my power, and for the honour of my majesty? 31 While the word was in the king's mouth, there fell a voice from heaven, saying, O king Nebuchadnezzar, to thee it is spoken; The kingdom is departed from thee. 32 And they shall drive thee from men, and thy dwelling shall be with the beasts of the field: they shall make thee to eat grass as oxen, and seven times shall pass over thee, until thou know that the most High ruleth in the kingdom of men, and giveth it to whomsoever he will.

DAN 4:17 This matter is by the decree of the watchers, and the demand by the word of the holy ones: to the intent that the living may know that the most High ruleth in the kingdom of men, and giveth it to whomsoever he will, and setteth up over it the basest of men.

Verse 22

2 CHRON 36:12 And he did that which was evil in the sight of the LORD his God, <u>and humbled not himself before ... the LORD</u>.

23 But hast lifted up thyself against the LORD of heaven; and they have brought the vessels of his house before thee, and thou, and thy lords, thy wives, and thy concubines, have drunk wine in them; and <u>thou hast praised the gods of silver, and gold, of brass, iron, wood, and stone, which see not, nor hear, nor know: and the God in whose hand thy breath is, and whose are all thy ways, hast thou not glorified:</u>

24 <u>Then</u> was the part of the hand sent from him; and this writing was written.

Daniel Reads the Writing on the Wall

25 And this is the writing that was written, MENE, MENE, TEKEL, UPHARSIN.

Verse 23

JER 50:29-30 Call together the archers against Babylon: all ye that bend the bow, camp against it round about; let none thereof escape: recompense her according to her work; according to all that she hath done, do unto her: for she hath been proud against the LORD, against the Holy One of Israel. 30 Therefore shall her young men fall in the streets, and all her men of war shall be cut off in that day, saith the LORD.

PS 115:4-8 <u>Their idols are silver and gold, the work of men's hands.</u> 5 They have mouths, but they speak not: eyes have they, but they see not: 6 They have ears, but they hear not: noses have they, but they smell not: 7 They have hands, but they handle not: feet have they, but they walk not: neither speak they through their throat. 8 They that make them are like unto them; so is every one that trusteth in them.

JER 10:23 O LORD, I know that the way of man is not in himself: it is not in man that walketh to direct his steps.

Verse 24

"Then" — gives reference to the moment when Belshazzar, in his drunkenness, gave way to praising his idol gods, and also drank from the consecrated golden vessels of the Jerusalem Temple. At *that moment* God pronounced judgment on Belshazzar with handwriting on the wall.

Verse 25

Note: Even though Daniel read the four Aramaic words on the wall, they could not be understood by Belshazzar because a whole truth was expressed in each word. Daniel was able to give the correct application.

Daniel Gives the Application for the Handwriting on the Wall

The Story of the Rise and Fall of Earthly Kingdoms

Daniel Interprets Mene:
Babylon is "Numbered"

26 This is the interpretation of the thing: <u>MENE</u>; God hath numbered thy kingdom, and finished it.

Verse 26

"MENE" — *Strong's* OT#4484 mene'; <u>numbered</u>: KJV - Mene.

JER 25:12 <u>And it shall come to pass, when seventy years are accomplished, that I will punish the king of Babylon,</u> and that nation, saith the LORD, <u>for their iniquity,</u> and the land of the Chaldeans, and will make it perpetual desolations.

JER.50:1-2 The word that <u>the LORD spake against Babylon</u> and against the land of the Chaldeans by Jeremiah the prophet. 2 Declare ye among the nations, and publish, and set up a standard; publish, and conceal not: say, <u>Babylon is taken,</u> Bel is confounded, Merodach is broken in pieces; her idols are confounded, her images are broken in pieces.

Daniel Interprets Tekel:
Babylon is "Weighed"

27 <u>TEKEL</u>; <u>Thou art weighed in the balances, and art found wanting</u>.

Verse 27

"TEKEL" — *Strong's* OT#8625 teqal; <u>to balance</u>: KJV - Tekel, <u>be weighed</u>.

JOB 31:6 <u>Let me be weighed</u> in an even balance, that God may know mine integrity.

PS 62:9 Surely men of low degree are vanity, and men of high degree are a lie: <u>to be laid in the balance,</u> they are altogether lighter than vanity.

JER 6:30 Reprobate silver shall men call them, because <u>the LORD hath rejected them.</u>

Belshazzar Was Found Lacking in Moral Worth by Profaning the Temple Vessels and His Own "Body Vessel"

Daniel Interprets Peres:
Babylon is "Divided"
Between the Medes and Persians

28 PERES; Thy kingdom is divided, and given to the Medes and Persians.

Belshazzar Fulfills His
Promise to Daniel

29 Then commanded Belshazzar, and they clothed Daniel with scarlet, and put a chain of gold about his neck, and made a proclamation concerning him, that he should be the third ruler in the kingdom.

The Fall of Babylon

30 In that night was Belshazzar the king of the Chaldeans slain.

(This verse repeated on the next page.)

Verse 28 (**Note:** *"UPHARSIN,"* from verse 25, and *"PERES"* are the same Aramaic word in the *Strong's Concordance*.)

"UPHARSIN" — *Strong's* OT#6537 perac; to split up: KJV - divide, [U-] pharsin.

"PERES" — *Strong's* OT#6537 perac; to split up: KJV - divide, [U-] pharsin.

ISA 47:5 Sit thou silent, and get thee into darkness, O daughter of the Chaldeans: for thou shalt no more be called, The lady of kingdoms.

ISA 44:28 — 45:1-2 28 That saith of Cyrus, He is my shepherd, and shall perform all my pleasure: even saying to Jerusalem, Thou shalt be built; and to the temple, Thy foundation shall be laid. 1 Thus saith the LORD to his anointed, to Cyrus, whose right hand I have holden, to subdue nations before him; and I will loose the loins of kings, to open before him [through Darius the Mede] the two leaved gates; and the gates shall not be shut; 2 I will go before thee, and make the crooked places straight: I will break in pieces the gates of brass, and cut in sunder the bars of iron.

Note: Daniel 5 teaches all nations and individuals that there is a limit to sin and blasphemy beyond which they are not permitted to pass.

The Troops of Cyrus the Great (King of Persia) Conquer Babylon

Verse 30

Note: The fall of the ancient capital city of Babylon was a brilliant execution of military strategy. The broad walls of the city appeared impregnable. The city was self-supporting and apparently seemed eternally secure from attack. The Euphrates River ran through the city, supplying water for gardens that were a "river of life." This river ran through the entire length of the city. Walls of great height and thickness protected the perimeter of the city and bordered both sides of the riverbed. Huge gates of brass were in these walls by the river. No one could enter the city of Babylon when these brass gates were closed and guarded. **But** on that fatal night, the gates were not shut as foretold in Isaiah 45:1. Darius the Mede (the uncle of Cyrus) captured Babylon in one night.

JER 50:18 Therefore thus saith the LORD of hosts, the God of Israel; Behold, I will punish the king of Babylon and his land.

Prophetic Key #12 Prophecy is understood near or at the time of fulfillment. Once the Babylonian king was slain, it was obvious that prophecy had been fulfilled.

The Fall of Babylon

30 In that night was Belshazzar the king of the Chaldeans slain.

The Rise of Medo-Persia — Darius the Mede Captures Babylon

31 And Darius the Median took the kingdom, being about three-score and two years old.

Darius the Mede Entered Through the Open Ishtar Gate in Babylon

Verse 30 (Continued)

JER 51:31, 39, 57-58   One post shall run to meet another, and one messenger to meet another, to shew the king of Babylon that his city is taken at one end. 39 In their heat I will make their feasts, and I will make them drunken, that they may rejoice, and sleep a perpetual sleep, and not wake, saith the LORD. 57 And I will make drunk her princes, and her wise men, her captains, and her rulers, and her mighty men: and they shall sleep a perpetual sleep, and not wake, saith the King, whose name is the LORD of hosts. 58 Thus saith the LORD of hosts; The broad walls of Babylon shall be utterly broken, and her high gates shall be burned with fire; and the people shall labour in vain, and the folk in the fire, and they shall be weary.

Verse 31

DAN 9:1   In the first year of <u>Darius</u> the son of Ahasuerus, of <u>the seed of the Medes, which was made king over the realm of the Chaldeans.</u>

Darius the Mede Takes the Kingdom of BABYLON in 538 BC

Note: Darius the Mede, a sixty-two year old military genius, brought the troops of Cyrus to Babylon. He commanded them to dig a lake bed beside the city and then channeled the water away from the city of Babylon into the lake bed, causing the river to dry up. Then at midnight, as Belshazzar desecrated the holy vessels at his banquet, Darius' troops marched through the dried up river bed. Darius entered Babylon through the two leaved gates that were left open, and took the city. The "drying up" of the River Euphrates brought about the final fall of ancient Babylon. (The drying up of the Euphrates River in Revelation 16:18 parallels the fall of that ancient city Babylon.)

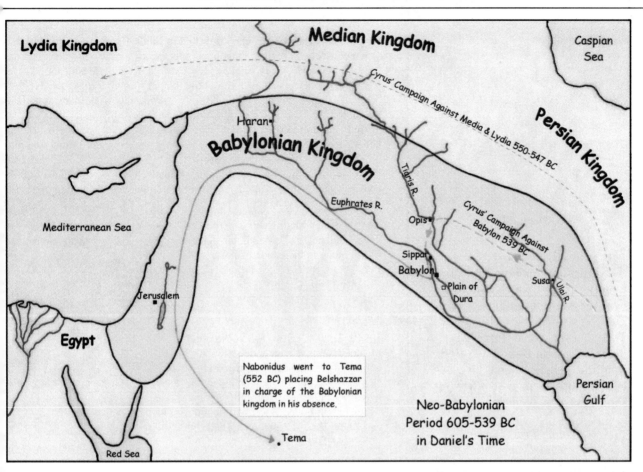

Map labels: Lydia Kingdom, Median Kingdom, Caspian Sea, Haran, Babylonian Kingdom, Cyrus' Campaign Against Media & Lydia 550-547 BC, Persian Kingdom, Tigris R., Euphrates R., Opis, Cyrus' Campaign Against Babylon 539 BC, Sippar, Babylon, Susa, Ulai R., Mediterranean Sea, Jerusalem, Plain of Dura, Egypt, Red Sea, Tema, Persian Gulf

Nabonidus went to Tema (552 BC) placing Belshazzar in charge of the Babylonian kingdom in his absence.

Neo-Babylonian Period 605-539 BC in Daniel's Time

Interesting Information

- Cyrus the Great (the Persian King) rose to power very quickly by taking over the kingdom of Media and Lydia in the far west.
- This alarmed Nabonidus and he returned to Babylon from Tema in 540 BC. On the way back he surrendered Sippar (50 miles north of Babylon) to Cyrus on October 10, 538 BC and fled south.
- In the meantime, Darius (King of the Medes) proceeded south to Babylon, and overtook the city on October 12, 538 BC.
- Darius the Mede (also known as Cyaxares) was the uncle to Cyrus the Great.
- Cyrus allowed Darius the Mede title to all of his conquests as long as he lived.
- Darius the Mede ruled in Babylon only two years before he died. Cyrus then ruled over Babylon and made provisions for the Jewish people to return to their homeland.

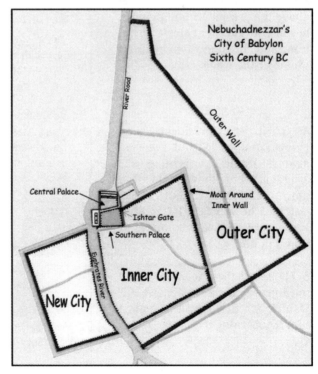

Nebuchadnezzar's City of Babylon Sixth Century BC

Labels: River Road, Outer Wall, Central Palace, Moat Around Inner Wall, Ishtar Gate, Outer City, Southern Palace, Euphrates River, Inner City, New City

DANIEL
The Story of the Rise and Fall of Earthly Kingdoms

Note: The setting of this chapter is that of Medo-Persia, the second of the seven consecutive earthly kingdoms. Darius, king of Medo-Persia, set up "an hundred and twenty princes" and over them, three presidents. These were the representatives of the entire kingdom and formed the highest council of government. (This "cabinet" represents a similar parallel in Revelation 17:12.) These jealous princes were of "one mind" and "sought to find occasion against Daniel" who was nearly ninety years old. Being united, they decided to find a method to legally condemn Daniel and put him to death. (This will also parallel with Revelation 13, 16, and 17.) However, there was no fault found in Daniel. This parallels the 144,000 who will face a final death decree just before the Second Coming of Jesus. Compare with Revelation 14:5.

CHAPTER 6

*Daniel Reigns Over
the Whole Kingdom Under
Darius the Mede*

1 It pleased Darius to set over the kingdom an hundred and twenty princes, which should be over the whole kingdom;

2 And over these three presidents; of whom Daniel was first: that the princes might give accounts unto them, and the king should have no damage.

*Jealous Presidents
Hate Daniel*

3 Then this Daniel was preferred above the presidents and princes, because an excellent spirit was in him; and the king thought to set him over the whole realm.

4 Then the presidents and princes sought to find occasion against Daniel concerning the kingdom; but they could find none occasion nor fault; forasmuch as he was faithful, neither was there any error or fault found in him.

5 Then said these men, We shall not find any occasion against this Daniel, except we find it against him concerning the law of his God.

Verse 2

1 SAM 2:30 Wherefore the LORD God of Israel saith, I said indeed that thy house, and the house of thy father, should walk before me for ever: but now the LORD saith, Be it far from me; for them that honour me I will honour, and they that despise me shall be lightly esteemed.

PROV 3:35 The wise shall inherit glory: but shame shall be the promotion of fools.

PROV 4:8 Exalt her [wisdom], and she shall promote thee: she shall bring thee to honour, when thou dost embrace her.

Verse 4

PHIL 2:15 That ye may be blameless and harmless, the sons of God, without rebuke, in the midst of a crooked and perverse nation, among whom ye shine as lights in the world.

1 PETER 2:12 Having your conversation honest among the Gentiles: that, whereas they speak against you as evildoers, they may by your good works, which they shall behold, glorify God in the day of visitation.

**Princes are Jealous
of Daniel**

Note: Despite Daniel's old age, he was well able to carry out his duties with no error or fault. He depended on his Heavenly Father for complete guidance.

DANIEL

CHAPTER 6   The Story of the Rise and Fall of Earthly Kingdoms

*The Jealous Presidents
Set a Trap for Daniel*

6 Then these presidents and princes assembled together to the king, and said thus unto him, King Darius, live for ever.

7 All the presidents of the kingdom, the governors, and the princes, the counsellers, and the captains, have consulted together to establish a royal statute, and to make a firm decree, that whosoever shall ask a petition of any God or man for thirty days, save of thee, O king, he shall be cast into the den of lions.

8 Now, O king, establish the decree, and sign the writing, that it be not changed, according to <u>the law of the Medes and Persians, which altereth not</u>.

Verses 7-8

Note: In Daniel's day it was common that kings were treated as gods. This particular decree would seem reasonable to the people as a test of their loyalty to a new leader.

**Fourth Death Decree —
"Lion's Den!"**

EST 1:19 let it be written among <u>the laws of the Persians and the Medes, that it be not altered</u>.

PS 118:9 It is better to trust in the LORD than to put confidence in princes.

**Death Decree Sealed
with the King's Ring**

---

*Daniel Continues His Fidelity
to God in Mode of Worship*

9 Wherefore king Darius signed the writing and the decree.

10 Now when Daniel knew that the writing was signed, he went into his house; and <u>his windows being open</u> in his chamber <u>toward Jerusalem</u>, he kneeled upon his knees three times a day, and prayed, and gave thanks before his God, as he did aforetime.

11 Then these men assembled, and found Daniel praying and making supplication before his God.

Verses 9-11

1 KINGS 8:44-45 If thy people go out to battle against their enemy … and shall <u>pray</u> unto the LORD <u>toward the city</u> which thou hast chosen, and toward the house that I have built for thy name: 45 Then hear thou in heaven their prayer and their supplication, and maintain their cause.

PS 5:7 But as for me, I will come into thy house in the multitude of thy mercy: and in thy fear will I <u>worship toward thy holy temple</u>.

PS 28:2 Hear the voice of my supplications, when I cry unto thee, when I lift up my hands toward thy holy oracle.

Note: To obey is better than sacrifice or compromise. (1 SAM 15:22)

PS 55:17
Evening, and morning, and at noon, will I pray, and cry aloud: and he shall hear my voice.

(Also see ACTS 2:1-2, 15; 3:1; 10:9; 1 THESS 5:17-18.)

King Darius is Coerced
Concerning Daniel's Worship

12 Then they came near, and spake before the king concerning the king's decree; Hast thou not signed a decree, that every man that shall ask a petition of any God or man within thirty days, save of thee, O king, shall be cast into the den of lions? The king answered and said, The thing is true, according to the law of the Medes and Persians, which altereth not.

13 Then answered they and said before the king, That Daniel, which is of the children of the captivity of Judah, regardeth not thee, O king, nor the decree that thou hast signed, but maketh his petition three times a day.

14 Then the king, when he heard these words, was sore displeased with himself, and set his heart on Daniel to deliver him: and he laboured till the going down of the sun to deliver him.

15 Then these men assembled unto the king, and said unto the king, Know, O king, that the law of the Medes and Persians is, That no decree nor statute which the king establisheth may be changed.

Verse 12

DAN 3:8 Wherefore at that time certain Chaldeans came near, and accused the Jews.

Verse 13

DAN 3:12 There are certain Jews whom thou hast set over the affairs of the province of Babylon, Shadrach, Meshach, and Abed-nego; these men, O king, have not regarded thee: they serve not thy gods, nor worship the golden image which thou hast set up.

Fourth Death Decree of the
Medes and Persians
Could Not Be Changed

Daniel Cast into the Lion's Den

16 Then the king commanded, and they brought Daniel, and cast him into the den of lions. Now the king spake and said unto Daniel, Thy God whom thou servest continually, he will deliver thee.

The Stone was Sealed

17 And a stone was brought and laid upon the mouth of the den; and the king sealed it with his own signet, and with the signet of his lords; that the purpose might not be changed concerning Daniel.

King Darius Laments Over Daniel

18 Then the king went to his palace, and passed the night fasting: neither were instruments of musick brought before him: and his sleep went from him.

19 Then the king arose very early in the morning, and went in haste unto the den of lions.

20 And when he came to the den, he cried with a lamentable voice unto Daniel: and the king spake and said to Daniel, O Daniel, servant of the living God, is thy God, whom thou servest continually, able to deliver thee from the lions?

Verse 16

ISA 41:10 Fear thou not; for I am with thee: be not dismayed; for I am thy God: I will strengthen thee; yea, I will help thee; yea, I will uphold thee with the right hand of my righteousness.

2 COR 1:10 Who delivered us from so great a death, and doth deliver: in whom we trust that he will yet deliver us.

1 PETER 5:6-8 Humble yourselves therefore under the mighty hand of God, that he may exalt you in due time: 7 Casting all your care upon him; for he careth for you. 8 Be sober, be vigilant; because your adversary the devil, as a roaring lion, walketh about, seeking whom he may devour.

Verse 17

LAM 3:53 They have cut off my life in the dungeon, and cast a stone upon me.

MATT 27:66 So they went, and made the sepulchre sure, sealing the stone, and setting a watch.

Note: The king's seal had a double purpose which guaranteed that Daniel would not be put to death by another method in case he was not harmed by the lions.

Verses 18-20

JER 32:17 Ah Lord GOD! behold, thou hast made the heaven and the earth by thy great power and stretched out arm, and there is nothing too hard for thee.

DAN 3:15 and who is that God that shall deliver you out of my hands?

Ps 34:7
The angel of the LORD encampeth round about them that fear him, and delivereth them.

King Darius Cannot Sleep

DANIEL

The Story of the Rise and Fall of Earthly Kingdoms

God Preserved Daniel From the Lions

21 Then said Daniel unto the king, O king, live for ever.

22 My God hath sent his angel, and hath shut the lions' mouths, that they have not hurt me: forasmuch as before him innocency was found in me; and also before thee, O king, have I done no hurt.

Verse 22

DAN 3:28 Blessed be the God of Shadrach, Meshach, and Abed-nego, who hath sent his angel, and delivered his servants that trusted in him.

PS 46:1 God is our refuge and strength, a very present help in trouble.

HEB 11:33 Who through faith subdued kingdoms, wrought righteousness, obtained promises, stopped the mouths of lions.

Daniel Released From the Lion's Den

Jealous Presidents Destroyed

23 Then was the king exceeding glad for him, and commanded that they should take Daniel up out of the den. So Daniel was taken up out of the den, and <u>no manner of hurt was found upon him</u>, because he believed in his God.

24 And the king commanded, and they brought those men which had accused Daniel, and they <u>cast them into the den of lions</u>, them, their children, and their wives; and the lions had the mastery of them, and brake all their bones in pieces or ever they came at the bottom of the den.

Verse 23

Note: The requirements of the royal decree that Daniel should be cast into the lion's den had been met. Beyond that, execution was not required and Daniel was delivered by another royal decree.

MARK 16:18 They shall take up serpents; and if they drink any deadly thing, <u>it shall not hurt them</u>.

Verse 24

DEUT 19:19 Then shall ye do unto him, as he had thought to have done unto his brother: so shalt thou put the evil away from among you.

PROV 11:8 The righteous is delivered out of trouble, and <u>the wicked cometh in his stead</u>.

DEUT 24:16 every man shall be put to death for his own sin.

Accuser's of Daniel are Thrown into the Lion's Den

DANIEL

The Story of the Rise and Fall of Earthly Kingdoms

*King Darius Decrees that the
Living God of Heaven
Shall be Worshipped*

25 Then king Darius wrote unto all people, nations, and languages, that dwell in all the earth; Peace be multiplied unto you.

26 I make a decree, That in every dominion of my kingdom men tremble and fear before the God of Daniel: for he is the living God, and stedfast for ever, and his kingdom that which shall not be destroyed, and his dominion shall be even unto the end.

27 He delivereth and rescueth, and he worketh signs and wonders in heaven and in earth, who hath delivered Daniel from the power of the lions.

*Darius the Mede and
Cyrus the Persian Rule*

28 So this Daniel prospered in the reign of Darius, and in the reign of Cyrus the Persian.

<u>Verses 25-28</u>

A New Decree is Written

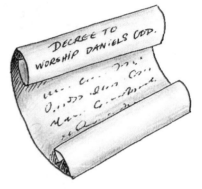

Note: Throughout Daniel's life in ancient Babylon, he never was indoctrinated into the systems of Babylon or Medo-Persia. Daniel prospered and was blessed when he heeded the command to separate himself for God alone. No death decree would move him from his resolve!

**King Darius Reinstates
Daniel to his Previous Office**

Daniel 6 **Ruling Kingdom**	Petition	Persons Involved	4th Death Decree	Deliverance
Medo-Persia through King Darius the Mede	ALL were commissioned to petition only Darius the king for 30 days.	Wicked princes and Daniel.	Those that prayed to any other than the king, would be thrown into the lion's den, including Daniel.	An angel was sent to shut the lion's mouths — The wicked princes were thrown to the lion's instead.

RECAPPING STRUCTURE CHART
Four Historic-Prophetic Outlines of Earthly Kingdoms in the Book of Daniel
The "Symbols" of Daniel 2, 7, and 8 (Image, Beasts, and Horns) and the "Literal" Kings of Daniel 11
Consistently Refer to the Progression of Persecuting Kingdoms Surrounding God's People.

Daniel 2 Symbolic	**Daniel 7** Symbolic	**Daniel 8** Symbolic	**Daniel 11-12:4** Litera
Vision 1 - Prophetic Outline 1	Vision 2 - Prophetic Outline 2	Vision 3 - Prophetic Outline 3	Vision 4 - Prophetic Outline

Kingdom #1   BABYLON   606 — 538 BC

DAN 2:38

Gold Head

DAN 7:4

Lion

Kingdom #2   MEDO-PERSIA   538 — 331 BC

DAN 2:39

Silver Breast
& Arms

DAN 7:5

Bear

Kingdom #3   GREECE   331 — 168 BC

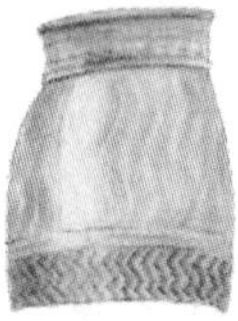

DAN 2:39

Brass Belly
& Thighs

DAN 7:6

Leopard

Kingdom #4   ROME (Pagan Imperial)   168 BC — AD 476

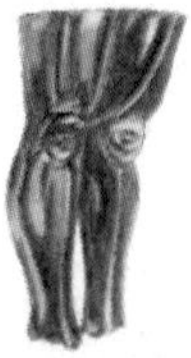

DAN 2:40

Iron Legs

DAN 7:7-8

Dreadful
Beast

Kingdom #5   ROME (Papal Supremacy No. 1 — Old Europe)   AD 538 — 1798

DAN 2:41

Feet
Part of Iron

DAN 7:8,
20-25
Little Horn

Kingdom #6

DAN 2:41

Feet
Part of Clay

Kingdom #7

DAN 2:42-43

Toes of
Iron & Clay

This chart shows the recapping of kingdoms in a "vertical" format.

DANIEL
The Story of the Rise and Fall of Earthly Kingdoms

CHAPTER 7

**HEAVENLY SCENE
VISION TWO**
(Symbolic Beasts
and Horns)

Daniel's Dream and Visions
(553 BC)

1 In the first year of Belshazzar king of Babylon Daniel had a dream and visions of his head upon his bed: then he wrote the dream, and told the sum of the matters.

2 Daniel spake and said, I saw in my vision by night, and, behold, the <u>four winds</u> of the heaven <u>strove</u> upon the <u>great sea</u>.

Introduction: See **The Structure of Daniel** Chart on page 135 for Vision Two. The second **Heavenly Scene** is given to Daniel in a night vision. The symbolic beasts are revealed in the first few verses. In Daniel 7:8 a symbolic horn appears. As noted on the previous page, the first four beasts will be a recapping of the identical earthly kingdoms brought forth in the symbolic image of Daniel 2. Additional information is presented, regarding characteristics of the beasts. A Fifth Kingdom, (the Little Horn), and a timeline are added, which moves the Outline forward in time from AD 476 to 1798. Daniel 2 dealt largely with <u>political matters</u> and God's plan for Babylon with Nebuchadnezzar as king. Daniel 7 is also political, but deals largely with <u>religious matters</u> and God's plan for the deliverance of His people from the Little Horn. Three times in this chapter there is a strong emphasis on God's judgment and His plan for deliverance — a theme that runs through the entire Book of Daniel. (See Appendix 7C, pages 124-125, for details.)

Review **Prophetic Keys #1-9** on pages 16-17.

Prophetic Key #6 This vision follows the same literary structure as the vision in Daniel 2.

Prophetic Key #9 Daniel 7 is the prophecy that begins to unfold John's prophecy in Revelation 13:1-2.

Prophetic Key #13 This vision adds additional information.

Prophetic Key #22 This vision contains a *timeline* within the Historic-Prophetic Outline section.

<u>Verse 1</u>

Nabonidus assigned the kingship to his son Belshazzar in 553 BC. (See table on page 26.)

<u>Verse 2</u>

"four winds ... strove" — symbol for strife, political commotion and war. Kingdoms rise and fall through political strife.

JER 25:32 Thus saith the LORD of hosts, Behold, evil shall go forth from nation to nation, and a <u>great whirlwind</u> shall be raised up from the coasts of the earth. (Also see JER 49:36-37.)

"great sea" — symbol for peoples, nations, and tongues. *The great sea* with it's tossing waves represent the wars and upheavals caused by the political rise and fall of nations; but *the earth* refers to the geographical areas from which these nations emerged.

REV 17:15 the <u>waters</u> which thou sawest ... are peoples, and multitudes, and nations, and tongues.

ISA 17:12 Woe to the multitude of many people, which make a noise like the <u>noise of the seas</u>.

HEAVENLY SCENE
DAN 7:2-14
LION
BEAR
LEOPARD
DREADFUL BEAST
LITTLE HORN

Note: Only God pulls back the curtain of time to reveal future events.

*Four Symbolic Beasts
Represent Four Consecutive
Earthly Kingdoms*

3 And four great beasts came up from the sea, <u>diverse</u> one from another.

*The Lion with Eagle's Wings
and a Man's Heart*

4 The first was like a lion, and had eagle's wings: I beheld till the wings thereof were plucked, and it was lifted up from the earth, and made stand upon the feet as a man, and a man's heart was given to it.

The Bear With Three Ribs

5 And behold another beast, a second, like to a bear, and it raised up itself on one side, and it had three ribs in the mouth of it between the teeth of it: and they said thus unto it, Arise, devour much flesh.

*The Leopard With
Four Wings and Four Heads*

6 After this I beheld, and lo another, like a leopard, which had upon the back of it four wings of a fowl; the beast had also four heads; and dominion was given to it.

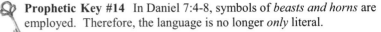

Prophetic Key #14 In Daniel 7:4-8, symbols of *beasts and horns* are employed. Therefore, the language is no longer *only* literal.

Prophetic Key #16 The symbols that are used are word pictures of something that is not real.

<u>Verse 3</u>

"diverse" — recaps on Daniel 2:38-40 in that the beasts are as diverse (or different) from one another as are the metals in the image.

<u>Verse 4</u>

<u>Verse 5</u>

<u>Verse 6</u>

*A Dreadful Beast
With Iron Teeth and Ten Horns*

7 After this I saw in the night visions, and behold a fourth beast, dreadful and terrible, and strong exceedingly; and it had great iron teeth: it devoured and brake in pieces, and stamped the residue with the feet of it: and it was diverse from all the beasts that were before it; and it had ten horns.

<u>Verse 7</u>

*A "Little Horn" Emerges from
Among the Ten Horns*

8 I considered the horns, and, behold, there came up among them another little horn, before whom there were three of the first horns plucked up by the roots: and, behold, in this horn were eyes like the eyes of man, and a mouth speaking great things.

<u>Verse 8</u>

(Change of Scenes)
Daniel Saw Thrones
Being Set in Place

9 I beheld till the <u>thrones were cast down</u>, and <u>the Ancient of days</u> [God the Father] **<u>did sit</u> ...**

Daniel Described
God the Father

9 ... whose garment was white as snow and the hair of his head like the pure wool: <u>his throne was like the fiery flame</u>, and his wheels as burning fire.

Daniel Saw the Number of Witnesses at a Judgment Scene Beginning in Heaven

10 A fiery stream issued and came forth from before him: <u>thousand thousands ministered unto him, and ten thousand times ten thousand stood before him</u> ...

Verses 9-10

In Revelation 4 and 5, John is Shown the Same Scenes Daniel was Shown

REV 4:2   And immediately I was in the spirit: and, <u>behold, a throne</u> was set in heaven, and <u>one sat on the throne</u>.

REV 4:4-6   And round about the throne were four and twenty seats: and upon the seats I saw four and twenty elders sitting, clothed in white raiment; and they had on their heads crowns of gold. 5 And <u>out of the throne proceeded lightnings and thunderings</u> and voices: and <u>there were seven lamps of fire burning before the throne</u>, which are the seven Spirits of God. 6 And before the throne there was a sea of glass like unto crystal: and in the midst of the throne, and round about the throne, were four beasts full of eyes before and behind.

John Saw the Same Number of Witnesses at the Same Scene

REV 5:11   And I beheld ... and <u>the number of them was ten thousand times ten thousand, and thousands of thousands</u>.

Prophetic Key #13 This vision introduces new information about the judgment. Daniel 8 continues to expand on the judgment theme.

*Daniel Saw the Books Opened
— the Investigative Judgment
Was Set
[The Court was Convened]*

10 … the judgment was set, and the books were opened.

<u>Verse 10</u>

God Appoints a Judgment Day

"the judgment was set" — **Acts 17:31** Because <u>he</u> [God] <u>hath appointed a day</u>, in the which he will judge the world in righteousness by that man [Jesus] whom he hath ordained; whereof he hath given assurance unto all men, in that he hath raised him from the dead.

God Appoints a Judge

JOHN 5:22 For the Father judgeth no man, but hath committed all judgment unto the Son.

ACTS 10:42 And he commanded us to preach unto the people, and to testify that it is <u>he which was ordained of God to be the Judge</u> of quick and dead.

Jesus, our Attorney and Judge

1 JOHN 2:1 if any man sin, we have an advocate with the Father, Jesus Christ the righteous.

1 TIM 2:5 For there is one God, and one mediator between God and men, the man Christ Jesus.

HEB 7:25 seeing he [Jesus] ever liveth to make intercession for them.

2 COR 5:10
For we must all appear before the judgment seat of Christ.

1 PETER 4:17
For the time is come that judgment must begin at the house of God.

*"the **books** were opened"* —

1. "The Book of Life"

REV 20:12 And I saw the dead, small and great, stand before God; and <u>the books were opened</u>: and another book was opened, which is the <u>book of life</u>: and the dead were judged out of those things which were written in the books, according to their works.

2. "The Book of Remembrance"

MAL 3:16 and a <u>book of remembrance was written</u> before him for them that feared the LORD, and that thought upon his name.

Note: The closing ministry of Christ's judgment is part of the heavenly sanctuary scene that will be addressed in Daniel 8:14. The first phase is the divine judgment (or Investigative Judgment) when *"the books were opened."*

Daniel Saw the Final Destruction of Pagan Imperial Rome and the Little Horn

11 I beheld then because of the voice of the great words which the [little] horn spake: I beheld even till the <u>beast was slain</u>, and his body destroyed, and given to the burning flame.

Four Empires Prolonged

12 As <u>concerning the rest of the beasts</u>, they had their dominion taken away: yet their lives were prolonged for a <u>season</u> and time.

Jesus Enters the Judgment Scene

13 I saw in the night visions, and, behold, one like the Son of man came with the clouds of heaven, and came to the Ancient of days, and they brought him near before him.

Jesus Receives Legal Title to the Kingdom in an Investigative Judgment

14 And there was given him dominion, and glory, and a kingdom, that all people, nations, and languages, should serve him: his dominion is an everlasting dominion, which shall not pass away, and his kingdom that which shall not be destroyed.

15 I Daniel was grieved in my spirit in the midst of my body, and the visions of my head troubled me.

Verse 11

The "Beast" Destroyed at the Second Coming

2 THESS 2:8 And then shall <u>that Wicked</u> [beast] be revealed, whom the Lord shall consume with the spirit of his mouth, and shall destroy with the brightness of his coming.

Verse 12

"concerning the rest of the beasts" — It should be noted that the kingdoms that lost their dominion to the succeeding kingdoms were not annihilated. Often, the conquerors adopted much of the culture, philosophy, and religion of the conquered. When Babylon was conquered by Medo-Persia, Babylon's subjects were permitted to live for a "season and time" under their own customs and traditions. The same applied to Medo-Persia, Greece, and Pagan Imperial Rome. However, under the rule of the Little Horn power, the new subjects were expected to conform to the customs and traditions of the new religious power. For those who refused, it resulted in severe persecution.

"season" — *Strong's* OT#2166 an *appointed occasion*:—KJV - season, time.

Verses 13-14

Note: These verses are closely connected to verses 9 and 10. Here Christ receives His kingdom at the close of His priestly work in the Heavenly Sanctuary. Then He will return to the earth to receive the redeemed of Revelation 14:4. The wicked of the earth will be destroyed at the brightness of His coming.

PS 2:9 Thou shalt break them with a rod of iron; thou shalt dash them in pieces like a potter's vessel.

MATT 11:27 All things are delivered unto me of my Father.

JOHN 3:35 The Father loveth the Son, and hath given all things into his hand.

INTERLUDE QUESTION
VISION TWO

*"What is the truth
of all this?"*

**16 I came near unto one of them
that stood by, and asked him the
truth of all this. So he told me,
and made me know the interpretation of the things.**

Reminder: See **The Structure of Daniel** Chart on page 135. Vision
Two is now moving from the **Heavenly Scene** to the **Interlude Question.**
The **Interlude** is an interruption between the **Heavenly Scene** and the
Historic-Prophetic Outline.   The **Interlude Question** addressed in
Daniel 7:16 is "What is the truth of all this?" meaning "What is the truth
of all these beasts, especially the Little Horn?" The rest of the chapter will
provide answers.

> **INTERLUDE QUESTION**
> **DAN 7:16**
> **WHAT IS THE
> TRUTH OF
> ALL THIS?**

> **HEAVENLY SCENE**
> **DAN 7:2-14**
> **LION**
> **BEAR**
> **LEOPARD**
> **DREADFUL BEAST**
> **LITTLE HORN**

> **INTERLUDE QUESTION**
> **DAN 7:16**
> **WHAT IS THE
> TRUTH OF
> ALL THIS?**

Verse 16

Daniel wished to know the "truth of
all this" and how God was planning to
save His people from all the earthly
persecuting kingdoms represented by
these symbolic beasts and horns.
What would bring the Little Horn to
its end and finally deliver the people
of God? The first part of the answer
has been addressed in Daniel 7:9-10
and will be reaffirmed in verses 22
and 26 with the Investigative Judgment.

It is important to understand that the
Investigative Judgment was to be the
main factor in the deliverance of
God's people. Through the judgment,
the righteous would be legally vindicated and the wicked would be legally
condemned.

Daniel's great desire was ***"when"***
would the great Investigative Judgment begin. Chapters 8 and 9 provide
the answer.

Note: This Investigative Judgment
takes place in a heavenly "courtroom"
scene. Daniel describes the beginning
of the Investigative Judgment for the
saints.   In Revelation 20 John describes the Investigative Judgment of
the wicked. The execution of the ver-
dict for the righteous, or the wicked, is
called the Executive Judgment, or the
execution of judgment.

Reminder: See **The Structure of Daniel** Chart on page 135. Following the **Interlude Question,** Daniel 7:17 begins the interpretation of the vision symbols in the **Historic-Prophetic Outline.** Daniel's focus in this vision is on the fifth earthly kingdom called the Little Horn. This Outline extends the time of earthly kingdoms from 606 BC to AD 1798.

**HISTORIC-PROPHETIC
OUTLINE
VISION TWO**

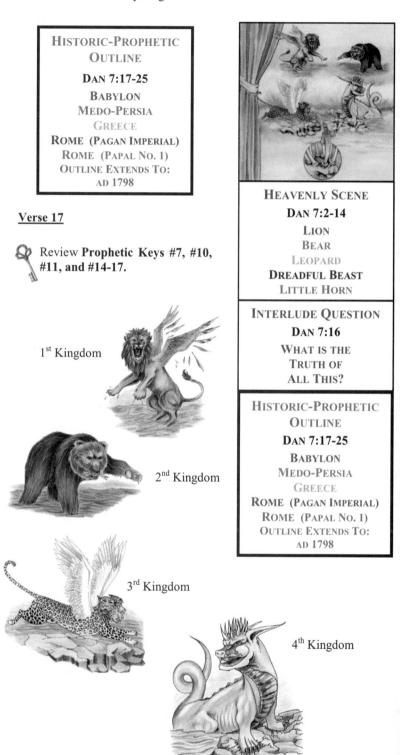

HISTORIC-PROPHETIC OUTLINE
DAN 7:17-25
BABYLON
MEDO-PERSIA
GREECE
ROME (PAGAN IMPERIAL)
ROME (PAPAL NO. 1)
OUTLINE EXTENDS TO:
AD 1798

HEAVENLY SCENE
DAN 7:2-14
LION
BEAR
LEOPARD
DREADFUL BEAST
LITTLE HORN

INTERLUDE QUESTION
DAN 7:16
WHAT IS THE TRUTH OF ALL THIS?

HISTORIC-PROPHETIC OUTLINE
DAN 7:17-25
BABYLON
MEDO-PERSIA
GREECE
ROME (PAGAN IMPERIAL)
ROME (PAPAL NO. 1)
OUTLINE EXTENDS TO:
AD 1798

*The Four Symbolic Beasts
are Interpreted as
Four Successive Kingdoms*

17 These great beasts, which are four, are four kings, which shall arise out of the earth.

(This verse will be repeated on the next several pages.)

Verse 17

🔑 Review **Prophetic Keys #7, #10, #11, and #14-17.**

1ˢᵗ Kingdom

2ⁿᵈ Kingdom

3ʳᵈ Kingdom

4ᵗʰ Kingdom

The Story of the Rise and Fall of Earthly Kingdoms

*The Four Symbolic Beasts
are Interpreted as
Four Successive Kingdoms*

17 These great beasts, which are four, are four kings, which shall arise out of the earth.

Verse 17 (Continued)

Prophetic Key #17 Each symbol must be <u>interpreted</u> by the Bible. (See Appendix 7A, on page 117, for extra help in decoding.)

*First Kingdom:
The **Lion** with Eagle's Wings
and a Man's Heart*

DAN 7:4 The <u>first was like a lion</u>, and had <u>eagle's wings</u>: I beheld till the <u>wings thereof were plucked</u>, and it was lifted up from the earth, and made stand upon the feet as a man, and a <u>man's heart</u> was given to it.

DEUT 28:49-50 The LORD shall bring a nation against thee from far, from the end of the earth, as <u>swift as the eagle flieth</u>; a nation whose tongue thou shalt not understand; 50 A nation of fierce countenance, which shall not regard the person of the old, nor shew favour to the young:

JER 4:7 The <u>lion</u> is come up from his thicket, and ... is on his way; he is gone forth from his place to make thy land desolate.

JER 50:17 Israel is a scattered sheep; the <u>lions</u> have driven him away: first the king of Assyria hath devoured him; and last this <u>Nebuchadrezzar king of Babylon</u> hath broken his bones.

JER 50:43-44 <u>The king of Babylon</u> 44 <u>shall come up like a lion</u> from the swelling of Jordan unto the habitation of the strong.

Prophetic Key #11 The **Lion** symbolizes the kingdom of **Babylon** with King Nebuchadnezzar as leader. This <u>recaps</u> with the **Head of Gold** in Daniel 2:38.

Prophetic Key #13 This vision adds extra information about the Kingdom of Babylon.

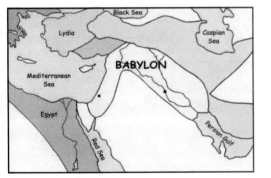

606 — 538 BC

"first was like a lion" — symbol of the "king of the beasts" and "king of Babylon." The lion is also noted for strength. (Note: The winged lion is commonly found on Babylonian art.)

"eagle's wings" — symbol of power, range of flight, and rapid conquest. The eagle was also a symbol of "king of the birds." (HAB 1:6, 8)

"wings plucked" — represent a time when less powerful rulers reigned and Babylon lost glory and power — not being able to fly anymore.

"man's heart" — represents Babylon's change of character from strength (through wealth and luxury), to weakness, in the declining years after the death of King Nebuchadnezzar.

CHAPTER 7   The Story of the Rise and Fall of Earthly Kingdoms

*The Four Symbolic Beasts
are Interpreted as
Four Successive Kingdoms*

17 These great beasts, which are four, are four kings, which shall arise out of the earth.

<u>Verse 17</u> (Continued)

🔑 **Prophetic Key #17**   Each symbol must be <u>interpreted</u> by the Bible. (See Appendix 7A, on page 118, for extra help in decoding.)

*Second Kingdom:
The Bear With Three Ribs*

DAN 7:5   And behold another beast, a second, like to a <u>bear</u>, and it <u>raised up itself on one side</u>, and it had <u>three ribs in the mouth</u> of it between the teeth of it: and they said thus unto it, Arise, <u>devour much flesh</u>.

🔗 **JER 51:11**   Make bright the arrows; gather the shields: the LORD hath raised up <u>the spirit of the kings of the Medes</u>: for his device <u>is against Babylon, to destroy it</u>; because it is the vengeance of the LORD, the vengeance of his temple.

DAN 5:28   Thy kingdom is divided, and given to the Medes and Persians.

🔑 **Prophetic Key #11**   The **Bear** symbolizes the Kingdom of **Medo-Persia**. This <u>recaps</u> with the **Silver Breast and Arms** in Daniel 2:39.

Prophetic Key #13   Extra information is given about Medo-Persia.

Note: Just as silver is inferior to gold, the bear's strength, speed, and prowess is inferior to the lion. The Medo-Persian kingdom was also inferior to the wealth and magnificence of Babylon.

"raised up itself on one side" — represents the Persians who became the more dominant power a few years before the dual kingdom conquered Babylon. The cruel characteristics of the bear represents the Medes.

🔗 **ISA 13:17, 19**   Behold, <u>I will stir up the Medes against them</u>, which shall not regard silver; and as for gold, they shall not delight in it. 19 <u>And Babylon</u>, the glory of kingdoms, the beauty of the Chaldees' excellency, <u>shall be as when God overthrew Sodom and Gomorrah.</u>

"three ribs in the mouth ... devour much flesh" — represents the three conquered territories of Babylon, Lydia, and Egypt (as noted on the map of page 97).

JER 51:28-29   Prepare against her the nations with the kings of the Medes, the captains thereof, and all the rulers thereof ... for every purpose of the LORD shall be performed against Babylon.

538 — 331 BC

CHAPTER 7 The Story of the Rise and Fall of Earthly Kingdoms

*The Four Symbolic Beasts
are Interpreted as
Four Successive Kingdoms*

17 These great beasts, which are four, are four kings, which shall arise out of the earth.

Verse 17 (Continued)

Prophetic Key #17 Each symbol must be <u>interpreted</u> by the Bible. (See Appendix 7A, on page 119, for extra help in decoding.)

*Third Kingdom:
The Leopard With
Four Wings and Four Heads*

DAN 7:6 After this I beheld, and lo <u>another, like a leopard</u>, which had upon the back of it <u>four wings of a fowl</u>; <u>the beast had also four heads</u>; and dominion was given to it.

Prophetic Key #11 In Vision Two the Leopard symbolizes the Kingdom of Greece. This <u>recaps</u> with the Brass Belly and Thighs in Daniel 2:39.

Prophetic Key #13 Vision Two adds extra information. Daniel 2 and secular history confirm the Third Kingdom is Greece. This vision moves forward to confirm the four divisions of Greece.

Note: Just as brass is inferior to silver, the kingdom represented by the leopard was also inferior to the kingdom of the bear, Medo-Persia. The leopard is a furtive but fierce, calculating, and carnivorous animal noted for its swiftness.

"four wings" — symbol of very, very rapid conquest as indicated by more than two wings. Alexander the Great's conquest of the greatest world kingdom (of that time) was achieved in only 12 years. This kingdom included Macedonia, Greece, Egypt, and all of the Persian Kingdom to the borders of India. The maps on page 37 point out that each successive kingdom also moves further west.

"four heads" — each head symbolizes one of the four generals under Alexander the Great. Alexander had no heir. After his death, Alexander's Grecian Kingdom was eventually divided between his four generals as listed below:

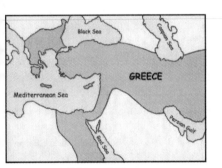

331 — 168 BC

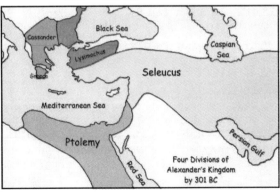

1. **Cassander** — Greece and Macedonia

2. **Lysimachus** — Asia Minor

3. **Seleucus** — Syria and Babylon

4. **Ptolemy** — Egypt and North Aftrica

(Note: "Greece" is an abbreviation for Alexander's "Greco-Macedonian" kingdom. Alexander's kingdom was united by the culture of Greek language, and thought.)

*The Four Symbolic Beasts
are Interpreted as
Four Successive Kingdoms*

17 These great beasts, which are four, are four kings, which shall arise out of the earth.

🗝 **Prophetic Key #17** Each symbol must be <u>interpreted</u> by the Bible. (See Appendix 7A, on page 120, for extra help in decoding.)

*Fourth Kingdom:
A **Dreadful Beast**
With Iron Teeth and Ten Horns*

DAN 7:7 After this I saw in the night visions, and behold a fourth beast, <u>dreadful and terrible</u>, and strong exceedingly; and it had great <u>iron teeth</u>: it devoured and brake in pieces, and <u>stamped the residue with the feet of it</u>: and it was <u>diverse from all the beasts that were before it</u>; and it had <u>ten horns</u>.

🗝 **Prophetic Key #11** In Vision Two the **Dreadful Beast** symbolizes the Kingdom of **Pagan Imperial Rome.** This <u>recaps</u> with the **Iron Legs** of Daniel 2:40. As the <u>dreadful beast</u> follows the leopard, Pagan Imperial Rome followed Greece. Iron is less valuable than brass; however, it is exceedingly strong.

Prophetic Key #13 This vision adds extra information regarding the ten horns.

"iron teeth" — represent cruelty and strength. Whole nations with their cities were torn to pieces and devoured. (PS 2:9)

"stamped the residue with the feet of it" — represents the *remnant* of those that did not hold the same political and religious preferences as Rome. Those not destroyed were made slaves of Pagan Imperial Rome.

"residue" — *Strong's* OT#7605 <u>a remainder</u>: KJV - other, <u>remnant</u>, residue, rest.

"The arms of the Republic, sometimes vanquished in battle, always victorious in war, advanced with rapid steps to the Euphrates, the Danube, the Rhine, and the ocean; and the images of gold, or silver, or brass, that might serve to represent the nations and their kings, <u>were successively broken by the iron monarchy of Rome</u>." Edward Gibbon, *The Decline and Fall of the Roman Empire,* Vol. III, p. 634. (Emphasis supplied.)

"diverse from all the beasts that were before it" — Rome's power to destroy was so intense that it surpassed all previous ruling earthly kingdoms.

"ten horns" — represent the kings of ten Barbaric tribes that fractured Pagan Imperial Rome into ten divisions between AD 351-476.

168 BC — AD 476

*The Saints Will
Inherit the Kingdom*

18 The saints of the most High shall take the kingdom, and possess the kingdom for ever, even for ever and ever.

Verse 18

Note: Once the Roman Kingdom (and all other earthly kingdoms) passes away, the Heavenly Kingdom, that endures forever, is presented to the saints. Daniel saw the Roman "Iron" Kingdom representing more than just Pagan Imperial Rome. The political system of the Little Horn (DAN 7:8, 24) is an *extension* of the Roman Kingdom that continues into the *iron feet.* Daniel 8 and 11 give further information on the following kingdoms represented in the toes of iron.

DANIEL

The Story of the Rise and Fall of Earthly Kingdoms

The Nature of
Pagan Imperial Rome
Described

19 Then I would know the truth of the fourth beast, which was diverse from all the others, exceeding dreadful, whose teeth were of iron, and his <u>nails of brass</u>; which devoured, brake in pieces, and stamped the residue with his feet;

Old Europe,
(Pagan Imperial Rome Divided)
— Symbolically Described —

20 And of the <u>ten horns</u> that were in his head ...

Verse 19

Additional Note: The transition from Greece to Rome was very gradual. By 168 BC, Rome had removed three of the four kings of Greece and forbade Macedonia to invade Egypt. By 30 BC, Egypt became a territory of Rome. Daniel 11 will expand on this historical aspect.

"nails of brass" — links with the Brass Belly on the Image of Daniel 2 and applies to the Greek philosophy that filtered down into the Pagan Roman Kingdom.

Verse 20

DAN 7:24 And the <u>ten horns</u> out of this kingdom <u>are ten kings</u> that shall arise ...

Ten Horns Represent the
Ten Divisions of Pagan Rome

1. Anglo-Saxons (England)
2. Franks (France)
3. Alamanni (Germany)
4. Lombards (Italy)
5. Seuvi (Portugal)
6. Visigoths (Spain)
7. Burgundians (Switzerland)
8. Ostrogoths (extinct)
9. Heruli (extinct)
10. Vandals (extinct)

(**Note:** The rise of the ten horns occurred between AD 351 and 476.)

Prophetic Key #7 Secular history will now assist in understanding the next portion of prophecy.

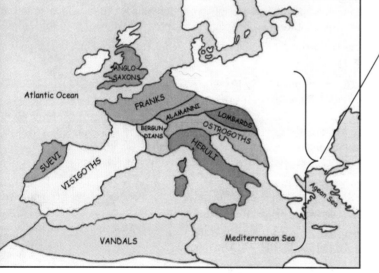

Ten Divisions of Pagan Imperial Rome by AD 476

Connecting Structure

The <u>Ten</u> Divisions of Pagan Imperial Rome from Vision One
— connect to —
the <u>Ten Horns</u> on the Dreadful Beast of Vision Two.

*The Fifth Kingdom Described
as the Little Horn
— it's Identity Defined*

20 ... and of the other which came up, and before whom <u>three</u> [horns] <u>fell</u>; even of that horn that had <u>eyes</u>, and a <u>mouth</u> that spake very great things, whose look was <u>more stout</u> than his fellows.

"more stout" — *Strong's* OT#7229 KJV - captain, chief, great, lord, master, stout. rib. See <u>OT#7378</u>.

<u>OT#7378</u> to toss, i.e. grapple; <u>mostly figuratively, to wrangle, i.e. hold a controversy</u>; to defend: KJV - adversary, chide, complain, contend, debate, ever, lay wait, plead, rebuke, strive, thoroughly.

Little Horn Rises AD 476 — 538
The Little Horn arose out of ten divisions of Rome. First it had to overcome the Vandals, the Ostrogoths, and the Heruli before assuming dominion over that part of the world.

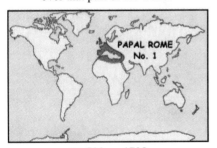

AD 538 — 1798

<u>Verse 20</u> (Concluded)

Prophetic Key #17 Each symbol must be <u>interpreted</u> by the Bible. (See Appendix 7A, on page 121, for extra help in decoding.)

Prophetic Key #7 Secular history will now assist in understanding the next portion of prophecy.

*Fifth Kingdom:
Emerges as the Little Horn*

DAN 7:8 I considered the horns, and, behold, there came up among them <u>another little horn</u>, before whom there were <u>three of the first horns plucked up</u> by the roots: and, behold, in this horn were <u>eyes like the eyes of man</u>, and <u>a mouth speaking great things</u>.

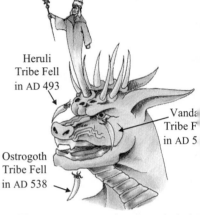

Heruli Tribe Fell in AD 493

Vanda[l] Tribe F[ell] in AD 5[...]

Ostrogoth Tribe Fell in AD 538

Prophetic Key #13 The Little Horn emerges as the next symbol representing **Papal Supremacy No. 1**. The prophecy has aligned perfectly with the first four kingdoms in Daniel 2. Verse 8 adds <u>extra information</u> on the succeeding Fifth Kingdom. The Little Horn aligns (or <u>recaps</u>) with the Roman Kingdom represented by the <u>iron in the feet</u> of Daniel 2:41. (See pages 122-123.)

Prophetic Key #10 All verses in this Outline have been kept in sequence, and have followed the same alignment of earthly kingdoms in Daniel 2.

Prophetic Key #11 Papal Supremacy No. 1 (Little Horn) follows the chronological order of secular historical events.

Prophetic Key #12 As the verses have "moved forward," time has also "moved forward."

Prophetic Key #5 The *Strong's Concordance* will aid to clarify the meaning of specific Biblical terms.

"another little horn" — is symbolic for another Roman kingdom, representing the apostate system of Papal Supremacy No. 1 which followed Pagan Imperial Rome. (See page 125 for identification of the Little Horn.)

Bible Definition: "Symbolic Horns" represent a king, kingdom, or power. (See DAN 8:20-21.)

"horn" — *Strong's* OT#7161 a horn (as projecting) ... <u>figuratively, power</u>: KJV - hill, horn.

"three of the first horns plucked up" — During the rise of the Little Horn (AD 476-538) three Barbarian tribes [horns], that supported Arianism, were uprooted due to theological differences with the Papal System. (Daniel 11 gives further details. See Glossary for Arianism.)

"plucked" — *Strong's* OT#6131 to pluck up (especially by the roots); specifically, to hamstring; <u>figuratively, [symbolically] **to exterminate**</u>: KJV - dig down, hough, pluck up, root up.

"eyes like the eyes of man" — are a symbol of intelligence, insight, and foresight. (See EPH 1:18.) The Barbarian tribes were largely illiterate.

"a mouth speaking great things" — represents official edicts given out in the context of political and religious matters combined with church tradition implying the Little Horn would be in opposition to the true God.

*The Little Horn —
a Continuing Persecutor
of God's People ...*

21 I beheld, and the same [little] **horn made war with the saints, and prevailed against them;**

22 Until [1]**the Ancient of days** [God the Father] **came ...**

... Until the Judgment Awards the Kingdom to the Saints

22 ... and [2]**judgment was given to the saints of the most High; and the time came that the** [3]**saints possessed the kingdom.**

Verses 21-22

Note: The vision takes Daniel over the previous scene of events again, giving more information on the Investigative Judgment. Three important events come forward:

1. *"the Ancient of days came"* — The coming of the Ancient of Days which opens the judgment scene of verses 9 and 10.
2. *"judgment was given to the saints"* — The Investigative Judgment process (by Jesus Christ) takes place before the Second Coming. After the Second Coming of Christ, the second phase of the Investigative Judgment begins when the saints sit with Jesus for a thousand years to confirm His judgment of the wicked. This enables the saints to understand the perfect judgment of God.

1 COR 6:2-3 Do ye not know that the saints shall judge the world? 3 Know ye not that we shall judge angels?

REV 19:21; 20:3-5 21 And the remnant [of the wicked] were slain with the sword of him that sat upon the horse 3 till the thousand years should be fulfilled. 4 And I saw thrones, and they [righteous] sat upon them, and judgment was given unto them: and I saw the souls of them that were beheaded for the witness of Jesus, and for the word of God, and which had not worshipped the beast, neither his image, neither had received his mark upon their foreheads, or in their hands; and they lived and reigned with Christ a thousand years. 5 But the rest of the dead lived not again until the thousand years were finished.

3. *"saints possessed the kingdom"* — When Jesus returns to the Earth the third time (after the 1000 years), the saints possess the kingdom of the New Jerusalem on the New Earth. The curse of sin and sinners will be wiped away forever in the everlasting fire. This is the Executive Judgment of the wicked. (See REV 20:7, 10, 14.)

MATT 25:33-34, 41 And he shall set the sheep on his right hand, but the goats on the left. 34 Then shall the King say unto them on his right hand, Come, ye blessed of my Father, inherit the kingdom prepared for you from the foundation of the world: 41 Then shall he say also unto them on the left hand, Depart from me, ye cursed, into everlasting fire, prepared for the devil and his angels.

DANIEL

The Story of the Rise and Fall of Earthly Kingdoms

Pagan Imperial Rome —
the Iron and Harsh Kingdom

23 Thus he said, The fourth beast shall be the fourth kingdom upon earth, which shall be diverse from all kingdoms, and shall devour the whole earth, and shall tread it down, and break it in pieces.

The Little Horn is
Diverse From
Pagan Imperial Rome

24 And the ten horns out of this kingdom are ten kings that shall arise: and another shall rise after them; and he shall be <u>diverse from the first</u>, and <u>he shall subdue three kings</u>.

Important Note: The Biblical references, in the Books of Daniel and Revelation, to the Little Horn are describing a counterfeit apostate <u>system</u> of worship. It does not blame the people that are deceived by it.

The fault is not aimed at our dear friends, neighbors, and even loved ones of our own families! This apostate system is a counterfeit because it mingled the worship of the Creator God with the degenerate forms of sun worship. It is arrogant, claiming to have changed times of worship and the very Commandments of God!

This apostate system has obscured the ministry of Christ by substituting a human process in place of divine intercession. It teaches false doctrines like the worship of dead saints, the fear of a vengeful, unforgiving God, and the infallibility of its leaders, "sitting in the temple of God, claiming to be god on earth." It is this apostate Pagan System of worship that is condemned, not its unfortunate worshippers who are instructed to "Come out of Babylon!"

<u>Verse 23</u> See comments on pages 100-101.

<u>Verse 24</u>

"diverse from the first" — the Papal Supremacy was an <u>ecclesiastical</u> kingdom ruled by a pontiff. The previous four kingdoms were <u>political</u> powers ruled by kings.

"he shall subdue three kings" — "The three tribes (Vandals, Heruli, and Ostrogoths) that were subdued were believers of the Arian teaching "that the Son was totally and essentially distinct from the Father; that He was the first and noblest of those beings whom the Father had created out of nothing, the instrument by whose subordinate operation the Almighty Father formed the universe, and therefore inferior to the Father, both in nature and dignity." John L. Mosheim, *An Ecclesiastical History, Ancient and Modern,* Vol. I, p. 412.

- Roman Emperor Justinian temporarily reunited Italy and parts of the western Roman Kingdom with some of the eastern parts of the former Roman Kingdom. He also gathered and organized the existing laws of the kingdom into a unified imperial code.
- AD 533: As part of the imperial code, Justinian confirms the Pope as "head of the church" and "corrector of heretics."
- AD 538: When the power of the last Arian tribe (Ostrogoths) was broken, the Papacy was then free to develop both its political power, conferred by Justinian <u>and</u> its religious authority. This formed the "<u>diverse</u>" religio-political kingdom [or nature] of Papal Rome. (As a result, the Pope of Rome became the most influential individual in Old Europe, as well as the head of a well organized church <u>system</u>.)
- Result: The remaining seven "horns" [kingdoms of Old Europe] became part of the Roman Catholic Papal political/religious system.
- The Kingdom of Pagan Imperial Roman was never conquered by another political-military force. It was <u>absorbed</u> into the rising religious force whose dominion would be even more cruel and lengthy.

Additional Notes and Definitions:
- "Catholic" was a term first introduced around AD 115 which referred to mainstream Christianity (in the 2nd and 3rd centuries) of the ancient undivided church. This term made a distinction between the orthodox and sectarian (or heretical).
- *"orthodox"* — Sound in the Christian faith; believing the genuine doctrines taught in the Scriptures; opposed to heretical. *Noah Webster 1828 Dictionary.*
- *"sectarian"* — One of a party in religion which has separated itself from the established church, or which holds tenets different from those of the prevailing denomination in a kingdom or state. *Noah Webster 1828 Dictionary.*
- *"heretical"* — Containing heresy; contrary to the established faith, or to the true faith. *Noah Webster 1828 Dictionary.*
- *"heretic"* — One who holds controversial opinions, esp. one who publicly dissents from the officially accepted dogma of the Roman Catholic Church. *American Heritage Dictionary.*
- "Roman Catholic" is a term that evolved when Pagan Imperial Rome declined through invasions of Germanic tribes. Today the term is specific to the Roman Catholic Church.

DANIEL

The Little Horn
Speaks Blasphemy

25 And <u>he shall speak great words against the most High</u>, and shall wear out the saints of the most High, and think to change times and laws: and they shall be given into his hand until a time and times and the dividing of time.

(This verse given on the next several pages.)

Additional Interesting Quotes

"The transfer of the emperor's residence to Constantinople was a sad blow to the prestige of Rome, and at that time one might have predicted her speedy decline. But the development of the church, and the growing authority of the Bishop of Rome, or the pope, gave her a new lease on life, and made her again the capital — this time the religious capital — of the civilized world." *Abbot's ROMAN History,* p. 236.

"The Popes filled the place of the vacant Emperors at Rome, inheriting their power, prestige and titles from paganism. Constantine left all to the Bishop of Rome ... The Papacy is but the ghost of the deceased Roman Empire sitting crowned upon its grave." *Stanley's HISTORY,* p. 40.

Verse 25

(See Appendix 7B, on pages 122-123, for supplemental documentation.)

Bible Definition: Blasphemy

MATT 12:31 Wherefore I say unto you, All manner of sin and blasphemy shall be forgiven unto men: but the <u>blasphemy</u> against the Holy Ghost shall not be forgiven unto men.

JOHN 10:33 The Jews answered him, saying, For a good work we stone thee not; but for <u>blasphemy</u>; and <u>because that thou, being a man, makest thyself God.</u>

LUKE 5:21 And the scribes and the Pharisees began to reason, saying, Who is this which <u>speaketh blasphemies</u>? Who can forgive sins, but God alone?

LUKE 5:24 But that ye may know that the Son of man hath power upon earth to forgive sins, (he said unto the sick of the palsy,) I say unto thee, Arise, and take up thy couch, and go into thine house.

"... he shall speak great words against the most High ..."

MARK 3:28-29 Verily I say unto you, All sins shall be forgiven unto the sons of men, and blasphemies wheresoever they shall blaspheme: 29 But he that shall blaspheme against the Holy Ghost hath never forgiveness, but is in danger of eternal damnation.

Papal Blasphemy

1. Usurping the Titles and Offices of God
2. Claiming to Offer Forgiveness of Sin

OFFICE OF GOD	PAPAL TITLE
GOD THE FATHER	THE HOLY FATHER
THE HOLY SPIRIT	THE VICAR OF CHRIST
JESUS CHRIST, MEDIATOR 1 TIM 2:5	MEDIATOR FOR FORGIVENESS OF SIN

Bible Definition: Man's Mediator

1 TIM 2:5 For there is one God, and <u>one mediator</u> between God and men, the man <u>Christ Jesus</u>.

2 THESS 2:4 Who opposeth and exalteth himself above all that is called God, or that is worshipped; so that he as God sitteth in the temple of God, shewing himself that he is God.

"antichrist" — *Strong's* NT#500 antichristos; from <u>**NT#473**</u>; <u>an opponent of the Messiah</u>: KJV - antichrist [a usurper].

<u>**NT#473 anti,**</u> an-tee a primary particle; opposite, i.e. *instead of* [Christ].

*The Little Horn
Wears Out the Saints*

25 And he shall speak great words against the most High, and <u>shall wear out the saints of the most High</u>, and think to change times and laws: and they shall be given into his hand until a time and times and the dividing of time.

Prophetic Key #7 Secular history assists in understanding this prophecy that was written over 1000 years in advance.

<u>Verse 25</u> (Continued)

(See Appendix 7B, on pages 122-123, for supplemental documentation.)

"shall wear out the saints of the most high" — (also described in verse 21.)

Papal Acknowledgment of Her Persecution

"In the Bull 'Ad exstirpanda' (1252) [Pope] Innocent IV says: 'When those adjudged guilty of heresy have been given up to the civil power by the bishop or his representative, or the Inquisition, the podesta or chief magistrate of the city shall take them at once, and shall, within five days at the most, execute the laws made against them.' . . . Nor could any doubt remain as to what civil regulations were meant, for the passages which ordered the burning of impenitent heretics were inserted in the papal decretals from the imperial constitutions

"… shall wear out the saints of the most High …"

'Commissis nobis' and 'Inconsutibilem tunicam.' The aforesaid Bull 'Ad exstirpanda' remained thenceforth a fundamental document of the Inquisition, renewed or re-enforced by several popes, Alexander IV (1254-61), Clement IV (1265-68), Nicholas IV (1288-92), Boniface VIII (1294-1303), and others. The civil authorities, therefore, were enjoined by the popes, under pain of excommunication to execute the legal sentences that condemned impenitent heretics to the stake." *The Catholic Encyclopedia,* Joseph Blotzer, art. "Inquisition," Vol. VIII, p, 34.

Protestant Acknowledgement of Papal Persecution

"Can anyone doubt that this is true of the papacy? The Inquisition, the 'persecutions of the Waldenses;' the ravages of the Duke of Alva; the fires of Smithfield; the tortures at Goa — indeed, the whole history of the papacy may be appealed to in proof that this is applicable to that power. If anything *could* have 'worn out the saints of the Most High' — could have cut them off from the earth so that evangelical religion would have become extinct, it would have been the persecutions of the papal power. <u>In the year 1208, a crusade was proclaimed by Pope Innocent III against the Waldenses and Albigenses, in which a million of men perished. From the beginning of the order of the Jesuits, in the year 1540, to 1580, nine hundred thousand were destroyed. One hundred and fifty thousand perished by the Inquisition in thirty years. In the Low Countries fifty thousand persons were hanged, beheaded, burned, and buried alive, for the crime of heresy, within the space of thirty-eight years from the edict of Charles V against the Protestants, to the peace of Chateau Cambreses in 1559. Eighteen thousand suffered by the hand of the executioner in the space of five years and a half during the administration of the Duke of Alva.</u> Indeed, the slightest acquaintance with the history of the papacy will convince any one that what is here said of 'making war with the saints' (verse 21), and 'wearing out the saints of the Most High' (verse 25), is strictly applicable to that power, and will accurately describe its history." Albert Barnes, *Notes on Daniel,* p. 328, comment on Daniel 7:25. (Emphasis supplied.)

The Little Horn
Will Change Times and Laws

25 And he shall speak great words against the most High, and shall wear out the saints of the most High, and think to change times and laws: and they shall be given into his hand until a time and times and the dividing of time.

Prophetic Key #7 Secular history assists in understanding this prophecy that was written over 1000 years in advance.

Verse 25 (Continued)

(See Appendix 7B, on pages 122-123, for supplemental documentation.)

"think to change times and laws"

"change" — *Strong's* OT#8133 KJV - alter, change, (be) diverse.

2 THESS 2:3-4 and that man of sin be revealed, the son of perdition; 4 Who opposeth and exalteth himself above all that is called God, or that is worshipped; so that he as God sitteth in the temple of God, shewing himself that he is God.

Note: Only the "man of sin" would exalt himself above God and "think to change times and laws."

"... think to change times and laws ... "

God's Commands for "times" —
the Holy Convocations

LEV 23:2 Speak unto the children of Israel, and say unto them, Concerning the feasts of the LORD, which ye shall proclaim to be holy convocations, even these are my feasts.

"times" — *Strong's* OT#2166 the same as **OT#2165:** KJV - season, time. **OT#2165**; an appointed occasion:

Note: The word translated *times* comes from a Chaldean word meaning *seasons*. The Daniel 7:25 passage predicts that all of God's Holy Days would come under attack by Satan who works through a religious/political system. When Satan (Lucifer) rebelled in heaven, (ISA 14:12-13; EZE 28:12-19), he said he would be like the Most High and would set his throne above God's throne. This includes, changing and casting down ALL of God's principles, **and the "daily"** of DAN 8:10-12. (See page 140.) Daniel 7:25 runs parallel to Daniel 8:12, demonstrating where Satan has attacked **ALL** of God's sacred principles.

Note: See Appendix 7D — The Change of "times" and "laws" on pages 126-134. Begin by reading the summary, ***"Resting in All of God Truths,"*** on page 134.

God's Commands for "laws" —
the Moral Law and Statues

DEUT 30:16 I command thee this day to love the LORD thy God, to walk in his ways, and to keep his commandments and his statutes and his judgments ...

"laws" — *Strong's* OT#1882 corresponding to **OT#1881;** decree, law. **OT#1881**; a royal edict or statute: KJV - commandment, commission, decree, law, manner.

Note: Although the Papal System has altered the Second, Fourth, and Tenth Commandments of the Moral Law, the Fourth Commandment of the Moral Law is desecrated the most today. The weekly Seventh-day Sabbath of Exodus 20:8-11, is determined by the daily cycle as set by the sun. The Scriptures do not command Sunday (the first day of the week) to be kept in honor of the resurrection. Rather, Jesus instituted the Lord's Supper in honor of His death, burial, and resurrection. (See 1 COR 11:24-25.)

Prophetic Key #5 Scripture is written in an ancient language. For the study given in Appendix 7D, a *Strong's Analytical Concordance*, and Bible Dictionary will be helpful to clarify meanings.

Thought Questions: God created everything in this universe. Can man dismiss anything created by God? God created ALL the Sabbaths, sanctifying and making them holy forever. How can man dismiss any of these Sabbaths which God has created and sanctified? According to Scripture, even God cannot (and does not) change His laws. Yet, the Papal System has attempted to alter ALL of God's Truths — not just Commandments 2, 4, and 10 as noted on page 130. In Daniel 7:25, the emphasis has been given to the changes of Sabbath day laws. This is the Papacy's direct attack against the authority of the Creator God of Heaven. (Review the material on page 57 regarding God's Seal.)

The Changeless Character of God

MAL 3:6 For I am the LORD, I change not.

HEB 13:8 Jesus Christ the same yesterday, and to day, and for ever.

The Little Horn
Will Persecute for 1260 Years

25 And he shall speak great words against the most High, and shall wear out the saints of the most High, and think to change times and laws: and they shall be given into his hand until a time and times and the dividing of time.

Verse 25 (Conclusion)

(See Appendix 7B, on pages 122-123, for supplemental documentation.)

"they shall be given into his hand until a time and times and the dividing of time" — see page 109 for calculation of this timeline.

"hand" — Strong's OT#3028 KJV - hand, power.

"time" — Strong's OT#5732 a set time; technically, a year: KJV - time.

"until" — Strong's OT#5705 corresponding to **OT#5704**; and, at, for, [hither-] to, on till, until, within.

OT#5704 as far (or long, or much) as, whether of space (even unto) or time (during, while, until) or degree (equally with) ...

"... they shall be given into his
hand until a time and times
and the dividing of time."

Prophetic Key #7 Secular history assists in understanding this prophecy that was written over 1000 years in advance.

Prophetic Key #8 This prophecy does not have a dual application to the future. This symbolic time equaled 1260 years and reaches "as far (or long) as" that time extended the power of the Papal hand.

Prophetic Key #13 The 1260 day timeline in this vision moves "time" forward to datable time of 1798.

Prophetic Key #26 The voices of this 1260 year timeline began with Justinian's decree and ended with Napoleon's voice of judgment.

Prophetic Key #27 The beginning of this timeline brought the unpleasant news or persecution to God's people. The ending of the timeline brought news of deliverance from persecution.

Historical Data Review: Papal Supremacy No. 1 extended over Old Europe from the time when the Roman Emperor, Justinian, wrote a decretal letter in AD 533 giving the Popes the ecclesiastical and political "power ... seat, and great authority." This became effective in AD 538 once the power of the Arian tribes was broken. That authority ended **1260 years later,** when Napoleon took Pope Pius VI captive in AD 1798. The Pope died in exile in France in 1799.

Note: Many sincere Christians were persecuted and put to death during the reign of the Papal Little Horn. The Papacy acknowledges this persecution and defends these acts as being granted from Christ. According to the church, those that were labeled as heretics were most often condemned to death — all in the name of the Lord.

JOHN 16:2-3 They shall put you out of the synagogues: yea, the time cometh, that whosoever killeth you will think that he doeth God service. **3** And these things will they do unto you, because they have not known the Father, nor me.

Counting out the "time and times and the dividing of time"

The word *time*, as used by the prophets Daniel and John is a prophetic term. It is unique to apocalyptic prophecy, referring to a year, as in Daniel 4:16, 23, 25, and 32 in the seven year timeline of the humiliation and insanity of Nebuchadnezzar. The word, *time*, is unique in that it refers to the Jewish solar year of only 360 literal days. When counting out the "time and times and the dividing of time," the word *time* refers to a 360 day-year.

Genesis 7:11 and 8:14, equate 150 days with five months of 30 days each. Therefore, 12 months of 30 days each would equal 360 days. (See page 60 for the calculations.)

Whenever Daniel, (or John in the Revelation), presented a timeline, they used the word *time* for a year of 360 days. Therefore, the phrase "time and times and a dividing of time," (when couched in symbolic language) is counted out using the Year-day Computation Principle as follows:

Time	=	360 (symbolic) days
Times	=	720 (symbolic) days (360x2 = 720)
Dividing of Times	=	180 (symbolic) days (360/2 = 180)
Total Length of DAN 7:25 Timeline	=	1260 (symbolic) days or 1260 literal years

The following three terms are often confused. (Reminder: The word *prophetic* is derived from the word *prophecy*.)

1. **Prophetic Time** simply means that the time element is found within a prophecy. Whether a timeline is written in a symbolic or literal setting — as long as it is couched in a prophecy — it is *prophetic time*.

2. **Literal Time** refers to a 24 hour day in a literal context.

3. **Symbolic Time** must lie within a symbolic context. Therefore, the symbolic time must be decoded correctly. See the following Prophetic Keys:

Prophetic Key #23 The prophetic timeline in Daniel 7:25 is contained within an Historic-Prophetic Outline using symbolism of "beasts and horns." Therefore, this timeline is *symbolic prophetic time.*

Prophetic Key #24a/b *Symbolic prophetic time* must be decoded using the Year-day Computation Principle of Numbers 14:34 and Ezekiel 4:6: "I have appointed thee each day for a year." In Daniel 7:25, the 1260 symbolic days = 1260 literal years.

Prophetic Key #13 The timeline in this vision has moved the Historic-Prophetic Outline forward to AD 1798 in datable time.

Prophetic Timeline #2: Details and Specifics

Timeline #2 (Length of Timeline)	Subject (of Timeline)	Prophetic Scripture For Timeline	Timeline Begins (with)	Speaking VOICE (Decree)	Timeline Ends (with)	Legislative & Judicial Action (Date)
1260 years DAN 7:25	Little Horn or Papal Rome No. 1 DAN 7:8, 20, 24, 25	DAN 7:25	Persecution of God's People by Papal Rome No. 1 DAN 7:25	Justinian's Decree Enacted in AD 538	Deliverance of God's People from Papal Rome No. 1	Napoleon's Voice of Judgment in AD 1798

Reminder: See **The Structure of Daniel** Chart on page 135. Following the **Historic-Prophetic Outline** of the Second Vision is the **Answer** given in Daniel 7:26, to the **Interlude Question** of Daniel 7:16. The answer to the "truth of all this" is that God makes provision for the redeemed to join Him in the Investigative Judgment of the wicked.

ANSWER TO QUESTION

("What is the truth of all this?")

VISION TWO

"Judgment Sits With the Ancient of Days!"

Through the Process of the Investigative Judgment the Little Horn Papacy Loses all Dominion to the Saints

26 But the judgment shall sit, and they shall take away his dominion, to consume and to destroy it unto the end.

ANSWER TO QUESTION
DAN 7:26
"JUDGMENT SITS WITH THE ANCIENT OF DAYS!"
ENDTIME EVENT
DAN 7:27
"KINGDOM GIVEN TO THE SAINTS"

Verse 26

Verse 25 brought the Historic-Prophetic Outline to AD 1798 — the end of the 1260 prophetic years of reign for the Little Horn kingdom. Between verses 25 and 26 there is another *gap* of time where no information is given between 1798 and the Investigative Judgment of the righteous. The Third Vision will give additional information that closes this gap of time.

Revelation supplies information on the Investigative Judgment of the wicked.

The "Beast" Destroyed For Eternity (Executive Judgment of Second Death)

REV 19:20 And <u>the beast</u> was taken, and with him the false prophet that wrought miracles before him, with which he deceived them that had received the mark of the beast, and them that worshipped his image. These both were <u>cast alive into a lake of fire</u> burning with brimstone.

REV 20:14 And death and hell were cast into the lake of fire. <u>This is the second death</u>.

HEAVENLY SCENE
DAN 7:2-14
LION
BEAR
LEOPARD
DREADFUL BEAST
LITTLE HORN

INTERLUDE QUESTION
DAN 7:16
WHAT IS THE TRUTH OF ALL THIS?

HISTORIC-PROPHETIC OUTLINE
DAN 7:17-25
BABYLON
MEDO-PERSIA
GREECE
ROME (PAGAN IMPERIAL)
ROME (PAPAL NO. 1)
OUTLINE EXTENDS TO: AD 1798

ANSWER TO QUESTION
DAN 7:26
"JUDGMENT SITS WITH THE ANCIENT OF DAYS!"
ENDTIME EVENT
DAN 7:27
"KINGDOM GIVEN TO THE SAINTS"

Prophetic Key #7 In this vision, as time moved forward, the prophecy unfolded and was clearly revealed.

Prophetic Key #13 The following prophetic visions in Daniel 8-12 will reveal information on future kingdoms. Dates will be established from secular historical data.

ENDTIME EVENT
VISION TWO

*The Saints Receive
the Heavenly Kingdom*

27 And the kingdom and dominion, and the greatness of the kingdom under the whole heaven, shall be given to the people of the saints of the most High, whose kingdom is an everlasting kingdom, and all dominions shall serve and obey him.

*The **End** of the Second
Historic-Prophetic Outline*

*"Tidy-Up" Verse for
Vision Two*

*The Dream and the
Visions Trouble Daniel*

28 Hitherto is the end of the matter. As for me Daniel, my cogitations much troubled me, and my countenance changed in me: but I kept the matter in my heart.

Reminder: (Continued) The **Endtime Event** is the establishment of the Heavenly Kingdom given to the saints. God's plan of judgment has delivered His people from all persecutors — forever!

Verse 27

HEB 1:8 But unto the Son he saith, Thy throne, O God, is for ever and ever: a scepter of righteousness is the scepter of thy kingdom.

LUKE 1:33 And he shall reign over the house of Jacob for ever; and of his kingdom there shall be no end.

DAN 7:14 And there was given him dominion, and glory, and a kingdom, that all people, nations, and languages, should serve him: his dominion is an everlasting dominion, which shall not pass away, and his kingdom that which shall not be destroyed.

Prophetic Key #29 The Historic-Prophetic Outline of earthly kingdoms ends with the establishment of Christ's kingdom. No indication as to the day and hour of this great event is given.

MATT 24:36 But of that day and hour knoweth no man, no, not the angels of heaven, but my Father only.

Verse 28

Note: In this chapter, Daniel's great desire was to know <u>when</u> the Investigative Judgment would begin. He was not to have this information until the next vision in chapters 8 and 9.

Prophetic Key #30 The last verse of this chapter is the "tidy-up" verse which indicates that the Historic-Prophetic Outline is completely finished and there is nothing more to be added.

ISA 25:9 And it shall be said in that day, Lo, this is our God; we have waited for him, and he will save us: this is the LORD; we have waited for him, we will be glad and rejoice in his salvation.

General Review and Theme of Vision Two: "Christ our Judge"

• Daniel 7 reviews the political scenes a second time, adding the 1260 years of the Dark Ages. The vision has traced the controversy between Christ and Satan from literal Babylon (the center of Satan's kingdom) to Spiritual Babylon, which is today's center of Satan's kingdom. Satan's kingdom succeeded in persuading people that the Law of God has been changed. But, the Judgment sits and Christ's kingdom will be eventually established and peopled by those who remain loyal to God. The vision climaxes with judgment in heaven, where Christ receives His kingdom and shares it with the saints that have received His forgiveness.

Daniel 7 — Review of the Historic-Prophetic Outline in Vision 2

1. Vision 2 uses some symbolic language to introduce a Symbolic Vision of Beasts and Horns.
2. Vision 2 describes and reveals **Five earthly kingdoms** surrounding God's people.
3. Vision 2 extends from 606 BC to the Establishment of Christ's kingdom in One Major Line of Prophecy.
4. Vision 2 <u>repeats</u> the former information of Vision 1. The Outline adds extra information of another kingdom and a timeline. Each successive vision will follow this procedure.
5. The symbols in Vision 2 must have a Biblical interpretation for the symbols because the "Bible is its own Interpreter." e.g. Daniel 7:17 "<u>These great beasts</u>, which are four, <u>are four kings</u> which shall arise out of the earth."
6. The Outline of Vision 2 is decoded according to secular history and continues to <u>recap and review</u> the Daniel 2 sequence of kingdoms: (Note the following new information given in red.)
   1st Kingdom = Lion Beast = BABYLON (606 — 538 BC)
   2nd Kingdom = Bear Beast = MEDO-PERSIA (538 — 331 BC)
   3rd Kingdom = Leopard Beast = GREECE (331 — 168 BC)
   - <u>New Information:</u> In Vision 2, Greece is divided into four divisions representing the four heads of the leopard beast.
   4th Kingdom = Dreadful Beast = PAGAN IMPERIAL ROME (168 BC — AD 476) **(This Beast has ten horns.)**
   - 5th **Kingdom** = <u>Little Horn</u> = <u>PAPAL SUPREMACY NO. 1</u> (AD 538 — 1798)
   - <u>New Information:</u> Vision 2 adds a timeline in Daniel 7:25 — "… a time and times and the dividing of time."
   a. **Prophetic Time:** The word *prophetic* comes from the word *prophecy*. Whether *time* in prophecy is written with or without symbolic language, the timeline is still considered **prophetic time**. Before attempting to decode any prophetic time, it must first be determined if the timeline is set within a *symbolic context* or a *literal context*.
   b. **Context:** The symbolic language or literal language establishes the context or setting to determine whether a timeline is to be understood as literal time OR symbolic time. Symbolic time is then interpreted by the Year-day Principle.
   c. WHEN the OUTLINE is written using <u>symbols</u>, (as in Vision 2) THEN the prophetic timeline in the Outline must be calculated as **prophetic symbolic time**.
   d. Just as symbolic beasts must be converted to literal kingdoms, the prophetic <u>symbolic</u> time must be converted to prophetic <u>literal</u> time.
   d. The Biblical conversion of *time* is found in Genesis 7 and 8. A time = 12 months; 1 month = 30 days.
   e. The Biblical conversion for prophetic symbolic time is found in Numbers 14:34 and Ezekiel 4:6 — one prophetic symbolic day = one prophetic literal year.
   f. Therefore: the timeline in Daniel 7:25 = 1260 prophetic symbolic days which = 1260 prophetic literal years.
   - **Extremely Important note:** This <u>1260 year timeline</u> is mentioned only **ONCE** in this vision and only **ONCE** in the Book of Daniel.

Note:
- **The ten horns on the Dreadful Beast represented the ten divisions of Pagan Imperial Rome** — the territory under the rule of Pagan Imperial Rome up until AD 476 when Rome was broken up by barbarous tribes into ten divisions.
- **Three of the ten horns (which are now extinct) were rooted out by Papal Roman Supremacy No. 1.**
- **In Daniel 2 the "Stone Kingdom" hits the <u>toes</u> which represents ten (or ALL the) kingdoms of the earth at the end of time or the Second Coming of Christ.**
- <u>**Therefore:**</u> the ten DIVISIONS or ten HORNS (of Pagan Imperial Rome) can <u>be compared with the TOES on the image ONLY in the "break up" of Pagan Rome and the "break up" of the endtime government on earth!</u>

7. **Datable Time:** Vision 2 extends to AD **1798** in **datable time** because the 1260 year timeline moves the vision forward in time from AD 538. The Little Horn power was wounded in 1798. (AD 538 + 1260 years = AD 1798.)
   - **VISION 2** reveals information for the large "gap" of time from AD 476 to 1798. Now the gap of time between 1798 and when the "saints receive the kingdom" has been reduced. Therefore, **this vision has MOVED FORWARD IN TIME.** All Outlines in the Visions following Daniel 2 move forward in time.
8. **Emphasis in Vision 2** is on Papal Roman Supremacy No. 1. This kingdom persecuted God's people the longest. It is an extension of Pagan Imperial Rome. Papal Supremacy No. 1 has the most exposure in the verses of this chapter.
9. **Vision 2 Tidy-up Verse:** Daniel 7:25 is the verse that ends the Historic-Prophetic Outline. There is nothing more to be added to the Outline.
10. **Endtime Event:** Vision 2 ends with the "saints receiving the kingdom" at the Second Coming.

THE STRUCTURE OF DANIEL'S <u>SECOND</u> OUTLINE
The Rise and Fall of Earthly Kingdoms Surrounding God's People
One Major Line of Prophecy From 606 BC — to the Establishment of Christ's Kingdom

DANIEL 7 (Vision 2 uses some Symbolic language for the following Historic-Prophetic Outline.)
The Symbolic <u>BEASTS and HORNS</u> represent Literal Kingdoms in the Outline.

LION
DAN 7:4

#1 BABYLON
606 — 538 BC

BEAR
DAN 7:5

#2 MEDO-PERSIA
538 — 331 BC

LEOPARD
DAN 7:6

#3 GREECE
331 — 168 BC

DREADFUL BEAST
DAN 7:7-8

#4 ROME
(Pagan Imperial)
168 BC — AD 476

DAN 7:20 "And of the ten horns that were in his head …" — These symbolic ten horns reveal the break up of the Pagan Imperial Roman Kingdom into ten nations by AD 476. The Little Horn uprooted three of these horns which were Arian tribes.

LITTLE HORN
DAN 7:20-25

#4A ROME
(Papal Supremacy No. 1)
AD 538 — 1798

DAN 7:20 "... and of the other which came up, and before whom three fell; even of that horn that had eyes, and a mouth that spake very great things, whose look was more stout than his fellows."

Symbolic Timeline (DAN 7:25)
"time and times and the dividing of time"
= 1260 years of literal time from
AD 538 — 1798

Vision Two
Time extends from
606 BC — AD 1798

VISION #

2

The Last Kingdom will be consumed and destroyed.
The "Heavenly Kingdom" shall be given
to the people of the saints. DAN 7:27

Connecting Structure

IRON LEGS
Dan 2:40

#4 ROME
(Pagan Imperial)
168 BC — AD 476

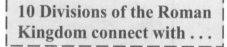

10 Divisions of the Roman Kingdom connect with . . .

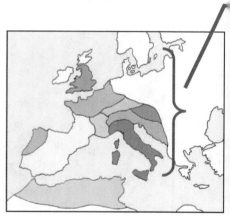

10 Divisions of Pagan Rome by AD 476

VISION #

1

Between Visions 1 & 2

DANIEL'S SECOND OUTLINE

┌─────────────────────────────┐
│ . . . the 10 "horns" on the │
│ Dreadful Beast of Rome.   │
└─────────────────────────────┘

**DREADFUL
BEAST**
DAN 7:7-8

#4 ROME
(Pagan Imperial)
168 BC — AD 476

DAN 7:20 "And of the ten horns that were in his head ..." — These symbolic ten horns reveal the break up of the Pagan Imperial Roman Kingdom into ten nations by AD 476. The Little Horn uprooted three of these horns which were Arian tribes.

VISION #

2

Daniel 7:3

3 And <u>four great beasts</u> came up from the sea, diverse one from another.

Application of Prophetic Key #17

SYMBOL: "four great beasts"

DECODING by Scripture:

- **DAN 7:17** "[four] great beasts are ... four kings"

APPLICATION: The four beasts represent four successive kingdoms that begin with Babylon which is represented by the first beast.

1. **BABYLON: JER 50:7, 17** The <u>lion</u> is come up from his thicket. 17 Israel is a scattered sheep; the <u>lions</u> have driven him away: first the king of Assyria hath devoured him [the northern kingdom of Israel]; and last this <u>Nebuchadrezzar king of Babylon</u> hath broken his bones [in the southern kingdom of Judah].

2. **MEDO-PERSIA: DAN 8:20** The ram which thou sawest having two horns are the kings of Media and Persia.

3. **GREECE: DAN 8:21** And the rough goat is the king of Grecia: and the great horn that is between his eyes is the first king.

4. **ROME: LUKE 2:1-7** ... there went out a decree from [Roman] Caesar Augustus, that all the world should be taxed. 4 And Joseph also went up ... into Judaea ... 5 To be taxed with Mary his espoused wife, being great with child. 7 And she brought forth her firstborn son ...

Daniel 7:2

2 Daniel spake and said, I saw in my vision by night, and, behold, the four <u>winds</u> of the heaven strove upon the <u>great sea</u>.

Application of Prophetic Key #17

SYMBOL: "great sea"

DECODING by Scripture:

- **REV 17:15** The waters which thou sawest ... are peoples, and multitudes, and nations, and tongues.

APPLICATION: *Seas* or *waters* are used to represent people. e.g. The *sea of humanity*.

Application of Prophetic Key #17

SYMBOL: "winds"

DECODING by Scripture:

- **JER 51:1** I will raise up against Babylon, and against them that dwell in the midst of them that rise up against me, a destroying wind.

- **JER 25:32** Thus saith the LORD of hosts, Behold, evil shall go forth from nation to nation, and a great whirlwind shall be raised up from the coasts of the earth.

APPLICATION: *Winds* represent war and strife. When Medo-Persia fought against the ancient city of Babylon and conquered it, Jeremiah 51:1 declares this war was a "destroying wind."

Note: The Bible was meant to be understood by those searching for truth. In Daniel 7:2 the prophetic symbols describe war among the inhabitants of the earth in the populated areas of that time. As a result of the wars in verse three, four great kingdoms sequentially appeared on the stage of history, each one different from the others.

Daniel 7:4

4 The <u>first was like a lion</u>, and <u>had eagle's wings</u>: I beheld till the wings thereof were plucked ...

Application of Prophetic Key #17

SYMBOL: "first was like a lion"

DECODING by Scripture:

- **JER 50:43-44** <u>The king of Babylon ... shall come up like a lion</u> from the swelling of Jordan unto the habitation of the strong.

APPLICATION: Babylon was represented by the first beast that was like a lion.

SYMBOL: "had eagle's wings"

DECODING by Scripture:

- **DEUT 28:49-50** The LORD shall bring a nation against thee from far, from the end of the earth, as <u>swift as the eagle flieth</u>; a nation whose tongue thou shalt not understand; 50 A nation of fierce countenance, which shall not regard the person of the old, nor shew favour to the young:

APPLICATION: The *eagle's wings* were a symbol of power, range of flight, and rapid conquest. The eagle was also a symbol of *king of the birds.*

- **HAB 1:6, 8** For, lo, I raise up the Chaldeans, [Babylonians] ... shall <u>fly as the eagle</u> that hasteth to eat.

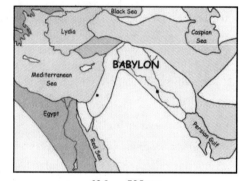

606 — 538 BC

Daniel 7:5

5 And behold <u>another</u> beast, a second, <u>like to a bear</u>, and it <u>raised up itself on one side</u>, and it had <u>three ribs in the mouth</u> of it between the teeth of it: and they said thus unto it, Arise, <u>devour much flesh</u>.

Application of Prophetic Key #17

SYMBOL: "another ... like to a bear"

DECODING by Concordance and Scripture: "*bear*" — *Strong's* OT#1680 a primitive root (compare **OT#1679**); to <u>move slowly</u>, i.e. glide.

<u>OT#1679</u> from an unused root (probably meaning to be <u>sluggish</u>, i.e. restful); <u>quiet</u>.

- JER 51:11 the LORD hath raised up <u>the spirit of the kings of the Medes</u>: for his device <u>is against Babylon, to destroy it</u>.

- DAN 5:28 Thy kingdom [Babylon] is divided, and given to the Medes and Persians.

APPLICATION: The Scriptures identified Babylon as the first beast. Medo-Persia succeeded Babylon and is likened to a bear. In a very slow and quiet manner, the Medes and Persians entered unprotected Babylon through the Ishtar Gate.

SYMBOL: "raised up itself on one side"

DECODING: One side of the bear was stronger.

APPLICATION: According to secular history, the Persians were stronger and more dominant just before the capture of Babylon.

538 — 331 BC

SYMBOL: "three ribs in the mouth"

DECODING by History: Altogether, the *bear* beast devoured a total of three territories.

APPLICATION: Secular history confirms these three territories as the provinces of Babylon, Lydia, and Egypt.

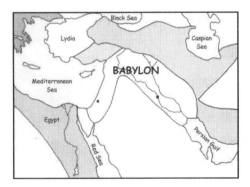

Appendix 7A — (Part 4) Decoding the "Leopard" Symbol in Daniel 7:6

Daniel 7:6

6 After this I beheld, and lo <u>another, like a leopard</u>, which had upon the back of it <u>four wings of a fowl</u>; <u>the beast had also four heads</u>; and dominion was given to it.

Application of Prophetic Key #17

SYMBOL: "another, like a leopard"

DECODING by Dictionary: The leopard is so rapacious that it will spare neither man nor beast. See extra note to the right.

APPLICATION: The Scriptures identified Babylon as the first beast and Medo-Persia as the second beast. Greece succeeded Medo-Persia and is represented as a leopard. This is confirmed by secular history and by the interpretation of Gabriel in Daniel 8:21.

SYMBOL: "four wings of a foul"

DECODING by Scripture: DEUT 28:49 designated that the lion of Babylon was swift with only two wings. This leopard beast has four wings which is a symbol of very rapid conquest.

APPLICATION: With great suddenness and rapidity, Alexander the Great conquered the greatest old world kingdom (of that time) in only 12 years. No other commander could parallel Alexander's suddenness and rapidity.

SYMBOL: "the beast had also four heads"

DECODING by Concordance: *"heads" — Strong's* OT#7217 … corresponding to OT#7218; the head; figuratively, the sum: KJV - <u>chief, head, sum</u>.

APPLICATION: The <u>sum</u> of <u>four heads</u> represents the <u>four chiefs</u> that ruled after the death of Alexander the Great known as Cassander, Lysimachus, Seleucus, and Ptolemy.

Note: In Daniel 7, Greece is represented by the symbolic leopard which is known by the following behavior: secretive; stealthy; stalking; and furtive (moving secretly behind the scenes). The leopard symbolism is named in Daniel 7 and in Daniel 8. These habits accurately describe the political maneuvers by which the rulers of the Grecian and Little Horn Kingdoms obtained power, seat, and great authority. This shrewd political maneuvering also comes forward in Daniel 8, Daniel 11, and Revelation 13.

331 — 168 BC

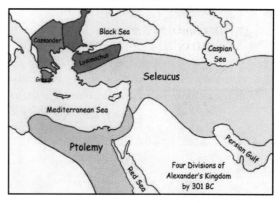

Four Divisions of Alexander's Kingdom by 301 BC

Daniel 7:7

7 After this I saw in the night visions, and behold <u>a fourth beast, dreadful and terrible, and strong exceedingly; and it had great iron teeth</u>: it devoured and brake in pieces, and <u>stamped the residue</u> with the feet of it: and it was <u>diverse from all</u> the beasts that were before it; and <u>it had ten horns</u>.

Application of Prophetic Key #17

SYMBOL: "a fourth beast, dreadful and terrible and strong exceedingly; and it had great iron teeth: ... stamped the residue ... diverse from all"

DECODING by Daniel 2: No beast in nature can be compared to this beast. However, the Fourth Kingdom in Daniel 2 had *iron legs* which compares to the *iron teeth* in this beast.

- **DAN 7:17** These great beasts, which are four, are four kings, which shall arise out of the earth.
- **LUKE 2:1-7** Jesus was born during the reign of this *iron kingdom*.
- **PS 2:9** Thou shalt break them with a <u>rod of iron</u>; thou shalt dash them in pieces like a potter's vessel.

APPLICATION: The fourth beast represented the Fourth Kingdom. The Fourth Kingdom that succeeded Greece was Pagan Imperial Rome. Secular history speaks of the dread and terror that Pagan Rome used to break anything that stood in its way. Nations were ground to dust by the brazen feet and devoured by *iron teeth*.

168 BC — AD 476

SYMBOL: "it [Rome] had <u>ten horns</u>"

DECODING by Scripture:
- **DAN 7:24** And the <u>ten horns</u> out of this kingdom <u>are ten kings</u> that shall arise.

APPLICATION: By AD 476 Pagan Imperial Rome was broken into *ten divisions represented by ten horns*.

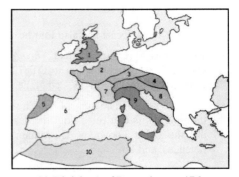

10 Divisions of Rome by AD 476

1.	Anglo-Saxons	6.	Visigoths
2.	Franks	7.	Burgundians
3.	Alamanni	8.	Heruli
4.	Lombards	9.	Ostrogoths
5.	Seuvi	10.	Vandals

Daniel 7:8

8 I considered the horns, and, behold, there came up among them <u>another little horn</u>, before whom there were <u>three of the first horns plucked up by the roots</u>: and, behold, in this horn were <u>eyes like the eyes of man</u>, and <u>a mouth speaking great things</u>.

Application of Prophetic Key #17

SYMBOL: "another <u>little horn</u>"

DECODING by Scripture:

* **DAN 7:24** And the <u>ten horns</u> out of this kingdom <u>are ten kings</u> that shall arise.

APPLICATION: The first ten horns that broke up Pagan Imperial Rome represented ten [Barbarious] kingdoms. Following Pagan Imperial Rome, another Little Horn also rises, representing *another kingdom,* known as Papal Supremacy No. 1.

SYMBOL: "three of the first horns <u>plucked up</u> by the roots"

DECODING by Concordance: *"plucked"* — *Strong's* OT#6131 to pluck up (especially by the roots); specifically, <u>to ... exterminate</u>.

APPLICATION: By AD 538 Papal Supremacy No. 1 had exterminated the three Barbarian tribes of the Heruli, the Ostrogoths, and the Vandals.

SYMBOL: "eyes like the <u>eyes of a man</u>"

DECODING by Concordance: *"eyes"* — *Strong's* OT#5869 an eye ... countenance ... knowledge ... think.

* **EPH 1:18** The eyes of your understanding being enlightened.

APPLICATION: The Barbarian tribes were largely illiterate. The *eyes* of the Little Horn represented intelligence, insight, and foresight which were strong characteristics of the Papal Supremacy Kingdom.

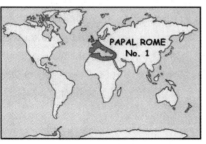

AD 538 — 1798

SYMBOL: "mouth speaking <u>great</u> things"

DECODING by Concordance and Scripture: *"great"* — *Strong's* OT#7260 from OT#7229; huge (in size); <u>domineering (in character)</u>.

* **DAN 7:20** And of the ten horns that were in his head, and of the other which came up, and before whom three fell; even of that horn that had eyes, and a mouth that <u>spake very great things</u>, whose look was more stout than his fellows.
* **DAN 7:24-25** and he shall subdue three kings. 25 And he <u>shall speak great words against the most High</u>, and shall wear out the saints of the most High, and think to [speak decrees to] change times and laws.
* **REV 13:5** And there was given unto him a <u>mouth speaking great things</u> and blasphemies.
* **JOHN 10:33** but for <u>blasphemy</u>; and because that thou, being a man, makest thyself God.
* **MARK 2:7** Why doth this man thus <u>speak blasphemies</u>? who can forgive sins but God only?
* **2 THESS 2:4** Who opposeth and exalteth himself above all that is called God, or that is worshipped; so that he as God sitteth in the temple of God, shewing himself that he is God.

APPLICATION: The "mouth speaking great things" belongs to the Papal Supremacy Kingdom who claims to be able to:

* Forgive sins;
* Stand in the place of Jesus the Son, and God the Father;
* Change God's Moral Law;
* Do away with the Lord's annual Feasts and Festival Sabbaths.

Appendix 7B — Characteristics of the "Little Horn"

Before reading any further, please refer to the **Important Note** on page 104 that addresses this counterfeit apostate system.

The Little Horn is a Diverse Power
DAN 7:24

1. The ten kingdoms of Pagan Imperial Rome were of a political power.
2. The Papacy has always been a religious power.
3. The Papacy is also a diverse power being religious _and_ political.

- "What the Pope himself thinks of the relationship of Rome to the Papacy is quite different. In his first Encyclical _Ubi Arcano_ (December 23, 1922) he wrote of 'Italy, our own dear native land, the country where the hand of God, who guides the course of history, _has set down the Chair_ of His Vicar on earth, in this city of Rome which, from being the capital of the wonderful Roman Empire, was made by Him the capital of the whole world, _because He made it the seat_ of a sovereignty which, since it extends beyond the confines of nations and States, embraces within itself all the peoples of the whole world.' " —Translated by Rev. James H. Ryan in _The Encyclicals of Pius XI_ (St. Louis: Herder, 1927), 44. Quoted by W. W. Rockwell in _Current History Magazine,_ August, 1929, p. 827. (Emphasis supplied).

- "The church has the right to require that the Catholic religion shall be the only religion of the state, to the exclusion of all others." _Pope Pius IV._

The Little Horn Subdues Three Kings
DAN 7:8, 20, 24

- The Little Horn begins to rise in AD 476 and subdues the Arian kings of the Heruli (AD 493); the Vandals (AD 534); and the Ostrogoths (AD 538).

The Little Horn Has Eyes Like a Man
DAN 7:8, 20

- This religious power is headed by a man recognized by the world as the Pope.

The "Holy See"

The Little Horn Speaks Against the Most High God
DAN 7:8, 20, 25

- "We hold upon this earth the place of Almighty God." Pope Leo XIII in an encyclical letter dated June 20, 1894.

- "For thou, [the Pope] art another God on earth." _History of the Councils_ p. 200.

- "The Pope is so great dignity and so exalted that he is not merely a man, but as it were, God, and the Vicar of God … The Pope is of such lofty and supreme dignity that, properly speaking, he has not been established in any rank of dignity, but rather has been placed upon the very summit of all ranks of dignities ..." _Loucious Ferraris, Prompta Bibliotheca (Catholic Dictionary),_ Vol. VI, pp. 438, 442.

- "The Pope is not only a representative of Jesus Christ but he is Jesus Christ himself hidden under a veil of flesh ..." _The Catholic National, July 1895._

- "The Pope is the Supreme Judge ... He is the vice-regent of Christ, who is not only a priest forever, but also King of Kings and Lord of Lords." _Vatican Council,_ p. 220.

- " 'He shall speak as if he were God.' So St. Jerome quotes from Symmachus. To none can this apply so well or so fully as to the popes of Rome. They have assumed infallibility, which belongs only to God. They profess to forgive sins, which belongs only to God. They profess to open and shut heaven, which belongs only to God. They profess to be higher than all the kings of the earth, which belongs only to God. And they go _beyond_ God in pretending to loose whole nations from their oath of allegiance to their kings, when such kings do not please them. And they go _against_ God when they give indulgences for sin. This is the worst of all blasphemies." Adam Clarke, _Commentary on the Old Testament,_ Vol. IV, p. 596, note on Daniel 7:25.

Appendix 7B — Characteristics of the "Little Horn"

The Little Horn Persecutes (with Power)
DAN 7:21, 25

- "That the Church of Rome has shed more innocent blood than any other institution that has ever existed among mankind, will be questioned by no Protestant who has a competent knowledge of history. The memorials, indeed, of many of her persecutions are now so scanty that it is impossible to form a complete conception of the multitude of her victims, and it is quite certain that no powers of imagination can adequately realize their sufferings ... These atrocities were not perpetrated in the brief paroxysms of a reign of terror, or by the hands of obscure sectaries, but were inflicted by a triumphant church with every circumstance of solemnity and deliberation." William E. H. Lecky, *History of the Rise and Influence of the Spirit of Rationalism in Europe*, Vol. II, pp. 35, 37.

- "The church has persecuted. Only a tyro in church history will deny that ... One hundred and fifty years after Constantine the Donatists were persecuted and sometimes put to death ... Protestants were persecuted in France and Spain with the full approval of the church authorities. We have always defended the persecution of the Huguenots, and the Spanish Inquisition. Wherever and whenever there is honest Catholicity, there will be a clear distinction drawn between truth and error, and Catholicity and all forms of heresy. When she thinks it good to use physical force, she will use it ... But will the Catholic Church give bond that she will not persecute at all? Will she guarantee absolute freedom and equality of all churches and all faiths? The Catholic Church gives no bonds for her good behavior." *The Western Watchman*, December 24, 1908.

- "There is no graver offense than heresy (opposition to the teaching and aims of the Catholic church) ... and therefore it (the heresy) must be rooted out with fire and sword." *The Catholic Encyclopedia 1911*, Vol. 4, pp. 776-778.

The Little Horn Attempts to Change God's Laws (Great Authority)
DAN 7:25

- "The pope has power to change times, to abrogate laws, and to dispense with all things, even the precepts of Christ." *Decretal de Translat*, Episcop. Cap.

- "The pope's will stands for reason. He can dispense above the law, and of wrong make right by correcting and changing laws." Pope Nicholas, Dis. 96.

- "Question. — Have you any other way of proving that the church has power to institute festivals of precept?"
  "Answer. — Had she not such power, she could not have done that in which all modern religionists agree with her, — she could not have substituted the observance of Sunday the first day of the week, for the observance of Saturday the seventh day, a change for which there is no Scriptural authority." Rev. Stephen Keenan, *A Doctrinal Catechism On the Obedience Due to the Church*, p. 174.

- "The Catholic Church for over one thousand years before the existence of a Protestant, by virtue of her divine mission, changed the day from Saturday to Sunday." *Catholic Mirror*, Sept. 23, 1893.

- "In reply to the letter of October 18, 1895, to Cardinal Gibbons, asking if the church claimed the change of the Sabbath as her mark, the following was received: 'Of course the Catholic church claims that the change was her act ... And the act is a mark of her ecclesiastical power and authority in religious matter.'" C.V. Thomas, Chancellor.

- "Sunday is a Catholic institution, and its claims to observance can be defended only on Catholic principles ... From the beginning to end of Scripture there is not a single passage that warrants the transfer of weekly public worship from the last day of the week to the first." Sydney, Australia, *The Catholic Press*, August 1966.

REV 13:2 The Dragon [Devil] gave him [Papal Rome] his power, seat, and great authority.

Appendix 7c — The Theme of Deliverance in the Book of Daniel

The theme of DELIVERANCE runs, like a thread, through the entire Book of Daniel. Persecution or a death decree and Providential deliverance are found seven times as follows.

1. **Nebuchadnezzar's Death Decree for the Wisemen**

   - **DAN 2:13** And the decree went forth that the wise men should be slain; and they sought Daniel and his fellows to be slain.
   - Daniel and his fellow friends desired "mercies" (verse 18) of the God of heaven. The secret of the dream was revealed and God's people were ***delivered***.

2. **Nebuchadnezzar's Death Decree in the Fiery Furnace**

   - **DAN 3:10-11** Thou, O king, hast made a decree, that every man ... shall fall down and worship the golden image: 11 And whoso falleth not down and worshippeth, that he should be cast into the midst of a burning fiery furnace.
   - When the three Hebrew worthies proved their allegiance to the God of heaven and were thrown into the furnace, the king looked into the furnace and said, "Lo, I see four men loose ... and the form of the fourth is like the Son of God." (DAN 3:25) It was God who brought ***deliverance***.

3. **Darius' Death Decree in the Lion's Den**

   - **DAN 6:9, 16** Wherefore king Darius signed the writing and the decree. 16 Then the king commanded, and they brought Daniel, and cast him into the den of lions.
   - The great question was: "O Daniel, servant of the living God, is thy God, whom thou servest continually, able to deliver thee?" (DAN 6:20)
   - After Daniel's deliverance, Darius wrote in Daniel 6:26-27 "the living God ... He ***delivereth*** and ***rescueth***."

4. **Babylonian Captivity of the Jews and Deliverance in 457 BC**

   - Whereas the first three deliverances concerned specific individuals, the fourth example concerned the entire nation of Israel. Taken captive by Babylon, the entire nation was doomed to slavery and extinction by assimilation — comparable to a death decree for an individual. Daniel prayed for the deliverance of the nation. (DAN 9:3-20)
   - Although the prince of Persia withstood the Lord's messengers, deliverance was finally secured by none other than Michael (the Son of God Himself). The decree was passed in 457 BC that the Jews should return to the holy land to restore and rebuild the holy city. God ***delivered*** the entire nation from a situation of hopeless doom. (DAN 10:13)

5. **Papal Captivity of the Christian Church and Deliverance in AD 1798**

   - In prophetic vision, Daniel foresaw the oppression of the Christian church in the rise of the Little Horn power. (DAN 7:8, 21, 25) Death decrees were multiplied through the 1260 years of Papal Supremacy.
   - **DAN 7:25** He shall wear out the saints of the most high.
   - Yet that period of oppression was to last only 1260 years and at its end, ***deliverance*** would come.
   - **REV 12:6** And the woman fled into the wilderness, where she hath a place prepared of God, that they should feed her there a thousand two hundred and threescore days.
   - Pope Pius VI was taken prisoner by Napoleon of France in 1798. Providentially, the Lord cut persecution short, before the end of the 1260 day-year period. Deliverance was granted to the emerging remnant.

Appendix 7C — The Theme of Deliverance in the Book of Daniel

6. Deliverance from the Power of Sin

- The next concept of deliverance broadens — encompassing the people of God of all ages. The entire human race is under the death penalty decree! "For all have sinned, and come short of the glory of God;" "the wages of sin is **death**." (ROM 3:23; 6:23)
- Daniel was given a vision of the legal procedure by which men can be delivered from that universal death decree. He saw "the judgment was set, and the books were opened" — a court room scene in which every sinner was condemned to a death penalty. (DAN 7:10)
- But "in the night visions … behold, one like the Son of man [Jesus Christ] came to the [judgment scene] before the "Ancient of Days," to deliver His people. None other than Michael — that great Prince which standeth for His people — that High Priest and Advocate — the greatest Lawyer of all time, comes to the **_rescue_**, and **_delivers_** His people.
- As each name, or case, is brought up, the Son of man [Jesus Christ] delivers from the death sentence and bestows eternal life — **_perfect and complete deliverance from the power and grip of sin and death._** He performs this service in fulfillment of the everlasting covenant [contract], the legal decision of final deliverance.
- Those who are living, when their names come up in the judgment, will experience deliverance from all aspects of sin involving the character and conscience. The Seal of God will be placed upon them making them eternally secure. (REV 14:1-5; REV 7)

7. Deliverance from the Grave — Immortality

- **DAN 12:1-3** And at that time shall Michael stand up … and at that time thy people shall **_BE DELIVERED_**, every one that shall be found written in the book. And many of them that sleep in the dust of the earth shall awake … to everlasting life … [to] shine as the brightness of the firmament … as the stars for ever and ever.

Daniel's vision in chapter seven, portrays the history of the world in a broad outline from his own day to the establishment of Christ's Kingdom. Using *beasts* as symbols of kingdoms, Daniel describes the consecutive rise and fall of the four earthly kingdoms that surrounded the people of God, namely — Babylon, Medo-Persia, Greece, and Pagan Imperial Rome. Using the beast's horns also as symbols, Daniel describes the division of the Roman kingdom of Old Europe. Out of this European setting, and specifically out of Pagan Rome, Daniel predicted the emergence of a Little Horn (a political-religious organization), easily identified by secular history as the Roman Papacy, or Daniel's fifth earthly kingdom.

Identification of the Little Horn

As noted in chapter seven, Daniel observed in his vision that this Little Horn Papal System would set up a counterfeit religion, persecute God's true saints, attempt to change God's Moral Law (and do away with the annual Feasts of the Lord). A combination of Scripture and historical fact identifies the Little Horn as Papal Supremacy No. 1 containing the following characteristics:

1. It would arise out of Pagan Imperial Rome once the ten barbarian tribes had separated.
2. It would arise after the ten horns had arisen in AD 476. (Imperial Rome ended, but the church did not.)
3. It would arise from among the ten horns (ten divisions of Old Europe), as its location.
4. Its seat of power was received from Pagan Imperial Rome.
5. It would be diverse from all other kingdoms when it combined church and state.
6. It would uproot *three horns* (the Heruli, Ostrogoths, and Vandals);
7. It would have *eyes* like the eyes of a man. (The Popes rose up as leaders.)
8. It would have a *mouth,* or be a spokesman, for Christendom.
9. It would be a blasphemous power — taking the place of God on earth and offering forgiveness of sins.
10. It would be a persecuting power. e.g. The Papacy set up the Inquisition and condemned heretics to death.
11. It would think to change times [Feast and Festivals] and laws [Ten Commandments or Moral Law];
12. The saints were given into his hand for 1260 years (time, times, and dividing of times).

War in Heaven

As noted in the Prologue, Lucifer was the angel that covered God's throne. This most trusted angel attempted a coup in heaven. The sad story is recorded in Isaiah 14:12-15 and Ezekiel 28:12-19. As the most exalted angel in God's kingdom, Lucifer decided to exalt himself above God's throne with the intent to convince the universe to worship him rather than God.

- **ISA 14:13** I will exalt my throne above the stars of God: I will sit also upon the mount of the <u>congregation</u>, in the sides of the north.

"congregation" — *Strong's* OT#4150 moed` from OT#3259; an appointment, i.e. <u>a fixed time or season</u>; <u>specifically, a festival</u>; conventionally a year; by implication, <u>an assembly</u> (as <u>convened for a definite purpose</u>): KJV - appointed (sign, time), (place of, solemn) assembly, congregation, (set, solemn) feast, (appointed, due) season, solemn (-ity), synogogue, (set) time (appointed).

Note: Before creation, when Lucifer desired to sit in the "mount of the congregation," — he planned to set up his own "appointed festivals in opposition to God's festivals." The many universes now had an issue to deal with. Whose appointed festivals would they honor — God's festivals, or Lucifer's counterfeit festivals? This transgression resulted in the expulsion of Lucifer and his followers to this earth, where the same battle continues.

The Lights in the Firmament Determine the Seventh-day Sabbath and the Feast Days

- **GEN 1:14** And God said, Let there be lights in the firmament of the heaven to divide the day from the night; and let them be for signs, and for seasons [OT#4150 moed`], and for days, and years.

Note: The sun determines the Seventh-day Sabbath — the weekly Holy Day. The moon determines when the yearly Holy Days are. Right from the point of creating the sun and moon, the Bible links the Seventh-day Sabbath and the yearly Holy Days together. Just as the moon reflects the light of the sun, so the yearly Feast days reflect the light of the weekly Sabbath Holy Day. Some other Bible versions have a clearer interpretation:

- **GEN 1:14** Then God commanded, "Let lights appear in the sky to separate day from night and <u>to show the time when</u> days, years, and <u>religious festivals begin</u>. TEV

The original word for moed` [OT#4150] is first found in Genesis 1:14 indicating God's Holy Days were in existence at Creation. The same word [moed`] is found in:

Ps 104:19 He appointed the moon for seasons. [OT#4150 moed`]

The Moral Law (Ten Commandments)

The Moral Law is found in Exodus 20:3-17. Jesus said:

- **MATT 22:37-40** Thou shalt love the Lord thy God with all thy heart, and with all thy soul, and with all thy mind. 38 This is the first and great commandment. 39 And the second is like unto it, Thou shalt love thy neighbour as thyself. 40 On these two commandments hang <u>all the law</u> and the prophets.

Note: Jesus said that all the Commandments and the Prophets hang on two great Commandments. The first four hang under LOVE TO GOD; the last six hang under LOVE TO MAN, illustrated as such:

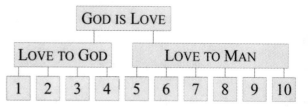

"all the law" — The word *law* comes from the original Greek word *nomos* which means *Mosaic Law or Torah*. The Mosaic Law is the Pentateuch, or the first five books of the Old Testament, which were given by God and written by Moses.

Statutes and Judgments

- **DEUT 11:1** Therefore thou shalt love the LORD thy God, and keep his charge, and his statutes, and his judgments, and his commandments, always.

Obedience to the Statutes and Judgments is commanded. Each of the Statutes in the Mosaic Law can be put under one of the Ten Commandments. The Statutes *further explain and guard the Commandments.* The only exceptions are the laws that the Bible specifically states were eliminated at the cross, such as the sacrificial Ceremonial Laws.

Mosaic Law Interprets the Ten Commandments

Some examples of how the Mosaic Law interprets the Ten Commandments are:

1. All the health laws in the Mosaic Law come under the Sixth Commandment, "Thou shalt not kill." God wants us to preserve life through healthful living.
2. Tithing is given in the Mosaic law and comes under the Eighth Commandment, "Thou salt not steal." We are not to withhold (steal) God's money from Him.
3. Statutes further defining the Seventh Commandment regarding adultery are:
   a. Do not lie with your father's wife. LEV 20:11
   b. Do not lie with your daughter-in-law. LEV 20:12
   c. Homosexuality is condemned. LEV 20:13
   d. Do not lie with a beast. LEV 20:15

Appendix 7D — The Change of "times" and "laws"

Examples of these Statutes can be illustrated this way:

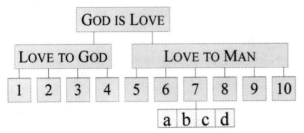

Note: If one of the Statutes "a" through "d" is broken, the Seventh Commandment is also broken. It is crucial to understand that the Statute that explains the Commandment has the same force of law as the Commandment that it further explains.

The Ten Commandments are similar to chapter titles of God's Law. The Statutes are the description, or further explanation, of what is included in each Commandment. ALL of the Commandments and the Statutes together make up God's Law.

The Fourth Commandment addresses the Seventh-day Sabbath, to remember to keep it holy. There are also seven annual Sabbaths, or Holy Days, that are called Holy Convocations — Feasts of the Lord. These special Sabbaths are kept according to the lunar movements. They can land on any day of the week.

- **LEV 23:4** These are the feasts [OT#4150 moed`] of the LORD, even holy convocations, which ye shall proclaim in their seasons. (Read the whole chapter.)

"feasts" — Strong's OT#4150 moed`; (2 Chron 8:13); also from OT#3259; properly, an appointment, i.e. a fixed time or season; specifically, a festival; an assembly (convened for a definite purpose): KJV - appointed (sign, time), (place of, solemn) assembly, solemn feast.

- **LEV 23:21** And ye shall proclaim on the selfsame day, that it may be an holy convocation unto you: ye shall do no servile work therein: it shall be a statute for ever in all your dwellings throughout your generations.

The above Scripture declares these *Holy Convocations* are Statutes that are to be kept forever. These *Holy Convocations* also included seven extra Sabbath days that were kept holy in the same way as the weekly Seventh-day Sabbath. Three specific Festivals were marked by the lunar cycle. God's people were invited to meet with Him at these times.

2 CHRON 8:12-13 Then Solomon offered burnt offerings unto the LORD … 13 … according to the commandment of Moses, on the sabbaths, and on the new moons, and on the solemn feasts, three times in the year, even in the feast of unleavened bread, and in the feast of weeks, and in the feast of tabernacles.

Note: The following Feasts belong to the LORD, and all of God's people today — not just the Jews. Leviticus 23 begins with the Seventh-day Sabbath, then explains God's other Holy Days. These Statutes are part of the Sabbath Commandment found in the Moral Law as noted in the following illustration:

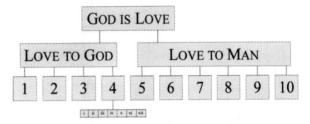

The Seven Annual Feasts and Seven Annual Sabbaths

i) Passover (LEV 23:5)

- Occurs on the 14th day of the first lunar month.
- It is <u>not</u> one of the Holy Days where no work is done.

ii) Feast of Unleavened Bread (LEV 23:6-8)

- Begins on the 15th day of the first lunar month.
- This Feast is seven days long.
- The 1st and 7th days are Holy Days. (Two Sabbaths.)

iii) Feast of Firstfruits (LEV 23:10-11)

- Occurs on the 16th day of the first lunar month — the day after the Sabbath of Unleavened Bread.
- A sheaf of the *Firstfruits* from the barley harvest was waved before the LORD.
- This Feast is <u>not</u> one of the Holy Days.

iv) Pentecost (LEV 23:15-16)

- Occurs 50 days from *Firstfruits*.
- This Feast is a Holy Day. (One Sabbath.)

v) Feast of Trumpets (LEV 23:25)

- Occurs on the 1st day of the seventh lunar month.
- The first day is observed as a Holy Day. (One Sabbath.)
- Announces that Day of Atonement will occur in ten days; a time to be ready for the judgment.

vi) Day of Atonement (LEV 23:27-32)

- Occurs on the 10th day of the seventh lunar month.
- Observed as a Holy Day, a Holy Convocation.
- This is the most solemn of God's Festivals as it represents the "day of judgment." (One Sabbath.)

vii) Feast of Tabernacles (LEV 23:34-39)

- Occurs on the 15th day of the seventh lunar month.
- This is a Feast for seven days unto the Lord.
- The 1st day is a Holy Day, as is the 8th day. (Last two Feast Sabbaths.)

Note: According to the lunar phases, the first month, (for the Feast Calendar of the Jewish Economy), is equivalent to March or April on the current calendar.

Leviticus 23 begins with the Seventh-day Sabbath, then explains God's other Holy Days which are part of the Sabbath Commandment found in the Moral Law. None of these Sabbaths have been done away with at the cross. All of these Sabbaths also had sacrifices attached to them. The "sacrificial" part of the Festivals was fulfilled through Jesus' sacrifice on the cross. However, the Festivals themselves are Statutes to be observed for ever in all generations. These Festivals will be observed in Heaven and the New Earth:

- **ISA 66:23** And it shall come to pass, that from one new moon to another, and from one sabbath to another, shall all flesh come to worship before me, saith the LORD.

Reminder: It is the new moon that determines the beginning of a new month, and how to calculate the Feasts and Festivals. (To calculate the New Moons, Feasts, and Festivals will require some self-study.)

In Review

All of God's Festivals are contained in Leviticus 23. His first Holy Day is the Seventh-day Sabbath, which occurs every week. Seven other Holy Days occur every year: the first and seventh days of Unleavened Bread, Pentecost, Feast of Trumpets, Day of Atonement, and the first and eighth days of Feast of Tabernacles. Passover and Feast of Firstfruits are Festivals, but are not Holy Days.

Response: Locating the Feasts in the Old Testament is very straightforward. If the Feasts are to be observed today, they must also be found in the New Testament, being kept by Jesus Christ (our prime Example) and by His disciples and apostles, especially after the cross.

Facts:
1. The ceremonial system that contained the sacrifices and oblations (meal offerings, etc.) that pointed forward to Jesus' death on the cross were no longer needed after the cross. Daniel 9:27 is clear that at the death of the Messiah, the sacrifices and oblations were to cease.
2. Leviticus 23 declares that the Festivals are Statutes that are to be in effect *forever.*
3. The weekly Seventh-day Sabbath Festival (Saturday) is closely associated with the seven annual Festivals.
4. All Festivals either *stand together or fall together!*

Paul's Teaching in the New Testament

Paul had been a student of Gamaliel, the preeminent teacher in the whole country of Israel. Through the instruction of the Jewish Economy, Paul kept the Ceremonial Laws, including the sacrifices and Feasts.

Paul (first known as Saul) was a Pharisee determined to stamp out Christianity that was infecting Judaism.

ACTS 9: Paul converted to Christianity. This conversion placed his life in danger. He fled to Arabia for safety for three years, where he was taught by Jesus what he was supposed to preach and teach to the heathen. (Also read Galatians 1:11-20.)

- **GAL 1:11-12** But I certify you, brethren, that <u>the gospel which was preached of me is</u> not after man. 12 For I neither received it of man, neither was I taught it, but <u>by the revelation of Jesus Christ</u>.

Paul certified that what he was teaching was truth. He commissioned the people to do as he did.

- **PHIL 4:9** <u>Those things, which ye have both learned,</u> and received, and heard, and seen in me, <u>do</u> ...

Paul was commissioned by Jesus to teach the Gentile converts. One of those teachings was to observe the Feasts, as his example was — so they were to do. Note the following examples:

- (1) **ACTS 18:21** But bade them farewell, saying, <u>I must by all means *keep* this feast that cometh in Jerusalem</u>: but I will return again unto you, if God will.

"keep" — *Strong's* NT#4160 to make or do; Compare NT#4238 <u>to</u> "<u>practise</u>", i.e. **perform repeatedly or habitually**.

<u>Paul states</u>, to his Gentile converts in Ephesus, that <u>he is going to keep, or perform, the Feast in Jerusalem</u>.

- (2) **ACTS 20:16** <u>For Paul had determined</u> to sail by Ephesus, because he would not spend the time in Asia: for he hasted, if it were possible for him, <u>to be at Jerusalem the day of Pentecost</u>.

Paul taught the Corinthian Gentile converts to not only observe the Festivals, but to also understand their deep spiritual meanings as noted:

- **1 COR 5:7-8** Purge out therefore the old leaven, that ye may be a new lump, as ye are unleavened. For even Christ our passover is sacrificed for us: 8 <u>Therefore let us keep the feast</u>, not with old leaven, neither with the leaven of malice and wickedness; but with the unleavened bread of sincerity and truth.

The Example of Jesus Christ — Passover

Jesus gave us a new example of how to celebrate ***Passover*** by observing Foot Washing and Communion at Passover time. It was celebrated in a home, on Passover evening. Notice that Jesus did not slay or eat a lamb:

LUKE 22:8, 15-19 And he sent Peter and John, saying, Go and prepare us the passover, that we may eat. 15 And he said unto them, With desire I have desired to eat this passover with you before I suffer: 16 ... I will not any more eat thereof, until it [Passover] be fulfilled in the kingdom of God. 18 ... I will not drink of the fruit of the vine, until the kingdom of God shall come. 19 And he took bread, and gave thanks, and brake it, and gave unto them, saying, This is my body which is given for you: this do in remembrance of me. 20 Likewise also the cup after supper, saying, This cup is the new testament in my blood, which is shed for you.

Note: Jesus is saying that Passover is *not fulfilled* until heaven.

- **MATT 5:18** For verily I say unto you, Till heaven and earth pass, one jot or one tittle shall in no wise pass from the law, till all be fulfilled.

- **1 PETER 2:21** Christ also suffered for us, leaving us an example, that ye should follow his steps.

Note: Since Passover is not yet fulfilled, it should still be observed, as Jesus did, with the Foot Washing and Communion meal, also known as "The Lord's Supper." It should also be observed at the correct time, not at the traditional time of Easter, a pagan holiday. (See point #6 in Appendix 8F on page 226.)

The Example of Jesus Christ — Feast of Tabernacles

- **JOHN 7:2, 10, 14** Now the Jews' feast of tabernacles was at hand. 10 ... then went he also up unto the feast ... 14 Now about the midst of the feast Jesus went up into the temple, and taught.

Note: Jesus did not sacrifice a lamb because:
1. He had no sin, therefore He did not need to take part in this ceremony;
2. He knew that when He died on the cross — then the sacrificial system, (which was the sacrificing of a lamb when someone sinned and which God commanded when sin entered this world), would end.

The Example of the Holy Spirit — Pentecost

Acts 2 records, fifty-two days after the crucifixion of Jesus, the disciples were gathered together on the Festival of Pentecost. This is when the Holy Spirit fell on them in a powerful way.

Question: If, as most Christians believe, the Festivals are part of the Ceremonial Law (the sacrificial system) that was done away with at the cross, then why did God choose to honor the Festival of Pentecost by sending His Holy Spirit to His disciples on that day? God has given evidence that His Festivals were not done away with at the cross and therefore are part of the *Moral Law* and not part of the *Ceremonial Law*. (See *Glossary* terms.)

In the days of the disciples and apostles, the Holy days were kept at the temple in Jerusalem. Today that temple

no longer exists. Jesus gave the instruction that God's true people can worship Him anywhere (and observe His Holy Days anywhere) through the Heavenly Sanctuary.

- **JOHN 4:21-23** Jesus saith unto her, Woman, believe me, the hour cometh, when ye shall neither in this mountain, nor yet at Jerusalem, worship the Father. 22 ... for salvation is of the Jews. 23 But the hour cometh ... when the true worshippers shall worship the Father in spirit and in truth: for the Father seeketh such to worship him.

- **MATT 18:20** For where two or three are gathered together in my name, there am I in the midst of them.

Summary

God has *one weekly* Festival Holy Day [Saturday], plus *seven yearly* Festival Holy Days. Paul was taught by Jesus to teach the Gentile converts to keep all of God's Holy Festivals long after the cross. Jesus is our example in all things. He observed God's Festivals. His death did not nail the Festivals to the cross. They are still valid today presenting special opportunities to worship the Lord. So, how were these special Holy Days done away with? The prophetic Scriptures have the answer.

1. The Little Horn Changed "laws"

DAN 7:25 And he shall speak great words against the most High ... and think to change ... laws ...

The following letter from T. Enright, CSSR, the Catholic Bishop of St. Alphonsus Church, St. Louis, Missouri (dated June 1905) clearly states the issue of changes under discussion.

> "Dear Friend, I have offered and still offer $1000 to any one who can prove to me from the Bible alone that I am bound, under grievous sin to keep Sunday holy. It was the Catholic Church which made the law obliging us to keep Sunday holy. The church made this law long after the Bible was written. Hence said law is not in the Bible. Christ, our Lord empowered his church to make laws binding in conscience. He said to his apostles and their lawful sucessors in the priesthood 'Whatsoever you shall bind on earth shall be binding in heaven.' Matthew 16:19. Matthew 18:17. Luke 16:19. The Cath. Church **abolished not only the Sabbath, but all the other Jewish festivals**. Pray and study. I shall be always glad to help you as long as you honestly seek the truth. Respectfully, T. Enright CSSR." (Emphasis supplied.)

Note: The astounding admissions made in this letter verify the change of worship from Sabbath [Saturday] to Sunday, and who is responsible for these changes. Changing Sabbath to Sunday was a *change in the Moral Law*. Worshipping on the day that the Papal System has attempted to make holy, places one in direct opposition against God who made the Seventh-day [Saturday] holy. Jesus Christ said, "Think not that I am come to destroy the [Moral] law, or the prophets: I am not come to destroy, but to fulfil. For verily I say unto you, Till heaven and earth pass, one jot or one tittle shall in no wise pass from the law, till all be fulfilled." (MATT 5:17-18)

2. The Little Horn Changed "times"

DAN 7:25 And he shall speak great words against the most High ... and <u>think to change times</u> ...

Note: There is an interesting sentence in Bishop Enright's quote. "The Cath. Church abolished not only the Sabbath, <u>but all the other Jewish festivals.</u>" How do these "other Jewish Festivals" fit into the idea of worship? Recall these Scriptures:

- **GEN 1:14** And God said, Let there be lights in the firmament of the heaven to divide the day from the night; and let them be for signs, and for <u>seasons</u>, and for days, and years.

- **PS 104:19** He appointed the moon for seasons.

Note: The admission by the Papal system is clear that they have tampered with the Seventh-day Sabbath *and* the Jewish Festivals, including the annual Feast Sabbaths. For further documentation, see Appendix 11D (page 357) and Appendix 11E (page 363).

- **JAMES 2:10** For whosoever shall keep the whole law, and yet offend in one point, he is guilty of all.

GOD'S MORAL LAW	COMMANDMENT	PAPAL CHANGE
Ex 20:4 Thou shalt not make unto thee any graven image ...	2	Dropped from the law.
Ex 20:8 Remember the sabbath day, to keep it holy ...	4	Command has been given to keep [Sunday] the first day holy.
Ex 20:17 Thou shalt not covet thy neighbour's house, thou shalt not covet thy neighbour's wife, nor his manservant, nor his maidservant, nor his ox, nor his ass, nor any thing that is thy neighbour's.	10	This commandment was divided in two: 9 Thou shalt not covet thy neighbour's wife. 10 Thou shalt not covet thy neighbour's goods.

Note: It is a very serious thing to break God's Moral Law which also includes the Statutes and Judgments.

Prophetic Key #1: Integrity, logic, and common sense are essential in understanding prophecy. It is <u>not</u> logical that the Papacy would do away with "anything" that was already cancelled at the cross.

God's Festivals Through History

Historians testify that the early Christian church observed all of God's Holy Days.

- "Far be it from us to charge John with foolishness, for he observed the precepts of the Law of Moses literally, at a time when the church still followed the Jews in many things; and the Apostles were not able suddenly to set aside the entire observance of the Law laid down by God ... So, John, according to the custom of the Law, began the celebration of the feast of Easter [Passover] on the evening of the fourteenth day of the first month, paying no attention to whether it fell on the Sabbath or on some other day." Bede's, *The Ecclesiastical History of the English People* for *The Great Histories Series* by Washington Square Press, N.Y., 1968.

The following quote shows that the early Christians still observed Passover, that it was the Roman Catholic system who did away with Passover, changing it to Easter.

- "While the 'living oracles' were neglected, the zeal of the clergy began to spend itself upon rites and ceremonies borrowed from the pagans. These were multiplied to such a degree, that Augustine complained that they were 'less tolerable than the yoke of the Jews under the law.' [4] At this period the Bishops of Rome wore costly attire, gave sumptuous banquets, and when they went abroad were carried in litters. [5] They now began to speak with an authoritative voice, and to demand obedience from all the Churches. Of this the dispute between the Eastern and Western Churches respecting Easter is an instance in point. The Eastern Church, following the Jews, kept the feast on the 14th day of the month Nisan [6] — the day of the Jewish Passover. The Churches of the West, and especially that of Rome, kept Easter on the Sabbath following the 14th day of Nisan. Victor, Bishop of Rome, resolved to put an end to the controversy, and accordingly, sustaining himself sole judge of this weighty point, he commanded all the Churches to observe the feast on the same day with himself. The Churches of the East, not aware that the Bishop of Rome had authority to command their obedience in this or in any other matter, kept Easter [Passover] as before; and for this flagrant contempt, as Victor accounted it, of his legitimate authority, he excommunicated them. [7] They refused to obey a human ordinance, and they were shut out from the kingdom of the Gospel. This was the first peal of those thunders which were in after times to roll so often and so terribly from the Seven Hills." J. A. Wylie's *History of Protestantism*, Chapter Two, *"Declension of the Early Church."*

- "From Rome there came now another addition to the sun-worshipping apostasy. The first Christians being mostly Jews, continued to celebrate, in remembrance

Appendix 7D — The Change of "times" and "laws"

of the death of Christ, the true Passover; and this was continued among those who from among the Gentiles had turned to Christ. Accordingly, the celebration was always on the Passover day, the fourteenth of the first month. Rome, however, and from her all the West, adopted the day of the sun as the day of this coloration. According to the Eastern custom, the celebration, being on the fourteenth day of the month, would of course fall on different days of the week as the years resolved. The rule of Rome was that the celebration must always be on a Sunday." A. T. Jones, *Great Empires of Prophecy,* 1898, p. 389.

- "The eastern churches celebrated the resurrection of Christ annually two days after the Passover feast. They commemorated the resurrection on whatever day of the week the sixteenth day of the month fell. This was in harmony with the way the Bible regulated the Old Testament Passover feast … In addition to their yearly spring festival at Easter time, sun worshippers also had a weekly festival holiday. As was previously pointed out, the first day of the week had widespread recognition as being sacred to the sun. The bishop of Rome, seeking to outrival pagan pomp, assaulted those churches which celebrated Easter as a moveable feast. He determined to force Easter to come on the same day of the week each year, namely, Sunday. By this he would create a precedent which only a devout and scholarly opposition could expose. By this he would appeal to the popular prejudices of his age, be they ever so incorrect. By this he would claim to be the lord of the calendar, that instrument so indispensable to civilized nations. By this he would assert the right to appoint church festivals and holy days. By this he would confuse and perplex other church communions more simple and scriptural than he. Only those who have read carefully the history of the growth of the papal power will ever know how powerfully the controversy concerning Easter served in the hands of the bishops of Rome … God had ordained that the Passover of the Old Testament should be celebrated in the spring of the year on the fourteenth day of the first Bible month. Heathenism in the centuries before Christ, had a counterfeit yearly holiday celebrating the spring equinox of the sun. It was called "Eostre" from the Scandinavian word for the goddess of spring, from whence we get our word 'Easter.' " B.G. Wilkinson, *Truth Triumphant,* pp. 123-125. (Notice that Wilkinson states that the heathen's celebration of Easter was a counterfeit of Passover.)

In the following quote, the term *Quartodecimans* is used, meaning: "fourteenth-day men" in reference to those who observed Passover because they observed this Holy Day on the fourteenth day of the first Jewish month, according to Exodus 12:2, 6.

- "Internal dissensions during this era affected the Church at Rome. The dispute over the celebration of Easter grew more acute. The Christians at Rome, who had come from the province of Asia, were accustomed to observe Easter on the 14th day of Nisan, whatever day of the week that date might happen to fall on, just as they had done at home. This difference inevitably led to trouble when it appeared in the Christian community of Rome. Pope Victor decided, therefore, to bring about unity in the observance of the Easter festival and to persuade the Quartodecimans to join in the general practice of the Church. He wrote, therefore, to Bishop Polycrates of Ephesus and induced the latter to call together the bishops of the province of Asia in order to discuss the matter with them. This was done; but in the letter sent by Polycrates to Pope Victor he declared that he firmly held to the Quartodeciman custom observed by so many celebrated and holy bishops of that region. Victor called a meeting of Italian bishops at Rome, which is the earliest Roman synod known. He also wrote to the leading bishops of the various districts, urging them to call together the bishops of their sections of the country and to take counsel with them on the question of the Easter festival. Letters came from all sides … These letters all unanimously reported that Easter was observed on Sunday. Victor, who acted throughout the entire matter as the head of the Catholic Christendom, now called upon the bishops of the province of Asia to abandon their custom and to accept the universally prevailing practice of always celebrating Easter on Sunday. In case they would not do this he declared they would be excluded from the fellowship of the Church." (Obtained from the *Catholic Encyclopedia* at www.newadvent.org).

- "Not until the council of Nicea in 325 A.D. decreed that Easter should be kept on the Sunday next after the first full moon on or after the vernal equinox was there a definite day for the observance of Easter. **Here is the evidence that it has a human origin,** as it was not known until after the fourth century just when Easter would be." Meyers, *Medieval and Modern History,* p. 4. (Emphasis supplied.)

In the following quote, the author is quoting the words of Constantine at the Council of Nicea in AD 325. Notice that the reason Constantine gives for changing Passover to Easter is because of hatred of the Jews, not because of any command from God. In AD 321, Constantine changed the weekly day of worship from the Sabbath on the Seventh-day to Sunday for the same reasons. God's Word should not be set aside due to hatred of anyone.

- "… it seemed to every one a most unworthy thing that we should follow the custom of the Jews in the celebration of this holy solemnity, who, polluted wretches! Having stained their hands with nefarious crime, are justly blinded in their minds. It is, therefore, that rejecting the practice of this people, we should perpetuate to all future ages the celebration of this rite, in a more legitimate order, which we have kept from the first day of our Lord's passion even to the present times … Let us then have nothing in common with the most hostile rabble of the Jews … and to sum up the whole in a few words, it is agreeable to the common judgment of all, that the most holy feast of Easter should be celebrated on one and the same day." *A Historical View of the Council of Nicea,* translation by Isaac Boyle, T. Madison, and G. Lane, New York, 1839, pp. 51, 54.

Waldenses Observed God's Holy Days

God has always had His people who observed His Holy Days. The Waldenses were converts of the apostles and maintained their faith until the nineteenth century.

- "The Reformers held that the Waldensian Church was formed about 120 A.D., from which date on, they passed down from father to son the teachings they received from the apostles." B. G. Wilkinson, *Our Authorized Bible Vindicated,* p. 33.

- "For this we have the confession of Raynerus, an inquisitor, who lived before the middle of the thirteenth century. He ingenuously acknowledgeth, 'That the heresy of those he calls Waudois, or poor people of Lyons, was of great antiquity. Mongst all sects, saith he, cap. 4. that either are or have been, there is none more dangerous to the Church than that of the Leonists, and that for three reasons: the first is, because it is the sect that is of the longest standing of any; for some say it hath been continued down ever since the time of Pope Sylvester, and others, ever since that of the Apostles. The second is, because it is the most general of all sects; for scarcely is there any country to be found, where this sect hath not spread itself.' " Peter Allix D.D., *The Ecclesiastical History of the Ancient Churches of the Piedmont and the Albigenses,* p. 185.

In addition to correctly believing that the Mosaic Law ought to be observed, the Waldenses also observed the Festivals, or God's Holy Days. Samuel Kohn, a Jewish rabbi, wrote a book about the Bosnian Cathars in Hungary (another name for the Waldenses). He said:

- "The hymnal was written in Hungarian. It consisted of one hundred and two hymns. Forty-four for the Sabbath, five for the New Moon, eleven for Passover and Unleavened Bread, six for the Feast of Weeks, six for Tabernacles, three for New Year, one for Atonement, and twenty-six for everyday purposes." (Bosnia Cathars) 1588-1623 Samuel Kohn:

Die Sabbatharier in Siebenburgen Ihr Geshichte, Literalur, and Dogmatik, Budapest, Verlag von Singer & Wolfer, 1894; Lipzig, Verlag von Franz Wager, p. 55. (Translated by Gerhard O. Marx.)

- "Furthermore they celebrated the three main Jewish Feasts: the celebration of the unleavened bread for a week and the Feast of Tabernacles, for which they had provided several songs which tell the history and the meaning of the celebration concerned. In particular the first of these celebrations, which they tended to call Passover in the *Hungarianised* Hebrew term, was held in great admiration among them. They ate only unleavened bread during the time ... They observed the first and seventh day as high holidays, and the days lying between them, which were designated weekdays of the Passover after the literal translation of the Hebrew designation usual 'with the Jews,' demi-feast days. This celebration had for them, apart from its direct Biblical meaning, in addition the significance of 'the future redemption' which Jesus will bring when he comes again to establish the millennial Kingdom of God ... They sanctified the Sabbath because one who does not do so does 'not participate with Christ in eternal life.' They celebrated 'the Feast of the Passover of Israel according to the instruction of our Christ,' and the Feast of Tabernacles, because whoever observes it 'belongs to Christ.' " *Ibid.,* pp. 106-107.

- "The Christian holiday's which, according to their opinion were not prescribed in the Bible, but were the 'inventions of the Popes' are left completely disregarded by them." *Ibid.,* p. 108.

Note: Historical records document very well that the Waldenses maintained the ancient faith, the same faith that Paul and John the Revelator had, and observed God's Holy Days just as they did. The Waldenses also observed the Seventh-day Sabbath and rejected the Pagan holidays, such as Christmas and Easter, which were brought into the Christian Church by the Papal system. They were taught their faith by the apostles and they maintained their faith for seventeen hundred years.

- **JER 6:16** Stand ye in the ways, and see, and ask for the old paths, where is the good way, and walk therein, and ye shall find rest for your souls.

- **JUDE 3** ... earnestly contend for the faith which was once delivered unto the saints.

God's Holy Days Observed in Heaven

Note: The context of the following Scriptures show that after the wicked are all destroyed at the Second Coming, God's people will observe His Sabbath forever in heaven. The Holy Days are part of the Fourth Commandment since they explain the Seventh-day Sabbath more fully and are included in the Sabbath mentioned in the Scripture.

- **ISA 66:23** And it shall come to pass, that from one new moon to another, and from one sabbath to another, shall all flesh come to worship before me, saith the LORD.

The context of Zechariah 14 is that of the new earth.

- **ZECH 14:16** And it shall come to pass, that every one that is left of all the nations which came against Jerusalem shall even go up from year to year to worship the King, the LORD of hosts, and to keep the feast of tabernacles.

The Feast of Tabernacles will be kept forever in Heaven. The weekly Sabbath will be kept in Heaven. The Passover is fulfilled in Heaven at the Marriage Supper of the Lamb. Therefore, it is understandable that all God's Holy Days will be observed in Heaven.

Objections to the Observance of the Seventh-day Sabbath and the Annual Feast Sabbaths

Consider this: The truths of the weekly Sabbath and the annual Feast Sabbaths of the Bible must harmonize between the Old and New Testaments. These "Sabbaths" were honored and observed in the Old Testament. Isaiah 66 reiterates that these "Sabbaths" will also be kept in Heaven and the New Earth. The majority of Christians have had objections, and rejected these "Sabbath" truths from AD 31 to the present day. Many have attempted to abolish the observance of God's Festivals by quoting several texts from the New Testament. These same Scriptures are also use to abolish the weekly Seventh-day Sabbath. Three passages of Scripture will be considered.

(1) Colossians 2:14-17

- **COL 2:14-17** Blotting out the handwriting of <u>ordinances</u> that was against us, which was contrary to us, and took it out of the way, nailing it to his cross; 15 And having spoiled principalities and powers, he made a shew of them openly, triumphing over them in it. 16 Let no man therefore judge you in meat, or in drink, or in respect of an <u>holyday</u>, or of the new moon, or of the sabbath ~~days~~: 17 Which are a shadow of things to come; but the body is of Christ.

"ordinances" — *Strong's* NT#1378 <u>a law</u> (civil, ceremonial <u>or</u> ecclesiastical): KJV - decree, ordinance.

Note: The word *ordinances,* simply means *law.* This text does not explain *which law.* The text does not say that either the weekly Sabbath or the Holy Days were nailed to the cross. Daniel 9:27 explains that the sacrificial system ended at the cross.

"holyday" — *Strong's* NT#1859 of uncertain affinity; a festival: KJV - feast, holyday.

Note: The word *holyday* in this text is a direct reference to the Feast days as these are the only Holy Days stated in the Bible. This text does not say that God's Holy Days or the Seventh-day Sabbath were abolished at the cross. Rather, it says that no one should judge another in these matters.

If Paul had not taught the Colossians to keep God's Holy Days, then he would not have addressed this issue as it would have been irrelevant. Obviously, the Colossians must have been judging one another as to how they kept God's Holy Days. Paul found it necessary to tell them not to judge one another. The Colossians were Gentile converts who did not observe God's Holy Days before their conversion. The very fact that Paul raises the subject of God's Holy Days shows that Paul had taught them to observe these <u>days</u>.

"days" — *Strong's* NT#9999 NOTE: inserted word (x); This word was added by the translators for better readability in the English. There is no actual word in the Greek text.

Note: Since the word *days* was added by the translators, the reference to the *Sabbath* is to the Seventh-day Sabbath, as the Holy Days were previously mentioned.

*"<u>Which are a shadow of things **to come**</u>"* — emphasizes God's Holy Days and the Seventh-day Sabbath point forward to events *yet in the future* — that will be kept in Heaven and the New Earth.

"shadow" — *Strong's* NT#4639 a primary word; "shade" or a shadow (literally or figuratively [an adumbration — to give a sketchy outline]).

Note: On this Earth, the Seventh-day Sabbath and God's Holy Days are but a *sketchy outline* of what Heaven will have to offer. Better *things are coming.*

(2) Ephesians 2:15

- **EPH 2:15** Having abolished in his flesh the enmity, even the law of commandments contained in ordinances; for to make in himself of twain one new man, so making peace;

At first glance this text appears to say that all ordinances are abolished, and since the Feasts are also ordinances, then God's Holy Days were also eliminated at the cross. This is not so! God is not the author of confusion. Therefore, His Word must harmonize from Genesis to Revelation. Consider the translation of the Messianic Jews for this verse:

- **EPH 2:15** Abolishing the *enmity to the Law,* the Commandments, and the Ordinances, through His own flesh, in order to create in Himself one new man from the two, making peace. *The Book of Yahweh.*

Appendix 7D — The Change of "times" and "laws"

Romans 7:14-25 describes a battle that is going on between good and evil in every individual. Romans 8:2 continues the discussion, "Jesus hath made me free from the law of sin and death." Jesus does this by "Abolishing the enmity (hatred) to the Law" as seen in Ephesians 2:15. Man, who has had his enmity (to God's Law) abolished, is left a "new creation."

- **EPH 2:16** And that he might reconcile both unto God in one body by the cross, having slain the enmity thereby.

Note: <u>The enmity to the law is slain, rather than the law being abolished.</u> Translating Ephesians 2:15 this way, places this text in harmony with other texts that say the law was *not abolished at the cross.* See Romans 3:31 and Matthew 5:17-18.

(3) Galatians 4:9-11

- **GAL 4:9-11** But now, after that ye have known God, or rather are known of God, how turn ye again to the weak and beggarly elements, whereunto ye desire again to be in bondage? 10 Ye observe days, and months, and times, and years. 11 I am afraid of you, lest I have bestowed upon you labour in vain.

This is another text that is used to prove God's Holy Days and the Seventh-day Sabbath were abolished. Both premises are false! The context of the quote must be considered. There is *no mention* of Holy Days, or the Seventh-day Sabbath. Luke 11:52 and the following Scriptures give stern counsel to those who take away (or add) to His Book:

- **DEUT 4:2** Ye shall not add unto the word which I command you, neither shall ye diminish ought from it, that ye may keep the commandments of the LORD your God which I command you.

- **REV 22:18-19** And if any man shall add unto these things, God shall add unto him the plagues that are written in this book. 19 And if any man shall take away from the words of the book of this prophecy, God shall take away his part out of the book of life, and out of the holy city, and from the things which are written in this book.

The Galatians were turning back to beggarly elements by observing certain days. (See GAL 4:3.) Paul was telling the Galatians that they were turning away from *what he had taught them*, turning back and following their *worldly ways* before they were Christians. Before they had heard Paul's teachings, they were keeping Pagan holidays — days *like* Easter, and Baal's birthday celebrated on December 25.

Acts 19:24-41 records how the Ephesians cried out for their heathen goddess, Diana. At Easter, Astarte conceived Tammuz, (another name for Baal), born on De-

cember 25. These were *some of the Pagan holidays* Paul was condemning in his letter to the Galatians.

There is no instruction in the Bible that God's Holy Days have been removed or changed or that God's people should no longer keep them.

God's Holy Days and the Sacrificial System

Some say that because sacrifices were done on the Feast days that they were abolished at the cross. *Twice as many sacrifices were done on the Seventh-day Sabbath as on other days.* (See NUM 28:9.) Using this argument to abolish the Feast Sabbaths, would also have to abolish the Seventh-day Sabbath. Abolishing one Commandment, but retaining the other nine of the Ten Commandments, which is what many Christians do when they say the Sabbath was changed to Sunday, is not logical! God declares that He does not change as noted in this Scripture:

- **MAL 3:6** For I am the LORD, I change not …

If nine Commandments are still binding, as the majority of the Christian world believes, then all ten of them are still binding. The sacrificial system ended at the cross (DAN 9:27), but God's Holy Days remain.

Resting in All of God's Truths

This appendix has addressed only **_some_** of God's Truths that have been turned upside down by mankind's customs and traditions. The reality is that ALL of God's Truths have been counterfeited by Satan, using one religious/ political system or another. "Man defined" economics, politics, education, and religion are but a few of the examples, within this system which are manufactured in the image of man. All of these "man defined" systems are designed with one thing in common — to glorify SELF. God's Laws were put in place to show mankind how to come out of SELF glorification and enter into His perfect rest. (HEB 4:10) Learning to enter into this rest of relationship, brings about a dependency upon the Creator, and at the same time, purges the human heart of rebellion. Luke 18:9-14 teaches this lesson well. The tax-collector learned that outside of relationship with God and His Provision, there was no hope for him. The Pharisee, clothed in his man made religion, had learned only "self dependency." Many Old Testament examples speak of coming out of "dependency on a system" and entering into relationship with the only One that can bring true meaning to life. (Review Appendices 3A and 3B, on pages 54-57. Also see pages 400-401 for further comment.)

~ ~ ~

Important Note: This appendix is only a very small portion of a large study. A personal study would require the use of a *Strong's Concordance* and the *King James Bible.*

THE STRUCTURE OF DANIEL

FOUR VISIONS REVEAL GOD'S PLAN TO SAVE HIS PEOPLE

The Major Line of Prophecy From 606 BC — to the Establishment of Christ's Kingdom

VISION 1 - DAN 2	VISION 2 - DAN 7	VISION 3 - DAN 8	VISION 4 - DAN 10-12
HEAVENLY SCENE DAN 2:1, 19 GOLD HEAD SILVER BREAST & ARMS BRASS BELLY & THIGHS IRON LEGS IRON & CLAY — FEET & TOES	**HEAVENLY SCENE** DAN 7:2-14 LION BEAR LEOPARD DREADFUL BEAST LITTLE HORN		
INTERLUDE QUESTION DAN 2:26 WHAT IS THE SECRET OF THE DREAM?	**INTERLUDE QUESTION** DAN 7:16 WHAT IS THE TRUTH OF ALL THIS?		
HISTORIC-PROPHETIC OUTLINE DAN 2:36-43 BABYLON MEDO-PERSIA GREECE ROME (PAGAN IMPERIAL) OUTLINE EXTENDS TO: AD 476	**HISTORIC-PROPHETIC OUTLINE** DAN 7:17-25 BABYLON MEDO-PERSIA GREECE ROME (PAGAN IMPERIAL) ROME (PAPAL NO. 1) OUTLINE EXTENDS TO: AD 1798		
ANSWER TO QUESTION DAN 2:44 GOD OF HEAVEN CONSUMES ALL THESE KINGDOMS! **ENDTIME EVENT** DAN 2:45 "STONE KINGDOM" SECOND COMING OF JESUS	**ANSWER TO QUESTION** DAN 7:26 JUDGMENT SITS WITH THE "ANCIENT OF DAYS!" **ENDTIME EVENT** DAN 7:27 "KINGDOM GIVEN TO THE SAINTS"		

Note: Only God pulls back the curtain of time in each vision to reveal future events.

RECAPPING STRUCTURE CHART
Four Historic-Prophetic Outlines of Earthly Kingdoms in the Book of Daniel

The "Symbols" of Daniel 2, 7, and 8 (Image, Beasts, and Horns) and the "Literal" Kings of Daniel 11
Consistently Refer to the Progression of Persecuting Kingdoms Surrounding God's People.

Daniel 2 Symbolic	**Daniel 7** Symbolic	**Daniel 8** Symbolic	**Daniel 11-12:4** Liter
Vision 1 - Prophetic Outline 1	Vision 2 - Prophetic Outline 2	Vision 3 - Prophetic Outline 3	Vision 4 - Prophetic Outlin

Kingdom #1 BABYLON 606 — 538 BC

DAN 2:38
Gold Head

DAN 7:4
Lion

Kingdom #2 MEDO-PERSIA 538 — 331 BC

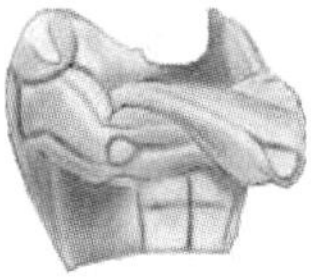

DAN 2:39
Silver Chest & Arms

DAN 7:5
Bear

DAN 8:3-4, 20
Ram

Kingdom #3 GREECE 331 — 168 BC

DAN 2:39
Brass Belly & Thighs

DAN 7:6
Leopard

DAN 8:5-8, 21
He Goat

Kingdom #4 ROME (Pagan Imperial) 168 BC — AD 476

DAN 2:40
Iron Legs

DAN 7:7-8
Dreadful Beast

DAN 8:9a
"... out of one of them ..."

Kingdom #5 ROME (Papal Supremacy No. 1 — Old Europe) AD 538 — 1798

DAN 2:41
Feet Part of Iron

DAN 7:8, 20-25
Little Horn

DAN 8:9b
Little Horn

Kingdom #6 ROME (Papal Supremacy No. 2 Rises and Rules) AD 1801 — Present

DAN 2:41
Feet Part of Clay

(Iron and Clay in the feet and toes, represents Rome's divided relationship with mankind. Atheistic France and Russian Communism represent Puppet Pawns Under Papal Rome.)

DAN 8:9c, 24-25
"king of fierce countenance waxed exceeding great"

Kingdom #7

DAN 2:42-43
Toes of Iron & Clay

This chart shows the <u>recapping</u> of kingdoms in a "vertical" format.

136

DANIEL
The Story of the Rise and Fall of Earthly Kingdoms

CHAPTER 8

**HEAVENLY SCENE
VISION THREE
(Part One)
(Symbolic Horns
and a "king")**

*Daniel's Vision
by the River Ulai
(551 BC)*

1 In the third year of the reign of king Belshazzar a vision appeared unto me, even unto me Daniel, after that which appeared unto me at the first [the First Vision dipicting beasts and horns in Daniel 7].

2 And I saw in a vision; and it came to pass, when I saw, that I was at Shushan in the palace, which is in the province of Elam; and I saw in a vision, and I was by the river of Ulai.

Introduction: See **The Structure of Daniel** Chart on page 233 to note the progression of Daniel's visions. The third **Heavenly Scene** given to Daniel reveals six of the seven persecuting earthly kingdoms. Some were *symbolic horns* (that follow Babylon) and one *king*. The chart on the previous page aligns these kingdoms with the former *symbolic beasts and image*. Vision Three supplies additional information regarding the symbols and the new *king*. Daniel's attention is quickly turned to the "king of fierce countenance." He saw the character of the Little Horn Kingdom transition into a kingdom having "a king of fierce countenance" as its leader. These two kingdoms make up the <u>main</u> persecuting powers from which God's people seek deliverance. In Daniel 7, the Little Horn was a main persecutor between AD 538-1798. In this chapter, the "king of fierce countenance" not only becomes the main persecutor of God's people, but he casts Christ's deity to the ground; he continues and he prospers. With Christ's office lowered to that of *just a man*, the Sanctuary and its message is destroyed. *Just a man* cannot die a substitutionary death for all of mankind. With this central truth destroyed, ALL Biblical Truth is cast down. Later, as the Loud Cry (Latter Rain) goes forth, this truth is raised to life again in the heart of the believer. This is the cleansing of the earthly sanctuary (vs 13) in the heart of the believer. No human power can bring these persecutors to judgment. Only God, through judgment, can overcome this counterfeit system and deliver His people. Note: The verses of Daniel 8:9-12 (included in the Heavenly Scene) will be given fuller explanation in the Historic-Prophetic Outline <u>between</u> the verses of Daniel 8:22-23.

Prophetic Key #6 Daniel 8 follows the same literary structure as the visions of Daniel 2 and 7.

Prophetic Key #22 This vision contains a *timeline* in Daniel 8:14. Daniel 9 includes more detail regarding this 2300 day-year timeline.

Verses 1-2

Note: This vision was given approximately two years after the Daniel 7 vision. Review the map on page 81 for the location of Susa [Shushan] and the River Ulai. During this time, Nabonidus was in Tema developing a trade center and reviving moon worship. Under Belshazzar's reign in Babylon, Daniel realized the economy was beginning to collapse, thus numbering the days of the Babylonian kingdom.

**HEAVENLY SCENE
DAN 8:2-14**

**RAM
HE GOAT
"OUT OF ONE OF THEM"
LITTLE HORN
"WAXED EXCEEDING GREAT"**

Note: Only God pulls back the curtain of time to reveal future events.

Prophetic Key #4 Remember the Hermeneutic Principle of ISA 28:9-13. The understanding of Scripture unlocks as a result of cross-reference Bible Study. **Note:** Not all the Prophetic Keys will be listed in this chapter in order to provide the Bible expositor with an opportunity to apply them.

JER 6:16a Stand ye in the ways, and see, and <u>ask for the old paths</u>, <u>where is the good way</u>, <u>and walk therein</u>, and ye shall find rest for your souls.

The "Two-Horned" Ram

3 Then I lifted up mine eyes, and saw, and, behold, there stood before the river a ram which had two horns: and the two horns were high; but one was higher than the other, and the higher came up last.

The "Ram" Kingdom Expanded and Became Great

4 I saw the ram pushing westward, and northward, and southward; so that no beasts might stand before him, neither was there any that could deliver out of his hand; but he did according to his will, and became great.

The Goat Kingdom with "One Notable Horn"

5 And as I was considering, behold, an he goat came from the west on the face of the whole earth, and touched not the ground: and the goat had a notable horn between his eyes.

He Goat Conquers the Ram

6 And [the] he [goat] came to the ram that had two horns, which I had there seen standing before the river, and ran unto him in the fury of his power.

7 And I saw him come close unto the ram, and he was moved with choler against him, and smote the ram, and brake his two horns: and there was no power in the ram to stand before him, but he cast him down to the ground, and stamped upon him: and there was none that could deliver the ram out of his hand.

 Prophetic Key #14 In Daniel 8:4-9, symbols of *horns* are employed. Verse 23 introduces the title "a king of fierce countenance."

Prophetic Key #16 The symbols that are used are word pictures of *horns* that are unusual.

<u>Verses 3-4</u>

"… became great …"

<u>Verse 5</u>

<u>Verses 6-7</u>

*He Goat Waxed Very Great
Before his Notable Horn
Was Broken*

8 Therefore the he goat waxed very great: and when he was strong, the great horn was broken; and ...

*Broken Horn Extends into
Four [Directions]*

8 ... for it came up four notable ones toward the four <u>winds</u> [four directions] **of heaven.**

*Another Kingdom
Addressed Briefly*

9a And <u>out of one of them</u> [Rome ---- one of the four winds/directions of verse 8] ...

Little Horn Kingdom Rises

9b ... <u>came forth a little horn</u> [Papal Supremacy No. 1] ...

*Little Horn Kingdom
Transitions to the
Kingdom that Waxes
With Exceeding Great Power
Expanding in all Directions*

9c ... which waxed exceeding <u>great</u>, [large in estate, honor, and pride] **<u>toward the south, and toward the east, and toward the pleasant land.</u>**

Verse 8

"... waxed very great ..."

"winds" — *Strong's* OT#7308 corresponding to <u>OT#7307</u>: KJV - mind, spirit, wind.

<u>OT#7307</u> wind ... by extension, <u>a region of the sky</u>.

Verse 9a

"out of one of them" — refers back to verse 8 which describes the *<u>four winds</u>* or *four directions*. (This is a very brief description identifying Pagan Imperial Rome.)

"... out of one of them ..."
Pagan Imperial Rome
emerged out of one of the
four winds (or directions)
of Greece.

Verse 9b

"came forth a little horn" — The Little Horn emerged out of Pagan Imperial Rome — one of the directions of the four winds.

Verse 9c

Note: The *latter time* of the antichrist Little Horn power unfolds the *exceeding great* kingdom of antichrist after the 1798 wound inflicted by Napoleon.

"great" — *Strong's* OT#1431 to be (causatively make) <u>large ... in estate, honor and in pride</u>. KJV - advance, <u>boast</u>, increase, <u>lift up, magnify</u>.

"toward the south ... east ... pleasant land" — these three directions have a similar link back to the three horns that were uprooted in DAN 7:20. In the endtimes, before civil power over the world can be exercised, the powers represented by these three directions must be subdued. Further explanations on pages 152 and 320.

"... waxed
exceeding
great ..."

"pleasant land" — *Strong's* OT#6643 in a sense of prominence; <u>splendor</u> ... (<u>as beautiful</u>). (OT#6643 relates to *glorious land* in Daniel 11:41.)

Note: For Daniel, the *pleasant land* was the dwelling place for God's people in the beautiful city of Jerusalem. Daniel 11:45 uses the term *glorious holy mountain* representing God's church. (Also see Ps 48:2.)

MATT 5:35 by Jerusalem; for it is the city of the great King.

Persecution of God's People

10 And it [the Papal Rome Persecutor] **waxed great, even to the host of heaven; and it cast down some of the host and of the stars to the ground, and stamped upon them.**

11 Yea, he [the Persecutor] **magnified himself even to the prince of the host, and by him the daily** ~~sacrifice~~ **was taken away, and the place of his sanctuary was cast down.**

12 And an host was given him [the Persecutor] **against the daily** ~~sacrifice~~ **by reason of transgression,** [wrong use of ruling power] **and it cast down [ALL] the truth to the ground; and it practiced, and prospered** [and extended itself over the world].

That Certain Saint, — Son of God — the Wonderful Numberer

13 Then I heard one <u>saint</u> speaking, and another saint said unto <u>that certain</u> ~~saint~~ [added word] **which spake ...**

The Pressing Questions — "How Long ...?"

13 ... How long shall be the vision concerning the daily ~~sacrifice~~**, and the transgression of desolation** [persecutor of God's people], **to give both the sanctuary** [in heaven and the heart of man] **and the host** [mass of God's obedient people] **to be trodden under foot** [and persecuted]?

Verse 10

Note: Extra study for this verse will be given in the Historic-Prophetic Outline on pages 153-154.

"... waxed great ..."

Verse 11

Note: Extra study for:
- the word *"sacrifice"* on page 155;
- the word *"daily"* on pages 156-157;
- transfer of *"the daily"* on page 158;
- *"the daily taken away"* on page 159.

Verse 12

"[ALL] the truth" — includes all Biblical, revealed truths in God's Word from Genesis to Revelation.

Note: Pages 160-161 give extra study on the "casting down of ALL truth."

A Promise to Claim

MARK 11:24 Therefore I say unto you, What things soever ye desire, when ye pray, believe that ye receive them, and ye shall have them.

"... practiced and prospered ..."
till he has the
whole world in his hands

Verse 13

"saint" — *Strong's* OT#6918 sacred (ceremonially or morally); (as noun) **God** (by eminence), an angel, a saint, a sanctuary: KJV - **holy (One),** saint.

"that certain" — *Strong's* OT#6422 palmowniy (pal-mo-nee'); probably for OT:6423; a certain one, i.e. so-and-so: KJV - certain.

Bible Margin Definition: *"pal-moh-nee"* — Palmoni: the numberer of secrets, or, the Wonderful Numberer.

The Pressing Questions of Daniel 8:13 — "How Long ...?"

1. How long shall be the vision [in Daniel 8:1—9:27]?
2. How long shall be the vision concerning the "daily"?
3. How long shall the transgression of desolation reign [the Papal system in its perversions of truth that desolates the people]?
4. How long shall the host of God's people be "trodden under foot [persecuted]?"
5. How long shall the sanctuary (in the heart of man and in heaven) be defiled or made unclean by the record of the sinful "persecutor" described in Daniel 8:10-12?

Note: Only questions 1 and 5 in the above list are answered in Daniel chapters 8 and 9. Questions 2, 3, and 4 are answered in Daniel 12, and explained more fully in the Book of Revelation.

"desolation" — further information is given in Daniel 11:31 describing this title as a persecutor.

The Answer to the
"How Long?" Question (No. 5)

14 And he said unto me, Unto two thousand and three hundred days [or 2300 Days of Atonement]; **then shall the <u>sanctuary</u> be cleansed** [in heaven and the heart of man].

Verse 14

🔑 **Prophetic Keys #23 and #24 a/b** The *2300 days* in Daniel 8 is a timeline contained within a *symbolic vision*. Therefore, this timeline of *symbolic days* is converted to *literal time* using the Year-day Computation Principle. The 2300 *symbolic* days equals 2300 *literal* years. Also see Expanded Note at the bottom of this page.

Prophetic Key #26 All timelines **_begin and end_** with voices or legislative decrees. The second part of Daniel's vision given in Daniel 9, fully explains how this timeline of 2300 literal years begins and ends. (Also see Timeline Table #3 below for extra help.)

Question No. 5: How long shall Christ's sanctuary, in heaven and the heart of man, be defiled or made unclean by the works of the sinful "persecutor?" (See DAN 8:13.)

Answer: Unto two thousand and three hundred days; then shall the <u>sanctuary</u> be cleansed. REV 20:12: Sins are destroyed in the lake of fire.

Note: Some of the interpretation for the 2300 days begins right away, but the interpretation is not completed until the last part of Daniel 9. (See page 161 for extra notes on verse 14 and Appendix 8C, on pages 182-183, for extra help in understanding some of the sanctuary service.)

"sanctuary" — *Strong's* OT#6944 qodesh; <u>a sacred place or thing</u>; rarely abstract, sanctity: KJV - consecrated (thing), dedicated (thing), hallowed (thing), holiness, holy, sanctuary.

DAN 7:10 the judgment was set, and the books were opened.

Prophetic Timeline #3: Details and Specifics

Timeline #3 (Length of Timeline)	Subject (of Timeline)	Prophetic Scripture For Timeline	Timeline Begins (with)	Speaking VOICE (Decree)	Timeline Ends (with)	Legislative & Judicial Action (Date)
2300 Years DAN 8:14	Investigative Judgment	DAN 8:14 and EZRA 7:11-26	Decree to Restore and Rebuild Jerusalem DAN 9:25	Artaxerxes' Decree of 457 BC	Cleansing of the Heavenly Sanctuary by Jesus Christ in AD 1844	1844 Voice of Judgment Must Begin at the House of God 1 PETER 4:17

Expanded Note: For those that know the Day of Atonement is the <u>yearly</u> day of judgment represented in the sanctuary services — to them it is significant that 2300 Days of Atonement are to be counted beginning at 457 BC. Therefore, the 2300th Day of Atonement would reach to the fall of 1844. At this time the "Great Day of Atonement" of the Heavenly Sanctuary was ushered in. Jesus Christ, as our High Priest, began His work of judgment in the Most Holy Place (beginning with the dead). The judgment of the living is soon to begin.

Note: The investigation which brings about judgment, in heaven and the heart of man, could not begin until the time of the cleansing of the Heavenly Sanctuary (i.e. Day of Atonement). Daniel was instructed that *2300 Years* of history had to unfold before the atrocities of the persecutor could be brought to judgment. Jesus Christ would then begin the work of removing the recorded sins from the sanctuary thereby cleansing it. This heavenly work began in AD 1844.

The Sanctuary is the Heavenly Temple

HEB 8:1-2 Now of the things which we have spoken this is the sum: We have such an high priest, who is set on the right hand of the throne of the Majesty in the heavens; 2 A minister of the sanctuary, and of the true tabernacle, which the Lord pitched, and not man.

HEB 9:11-12 But Christ being come an high priest of good things to come, by a greater and more perfect tabernacle, not made with hands, that is to say, not of this building; 12 Neither by the blood of goats and calves, but by his own blood he entered in once into the holy place, having obtained eternal redemption for us.

Reminder: See **The Structure of Daniel** Chart on page 233. Vision Three is now moving from the **Heavenly Scene** to the **Interlude Question.** The **Interlude** is an interruption between the **Heavenly Scene** and the **Historic-Prophetic Outline.** When Daniel had seen the vision, he then sought for the meaning of the vision. He also heard questions being asked in verse 13 which troubled him. One of the answers in verse 14 didn't seem reasonable to him. Therefore, in verse 15 Daniel asks the meaning of everything he has just experienced, likely wondering how this vision will end. The answer to Daniel's question will be given at the <u>end</u> of the **Historic-Prophetic Outline.**

INTERLUDE QUESTION
DAN 8:15
WHAT IS THE MEANING OF THIS VISION?

HEAVENLY SCENE
DAN 8:2-14

RAM
HE GOAT
"OUT OF ONE OF THEM"
LITTLE HORN
"WAXED EXCEEDING GREAT"

INTERLUDE QUESTION
DAN 8:15
WHAT IS THE MEANING OF THIS VISION?

INTERLUDE QUESTION VISION THREE

"What is the meaning of this vision?"

*Interpretation of the Vision Commanded by **Him** Who Walks Upon the Water*

15 And it came to pass, when I, even I Daniel, had seen the vision, and sought for the meaning, then, behold, there stood before me as the appearance of a <u>man</u> [Michael the Archangel].

16 And I heard a man's voice between the banks of Ulai, which called, and said, Gabriel, make this man to understand the vision.

Verses 15-16

Note: Compare the *Strong's Concordance* definitions of *"man"* and *"Michael"* to have a fuller understanding of who this "man" really is.

"man" — *Strong's* OT#1397 **a valiant man or warrior**; generally, a person simply: KJV - every one, man, **mighty**.

"Michael" — *Strong's* OT#4317 Mi-yka'el (me-kaw-ale'); from **OT:410**; **who (is) like God?**; Mikael, **the name of an archangel**: KJV - Michael.

OT#410 shortened from OT#352; strength; as adjective, **mighty; especially the Almighty**: KJV - **God**, goodly, great, mighty one, power, strong.

A Theophany (Vision of Michael the Archangel)

Note: In these two verses, Daniel saw a Being that "appeared" as a man, and called with a man's voice, giving a command to the angel Gabriel to instruct Daniel in the vision. This Being would be One superior to Gabriel — known as Michael the Archangel. The concordance definition for this *"man"* is **a valiant, mighty man or warrior**. "Michael" is defined as **"mighty, especially the Almighty."** (See Daniel 3:15 where King Nebuchadnezzar also recognized the Son of God.)

Daniel did not understand the meaning of the timeline he had seen nor how to count out the 2300 day-years. He had to wait about thirteen years to receive this information from Gabriel given in Daniel 9, the second part of the vision.

*The Answer to the
"How Long?" Question (No. 1)*

*The Vision Extends
to the Very Endtime*

17 So he [Gabriel] **came near where I stood: and when he came, I was afraid, and fell upon my face: but he said unto me, Understand, O son of man: for at the time of the end** [#7093 utmost border end of time] **shall be the vision.**

*The Physical Manifestations
of a True Prophet in Vision
(Daniel was not
in a mode of worship.)*

18 **Now as he was speaking with me, I was in a deep sleep on my face toward the ground: but he** [Gabriel] **touched me, and set me upright.**

*The End of This World
Has an Appointed Time*

19 **And he** [Gabriel] **said, Behold, I will make thee know what shall be in the last end** [OT#319] **of the indignation: for at the <u>time appointed</u> the <u>end</u>** [OT#7093] **shall be.**

Verse 17

<u>Question No. 1 from DAN 8:13</u>: "How long shall be the vision of Daniel 8:1-9:27?"
<u>Answer</u>: <u>The vision of Daniel 8 extends from Medo-Persia (331 BC) to the utmost "end" or extremity of time</u> where the desolating/persecuting kingdom will eventually be "broken without hand." (DAN 8:25) This event is associated with the Second Coming of Jesus.

"end" — *Strong's* OT#7093 qets (kates); contracted from **<u>OT#7112</u>**: an extremity; adverbially (with prepositional prefix) after: KJV - after, (**utmost**) **border, end**.

<u>OT#7112</u> qatsats (kaw-tsats'); **to chop off** (literally or figuratively): KJV - cut (asunder, in pieces, in sunder, off), utmost.

DAN 7:26 But the judgment shall sit, and they shall take away his [Papal] dominion, to consume and to destroy it unto the [very] <u>end</u> [of time]. ["*end*" — *Strong's* OT#5491, 5490.]

"end" — *Strong's* OT#5491 corresponding to **<u>OT#5490</u>**: - end.

<u>OT#5490</u> a termination: KJV - **conclusion**, end.

Verse 18

REV 22:8-9 And I John ... fell down to worship before the feet of the angel ... 9 Then saith he unto me, See thou do it not: for I am thy fellowservant, and of thy brethren the prophets.

Verse 19

"end" — *Strong's* OT#319 **the last or end, hence**, **the future**; also posterity: KJV - (last, latter) end (time), hinder (utter) -most, length, posterity, **remnant**, residue, reward. (Note: This is the definition for the word "end" through the *Strong's Concordance* computer program. There is <u>no</u> <u>entry</u> for the word "end" in the *Strong's Concordance* handbook.)

"indignation" — *Strong's* OT#2195 from **<u>OT#2194</u> strictly froth at the mouth**, i.e. (figuratively) **fury** (especially of God's displeasure with sin): KJV - angry, **indignation**, rage.

<u>OT#2194</u> properly, to foam at the mouth, i.e. **to be enraged**: KJV - abhor, *abominable, be angry, defy, have indignation.

"indignation" — Anger or extreme anger, mingled with contempt, disgust or abhorrence. *Noah Webster 1828.*

Note: *Indignation* is a direct attack which is <u>intended</u> to bring down the dignity of a person, in this case, Jesus Christ!

"abominable" — very hateful, detestable. *Noah Webster 1828.*

"time appointed" — *Strong's* OT#4150 moed`; an appointment, i.e. <u>a fixed time or season</u>; specifically, a festival; conventionally a year; also a signal (<u>as appointed beforehand</u>): KJV - (set) time (appointed).

Note: God has a *fixed appointed time* for the very end of sin on this earth just as the 2300 day-year timeline had an appointed time to end.

The Story of the Rise and Fall of Earthly Kingdoms

Reminder: See **The Structure of Daniel** Chart on page 233. Following the **Interlude Question,** Daniel 8:20 begins the interpretation in the **Historic-Prophetic Outline.** The interpretation of the *horns* and *"waxed exceeding great"* from the **Heavenly Scene** are given in the Outline with the focus on the "king of fierce countenance" that rules at the present time. This Outline extends the datable time of earthly kingdoms from 538 BC to AD 1844 bringing the vision to the beginning of the Investigative Judgment. Daniel 9 offers the explanation for calculations of the 1844 date. **Note:** Between verses 22 and 23 there will be a slight interruption using several pages to address and enlarge on information given in Daniel 8:9-12 — comparing the two Papal Supremacies as one entity but two separate kingdoms, ruling during separate time periods.

HISTORIC-PROPHETIC OUTLINE
VISION THREE

HISTORIC-PROPHETIC OUTLINE

DAN 8:20-25

(BABYLON IS REIGNING)
MEDO-PERSIA
GREECE
ROME (PAGAN IMPERIAL)
ROME (PAPAL NO. 1)
ROME (PAPAL NO. 2)
OUTLINE EXTENDS TO:
AD 1844

HEAVENLY SCENE
DAN 8:2-14

RAM
HE GOAT
"OUT OF ONE OF THEM"
LITTLE HORN
"WAXED EXCEEDING GREAT"

INTERLUDE QUESTION
DAN 8:15

WHAT IS THE MEANING OF THIS VISION?

Gabriel Begins to Interpret the Vision

20 The ram which thou sawest having two horns are the kings of Media and Persia.

(This verse will be repeated on page 145 revealing more information.)

21 And the rough goat is the king of Grecia: and the great horn that is between his eyes is the first king.

(This verse will be repeated on pages 146-147 revealing more information.)

Verses 20-21

Review **Prophetic Keys #7, #10, #11, and #14-17.**

2nd Kingdom
MEDO-PERSIA
Darius-Cyrus
538 — 331 BC

3rd Kingdom
GREECE
Alexander the Great
331 — 168 BC

Note: In the thumbnail for the Historic-Prophetic Outline, "Babylon is Reigning" has been placed in brackets to indicate Babylon has not been specifically mentioned in this vision. This Historic-Prophetic Outline reveals kingdoms that will follow the First Kingdom of Babylon, which is soon to pass off the scene.

HISTORIC-PROPHETIC OUTLINE
DAN 8:20-25

(BABYLON IS REIGNING)
MEDO-PERSIA
GREECE
ROME (PAGAN IMPERIAL)
ROME (PAPAL NO. 1)
ROME (PAPAL NO. 2)
OUTLINE EXTENDS TO:
AD 1844

Thumbnail including Historic-Prophetic Outline for Daniel 8.

DANIEL

CHAPTER 8   The Story of the Rise and Fall of Earthly Kingdoms

*Gabriel Begins to
Interpret the Vision*

**20 The <u>ram which thou sawest
having two horns</u> are the kings
of Media and Persia.**

🔑 **Prophetic Key #17** Each symbol must be <u>interpreted</u> by the Bible.
(See Appendix 8B (Part 1), on page 176, for extra help in decoding.)
Note: Daniel 2:38 named Babylon as the First Kingdom. (In this
vision Babylon is still reigning, but is no longer the main focus.)
Verse 20 names Medo-Persia as the second earthly kingdom.

Verse 20

*The "Two-Horned" Ram
Represents Medo-Persia
(538 BC)*

DAN 8:3 Then I lifted up mine eyes,
and saw, and, behold, there stood before the river <u>a ram which had two
horns</u>: and the two horns were high;
but <u>one was higher</u> than the other, and
the higher came up last.

"<u>one [horn] was higher</u>" — aligns
with the bear raising higher on one
side and represents the kingdom of
Persia that became the dominating
kingdom. See:

DAN 7:5 a second, like to a bear, and
it <u>raised up itself on one side</u>.

*The Kingdom Expanded
Under the Reign of Persia*

DAN 8:4 I saw the ram <u>pushing westward, and northward, and southward</u>;
so that no beasts might stand before
him, neither was there any that could
deliver out of his hand; but he did according to his will, and <u>became great</u>
[large in estate, hono,r and pride].

🔑 **Prophetic Key #11** This
vision aligns with the previous visions of Daniel 2
and 7. Since the kingdom
of **Babylon** is in the last
years of its reign this vision begins with the Sec-
ond Kingdom. (See the
chart on page 136.)

The two **horns** of the
Ram represent the king-
dom of **Medo-Persia**,
which aligns with the two
sides of the **Bear** in
Daniel 7:5 and the **Silver
Breast** and two **Arms** in
Daniel 2:39.

"<u>pushing westward, and northward, and southward</u>" — represents the
literal directions that Medo-Persia pushed: westward into Lydia; northward against the Scythians [in the southern parts of Russia]; southward
into Egypt and Ethiopia. The eastern boundaries reached unto India. (See
map on page 81.)

EST 1:1 Now it came to pass in the
days of Ahasuerus [Persian King
Xerxes I], (this *is* Ahasuerus [Queen
Esther's husband], which reigned,
from <u>India even unto Ethiopia, *over* an
hundred and seven and twenty prov-
inces</u>:)

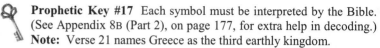

*Gabriel Continues the
Interpretation of the Vision*

21 And the rough goat is the king of Grecia: and the great [notable] **horn** [of agreement] **that is between his eyes is the first king** [Alexander the Great].

(This verse is repeated on the next page.)

Prophetic Key #17 Each symbol must be interpreted by the Bible. (See Appendix 8B (Part 2), on page 177, for extra help in decoding.) **Note:** Verse 21 names Greece as the third earthly kingdom.

Verse 21

*The He Goat with
"One Notable Horn"*

DAN 8:5   And as I was considering, behold, an <u>he goat came from the west</u> on the face of the whole earth, and <u>touched not the ground</u>: and the goat had a [great] <u>notable</u> horn [of agreement] between his eyes.

"he goat came from the west" — Greece lays west of Persia and attacked from that direction.

"first king" — Alexander the Great [the first king of Greece] received authority to rule over the fiercely independent Greek City States through skillful diplomacy which yielded their *agreement*. Alexander is represented by the notable horn on the He Goat.

Prophetic Key #11 This vision continues to align with the previous visions of Daniel 2 and 7. (See chart on page 136.)

The horn of the He Goat is a symbol of Greece. This aligns with the Leopard in Daniel 7:6 and the Brass Belly and Thighs in Daniel 2:39.

"touched not the ground" — Alexander's movements were as swift as the wind which has the same characteristics of speed indicated by the four wings on the leopard of Daniel 7.

"notable" — *Strong's* OT#2380 a look; striking appearance, revelation: KJV - <u>agreement</u>, notable (one).

*Greece Attacks Persia
at the Battle of Arbela
(331 BC)*

DAN 8:6   And he [Alexander the Great] came to the ram [Persian Kingdom] that had two horns, which I had there seen standing before the river, and <u>ran unto him in the fury</u> of his power.

"ran unto him in the fury" — Alexander the Great easily defeated Persia with fury in three different battles.
1.   334 BC — River Grancius in Phrygia
2.   333 BC — Issus, Cilicia
3.   331 BC — Plain of Arbela in Syria

"fury" — *Strong's* OT#2534 heat; anger, poison (from its fever): KJV - hot displeasure, furious, **indignation**, poison, rage, **wrath**.

*Gabriel Continues the
Interpretation of the Vision*

**21 And the rough goat is the king
of Grecia: and the great** [notable]
horn [of agreement] **that is between his eyes is the first king**
[Alexander the Great].

*The Fall (323 BC)
and Division (301 BC)
of Greece*

22 Now that being broken [323
BC], **whereas four stood up for it**
[301 BC] ...

Verse 21 (Continues the interpretation for the Kingdom of Greece, using
the verses from the Heavenly Scene section.)

*Greece Conquers Persia
at the Battle of Arbela
(331 BC)*

DAN 8:7 And I saw him come close
unto the ram, and he was moved with
choler against him, and smote the ram,
and brake his two horns: and there was
no power in the ram to stand before
him, but he cast him down to the
ground, and stamped upon him: and
there was none that could deliver the
ram out of his hand.

"choler" — *Strong's* OT#4843 to be (causatively, make) bitter: KJV -
bitter, be moved with choler, grieved, provoke, vex.

"cast him down to the ground, and stamped upon him" — Alexander totally subdued Persia; cut their armies to pieces and scattered them; plundered the cities and ravaged the country. The royal city of Persepolis was
sacked and burned. The Ram had no power to stand against this He Goat.

Verse 22

*The Notable Horn of Greece
is Broken (323 BC)*

DAN 8:8 Therefore the he goat waxed
very great: and when he was strong,
the great horn was broken; and ...

Note: Alexander the Great consumed a great deal of alcohol and encouraged those in his army to do the same. Having sat through one long drinking spree, he was invited to another. According to history, after drinking
to each of twenty guests, he twice drank the full Herculean cup containing
the equivalent of about six quarts. At the age of thirty-two years, he never
recovered and died eleven days later on June 13, 323 BC. Thus the notable
horn was broken in the prime of his strength and height of his power.

*Greece Divided Toward
Four [Directions]
(301 BC)*

DAN 8:8 ... for it came up four notable ones toward the four winds [four
directions] of heaven.

"winds" — *Strong's* OT#7308 ruwach; corresponding to **OT#7307**: KJV
- mind, spirit, wind.

OT#7307 ruwach; wind ... by extension, a region of the sky.

Prophetic Keys #11, #12, and #13 The vision continues to move
"forward in time" and aligns with secular history. Verse 8 confirms
the information in the previous vision, namely, Greece would have
four divisions. See Daniel 7:6 and review page 99 for Vision Two
details.

Greece Divided Between Four Generals

22 ... four kingdoms shall stand up out of the nation, but <u>not in his power</u>.

<u>Verse 22</u> (Concluded)

Third Kingdom
"Alexander the Great"
Dies in 323 BC

"not in his power" — The four divisions of Alexander's kingdom did not stand in his power. None of them possessed the strength of Alexander's original kingdom. Eventually, the four divisions were slowly absorbed by Pagan Imperial Rome. However, the Hellenistic culture of Greek language, thought, and civilization was still very prominent. Alexander had set up fine public buildings, gymnasiums, and open-air theatres that have had a lasting influence. He also encouraged his subjects to take Greek names, use the Greek language, and adopt Greek dress — in short, to become Hellenized. The process of Hellenization cast a great influence over God's people during the rule of Rome.

"Hellenist" — A Grecian Jew; a Jew who used the Greek language.

"Hellenistic" — Pertaining to the Hellenists. The *Hellenistic* language was the Greek spoken or used by the Jews who lived in Egypt and other countries, where the Greek language prevailed. *Noah Webster 1828.*

"Grecian" — *Strong's* NT#1675 <u>an Hellenist</u> or Greek-speaking Jew: KJV - Grecian.

ACTS **9:29**   And he spoke boldly in the name of the Lord Jesus and disputed against the <u>Hellenists</u>, but they attempted to kill him. NKJV

ACTS **11:20**   But some of them were men from Cyprus and Cyrene, who, when they had come to Antioch, spoke to the <u>Hellenists</u>, preaching the Lord Jesus. NKJV

Succession of Kingdoms

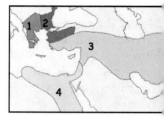

**# 3 — Greece
Four Divisions by 301 BC**

1. Cassander: Macedonia
2. Lysimachus: Thrace
3. Seleucus: Syria
4. Ptolemy: Egypt

Prophetic   Key   #13
This vision has given extra information regarding the kingdom of Greece. The Outline in the next vision (DAN 11:3-4) will expand with further details regarding the "kings of the north and south" concerning fragmented Greece.

Important Note:

It is necessary to have a review between verses 22 and 23 of Daniel 8. This review will transition the reader from verse 22 to verse 23. Greece represented the third earthly kingdom. Daniel 8:22 ended with the "notable horn" of Greece being broken. Daniel 8:23 introduces endtime prophecy, focusing on the <u>sixth</u> earthly kingdom. Verses 9-12 in Daniel 8 provide most of the information that is needed to make this transition from the Third Kingdom to the Sixth Kingdom. The explanations of these verses are best suited within the Historic-Prophetic Outline portion of the vision given on the following pages.

Up to the first part of Daniel 8:9 (in the Heavenly Scene), the verses in Daniel 8 have moved the vision forward, describing three of the four earthly kingdoms following Babylon. (Notice how these kingdoms have aligned with Visions 1 and 2 on page 136.) Beginning with the last part of Daniel 8:9c to 8:12, the vision moves rapidly forward to reveal information on the sixth earthly persecuting kingdom which occurs at the <u>latter end</u> of the Little Horn Kingdom, that ruled for 1260 years (AD 538-1798). Scripture reveals **the "latter end"** of this Little Horn Kingdom — **"waxes exceeding great."** These two kingdoms have identical characteristics. The only difference is: the Little Horn ruled during the Dark Ages, and the kingdom that "waxes exceeding" begins to rise and wax great after AD 1801. The following pages will give:

- The application for the kingdom that "waxes exceeding great;"
- The "king of fierce countenance" as the title for the ruler of this sixth earthly kingdom.

The next section focuses on the application for Papal Supremacy No. 2 from 1801 to the present. The Little Horn, as Papal Supremacy No. 1, was the focus of Daniel 7. The focus of Daniel 8 is on the Sixth Kingdom with a ruler titled "king of fierce countenance" that currently rules by craft and deceit through its system of Secret Societies. (A short comparison of the two Papal Supremacies is given on page 154.)

This is a very large study. Extra personal research is necessary for a full and complete understanding, through books, video presentations, and the web. (Appendices 8D and 8E present *some* secular historical information that lays the foundation for the prophecy regarding the sixth earthly kingdom.)

No other vision in the Book of Daniel has a shift such as this. Review of the material will be advantageous when coupled with personal research.

Transition From
Greece to
Pagan Imperial Rome

Prophetic Key #11 By 168 BC Pagan Imperial Rome was established as the fourth earthly kingdom surrounding God's people. This prophecy aligns perfectly with the first four kingdoms in Daniel 2 and 7.

Third Kingdom
Greece
"Alexander the Great"
Dies in 323 BC — the Kingdom is Divided in Four Directions by 301 BC

DAN 8:8 Therefore the he goat waxed very great: and when he was strong, the great horn was broken; and for it came up four notable ones toward the four winds [four directions] of heaven.

Succession of Kingdoms

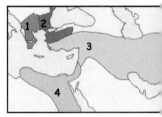

 # 3 — Greece
Four Divisions by 301 BC

1. Cassander: Macedonia
2. Lysimachus: Thrace
3. Seleucus: Syria
4. Ptolemy: Egypt

The Fourth Kingdom
Addressed Briefly:
— Pagan Imperial Rome —

DAN 8:9a And out of one of them [one of the four winds of verse 8] ...

There is a gradual transition from the Grecian Kingdom to Pagan Imperial Rome

"out of one of them" — refers back to Daniel 8:8 which describes the *four winds* or *four directions* of the compass. Pagan Imperial Rome was to the west direction of Greece. It arose gradually and attained supremacy only after the divisions of the Grecian kingdom had weakened. (From now on, any kingdom that is connected with Rome will also rise gradually to power.)

Note: Pagan Imperial Rome has had mere mention in Daniel 8:9. This presents enough information to align with the previous two visions. The characteristics of an *iron rule* will continue until the end of time. The iron in the Daniel 2 image continued from the legs, through the feet and into the toes.

Iron in the Legs —
Pagan Imperial Rome

Note the Alignment: The *iron* in the legs of Daniel 2:40 represented the kingdom of Pagan Imperial Rome which is known to have broken, bruised, and killed many of God's people — including the Messiah. Daniel 8 will continue to follow the *iron* kingdom that succeeded Pagan Rome. (Each symbol must be interpreted by the Bible. See Appendix 8B (Part 3), on page 178, for extra help in decoding.)

#4 — Pagan Imperial Rome
168 BC — AD 476

Transition From Pagan Imperial Rome to Papal Supremacy No. 1

Prophetic Key #11 Pagan Imperial Rome broke up into ten divisions by AD 476. In AD 538 the **Little Horn** emerged as the next symbol representing the Kingdom of **Papal Supremacy No. 1**. The prophecy aligns perfectly with the first four kingdoms in Daniel 2 and the first five kingdoms in Daniel 7. (See Appendix 8B (Part 4), on page 179, for extra help in decoding Papal Supremacy No. 1.)

Fourth Kingdom Pagan Imperial Rome

DAN 8:9a And out of one of them [one of the four winds of verse 8] …

A New Fifth Kingdom Rises Out of Pagan Imperial Rome — The Little Horn Kingdom Expands in all Directions

DAN 8:9b … came forth a little horn … [The Little Horn emerged from the west out of Pagan Imperial Rome.]

Succession of Kingdoms

#4 — Pagan Imperial Rome 168 BC — AD 476

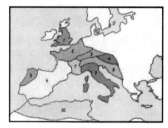

10 Divisions of Pagan Imperial Rome by AD 476

There is a gradual transition from **Pagan Imperial Rome** to **Papal Supremacy No. 1**.

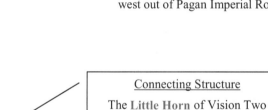

Little Horn Rises (AD 476-538)

Iron in the Feet — Papal Supremacy No. 1

Connecting Structure

The **Little Horn** of Vision Two — connects to — the **Little Horn** of Vision Three.

DAN 7:8 I considered the horns, and, behold, there came up among them another little horn … in this horn were eyes like the eyes of man, and a mouth speaking great things.

Note the Alignment: The *iron* in the feet of the Daniel 2 image succeeded the *iron* in the legs just as Papal Supremacy No. 1 succeeded Pagan Imperial Rome. (See Appendix 8B (Part 4), on page 179.)

#5 — Papal Supremacy No. 1 Little Horn Rules (AD 538-1798)

Transition From Papal Supremacy No. 1 (Little Horn) to Papal Supremacy No. 2 (king of fierce countenance)

Prophetic Key #13 In AD 1798 the power of the **Little Horn** appears to be broken. The "latter end" of this kingdom emerges again at the end of time, and is known as **Papal Supremacy No. 2.** Daniel 8:9c adds <u>extra information</u> on the sixth earthly persecuting kingdom. (See parts 4 and 5 of Appendix 8B, on pages 179-181, for extra help in decoding these two Papal Supremacies.)

How Papal No. 2 Begins to Rise and Wax Exceeding Great

1798: Napoleon declared there shall be no more Popes on the Vatican throne. He took Pope Pius VI captive back to France. Upon his death, the cardinals in Rome immediately elected a new Pope — Pope Pius VII. He began his urgent and serious reign with a determined effort to have Napoleon as an ally once again.

1801: "Accordingly we find that he [Napoleon] now <u>began negotiations with the Pope, which issued in a Concordat in July, 1801, whereby the Roman Catholic religion was once more established in France.</u>" Arthur Robert Pennington, *Epochs of the Papacy,* pp. 450-452. (Emphasis supplied.) See Appendix 8D, pages 191-192.

Fifth Kingdom Papal Supremacy No. 1

DAN 8:9b … came forth a little horn … [The Little Horn emerged from the west out of Pagan Imperial Rome.]

Little Horn Kingdom Transitions to the Kingdom that Waxes With Exceeding Great Power Expanding in all Directions in the Latter Times — A Gradual Transformation From Papal No. 1 to Papal No. 2 (AD 1798-1801)

DAN 8:9c … which waxed exceeding great, [Papal Supremacy No. 2 gradually becomes large in estate, honor, and pride] toward the south, [representing Atheism] and toward the east, [representing godless nations of paganism] and toward the <u>pleasant</u> land [representing Protestant nations that stemmed from the teachings of Jesus in Judah].

"pleasant" — *Strong's* OT#6643 in the sense of prominence; splendor; also a gazelle (as beautiful): KJV - glorious, goodly, pleasant.

Note: The word *glorious* in Daniel 11:41 is also OT#6643. Further explanation will be given on page 320.

#5 — Papal Supremacy No. 1 **(AD 538-1798)**
(Little Horn ruled Old Europe)

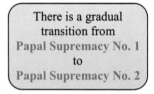

There is a gradual transition from **Papal Supremacy No. 1** to **Papal Supremacy No. 2**

The "king" of Papal No. 2 will "pu all the earthly nations, beginning v Atheistic France and Communistic Russia.

#6 — Papal Supremacy No. 2
(Begins to rise in AD 1801, expan to Russian Communism. Current uses Secret Societies as a Papal towards world dominion.)

Clay in the Feet — Mankind under the manipulation of the Papal Supremacies

Note the Alignment: The *iron in the feet* of Daniel 2 represents Papal Supremacy No. 1. The *clay in the feet,* represents mankind. (See ISA 64:8 and page 208.) <u>Papal Supremacy No. 1 has not perished, but has merely undergone a transformation into the sixth ruling kingdom as Papal Supremacy No. 2,</u> with the "king of fierce countenance" as its leader (vs 23-25). This system manipulates the clay of mankind through Atheistic, Communistic, and Protestant nations. Just as the iron gradually transitions from the feet into the toes, so it is with the Papal Kingdom that will gradually transition throughout all the world as the last Papal Roman kingdom. More information on the Sixth Kingdom is given on pages 162-167.

Sixth Kingdom
Papal Supremacy No. 2

Prophetic Key #13 Daniel 8 adds <u>extra information</u> regarding the persecution through Papal Supremacy No. 2 which is the major focus of this vision. This kingdom manifests the same characteristics as the Little Horn Kingdom. (Review pages 102-108 and 122-123 on the Little Horn and Appendix 8D, pages 199-201.)

Papal Supremacy No. 2
Persecutes God's Faithful People
(AD 1801 — Present)

DAN 8:10 And it [the Papal Supremacy No. 2 of verse 9] waxed great, [large in estate, honor, and pride] even to [against] the host [inhabitants] of heaven; and it cast down some of the <u>host</u> [mass of persons in God's army] and of the <u>stars</u> [modern luminous reformers like Wycliffe] to the ground, and <u>stamped</u> [trampled] upon them.

Persecution by the Papal king that "waxes exceeding great" is given the title "king of fierce countenance" in Daniel 8:23.

"host" — *Strong's* OT#6635 <u>a mass of persons</u>, especially organized for war (an army); <u>a campaign</u>, (specifically, <u>hardship</u>, worship): KJV - <u>appointed time</u>, army, battle, company, host, service, soldiers, waiting upon, war fare.

Note: This "mass of persons ... especially organized for war" represent "God's organized army for truth" and not an army against truth. This army goes forth to the whole world with the "Loud Gospel Cry" of Jesus Christ. The Papal Kingdom has persecuted many of God's host (through Atheistic-Communistic nations as noted on pages 199-201) just as the Little Horn persecuted God's people in the Dark Ages. See the first verse in the Scriptures that uses "host" to denote "all created beings."

GEN 2:1 Thus the heavens and the earth were finished, and all the **host** [OT#6635] of them.

"stars" — *Strong's* **OT**#3556 (in the sense of blazing); a star (as round or as shining); <u>figuratively, a prince</u>.

NUM 24:17 there shall come a <u>Star</u> [a Prince, OT#3556] out of Jacob, and a Sceptre shall rise out of Israel.

REV 2:1 he that holdeth the seven <u>stars</u> in his right hand.

"star" — In Scripture, Christ is called the *bright and morning star,* the star that ushers in the light of an eternal day to his people. REV 22:16. Ministers [God's people] are also called *stars in Christ's right hand,* as, being supported and directed by Christ, they convey light and knowledge to the followers of Christ. REV 1:20; 2:1. *Noah Webster 1828.*

2 PETER 1:19 We have also a more sure word of prophecy; whereunto ye do well that ye take heed, as unto a light that shineth in a dark place, until the day dawn, and the day <u>star</u> [NT #5459] arise in your hearts:

"stars" — *Strong's* **NT**#5459 phosphoros; from **NT#5457** and NT#5342; **light-bearing** ("phosphorus"), i.e. (specifically) the morning-star (figuratively): KJV - day star.

NT#5457 phos; (to shine or make manifest, especially by rays; compare NT#5316, NT#5346); **luminousness (in the widest application)**. KJV - fire, light.

DAN 7:25 And he ... shall <u>wear out</u> [cast down and stamped upon] <u>the saints</u> of the most high ... and they shall be given into his hand.

Note: The characteristics of the Papal System continue to remain unchanged.

Note: Through His *stars,* His light is to shine forth. In England during the fourteenth century, John Wycliffe was the herald of reform for all of Christendom. He was known as the "morning <u>star</u> of the Reformation." In the endtimes, many *stars* will shine and proclaim all Biblical truth.

"stamped" — *Strong's* OT#7429 ... to tread upon. KJV - oppressor, stamp upon, trample (under feet), tread (down, upon).

Comparison Between Papal Supremacy No. 1 and Papal Supremacy No. 2

Fifth Kingdom
Little Horn Papal Supremacy No. 1
Rises from: AD 476 — 538
Rules from: AD 538 — 1798
(1260 Literal Years)

1. Rises from the fall of Pagan Imperial Rome: AD 476-538.
2. Roots out three tribes of Arianism.
3. Rules 1260 years from AD 538-1798.
4. Bishops gain control in Old Europe.
5. Use of Jesuit Order to counter the Reformation.
6. Gains obeisance of Caesars/Emperors through manipulation and coercion.
7. Church and State combined in Old Europe.
8. Changes times and laws.
9. Calling backslidden members back to the mother church.
10. Mary worship instituted in the Roman Catholic Church.

Sixth Kingdom
"king of fierce countenance" Papal Supremacy No. 2
Rises from: AD 1798 — 1801
"Waxes Exceeding Great" from: AD 1801— Present

1. Rises from the wound of the Little Horn in AD 1798 to AD 1801 when Pope Pius VII signed a Concordat with Napoleon to re-instate the Catholic religion back into France. (This is the beginning of future Fascist, totalitarian laws.)
2. Roots out Atheism in France with the AD 1801 Concordat between Pope Pius VII and Napoleon. (Later in 1989 Communism is rooted out in Russia and the European Bloc. Next to be subjugated will be the Protestant nations, and the remainder of godless nations around the world. DAN 11:41-43)
3. Begins to rule through Secret Societies and Atheistic-Communistic countries (i.e. Russia). (See Appendices 8D, pages 185-209; 8E, pages 210-225.)
4. Popes gain world respect through political manipulation, Vatican Councils, and ecclesiastical encyclicals. (See Appendix 11A, page 352.)
5. Use of the Illuminati, Communist Manifesto, and many Secret Societies to destroy Christianity. (See Appendix 8D, pages 186-189.)
6. Gains respect of world political and religious leaders. (See Daniel 8:25, page 169.)
7. Papal Church and Communist States work together. (See Appendix 8D, pages 206-207.)
8. Conditions the nations to accept future changes of "times and laws" on a universal basis. (Refer to Daniel 7:25, page 107 and Appendix 7D, pages 126-134.)
9. Calling Protestant churches back to the mother church. (See quotes in Appendix 11D, pages 357-362.)
10. Mary worship for the world. (See Appendix 8G, page 230.)

Explanation of the word *"sacrifice"* in
Daniel 8:11, 12, 13;
Daniel 11:31 and
Daniel 12:11.

Note: At this juncture, the Scriptures take a break from giving new information on the kingdoms, to enlighten the reader on some new terminology.

Prophetic Key #13 Beginning with Daniel 8:11, <u>extra information</u> is introduced. This page of study will focus on the word *sacrifice*.

The Word, "sacrifice"

DAN 8:11 Yea, he magnified himself [in his "waxed great" or ecclesiastical character of verse 10] even to the prince of the host, and by him the daily ~~sacrifice~~ was taken away, and the place of his sanctuary was cast down.

(This verse is repeated on the next several pages.)

Note: Before any further work is done on this verse, the word *"sacrifice"* needs to be examined.

The Word, *"sacrifice"*

"sacrifice" — *Strong's* OT#9999 NOTE: inserted word (x); This word was added by the translators for better readability in the English. There is no actual word in the Hebrew text. The word may be displayed in italics, or in parentheses or other brackets, to indicate that it is not in the original text.

- In most Bibles the word *"sacrifice"* is in *italics* showing that it was <u>not</u> in the original Hebrew manuscript. Therefore, having the word *sacrifice* will cause *confusion* and it would be wise to remove it. The following five Daniel texts also have the inserted word *sacrifice:*
  1. Daniel 8:11
  2. Daniel 8:12
  3. Daniel 8:13
  4. Daniel 11:31
  5. Daniel 12:11

- The word *sacrifice* was **added** to the word "daily" by the translators.

- The Hebrew word, ***"tamiyd,"*** translated "daily" as it was used in the Books of Leviticus and Numbers is an adjective or an adverb, always <u>describing</u> the continual or daily sacrifices offered in the Hebrew worship service. Therefore, the translators took the liberty to <u>add</u> the word, *sacrifice,* in the Book of Daniel. This insertion was an unintentional error. The translators thought the sentences about **the** "daily" in the Book of Daniel lacked a noun.

- The addition of the word *sacrifice* may have been allowed by the providence of God, to <u>lock up the meaning of the Hebrew word,</u> "tamiyd," **until the endtime**.

- If the word ***"tamiyd"*** had been correctly understood, the endtime prophecies would have <u>opened up too soon</u>. God's people would have given premature warning messages before the appointed time in history had come.

Titles Usurped
**by the Little Horn
and king of fierce
countenance**

"The Holy Father"
"Highest Priest and Pontiff"
"Head of the Churches"
"Vicar of Christ"

Understanding of the word "daily"
in Daniel 8:11.

Prophetic Keys #5 and #13 Correct information for this term will be explained with definitions from the *Strong's Concordance.* An accurate understanding of the term "daily" is crucial to the whole theme of Daniel's Book.

*The Little Horn Took the Titles
and Offices of God —
The king of fierce countenance
Maintains These Titles*

DAN 8:11 Yea, he [king of fierce countenance] magnified [exalted] himself even to the prince of the host ...

"magnified" — *Strong's* OT#1431 to be large in ... estate or honor, also in pride): KJV - advance, boast, increase, lift up, magnify **Note:** This is the same word number as *great* in Daniel 8:9.

"prince of the host" — This "king of fierce countenance" power stands up against the Prince of princes [Son of God] and a numerable host of God's reformers just at the Little Horn did. (Review Daniel 8:25 comments on page 166.)

DAN 7:20 even of that [little] horn that had eyes, and a mouth that spake very great things [blasphemy], whose look was more stout than his fellows.

JOHN 10:33 The Jews answered him, saying, For a good work we stone thee not; but for blasphemy; and because that thou, being a man, makest thyself God.

The Meaning of the "daily"

DAN 8:11 ... and by him [the "papal supremacy"] the daily [sceptre of power, seat, and authority] ~~sacrifice~~ was taken away ...

- The original meaning of the word "daily" ("tamiyd") must be investigated with a *Strong's Analytical Concordance.*

"daily" — *Strong's* OT#8548 tamiyd (taw-meed'); from an unused root meaning to stretch; properly, continuance (as indefinite extension); but used only (attributively as adjective) constant (or adverbially, constantly); ellipt. the regular (daily) sacrifice [as in the Books of Leviticus and Numbers]: KJV - alway (-s), continual (employment, -ly), daily, **perpetual [lasting for eternity].**

- The original "tamiyd" translated to "daily" means "something which stretches indefinitely in both directions."
- It is the Bible itself which tells what stretches in both directions indefinitely, that is, into eternity — past and future.

Question: In each of the five references to the "daily" in the Book of Daniel, it is not the "daily *sacrifice"* that is taken away, but always the "daily" that is **"taken away".** **The Hebrew word for "daily" is "tamiyd."** So what is the correct meaning of "tamiyd" in Daniel? As an adjective, adverb, or a noun?

Answer: The word, "daily" or "tamiyd," was used in Leviticus and Numbers as an adjective or adverb describing the **continual sacrifices** and worship which happened every day.

The sacrifices were "daily sacrifices" — or "continual sacrifices."
In the original manuscript of the Book of Daniel the word,
"daily" (tamiyd) is used as a **noun!**
The meaning therefore changes from "continual" to a "continuum."

Understanding of the word "daily"
in Daniel 8:11 (Continued)

Prophetic Keys #4 and #13 Other Scriptures will assist in unlocking the deeper meaning of the word "daily."

CROWN
=
POWER

THRONE CHAIR
=
SEAT

SCEPTRE
=
AUTHORITY

The Sceptre of
Charles V of France
*(Heritage Illustrated
Dictionary)*

DAN 8:11 Yea, he magnified himself even to the prince of the host, and by him [the "papal supremacy"] the <u>daily</u> [scepter of power] ~~sacrifice~~ was taken away ... (*See additional note below.)

Ps 45:6 Thy throne, O God, is for ever and ever: the sceptre of thy kingdom is a right sceptre.

The "Daily" Refers to the Sovereignty of the Throne of God

- God exists from eternity in the past, to eternity in the future. **God is eternal.** His government over the universe, represented by His throne or His **Sovereignty**, is encompassed in the word, "daily" or "tamiyd."
- His Rulership (a "continuum") is that which stretches in both directions indefinitely, past and future, and defines His <u>perpetual</u> power, seat, and authority.

"The Daily" is Represented in the Sceptre as "Power, Seat, and Authority"

The sovereignty of kings is represented as a
crown, a **throne**, and a **sceptre**,
spoken of in Revelation 13:2 as **"power, seat, and authority."**
This is also the "<u>daily</u>" spoken of in the Book of Daniel.

Note: The "sceptre" — an emblem of authority, may be seen in the hand of a king, or a baton in the hand of a music instructor; or a rod in the hand of Moses as he parted the Red Sea; or as a walking stick in the hand of a tribal chief. It was the rod, or "branch" of Aaron, the symbol of his priesthood, which flowered, budded, and bore almonds. Such a rod or staff was often formed from the **"branch"** of a tree. From ages past, the concept of rulership was connected to a **branch**. The sceptre of power and rulership originated at the throne of God. In Zechariah 6:12-13, Christ is referred to as THE BRANCH or THE MAN WHOSE NAME IS THE BRANCH. In Daniel (as well as the whole Bible) the story is told of the lost **dominion** (lost sceptre) and its restoration! The whole Book of Daniel is this story of the sceptre passing from nation to nation until at last: ... the saints of the most High shall take the kingdom, and possess the kingdom for ever, even for ever and ever. (DAN 7:18) This restoration is also the theme of the Book of Revelation.

*Additional Note: The outright and aggressive attempt to destroy Protestantism took on great strength at the time of the establishment of the Jesuit Order in the 1500s. Prior to this, the Papal System took somewhat of a defensive posture. Now it was about to become downright "fierce." The Jesuit authored Illuminati and Freemasonry, began to infiltrate political and religious systems around the middle of the 1700s. Their purpose was to destroy Protestantism. At the same time, the Secret Societies brought about a change in the Protestant understanding of the Word with the introduction of Preterism and Futurism (a Jesuit prescription for casting down truth; see Appendix 12B, pages 386-387). The Bible has been "manhandled" since the turn of the 1900s. The Word now reflects the Papal perspective of Biblical interpretation which accomplishes the following: 1) Christ's "power, seat, and authority" being taken away; 2) Christ's blood sacrifice and atonement in the sanctuary of the human heart is cast down.

Daniel 8:11 — Understanding the *"transfer of the daily"*

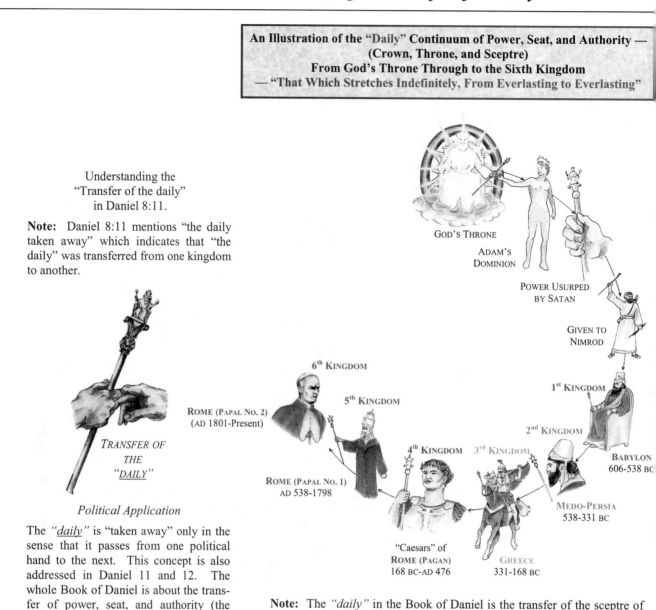

GOD'S THRONE

ADAM'S DOMINION

POWER USURPED BY SATAN

GIVEN TO NIMROD

1st KINGDOM

BABYLON 606-538 BC

2nd KINGDOM

MEDO-PERSIA 538-331 BC

3rd KINGDOM

GREECE 331-168 BC

4th KINGDOM

"Caesars" of ROME (PAGAN) 168 BC-AD 476

5th KINGDOM

ROME (PAPAL NO. 1) AD 538-1798

6th KINGDOM

ROME (PAPAL NO. 2) (AD 1801-Present)

TRANSFER OF THE "DAILY"

Understanding the
"Transfer of the daily"
in Daniel 8:11.

Note: Daniel 8:11 mentions "the daily taken away" which indicates that "the daily" was transferred from one kingdom to another.

Political Application

The *"daily"* is "taken away" only in the sense that it passes from one political hand to the next. This concept is also addressed in Daniel 11 and 12. The whole Book of Daniel is about the transfer of power, seat, and authority (the "daily") from nation to nation. (The transfer of the "daily" to the Seventh Kingdom will be addressed in Daniel 11.)

Spiritual Application

Ultimately, Jesus Christ holds the "daily" (or power, seat, and authority) over all the universe. His desire is to plant this "daily" within the hearts and minds of all mankind so that they may take on His mind, character, and personality. The persecuting earthly kingdoms are determined to usurp this authority and have rule over ALL mankind on the earth.

Note: The *"daily"* in the Book of Daniel is the transfer of the sceptre of power from nation to nation until it is finally restored to the saints and to Christ in God's new kingdom. The sceptre of power originated in the eternal throne of God. It was delegated to Adam when he was given dominion (the sceptre of power) over this earth. (GEN 1:26) At the fall of man, the devil usurped that dominion and has delegated it, as far as God permits, to those nations whom he seeks to control. Using these nations, he harasses and attempts to destroy the people of God. Immediately after Noah's flood, Nimrod grasped the sceptre of power and built Babel, which developed into the Kingdom of Babylon with its counterfeit system of sun worship. (Review the Prologue on pages 7-10.) The Book of Daniel traces this sceptre of power from nation to nation until, at the end of time, it will revert back to Christ's Stone Kingdom. (Daniel 8:9b takes the *"daily"* as far as the Fifth Kingdom. The last part of Daniel 8:9c moves the scepter to the Sixth Kingdom.) Like a great circle, this sceptre of power is from everlasting to everlasting. It is the great *"tamiyd,"* — *"daily,"* or continuum which stretches from eternity to eternity.

*The **Little Horn** and
king of fierce countenance
Claim the Titles
and Offices of God*

DAN 8:11 Yea, he [papal supremacy] magnified himself even to the prince of the host …

*The "daily taken away"
by the
king of fierce countenance
(Papal Supremacy No. 2)*

… and by him [the "king of fierce countenance"] the daily [sceptre of power] ~~sacrifice~~ was <u>taken away</u>, [absorbed and exalted from the Fifth Kingdom] and the place of his [the LORD'S] sanctuary [host of the Christian church] was <u>cast down</u> [trampled upon during endtime persecution].

DAN 7:25 and they shall be given into his hand [cast down] until a time and times and the dividing of time [1260 years].

In the *latter time* of the Little Horn kingdom, the "king of fierce countenance" will manifest the same persecuting spirit.

Note: This *endtime persecution* is a <u>continuance</u> of the Little Horn power in the Dark Ages. (Further study will be given in Daniel 11-12 and Revelation 13:5.)

Verse 11 (Concluded)

"taken away" — *Strong's* OT#7311 ruwm; to rise or raise. KJV - bring up, [to] exalt, [to] take up [absorb].

Note: In Daniel 8, the Hebrew word "**RUWM**," translated as "taken away," **has the meaning of absorption, or to be exalted**. The same word in Daniel 12:11 has a different meaning.

"In the West, the Church took over the defenses of Roman civilization. The emperor gave up the [Pagan] title of Pontifex Maximus [high priest] because the Roman gods were no longer worshipped. **The bishop of Rome assumed these priestly functions, [a process of absorption],** and this is why the Pope today is sometimes referred to as the Pontiff … It was the Pope and not the emperor which stood at the gates of Rome. The Roman Empire had become the Christian church." Harry A. Dawe, *Ancient Greece and Rome, World Cultures in Perspective,* p. 188. (Emphasis supplied.)

"When Rome through the neglect of the Western emperors was left to the mercy of the barbarous hordes, the Romans turned to one figure for aid and protection and asked him to rule them; and thus … commenced the temporal sovereignty of the popes. And meekly stepping to the throne of Caesar, the vicar of Christ **TOOK UP THE SCEPTER**." *American Catholic Quarterly Review,* April 1911. (Emphasis supplied.)

As noted in the illustration on page 158, the succession from Pagan Imperial Rome to Papal Rome was just one step in the continuum of passing the *"daily"* or the *"sceptre of power."* It is important to understand that the Roman Kingdom was a church-state union of political and religious power. Its religion was Paganism or sun worship. Therefore, when the "sceptre of power" was transferred, Paganism was a part of the transaction! It was by the <u>absorption of Pagan worship and an exaltation of it</u> that the

Papacy gained favor in the Pagan Imperial Roman Kingdom and thereby acquired the sceptre of power! This is how the "daily" — sceptre of power, seat, and authority (with its Pagan culture and religion) was <u>absorbed and exalted by Papal Rome</u>. It was all one package! Therefore, in Daniel 8:11, the word, RUWM, is used to indicate that the "daily" — sceptre of power — was "taken away" from Pagan Rome by **absorption and exaltation** of the Pagan culture and worship into Papal Rome. Roman Catholicism has been called baptized Paganism. "The mighty Catholic Church was little more than the Roman Empire baptized." Alexander Clarence Flick, *The Rise of the Mediaeval Church,* p. 148. (Also see Appendix 8B, Parts 4 and 5, on pages 179-181.) **In like manner** the <u>king of fierce countenance</u> seized the "daily" by similar methods of absorption and exaltation.

"cast down" — for 1260 years the Christian church endured persecution. The remnant Christian church will also endure persecution at the very end of time.

Daniel 8:12 — Understanding the Unchanging Character of the Papacy

*The **Papal** Persecutor*
(king of fierce countenance)

DAN 8:12 And an <u>host</u> [mass of person's in God's army] was given him [the Papacy] ...

Persecution by the
Power of the State

... <u>against</u> the daily ~~sacrifice~~ by reason of <u>transgression</u>, [wrong use of ruling power] ...

*The **Papacy** Will Merge*
Christianity with Sun Worship
(as in the Dark Ages)

... and it <u>cast down the truth</u> [Christ and the Word] to the ground; and it <u>practiced</u>, and <u>prospered</u> [and extended itself over the whole world].

Communistic Russia a Puppet Kingdom
Papal Secret Societies managed the persecuting affairs of the Russian Revolution. Millions died through this puppet kingdom in the 20th century.

The Pressing Question —
"How Long...?"

DAN 8:13 ... How long shall be the vision concerning the daily ~~sacrifice~~, and the transgression of desolation [persecutor of God's people], to give both the [heavenly] sanctuary and the host [mass of God's obedient people] to be trodden under foot [and persecuted]?

Verse 12

Reminder: *"host"* — *Strong's* OT#6635 has the definition of *"mass of persons."* Verse 12 repeats many concepts of verse 11.

Note: During the reign of this kingdom, a *"mass"* (large number) of persons, referring to millions of martyrs, have been martyred under the Papal system. This persecution was an attempt to dethrone Christ, making Him the same as any man like Mohammed or Buddha, etc. Mankind will be exalted above deity.

"against" — *Strong's* OT#5921 the same as **OT#5920** used as a preposition ... above, over, upon, or against (yet always in this last relation with a downward aspect) in a great variety of applications (as follow): KJV - above ... <u>because of</u> ... and, by (reason of).

OT#5920 from OT#5927; properly, the top; specifically, the highest (i.e. God); also (adverb) **aloft, to Jehovah**: KJV - above, high, Most High.

Note: In the past, the Papacy was able to persecute because it had wrested the "daily" (or power to rule) from the Caesars, by reason of "transgression" (the wrong use of ruling power). The church used the civil authority to enforce its will and its dogma, and to initiate persecution against dissenters. <u>The king of fierce countenance has repeated this action</u> through the Atheistic-Communistic revolutions of France and Russia. Millions died! See Appendix 8D, pages 199-201.

"transgression" — *Strong's* OT#6588 from **OT#6586**; <u>a revolt</u> (national, moral or religious): KJV - <u>rebellion</u>, sin, transgression, trespass.

OT#6586 ... <u>to break away (from just authority)</u>, i.e. trespass, apostatize, quarrel: KJV - offend, rebel, revolt, transgress (-ion, -or).

"cast down the truth" — **The Papacy Incorporated Pagan Deities When Expedient** — "For example, the earliest known Christian mosaic, found in the 1940s underneath St. Peter's Basilica, uses gold mosaic in its representation of Christ as the sun God, 'Helios.' " Michael Collins and Matthew A. Price, *The Story of Christianity, A Celebration of 2000 Years of Faith,* p. 73.

Note: Throughout the ages, the Papacy has mixed and obscured ALL Bible truth with Pagan tradition and superstition. This has been accomplished under the disguise of a pure and undefiled religion.

2 THESS 2:7 For the mystery of iniquity doth already work.

"practiced" — *Strong's* OT#6213 **to do or make, in the broadest sense and widest application**.

"prospered" — *Strong's* OT#6743 **to push forward**, in various senses: KJV - break out, <u>come (mightily)</u>.

Verse 13

This verse is a further explanation of the previous verses with the introduction of the time element of how long will this transgression continue. It is true that the verse has application to what is taking place in the Heavenly Sanctuary. However, since the mid-1800s the movement for the Second Coming of Jesus to this earth, began the process of bringing man's heart into a relationship with the Lord or Satan. JOSH 24:15 "Choose you this day whom ye will serve."

Important Note: The manuscript will return to Daniel 8:23 on page 162.

Understanding the Heavenly Scene Verses of Daniel 8:10-14

Daniel 8:10-14

The verses below are part of the Heavenly Scene in Vision 3 describing the Sixth Kingdom which "waxed exceeding great."

10 And it waxed great, **even to the host of heaven;** and it **cast down some of the host and of the stars to the ground, and stamped upon them.**

11 Yea, he magnified himself even to the **prince of the host,** and by him the **daily** *sacrifice* **was taken away, and the place of his sanctuary was cast down.**

12 And an host was given him **against the daily** *sacrifice* by reason of transgression, and it **cast down the truth to the ground;** and **it practised, and prospered.**

13 Then I heard one saint speaking, and another saint said unto that certain saint which spake, How long shall be the vision concerning the daily *sacrifice,* and the transgression of desolation, to give both the **sanctuary and the host to be trodden under foot?**

14 And he said unto me, Unto two thousand and three hundred days [or 2300 Days of Atonement]; then shall the Sanctuary* be cleansed.

*Sanctuary: the cleansing includes the heavenly sanctuary, as well as the "sanctuary" in the hearts of God's people.

Note: Papal Supremacy No. 2 is an interchangeable term with "waxed exceeding great" (vs 9c) or the title of "king of fierce countenance" (vs 23). Notice how many similar ideas are repeated over and over in these few verses.

DAN 8:10-11 Papal Supremacy No. 2 will elevate himself through self-glorification, **daring to call himself "King of kings and Lord of lords" — a title that belongs only to the Lord Jesus Christ. He will take away the "daily" which is the power, seat, and authority of Christ in order to elevate self.** This in effect is **meant to dethrone Christ,** placing Him on the same level of authority as Mohammad, Buddha — or just another prophet. **The sanctuary (salvation of Christ in man's heart) is cast down.** This will deceive many, causing the great falling away spoken of in 2 THESS 2:10-11. The result separates the sheep from the goats; a pure remnant is brought forth. (See REV 12:17.)

DAN 8:12 Papal Supremacy No. 2 will receive an host (army) against the "daily." The goal of the **Jesuit Order** (formed in the mid 1500s) was **to counter the Reformation.** A great Counter Reformation assault, resulted in a host of martyrs. Many of the Protestant churches, because of a lack of love for the Truth, have slipped back into apostasy. **Truth was cast down to the ground all through the Dark Ages.** During the French Revolution **Bibles were burned.** In the current age, **Truth has been cast down with the introduction of many apostate Bible versions. This prosperous, fallen, anti-christ system must cast Truth down to the ground** so that false worship can be lifted up. (See Appendix 8D on pages 186-189 on the beginnings of Secret Societies. Review Appendices 8F, 8G, and 8H on pages 226-231 for information on how paganism has displaced Truth.)

DAN 8:13 The "one saint" is Palmonee (Christ, the Wonderful Numberer). He is speaking to another saint regarding the attempted removal of power, seat, and authority of Christ that resulted in the great falling away spoken of in the previous verse. When the Gospel message of Christ is given to the whole world, God's people will come out of this fallen system. **Many of the host will be trampled and persecuted.** Babylon will become so full of iniquity, that there is no turning back to repentance. This will usher in the "judgment" of all mankind, who did not receive the love of the Truth.

DAN 8:14 The promise is two-fold:
1. The cleansing of the sanctuary, in heaven and the heart of man, will begin after 2300 years. It will deal with the sin problem, and bring the evil kingdoms to judgment.
   a) The ending of the 2300 year timeline (in 1844) commenced the judgment of the dead with the cry to "come out of [apostate] Babylon." (The dates of the 2300 year timeline are thoroughly explained in Daniel 9.)

2. The first phase of judgment (since 1844) will continue until the Loud Cry (from REV 14) reaches its climax to "come out of fallen Babylon."
   a) This commences the phase of judgment for the living.
   b) Those that don't take sanctuary in Christ will be cast (or shaken) out.
   c) Those who take sanctuary in Christ will be cleansed and become known as the Biblical Remnant of Revelation 12:17.
   d) This Remnant is purified and prepared by the Holy Spirit to give the message of Revelation 14 to "come out of Fallen Babylon," before probation closes.

An Endtime Prophecy:
Rule of the
"king of fierce countenance"
(AD 1801—Present)

23 And in the <u>latter time</u> of their [Papal Supremacy No. 1] **kingdom, when the   transgressors are come to the <u>full</u>** [with iniquity], **a king of fierce countenance, and understanding dark sentences** [Papal Supremacy No. 2], **shall stand up** [and assume power over the whole world].

(This verse repeated on the next page.)

#6 — Papal Supremacy No. 2
(Begins to rise in AD 1801, expanding to Russian Communism. Currently it uses Secret Societies as a papal tool towards world dominion.)

Verse 23

Note: The verses of Daniel 8:23-25 are entering into unfulfilled prophecy. The information given on page 319 is also applicable here.

Prophetic Key #10   The Daniel 8:9-12 verses from the Heavenly Scene section have been reviewed and interpreted in the Historic-Prophetic Outline. All verses in this Outline have been kept in sequence, and have followed the same alignment of earthly kingdoms in Daniel 2 and 7.

Prophetic Key #12   As the verses in the Outline have "moved forward," time has also "moved forward." Prophecy is usually understood at the time of fulfillment.

Prophetic Key #13   Papal Supremacy No. 2 emerges as the Sixth Kingdom. The prophecy has aligned perfectly with the first five kingdoms in Daniel 2 and 7. Vision Three adds <u>extra information</u> on the sixth ruling earthly kingdom, giving the clue that the very last kingdom is also part of the "latter end" of Papal Supremacy No. 1. This information will be verified in the Fourth Historic-Prophetic Outline of Daniel 11.

DAN 8:17, 19   Understand, O son of man: for at <u>the time of the end</u> [the latter time] shall be the vision. 19 I will make thee know what shall be in <u>the last end of the indignation</u>: for at the time appointed the end shall be.

"latter time" — *Strong's* OT#319 **the last or end**, hence, **the future**; also posterity: KJV - (last, latter) **end (time)**, hinder (utter) -most, length, posterity, **remnant**.

Note: In the context of the succession of kingdoms, the *latter times* is at the end of the succession, or the end of earth's history. The end of the *iron* kingdom is indicated in the iron toes of Daniel 2. Gabriel assured Daniel of the proper timeframe.

1 TIM 4:1   Now the Spirit speaketh expressly, that in the latter times some shall depart from the faith, giving heed to seducing spirits, and doctrines of devils.

Review: Question No. 1, in Daniel 8:13, asked "How long shall be the vision?" Verse 17 answered: "The vision of Daniel 8 extends from Medo-Persia (331 BC) to the utmost *end* or *extremity of time* in the future." Verse 23 now affirms that a king of fierce countenance will be ruling and usher in the endtime just before the Second Coming of Jesus.

"full" — **GEN 15:16**   for the <u>iniquity</u> [mischief and sin] of the Amorites is not yet <u>full</u> [complete].

"iniquity" — *Strong's* OT#5771 perversity, i.e. (moral) <u>evil</u>: KJV - fault, iniquity, <u>mischief</u> … <u>sin</u>.

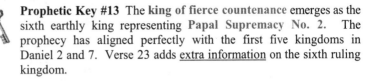

*An Endtime Prophecy Predicts
the Sixth Earthly "king"
With the Title
"king of fierce countenance"
(Papal Supremacy No. 2)*

23 And in the latter time of their kingdom, when the [1]**transgressors are come to the full** [with iniquity], [2]**a king of fierce countenance, and understanding dark sentences** [defining absolute apostasy], [2a]**shall stand up** [and assume power].

---

*Verse Linkage and Comparisons for
"king of fierce countenance"*

[1] *"transgressors are come to the full"*-
- DAN 8:12 *"by reason of transgression"*
- DAN 8:13 *"transgression of desolation"*

[2] *"a king of fierce countenance"* and
[2a] *"shall stand up"* —
- DAN 8:9 *"waxed exceeding great"*
- DAN 8:10 *"waxed great"*
- DAN 8:11 *"he magnified himself"*

(Further comment on page 167.)

Note: All the Scriptures in these boxes on pages 165 and 169 have further comparison with the verses in Daniel 11:36-39. Also see Appendix 11B on page 353.

Verse 23 (Concluded)

Prophetic Key #13 The **king of fierce countenance** emerges as the sixth earthly king representing **Papal Supremacy No. 2**. The prophecy has aligned perfectly with the first five kingdoms in Daniel 2 and 7. Verse 23 adds extra information on the sixth ruling kingdom.

DAN 2:44 And in the days of these kings [including the "king of fierce countenance"] shall the God of heaven set up a kingdom, which shall never be destroyed … it shall break in pieces and consume all these kingdoms.

Note: "in the days of these kings" has a further explanation in Daniel 11:41-45. The following text explains *"fierce countenance."*

DEUT 28:50 A nation of fierce countenance, which shall not regard the person of the old, nor shew favour to the young.

JOHN 16:2 yea, the time cometh, that whosoever killeth you will think that he doeth God service.

The "king of fierce countenance" will understand how to solve the riddle of gaining power, seat, and authority over the whole world.

"dark sentences" — *Strong's* OT#2420 **a puzzle**, hence, **a trick**, conundrum, sententious maxim: KJV - dark saying (sentence, speech), hard question, proverb, **riddle**.

"a king of fierce countenance and understanding dark sentences" — is the ruler of the Sixth Kingdom. The Papacy shall again solve the puzzle of how to gain power, seat, and great authority (or the "daily") over the entire world. Once this kingdom reaches absolute apostasy, he will transition to the iron fisted persecutor of the Seventh Kingdom. At this time his deadly wound will be completely healed as described in Daniel 12 and Revelation 13-20. Revelation 13:5, 7-8 reveals that the "king of fierce countenance" is a continuance of the Papal entity that reigned from AD 538-1798. The alignment of kings and kingdoms will be the subject of the Fourth Historic-Prophetic Outline in Daniel 11. This "puzzle" also involves the mysteries of Secret Societies and the occult — so prevalent in today's world.

"shall stand up" — refers to the act of taking up the "power, seat, and great authority" to reign over the world as one kingdom. This phrase is used in the same sense in Daniel 11 and 12.

A Brief Summary of Verse 23

Daniel 8:23 reveals that the ruler of the Sixth Kingdom will rule from "behind the scenes" through Secret Societies over much of the world. A brief summary of events during the rise and rule of the "king of fierce countenance" can be found in Appendix 8D, pages 185-209, and Appendix 8E on pages 210-225. These pages give concise information covering a period of more than 500 years. It is a very large study. Be prepared to do some extra work in this area to understand the prophecy in Daniel 8.

Daniel 8:23

This verse is part of the Historic-Prophetic Outline in Vision 3 describing the Sixth Kingdom ruled by the *"king of fierce countenance"*

23 And in the latter time of their kingdom, when the transgressors are come to the full, a king of fierce countenance, and **understanding dark sentences,** shall stand up.

Note: Papal Supremacy No. 2 is an interchangeable term with the terms: "waxed exceeding great" (vs 9c), "waxed great" (vs 10), and the "king of fierce countenance" (vs 23). Again, similar ideas are repeated, with different words, over and over in these few verses.

Some of the information given in the following comments is new and will be expanded upon in Appendices 8D and 8E. Secular history verifies how the Sixth Kingdom of Papal Rome No. 2 set up a "behind the scenes" kingdom (through the use of Secret Societies) totally undetected by much of the world. The Papal wound of AD 1798 directed the eyes of the Protestant world <u>away from the plans of the Papal System</u>. As a result, the Protestants let down their guard and didn't see the Papal threat forming. In the meantime, the "Puppeteer" of the Papal System has been diligently "planning their work and working their plan" to understand the dark sentences of generating a New World Order, or One World Government — the seventh and last kingdom of the Papal Roman System. (Please note: this topic is a very large study. It will be addressed briefly in this manuscript to link the progression of Daniel's visions. Excellent resources are listed in Appendix 12C on page 388.)

DAN 8:23 In the latter time of the Papal Supremacy No. 1 kingdom (in AD 1798), Papal Supremacy No. 2 began to rise (in 1801) with the signing of the Concordat between Pope Pius VII and Napoleon. To re-instate the Roman Catholic religion back into France, was its focus. Both Roman Kingdoms maintain identical agendas — <u>to obtain and hold "power, seat, and authority" over ALL the world</u>. From approximately AD 1801 to the Russian Revolution (of AD 1917), the Roman Kingdom waxed greater and greater. Through the Russian Revolution, many Christians (and others) were martyred — fully developing the transgressions of this kingdom. The Scriptures teach that once the "age of the gentiles" is fulfilled, the character of Satan will be fully formed in the mind, character, and personality of the unbeliever.

- See GEN 15:16 to compare the "age of the gentiles" with how "the iniquity of the Amorites is not yet full." The Amorites and/or the Gentiles receive an extension of their day of grace until they have proven they want nothing to do with the saving grace of Christ. If this day of grace was cut short, God could be charged with unfairness when the time comes to destroy all iniquity. For the Gentiles, there is a fixed degree of iniquity — and when they go beyond that point, they will receive the judgments of God — encompassed in the Seven Last Plagues.

- Since 1801, this "king of fierce countenance" has been progressively rising to world dominion. When this king stands up, <u>he will progressively move towards full control over ALL the nations, tongues, and peoples of the world</u>. Several events happen at the same time.

a) While the Heavenly Sanctuary is cleansed of all confessed and forgiven sins, other events are also taking place:

1. Age of the Gentiles is being fulfilled;
2. The Sealing process is taking place;
3. The Heavenly Courtroom judgment is being finalized;
4. Separation of the sheep and the goats.

b) The sanctuary in the heart of man is also cleansed. Both events are connected. One, is the other. They are the same.

"__understanding dark sentences__" — under the canopy of the "king of fierce countenance," the Illuminati was firmly established in the mid 1700s through Adam Weishaupt. His mandate was to destroy Christianity by dethroning Christ, and destroying the Christian Gospel. Beginning with <u>the evil systems of Atheistic-Communism</u>, the Sixth Kingdom will eventually involve all western nations. (See Appendix 8D, on pages 187-188, for information on Weishaupt and western nations.)

The Persecutor of the Sixth Kingdom
(king of fierce countenance)
is Permitted to Destroy
(Present)

24 And [1]**his power** [to rule a one world government] **shall be mighty, but not by his own power: and he shall** [2]**destroy wonderfully, and shall** [3]**prosper** [push his aims forward], **and practice** [accomplish his aims], **and** [2a]**shall destroy the mighty and the holy people.**

Verse Linkage and Comparisons for "king of fierce countenance"

[1]*"his power shall be mighty"* —
- DAN 8:9 *"waxed exceeding great"*
- DAN 8:10 *"waxed great"*
- DAN 8:11 *"he magnified himself"*

[2] *"destroy wonderfully"* and
[2a] *"shall destroy the mighty and the holy people"* —
- DAN 8:10 *"cast down some of the host and of the stars to the ground, and stamped upon them"*
- DAN 8:11 *"daily was taken away ... sanctuary was cast down"*
- DAN 8:12 *"against the daily ... cast down the truth to the ground"*
- DAN 8:13 *"sanctuary and the host trodden under foot"*

[3] *"prosper and practice"* —
- DAN 8:12 *"it practiced, and prospered"*

(Further comment on page 166)

Verse 24

"but not of his own power" — Through all of its existence, the Papacy has depended on the power of the dragon [Satan in REV 13:2], and kings and nations, to extend its influence and to enforce its dictates. At the very end-time, the Papacy will join with *another power* to finalize the plans for a One World Government. (Revelation 13:11 gives the description for this *another power*. See Appendix 8B (Part 5), on pages 180-181, for further help.)

"destroy wonderfully" — *Strong's* OT#6381 **to separate**, i.e. **distinguish**.

Note: This "king of fierce countenance shall destroy" (or persecute) *"selectively"* those who refuse to come under his spiritual dictates.

"prosper" — *Strong's* OT#6743 **to push forward**, in various senses.

"practice" — *Strong's* OT#6213 to do or make, **in the broadest sense** and widest application: KJV - accomplish, advance.

"shall destroy the mighty and the holy people" — The "king of fierce countenance" has persecuted and destroyed God's holy people in various ways through the use of Secret Societies in the Communist countries. Millions were killed by Stalin alone, just as the Little Horn in Daniel 7 persecuted the holy people during the Dark Ages. Both persecutors are rulers of the Papal system. This is the spirit of antichrist.

1 JOHN 2:18 Little children, it is the last time: and as ye have heard that antichrist shall come, even now are there many antichrists; whereby [can] we know that [or when] it is the last time [or end time].

2 THESS 2:3-4 Let no man deceive you by any means: for that day shall not come, except there come a falling away first, and that man of sin [king of fierce countenance] be revealed, the son of perdition; 4 Who opposeth and exalteth himself above all that is called God, or that is worshipped; so that he as God sitteth in the temple of God, shewing himself that he is God.

- Note how this Scripture has very similar wording as recorded in DAN 8:10-13; 23-25.

The Antichrist Seeks Power to Rule the World and Destroy the Holy People

Note: The word "antichrist," as used in Scripture, does not convey that the Papal power is negative toward the legitimate offices of Christ. Rather, Scripture declares that one, such as this, would **appear** and **usurp the office of Christ by means of self exaltation**. (Review the Daniel 7:25 material.) This power "wants" Christ's office for itself.

Note: Verses 23 and 24 warn that the Papacy, in its rising posture as the "king of fierce countenance," does conduct persecutions against God's people. The characteristics of this king are also found in:
- "king of the north" in Daniel 11:41-45;
- "the beast" in Revelation 13:1-10.

Understanding the Historic-Prophetic Outline Verses of Daniel 8:24-25

Daniel 8:24-25

These verses are part of the Historic-Prophetic Outline in Vision 3 describing the Sixth Kingdom ruled by the "king of fierce countenance"

24 And
his power shall be mighty,
but not by his own power:
and
he shall destroy wonderfully,
and
shall prosper, and practise,
and
shall destroy the mighty and the holy people.

25 And through his policy also he **shall cause craft to prosper in his hand;**
and
he shall magnify himself
in his heart,
and
by peace shall destroy many: he shall also stand up against the Prince of princes;
but he shall be broken without hand.

2 THESS 2:3-9 Let no man deceive you by any means: for that day shall not come, except there come a falling away first, *and that man of sin be revealed, the son of perdition*; 4 *Who opposeth and exalteth himself above all that is called God*, or that is worshipped; *so that he as God sitteth in the temple of God, shewing himself that he is God.* 6 ... that he might be revealed in his time. 7 For the mystery of iniquity doth already work: ... 8 And then shall that Wicked be revealed, whom the Lord shall consume with the spirit of his mouth, and shall destroy with the brightness of his coming: 9 Even him, *whose coming is after the working of Satan with all power and signs and lying wonders*.

Reminder: Appendices 8D (pages 185-209) and 8E (pages 210-225) provide secular history information to aid in understanding the verses of Daniel 8:23-25.

DAN 8:24 This "king of fierce countenance," worked through the mighty power of agents such as the Jesuits, Freemasons, Weishaupts's Illuminati, Marx's Communist Manifesto, Darwin's theory of evolution, New Age Movement, etc. These agents are all inspired by Satan himself and geared towards Luciferian worship. As time has progressed, these Protestant Nations [who claim to worship the true God] have become "fat" through the Industrial Revolution. GEN 31:15 records how "fatness" can lead a nation to forsake God. Protestant nations have joined hands with these agents and their movements. Thus, the "age of the gentiles" is being fulfilled.

- **Many of God's people will** endure the wrath of Satan through an evil world system and **be penalized, imprisoned, and martyred** for not surrendering their inalienable rights to the rule of the "king of fierce countenance."
- The remnant of God's people parallels the three Hebrews in Daniel 3 that would not bow down to the image erected by the king. **They incurred the wrath of the king and the death penalty** of the fiery furnace. They were delivered through the fiery furnace because of their relationship with their God.

DAN 8:25 The Roman Papal system holds the strings of the puppeteer. **Through the workings of the Papacy — the Jesuits, Freemasons, and many other Secret Societies have formed a web which has been integrated throughout the political and religious world.** In due time, ALL the kings of the earth will hand over their sovereignty to this fierce system and ALL the world will wonder after the beast. (See page 209.)

- With this action, he will magnify himself in his heart — and magnify himself above every god, to be worshipped as God. DAN 3:5; 14; DAN 11:36; 2 THESS 2:3-9.
- The result of this exaltation produces **persecution and destruction of many of God's people. By statements of peace and political manipulation he will bring all under his control.** The New World Order, under Papal control, **will attempt to universally exert itself above the Creator God,*** "but he shall be broken without hand." At the Second Coming of Jesus this Roman Papal power will be broken forever.

"he shall also stand up against the Prince of princes" — Compare the following quotes with 2 THESS 2:3-9 of how this "king of fierce countenance" will determine to "stand up against the Prince of princes."

- "1. ***The Pope is*** of so great dignity and so exalted that he is not a mere man, but as it were ***God, and the vicar of God*** ... 13. Hence ***the Pope is*** crowned with a triple crown, as ***king of heaven and of earth and of hell*** ... 18. As to papal authority, the pope is as it were God on earth, Sole sovereign of all the faithful of Christ, chief king of kings, having plentitude of unbroken power, entrusted by the omnipotent God to govern the earthly and heavenly kingdoms ... 30. The ***Pope is of so great authority and power, that he is able to modify, declare, or interpret even divine laws.***" — Lucius Ferraris, *Prompta Bibliotheca Canonica*, Vol. 5, Petit-Montrouge: Jp. P. Migne, 1858, "Papa," Article 2, Cols. 1823, 1824. Cited in http://www.biblelight.netprompta.htm. (Emphasis supplied.)
- "***The Pope is*** not only the representative of Jesus Christ, but he is ***Jesus Christ Himself***, hidden under the veil of the flesh. Does the pope speak? It is Jesus Christ who speaks. Does the pope accord a favour or pronounce an anathema? It is Jesus Christ who accords the favour or pronounces that anathema. So that ***when the pope speaks we have no business to examine***." — *Catholique Nationale*, Paris, July 13, 1895. Cited in http://biblelight.net/claims.htm. (Emphasis supplied.)

The Roman Pontiff [Antichrist]
(Papal Supremacy No. 2)
Seeks the Office of Christ
in the Hearts of Men

25a And through his policy [political maneuvers] **also he shall cause** [use] **craft** [deception] **to prosper** [push his agenda forward] **in his hand** [his own diplomacy]; **and he shall magnify himself in his heart, and by peace** [using political and diplomatic means] **shall destroy many ...**

(The last part of this verse is given again on the next page.)

Verse 25a

"policy" — *Strong's* OT#7922 **intelligence**; success: KJV - discretion, knowledge, policy, prudence, sense, understanding, wisdom, wise.

"craft" — Skill in evasion or deception; cunning; guile. *American Heritage Dictionary of the English Language.*

"craft" — *Strong's* OT#4820 from **OT#7411** in the sense of **deceiving**; **fraud**: KJV - craft, deceit (-ful, -fully), false, feigned, guile, subtilly, treachery.

OT#7411 to hurl; **specifically, to shoot**; figuratively, **to delude or betray** (as if causing to fall): KJV - beguile, betray, deceive, throw.

"prosper" — *Strong's* OT#6743 **to push forward**.

"shall magnify himself in his heart, and by peace"

Note: The apostate "Papal System" depends on the secular power of the nations for protection and for the implementation of its aims and dictates. To orchestrate the political climate, to achieve its temporal goals, this Papal System commonly uses encyclicals, diplomacy, manipulative political pressure, religious doctrines and policy, and subversion of political processes to achieve its desired goals. Manipulated wars and international strife have always created an excellent climate for the Papacy to further its goals.

"shall destroy many" — **JOB 34:20**
In a moment shall they die, and the people shall be troubled at midnight, and pass away: and the mighty shall be taken away without hand.

Reminder: (for the next page) See **The Structure of Daniel** Chart on page 233. Following the **Historic-Prophetic Outline** of the Third Vision is the **Answer** given in the last part of Daniel 8:25, to the **Interlude Question** of Daniel 8:15. The answer to "what is the meaning of this vision" is: "he" (Roman Papal System or the Antichrist) will stand up against the "Prince of princes" [Jesus Christ]. At that moment, the Antichrist system with its leadership is "broken without hand." This action ends all earthly kingdoms. (The **Answer** is in the last part of Daniel 8:25, given on the next page.)

DANIEL

The Story of the Rise and Fall of Earthly Kingdoms

ANSWER TO QUESTION

("What is the meaning of this vision?")

VISION THREE

*The Antichrist Will Reign and —
"he shall also stand up against the Prince of princes"*

25b ... he shall also stand up [govern and reign over ALL people] **against** [in place of] **the Prince of princes** [Jesus Christ] ...

ENDTIME EVENT
VISION THREE

The End of the Antichrist

25c ... but he [Antichrist] **shall be broken without hand** [come to his end].

(This verse given again on the next page.)

*The **End** of the Third Historic-Prophetic Outline*

**ANSWER TO QUESTION
DAN 8:25
"HE [PERSECUTOR]
SHALL STAND UP
AGAINST THE PRINCE!"**

Verse 25b (Continued)

"stand up" — the Sixth Kingdom has the same characteristics and persecuting spirit as Papal Supremacy No. 1.

DAN 8:11 Yea, <u>he magnified himself even to the prince of the host.</u>

DAN 7:25 And <u>he shall speak great words against the most High</u>, and <u>shall wear out the saints.</u>

1 JOHN 2:18 Little children, it is the last time: and as <u>ye have heard that antichrist shall come</u>, even now are there many antichrists; whereby we know that it is the last time.

2 THESS 2:3-4 Let no man deceive you by any means: <u>for that day shall not come, except there come a falling away first, and that man of sin be revealed</u>, the son of perdition; 4 <u>Who opposeth and exalteth himself above all that is called God, or that is worshipped</u>; so that he as God sitteth in the temple of God, shewing himself that he is God.

**ENDTIME EVENT
DAN 8:25
"PERSECUTOR BROKEN
WITHOUT HAND"**

Verse 25c (Concluded)

"shall be broken without hand" —
DAN 2:34 Thou sawest till that a stone was cut out <u>without hands</u>, which smote the image upon his feet that were of iron and clay, and <u>brake them to pieces.</u>

DAN 7:26 and they shall take away his dominion, to <u>consume and to destroy it unto the end.</u>

🔑 **Prophetic Key #29** Even though this antichrist comes to his end, there is no indication as to the day and hour of the Second Coming of Jesus. (See MATT 24:36.)

**HEAVENLY SCENE
DAN 8:2-14**

**RAM
HE GOAT
"OUT OF ONE OF THEM"
LITTLE HORN
"WAXED EXCEEDING GREAT"**

**INTERLUDE QUESTION
DAN 8:15
WHAT IS THE
MEANING OF
THIS VISION?**

**HISTORIC-PROPHETIC
OUTLINE
DAN 8:20-25
(BABYLON IS REIGNING)
MEDO-PERSIA
GREECE
ROME (PAGAN IMPERIAL)
ROME (PAPAL NO. 1)
ROME (PAPAL NO. 2)
OUTLINE EXTENDS TO:
AD 1844**

**ANSWER TO QUESTION
DAN 8:25
"HE [PERSECUTOR]
SHALL STAND UP
AGAINST THE PRINCE!"**

**ENDTIME EVENT
DAN 8:25
"PERSECUTOR BROKEN
WITHOUT HAND"**

The Antichrist Will Reign and—
"he shall also stand up against the Prince of princes"

25 And through his policy also he [1]shall cause craft to prosper in his hand; and [2]he shall magnify himself in his heart, **and** [3]by peace shall destroy many: [4]he shall also stand up against the Prince of princes; but he shall be broken without hand.

<u>Verse 25</u> (Concluded)

Note: This verse emphasizes the main persecuting power at the present time. Currently, this power is hidden behind Secret Societies. The people of God will have to deal directly with this power in the final crisis leading up to the Seventh Kingdom. Only God can overcome this counterfeit system and deliver His people for eternity. The intent of this powerful kingdom will be further explained in Daniel 11 and 12, and Revelation 13-18.

Verse Linkage and Comparisons for
"king of fierce countenance"

[1] *"shall cause craft to prosper in his hand"* —
- DAN 8:12 *"practiced, and prospered"*

[2] *"he shall magnify himself in his heart"* —
- DAN 8:9 *"waxed exceeding great"*
- DAN 8:10 *"waxed great"*
- DAN 8:11 *"he magnified himself"*

[3] *"by peace shall destroy many"* —
- DAN 8:10 *"cast down some of the host and of the stars to the ground, and stamped upon them"*
- DAN 8:11 *"daily was taken away"*
- DAN 8:11 *"his sanctuary was cast down"*
- DAN 8:12 *"against the daily"*
- DAN 8:12 *"it cast down the truth to the ground"*
- DAN 8:13 *"the sanctuary and the host trodden under foot"*

[4] *"he shall also stand up against the Prince of princes"* —
- DAN 8:10 *"even to the host of heaven"*
- DAN 8:11 *"he magnified himself even to the prince of the host"*

(Further comments were given on page 166.)

THE ROMAN PONTIFF GAINS ACCEPTANCE BY WORLD LEADERS

President Ronald Reagan with Pope John Paul II

Prime Minister Tony Blair with Pope John Paul II

President George Bush with Pope John Paul II

President William Clinton with Pope John Paul II

Billy Graham with Pope John Paul II

President Yeltsin with Pope John Paul II

Queen Elizabeth with Pope John Paul II

Iranian President Khatarni with Pope John Paul II

Pope John Paul II kisses the Koran

The 2300 Day Prophecy of Daniel 8:14 is the Longest Timeline in the Bible

26 And the vision of the <u>evening and the morning</u> which was told is true: wherefore shut thou up the vision; for it shall be for many days.

"Tidy-Up" Verse for Vision Three

27 And I Daniel fainted, and was <u>sick certain days</u>; afterward I rose up, and did the king's business; and I was astonished at the vision, but none understood it.

Verse 26

"evening and morning" —
GEN 1:4-5 and God divided the light from the darkness. 5 And God called the light Day, and the darkness he called Night. <u>And the evening and the morning were the first day</u>.

Prophetic Key #24 The *evening and morning* of this verse is the same as the *days* of Daniel 8:14. However, the symbolic horns of the Ram and He Goat, also places the 2300 days timeline in a symbolic context, to which the Year-day Computation Principle is applied. Therefore, the 2300 *symbolic* days is interpreted as 2300 *literal* years. Daniel 9 explains when the 2300 years began and how they ended in 1844. Gabriel assures Daniel the vision is true and extends far into the future.

Note: Daniel 8:14 brought the Historic-Prophetic Outline to AD 1844 — datable time for the beginning of the Heavenly Judgment. Appendices 8D and 8E supply some of the historical information from 1844 to the current day. The Fourth Vision will reveal the Seventh Kingdom, closing the gap of time.

Verse 27

Note: As Daniel viewed the powerful work of the Little Horn and the "king of fierce countenance," he fainted and was *sick certain days*. Daniel was worried sick over many things — some of which will be reviewed in the next chapter.

Prophetic Key #30 The last verse of this chapter is the "tidy-up" verse which indicates that the Historic-Prophetic Outline is completely finished and there is nothing more to be added to this vision.

General Review and Theme of Vision Three:
"Christ our High Priest"

- Daniel 8 again reviewed the political kingdoms of history. This vision omitted Babylon since it was in the declining years of its reign. The vision touched on medieval Christianity and pointed directly to Christ's work of atonement (in the Heavenly Sanctuary) and salvation from sin.
- This chapter includes the longest timeline in the Bible which is connected to the Heavenly Sanctuary where Christ is abiding as our High Priest. Daniel 9 gives further comment regarding this timeline.

A Brief Comment for Daniel 8
Daniel 8:13-14 has two applications — spiritual and political.

Spiritual	*Political*
The ending of the 2300 year-days time prophecy points to the beginning of Christ's work in the Heavenly Sanctuary when all peoples and kingdoms will come to judgment — their motives investigated, and their reward or fate determined. This work of judgment begins with the dead.	The chapter describes how the great rulers from the Third to the Sixth Kingdoms obtain power to rule. The symbolic Leopard, introduced in Daniel 7:6 and continuing in Revelation 13:2, characterized by its *__stealth__*, its habit to stalk and unexpectedly seize its prey. The Leopard symbol, describes the manner by which the Fifth Kingdom was established and warns that the Sixth Kingdom will be established in the same manner — by stealth! *"stealth"* — The act of moving, proceeding, or acting in a covert way or <u>secret movement</u>; avoiding notice. The act of stealing. *The Heritage Dictionary of the English Language.*

Appendix 8A — Other Translations for Daniel 8:23-25

Today's English Version

23 When the end of those kingdoms is near and they have become so wicked that they must be punished, there will be a stubborn, vicious, and deceitful king.

24 He will grow strong--but not by his own power. He will cause terrible destruction and be successful in everything he does. He will bring destruction on powerful men and on God's own people.

25 Because he is cunning, he will succeed in his deceitful ways. He will be proud of himself and destroy many people without warning. He will even defy the greatest King of all, but he will be destroyed without the use of any human power.

Today's Living Bible

23 Toward the end of their kingdoms, when they have become morally rotten, an angry king shall rise to power with great shrewdness and intelligence.

24 His power shall be mighty, but it will be satanic strength and not his own. Prospering wherever he turns, he will destroy all who oppose him, though their armies be mighty, and he will devastate God's people.

25 He will be a master of deception, defeating many by catching them off guard as they bask in false security. Without warning he will destroy them. So great will he fancy himself to be that he will even take on the Prince of Princes in battle; but in so doing he will seal his own doom, for he shall be broken by the hand of God, though no human means could overpower him.

Revised Standard Version

23 And at the latter end of their rule, when the transgressors have reached their full measure, a king of bold countenance, one who understands riddles, shall arise.

24 His power shall be great, and he shall cause fearful destruction, and shall succeed in what he does, and destroy mighty men and the people of the saints.

25 By his cunning he shall make deceit prosper under his hand, and in his own mind he shall magnify himself. Without warning he shall destroy many; and he shall even rise up against the Prince of princes; but, by no human hand, he shall be broken.

New Living Translation

23 At the end of their rule, when their sin is at its height, a fierce king, a master of intrigue, will rise to power.

24 He will become very strong, but not by his own power. He will cause a shocking amount of destruction and succeed in everything he does. He will destroy powerful leaders and devastate the holy people.

25 He will be a master of deception, defeating many by catching them off guard. Without warning he will destroy them. He will even take on the Prince of princes in battle, but he will be broken, though not by human power.

New American Standard Bible-Updated Edition

23 In the latter period of their rule, When the transgressors have run their course, A king will arise, Insolent and skilled in intrigue.

24 "His power will be mighty, but not by his own power, And he will destroy to an extraordinary degree And prosper and perform his will; He will destroy mighty men and the holy people.

25 "And through his shrewdness He will cause deceit to succeed by his influence; And he will magnify himself in his heart, And he will destroy many while they are at ease. He will even oppose the Prince of princes, But he will be broken without human agency.

New International Version

23 In the latter part of their reign, when rebels have become completely wicked, a stern-faced king, a master of intrigue, will arise.

24 He will become very strong, but not by his own power. He will cause astounding devastation and will succeed in whatever he does. He will destroy the mighty men and the holy people.

25 He will cause deceit to prosper, and he will consider himself superior. When they feel secure, he will destroy many and take his stand against the Prince of princes. Yet he will be destroyed, but not by human power.

Daniel 8 — Review of the Historic-Prophetic Outline in Vision 3

1. Vision 3 uses some symbolic language introducing a Symbolic Vision of Horns and a "king."
2. Vision 3 describes and reveals **Six earthly kingdoms** surrounding God's people.
3. Vision 3 extends from 538 BC to the Establishment of Christ's Kingdom in One Major Line of Prophecy.
4. Vision 3 <u>repeats</u> the former information from previous visions. The Outline adds extra information of another kingdom and <u>one</u> timeline. Several other timelines in the second part of Vision 3 (found in Daniel 9:24-27) <u>follow</u> the Outline of Daniel 8.
5. The symbols in Vision 3 for the Second and Third Kingdoms have a Biblical interpretation — as the "Bible is its own Interpreter." e.g. Daniel 8:20-21 "<u>the two horns are the kings of Media and Persia ... and the rough goat is the king of Grecia: and the great horn that is between his eyes is the first king.</u>" The Bible has now named the first three kingdoms of the first three visions.
6. The Outline of Vision 3 is decoded according to secular history and continues to <u>recap and review</u> the sequence of kingdoms found in Daniel 2 and 7.

    (**1ˢᵗ Kingdom**) = BABYLON is still reigning even though it is not mentioned in this vision. (606 — 538 BC)

    2ⁿᵈ Kingdom = Ram with higher horn = MEDO-PERSIA. (538 — 331 BC)

    3ʳᵈ Kingdom = Goat with Notable Horn = GREECE. (331 — 168 BC)

    4ᵗʰ Kingdom = "... out of one of them ..." = PAGAN IMPERIAL ROME. (168 BC — AD 476)

- <u>Limited Information</u>: Daniel 8:9 "And out of one of them" is the only reference made in this chapter to Pagan Imperial Rome. Everything the reader needed to know about Pagan Rome was in the previous two visions, and verified with secular history. There is no need for the Bible verses to enlarge upon the information again.

    5ᵗʰ Kingdom = Little Horn = PAPAL SUPREMACY NO. 1. (AD 538 — 1798)
- <u>New Information</u>: A **6ᵗʰ Kingdom** is revealed titled as "waxed exceeding great" and "king of fierce countenance" = PAPAL SUPREMACY NO. 2. This kingdom began to rise in AD 1801 when Pope Pius VII signed a Concordat with Napoleon. This kingdom's ruling power presently works through many Secret Societies to persecute many that will not fall into line with its dogma. Many lost their lives under the rule of Stalin and Hitler and the "planned" wars.

- <u>New Information</u>: <u>Vision 3 adds a new timeline of 2300 days as given in Daniel 8:14</u> — "unto two thousand and three hundred days."
a. This prophetic timeline is encased within a symbolic context of symbolic horns.
b. Therefore: the symbolic timeline is converted to literal time using the "Year-day" Computation principle.
c. The Biblical conversion for prophetic symbolic time is found in Numbers 14:34 and Ezekiel 4:6 — one prophetic symbolic day = one prophetic literal year.
d. Therefore: the timeline of Daniel 8:14 = 2300 prophetic literal years.
e. The explanation for this timeline is given in Daniel 9:25. Gabriel explains how this timeline begins with the voice of Artaxerxes in 457 BC — a decree to rebuild and restore Jerusalem. (Daniel 9:24-27 also includes several other timelines in the Second Part of Vision 3.)
f. The information in Daniel 9 allows the correct interpretation for the 2300 day-year timeline — which ends in AD 1844 (remembering the necessary adjustment because there is no zero year. e.g. 457 BC + 2300 day-years = AD 1844).

- **Extremely Important Note:** The 2300 day-year timeline is mentioned only **ONCE** in this vision. There are several other timelines in Daniel 9 (contained within the 2300 day-year timeline). Each of them is also mentioned only once.

7. **Datable Time:** Vision 3 extends to AD **1844** in **datable time** because the 2300 day-year timeline moved the Outline forward in time. 1844 is when a) [the beginning of] judgment is promised for the saints; b) the evil Papal Kingdom is also brought to judgment.

- **VISION 3** reveals information for the "gap" of time between AD 1798 — 1844. The gap of time, between 1844 and when the "king of fierce countenance comes to his end," is again reduced. **Note: Each kingdom has <u>moved forward in time — a concept that cannot be violated in prophecy</u>.**

8. **Emphasis in Vision 3** is on the "king of fierce countenance" — representing <u>Papal Roman Supremacy No. 2</u> that is so prevalent in today's events.
9. **Vision 3 Tidy-up Verse:** Daniel 8:27 completes the Historic-Prophetic Outline. However, the Second Part of the vision in Daniel 9:24-27 still includes several timelines that are connected to the Outline in Daniel 8. This structure prepares the reader for what happens in Vision 4 where there are three timelines in Daniel 12:7-13 that follow the Outline of Daniel 11.
10. **Endtime Event:** Vision 3 ends when the system of the "king of fierce countenance is broken without hand" at the Second Coming of Jesus.

THE STRUCTURE OF DANIEL'S THIRD OUTLINE
The Rise and Fall of Earthly Kingdoms Surrounding God's People
One Major Line of Prophecy From 606 BC — to the Establishment of Christ's Kingdom

DANIEL 8 (Vision 3 uses some Symbolic language for the following Historic-Prophetic Outline.)
The Symbolic HORNS and KING represent Literal Kingdoms in the Outline.

(Date of Vision 3: 551 BC)
(Now Under Belshazzar)

(#1 BABYLON IS REIGNING)
606 — 538 BC

RAM

ONE HORN HIGHER
DAN 8:3-4

#2 MEDO-PERSIA
538 — 331 BC

HE GOAT

NOTABLE HORN
DAN 8:5

#3 GREECE RULES
(Alexander the Great)
331 BC

NOTABLE HORN BROKEN
DAN 8:8

GREECE BROKEN
(Alexander the Great Dies)
323 BC

FOUR NOTABLE ONES
(Greece divided between the four "winds/directions.")

GREECE DIVIDED
(Between the Four Generals)
311 — 168 BC

FOUR DIVISIONS OF GREECE
(Illustrated on the Map)   DAN 8:8

(Addressed on the Map as
"… out of one of them … "
or out of "one direction"
of the "four winds" of Greece.)
DAN 8:9a

#4 ROME
(Pagan Imperial)
168 BC — AD 476

LITTLE HORN

Little Horn arose out of
the 10 Divisions of Rome.

LITTLE HORN
Rises and Rules
DAN 8:9b

#5 ROME
(Papal Supremacy No. 1)
Rises (AD 476-538) and
Rules (AD 538-1798)

Symbolic Timeline (DAN 8:14)
"Unto two thousand and three hundred days"
= 2300 years of literal time from
457 BC — AD 1844

Vision Three
Time extends from
538 BC — AD 1844

Papal No. 2 as
Puppeteer

"WAXES EXCEEDING GREAT"
DAN 8:9c

#6 ROME
(Papal Supremacy No. 2)
Rises (AD 1801) and
Rules (Present)

VISION #

3

"he" [king of fierce countenance]
is broken "without hand"
at Jesus' Second Coming
DAN 8:25

Connecting Structure

DANIEL'S <u>SECOND</u> OUTLINE

The Little Horn of Vision 2 is
Papal Rome No. 1 (538-1798)
and this connects with . . .

DAN 7:20 "And of the ten horns that were in his head ..." —
These symbolic ten horns reveal the break up of the Pagan Imperial Roman Kingdom into ten nations by AD 476.   The Little
Horn uprooted three of these horns which were Arian tribes.

LITTLE HORN
DAN 7:20-25

#5 ROME
(Papal Supremacy No. 1)
AD 538 — 1798

Between Visions 2 & 3

DANIEL'S THIRD OUTLINE

> ... the Little Horn of Vision 3
> which is <u>also</u>
> Papal Rome No. 1 (538-1798).

LITTLE HORN

Little Horn arose out of
the 10 Divisions of Rome.

LITTLE HORN
Rises and Rules
DAN 8:9b

#5 ROME
(Papal Supremacy No. 1)
Rises (AD 476-538) and
Rules (AD 538-1798)

VISION #

3

Daniel 8:3

3 Then I lifted up mine eyes, and saw, and, behold, there stood before the river <u>a ram which had two horns</u>: and the two horns were high; but one was higher than the other, and the higher came up last.

Application of Prophetic Key #17

SYMBOL: "a ram which had two horns"

DECODING by Scripture:

- **DAN 7:24** And the … horns are … kings that shall arise.

APPLICATION:

- **DAN 8:20** The ram which thou sawest having two horns are the kings of Media and Persia.

SYMBOL: "one [horn] was higher than the other, and the higher [horn] came up last."

DECODING by Scripture:

- **DAN 8:20** The ram which thou sawest having two horns are the kings of Media and Persia.

APPLICATION: Secular history notes Persia in the beginning was only an ally of the Medes, but later became the dominating power.

Daniel 8:4

4 I saw the <u>ram pushing westward, and northward, and southward</u>; so that no beasts might stand before him, neither was there any that could deliver out of his hand; but he did according to his will, and became great.

SYMBOL: "ram pushing westward, and northward, and southward"

DECODING by History: Medo-Persia came from the east and pushed in all directions trying to extend their territory.

APPLICATION: The literal directions that Medo-Persia pushed were westward into Lydia; northward against the Scythians [in the southern parts of Russia]; southward into Egypt and Ethiopia. The eastern boundaries reached unto India. The Persian king, Ahasuerus, was the last king to stir up trouble with Greece.

- **EST 1:1** Now it came to pass in the days of Ahasuerus [Persian King Xerxes I], (this *is* Ahasuerus [Queen Esther's husband], which reigned, from <u>India even unto Ethiopia, *over* an hundred and seven and twenty provinces</u>:)

"Great"

Persia consisted of one hundred twenty-seven provinces and is simply called "great."

Historical Note

During the period 539-465 BC, two lines of kings ruled the kingdom together. One line was a <u>Mede</u> and the other was a <u>Persian</u>. Daniel first served in the Median part of the kingdom under King Darius the Mede. However, the Persian Kingdom was stronger. The "higher horn" of Persia came up last. At first Persia was an ally of the Medes, but later became the dominant power when Cyrus defeated his grandfather, King Astyages of Media in 553 BC. In 547 BC, Cyrus annexed Lydia to his realm, which had been a province of Babylon. In 538 BC, Cyrus added Babylon to his territory. In this way the horn that came up second became taller than the first one. In the end, the Medes were allies to the Persians rather than subjects.

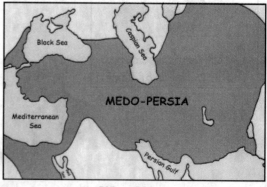

538 — 331 BC

Daniel 8:5

5 And as I was considering, behold, <u>an he goat came from the west</u> on the face of the whole earth, and touched not the ground: and <u>the goat had a notable horn</u> between his eyes.

Application of Prophetic Key #17

SYMBOL: "an he goat came from the west"

DECODING by Scripture:

- **DAN 8:21** And the rough goat is the king of Grecia.

APPLICATION: Greece and Macedonia are represented by the rough goat.

- **Note:** The rough goat is a very fitting symbol to represent Greece or the Macedonian people. About 200 years before Daniel's time, the Macedonians were known as the "goat's people." Edess was the seat of the kingdom and known as the "goat's town." Alexander's son was named Ægus, or the "son of the goat." Some of Alexander's successors had coins with goat's horns.

SYMBOL: "the goat had a notable horn"

DECODING by Scripture:

- **DAN 8:21** and the great horn that is between his eyes is the first king.

APPLICATION: Secular history confirms the first great king was Alexander the Great.

Daniel 8:8

8 Therefore the he goat waxed very great: and when he was strong, <u>the great horn was broken</u> ...

SYMBOL: "the great horn was broken"

DECODING by Concordance:
"broken" — OT#7665 to ... crush, destroy, hurt, quench, tear.

APPLICATION: Secular history confirms that Alexander the Great died suddenly, shortly after all his victories.

"Very Great"

Grecia was more extensive than Persia and is called "very great."

Daniel 8:8

8 ... and for it [Alexander the Great] **came up <u>four notable ones</u> toward the four winds of heaven.**

SYMBOL: "four notable ones"

DECODING by History: By 301 BC Alexander's Kingdom had been divided into four parts.

APPLICATION: Secular history confirms that Alexander's territory was finally divided between four of his army generals into four directions as noted in the following map.

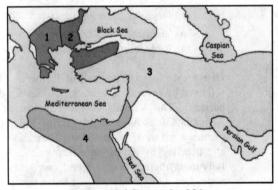

Divisions of Greece by 301 BC

1. **Cassander:** Greece, Macedonia
2. **Lysimachus:** Thrace
3. **Seleucus:** Syria including Babylon
4. **Ptolemy:** Egypt

Daniel 8:9a

9a And <u>out of one of them</u> ...

Application of Prophetic Key #17

SYMBOL: "out of one of them"

DECODING by Concordance: *"them"* — refers back to verse 8 which describes the *four winds* or four directions.

- *"winds"* — *Strong's* OT#7307 a region of the sky.

APPLICATION: One of those *winds* was the west direction. According to secular history, by 168 BC, Pagan Imperial Rome had come from the west of Greece and set up their rule over most of the Grecian territory. Egypt, the last province of Greece, became part of the Roman Kingdom by 30 BC. The remainder of verse 9 refers to what happened after Pagan Imperial Rome was divided in AD 476.

- **Note:** This chapter does <u>not</u> give extra information about Pagan Imperial Rome. All the necessary information about this Kingdom was given in Daniel 7. In chapters 7 and 8, Daniel's focus is turned toward the activities of Papal Rome which arose out of Pagan Imperial Rome. Therefore, Pagan Imperial Rome is mentioned very slightly, thus keeping the alignment of the kingdoms that are addressed in the Book of Daniel.

168 BC — AD 476

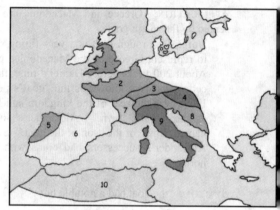

10 Divisions of PAGAN IMPERIAL ROME by AD 476

The Story of Christianity,
a Celebration of 2000 Years of Faith
Michael Collins and Matthew A. Price

Historical Note: "The sack of Rome in 410 was followed by several significant victories for the barbarians. The Vandals conquered most of North Africa in 430 as Augustine lay dying in Hippo, and Carthage fell in 439. In 452 the Huns, and an Asiatic tribe led by Attila, crossed over the Alps into Italy in an attempt to march on Rome, although the pope, Leo the Great, managed to persuade them to turn back. *The fact that the pope had successfully averted the disaster increased the political position of the papacy immeasurably. Leo took every opportunity to underline the supremacy of the bishop of Rome, especially after 451, when the bishops at the Council of Chalcedon had voted that the city of Constantinople be regarded as second only to* Rome. "Due to the preeminence of the Apostolic See," wrote Leo, "made certain by the merits of the prince of bishops, St. Peter, and by the prime position of the city of Rome, let nobody presume to attempt anything to the contrary. Thus will the peace of the churches be preserved if the whole body acknowledge its ruler ... successive popes made ever more explicit claims to their universal role as chief pastor of the church. *The fact that the emperors continued to endow the papacy with funds, despite the threats to the empire, demonstrates the high esteem in which the papacy was held ...*" p. 71. (Emphasis supplied.)

Daniel 8:9b

(9a   And out of one of them …)
9b … came forth <u>a little horn</u> …

Application of Prophetic Key #17

SYMBOL: "out of one of them [direction of the west wind] came forth <u>a little horn</u>"

DECODING from Scripture: Daniel chapter 7 identifies the Little Horn as the Fifth Kingdom that succeeded Pagan Imperial Rome after AD 476.

APPLICATION: The Little Horn Kingdom in Daniel 8 is the <u>same</u> as the Little Horn Kingdom in Daniel 7 which is identified in secular history as Papal Supremacy No. 1. This kingdom ruled for 1260 years from AD 538-1798.

The Little Horn surpassed both Persia and Greece.
AD 538 — 1798

The Story of Christianity, a Celebration of 2000 Years of Faith
Michael Collins and Matthew A. Price

Transfer of Power to Papal Rome

"During his reign, Constantine had organized the church along the lines of his civil administration, with territories divided up into areas called dioceses, each one supervised by a bishop. The bishop resided in a town, and the building - called a cathedral - where his "see," or official seat (Latin, *cathedra*, meaning "chair") was located was a place not only of worship, but of bureaucratic power. With the breakdown of civil administration during the fifth century, people turned to the bishop and his court for help. The church was the only institution that would defend and sustain them.

"These bishops felt the impact of such disarray strongly, finding it difficult to deal with an emperor far away … In Rome, when Leo assumed the title *"Pontifex Maximus,"* he also assumed the duties of the emperor in the maintenance of public monuments. The claims of the bishops of Rome were increasingly unambiguous [or, poorly defined] …

"At the end of the fifth century, Pope Gelasius I (AD 492-496) was to claim that the pope was the ruler of the spiritual sphere, while the emperor was ruler of the temporal sphere: a clear statement that popes would not accept imperial directions on spiritual matters." p. 72.

"The Christian architects adapted the pagan plan, installing an alter near the large, rounded recess, or apse, at one end of the edifice, where the king or judge sat; the bishop was now to take the place of the pagan dignitary."
p. 64.

AMBROSE OF MILAN

"Since the time of Constantine, bishops have worn purple as their official color. Pure purple, which is a special dye, was worn only by the emperor himself. The bishops had all the rights and privileges of senators and, as senators wore a purple band to show their imperial dignity, so did the bishops."
p. 65.

Ambrose had a high view of his office, saying, "Christ gave to his apostles the power of remitting sins, which has been transmitted by the apostles to the sacerdotal [priestly] office."
Op. cit., p. 64.

Daniel 8:23

23 And in the latter time of their kingdom, when the transgressors are come to the full, a king of fierce countenance, and understanding dark sentences, shall stand up.

Application of Prophetic Key #17

SYMBOL: "in the latter time of their [Papal Supremacy No. 1] kingdom"

DECODING from Scripture: Daniel 7 and 8 have identified the Little Horn as the Fifth Kingdom that reigned during the Dark Ages between 538-1798.

- The Sixth Kingdom rises in 1801 just after the 1798 wound of the Fifth Kingdom.
- Daniel 11 provides further information on the linkage between the Fifth, Sixth, and [latter] Seventh Kingdom.

APPLICATION: The Little Horn Kingdom represented Papal Supremacy No. 1. This latter [similar] kingdom of Papal Supremacy No. 2 will give rise to the Seventh Kingdom.

"Feet of Iron" = Little Horn Papal Supremacy No. 1
(AD 538-1798)

"Feet of Clay" = *Mankind* under the reign of the "Waxes Exceeding Great" Kingdom
(or "king of fierce countenance")
Papal Supremacy No. 2 (AD 1801-Present)

The "king of fierce countenance" coordinates the activities of world Secret Societies manipulating the Atheistic, Communistic, and Protestant countries towards the New World Order.

SYMBOL: "a king of fierce countenance ... shall stand up"

DECODING by Scripture:
- DEUT 28:50 A nation of fierce countenance, which shall not regard the person of the old, nor shew favour to the young.

APPLICATION: The present "king of fierce countenance" stood up fiercely during the Russian Revolution of 1917, persecuting many, many Christians among others. This power has continued severe persecution through every war to date, invading every country and religion of the world. In 1980 the ecumenical movement had successfully wiped out Protestantism. At this time the "king of fierce countenance" had a solid grasp on the political and religious world. See the **"1980"** note, and quote, on page 207.

The 1917 Russian Revolution gives evidence of the strong rule of this king. Since then, it has continued to *wax exceeding great*. The world is in his hands. With a few more planned world events, the New World Order will be in total control, globally.

Daniel 8:24

24 And his power shall be mighty, but <u>not by his own power</u>: and he shall destroy wonderfully, and shall prosper, and practise, and shall destroy the mighty and the holy people.

Application of Prophetic Key #17

SYMBOL: "but <u>not in his own power</u>"

DECODING by Scripture:

• **REV 13:11-12** And I beheld <u>another beast</u> coming up out of the earth; and he had two horns like a lamb, and he spake as a dragon. 12 And he exerciseth <u>all the power of the first beast before him</u>, and causeth the earth and them which dwell therein to worship the first beast, whose deadly wound was healed.

APPLICATION: Revelation 13 reveals *another beast* that will exercise the same power as the "king of fierce countenance" [a head on the composite beast of REV 13:1-10]. The ultimate goal of these two powers is to set up the New World Order under the Seventh Kingdom. Both these kingdoms receive their power from the "great red dragon" [scarlet coloured beast]. See REV 13:4.

Daniel 8:25

Dan 8:25 And through his policy also he shall cause craft to prosper in his hand; and he shall magnify himself in his heart, and by peace shall destroy many: he shall also stand up against the Prince of princes; but <u>he shall be broken without hand</u>.

Application of Prophetic Key #17

SYMBOL: "<u>he shall be broken without hand</u>"

DECODING by Scripture:

• **REV 13:10** He that leadeth into captivity shall go into captivity: he that killeth with the sword must be killed with the sword.

APPLICATION: Papal Supremacy No. 2 and all other antichrist kingdoms will end at the Second Coming of Jesus.

• **DAN 11:45** he shall come to his end, and none shall help him.

Two Powers Work Together

"king of fierce countenance"
Daniel 8:24

"another beast"
Revelation 13:11

= NEW WORLD ORDER!

(Under the Rule of the Seventh Kingdom)

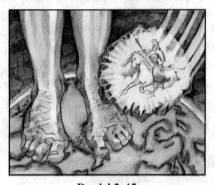

Daniel 2:45
Forasmuch as thou sawest that the stone was cut out of the mountain <u>without hands</u>, and that it brake in pieces the iron, the brass, the clay, the silver, and the gold.

The last "king is broken" <u>without hand</u>
by the Stone Kingdom that is cut out
of the mountain <u>without hands</u>.

Appendix 8c — The Heavenly Sanctuary

Note: In the wilderness, God commanded Moses to construct a Sanctuary. Each of the services contained deep spiritual meaning. All of these symbolic rites and ceremonies pointed forward to the Messiah, Jesus Christ, as the Savior. Upon His ascension, in AD 31, Jesus Christ has been ministering as our High Priest in the Heavenly Sanctuary.

God's Command

EX 25:8 And let them make me a sanctuary; that I may dwell among them.

Offerings in the Sanctuary

HEB 9:9 in which were offered both gifts and sacrifices.

Apartments of the Sanctuary

EX 26:33 and the vail shall divide unto you between the holy place and the most holy.

First Apartment: The Holy Place

HEB 9:2 For there was a tabernacle made; the first, wherein was the candlestick, and the table, and the shewbread; which is called the sanctuary.

EX 40:26 And he put the golden altar in the tent of the congregation before the vail. (See EX 30:1-6.)

Second Apartment: The Most Holy Place

HEB 9:3-4 And after the second veil, the tabernacle which is called the Holiest of all; 4 Which had the golden censer, and the ark of the covenant overlaid round about with gold, wherein was the golden pot that had manna, and Aaron's rod that budded, and the tables of the covenant. (See EX 40:20-21.)

Name of the Cover of the Ark

EX 25:21 And thou shalt put the mercy seat above upon the ark; and in the ark thou shalt put the testimony that I shall give thee.

God's Meeting Place With Israel

EX 25:22 And there I will meet with thee, and I will commune with thee from above the mercy seat, from between the two cherubims which are upon the ark of the testimony.

Contents of the Ark Under the Mercy Seat

DEUT 10:4-5 And he wrote on the tables, according to the first writing, the ten commandments ... 5 And I turned myself and came down from the mount, and put the tables in the ark which I had made; and there they be, as the LORD commanded me.

First Apartment Ministry —The Holy Place

HEB 9:6 These preparations having thus been made, the priests go continually into the outer tent, performing their ritual duties. RSV

Second Apartment Ministry — The Most Holy Place

HEB 9:7 But into the second went the high priest alone once every year [on the Day of Atonement], not without blood, which he offered for himself, and for the errors of the people.

The Daily Service for Sinners

LEV 4:27-29 And if any one of the common people sin through ignorance, while he doeth somewhat against any of the commandments of the LORD ... 28 then he shall bring his offering, a kid of the goats, a female without blemish, for his sin which he hath sinned. 29 And he shall lay his hand upon the head of the sin offering, and slay the sin offering in the place of the burnt offering.

The Blood Offering

LEV 4:30 And the priest shall take of the blood thereof with his finger, and put it upon the horns of the altar of burnt offering, and shall pour out all the blood thereof at the bottom of the altar.

The Yearly Day of Atonement

LEV 16:29-30 And this shall be a statute for ever unto you: that in the seventh month, on the tenth day of the month, ye shall afflict your souls ... 30 For on that day [of Atonement] shall the priest make an atonement for you, to cleanse you, that ye may be clean from all your sins before the LORD.

How Was the Sanctuary Cleansed?

LEV 16:5, 7-8 And he [the high priest] shall take of the congregation of the children of Israel two kids of the goats for a sin offering. 7 And he shall take the two goats, and present them before the LORD at the door of the tabernacle of the congregation. 8 And Aaron shall cast lots upon the two goats; one lot for the LORD, and the other lot for the scapegoat [or Azazel, representing Satan].

Appendix 8C— The Heavenly Sanctuary

The Lord's Goat

LEV 16:15 Then shall he kill the goat of the sin offering, that is for the people, and bring his blood within the vail … and sprinkle it upon the mercy seat, and before the mercy seat.

The Necessity of Sprinkling the Blood

LEV 16:16 And he shall make an atonement for the holy place, because of the uncleanness of the children of Israel, and because of their transgressions in all their sins: and so shall he do for the tabernacle of the congregation, that remaineth among them in the midst of their uncleanness.

Note: Sins were transferred to the sanctuary during the year by the blood and flesh offerings. These sins remained in the sanctuary until the Day of Atonement. Then the high priest went into the Most Holy Place with the blood of the Lord's goat, symbolically bearing the accumulated sins from the whole year. Before the mercy seat, the high priest atoned for the sins of the people. This process symbolically cleansed the sanctuary.

The Scapegoat

LEV 16:20-22 And when he hath made an end of reconciling the holy place, and the tabernacle of the congregation, and the altar, he shall bring the live goat: 21 And Aaron shall lay both his hands upon the head of the live goat, and confess over him all the iniquities of the children of Israel, and all their transgressions in all their sins, putting them upon the head of the goat, and shall send him away by the hand of a fit man into the wilderness: 22 And the goat shall bear upon him all their iniquities unto a land not inhabited: and he shall let go the goat in the wilderness.

Note: The offering of the Lord's goat cleansed the sanctuary. Through that offering all the sins of the people were atoned for (in type). This offering did not "destroy" the sins. The scapegoat (symbolizing Satan) received the "already atoned for sins" upon his head. The sins were forever separated from the sanctuary when the goat was led into the wilderness.

The Earthly Sanctuary was a "Type or Figure" of the Heavenly Sanctuary

HEB 9:9 Which was a figure for the time then present.

Heavenly and Earthly Sanctuaries Related

HEB 8:5 Who serve unto the example and shadow of heavenly things, as Moses was admonished of God when he was about to make the tabernacle: for, See, saith he, that thou make all things according to the pattern shewed to thee in the mount.

Christ as High Priest in the Heavenly Sanctuary

HEB 8:2 A minister of the sanctuary, and of the true tabernacle, which the Lord pitched, and not man.

Note: Upon Christ's ascension in AD 31, His work of High Priest began in the Holy Place (or first apartment) of the Heavenly Sanctuary. At the end of the 2300 years, His priestly work was continued in the Most Holy Place where He began the work of the Investigative Judgment of the righteous dead. (See DAN 7:9-10.) Daniel 9 explains the beginning date of this Heavenly Day of Atonement.

Earthly Sanctuary Services End at Christ's Death

MATT 27:50-51 Jesus, when he had cried again with a loud voice, yielded up the ghost. 51 And, behold, the veil of the temple was rent in twain from the top to the bottom.

Cleansing of the Heavenly Sanctuary

HEB 9:23 It was therefore necessary that the patterns of things in the heavens should be purified with these; but the heavenly things themselves with better sacrifices than these [Christ's sacrifice].

THE JUDGMENT HOUR MESSAGE

Who Must Stand in the Judgment?

2 COR 5:10 For we must all appear before the judgment seat of Christ; that every one may receive the things done in his body, according to that he hath done, whether it be good or bad.

What is the Standard for the Judgment?

JAMES 2:10-12 For whosoever shall keep the whole law, and yet offend in one point, he is guilty of all. 11 For he that said, Do not commit adultery, said also, Do not kill. Now if thou commit no adultery, yet if thou kill, thou art become a transgressor of the law. 12 So speak ye, and so do, as they that shall be judged by the law of liberty.

Counsel Regarding the Judgment

ECCL 12:13-14 Let us hear the conclusion of the whole matter: *Fear God, and keep his commandments:* for this is the whole duty of man. 14 For God shall bring every work into judgment, with every secret thing, whether it be good, or whether it be evil.

Note: Compare Revelation 14:7 which confirms the way to give glory to God is to keep His Commandments through a converted, God dependent heart. While the "judgment-hour message" goes to all the world, the duty of keeping the Commandments is emphasized. (Also see REV14:12.)

Appendix 8D — Secular Historical Events From the 1500s — Present

INDEX

Secular History Comments for Loyola and the Jesuit Order

Note: The verses of Daniel 8:23-25 focus mainly on the spiritual events surrounding God's people under the rule of Papal Supremacy No. 2 or the "king of fierce countenance." Following is a brief review of political/secular, historical events that occurred within the structure of the organized Papal church, beginning in the 1500s under Papal Supremacy No. 1. (Review DAN 7:25 on page 106.)

Loyola

Loyola's Plan in 1534 to Counter the Reformation Through the Jesuit Order

- At first the Papacy underestimated the power of the Protestant Reformation until they saw it spreading quickly from one community to another.
- Ignatius <u>Loyola</u> set up the <u>Jesuit order</u> in 1534. It was sanctioned by the Pope in 1540. The Jesuit members took the role of a subversive military company to combat heresy and counter the Reformation.
- From 1545-1563, the Council of Trent tried to reaffirm the doctrines and traditions of the church by implementing the Inquisition. Corrections included fines, imprisonment, torture, and death.
- Many did recant, but millions gave their lives and furthered the cause of the Reformation. The result of the protests was the separation of the Protestant Church from the Roman Catholic Church.
- These protests were as a "thorn in the side" of the Papacy causing a wound that eventually led to an "apparent" deadly wound for the Papacy in 1798.

Definitions

The Heritage Dictionary of the English Language

"*Jesuit*"   A member of the Society of Jesus, a Roman Catholic order founded by Ignatius Loyola in 1534.

Noah Webster 1828

"*Jesuit*"   1. Pertaining to the Jesuits or their principles and arts. 2. Designing; cunning; deceitful; prevaricating.

Part of Loyola's Ceremony of Induction and Extreme Oath of the Jesuits

"You have been taught to insidiously plant the seeds of jealousy and hatred between communities, provinces and states that were at peace, and incite them to deeds of blood, involving them in war with each other, and to create revolutions and civil wars in countries that were independent and prosperous ... To take sides with the combatants and to act secretly in concert with your brother Jesuit, who might be engaged on the other side, but openly opposed to that with which you might be connected; <u>only that the Church might be the gainer in the end</u>, in the conditions fixed in the treaties for peace <u>and that the end justifies the means</u>."
Library of Congress Catalog Card Number 66-43354. (Emphasis supplied.)

The "Jesuits" — Who are they?

Note: Most people know very little about the Jesuits, also known as the Society of Jesus. This is a very secretive society that functions as the Papacy's secret world-wide police. Every attempt is made to keep their operations out of the public view. Much has been written about this Order, their principles, and their plan.

Reminder: Just after the founding of the Reformation in 1516 by Martin Luther, the Jesuit Order of 1534 was formed by **Ignatius Loyola**. The position of this order was solidified at the Council of Trent (1545-1563) <u>with one great goal: to counter the Protestant Reformation</u>. The Jesuits became the Secret Society of the Roman Catholic Church, to undo and destroy, every trace of Protestantism wherever it was found. It may be said that the Reformation was the beginning of the Papal wound as mentioned in Revelation 13:3, "And I saw one of his heads as it were wounded." This *wound* forced the Jesuits to realize that if the Reformation were not stopped, it would eventually undermine the position of the Catholic Church and destroy the absolute political power and religious authority they had put in place over the centuries.

The Jesuits have two main purposes:
1. To destroy every trace of Protestantism and its principles, relating to religious freedom;
2. To expand the power and control of the Papacy, throughout the entire world, culminating in a New World Order.

Note the following quote:
"I cannot too much impress upon the minds of my readers that the Jesuits, by their very calling, by the very essence of their institution, are bound to seek, by every means, right or wrong, the *destruction of Protestantism*. This is the condition of their existence, the duty they must fulfill, or cease to be Jesuits ... In the first instance, they must be considered as the bitterest enemies of the Protestant faith; in the second, as bad and unworthy priests; and in both cases, therefore, to be equally regarded with aversion and distrust." — G. B. Niccolini, *History of the Jesuits: Their Origin, Progress, Doctrine, and Design,* Henry G. Behn, preface. (Emphasis supplied.)

Secular History Comments for Weishaupt and the Illuminati

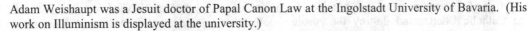

Note: The plan of the Jesuit Order to counter the Reformation was not as successful as anticipated. Following, is a brief review of secular historical events that occurred within the structure of the organized Papal church from the 1700s. This plan was meant to <u>destroy</u> Christianity, not just <u>counter</u> it.

Weishaupt's Plan in 1776 to Destroy Christianity Through the Illuminati

Weishaupt

> .. continued
> he Jesuit oath
> only that the
> Church might
> be the gainer
> n the end …
> nd that the
> nd justifies
> he means."
> *(Part of the
> Jesuit Oath.)*

- Adam Weishaupt was a Jesuit doctor of Papal Canon Law at the Ingolstadt University of Bavaria. (His work on Illuminism is displayed at the university.)
- Weishaupt and his "Inner Circle" were not Atheists; they believed in a god. However, this god was not Jesus Christ, but Lucifer. Communism is an anti-Christian, atheistic force, designed to destroy Christianity and all world governments by modern day Luciferianism.
- Adam <u>Weishaupt</u> determined to wipe out Christianity, not just counter it. His establishment of the <u>Illuminati</u> on May 1, 1776, planned the French Revolution, planted the seeds for Atheism and Communism and lay the foundation to prepare the world to receive the Pope as a world leader. He also lead Jacobinism, founded in 1789.
- The design of this plan was to enlist many world bankers and leaders into its framework. As a result, the French Revolution set up a kingdom based on Atheism (including the concepts of Humanism), which eventually evolved into the political system of Communism.
- This godless kingdom of Atheism in France looked independent, but was fully under the control of the Papal System. Behind the scenes, the Papacy <u>pulled the strings</u>. Today many political and religious leaders are now "puppets" under the masteries of the Papal controlled Secret Societies. (See pages 194, 202, 205, 206 and 207 for some details on Papal Puppets.)

Beginning in the 1600s, the <u>Jesuits created a **communist regime**</u> in Paraguay. This was a test to see if Communism would work. It did!!

Definitions

The Heritage Dictionary of the English Language

"Freemason" 1. A member of a guild of skilled, itinerant masons of the Middle Ages. 2. A member of the Free and Accepted Masons, an international secret fraternity. In this sense, also called "Mason."

Noah Webster 1828

"Jacobin" The *Jacobins,* in France, during the late revolution, were a society of violent revolutionists, who held secret meetings in which measures were concerted to direct the proceedings of the National Assembly. Hence, a *Jacobin* is the member of a club, or other person, who opposes government in a secret and unlawful manner or by violent means; a turbulent demagogue.

"Jacobinism" unreasonable or violent opposition to legitimate government; an attempt to overthrow or change government by secret cabals or irregular means.

"Jacobine" A monk of the order of Dominicans. The Jacobins of France were turbulent; discontented with government, holding democratic principles.

"Dominicans" Dominican Friars, are an order of religious monks, called also *Jacobins,* or Predicants, preaching friars; an order founded about the year 1215.

On May 1, 1776, **Freemason Adam Weishaupt established the Illuminati** which later also became known as **Communism**. Next, his efforts established the French Revolution as a birth mother for Communism. The Jesuits also used Karl Marx to write the *Communist Manifesto* in 1844, which codified the Illuminati's plans. The teachings of Marx were then passed down to Lenin, Stalin, and Trotsky. (Napoleon was also a high degree Freemason carrying out the plans of the Jesuits during the French Revolution.)

During the time of the French Revolution, and the years of Communism, millions of Christians lost their lives through the murderous rages of these men who claimed that there was "no god to worship" except the "Goddess of Reason." Papal Supremacy No. 1 was never able to control the Protestant Reformation. <u>Once the Jesuits were formed, the Papal Plan to destroy Protestantism went underground — working through many Secret Societies</u>. They planned the French Revolution and set up Communism as a means of establishing a New World Order — another way to establish universal dominion. The "iron fist of Rome" has always sought to be in control.

When the Pope was taken captive in 1798 by Napoleon, it "looked like" the Papacy had received a deadly wound. This well-devised smokescreen has deceived the world. Even though it appeared that the "iron and clay" would not mix — the "iron" was still in control as noted in the image of Daniel 2. (More information with historical facts surrounding Napoleon to follow.)

Quotes: The Jesuit / Adam Weishaupt Connection

Review: Who are the Jesuits?

"By the 1550s the Reformation had become so extensive in Europe that the papacy began to realize that they must do something to try to stop it. They realized that if it were not stopped, it would eventually undermine the position of the Catholic Church and destroy the absolute political power they had achieved. In order to accomplish the destruction of the Reformation, a new secret organization was formed within the Vatican called the Jesuits. ... One of the major purposes of the Jesuits was to destroy every trace of Protestantism and its principles, including religious freedom, republicanism, representative government, and an economy built around a strong middle class. Another purpose of the Jesuits was to greatly expand the power and control of the papacy throughout the entire world ... The Jesuits used deception in the extreme to bring about the St. Bartholomew's Day Massacre in 1572, where 70,000 Protestant Huguenots, including women and children, were slain in one night. They also created the 30 Years War from 1618-1648 in order to destroy the Lutherans of Europe. The blood that reddened European soil for centuries can all be traced back to the murderous Jesuits." Bill Hughes, *The Enemy Unmasked,* p. 10.

Review: What is the aim of the Jesuits?

"At what then do the Jesuits aim? According to them, they only seek the greater glory of God; but if you examine the facts you will find that they aim at universal dominion alone. They have rendered themselves indispensable to the Pope, who, without them, could not exist, because Catholicism is identified with them. They have rendered themselves indispensable to governors and hold revolutions in their hands; and in this way, either under one name or another, *it is they who rule the world* ..." Luigi Desanctis, *Popery, Pusyism and Jesuitism,* (London, D. Catt, 1905; translated by Maria Betts from the original Italian edition published as *Roma Papale* in 1865) p. 139. (Emphasis supplied.)

Review: Who Was Adam Weishaupt?

Weishaupt

"During the [Jesuit] Order's suppression from 1773 to 1814 by Pope Clement XIV, General Ricci [the head of the Jesuits] created the Illuminati with his soldier, **Adam Weishaupt**, the Father of modern Communism, who with his Jacobins [Dominican Friars], conducted the French Revolution. ... For the Sons of Loyola punished all their enemies including the Dominican priests, perfected the inner workings between themselves and Freemasonry, created an alliance between the House of Rothschild in establishing the Illuminati. ... The Jesuit General was in control of Scottish Rite Freemasonry and now sought an alliance with the Masonic Baron

of the House of Rothschild. To accomplish this he chose a Jesuit who was a German Gentile (not a Jew) by race and a Freemason by association — Adam Weishaupt. ... *Weishaupt established the Illuminati in [May 1] 1776* and joined the Grand Orient Masonic Lodge in 1777. He united the magnificent financial empire of the Masonic Jewish House of Rothschild with the opulence of the international secret, anti-Jewish Race, Gentile Society of Jesus." Eric Phelps, *Vatican Assassins,* pp. 206, 205, 213, 215. (Emphasis supplied.)

Note: The House of Rothschild financed Weishaupt in his creation of the Illuminati which later became known as Communism. Phelps alluded to this several times in the preceding paragraph. He is not alone in his assertion that the Jewish House of Rothschild worked hand in hand with the Jesuits in creating and funding the Illuminati.

"At that time (1789) France was the richest and most populous nation on the continent of Europe; and it was here that the 'Great Experiment in Democracy' began. The battle cry was 'liberty, equality, and fraternity.' The vehicle was Socialism." Dee Zahner, *The Secret Side of History,* LTAA Communications Publishers, p. 34.

The French Revolution and the Russian Communism Connection

"The French Revolution was a source for communist, anarchist, and socialist conceptions; conceptions that, when carried to conclusion, resulted in the necessity of installing drainage systems to carry away the torrents of blood that flowed from French guillotines. These same 'conceptions' applied during the twentieth century have resulted in the murder of well over one hundred million human beings. There is much to learn from the Great Revolution." — Dee Zahner, *The Secret Side of History,* LTAA Communications, p. 35.

Understanding the "Craftiness" of the Hegelian Principle

Who was Georg Wilhelm Friedrich Hegel

Hegel (1770-1831) was the founder of the Hegelian Principle (or Hegelian Dialectic). In his book, *The Rise and Fall of the Third Reich*, author/historian William Shirer quotes (on page 144) Georg Hegel as saying, "… the State 'has the supreme right against the individual, whose supreme duty is to be a member of the State … for the right of the world spirit is above all special privileges.' " In 1847 Karl Marx and Frederick Engels, of the London Communist League, used Hegel's theory of the dialectic thinking to back up their economic theory of Communism. Today, in the 21st century, the Hegelian-Marxist thinking affects the entire social and political structure of the world. This Hegelian Dialectic Principle is the framework for guiding every individual's thoughts and actions into conflicts that will lead to a predetermined solution. It is extremely important to understand how the Hegelian Dialectic Principle shapes the individual perception in order to implement the ultimate synthesis. Secret Societies, (through the current "king of fierce countenance"), use the Hegelian Principle as one of the elements towards world control.

> DAN 8:23-25 … when the transgressors are come to the full, a king of fierce countenance, and understanding dark sentences, shall stand up. 24 … he shall destroy wonderfully, and shall prosper, and practice … 25 … he shall cause craft to prosper in his hand; and he shall magnify himself in his heart, and by peace shall destroy many …

This is the Hegelian Principle, explained in a few steps:
1. Take two opposing viewpoints;
2. Use Dialectic [argumentative] Thinking;
3. War the one with the other and rub them up against each other until there is nothing left.
4. This is called "Thesis" verses "Antithesis." The resulting clash brings about "Synthesis" — the desired end result. In this way the Secret Societies can be equally active on both sides to bring about the Synthesis — using "craft to prosper." (DAN 8:25)

An example of the Hegelian Philosophy would be:
- First, there is *thesis*, then, *anti-thesis* — these opposites are rubbed together to create a desired *synthesis*.
- Create a problem such as WWI or WWII, with two or more opposing sides.
- Then, out of war, provide stability and World Peace — through the vehicle of the United Nations which has been marketed as a peacekeeping operation.
- Synthesis: The United Nations is accepted in the world, but is slowly changed from a "peacekeeping force" to a "global police force."
- The Masonic (Secret Society) Motto used to describe this philosophy is "Ordo Ab Chao" or "order out of chaos."

This is the principle that is being used worldwide to successfully set up and take down rulers. Papal Rome's ultimate goal is a synthesized New World Order or One World Government, free of all dissenters. Papal Rome believes it has Divine right to use this principle to attain its goal.

Thomas Aquinas (Great Philosopher of the Roman Catholic Church) said:
- "The Pope, by Divine Right, hath spiritual and Temporal Power, as supreme King of the World … the Pope of Rome, as Head of the Papal Government, claims absolute sovereignty and supremacy over all the governments of the earth." Luther S. Kauffman, *Romanism as a World Power,* pp. 30, 31.

Cardinal Henry Manning, 1892, Archbishop of Westminister said:
- "The right of deposing kings is inherent in the supreme sovereignty which the Popes, as vice-regents of Christ exercise over all Christian nations." Hector Macpherson, *The Jesuits in History,* p. 115.

Another quote:
- "Its [the Jesuit Order's] objective was, and still is, to destroy the effects of the Reformation and to re-establish the Holy Roman Empire of the German nation … A Greater Germany, in other words, must be made again the center of a revived Holy Roman Empire." Leo H. Lehmann, *Behind the Dictates,* p. 26.

Many orders of the Secret Societies have successfully used the Hegelian Principle to begin the break down of Protestantism. The ultimate goal is about a New World Order that will rule over all nations and all religious sects. In the latter part of the Dark Ages, the Jesuit Secret Societies craved the power to control the monarchs of Europe, the individual states, and keep the religious expansion of Protestantism under its control. Many times the Jesuit Orders would not be tolerated (even in Roman Catholic countries) and were banned by many kings from their countries. Finally the Jesuits were suppressed during the period of 1773-1814. However, their underground plan directed the Illuminati and Freemasons to set up the godless kingdom of Atheistic France. Events that occurred during that time period were:
1. The Illuminati was raised up in 1776;
2. French Revolution of 1789-1798 was planned in an effort to destroy Christianity, including Catholicism;
3. Dethronement of the Papacy in 1798 — an act to remove it from center stage.

> In the Hegelian Principle it matters not how many of one's own people are sacrificed, as long as the "Synthesis" is achieved and that "the church [system] is the gainer in the end … and that the end justifies the means." *(Part of the Jesuit Oath.)*

Napoleon's Atheistic French Revolution

- Napoleon was the leader in France during the French Revolution beginning approximately 1788-1789.

- **July 14, 1789:** Atheism replaced Catholicism as the faith of the nation. Prelates, priests, and Roman Catholic laity all suffered under this new revolutionary rule.

- The bloody French Revolution destroyed the clergy and religious orders of France. Roman Catholic property was confiscated.

- Some of the clergy of France "flung away their sacred vestments, proclaimed that their whole life had been an imposture, insulted and persecuted the religion of which they had been ministers, and <u>distinguished themselves even in the Jacobin Club</u> and the Commune of Paris, by the excess of their impudence and ferocity." Baron Macauley, *History of the Popes,* 1846, p. 89.

- **1792:** Divorce was established. Atheism determined that *marriage* was a mere civil contract and *could be broken at will* by the parties concerned.

- In 1793, official action was taken to *abolish all religion* in the capital of France. Even though this action was eventually reversed, (1801), it illustrates the influence to which Atheism attained during this period.

- Death was declared an *eternal slumber.* This concept abolished heaven and hell alike.

- In France at this time the Roman Catholic Church was disgracefully corrupt within the realm of church leadership. The people were anxious to shed the yoke of ecclesiastical oppression.

- **1793:** As a result, the Atheists spoke boastful words to abolish all religion and set up the worship of the *Goddess of Reason* as the national religion in France.

- **1793:** The *reign of terror* culminated with the discarding of all Bibles and denying the existence of the Creator God. All churches were closed.

- Atheism spread from France all through Europe taking hold in many Catholic communities. Originally the Reformation had been crushed in France, but now Catholicism was being crushed by Atheism. This was a real *blow* to the Holy See. Ruling Pope Pius VI had no control over rebellious France.

- With Napoleon's rise to power, the Papacy worsened. By 1797, he determined to eliminate the Papal line.

- "When in 1797, Pope Pius VI fell grievously ill, <u>Napoleon gave orders that in the event of his death no successor should be elected to his office, and that the Papacy should be discontinued.</u>" Joseph Rickaby, *Lectures on the History of Religion,* Vol. 3, Lecture 24, p. 1. (Emphasis supplied.)

- Pope Pius VI made a remarkable recovery and chose to celebrate the anniversary of his election, to the sovereignty, on February 10, 1798.

Napoleon — <u>**pushed at**</u> — Pope Pius VI

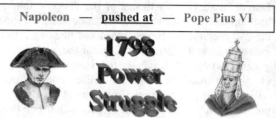

- Napoleon commissioned General Berthier to enter Rome on February 10, <u>1798</u>. Upon arrival he proclaimed a Republic and took the Pope captive back to Valence, France.

- "Berthier entered Rome on the tenth of February, 1798, and proclaimed a republic … Half of Europe thought Napoleon's veto would be obeyed, and that with the Pope the Papacy was DEAD." Rev. Joseph Rickaby, *The Modern Papacy,* p. 1.

- "Whilst he [Pope Pius VI] was according to custom, in the Sistine Chapel, celebrating his accession to the papal chair, and receiving the congratulations of the Cardinals, Citizen Haller, the commissary-general, and Cervoni, who then commanded the French troops within the city, gratified themselves in a peculiar triumph over this unfortunate potentate. During that ceremony they both entered the chapel, and Haller announced to the sovereign Pontiff on his throne, that <u>his reign was at an end</u> … his Swiss guards were dismissed, and Republican soldiers put in their place." Richard Duppa, *A Brief Account of the Subversion of the Papal Government, 1798*, pp. 46, 47. (Emphasis supplied confirms the end of the 1260 year timeline given in Daniel 7:25.)

- The Fifth Kingdom no longer held the "power, seat, and authority." The new emerging kingdom with a "king of fierce countenance" will hold the ruling powers next. At this time most of the Protestants relaxed, believing the Papacy was no longer a threat.

Secular Historical Facts For Napoleon From AD 1798 — 1801

- "The Papacy was extinct: not a vestige of its existence remained and among all the Roman Catholic powers not a finger was stirred in its defense. The Eternal City had no longer prince or pontiff; its bishop was a dying captive in foreign lands, and the decree was already announced that *no successor would be allowed in his place.*" George Trevor, *Rome: From the Fall of the Western Empire,* London: The Religious Tract Society, 1868, p. 440. (Emphasis supplied.)

- **Fact:** Pope Pius VI died in Valence, France on August 29, 1799. By March 14, 1800, (only 197 days later), Pope Pius VII was elected against the former direction of Napoleon.

- "Many of the men in those days [of 1798] imagined that the dominion of the Pope had come to an end, and that the knell of the temporal power was then sounding among the nations. This supposition, however, proved to be erroneous. The French republicans were very anxious that Rome should not have another Pope. But as the reverses of the revolutionary armies had left Southern Italy to its ancient masters, the cardinals were able to proceed to an election at Venice. They elected, on March 14, 1800, Barnabas Chiaromonti, who assumed the name of Pius VII.

"The first transaction of this Pope was a negotiation with the government of France, of which Napoleon Buonaparte, was the First Consul ...

"He [Napoleon] felt that, as the large majority of the inhabitants of France knew no other form of faith than Romanism, it must become the established religion of the country. Accordingly we find that he now began negotiations with the Pope, which issued in a Concordat in July, 1801, whereby the Roman Catholic religion was once more established in France. He also left Pius in possession of his Italian principality." Arthur Robert Pennington, *Epochs of the Papacy,* pp. 450-452. (Emphasis supplied.)

Facts of History

- Joseph Bonaparte (1768-1844) was King of Spain, and a Grand Master. His brother, Napoleon, was also a high degree Freemason and is known for his warring in Europe cleaning up the monarchies that rebelled against Rome during the Protestant Reformation.

- Sometimes the Jesuit Order was banned even in the Roman Catholic countries. e.g. The Jesuit Order was suppressed by Pope Clement XIV from 1773-1814. During this time the Illuminati was raised up to precipitate the French Revolution, dethrone the Papacy, and bring the world one step closer to the New World Order.

Napoleon Bonaparte made this statement: "The Jesuits are a military organization, not a religious order. Their chief is a general of an army, not the mere father abbot of a monastery. **And the aim of this organization is:** POWER. Power in its most despotic exercise. **Absolute power, universal power, power to control the world by the volition of a single man**. *Jesuitism is the most absolute of despotisms; and at the same time the greatest and most enormous of abuses ...* The general of the Jesuits insists on being master, sovereign, over the sovereign. Wherever the Jesuits are admitted they will be masters, cost what it may. Their society is by nature dictatorial, and therefore it is the irreconcilable enemy of all constituted authority. **Every act, every crime, however atrocious, is a meritorious work, if committed for the interest of the Society of Jesuits, or by the order of the general**." — General Montholon, *Memorial of the Captivity of Napoleon at St. Helena,* pp. 62, 174. (Emphasis supplied.)

> In the Hegelian Principle it matters not how many of one's own people are sacrificed, as long as the "Synthesis" is achieved and that "the church [system] is the gainer in the end ... and that the end justifies the means." *(Part of the Jesuit Oath.)*

- "General Ricci created the Illuminati with his soldier Adam Weishaupt, the Father of Modern Communism, who, with his Jacobins, conducted the French Revolution. Years later, Jesuit General Ledochowski, with his Bolsheviks, conducted the Russian Revolution in 1917, it being identical to the upheaval of 1789." G. M. Nicolini of Rome, *History of the Jesuits, Their Origin, Progress, Doctrines and Designs,* pp. 356, 357.

- "The truth is, the Jesuits of Rome have perfected Freemasonry to be their most magnificent and effective tool, accomplishing their purposes among Protestants' ..." John Daniel, *The Grand Design Exposed,* p. 302.

Conclusion: The first godless kingdom brought to the forefront under the manipulation of the Secret Societies, was Atheism in France. By 1801, the "king of fierce countenance" began to surface and rise to prominence with the signing of the Concordat between Pope Pius VII and Napoleon. Its purpose was to re-instate the Roman Catholic religion in place of Atheism. Atheism eventually evolved into Russian Communism. Both these puppet kingdoms were brought to power by use of the Hegelian Principle. Their purpose was to destroy many Christians *and* Roman Catholics that would not fall into line with Roman dogma. At present, the "king of fierce countenance" is still in control through many Secret Societies. (The French Revolution was not only anticlerical but its atheistic philosophy has had *far-reaching effects* in the 19th and 20th centuries.)

Review

- In the 1700s, the Papal power progressively weakened as a result of the spreading of Protestantism. It was a time when the Roman Catholic church and its leadership were very corrupt.

- The Protestant Reformation continues to gain strength and numbers as a result of persecution from the Holy See and its Jesuits.

- The Secret Society of the Jesuits became very strong and was detested by many Catholic countries and their monarchs. The Jesuit Order was suppressed by Pope Clement XIV from 1773-1814.

- During this time period, Adam Weishaupt raised up the Illuminati to precipitate the French Revolution and continue the work of the hated Jesuits.

- This resulted in an exchange of Atheism for Catholicism in France. At the same time the Catholic church was purged of dissenters.

- The Papacy is dethroned by Napoleon in 1798.

- In 1801, Napoleon signs a Concordat with the new Pope (Pius VII) which re-instates the Roman Catholic religion in France. This was a planned transfer of power from the Fifth Kingdom to the Sixth Kingdom.

- The scepter had been successfully passed from Papal Supremacy No. 1 to Papal Supremacy No. 2 — referred to as "king of fierce countenance" in Daniel 8.

- This new Papal "king" works underground with many different Secret Societies in an effort to destroy Protestantism.

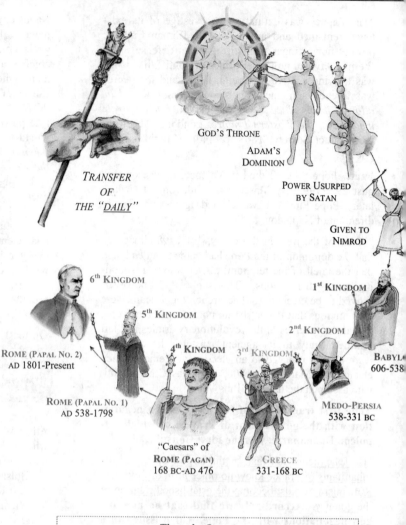

TRANSFER OF THE "*DAILY*"

GOD'S THRONE

ADAM'S DOMINION

POWER USURPED BY SATAN

GIVEN TO NIMROD

1st KINGDOM

2nd KINGDOM

BABYL 606-538

6th KINGDOM

5th KINGDOM

4th KINGDOM

3rd KINGDOM

MEDO-PERSIA 538-331 BC

ROME (PAPAL NO. 2) AD 1801-Present

ROME (PAPAL NO. 1) AD 538-1798

"Caesars" of ROME (PAGAN) 168 BC-AD 476

GREECE 331-168 BC

Thought Questions:

1. Why would Jesuit Weishaupt, set up the Illuminati, to use Freemason Napoleon to wound the Papacy?

2. Why would Napoleon re-instate the Catholic religion in France, signing a Concordat with the new Pope?

3. Was this Papal *wound* a smokescreen to usher in an underground Papal Supremacy No. 2 named as "king of fierce countenance?"

4. How was the Hegelian Dialectic Principle being used then? Today?

Note of Interest: Napoleon was captured by the English and banished to the island of St. Helena. His *Memoirs* describe his masters, the Jesuits.

The "king of fierce countenance" Used "Craft" to Set Up Atheism

*Atheism, Communism,
Godless Nations and
Secret Societies*
A system of world dominion
and control
founded on Luciferian worship.

"The devil is the personification of Atheism or Idolatry."
Albert Pike, *Morals and Dogma*, p. 102.

The Emergence of Atheism
— a Godless Kingdom

- Paganism worshipped *many* gods.

- Arianism denies the divinity of Christ.

- True Biblical Christianity accepts the teachings and divinity of Jesus Christ, the Creator God of heaven and earth.

- Atheism is a disbelief in the existence of deity — the doctrine that there is no deity. This belief system is one of total denial and defiance of any Supreme God. "Atheism is a ferocious system that leaves nothing above us to excite awe, nor around us, to awaken tenderness." Rob Hall. *Noah Webster 1828 Dictionary*.

- The Illuminati used Atheism, through Napoleon and the French government, to bring down Papal Rome No. 1. Atheism is a promoter of:
  1. The theories of evolution;
  2. Exalting man above God and thereby denying the existence of the Creator God;
  3. Worshipping the "Goddess of Reason" which is "Humanism."

Reminder: The ultimate plan of the great deceiver is to set up an antichrist system of Luciferian worship throughout the whole world (New World Order). The ultimate tool of the Papacy is to use the Hegelian Principle to craft this One World Government. In order to succeed with this plan, craft and deceit were used (such as the Hegelian Principle) throughout all systems of world governments. Whether it is realized or not, the Papacy and unsuspecting godless nations, are intricately woven together to bring this plan to pass. Secular history brings on stage the players, or puppets, on the strings of the puppeteer. Observe the Hegelian Principle at work and the frequency of use throughout history.

Eastern Hemisphere Events (Review)

*Atheism as a Puppet
Under the "king of fierce countenance"*

Note: Atheism, as established in France, was the tool used to move the world one step closer to a New World Order or an "image to the beast." Napoleon was one of the many pawns used in the progressive move towards a man-centered, humanistic system that totally denies the power, seat, and authority of Christ (the "daily" of DAN 8:11). Intended result: When the power, seat, and authority of Jesus Christ is destroyed, through humanism — and Christ is brought down to being just another man, the salvation message presented in the Sanctuary typology explodes and becomes meaningless. All becomes a denial of Christ and His deity.

"At that time (1789) France was the richest and most populous nation on the continent of Europe; and it was here that the 'Great Experiment in Democracy' began. The battle cry was 'liberty, equality, and fraternity.' The vehicle was Socialism." Dee Zahner, *The Secret Side of History*, p. 34.

The Strong Will of Napoleon in France

- Napoleon of France did what he wanted and threatened to do. He entered the Vatican and took the Pope off his throne in 1798.

- Even though this was a plan from "inside the Secret Society," Napoleon acted out the taking of "power, seat, and authority" away from the Papacy. This action moved the Pope off the stage and into the background where the Papacy could work with craft and deception.

The Exaltation of Napoleon

- In taking the Pope captive, Napoleon exalted and magnified himself above the Pope.

- The "Goddess of Reason" was set up in the vacancy left. This is the beginning of Humanism.

- This paves the way for the ultimate plan to set up a Fascist New World Order which is a system based on Luciferianism.

Atheism Introduces Many New Changes to France

- God's gospel and sanctuary message of truth was cast down; Bibles were burned.

- Times and Laws were changed: The seven day week was changed to a ten day week. God's institution of marriage was disregarded and divorce permitted.

- The whole system speaks of the glorification of mankind.

Thesis + Antithesis = Synthesis

Thesis: Established Monarchs of Europe
+
Antithesis: Napoleon and French Revolution
=
Synthesis: Napoleonic Kingdom to Control Europe and to Lay the Groundwork for Communism and the Next "Synthesis" Struggle

The Fury in France

- "The French Revolution was a source for communist, anarchist, and socialist conceptions; conceptions that, when carried to conclusion, resulted in the necessity of installing drainage systems to carry away the torrents of blood that flowed from French guillotines. These same 'conceptions' applied during the twentieth century have resulted in the murder of well over one hundred million human beings. There is much to learn from the Great Revolution." Dee Zahner, *The Secret Side of History*, p. 35.

- "History books will tell us that the French Revolution first began in 1787 or 1789, depending on which book you read. However, it was actually planned by Dr. Adam Weishaupt and the House of Rothschild almost 20 years before the Revolution took place." William Sutton, *The New Age Movement and The Illuminati 666*, pp. 172, 173.

Note: Atheism was fulfilled in France — but this was just the beginning of Lucifer's kingdom. What happened in France is a forerunner of what will happen in the near future throughout the whole world.

1. The French Revolution set up a new standard called the Manifesto of Human Rights.
2. After the French Revolution and Papal wound of 1798, the Papacy became insignificant in the eyes of Protestants.

What happened to Napoleon? He was used as a pawn until not needed anymore! The circumstances around the Battle of Waterloo in June 1815 explain how the Jesuits used the country of Britain, and other events, to gain control over Britain and its financial market. (See: "Rothschild Strategy at Waterloo" in Appendix 8E, page 214.)

France was in its prime in 1798 when the United States was founding a Republic on a set of laws that govern what the majority can, and cannot do. The USA Republic is based on the Constitution. The word "democracy" cannot be found in the Constitution, or in the Declaration of Independence.

1798
Atheism Dethrones Papacy

Weishaupt was a major player in setting up the Atheistic puppet kingdom. The "king of fierce countenance" briefly passes the scepter of power to his Atheistic pawn, to rule with the fist of iron.

> **DAN 8:23, 25** ... a king of fierce countenance, and understanding dark sentences ... shall cause craft to prosper in his hand ...

Western Hemisphere Events (New)

- **July 1, 1776** — Declaration of Independence and signing of the Constitution in the USA was based on the ideas of a Republic, not a Democracy. They are different!

- Charles Chiniquy says: "Long before I was ordained a priest, I knew that my church was the most implacable enemy of this republic. My professors ... had been unanimous in telling me that the principles and laws of the Church of Rome were absolutely antagonistic to the principles which are the foundations stones of the Constitution of the United States of America." Charles Chiniquy, *Fifty Years in the Church of Rome*, p. 283.

- "The Vatican condemned the Declaration of Independence as 'wickedness' ... and called the Constitution of the United States 'a Satanic document.' " Avro Manhattan, *The Dollar and the Vatican*, p. 26.

- **1791** — Bill of Rights (Note the First Amendment to the Constitution:)

> **Congress shall make no law respecting an establishment of religion, or prohibiting the free exercise thereof; or abridging the freedom of speech, or of the press; or the right of the people peaceably to assemble, and to petition the government for a redress of grievances.**

- **1832** — Skull and Bones Order Founded at Yale. (On the surface this is just an exclusive fraternity. In reality, this order is an entry point into the Illuminati.)

Napoleon and Pope Pius VII

- The Papal wound of 1798 took the Papacy off the stage.
- Pope Pius VII was elected soon after the death of Pope Pius VI.
- Pope Pius VII began his reign by taking very bold steps to secure a satisfactory settlement with his French enemy.
- The plan was successful with the signing of the 1801 Concordat which allowed Catholicism back into Atheistic France.
- The action of this restoration was to demonstrate to Papal successors that prestige and influence could be recovered and exert Roman Catholic influence on these territories.
- Papal States had been devastated by France, Austria, and Naples. Pius VII requested that France, Austria, and Naples evacuate the Papal territories. France totally ignored this request.
- Even though the 1801 Concordat placed Roman Catholicism back into France as the state religion, Napoleon, in 1802, greatly restricted Papal intervention in the church affairs of France.
- However, Napoleon's next move was interesting. He invited Pius VII to attend his coronation as Emperor in Notre Dame Cathedral in Paris on December 2, 1804 and perform the coronation.
- Pius VII agreed to this request which proved to be a great humiliation. Just as he was about to crown the new Emperor, Napoleon snatched the crown from the Pope's hands and crowned himself.
- By 1809 Pius VII had commenced a five year-period of confinement. It was quite apparent that Napoleon was not reluctant to use his military power in settling disputes.
- Napoleon demanded that the Papal States assist France in blocking England. The Papacy did not cooperate, so Napoleon sent his forces to occupy Rome. By May 1809, the Papal States were captured.

Napoleon — **pushed at** — Pope Pius VII

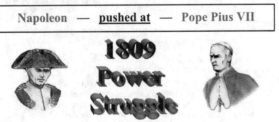

- Napoleon incurred the wrath of Pope Pius VII and was excommunicated. This was all that was needed for Napoleon to arrest Pope Pius VII in 1809. The Pope was eventually imprisoned in 1812 at Fontainbleau, just southeast of Paris.
- Pope Pius VII became ill and discouraged. In January 1813 he signed the Concordat of Fountainbleau where he renounced control over the Papal States. These Papal States were surrendered to France — another Papal wound.
- Between 1804-1813, Napoleon had taken France to a position of supremacy in Europe. By **1806** Napoleon's confederation was so well established, that it put an end to the Holy Roman Empire and brought most of Germany under his control. By **1808** Napoleon was master of all Europe except Russia and Britain.
- By **1814**, the major powers of Prussia, Russia, Britain, and Austria defeated Napoleon's plans to engulf all of Europe in his realm. He was deposed and exiled to the island of Elba. Louis XVIII was made the ruler of France.
- The Congress of Vienna, in September **1814**, met to discuss the problems that were rising from the defeat of France and to redistribute the territories in Europe. However, while this Congress was still in session in February **1815**, Napoleon escaped from Elba and returned to France.
- With the aid of former veterans, Napoleon again ascended the throne of France in March **1815**. The Congress of Vienna was very alarmed and made plans to invade France on July 1 of that year.
- Napoleon's reaction to the decision of this Congress was to attack. This began the Battle of Waterloo, which ended in defeat of Napoleon on **June 18, 1815**. His troops were no match for Prussia, Russia, Austria, and Britain. This battle was the final and decisive action of the Napoleonic Wars. It effectively ended French domination of Europe and brought about drastic changes in political boundaries. This battle was a great turning point in modern history.
- _But, that's not the end of the story_! Below are two important quotes that site another side of history; that of the Jesuits. Consider the Hegelian Dialectic Principle that was successfully used during the years of Napoleon's reign.
- "Weishaupt and his fellow Jesuits cut off the income to the Vatican by launching and leading the French Revolution; by directing Napoleon's conquest of Catholic Europe; [and] ... by eventually having Napoleon throw Pope Pius VII in jail at Avignon until he agreed, as the price of his release, to reestablish the Jesuit Order. This Jesuit war on the Vatican was terminated by the congress of Vienna and by the secret, 1822, Treaty of Verona." Emanuel M. Josephson, _The Federal Reserve Conspiracy and Rockefellers,_ pp. 4, 5. (Emphasis supplied.)
- "After Pope Pius VII was released from Napoleon's prison he formally restored the Jesuit order with a Papal Bull in 1814." Ian R. Paisley, _The Jesuits,_ pp. 9, 10. (See Appendix 8E, page 214, regarding Rothschild's Strategy at the Battle of Waterloo.)

Karl Marx Combines Atheism and the Hegelian Principle AD 1848

Karl Marx
Rise of Communism and
"Marxism"
"Communist Manifesto"
AD 1848

1848: Karl Marx first published his pamphlet on Communism called *"Communist Manifesto."* This pamphlet updated and codified the very same revolutionary plans and principles set down seventy years earlier by Adam Weishaupt, the founder of the Order of the Illuminati in Bavaria. Marxism tells the poor that if they would establish a dictatorship of the proletariat, (setting up a classless Communist society) everyone would live in peace, prosperity, and freedom. There would be no more need for governments, police, or armies — which naturally sounded good to the poor and starving. This was the beginning of the rise of Communism worldwide — the natural extension of Napoleon's "Atheism" in France. However, the working people weren't told that the Communist leaders would be exempt from equally sharing the wealth of their nation. The Communist Party is a front for the super-rich, an instrument to gain and use power. Who is really behind this system?

- "Karl Marx, 'the Father of Modern Communism' ... was privately tutored by Jesuits in the huge Reading Room of the British Museum while writing *The Communist Manifesto* based upon the ten maxims or 'planks' the Order had perfected on its Paraguayan Reductions ... <u>A Jew was chosen for this task; for, the Order anticipated blaming all the evils of their Communist Inquisition on the Jewish Race.</u>" Eric Phelps, *Vatican Assassins,* p. 293. (Emphasis supplied.)

Definitions

Heritage Illustrated Dictionary of the English Language

"Marx" (Karl). 1818-1883. German philosopher and political economist; founder of world Communism.

"Marxism" The political and economic ideas of Karl Marx and Friedrich Engels as developed into a system of thought that gives class struggle a primary role in leading society from bourgeois democracy under capitalism to a socialist society and thence to communism.

"Communist Manifesto" A pamphlet, issued (February 1848) by Karl Marx and Friedrich Engels, constituting the first statement of the principles of modern Communism.

"Manifesto" A public declaration of principles or intentions, especially of a political nature.

"Communism" A system characterized by the absence of social classes and by common ownership of production means.

Atheism had spread quickly from France all through Europe. Atheism —

- " ... became conqueror in its turn; and not satisfied with the Belgian cities, went raging over the Rhine and through the passes of the Alps ... Spain was now the obsequious vassal of the infidels. Italy was subjugated to them." Baron Macauley, *History of the Popes,* pp. 89, 90.

The political arm of Atheism emerged and grew as men, such as Karl Marx, (early 1800s), studied the French Revolution and Hegel's idea of the Hegelian Dialectic Principle. In 1847 the London Communist League (Marx and Frederick Engels) used Hegel's theory of the dialectic to back up their economic theory of Communism. Marx's ideas were in turn picked up by Lenin, Trotsky, and Stalin. An example of Marx's theory can be shown as follows: *(From: www.calvertonschool.org/waldspurger/pages/hegelian_dialectic)*

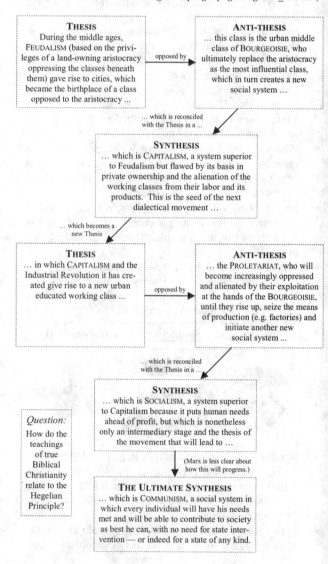

196

The "king of fierce countenance" Uses "Craft" on the USA

The War Against the USA Constitution and its Leaders

- "Two years after the Constitution of the United States was ratified, the Jesuits carried out their principles of government in the French Revolution. These two antagonistic forms of government were laid open for all the world to see. The constitution guaranteed Republican government where the government was founded on law, and every citizen was equal before the law. In France, however, the great cry was for democracy." Bill Hughes, *The Enemy Unmasked,* p. 32. (Emphasis supplied.)

- "Protestantism must therefore be utterly abolished … Catholics shall be imbued with hatred for all heretics [A heretic is anyone who does not believe the Catholic religion, anyone who opposes the Pope, and anyone who believes the Pope is the anti-Christ] … We shall strike deadly blows at heresy … They little think that Jesuits have in store for them the censorship gags and flames and will one day be their masters." Hector Macpherson, *The Jesuits in History,* Appendix 1.

- "Liberty of conscience is proclaimed by the United States a most sacred principle, which every citizen must uphold … But liberty of conscience is declared by all the popes and councils of Rome, a most godless, unholy, and diabolical thing, which every good Catholic must abhor and destroy at any cost." Charles Chiniquy, *Fifty Years in the Church of Rome,* p. 284.

- "We will rule the United States, and lay them at the feet of the vicar of Jesus Christ [the Pope], that he may put an end to their Godless system of education, and *impious laws of liberty of conscience which are an insult to God and man."* Charles Chiniquy, *Fifty Years in the Church of Rome,* p. 282. (Emphasis supplied.)

The "king of fierce countenance" reasserted its authority over nations and all of mankind, in the following quote by Pius XI. The 1925 encyclical, *Quas primas,* declared that the Roman Catholic Church —

- " … not only symbolizes the definitive reign of God over the universe, but actuates, if by gradual degrees, the sovereignty of Christ in the world, including men and peoples to its laws of justice and peace."

Peter de Rose reported that, "… Pope Leo XIII said that politically 'it is always urgent, indeed, the chief preoccupation, to think *how best to serve the interests of Catholicism."* *Vicars of Christ,* p. 208. (Emphasis supplied.)

Western Hemisphere Events

(Attacks on the USA)

- **1835:** Attempted assassination on <u>President Jackson</u> for overriding the plans for a Central Bank in the USA.

- **1841:** <u>President William Harrison</u> poisoned for declaring that the United States would not submit to the Pope's control.

- **1850:** <u>President Zachary Taylor</u> poisoned for speaking passionately about preserving the Union rather than having it split in two.

- **1857:** <u>President James Buchanan</u> survived attempted poisoning for making his intention known regarding the question of Slavery in the Free States — to the satisfaction of the people in those States.

- **1865:** <u>President Abraham Lincoln</u> assassinated for his presidential loyalty to the Constitution and for being the defense lawyer for Father Charles Chiniquy. Chiniquy had been attacked in a series of court cases by the Bishop of the Chicago Diocese for speaking out on the evils of liquor abuse by the priests. At the same time, assassination attempts were made on William Seward, Ulysses S. Grant, and vice-president Andrew Johnson to bring the US government into total chaos.

- **Later in 1912:** Destruction of the Titanic for those on board that opposed the Federal Reserve System.

This map illustrates the general godless nations [in green] and Protestant nations [in light yellow] of the world today. Once the Papacy gains control over all the godless nations, it will not be difficult to have complete rule of the remaining Protestant nations, bringing ALL together under a united world religion.

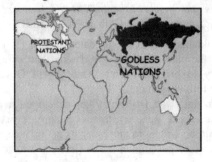

Secular History Link: Albert Pike Uses "Craft" in AD 1871

The Prologue on pages 7-10 explain that there is a great controversy between two systems on this planet — good and evil. Beginning in heaven, Lucifer desired to secure worship that belonged only to God. As a result, Lucifer [Satan] and his followers were banished to earth. In the form of a serpent, Satan began to work his evil system through mankind — coveting the worship which Adam and Eve gave to the Creator God. This has been Satan's plan all through the ages — to have all of mankind on this earth worshipping only him.

Secular history records how Loyola established the Jesuit order in 1534 to counter the Reformation. Just two hundred years later in 1776, former Jesuit Weishaupt formed a Secret Society called the Illuminati, whose mandate was to completely destroy every trace of Protestantism. Satan has been very successful in working through these societies, infiltrating practically every political and religious entity in the world. The Jesuits aim is universal domination.

> "At what then do the Jesuits aim? According to them, they only seek the greater glory of God; but if you examine the facts you will find that they aim at universal dominion alone. They have rendered themselves indispensable to the Pope, who, without them, could not exist, because Catholicism is identified with them. They have rendered themselves indispensable to governors and <u>hold revolutions in their hands</u>; and in this way, either under one name or another, <u>it is they who rule the world</u> …" Luigi Desanctis, *Popery, Puseyism & Jesuitism,* (London, D. Catt, 1905; translated by Maria Betts from the original Italian edition published as *Roma Papale* in 1865) p. 139. (Emphasis supplied.)

Who was Albert Pike?

Albert Pike was a known Satanist and leading Freemason. His plan was to foment three world wars with the third and final war leading the way for the introduction of a new global faith or religion, that would have Lucifer as its focus. In the 19th century

Pike

Pike wrote out a blueprint of events that would play themselves out in the 20th century thereby bringing about a One World Government. Pike was deeply involved in Freemasonry. One of the major sourcebooks of masonic doctrine is *Morals and Dogma of the Ancient and Accepted Scottish Rite of Masonry* written by Albert Pike in 1871.

Albert Pike had written a letter dated August 15, 1871 that outlined the plans for three world wars that were seen as necessary to bring about the One World Government. Note the following quote:

- "Mazzini, with [Albert] Pike, developed a plan for three world wars so that eventually every nation would be willing to <u>surrender its national sovereignty</u> to a world government. The **first** war was to end the Czarist regime in Russia, and the **second** war was to allow the Soviet Union to control Europe. The **third** world war was to be in the Middle East between Moslems and Jews and would result in Armageddon." *Now is The Dawning of the New Age New World Order* (Hearthstone Publishing, Ltd. 1991), p. 42. (Emphasis supplied.)

What is the "missing piece" of the puzzle?

Because Napoleon was a Freemason, he was under the control of the Jesuit Order. So, who sent Napoleon to Rome to take the Pope captive? <u>The Jesuit Order!</u> Why?

At this time there were numerous secret orders within the Roman Catholic church that did not exist in perfect harmony. In fact, the Jesuit order slowly took control of all the other orders. Tremendous tension was created when the Papacy took the Inquisition away from the Jesuits and gave it to the Dominicans. In the French Revolution it was the Dominican Order that was destroyed — not the Jesuits. There were also other issues in the church that had to be sorted out. At the Council of Trent (1545-1563) many Roman Catholics stood up and said, "The Word and the Word alone!" Not everything in the Roman Catholic church has been negative towards the Word even though Luther had had a tremendous impact within the walls of the church. During his time, there had been many that were not "in line" with Papal church dogma. The church itself needed to be purged of dissenters!

There was **another problem**. The Reformation had fingered Rome as the anti-christ. Hence, any move that seemed to be emanating from Rome would be looked upon with suspicion. **Rome's Solution?** Why not destroy the Papacy (apparently) and then resurrect it <u>and</u> at the same time purge it of everything that is contrary <u>and</u> finally resurrect a power that is in complete control of these organizations. **Rome's Desired Outcome?** <u>Then</u> anything that happened thereafter "with the weak little Papacy over there" would be disregarded. Certainly, any distasteful events could not come from the Papacy? — it has to come from elsewhere! (That is how the Secret Societies worked — and their plan met with great success! They worked behind many fronts, in extreme secrecy.) **Result:** The Protestants literally relaxed and were put off guard. Atheism and Communism were easily set up <u>as the beginning of a godless kingdom under Papal control</u> to persecute and help destroy Protestants without any blame being placed on the Papacy. Behind the scenes, the Papal "king of fierce countenance" was in full control through the use of Secret Societies.

> Satan's plan to work through earthly leaders and godless systems, constantly moves steadily forward "only that the Church [system] might be the gainer in the end … and that the end justifies the means." *(Part of the Jesuit Oath.)*

The "king of fierce countenance" Continues to Use "Craft to Prosper"

The Emergence of Atheistic-Communism — Another Godless Kingdom

Historical Note: The plan of the great deceiver continued as Atheism moved eastward and later culminated in the Communist Bolshevik Revolution of 1917. Communist Russia was determined to crush out all forms of religion.

Marx

Karl Marx's pamphlet *(Communist Manifesto)* updated and codified the very same revolutionary plans and principles set down seventy years earlier by Adam Weishaupt. The Hegelian Principle of thesis/antithesis was used successfully to implement Communism. Marx's teachings were in turn passed to Lenin, Trotsky, and Stalin. At this time in Russia, the Czars were the "protectorate" of the Orthodox church. Since the year AD 1054, the Papacy had been waging war against the Orthodox Christians to bring them into line. (See DAN 11:24 on page 293 regarding the beginning of the Easter Controversy.)

- "One may say quite specifically that in 1914, the Roman Catholic Church started the series of hellish wars [in Russia]." Edmund Paris, *The Vatican Against Europe,* p. 14.

Finally, in 1917, the last Czar, and all his family were murdered. Never again would an Emperor from the House of the Romanoff rule Russia or protect the Orthodox Church.

- "The overthrow of the Czarist system therefore, brought with it the inevitable overthrow of the established Orthodox Church. To the Vatican, which had waged war against the Orthodox Church since the eleventh century, the downfall of her millenarian rival was too good to be true." Avro Manhattan, *The Vatican Billions,* pp. 120, 121.

How was the Russian revolution financed and who backed Lenin, Trotsky, and Stalin as they created revolution and bloodshed throughout Russia? (See Appendix 8E, pages 220, 223.)

Lenin   Trotsky   Stalin

- "The instruments of this new alliance between the Soviets and the Vatican were to be the Jesuits, described as the hereditary enemies of the Orthodox Church. Reportedly, there were large numbers of representatives of the Jesuit Order in Moscow during the Revolution." James Zatko, *Descent into Darkness,* p. 111.

> **DAN 8:23, 25** ... a king of fierce countenance, and understanding dark sentences ... shall cause craft to prosper in his hand ... "only that the Church [system] might be the gainer in the end ... and that the end justifies the means." *(Part of the Jesuit Oath.)*

Eastern Hemisphere Events
Atheistic-Communism as a Puppet Under the "king"
The Overthrow of Religion

- The people of Russia were taught to worship the state — a very unusual and strange god.
- In Russia, even Catholic Christians were destroyed to further the aims of the church. (See Appendix 8E, top of page 217.) Also note the following quote:
- "Among the 1,766,188 victims up to the beginning of 1922, figures obtained from the Soviet documents, nearly five thousand were priests, teachers, nuns, etc. of the Orthodox Church ... Nearly 100,000 Lutherans banished ... Whole villages were wiped out ... Thousands of churches of the different branches have been demolished and the work of destruction goes on ..." Arno Gaebelien, *Conflict of the Ages,* pp. 103-106.

The Destruction of the Family

- In Atheism, the family was downplayed with France's introduction of divorce.
- Modern day Protestant countries are now promoting, and allowing, same-sex marriages through the Gay Rights Movement.

> **MATT 19:5-6** For this cause shall a man leave father and mother, and shall cleave to his wife ... 6 What therefore God hath joined together, let not man put asunder.

- This destruction of the marriage unit, is man's attempt at changing the times and laws of God's perfect plan for humanity. The following Scriptures indicate that men of the Old Testament had understanding of *times* and *laws*.

> **1 CHRON 12:32** And of the children of Issachar, which were men that had understanding of the times, to know what Israel ought to do ...

> **DEUT 32:28** For they are a nation void of counsel, neither is there any understanding in them.

Note: How did Atheism begin in France and culminate in Russia? After the French Revolution, the philosophy of Atheism began to grow and be refined. The government of France moved away from Atheism as the fundamental principle of its philosophy of government when Napoleon signed a Concordat in 1801 with Pope Pius VII restoring Catholicism in France. Atheism spread across parts of Europe and the world, gaining a foothold in the government of Russia and other countries. By 1917 the "king of fierce countenance" was re-established and continued its ongoing battle against the forces of Biblical Christianity.

Vladmir Lenin
USSR Communism
Continues to Rise through the
"Bolshevik Revolution" in Russia
AD 1903 — 1917

The Birth of Communism

"Adam Weishaupt and the Rothschild family created the Illuminati. Then both Wesihaupt and the Rothschilds united their efforts to <u>foment the French Revolution and the roots of Communism. The Jesuits next used Karl Marx to write the Communist Manifesto, which codified the Illuminati's plans. The teachings of Marx were then passed to Lenin, Stalin, and Trotsky."</u> Bill Hughes, *The Enemy Unmasked,* p. 32. (Emphasis supplied.)

As Atheism moved eastward, it culminated in the Bolshevik Revolution of AD 1917, forming the Atheistic-Communist USSR. That nation was determined to crush out all forms of religion, declaring it to be the "opiate of the people."

Vladmir Lenin (1870-1924) was a Russian revolutionary statesman, the founder of Bolshevism and the major force behind the Russian Revolution of October 1917. The USSR was formed in 1922, with Lenin as the first premier from 1918-1924. (The Bolshevik Party was financed by Capitalists from America, England, and Germany to promote the Russian Revolution. Later the Bolshevik Party was renamed as the Communist Party.)

Definitions

Heritage Illustrated Dictionary of the English Language

"*Leninism*" The theory and practice of proletarian revolution as developed by Lenin.

"*Marxism-Leninism*" The expansion of Marxism to include Lenin's concept of imperialism as the final form of capitalism, and a shift in the focus of struggle from the developed to the underdeveloped countries.

"*Bolshevik*" **1. a.** A participant in the Russian Revolution belonging to the Communist Party of the Soviet Union. **b.** A member of the left-wing majority group of the Russian Social Democratic Party adopting Lenin's theses on party organization (1903). (Note: The Bolsheviks sought to bring down the government and replace it with a so-called "dictatorship of the proletariat" — in other words, a government ruled by the Bolsheviks on behalf of Russia's industrial workers and peasants.)

"*Bolshevism*" **1.** The strategy developed by the Bolsheviks between 1903 and 1917 with a view to seizing state power and establishing the dictatorship of the proletariat. **2.** Soviet Communism.

"*Proletariat*" **1. a.** The class of industrial wage earners who, possessing neither capital nor production means, must earn their living from their labor power. **b.** Marxists' name for the poorest class of working people. **2.** The non-possessing class of ancient Rome constituting the lowest class of citizens.

"*Proletarian*" Of, pertaining to, or characteristic of the proletariat. —n. A member of the proletariat. From Latin *proletarius,* Roman citizen of the lowest class (who serves the state only by producing offspring).

Leon Trotsky
USSR Communist Revolutionist
and Soviet Statesman
AD 1903 — 1917

- Trotsky was a fanatical supporter of Marxism and Darwinism.
- Trotsky believed the building of socialism could begin in Russia alone. He joined the Bolsheviks in 1917 when he saw they were agreeing with Lenin's call for an insurrection and was militarily and organizationally important in organizing the 1917 revolution.
- After the revolution, Trotsky took over the Red Army and used them to crush out any enemies of the Soviet State and establish the revolution.
- Trotsky argued that the working class could rise directly after the fall of an imperial ruling class. He believed that a revolution in Russia would constitute the first step in a revolution that would spread in stages to the entire world.
- Trotsky formed the Left Opposition after Stalin seized the leadership of the Party but was ousted for his opposition to Communist Party leader Stalin in 1925. He was deported by Stalin and assassinated in 1940.

Definition

Heritage Illustrated Dictionary of the English Language

"*Trotskyism*" — The theories of Communism advocated by Leon Trotsky and his followers, who argued for worldwide revolution and bitterly opposed the leadership of Stalin.

"From the days of Adam Weishaupt to Karl Marx, to those of Trotsky, … this world-wide conspiracy has been steadily growing. This conspiracy has played a definitely recognizable role in the tragedy of the French Revolution. It has been the mainspring of every subversive movement during the 19th century; and now at last, this band of extraordinary personalities from the underworld of the great cities of Europe and America have gripped the Russian people by the hair of their heads, and have become practically the undisputed masters of that enormous empire." Winston Churchill, *Illustrated Sunday Herald,* February 8, 1920.

Secular Historical Facts For Stalin From AD 1929 — 1953

History of Russia's Conquests

Many countries came under the control of this puppet kingdom through revolution. Communism's design was to infiltrate, indoctrinate, and bring about a revolution. Most of the countries which were brought into Russia had previously been Catholic-dominated nations. As a result, Catholicism began to loose its power base.

As Communist revolutions spread over the world, the Papacy was provided with a tool in Russia. As a common enemy to themselves and an (USA) ally in the Western Hemisphere, the way was prepared for strong alliances. The way has now been opened for the "king of fierce countenance" to work through the arm of Communism in Russia.

Joseph Stalin
"Man of Steel" in Russia
USSR Communism
is Well Established
AD 1929 — 1953

- Stalin became an Atheist upon reading the works of Charles Darwin. With God out of his way, he had no restrictions of conscience or morals. Darwin's ideas shaped Stalin's approach to society in a powerful way.
- Stalin was always a supporter of Lenin from the beginning, and politically prominent in the 1917 revolution.
- Stalin believed in 'Revolution in one country' by establishing power in Russia first, and then perhaps conquering the world. He took control of the USSR after the death of Lenin.
- Stalin was utterly ruthless in the pursuit of power and ruled with an "iron fist" for 24 years. He became one of the most influential totalitarian dictators of the 20th century.
- Stalin, through war, defeated Hitler; established Communist regimes throughout eastern Europe; and was responsible for the death of millions of people, including Leon Trotsky.
- Under Stalin, many people lived in fear of his totalitarian regime.
- Stalin was in power when the Cold War began in 1945.

Description of the USSR, Under the
Sixth Kingdom of "king of fierce countenance"

Size: The USSR was a very large kingdom under Papal control. From west to east it covered 11 of the 24 time zones.

Expansion: The USSR also had an objective to rule the entire world. From Russia, Communism spread quickly to many parts of the world.

- Its military attempted to push into Europe. The Berlin airlift stopped its intrusion into Germany.
- Sweden prevented its extension from Finland into Scandinavian countries.
- The USA protected its Alaskan borders, the North Pole, and Canadian lands by setting up the DEW line in which planes were in the air 24 hours a day, year after year. The entire western world was threatened.
- Communism entered Cuba and pushed into Central and South America. Most of east and north Africa, except Kenya, was affected.
- The USSR finally sent up Sputnik.
- No puppet kingdom before it had achieved such great expansion and even began to push into outer space.

Ideology: The worth of the individual is the cornerstone of democracy, and was instituted by Christianity.

- Contrary to these ideals, Atheistic Communism places all individuals in subjugation to the state.
- (Where the military could not penetrate, subversive groups spread the ideology of Communism as in Central and South America, and China. A Communist party was even formed in the USA.)

Persecution: Prophecy always centers around God's people. Daniel's prophecies, and secular history, show how all the kingdoms were persecutors of God's people including the USSR puppet.

- The USSR harassed Christians, used their churches for other purposes, sent them to prison or to work in the mines in Siberia, and put many of them to death.
- Atheism was the forced religion of the state. Failure to comply with the rules of the state resulted in the death of millions.

Thesis + Antithesis
= Synthesis

Thesis: Czarist Monarchy in Russia
+

Antithesis: Karl Marx's *Communist Manifesto,*
Lenin, Trotsky, Stalin, Russian Revolution
=

Synthesis: Establishment of Communist Russia
to Lay the Groundwork for the Next
"Synthesis" Struggle
Which in Turn, Progressively Moves Mankind
Towards a New World Order

1917
Overthrow of
Orthodox Church and
Communism Set Up

Who is Magnified in Russia?

"The Papacy through godless kingdoms has complete control over land, commerce, people, beliefs, education, medicine and pharmacy, media, politics, sports, etc. 'The pope is the ruler of the world. All the emperors, all the kings, all the princes, *all the presidents of the world are as these altar boys of mine'.*" Priest D. S. Phelan, *Western Watchman,* June, 27, 1912.

Note: Even though Atheism, Communism, and all the godless nations include most of the world's population today, God's faithful remnant are found scattered throughout all the nations. At the appointed time, the Shepherd will call His sheep out of every system of Babylon.

JOHN 10:16 And other sheep I have, which are not of this fold: them also I must bring, and they shall hear my voice; and there shall be one fold, and one shepherd.

JOHN 6:37 All that the Father giveth me shall come to me; and him that cometh to me I will in no wise cast out.

REV 3:20-21 Behold, I stand at the door, and knock: if any man hear my voice, and open the door, I will come in to him, and will sup with him, and he with me. 21 To him that overcometh will I grant to sit with me in my throne, even as I also overcame, and am set down with my Father in his throne.

Reminder: France and Russia were the first two main godless kingdoms that came onto the stage, after 1798. As time progresses, other godless nations became more powerful and influential. The map below illustrates only the Kingdom of Communist Russia. However, if all Communist Kingdoms were included on the map, a large portion of the earth's land masses would have to be included, such as — Eastern Europe, Asia, Central and South America, the Caribbean, and Africa. Communism became a mighty worldwide force against the true church of God. Meanwhile, the western, industrialized world is moving quickly towards the glorification of "self" — a characteristic of Satan found in Isaiah 14 — the epitome of godlessness.

Atheism evolved into Communism and eventually controlled eleven time zones of the world, spreading everywhere at an alarming rate. Ultimately, it became a world power, threatening the other nations of the world. In Communism, man's dignity was destroyed. His inalienable right to worship the Creator God was totally disregarded. Russia invested a large portion of its wealth in the military and the space program in an effort to rule the world. This set the stage for the next thesis/antithesis struggle between the East and the West — the ultimate synthesis is a New World Order.

Maps Define the Progression of Godless Kingdoms

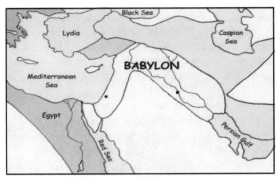

1st Kingdom   606 — 538 BC

2nd Kingdom   538 — 331 BC

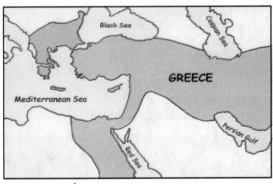

3rd Kingdom   331 — 168 BC

4th Kingdom   168 BC — AD 476

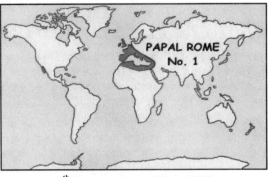

5th Kingdom   AD 538 — 1798

6th Kingdom   AD 1801 — Present

**Current Transition Between the 6th & 7th Kingdoms
of Atheistic-Communism and Godless Nations**

Note: Now in the 21st century, Hegelian-Marxist thinking affects the entire social, political, and religious structure in the world. The Hegelian Dialectic is the framework for guiding our thoughts and actions into conflicts that will lead to the predetermined solution. If individuals and communities in the world do *not* understand, how the Hegelian Dialectic shapes the perceptions of the world, then they actually play an important role, implementing the vision towards the ultimate synthesis of a New World Order. How would that last power be displayed on the map? (Refer back to page 189.)

Eastern Hemisphere Events

Honor Given to the God of Forces

- **France:** The worship of the Goddess of Reason was instituted at Paris in 1793. This was later followed by worshipping nature deified, also considered a *"god of forces."* Lucifer is also known as the "god of forces."

- **Russia:** Communism honored the military for their strength. All other godless nations follow the same pattern. Atheism was the forced religion of the state.

The God of Atheism

- Secret Societies of the Papacy promote the worship of Lucifer which was a foreign idea to their forefathers.

> "The devil is the personification of Atheism or Idolatry. For the Initiates, this is not a Person, but a Force, created for good, but which may serve for evil ..." Albert Pike, *Morals and Dogma*, p. 102.

1 TIM 4:2 Now the Spirit speaketh expressly, that in the latter times some shall depart from the faith, giving heed to seducing spirits, and doctrines of devils.

- Promoting the worship of Lucifer (or angels and/or the Virgin Mary) is an effort to <u>destroy</u> Christianity.

> "Catholics, however, have an answer for the "you worship Mary" charge by pointing out the different levels of worship used in the Catholic church: *latria,* adoration for the triune God alone; *dulia,* veneration due the angels and canonized saints; and *hyperdulia,* a category reserved for Mary alone in which she is given 'superveneration'." Fritz Ridenour, *So What's the Difference?*, p. 46, referenced from Colacci, *Conflict*, pp. 188, 189.

COL 2:18 Don't let anyone declare you lost when you refuse to worship angels, as they say you must. TLB

Honour Given to Wealth

- In Communism, the state had the power over the wealth of the land. None of it belonged to the people.

- Godless nations often deck their images with costly ornaments just as the images of the Virgin Mary and saints are decked with priceless gifts as mentioned in Daniel 11:38 on page 311.

Ps 97:7 Confounded be all they that serve graven images, that boast themselves of idols.

Note: Atheistic-Communism was also developed as an <u>antithesis</u> to true Biblical Christianity (the <u>thesis</u>) to bring about an eventual confrontation on a global scale. The end result will be a synthesis or one world religion under a New World Order, with a Papal political/religious head.

- **1929:** This was the year Mussolini restored Vatican City to the Papacy which sealed the union of Fascism with the Papacy. "The state of Vatican City was constituted by the Lateran Treaty signed by Pietro Cardinal Gasparri and Benito Mussolini in 1929, which assured the Holy See absolute independence and guaranteed it sovereignty also in international relations." (*Encyclopedia Britannica*, Vol. 22, p. 905, 1971 edition.) The Papal throne over the state was restored. This *began* the healing of the 1798 wound to the Papal system.

Mussolini

Another Thesis/Antithesis

- **1943-1945:** World War II was planned to accomplish the following goals:
1. Destroy German Communists through the power of Hitler;
2. Destroy Russian Orthodox Christians;
3. Destroy many of the Jews through Hitler's power;
4. Entice the remainder of the Jewish race to return to Palestine — many did return;
5. Condition the world to accept the United Nations in place of the League of Nations, created at the end of World War I;
- Discipline Japan for expelling Catholics with their Exclusion Edict in 1639.

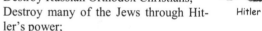
Hitler

Review of Albert Pike's Blueprint

- "Mazzini, with [Albert] Pike, developed a plan for three world wars so that eventually every nation would be willing to <u>surrender its national sovereignty</u> to a world government. The **first** war was to end the Czarist regime in Russia, and the **second** war was to allow the Soviet Union to control Europe. The **third** world war was to be in the Middle East between Moslems and Jews and would result in Armageddon." *Now is The Dawning of the New Age New World Order* (Hearthstone Publishing, Ltd. 1991), p. 42. (Emphasis supplied.)

> **DAN 8:23, 25** ... a king of fierce countenance, and understanding dark sentences ... shall cause craft to prosper in his hand ... "only that the Church [system] might be the gainer in the end ... and that the end justifies the means." *(Part of the Jesuit Oath.)*

Thesis + Antithesis = Synthesis

Thesis: Communism in the East

+

Antithesis: Democracy in the West

=

Synthesis: Establishment of Communism in South East Asia

Western Hemisphere and Other Events
(Continued)

- **1962-1972:** Vietnam War planned to plant a Vatican power base in southeast Asia to take over all of Asia.

- **1963:** President John F. Kennedy was assassinated for:

Kennedy

1. Attempting to dismantle the Federal Reserve System in the United States which is the central bank of the United States, a creation of the Jesuits.

- "When Kennedy called for a return of America's currency to the gold standard, and the dismantling of the Federal Reserve System — he actually minted non-debt money that does not bear the mark of the Federal Reserve; when he dared to actually exercise the leadership authority granted to him by the U.S. Constitution … Kennedy prepared his own death warrant. It was time for him to go." Colonel James Gritz, *Called to Serve: Profiles in Conspiracy from John F. Kennedy to George Bush,* pp. 511, 512.

- **Note:** The Constitution of the United States gives to Congress the power to coin money. Eventually this would eliminate the hundreds of billions of dollars of interest that the USA now pays each year to the bankers for the national debt, for money that came out of nothing. Kennedy wanted to free his country of this enormous debt. In this way, Roman Catholic <u>Kennedy acted as the President of the USA and not as a puppet for the Jesuits</u>! He put the welfare of the United States before the desires of the Papacy. He was not as the Jesuits, who use the wealth created by the Federal Reserve Bank to finance their murderous deeds. (See Appendix 8E, pages 221 and 223.)

1962-1972
Communism Established in South East Asia

"The pope is the ruler of the world. All the emperors, all the kings, all the princes, *all the presidents of the world are as these altar boys of mine."* Priest D. S. Phelan, *Western Watchman,* June 27, 1912.

> **DAN 8:23, 25** … a king of fierce countenance, and understanding dark sentences … shall cause craft to prosper in his hand … "only that the Church [system] might be the gainer in the end … and that the end justifies the means." *(Part of the Jesuit Oath.)*

- Kennedy was Roman Catholic. The Jesuits are Roman Catholic. If the Jesuits issue a death sentence against one of their own, it is carried out. Notice a section from the secret instructions of the Jesuit Order, written by their founder, Ignatius Loyola:

> "Finally, let all with such artfulness gain the ascendance over princes, noblemen and the magistrates of every place <u>that they may be ready at our beck and call, even to sacrifice their nearest relatives and most intimate friends when we say it is for our interest and our advantage</u>." W. C. Brownlee, *Secret Instructions of the Jesuits,* p. 47. (Emphasis supplied.)

2. Wanting to end the Vietnam war.

- "With this report [of McNamara-Taylor Mission to South Vietnam] in hand, President Kennedy had what he wanted. It contained the essence of decisions he had to make. He had to get re-elected to finish programs set in motion during his first term; he had to get Americans out of Vietnam." Col. L. Fletcher Prouty, *JFK: The CIA, Vietnam, and The Plot to Assassinate John F. Kennedy,* p. 264. (Note: The day after Kennedy was killed, the decision to stop America's involvement in Vietnam was reversed and the Vatican's program continued as planned.)

3. Wanting to end the international drug trade connected with that war.

- "Since the original Jesuit mission had established itself in Beijing in 1601, the Society of Jesus [the Jesuits] had held the key to the Far East Trade — including the drug trade." Assorted Authors, *Dope, Inc.: The Book that Drove Kissinger Crazy,* p. 117.

Eastern Hemisphere Events

- **1978:** Pope John Paul II elected as the Vatican world leader.

John Paul II

- **1979:** Pope John Paul II visits his homeland of Poland. This visit was the prelude catalyst to the collapse of Communism.

- The Pope used President Reagan as an ally to overthrow the Soviet kingdom even though Poland was under martial law in the 1980s. Papal Rome secretly worked together with the United States to bring down Communism. This alliance was propelled with a meeting on June 7, 1982. The first time these two leaders met, they immediately "agreed to undertake a clandestine campaign to hasten the dissolution of the communist empire."

Pope & Reagan

- **1980:** Lech Walesa was the founder of the Solidarity Labor Movement in Poland. Negotiations between Welesa and Pope John Paul II eventually brought democracy to Poland and produced the downfall of Communism in Eastern Europe, including Russia.

John Paul II & Walesa

Walesa

- **1986:** In February 1986, Mikhail Gorbachev, became the Soviet leader. He was also known as the father of *glasnost* (openness), *perestroika* (restructuring), and *uskorenie* (acceleration of economic development), which unleashed the powerful forces that led to the breakup of the Soviet Union.

Gorbachev

Albert Pike planned three world wars (in a letter dated August 15, 1871 to Mazzini), and until recently the letter was on display in the British Museum. He wrote:

> "We shall unleash the nihilist and the atheists, and we shall provoke formidable social cataclysm which in its horror will show clearly to the nations the effect of absolute atheism, origin of savagery and the most bloody turmoil. Then everywhere, the citizens, obliged to defend themselves against the minorities of revolutionaries, will exterminate those destroyers of civilization, and the multitude, disillusioned with Christianity … will receive the pure light through the universal manifestation of the pure doctrine of Lucifer … the destruction of Christianity and atheism. <u>Both conquered and exterminated at the same time</u>." Griffin, *Forth Reich of the Rich*, pp. 70, 71. (Emphasis supplied.)

> A man behind the Pope — Who might it be?

World Religions | World Politics

- "On June 7, 1982, the United States and the Vatican, in 'one of the great secret alliances of all time,' had agreed to undertake a clandestine campaign to hasten the dissolution of the Communist empire. On December 27, 1989, the *Catholic Weekly* has revealed that behind the scenes the Pope and his men really did most of it. In 1990, one-time Jesuit and Vatican insider [Malachi Martin in his book *The Keys of This Blood*] had announced that, of the three contestants for world dominion (the Papacy, Communism and Western capitalism), <u>the Pope held the trump card. He saw himself as the coming leader of the New World Order</u>." Jonathan Gray, *Ark of the Covenant*, pp. 504, 505. (Emphasis supplied.)

Thought Questions

Should true Biblical Christians be members of Secret Societies?

- **JAMES 4:4** know ye not that the friendship of the world is enmity with God? whosoever therefore will be a friend of the world is the enemy of God.

Can there be unity of purpose and action between Secret Societies and God's people?

- **LUKE 16:13** No servant can serve two masters: for either he will hate the one, and love the other; or else he will hold to the one, and despise the other. Ye cannot serve God and mammon.

- **EPH 5:11-12** And have no fellowship with the unfruitful works of darkness, but rather reprove them. 12 For it is a shame even to speak of those things which are done of them in secret.

Should God's people understand the ultimate mandate of these Secret Societies? Why?

The artwork depicts a puppeteer. Who might that be? Is there a "black pope" behind the "white pope"?

Thesis + Antithesis = Synthesis

Thesis: Papacy in the East
+
Antithesis: Republicanism in the West
=
Synthesis: Worldwide Progression to the New World Order

1989-1991
Communism Collapses in the Eastern European Bloc and Russia

> **DAN 8:23, 25**
> ... a king of fierce countenance, and understanding dark sentences ... shall cause craft to prosper in his hand ... "only that the Church [system] might be the gainer in the end ... and that the end justifies the means."
> *(Part of the Jesuit Oath.)*

Pope John Paul II and President Reagan form an "Holy Alliance" to Collapse Communism

Western Hemisphere and Other Events
(Continued)

- **1981-1989:** Ronald Reagan, USA President.

- **1980:** Infiltration of religious organizations in the USA is complete. By this year all major religious organizations have been infiltrated and taken over by the Jesuits. They want everyone to stay in the mainstream organizations so that they can more easily be indoctrinated. Anyone outside the main churches will be more difficult to brainwash. According to Ex-Jesuit priest, Alberto Rivera, all the mainstream churches were taken over by 1980. Under extreme oath of the Jesuits, he was told that a secret sign was to be given to the Jesuits world-wide when the ecumenical movement had successfully wiped out Protestantism. "The sign was to be when a President of the U.S. took his oath of office facing an obelisk. For the first time in U.S. history, the swearing in ceremonies were moved to the West front of the Capitol, and President Reagan faced the Washington Monument. This happened January 20, 1981." Jack Chick, *The Godfathers, Alberto Part Three*, p. 26.

Reagan

- President Reagan also shared Pope John Paul's strong convictions about Communism. Both believed Communism was a moral evil, not simply bad economics, and both remained confident that free peoples could overcome the challenge of Communism.

- **1982:** A five-part strategy emerged that was aimed at bringing about the collapse of the Soviet economy. Elements of that strategy included:
a) The USA defense buildup was already under way and aimed at making it too costly for the Soviets to compete militarily with Reagan's Strategic Defense Initiative (Star Wars). This became the centerpiece of the strategy.
b) Secret operations to encourage reform movements in Hungary, Czechoslovakia, and Poland.
c) Financial aid was to be given to the Warsaw Pact nations in relationship to their willingness to protect human rights and undertake political and free-market reforms. (During Reagan's presidency, these nations included: Soviet Union, Bulgaria, Romania, Hungary, Poland, Czechoslovakia, and East Germany.)
d) Isolate the Soviet Union economically by withholding Western and Japanese technology from Moscow.
e) Transmit the messages of the Administration to the people of Eastern Europe through the use of radio.

Thought Questions

- At the same time that the Papal System was creating Atheistic-Communism, was it creating a western world that was looking more and more like the system under Nebuchadnezzar?
- Totally antichrist in every aspect of its existence?
- A system formed in the image of man, powered by the dragon?

207

GOLD HEAD
Dan 2:38

#1 BABYLON
606 — 538 BC

SILVER ARMS
DAN 2:39

#2 MEDO-PERSIA
538 — 331 BC

BRASS BELLY
DAN 2:39

#3 GREECE
331 — 168 BC

IRON LEGS
DAN 2:40

#4 ROME (Pagan Imperial)
168 BC — AD 476

> The iron of the legs continues down into the feet and toes as the Roman kingdom in one form or another. The last form of the Roman kingdom is found at the end of the toes — a New World Order.

IRON in the FEET
DAN 2:41

#5 ROME
(Papal Supremacy No. 1)
AD 538 — 1798

CLAY in the FEET
DAN 2:41

#6 ROME
(Papal Supremacy No. 2)
Rules the
GODLESS KINGDOM
of Atheistic-Communism
AD 1801 — Present

ROM 9:21 Hath not the potter power over the clay, of the same lump to make one vessel unto honour, and another unto dishonour?

Note: The "clay vessels of honour" represent God's remnant on earth.

JOHN 16:2 yea, the time cometh, that whosoever killeth you will think that he doeth God service.

DANIEL 3:2-7 SPEAKS

2 Then Nebuchadnezzar the king sent to gather together the princes, the governors, and the captains, the judges, the treasurers, the counsellers, the sheriffs, and all the rulers of the provinces, to come to the dedication of the image which Nebuchadnezzar the king had set up.
3 ... and they stood before the image that Nebuchadnezzar had set up.
4 Then an herald cried aloud, To you it is commanded ...
5 That at what time ye hear the sound of all kinds of musick, ye fall down and worship the golden image that Nebuchadnezzar the king hath set up:
6 And whoso falleth not down and worshippeth shall the same hour be cast into the midst of a burning fiery furnace.
7 Therefore at that time, when all the people heard the sound ... all the people ... fell down and worshipped the golden image that Nebuchadnezzar the king had set up.

Clay, an element of the earth, is more easily molded than any metal. In Daniel 2, the clay represents *mankind*, as made from the dust of the earth. Part of the clay (e.g. Atheistic-Communism) was molded for evil purposes by the Jesuit Order (under the reign of the "king of fierce countenance") to destroy Protestantism. This system, along with ALL other godless systems, will form the future New World Order (N.W.O.) with a Papal head over ALL the kings of the earth. The "clay vessels of dishonour" will succumb to the pressures of the *iron* — but the iron and the clay will not cleave together. (REV 17:16)

Rule of Papal Supremacy No. 1
AD 538 — 1798

Ignatius Loyola
1534

DAN 8:23-25
This system understands dark sentences and causes craft to prosper in its hands.

Adam Weishaupt
1776

Plans of the Illuminati carried forward through the evil Puppet Kingdom of Atheistic-Communism.

Ten faces represent the "toes or 10 kings" or ALL the world that follows the top "antichrist" commands. REV 17:12

"Then the princes, the governors, and captains, the judges, the treasurers, the counsellers, the sheriffs, and all the rulers of the provinces, were gathered together unto the dedication of the image that Nebuchadnezzar the king had set up." DAN 3:2

Appendix 8E — Unmasking the Enemy

INDEX

1 THESS 5:5-6 Ye are all the children of light, and the children of the day: we are not of the night, nor of darkness. 6 Therefore let us not sleep, as do others; but <u>let us watch</u> and be sober.

Appendix 8E — Unmasking the Enemy

Divine Hand Over the United States

The United States of America is on the brink of total collapse. Once a great and powerful nation, the United States is now in a free fall. A few more steps in its decline and it will be ruined. These are not easy words for patriotic Americans to read, but, nevertheless, they are absolutely true. Tragically, it need not have come to this.

As one looks at the history of nations, from Babylon to Rome to America, it is evident that a Divine hand has been protecting and guiding America. This country began as a few colonies on the Eastern seaboard of this vast land and became a great nation.

In her youth, the United States was very good. On her money, her trust in God was proclaimed, and the great blessing of God rested upon this nation. As the United States grew to greatness, she gradually abandoned the principles that made her great, and today she is approaching a very tragic end. The process of the decline of America is similar to the decline and fall of the Roman Kingdom. Let us examine a little of the history of ancient Rome and see the parallels.

As the early Roman Kingdom was beginning to develop, it was building on the solid premise that the family unit was the cornerstone of society. Morality and discipline were the cornerstones! As the kingdom developed, liberalism crept in, and the morality and discipline that protected society began to wane. By the beginning of the 2nd century AD, most families had given into the liberal trends, and their children were allowed to do pretty much as they pleased.

It is obvious to most, that the moral fabric of America today is where the morality of the Roman Kingdom was nearly 2000 years ago. Do we not see the: a) breakdown of the home; b) a strong women's rights movement; c) a deterioration in the school system; d) moral decay as espoused by the news and entertainment media; e) and the schools, and welfare eating the heart out of the American economy? With regard to these problems, how are we any different from the Roman Kingdom during its decay? Why are these things happening in America? But, that's the wrong question. The question should be: Who has brought America to the brink of destruction?

As mentioned earlier, Providence had its eye on the United States. It was the land of opportunity. It was the place where those who were being persecuted for their faith could come and worship God according to the dictates of their own conscience. It was a land without a king where one could come and breathe the air of civil liberty. It was the place where one could come and earn a good living for himself and his family. America was the place where dreams came true. There once was a Divine Hand over America.

In 1759, twenty-five years stood between the thirteen colonies and their freedom from the British. Twenty-five years and the greatest Protestant nation to ever exist in the history of nations would fly its flag. Twenty-five years and the groundwork for the Constitution — Republicanism, inalienable rights, and a government of the people, by the people, and for the people — was in sight. An experiment in government, never before tried in history, was to become a reality.

Many said such a government would not work. The Papal System had ruled the world through the Dark Ages and sought to keep the world under her dictatorial control. She was, and still is, deathly afraid of such an experiment. For over 200 years, the Protestant Reformation had challenged the Papacy's authority. The Papacy gradually began losing her power. An experiment like America was certainly not in the game plan of the Papal System. No nation would be allowed to espouse such freedom of conscience principles that were the direct antithesis of Papal dogma.

What of the monarchs of Europe? They ruled by permission of the Papacy. The Papacy had wielded tyrannical control for ages, that no one could oppose them. Were they now ready to watch the development of a government of the people, by the people, and for the people? She would not stand by and allow this threat to her sovereignty develop.

Earlier in the 1550s, the Reformation Movement had become so powerful in Europe that the Papacy realized something must be done to stop it from spreading. If it were not stopped, it would eventually undermine the position of the Papal System and destroy its absolute political and religious control. In order to accomplish the destruction of the Reformation, a new secret organization was formed within the Vatican, called the Jesuits.

Attempt to Overthrow Protestantism

The major purpose of the Jesuits was to destroy every trace of Protestantism, its principles of religious freedom, Republicanism, representative government, and the economy built around a strong middle class. The other purpose of the Jesuits, was to greatly expand the power and control of the Papacy throughout the entire world.

> "I cannot too much impress upon the minds of my readers that the Jesuits, by their very calling, by the very essence of their institution, are bound to seek, by every means, right or wrong, *the destruction of Protestantism.* This is the condition of their existence, the duty they must fulfill, or cease to be Jesuits."
> G.B. Nicolini, *History of the Jesuits: Their Origin, Progress, Doctrine, and Design,* preface. (Emphasis supplied.)

Appendix 8E — Unmasking the Enemy

70,000 Slain in One Night

The Jesuits used extreme deception to bring about the 1572 St. Bartholomew's Day Massacre. 70,000 Protestant Huguenots, men, woman, and children were murdered in one night. They also planned and implemented the 30 Years War (1618-1648) in an attempt to destroy all the Lutherans of Europe. The blood that reddened European soil for centuries can all be traced back to these murderous Jesuits.

By the middle of the 1700s, the Jesuit Order had become the powerhouse of Europe. According to Barrett, —

> "... the Jesuit Order at last reached the pinnacle of its power and prestige in the early eighteenth century. It had become more influential and wealthier than any other organization in the world. It held a position in world affairs that no oath-bound group of men has ever held before or since ... nearly all the Kings and Sovereigns of Europe had only Jesuits as directors of their consciences, so that the whole of Europe appeared to be governed by Jesuits only."
> Boyd Barrett, *The Jesuit Enigma*, p. 209.

America Under Divine Care

The Jesuits ruled the world. The monarchs of Europe, and the Pope himself had Jesuits as their confessors. The plans and plots were all known to them. Besides this, they were amassing a vast amount of wealth that allowed them to do as they chose. With them controlling the world, how could the little colonies of America have had a chance to stand against Jesuit controlled Europe? In an instant, the Jesuits could utilize any army at its disposal and crush the colonies.

Nations Ban Jesuits in 1759

It was at this juncture in 1759 that something strangely divine began to happen. It began in Portugal. The Portuguese king, Joseph I, banished the Jesuits from his realm. Catholic France banished them in 1762. The decree of Louis XV and the French Parliament reads as follows:

> "It denounced their doctrines and practices 'as perverse, destructive of every principle of religion, and even of probity; as injurious to morality, pernicious to civil society, seditious, dangerous to rights of the persons of the sovereigns; as fit to excite the greatest troubles in States, to form and maintain the most profound corruption in the hearts of men ... that the institutions of the Jesuits should forever cease to exist throughout the whole extent of the kingdom.' " *Ibid.*, p. 219.

The third sovereign to drive the Jesuits from their realm was King Charles III of Spain. He banished the Jesuits in 1767.

The mightiest Papal nations of Europe had banished the Jesuits from their realms. These Papal monarchs demanded that the Papal System abolish the society forever. Clement XIII, the Pope at that time, resisted the pressure of the European monarchs, but finally capitulated. The night before he planned to abolish the Jesuits, he was poisoned to death.

Four years later in 1773, three years before the Declaration of Independence, Pope Clement XIV issued an order, the purpose of which was to abolish the Jesuits forever. **Unfortunately, a later Pope, in 1814, re-established them.**

The Jesuit Ban Removed in 1814

The timing of these events in Europe is fascinating. Papal Europe was in disarray. The Papal monarchs were preoccupied with taking care of the problems with the Jesuit Order. The Jesuits were reeling, as one Catholic country after another drove them from their realms. While Europe was shaking, thirteen colonies across the Atlantic were looking at the possibility of war with England. The thirteen colonies were instituting principles of government never before heard in the annals of human history. Documents would soon be written that would codify such things as inalienable rights, government of the people, by the people, and for the people, free exercise of religion, and the right to keep and bear arms. These documents would soon be the hope of mankind throughout the whole world.

Colonies Escape the Jesuits

What if the Papal monarchs were not distracted by their dealings with the Jesuits? What if the Jesuits were not reeling by their banishment from Europe? The monarchs and the Jesuits would have utilized their wealth and military power to bludgeon the American colonies in the New World. The Protestant dream in America would have never come to a reality. Without a doubt, there was a Divine Hand over America!

The Illuminati-Jewish Front

"It is an unshakeable fact that the founder of the modern Bavarian Illuminati was a trained Jesuit named Adam Weishaupt from Ingolstadt, Bavaria. Weishaupt was a professor at Ingolstadt University, which was the center of the Jesuit counter-reformation." (See Encyclopedia Britannica, Volume 12, page 251.)

"Ingolstadt was the center where the Jesuits were flourishing in 1556." (See *History of Protestantism* by Wylie, Volume 2, p. 413.)

"The Apostle of Lucifer, Adam Weishaupt was born a Jew, converted to Catholicism, then turned to Witchcraft, where he became an expert, and founded another sect of the Illuminati. This sect of Illuminati was founded May 1st, 1776." William Josiah Sutton, *The New Age Movement*, p. 173.

Canon law was the result of the infamous Council of Trent, which met from 1545-1563. This law revealed the Catholic Church's stand against the Protestant Reformation and is known as the beginning of the Catholic Counter-Reformation. This council not only revealed the church's hostility toward the Reformation, but also how she would attack and destroy it.

Secret Fronts of the Jesuits

Weishaupt

Weishaupt established the Illuminati specifically to be a front organization behind which the Jesuits could hide. After being abolished by Clement XIV in 1773, the Jesuits used the Illuminati and other organizations to carry out their operations. Thus the front organizations would be blamed for the trouble caused by the Jesuits. Having so many front organizations would confuse the people to the point that it would be virtually impossible to know who was actually manipulating the wars, politics, and trouble. The methods of many of these front organizations, such as the Illuminati, are examples of the Jesuits methods and techniques.

The Jewish belief principles, that the Messiah will one day come and rule the world, caused the Vatican to shudder. The Vatican believed that if hatred for the Jews could be promoted, as took place in Hitler's Germany, then the Jews would be ruthlessly eliminated. The Vatican believed that if all Jews are killed, the Messiah would not come. As a result, the Vatican's aim to rule the world would remain intact. Avro Manhattan says it this way:

"It is important, although it may be difficult for some to recognize the religious nature of the Communist/ Zionist/Catholic political configuration. Although deliberately muted in public pronouncements, behind the Zionist banner there was to be found the ancient Messianic hope for the coming of a global theocracy, as predicted by all the seers and prophets of Zion. It was to be a theocracy in which Jehovah, not Christ, was to be King.

"The spectre of the creation of such a theocracy has haunted the inner chambers of the Catholic church from her earliest inception, and still is a dominant fear." Avro Manhattan, *The Vatican Moscow*, pp. 169, 170.

Jesuits Use Jewish Front

Why would the Jesuits use their implacable enemy, the Jews, to further their designs for world dominion? The Jesuits never do anything out in the open where they can be exposed. If they are recognized as the culprits, they will be blamed and suffer the consequences, but if they can use someone else as the cause of the world's problems, especially an enemy they can destroy in the process, then they have simultaneously accomplished two of their objectives. The Jewish people are the perfect scapegoat. Since the Rothschilds are Jesuit agents, operating under a Jewish cover, using them (in forming the Illuminati back in 1776), effectively throws the onus of this conspiracy on the Jews. The Rothschilds are certainly not the only Jesuit agents that operate under a Jewish front.

The following sources indicate that Adam Weishaupt and the Rothschilds were the brains and the wealth behind the French Revolution.

"History books will tell us that the French Revolution first began in 1787 or 1789, depending on which book you read. However, it was actually planned by Dr. Adam Weishaupt and the House of Rothschild almost 20 years before the Revolution took place." William Sutton, *The New Age Movement and The Illuminati 666*, pp. 172, 173.

The Jesuits Promote Communism

The Jesuits, Weishaupt, and the Rothschilds, managed to cast the blame for the French Revolution on their front organization, the Illuminati!!

The Communistic ideals that came from the Reductions (communes) in Paraguay, and exalted in France, had their fruition in the writings of **Karl Marx.**

Marx

"Karl Marx, 'the Father of Modern Communism' … was privately tutored by Jesuits in the huge Reading Room of the British Museum while writing *The Communist Manifesto* based upon the ten maxims or 'planks' the Order had perfected on its Paraguayan Reductions … A Jew was chosen for this task; for, the Order anticipated blaming all the evils of their Communist Inquisition on the Jewish Race." Eric Phelps, *Vatican Assassins*, p. 293.

Adam Weishaupt and the Rothschild family created the Illuminati. Both Weishaupt and the Rothschilds united their efforts to foment the French Revolution and inspire Communism. The Jesuits used Karl Marx to write the *Communist Manifesto*, which codified the Illuminati's plans. The teachings of **Marx** were then passed to **Lenin**, **Stalin**, and **Trotsky**. The financiers of all of these men were the Rothschilds, or Rothschild agents, such as

Lenin

Stalin

Trotsky

Paul **Warburg**, the first chairman of the Federal Reserve Bank, Jacob **Schiff**, and Armand Hammer. Each of these men, being Jesuits, were Jews and operated under a Jewish front. Is it any wonder that the Jews are usually blamed for all the conspiracies?

Warburg

Schiff

In the Jesuit's relentless pursuit to destroy America, she would use the Jewish House of Rothschild to gain control of the American banking system.

Appendix 8E — Unmasking the Enemy

The Bank Bandits

Because Pope Clement XIV and the Catholic Emperors across Europe were busy abolishing the Jesuits, they were not able to cooperate with each other well enough to stop the Protestant American experiment. If a Divine Hand had not intervened to protect the thirteen colonies, there would never have been a United States with its God-given Constitution!

The Jesuits were greatly troubled because of their expulsions around the world. They were forced to go underground. We have seen that they used their agent, Adam Weishaupt, to create the Illuminati and the Jesuit House of Rothschild to finance it. It was not just here, however, where Rothschild wealth was very helpful. America was becoming a giant of financial affluence and prosperity. Already, the Rothschilds were involved in extensive trading in the Americas. Besides their financial and mercantile empires, the Rothschilds were utilizing their wealth to gain political and religious control in an effort to further the ends of the Jesuits.

The Jesuits used all their resources in their attempt to destroy America. They used the powerful financial empire of the Rothschilds to obtain control over finances. Biographer Frederick Morton concluded that, through the effective use of money the Rothschilds had successfully —

"... conquered the world more thoroughly, more cunningly, and much more lastingly than all the Caesars before or all the Hitler's after them." Frederick Morton, *The Rothschilds: A Family Portrait*, p. 14.

The Rothschilds believed that if they could control a nation's money, then they could control that country. This is clearly pointed out in the following statement from biographer Derek Wilson.

"It commanded vast wealth. It was international. It was independent. Royal governments were nervous of it because they could not control it. Popular governments hated it because it was not answerable to the people." Derek Wilson, *Rothschild: The Wealth and Power of a Dynasty*, pp. 79, 98, 99.

Using the vast wealth of the Rothschilds, the Jesuits equipped armies to destroy countries that would not do their bidding. They could buy politicians, and through them change the very laws of a nation. This is exactly what they did in America and are still doing today! The Jesuits have been using the Rothschild wealth to control major events behind the worldwide scenes over the last few

Rothschilds

centuries. This was true when they first started, and true today. They have the Central Banks in each country, including the Federal Reserve Bank, supplying them with funds.

Rothschild Strategy at Waterloo

To illustrate how the Jesuits and the Rothschilds have used countries and events to gain domination over nations and their financial markets, we must look at the Battle of Waterloo between France and England on June 18, 1815.

"As the two huge armies closed in for the battle to the death, Nathan Rothschild had his agents working feverishly on both sides of the line to gather the most accurate possible information as the battle proceeded. Additional Rothschild agents were on hand to carry the intelligence bulletins to a Rothschild command post strategically located nearby.

N. Rothschild

"Arriving at the Exchange amid frantic speculation on the outcome of the battle, Nathan took up his usual position beside the famous 'Rothschild Pillar.' Without a sign of emotion, without the slightest change of facial expression the stony-faced, flint eyed chief of the House of Rothschild gave a predetermined signal to his agents who were stationed nearby.

"Rothschild agents immediately began to dump consuls on the market. As hundreds of thousands of dollars worth of consuls poured onto the market their value started to slide. Then they began to plummet.

"The selling turned into a panic as people rushed to unload their 'worthless' consuls or paper money for gold and silver in the hope of retaining at least part of their wealth. Consuls continued their nosedive towards oblivion. After several hours of feverish trading the consul lay in ruins. It was selling for about five cents on the dollar.

"Nathan Rothschild, emotionless and expressionless as ever, still leaned against his pillar. He continued to give subtle signals. But these signals were different. They were so subtly different that only the highly trained Rothschild agents could detect the change. On the cue from their boss dozens of Rothschild agents made their way to the order desks around the Exchange and bought every consul in sight for just a 'song.'

"Napoleon had 'met his Waterloo.' Nathan had bought control of the British economy. Overnight his already vast fortune was multiplied twenty times over." Des Griffin, *Descent Into Slavery*, pp. 27, 28.

Napoleon

By 1815, the Jesuits had complete control over England. If a leader did not do as he was told, money would be used to kill, smear, destroy, blackmail, or just drive the person from office. This procedure is being used today to control people like George Bush and Tony Blair. What was done in England is being done in many countries today.

Appendix 8E — Unmasking the Enemy

The Federal Reserve Bank

The Central Banks established by the Jesuits and the Rothschilds are in NO WAY similar to the neighborhood banks that we all use to manage our money. Let us take a closer look at the Central Bank and see why it is so dangerous. We will use the Federal Reserve Bank as an example. Here is a very simplified scenario that explains the principle of operations of the Federal Reserve Bank.

It is necessary to understand that the Federal Reserve Bank is not owned by the United States government as many believe. The Central Bank, the Federal Reserve Bank, is a private bank, owned by some of the richest and most powerful people in the world. This bank has nothing to do with the United States government other than the connection, which allows the operation described below. The private Federal Reserve Bank has a total, government-enforced monopoly on money. Before we had the Central Bank, each individual bank competed with other banks; the customers, or consumers, got the best deal. Not any more.

We all know today, the United States government borrows money and operates under astronomical debt. Why is this? Common sense dictates that a policy of such enormous debt will sooner or later destroy the organization that practices it, because the interest on its debt must increase beyond its income, making payoff impossible.

Now to our scenario. Here, roughly, is how the operation proceeds. Suppose the United States government wants to borrow a billion dollars. The government issues a bond for this amount, much as a water company does when it wants to raise money for a new pipeline or a new dam. The government delivers this bond for the billion dollars to the Federal Reserve Bank. The Federal Reserve Bank takes the bond and writes an order to the Department of Printing and Engraving to print the billion dollars' worth of bills. After about two weeks or so, when the bills are printed, the Department of Printing and Engraving ships the bills to the Federal Reserve Bank, which then writes a check for about two thousand dollars to pay for printing the billion dollars' worth of bills. The Federal Reserve Bank then takes the billion dollars and lends the billion dollars to the United States government, and the people of the country pay interest each year on this money, which came out of nothing. The owners of the Federal Reserve Bank only put up about $2000.00 for all this money.

We see, therefore, that when the United States government goes into debt one dollar, a dollar plus the interest goes into the pockets of the owners of the Federal Reserve Bank. This is the largest, the most colossal theft ever perpetrated in the history of mankind, and it is so slick, so subtle, and so obscured by propaganda from the news media that the victims are not even aware of what is happening. You can see why the Jesuits want to keep this operation secret.

Dangers of the Central Bank

Thomas Jefferson clearly saw what a central bank would do to America. He declared, —

"A private central bank issuing the public currency is a greater menace to the liberties of the people than a standing army." Jefferson
The Writings of Thomas Jefferson, Volume X, p. 31.

Jefferson realized that if a Central Bank was ever set up in America, the bankers would have virtually unlimited amounts of money to control how lawmakers voted, and to control the media and what they said. Within a short time, these bankers would essentially rewrite the Constitution and the Bill of Rights substituting unconstitutional laws for the original. Thomas Jefferson was completely correct. Today America has enough laws, such as the USA Patriotic Act and the Homeland Security Act, to literally convert the United States into a police state.

Just like the old Bank of North America, the new Bank of the United States had eighty percent of its initial funding capital provided by 'secret' investors, while the government put up only twenty percent. Whoever these 'secret' investors were, they had tremendous power in America. Many books, written about this time period, tell us who these people were.

The Rothschilds and the Jesuits have been using their vast wealth to take over the United States for a great many years. The Jesuits and the Rothschilds would settle for nothing less.

After the Hamilton Central Bank failed, the Jesuits were able to establish a third Central Bank in 1816 using **Nicholas Biddle** as their agent. The charter for this bank ran until 1836. Biddle then attempted to renew the charter of this third bank during the Presidential campaign of 1832. Biddle — during the Presidential campaign of 1832.
Biddle believed that Andrew Jackson would not dare risk his second term in office by opposing him, so Biddle felt this was the perfect time to renew the banks charter. **Andrew Jackson** understood the dangers of the Central Bank and vetoed the bill to renew the bank's charter. Jackson's argument was very simple. Jackson

"Controlling our currency, receiving our public monies, and holding thousands of our citizens in dependence, it would be more formidable and dangerous than a naval and military power of the enemy." Herman E. Kross, *Documentary History of Banking and Currency in the United States,* pp. 26, 27.

Jackson feared that the foreigners, who wanted to dominate and control America, would use the Central Bank to destroy her. The Rothschilds and the Jesuits have been doing just that for many years. The following quote shows how Nicholas Biddle manipulated the Congress.

Appendix 8E — Unmasking the Enemy

> "Biddle had one powerful advantage over his adversary. For all practical purposes, Congress was in his pocket. Or, more accurately, the product of his generosity was in the pockets of Congressmen. Following the Rothschild Formula, Biddle had been careful to reward compliant politicians with success in the business world. Few of them would bite the hand that fed them. Even the great Senator, Daniel Webster, found himself kneeling at Biddle's throne." G. Edward Griffin, *The Creature from Jekyll Island,* p. 351.

Webster's record in Congress had previously been on behalf of sound money. When Biddle bought Webster with money and other enticements, he succumbed and became a supporter of the corrupt banking objectives of Biddle. Webster became one of the Central Banks most avid supporters. How tragic that Daniel Webster did not have the moral courage to withstand Biddle's bribes! In the early 1830s, Congress had many Jesuits seeking to secretly undermine the great principles of the Constitution.

When Andrew Jackson finally ousted Nicholas Biddle and the Central Bank, he had to face other things such as Jesuit assassins.

"With these accomplishments close on the heels of his victory over the Bank, the President had earned the undying hatred of monetary scientists, both in America and abroad. It is not surprising, therefore, that on January 30, 1835, an assassination attempt was made against him. Miraculously, both pistols of the assailant misfired, and Jackson was spared by a quirk of fate. It was the first such attempt to be made against the life of a President of the United States." *Ibid.,* p. 357.

The Civil War and Assassinations

The Rothschilds and the Jesuits needed to regroup. For the next 20 years, the name of the game was assassination. Two presidents were poisoned and one almost killed by poisoning. Then, the guns of war were heard, as the Civil War reddened American soil. According to German Chancellor, Otto von Bismarck, all this was carefully planned.

"The division of the United States into federations of equal force was decided long before the Civil War by the high financial powers of Europe. These bankers were afraid that the United States, if they remained in one block and as one nation, would attain economic and financial independence, which would upset their financial domination over Europe and the world. Of course, in the 'inner circle' of Finance, the voice of the Rothschilds prevailed." *Ibid.,* p. 374.

The Rothschilds and Jesuits used the Civil War to divide the United States into two contending countries. This would make America weak and much easier to control.

President Lincoln understood the insidious hand of the Rothschilds and the Jesuit schemers in the Civil War. He understood the massive destructive power of these people. He knew that they were relentless in their pursuit of the destruction of the United States. Lincoln greatly feared for the survival of America and did everything he could to defeat their purposes.

Lincoln

Greed, selfishness, and financial gain are used to compromise politicians to pass laws defeating the purpose of the Constitution, and to take America down a path never intended by the Founding Fathers. These politicians adopted governing principles like those of Communism and the French Revolution. Following the awful bloodbath called the Civil War the nation was bleeding, and things were in disarray. The country was quite vulnerable to more Jesuit mischief, and they took good advantage of it.

Trashing the Constitution

Any observer of Congress in the 1860s would declare that **Thaddeus Stevens** was undeniably in charge. This radical, Thaddeus Stevens, controlled Congress and applied all his overbearing and caustic manner to bring about one of the greatest revolutions in America since 1776. By his influence, certain hidden changes were implemented into the Reconstruction Amendments which did so much more than provide freedom and equality for the slaves. The Reconstruction Amendment attacked the very rationale behind the Bill of Rights.

Republic Versus Democracy

The United States of America is not a Democracy. It is a Republic, and there is a big difference between the two. A pure Democracy is based solely on the majority, without any restrictions on what they can do. An excellent example of a Democracy is a lynch mob. The majority wants to hang the person, and the minority, the person to be hanged, does not want to be hanged. They have a vote, and then, hang the person. In a pure Democracy, the minority is the victim of the majority.

In contrast, a Republic is founded on a set of laws that govern what the majority can and cannot do. The law on which the United States' Republic is founded is the Constitution. Part of the Constitution states, —

> **Congress shall make no law respecting an establishment of religion, or prohibiting the free exercise thereof; or abridging the freedom of speech, or of the press; or the right of the people peaceably to assemble, and to petition the government for a redress of grievances. — First Amendment to the Constitution.**

Appendix 8E — Unmasking the Enemy

150 Million Martyrs and the Dark Ages

If a law was proposed in Congress to set up a national religion, and everyone in Congress voted for it, it still cannot be done, because the Constitution prohibits this type of law. The Constitution says that the government is not permitted to pass any law concerning religion. During the Dark Ages, over 150 million Christians were put to death because they would not abide by the universal religion of the time. The same thing could happen in America, if America were a pure Democracy.

The word *Democracy* cannot be found in the Constitution or in the Declaration of Independence, or in any of the State's constitutions. Many of the Founders of the United States tried to warn about the dangers of a pure Democracy.

"Remember, democracy never lasts long. It soon, exhausts, and murders itself. There never was a democracy yet that did not commit suicide." John Adams, *The Works of John Adams,* Volume 6, p. 484.

If America had been established as a pure Democracy, it would have long since ceased to exist.

100 Million Die in the 20th Century

> **"The French Revolution was a source for communist, anarchist, and socialist conceptions; conceptions that, when carried to conclusion, resulted in the necessity of installing drainage systems to carry away the torrents of blood that flowed from French guillotines. These same 'conceptions' applied during the twentieth century have resulted in the murder of well over one hundred million human beings. There is much to learn from the Great Revolution."** Dee Zahner, *The Secret Side of History,* p. 35.

Afro-America Denied

The principles of Democracy or mob rule have filled this world with blood. Thaddeus Stevens was most instrumental in bringing the ideals of the French Revolution to

America under the guise of bringing freedoms to the downtrodden slaves.

As we have seen, the ideas of **Karl Marx** were nothing new. He simply took the ideas of the Jesuits and Weishaupt and codified them into the *Communist Manifesto*.

Marx

The principles of Democracy, Communism, and the French Revolution, codified by Karl Marx, are seen in countless countries in the twentieth century. From the purges in Russia by **Joseph Stalin**, to **Mao Tse Tung's** Reign of Terror in China, to **Pol Pot** in Cambodia and numerous others, the results of Jesuitism have filled this world with misery, pain, suffering, and death. Will the United States, the greatest bastion of Republican government, fall as well?

Stalin

Mao Tse Tung

Pol Pot

It became clear that freedom and equality for the Afro-American free man was used to create an entirely new citizenship, which broadened the powers of the national government and attacked the Bill of Rights. This was the same method used in France; the peasants were struggling under horrible difficulties, so the reign of terror granted them liberty and equality. Hidden beneath this was a drive to expand the power of the government and further entrench the peasants in bondage.

A professor at Columbia University recognized that the Thirteenth, Fourteenth, and Fifteenth Amendments brought about a completely different Constitution than the one established in 1787. He declared that these Amendments created a new Constitution. As we have seen from subsequent court cases after the passing of those Amendments, it is clear that that is exactly what Stevens and Rome wanted to do.

"Summing it up, by 1868 the Jesuits, with their radicals Thaddeus Stevens and Charles Sumner, had forced the Fourteenth Amendment on the peoples of the States, North and South. They had created a new nation as a result of a new citizenship. By 1872 the Jesuits, with their radicals on the Supreme Court, had made the powers of both the Federal and State governments absolute, limited only by decisions of their respective King's benches — the Federal and State Supreme Courts. The transition from a Presbyterian form of government to a Roman Catholic form of government has been accomplished. And how did they do it? By declaring that the Bill of Rights were not privileges and immunities of Fourteenth Amendment citizenship, thereby overthrowing the ancient liberties." Eric Phelps, *Vatican Assassins,* p. 327.

In light of the heinous and destructive work of Thaddeus Stevens and the Radical Republicans, it is easy to conclude that they were the tools of Rome in destroying the great Protestant Constitution. No more wicked, and diabolical men, ever walked the land of the free and the home of the brave.

Appendix 8ᴇ — Unmasking the Enemy

Tightening the Noose

After the Jesuits' attempts to destroy the fledgling United States, they concentrated on another goal that had eluded them for many years. They had desperately tried to establish a Central Bank under Robert Morris, Alexander Hamilton, and Nicholas Biddle, but each attempt had failed. During the devastating Civil War, Augustus Belmont, a rabid Jesuit and Rothschild agent, tried to coerce Lincoln into establishing a Central Bank, but Lincoln understood the damage a Central Bank would cause to the country, and he refused.

With new gusto and a different approach, the Jesuits and the Rothschilds tried again. They realized, as Lenin had:

"… that the establishment of a central bank was 90% of communizing a nation." Fritz Springmeier, *Bloodlines of the Illuminati,* p. 268.

In the mid 1750s, the Rothschilds and the **Schiffs** moved into the same residence, a large duplex house in Frankfurt, Germany, where their families lived together.

About 100 years after the two families lived together in Frankfurt, Germany, Jacob Schiff was born. He was a wizard at finances and developed the underhanded shrewdness of the Rothschilds. In 1865, as the Civil War was ending, young 18-year-old Jacob left Germany and came to America.

USA's Financial Empires

Schiff

Warburg

"Schiffs 'important financial connections in Europe' were the Rothschilds and their German representatives, the M. M. Warburg Company of Hamburg and Amsterdam. Within twenty years the Rothschilds, through their Warburg-Schiff connection, had provided the capital that enabled John D. Rockefeller to greatly expand his Standard Oil empire. They also financed the activities of Edward Harriman (Railroads) and Andrew Carnegie (Steel)." Des Griffin, *Descent Into Slavery,* pp. 36, 37.

Couple that with this statement: **"He came to New York first for the sole purpose of getting control of the United States monetary system. He eventually became the head of the banking firm of Kuhn, Loeb and Company. He bought Kuhn & Loeb out later with Rothschild money."**

"Using charity as a front to hide his Illuminati One World Government activities, Jacob Schiff became one of the most important successors of Albert Pike in leading the United States toward anarchy. As stated by Lenin earlier, one of the first goals of the communists is to get control

Pike

of all monetary systems of the world. And this was to be Jacob Schiff's first achievement." William Sutton, *The New Age Movement and Illuminati 666,* pp. 234, 235.

Absolute Monetary Control

Thus, we see that the Jesuits-Rothschilds sent Jacob Schiff to the United States at the end of the Civil War to gain

Morgan

Rockefeller

enough control over the American financial system that it would be impossible for America to refuse a Central Bank. Schiff used Jesuit-Rothschild money to finance **J. P. Morgan, John D. Rockefeller, Edward Harriman, and Andrew Carnegie.** Through the companies owned by these four individuals, shipping, energy, oil, transportation, railroads, import, exports, and steel with its associate businesses, would be involved.

Harriman

Carnegie

These financial giants branched off into so many other business enterprises that it simply boggles the mind. To say the least, the financial power gained by Jacob Schiff by 1900 was absolutely staggering! We must keep in mind the statement of F. Tupper Saussy, which says, —

Vatican Treasury Guardian

"Aware that the Rothschilds are an important Jewish family, I looked them up in Encyclopedia Judaica and discovered that they bear the title 'Guardians of the Vatican Treasury' … The appointment of Rothschild gave the black papacy absolute financial privacy and secrecy. Who would ever search a family of orthodox Jews for the key to the wealth of the Roman Catholic Church?" F. Tupper Saussy, *Rulers of Evil,* pp. 160, 161.

Saussy's reference to the Black Papacy is a reference to the Jesuits. The head Jesuit, the Jesuit general, is referred to quite frequently as the **Black Pope.**

Kolvenbach

In their relentless drive to abolish freedom in America without firing a shot, the Jesuits used their financial agents to so dominate American business and the banking system that they were able to push a central bank on the unsuspecting American people. This time, the Central Bank did not fail.

Bank Panic Ruins Thousands

"Early in 1907, Jacob Schiff, the Rothschild-owned boss of Kuhn, Loeb and Co., in a speech to the New York Chamber of Commerce, warned that 'unless we have a Central Bank with adequate control of credit resources, this country is going to undergo the most severe and far reaching money panic in its history.'

Appendix 8E — Unmasking the Enemy

"Shortly thereafter, the United states plunged into a monetary crisis that had all the earmarks of a skillfully planned Rothschild 'job.' The ensuing panic financially ruined tens of thousands of innocent people across the country, and made billions for the banking elite. The purpose for the 'crisis' was two-fold:

1. To make a financial 'killing' for the Insiders, and
2. To impress on the American people the 'great need' for a central bank.

Warburg

Paul Warburg told the Banking and Currency Committee: 'In the Panic of 1907, the first suggestion I made was, 'let us have a national clearing house' [Central Bank].' The Aldrich Plan [for a Central Bank] contains many things that are simply fundamental rules of banking." Des Griffin, *Descent Into Slavery*, p. 37.

The [Jesuit] Illuminati interests wanted to create a Central Bank in America. They wanted to build the Federal Reserve. First, they needed a banking crisis' that would push public opinion towards a Federal Reserve system. These were provided by the Illuminati, including J. P. Morgan's Knickerbocker Panic of 1907. Second, they needed a favorable U. S. president in office.

House

"Rothschild agent Colonel House provided this by getting Woodrow Wilson elected." Fritz Springmeier, *Bloodlines of the Illuminati*, p. 273.

Wilson

The engineered banking panic of 1907 did just what the Jesuits and the Rothschilds wanted it to do. It was made to appear that the only way to avoid another depression was to have a Central Bank.

Central Bank Deception

"To convince Congress and the public that the establishment of a banking cartel was, somehow, a measure to protect the public, the Jekyll Island strategists laid down the following plan of action:

1. Do not call it a cartel nor even a central bank.
2. Make it look like a government agency.
3. Establish regional branches to create the appearance of decentralization, not dominated by Wall Street banks.
4. Begin with a conservative structure including many sound banking principles, knowing that the provisions can be quietly altered or removed in subsequent years.
5. Use the anger caused by recent panics and bank failures to create popular demand for monetary reform.
6. Employ university professors to give the plan the appearance of academic approval." G. Edward Griffin, *The Creature from Jekyll Island*, p. 438.

The Central Bank is Not Federal

Under these pretenses, the American people were ready for the Federal Reserve Bank. The name sounds very official as if it were an entity of the American government. If people understood how the Federal Reserve Bank was going to operate, and that it would be controlled by a few of the richest bankers, they would not have tolerated its creation. The dream the Jesuits had of a Central Bank in America took shape at Jekyll Island. The operators and controllers of this bank are from the same groups as those who were behind the Central Bank in the 18th and 19th centuries: the Jesuits and the Rothschilds!

The Central Bank a Reality

Only one step remained to complete the project. The Jesuits needed certain men in the White House and the government to pass the Federal Reserve Act. By 1912, they had their man in the White House, **Woodrow Wilson**. Since **Jacob Schiff** was already deeply into the financial scam, the Jesuits needed another man whose expertise was politics. The man they found was **Edward Mandel House**. It was he who controlled Wilson in the White House.

House hoped to see the teachings of **Karl Marx** become a living reality in America. Remember that the teachings of Marx were the codified writings of **Adam Weishaupt**, the Illuminist and Jesuit agent. According to Woodrow Wilson's own words, he was dominated by House while he was president! How deceitful that the man sitting in the White House portrayed himself to the American people as a loyal American, when in fact, he did the bidding of America's greatest enemy — the Jesuits of Rome! Several books reveal the control that House had over Wilson while he was in the Oval Office.

Wilson

Roosevelt

"A key individual of the New York Archbishop's control of the Democratic Party through Tammany Hall, Colonel House, known as 'the holy monk,' was directly involved in making Woodrow Wilson and Franklin Roosevelt presidents of the American empire. As Wilson's advisor and 'alter ego,' he pressed for the passage of Morgan's Federal Reserve Act." Eric Phelps, *Vatican Assassins*, p. 447.

Kolvenbach

In their efforts to create a Jesuit empire in America, **Jacob Schiff, J. P. Morgan, the Rockefellers,** and **Edward House** were their agents. So many books refer to them as Illuminists, international bankers, or as Marxists, but we have seen that all of these organizations were being used as fronts for the Jesuits. All of them do the bidding of the **Black Pope**, the Jesuit general!

The early 1900s were very busy years indeed. The Federal Reserve Act and a Central Bank, World War One, and the sinking of the Titanic were just a few of the events transpiring at that time. Two other unfortunate events were, the toppling of Czarist Russia, and the attempt to establish a League of Nations.

Russia is Victim of USA Funds

When the Czar of Russia, Alexander I, rejected the Jesuits' effort to create a League of Nations in Europe, the Jesuits sought to destroy him and the system of government he represented.

"Jacob Schiff, head of the New York based Kuhn, Loeb and Co., spent $20 million on the revolution. Federal Reserve Director, William Boyce Thompson, gave the Bolsheviks $1 million. In the summer of 1917, fifteen Wall Street Financiers and attorneys, led by Thompson, went to Petrograd, the center of revolutionary activity." Dee Zahner, *The Secret Side of History,* p. 93.

There are numerous other references to these facts that could be quoted. These people were American citizens, and most of them took an oath swearing allegiance to the Constitution. Their acts in supporting a government whose principles are diametrically opposed to the Constitution is treason. How could these people do this? How could **Woodrow Wilson** and **Franklin D. Roosevelt** support Communist Russia? They were all Jesuits working to destroy the United States. They worked together and supported each other because their masters in the Vatican told them to do this.

League of Nations Failed

The establishment of the League of Nations after World War One was very important for the Jesuits. They had been trying to establish the League ever since the early 1800s. When **Woodrow Wilson,** under the direction of Jesuit agent, **Edward Mandel House,** failed to convince the American people and the United States Senate that they should join the League of Nations, the Jesuits realized that they had to make sure this refusal never happened again.

Another Jesuit Front

For fifty years the Jesuits had been planning World War Two. This next war was planned to make sure that America would join their next League of Nations. This time it would be called the United Nations. In order to accomplish this, the Jesuits knew that they had to have greater control of the mass media outlets, more Congressmen in their pocket, more businesses had to be dominated, and the office of the President had to be controlled.

United Nations Set Up

When these things were accomplished, the Jesuits knew that they would have no trouble convincing a blinded and deluded American people into eventually surrendering their sovereignty to the United Nations. In order to accomplish these things, the Jesuits created the Council on Foreign Relations. This was to be another front behind which they would hide while accomplishing their subversion in America. In England they created a similar sister organization called the Royal Institute of International Affairs.

"The Council on Foreign Relations was a spin-off from the failure of the world's leaders at the end of World War I to embrace the League of Nations as a true world government. It became clear to the master planners that they had been unrealistic in their expectations for rapid acceptance." G. Edward Griffin, *The Creature from Jekyll Island,* p. 273.

USA Diocese Housed the Council on Foreign Relations

"The agents of the Jesuits created the Council on Foreign Relations [CFR]. The locations would be in the two most powerful Roman Catholic Dioceses in the American Empire, New York and Chicago. The CFR would control the Empire's finance, government, industry, religion, education, and press. No one could be elected to the Presidency of the United States without the Council's consent, as the office would be a tool for the Archbishop of New York subject to 'the Vicar of Christ' [the Pope] in Rome. (One of the founders of the CFR also aided in the creation of the Federal Reserve Bank. He was the 'holy monk,' a Shriner Freemason and agent of the Jesuit General, Edward M. House). Its purpose was to return the world to the Pope's Dark Ages with an economically socialist world police state." Eric Phelps, *Vatican Assassins,* pp. 464, 465.

House

"At least FORTY-SEVEN C.F.R. [Council on Foreign Relations, Inc.] members were among the American delegates to the founding of the United Nations in San Francisco in 1945." Gary Allen, *None Dare Call It Conspiracy,* p. 86.

Controlled News Media

"To guard against exposure, and to mold public opinion, as far back as 1915 the powerful men in America working in world government set out to control the news media. They accomplished this by employing 12 leading men in the newspaper field to find out what was necessary to control the general policy of the daily press throughout the country. It was decided that this could be accomplished by purchasing control of 25 of the greatest papers.

Appendix 8E — Unmasking the Enemy

"For decades many top officials of the United States Government have been members of the Council on Foreign Relations. This includes many presidents, fourteen secretaries of state, fourteen treasury secretaries, eleven defense secretaries, and scores of other federal department heads." Dee Zahner, *The Secret Side of History,* p. 91.

Most Americans have never heard of the Council on Foreign Relations. Although unseen and unknown, it has exerted tremendous power and control over the decision making process in America throughout most of the 20th century. Some of the media organizations that show up repeatedly as being run and controlled by CFR members include NBC, CBS, New York Times, Washington Post, Des Moines Register, Los Angeles Times, Time magazine, Newsweek, Fortune, Business Week, U.S. News and World Report, the news services such as Associated Press, and many of the large, influential television stations. At least 170 journalists are controlled by the CFR. The influence of these media giants on public opinion is phenomenal, and it is done in such a subtle way that the people are not aware that they are being "told" what to think. The people generally believe that they are independent thinkers.

New York Times Chief Confesses

John Swinton, Chief of Staff for the New York Times, who was considered to be the dean of his profession, made a most revealing statement in 1953. At a New York Press Club dinner, Swinton declared, —

> **"If I allowed my honest opinions to appear in one issue of my newspaper, before twenty-four hours my occupation would be gone. *The business of the journalists is to destroy the truth; to lie outright; to pervert; to vilify; to faun at the feet of mammon, and to sell his country and his race for his daily bread. You know it, and I know it and what folly is this toasting an independent press? We are the tools and vassals of rich men behind the scenes. We are the jumping jacks; they pull the strings and we dance. Our talents, our possibilities and our lives are all the property of other men. We are intellectual prostitutes."* Multiple contributors, The American Citizens and Laumen Association, *A U.S. Police Action: Operation Vampire Killer,* pp. 18, 19. (Emphasis supplied.)

Swinton was honest enough to admit that he and most other journalists are told to write the things that are in harmony with the plans and purposes of the CFR. Ultimately, the world's wealthy, like the Rothschilds, Rockefellers, and Morgans, who founded and run the CFR, are under the control of the Black Pope, the Jesuit General. <u>The Jesuits are using the media to prepare the world to receive the Pope as the great man of peace</u>, to receive the Pope as the ruler of the world from Jerusalem, to accept the destruction of the U. S. Constitution, and to bring the world back to the feudalism of the Dark Ages.

Job Loss Since NAFTA

We were emphatically told by the CFR that the North American Free Trade Agreement, [NAFTA], was in the best interests of the American people. Instead, NAFTA has destroyed thousands of middle class jobs in America and moved those jobs to Mexico and Red China. NAFTA is devastating the industrial manufacturing base in the United States. We have seen all the Jesuits are behind the effort to destroy the middle class in America and return to the structure that existed during the Dark Ages. The Jesuits want to undo everything that Protestantism and freedom has done for America. NAFTA is part of that process.

Vietnam: Why Did We Go?

"At 8:30 a.m., Saturday, the 23rd of November, 1963, the limousine carrying CIA director John McCone pulled into the White House ... He was also there to transact one piece of business prior to becoming involved in all the details entailed in a presidential transition, and the signing of National Security Memorandum 278, a classified document which immediately reversed John Kennedy's decision to withdraw from the war in Vietnam. The effect of memorandum 278 would give the Central Intelligence Agency carte blanc to proceed with a full-scale war in the Far East ..." Robert Morrow, *First Hand Knowledge,* p. 249.

Kennedy Withdraws Troops

This war eventually involved over half a million Americans in a life-and-death struggle without the Constitutional requirement of congressional approval. Eventually, President Kennedy began pulling troops from South Vietnam. The Papacy strongly objected to this, and **President Kennedy** was gunned down. The very next day, Memorandum 278 was signed, which reversed Kennedy's decision to deescalate the war in South Vietnam.

Kennedy

At Death, Order Reversed

Vietnam was a Jesuit war designed to create a Catholic super-power in Southeast Asia. The only way this could occur was by the bitter persecution of a religious giant already in the area, the Buddhists. **Ngo Dinh Diem**, a tyrannical Catholic dictator, was put into power. The Jesuit controlled American press said almost nothing about the terrible religious persecutions taking place in Southeast

Diem

Asia. John Kennedy began pulling America out of Vietnam but was gunned down by Jesuit assassins before he could accomplish much. The no-win war went on for another ten years, ending in ignominious defeat for America. What remains is, a winding wall in Washington, D. C., listing 58,000 Americans that lost their lives and millions of others not listed who have lived retarded lives as a result of wounds and afflictions received in this religious war.

Jesuit wars to destroy religious enemies continue today. Next we will look at the Middle East and why so many die near the city of peace — Jerusalem.

Won't They Ever Stop Fighting?

During the last two generations, there has been continual conflict in the Middle East. The six-day Israeli-Egyptian war of 1967, and the Yom Kippur Arab-Israeli war of 1973 are more prominent than the others. The bombings, bloodshed, crying, and the misery of war never seem to stop. Why do they continue fighting? What is the purpose of continuing this senseless killing?

The land of Israel lies at the center of an area that is completely hostile to it. Israel is of great religious and historical significance because the Messiah, Jesus Christ, walked the land of Israel for three and a half years of public ministry.

Catholics Eye Jerusalem

"A Jesuit cardinal named Augustine Bea showed us how desperately the Roman Catholics wanted Jerusalem at the end of the third century. Because of its religious history and its strategic location, the Holy City was considered a priceless treasure. A scheme had to be developed to make Jerusalem a Roman Catholic city.

"The great untapped source of manpower that could do this job was the children of Ishmael. The poor Arabs fell victim to one of the most clever plans ever devised by the powers of darkness ..." Jack Chick, *The Prophet Part 6*, pp. 5, 18.

Muslims Keep Jerusalem

The Pope's plans failed miserably. Instead of giving Jerusalem to the Pope, the Moslems built their sacred, Dome of the Rock, in Jerusalem, on the very site of the old Jewish temple, making Jerusalem the second most holy place, next to Mecca, in the whole Islamic world. There was no way that the victorious and powerful Arab armies would give Jerusalem to the Pope. Now the Arab leaders turned to new lands to conquer.

"The Muslim generals were determined to conquer the world for Allah ... so they turned their eyes towards Europe. The Islamic ambassadors approached 'His Holiness' in the Vatican and asked for papal bulls to give them permission to invade European countries. The Vatican was outraged. War was inevitable. Temporal power and control of the world was considered the basic right of the pope. He wouldn't think of sharing it with what he considered heathens. The pope raised up his armies and called them *crusades* to hold back the children of Ishmael from grabbing Catholic Europe. The wars continued for centuries ... and Jerusalem slipped out of the pope's grasp." *Ibid.,* p. 23. (Emphasis supplied.)

Will there ever be peace in Israel? There will probably be peace for a brief interval when the Pope is enthroned there. But the Pope will soon start to exercise his authority to force the entire world to become Catholic as he did during the Dark Ages when he controlled that part of the world. This will bring about terrible persecution and destruction throughout the earth. Only those who are in submission to God's control will find safety in that awful time.

America No Longer Free

The Skull and Bones Order is an entry point into the Illuminati. The Illuminati, which we have seen, is a front for the Jesuit Order. Anyone, who is working for (or a part of) the Illuminati, is connected to the Jesuits, the greatest foe of Protestant religious and civil liberty. To be part of the Illuminati and the Jesuits makes it *impossible* to love the Constitution or to uphold its principles. Those groups exist for the destruction of the Constitution.

Are you aware of any leaders or Presidents that have ever held office who have been part of the Skull and Bones Order of Yale University?

"George Bush (father and son) was a Skull and Bonesman." *Ibid.,* p. 320.

George Bush [the father], and George Bush [the son], have both attended Yale University and are both a part of the Skull and Bones Order. Both of these men are part of the Illuminati and the Jesuits.

Bush Sr.

Bush Jr.

The Bush family's connection to the Harriman's/Illuminati/Jesuits, goes way back.

President Would Obey the Pope

Bush Jr.

Before George Bush ever entered the White House (January 2001), he was availing his support to the work of the Catholic Church in America. He demonstrated that his allegiance would be counter to the Constitution, and supportive of a system whose position, over the last 200 plus years has been opposed to the American Constitution.

Appendix 8E — Unmasking the Enemy

Kennedy Disobeys the Pope

Kennedy

"In 1960, John Kennedy went from Washington to Texas to assure Protestant preachers that he would not obey the pope. In 2001, George Bush came from Texas up to Washington to assure a group of Catholic Bishops that he would obey the pope." *Washington Times, April 16, 2001.*

From another document, a Catholic paper called *Peter's Voice*; the following was also quoted in Reuters News service of March 22, 2001 — for the cultural center in Washington D.C. dedicated to **Pope John Paul II.** This is what President Bush declared, **"The best way to honor Pope John Paul II, truly one of the great men, is to take his teachings seriously, to listen to his words and put his words and teachings into action here in America."**

Pope John Paul

Compare this quote and recognize the contrast between the words of the Constitution and the words of the Church of Rome.

Equality At Law Denied

"The most sacred principle of the United States Constitution is the equality of every citizen before the law. The fundamental principle of the Church of Rome is the denial of that equality. Liberty of conscience is proclaimed by the United States, a most sacred principle which every citizen must uphold ... But liberty of conscience is declared by all the popes and councils of Rome, a most godless, unholy, and diabolical thing, which every good Catholic must abhor and destroy at any cost." Charles Chiniquy, *Fifty Years in the Church of Rome*, p. 284.

George Bush's very statements, at the dedication of the cultural Center, declare he would destroy and abolish the First Amendment to the Constitution of the United States.

Church and State Combine

"The American Constitution assures the absolute independence of the civil from the ecclesiastical or church power; but the Church of Rome declares through all her pontiffs and councils that such independence is an impiety and revolt against God." *Ibid.*, p. 284.

The American Constitution assures the separation of the church from the State, but the Catholic Church throughout the Dark Ages, and today, has been trying to force them together. The result of such a union has always been terrible bloodshed and persecution. Because the Founding Fathers of America realized the evils of church/state union, they made sure in the Bill of Rights that the church and state would remain separate.

"The Constitution of the United States denies the right in anybody to punish any other for differing from him in religion. But the Church of Rome says that she has the right to punish with the confiscation of their goods, or the penalty of death, those who differ in faith from the pope." *Ibid.*, p. 284.

Popes Not Infallible

As we go down through history and see how one Pope after another differed from previous Popes, arguing, and disagreeing with each other, — the concept of Papal infallibility becomes meaningless! How many beliefs of the Pope and of the Church of Rome are even found in the Word of God? Is purgatory? Is worship of the Virgin Mary? Is turning the bread in the Communion Service into the actual body of Christ? These are the Pagan principles, handed down through the ages, that the Church of Rome declares valid.

War on Terror Planned

The basis for this section is a letter that was written on August 15, 1871 by Albert Pike to Giusseppe Mazzini quoted in the book *Descent Into Slavery*.

Pike

Pike declared that the First World War would be used to destroy Czarist Russia and then to place that land under the control of Illuminati agents. That Czarist Russia was destroyed in WWI is a fact of history. Czar Nicholas and his wife, Alexandra, along with their many children, were all slain while posing for a picture in 1917. The reasons why Czarist Russia was targeted are more skewed elements in history. The Czars of Russia had for well over 100 years been a thorn in the side of the Jesuits.

Russia Removed Jesuits in 1820

"The Russian emperor, Alexander, was currently compelled to issue a royal decree in 1816, by which he expelled them [the Jesuits] **from St. Petersburg and Moscow. This proving ineffectual, he issued another in 1820, excluding them entirely from the Russian dominions."** R. W. Thompson, *The Footprints of the Jesuits*, pp. 245, 246.

Alexander

The same Czar, who had the audacity to bring a Constitution to the Russian people, also did something else for which the Jesuits would not forgive him. At the height of the Civil War, when the balance of the war could go either way, Alexander II came to the aid of Abraham Lincoln.

"The presence of the Russian Navy helped the Union enforce a devastating naval blockade against the Southern states which denied them access to critical supplies from Europe ... Without the inhibiting effect of the presence of the Russian fleet, the course of the war could have been significantly different." G. Edward Griffin, *The Creature from Jekyll Island,* pp. 377, 378.

Civil War / Russian Blockade

By driving the Jesuits from Russia, refusing to establish a Central Bank, planning a constitution, and aiding the North during the Civil War, the Czars of Russia had incurred the undying wrath of the Jesuit Order. Payback was imminent. The other no-no of the Czars was their protection of the Russian Orthodox Church, the implacable enemy of Rome for over 1000 years.

Communism's Reign of Terror

Not only was the Czarist system in Russia to be destroyed, but the Orthodox Church would be toppled as well. Pike revealed that Illuminati agents would be put into positions of power in Russia. Illuminati agents, acting as a front for the Jesuits, would bring a reign of terror to that great land for several generations. Starting with **Lenin, Trotsky**, and **Stalin**, the Jesuits used them to have 60 million Russians obliterated over the next 30 years. **Kruschev** and **Breshnev** continued the onslaught to a lesser degree for several more years. All of this was done in the name of Communism. *In truth, the Jesuits used the Communist front to carry out heinous crimes in Russia.*

Trotsky

Kruschev

Lenin

Stalin

Breshnev

Terror Attacks Start Wars

In order to bring America into this conflict and violate the famed Monroe doctrine, (which stated that Europe could fight her own wars and America would stay out of them), there was a planned 'terrorist' attack that caused the loss of many Americans lives. This brought America into the war. The terrorist attack that was carried out against Americans was the torpedoing of the Lusitania.

"The deed had been done, and it set in motion great waves of revulsion against the Germans. These waves eventually flooded through Washington and swept the United States into war." *Ibid.,* pp. 260, 261.

Does that sound familiar? Is the author talking about WWI or WWII (Pearl Harbor), or about September 11, 2001 and the war on terror? In every case, the situation has been nearly identical. Create a fervor of anger against a foreign power and America goes to war. It was all

planned that way! The Jesuits, who pre-planned the wars, planned for these terrorist attacks in order to bring America into the battle.

Russian Expansion World War II

Illuminist-Jesuit, **Albert Pike,** declared that the second war would result in an expansion of Russian influence and the creation of a state of Israel in Palestine. Did the Second World War do those things? The influence of Russia worldwide was certainly seen following the Second World War. Due to the war, Russian expansion was certainly seen as the Russian government brought under her control several satellite countries. The Second World War also brought about the creation of Israel in Palestine. The Jews were given the strip of land along the eastern shores of the Mediterranean Sea. *Albert Pike is batting 100%. Who is listening?*

World War III, Zionist, and Arabs

According to **Albert Pike**, the third war would be stirred up by Illuminati agents between the Zionists and the Arabs. Since the Illuminati is a front organization for the Jesuits, the Jesuits created the current war on terror. What event was it that ignited the involvement of America in this conflict? It was the tragic events of September 11, 2001. Could it be that the World Trade Center attacks, just like the Lusitania and Pearl Harbor, were orchestrated to bring America into this conflict?

This conflict was to originate between the Zionists and the Arabs. Who are Zionists? They are Jews, or those who are pro-Israel. In the current war on terror, who is fighting? The Americans and the English, the two most pro-Israeli nations on the earth, are at war against the Arabs of Afghanistan and Iraq. The conflict, according to Pike, was planned to extend worldwide. After a time of death and devastation, the world would become so fed up with the horrors of war that they would welcome anything. At that moment, the 'pure doctrine of Lucifer' can be manifested on the earth.

Doctrine of Lucifer

What is the pure doctrine of Lucifer? Lucifer is the name that originally was given to the angel that was closest to

God in Heaven. After a time, Lucifer, the bearer of light, became so proud of his powers, given to him by his Creator, that he rebelled and tried to bring all the angels and created beings to his side. Eventually, there was war in heaven (REV 12:7-9) and Lucifer, now the devil, was cast to the earth. He devilishly sought to possess worship and honor of all created beings.

Appendix 8E — Unmasking the Enemy

Introducing Sun Worship

Lucifer sought the worship that belonged to God and God alone!! For finite beings that had cast off their allegiance to their Creator, the devil had the perfect and most ready object for men to adore and worship. He chose the most powerful thing in man's visible universe, the sun. Through **Nimrod**, the great grandson of Noah, sun worship was introduced. As generations passed, the devil's sun worshippers began to make monuments in honor of the sun.

Nimrod

Stonehenge in England and the Parthenon in Rome were just a few of the memorials in the sun's honor. After millennia, the building of **St. Peter's Basilica** in Rome

Stonehenge

was shaped in the form of the sundial, in honor of the sun.

Towards the end of the war on terror, there would be a universal manifestation of Lucifer's doctrine of sun worship; it will be seen in the honoring of the day that honors the sun. It is called Sunday. Laws to worship on the day of the sun will spread all over the earth because the devil, (or dragon of REV 13:4), wants everyone to worship him. Most of the earth will choose to honor this pagan day — the day that is steeped in devil worship.

World Honoring the Day of the Sun

There are so many dear, dear people who have no idea that by worshipping on the day of the sun that they are honoring the devil's counterfeit. They have honored this day, in ignorance, all of their lives. This is what they have been taught, and seen practiced, by their parents, grandparents, and their religious institutions.

Honor God or Lucifer?

This universal manifestation will be brought out in the public view in full display, before all of mankind. All the world will be brought to honor the doctrines of Lucifer or the One who deserves worship. Throughout the Bible, it is clear that worship of God is due Him because He is the Creator.

"O come, let us worship and bow down: let us kneel before the Lord our maker. (PS 95:6) Know ye that the Lord he is God: it is He that hath made us, and not we ourselves; we are His people, and the sheep of His pasture." (PS 100:3)

The Creator's Sabbath

Only one Commandment reveals God as the Creator.

"Remember the Sabbath day to keep it holy. Six days shalt thou labor, and do all thy work, but the seventh day is the Sabbath of the Lord thy God ... for in six days the Lord make heaven and earth, the sea, and all that in them is, and rested the seventh day: wherefore the Lord blessed the Sabbath day, and hallowed it." (EX 20:8-11)

The Seventh-day Sabbath, that we call Saturday, reveals God as the Creator. As we honor His day of rest, we are acknowledging that He alone deserves our worship.

As we rest in relationship with Him on His Sabbath day, we are reminded of God's great power in His creating the world. As we behold God's mighty and majestic power displayed in creation, it cheers our hearts to know that the same Creator can speak peace, hope, and joy to our troubled, restless, and weary hearts and minds. The same Creator/Redeemer is willing to manifest His creative power to make us new creatures. So, while the Sabbath speaks of Christ's great power in creation, it also speaks to us of His wonderful strength to restore in us His gracious character.

God Still Intervenes

It is remarkable to learn that the Bible talks about much of the subject matter covered so far. It has considerable information about the Papacy, its associates, and what the Papal System will accomplish in the near future in its efforts to regain the extensive political power they enjoyed during the Dark Ages.

(Thoughts in this Appendix are used by permission from Truth Triumphant "Special Edition" tabloid on *The Enemy Unmasked.)*

Understanding Bible Prophecy

One of the problems people have with the Bible, especially the Books of Daniel and Revelation, is that it uses many symbols. This does not need to be a problem, because the Bible clarifies what the symbols mean. When the symbols are understood, the Bible can be read as clearly as reading plain text. Each reader that studies prophecy, linked with secular history and current events, will be aware of what to expect next. It is the plan of the enemy, that no one understand these symbols, which unravel prophecy. The Fourth, and last, Vision of Daniel brings everything into focus. The Book of Revelation gives still greater detail.

Appendix 8F — Paganism in the Church

Babylonian Pagan Worship

1. The nativity of the Sun, the birth of Tammuz on December 25.

2. The assumption of Semiramus who became the mother goddess.

3. The mother goddess was worshipped as the Queen of Heaven. JER 7:18

4. Cakes decorated to the goddess with a "T" drawn on them. JER 44:17, 19

5. 40 days of fasting for Tammuz. EZE 8:16

6. Festival of Easter. EZE 8:16

7. The resurrection of Tammuz at Easter and the procession of graven images during the holy week.

8. Veneration of graven images of Baal, Ishtar, Tammuz, and lesser gods in the heavens.

9. The belief of immortality of the soul and burning place of torment.

10. The doctrine of purgatory.

11. The belief of the dead visiting the living; feast held for all in November ("all souls day").

12. Burning incense and candles. JER 11:17; EZE 8:11

13. Chants and repetitive prayers; beaded prayer chains.

14. Symbol of the cross as symbol of Sun worship.

15. Amulets and idols to scare away evil spirits.

16. Transubstantiation practiced by Babylonian priests from 1200-600 BC. They believed the sun god entered the wafer, and the round wafer was to be worshipped and eaten as food for the soul.

17. The round disk "sun" wafer with IHS symbol of Isis, Horus, and Seb eaten as food for the soul.

18. Painting of the child (Tammuz) and mother (Semiramus) with the glory of the sun around their heads.

19. Infant baptism and sprinkling of holy water.

20. Necromancy — talking to the dead.

21. House for the virgin priestesses (prostitutes) to be employed at Pagan temples.

22. The first day of the week kept sacred to honor the Persian sun god Mithra. "SUN"day.

Catholic Doctrines of the Vatican

1. The nativity of Jesus, Christmas day, December 25.

2. In 1950 Pope Pius XXI adopted the Pagan belief and proclaimed the assumption of Mary (Bodily ascension to Heaven without dying) to be Catholic doctrine. The first exultation of Mary as the "Mother of God" was applied by the Council of Ephesus.

3. The Virgin Mary worshipped as the Queen of Heaven.

4. Hot Cross Buns with a cross drawn on them.

5. 40 days of Lent.

6. The Festival of Easter.

7. The procession of graven images of Jesus, Mary, and Peter, and of the saints.

8. Veneration of graven images of Jesus, Mary, Peter, and of the "lesser" saints in the heavens.

9. The belief of immortality of the soul and burning place of torment.

10. The doctrine of purgatory adopted from pagan beliefs in AD 593.

11. The festival of "all souls day" held November 2, and "all saints day" held November 1.

12. The burning of incense and candles.

13. Gregorian chants and the Rosary, adopted from Pagan beliefs by Peter the Hermit in AD 1079.

14. The crucifix.

15. The wearing of crucifixes and medals displayed for protection. (e.g. Scapular)

16. Transubstantiation adopted from Paganism by the Catholic Church in the 11th Century.

17. The wafer used in the Eucharist is round with IHS engraved on it.

18. Paintings of the child (Jesus) and mother (Mary) with "halos" or of the "sun" around their heads.

19. Infant baptism and sprinkling of holy water.

20. Mysticism — novenas to the dead.

21. Convents for nuns.

22. The change of the seventh day Sabbath to "SUN"day.

23. Title Pontifex Maximus is the name for the chief head of the Pagan Babylonian system of idolatry, later claimed by the Caesars. It means 'The Great Bridge Builder' intending he has the power to bridge the gap between death and life!

23. Pontifex Maximus one of the first names for the Pope!

24. Janus and Cybele were holders of the keys to Heaven and Hell.

24. The Pope claims to have the keys of Peter.

25. The high priest kings carried on a throne to the temple of his god.

25. The Pope carried on a portable throne to the Basilica of St. Peter.

26. The Pagan high priest king believed to be the incarnate of the Sun god.

26. The Pope proclaims to be Christ's Vicar here on Earth.

27. Offerings of "good works" to appease the gods.

27. Penance, and indulgences, as salvation by works.

28. Human sacrifices burned by fire as offering to appease the Sun god.

28. Those who opposed the doctrines of the Roman Catholic church were often burned at the stake.

29. Gold was considered the flesh of the "Sungod."

29. The Vatican is drenched in gold throughout.

30. Gargoyles = a pagan god.

30. Vatican as well as thousands of Catholic churches have gargoyles on their roofs.

31. Phallic symbol of the male sex organ placed on roofs.

31. Largest phallic symbol is in the center of St. Peter's square as well as steeples on all Catholic churches.

32. Symbol of serpent on numerous Roman bath houses.

32. Symbol of serpent on numerous Catholic church door handles, Papal crests, etc. (See #57.)

33. Atlas carries the universe on his shoulders.

33. Numerous Popes depicted in paintings in the same manner.

34. Solar wheel as symbol for Baal worship can be found carved into ancient as well as modern Buddhist temples — carved into ancient ornament representing Osiris. Stone carvings showing a wheel to represent an Assyrian Babylonian altar. (See #53.)

34. St. Peter's square (See #54) has the largest solar wheel on the planet. ALL Catholic churches have numerous solar wheels in stain glass windows as well as many other areas of the church. Notre Dame Cathedral in Paris sports a very huge one on it's face. There is a great one in the ceiling as well as the floor tiles of the monastery of St. Ignatius Loyola in Spain. Numerous paintings, statues, ornaments, and letterheads of all Catholic churches have one or more "solar wheels" depicted upon them. And the ONE WORLD CHURCH that started June 26, 2000 uses the solar wheel as its official logo.

35. Symbols of the "Unicorn, Peacock, and Phoenix" used to signify the Sun god.

35. Symbols of the "Unicorn, Peacock, and Phoenix" used to symbolize the "communion" of Christ in many churches on doors or chapels as well as sanctuaries.

36. Crescent moon used to signify moon goddess, "Nanna."

36. Crescent used to cradle Eucharist in the Monstrance of the Catholic church. As well, it is depicted in numerous paintings and sculptures.

37. Three letters "S.F.S." within a small blaze is used to represent the universal number "6" in the Pagan mysteries.

37. "S.F.S." in a small blaze is carved into the Vatican Monstrance in the Vatican museum as well as many monstrances the world over. (See #56.)

38. Alternating rays of the sun burst used to represent unity of "man and woman" common in all aspects of Paganism. (Curved ray = female "yonic;" Straight ray = male "phallic.")

38. Monstrance of Catholicism, as well as many paintings and sculptures, all depict same rays of both the "phallic and yonic" symbolism can be found literally all over the Roman Catholic church.

39. Carvings of "nature spirits" (fauns or satyrs) depicting a horned, hoofed-god were a common feature in all Pagan cults.

39. Carvings of "nature spirits" (fauns or satyrs) depicting a horned, hoofed-god are found all over the Treasury of the Vatican beneath St. Peters Square and Cathedrals.

40. Statues of a "Modonna" found in all Pagan cults as well as Egyptian Madonna Isis with her son Horus, or Hindu cults with Davaki, and her son Krishna.

40. Mary found in all Catholic churches holding baby Jesus.

41. Statue of Zeus holds a symbol of thunder and a lightening bolt to symbolize his position as a god.

41. Mary depicted in many statues in the same manner.

42. Demi-gods holding crooked diving staff representative of the serpent and lightening bolt.

42. Pope carries exact same staff (serpent crosiers).

43. Adad, Enlil, Baal, Neptune, Poseidon and other "gods" of storm and sea were depicted as carrying tridents.

43. Crosses, as well as statues of Jesus and Mary, in Cathedrals all over the world are carved with tridents on them.

44. Hand gestures in the form of a trident found depicted in Jupiter, Buddha, Apollo, Hindu deities, as well as "votive hands" in Pagan temples.

44. Statue of St. Peter as well as millions of other statues, paintings, photos, and videos of everyone from Jesus and Mary to priests, cardinals, bishops, all the Popes, Vatican guards and even lay people in the Catholic church can be seen holding up the three finger trident salute of Pagan Rome. (Now called the salute to the Trinity.)

45. Pine cones used to represent the deity of a solar god Osiris, Bacchus, Dionysus, as well as Mexican gods, Hindu gods, and Assyrian gods.

45. Largest pine cone sculpture in the world found in the "Court of the Cone" at the Vatican. The pine cone is also found carved into the crooked pagan staff (serpent crosier) of the Popes of Rome. In fact, the pine cone is found throughout the Vatican, as well as in Cathedrals as decoration.

46. Oanne, Babylonian fish-god (half man, half fish) was depicted by Pagan high priests by wearing a fish head mitre (head dress) upon a man's head to symbolize man and fish joining when "sun god" set into the ocean. One particular Biblical deity = Dagon. Dag = fish; On = sun.

46. Mitres are worn by all Popes of Catholicism.

47. The Roman sun-god with the alternating yonic and phallic symbols surrounding his head was found carved in excavated Roman bath houses in England. It is also found as "Apollo" on the façade of the Pergamum Museum in East Berlin.

47. Almost all Catholic churches have the exact same carving above their pulpits, pillars, on statues, as well as carved into ceilings above altars. Some Catholic churches actually have it carved into the Eucharist itself.

48. Statues of the Romanized Egyptians Isis with globes in hand, Hercules as a solar deity carried the very same globe in hand, and the Persian sun-god Mithra is also depicted with the globe in hand as a sign of a ruler of the Universe.

48. The Vatican has a solid gold statue of Jesus with the globe in hand, a black marble statue called "the black virgin of Montserrat" and a statue of a "child Jesus" with globe in hand.

49. Coptic shells were carved to symbolize the Universe. Roman grave stones used them to represent the Heavens. Statues of Atlas can be found carrying the "universe" shell upon its shoulders. Pagan Rome carved Poseidon with the shell in his head. Venus was said to be born IN a Coptic shell.

49. St. Peter's Basilica in the Vatican has the Pagan symbols within the Papal Crest upon the wall. The coptic shell is found over the crypt of St. Paul's Cathedral in London. This cosmic symbol is often used as a font for holy water in Catholic churches the world over. They even have statues of angels holding the Pagan symbol.

50. Large evil eye can be found carved on a Roman sarcophagus in the National Archaeological Museum in Rome, Italy. Masonic pendants have them as well. Hathor, the "eye of Osiris," can be found all over Egyptian temples. It was commonly used as protection against evil magic.

50. This very same evil eye within the pyramid is found on Roman Catholic pulpits, ceilings, altars, doors, pendants, medals, etc.

It is also on the back side of the USA dollar bill.

51. The multi-level crown was first worn by old Babylonian gods in 1800 BC. The horned tiara was carved atop Assyrian winged-bull cherubims. The Jewish Kabbalistic solar deity wore this very same tiara, as did Krishna.

51. The bronze tomb of Pope Sixtus has this three ringed tiara on his head. On that tiara you can also see six serpents upon it. All the Popes have worn the tiara as a symbol of their authority as "gods of the earth, heaven, and hell." Hence, the "three rings" upon it. The Vatican has a solid gold tiara on display in the Vatican treasury. This could be the very crown the Pope will hand to Antichrist when he arrives to personate Jesus Christ in the days ahead.

52. Quetzalcoatl, the lord of life and death in the Aztec and Toltec cultures of AD 1000 had an open chest with an exposed heart displayed. This was believed to be nourishment offered to the sun gods.

52. Literally hundreds of thousands of statues, paintings, posters, lithographs, etc. have Jesus as well as Mary depicted in the same manner with what the Catholic church calls "The Sacred Heart." Notice that these "sacred hearts" also have the symbols of the sun god, Mithra, glowing rather boldly behind them.

53. Assyrio-Babylonian Altar

54. St. Peters Square in the Vatican has the largest symbol of Baal in the world.

55. Statue of St. Peter, in St. Peter's Basilica, Rome. The gods from the Pantheon are in the Vatican museum with the exception of Jupiter which has been modified, retitled as St. Peter, and seated on a throne in St. Peter's Basilica.

56. This monstrance (the case used to display the wafer-god of the mass) in the Vatican Museum has the three letters S.F.S. within a small blaze. Each of these letters is a universal symbol for the number "6" in the Papal mysteries. To the eye of the initiate it simply reads 666.

57. Dragon Papal Crest, Vatican Museum in Rome.
(Vatis = diviner; can = serpent)
Vatican = divining serpent (in Latin).

Note: Appendix Information compliments of websites:
www.harrypottermagic.org/Paganism-charts.htm
www.harrypottermagic.org/tradition.htm
www.members.tripod.com/sword_of_the_spirit/id3.htm

Appendix 8G — Parallels Between Mary Worship and Wicca Goddess Worsh

BIBLICAL MARY	ROMAN CATHOLIC MARY	THE WICCA GODDESS
1. Humble and obedient. Calls herself "the handmaid of the Lord."	1. The Pope officially gave Mary the title "Queen of Heaven" and established a feast day honoring Mary as the Queen of Heaven.	1. Wiccans call their goddess the "Queen of Heaven."
2. Knew she needed a Savior: "And my spirit hath rejoiced in God my Saviour." LUKE 1:47	2. "Immaculate Conception" (Mary was conceived sinless, without original sin) and "All-Holy" (Mary lived a sinless life).	2. Goddesses don't need salvation. They make the rules.
3. Normal wife and mother.	3. "Perpetual Virginity."	3. Goddess don't have human children.
4. No Biblical evidence that Mary didn't die like a normal person.	4. "Glorious Assumption," (Mary was bodily taken up into Heaven.)	4. Goddesses don't die.
5. Jesus told John to take Mary into his home and take care of her as if she was his own mother.	5. Catholics are the adopted children of Mary. "Woman behold your son" (JOHN 19:26) is taken to apply literally to every Catholic.	5. Witches are the adopted, "hidden children" of the Queen of Heaven.
6. Normal woman.	6. Sometimes pictured standing on a crescent moon, wearing a crown, or with a circle of stars around her head.	6. Moon goddess.
7. Normal woman.	7. Supernatural (apparitions accompanied by miracles and healings).	7. Supernatural.
8. Points people to Jesus. Mary said, "Whatsoever he saith unto you, do it." JOHN 2:5	8. Can make Jesus do things. A full page newspaper ad showing Mary and Jesus says, "He hasn't denied her anything in 2,000 years. What would you have her ask Him?" This is not official Catholic doctrine but it is a widespread attitude which is encouraged by pious literature.	8. Points to herself. Wants to be worshipped.
9. Knew that she needed a Saviour.	9. Apparitions of "Mary" have promised that if people wear certain objects (such as a Scapular or Miraculous Medal) or say certain prayers, then they are guaranteed to go to Heaven. The Catholic Church has not officially approved of these practices, but it has also not discouraged them.	9. Invoked to make supernatural things happen through witchcraft (the use of special objects and special verbal formulas). Goddesses don't need a Saviour.

Appendix 8H — Christianity Steps Downward to Paganism

Note: The following list reveals strange practices that have entered many "Christian" denominations. None of these practices have their roots in the Bible, or the teachings of Christ! All of them have come from Sun Worship or Paganism.

1. Prayers for the dead began about AD 300.

2. Making the sign of the cross — AD 300.

3. Wax candles — AD 320.

4. Veneration of angels and dead saints and the use of Images — AD 375.

5. The Mass, as a daily celebration — AD 394.

6. Beginning of the exaltation of Mary, the term "Mother of God," first applied to her by the Council of Ephesus -AD 431.

7. Priests began to dress differently from laymen — AD 500.

8. Extreme Unction — AD 526.

9. Purgatory doctrine established by Gregory I in AD 593.

10. Latin language, used in prayer and worship, imposed by Gregory I in AD 600.

11. Prayers directed to Mary, dead saints, and angels around AD 600.

12. Title of Pope, or universal bishop, given to Boniface III by Emperor Phocas in AD 607.

13. Kissing the Pope's foot, began with Pope Constantine in AD 709.

14. Temporal power of the Popes, conferred by Pepin, king of the Franks — AD 750.

15. Worship of the cross, images, relics, authorized in 786.

16. Holy water, mixed with a pinch of salt and blessed by a priest — AD 850.

17. Worship of St. Joseph — AD 890.

18. College of Cardinals established in AD 927.

19. Baptism of bells, instituted by Pope John XIII in AD 995.

20. Canonization of dead saints, first by Pope John XV, in AD 995.

21. Fasting on Fridays and during Lent — AD 998.

22. The Mass, developed gradually as a sacrifice, attendance made obligatory in the 11th century — AD 1050.

23. Celibacy of the priesthood, decreed by Pope Gregory VII (Hildebrand) — AD 1079.

24. The Rosary, mechanical praying with beads, invented by Peter the Hermit — AD 1090.

25. The Inquisition instituted by the Council of Verona — AD 1184.

26. Sale of Indulgences — AD 1190.

27. Transubstantiation, declared by Pope Innocent III — AD 1215.

28. Auricular Confession of sins to a priest instead of to God, instituted by Pope Innocent III, in Lateran Council — AD 1215.

29. Adoration of the wafer (Host), decreed by Pope Honorius III — AD 1220.

30. Bible forbidden to laymen, placed on the index of Forbidden Books by the Council of Valencia — AD 1229.

31. The Scapular, invented by Simon Stock, an English monk — AD 1251.

32. Cup forbidden to the people at Communion by Council Constance — AD 1414.

33. Purgatory proclaimed as a dogma by the Council of Florence — AD 1439.

34. The doctrine of Seven Sacraments affirmed — AD 1439.

35. The Ave Maria (part of the last half) was completed 50 years later and approved by Pope Sixtus V at the end of the 16th century — AD 1508.

36. Jesuit order founded by Ignatius Loyola — AD 1534.

37. Tradition declared of equal authority with the Bible by the Council of Trent — AD 1545.

38. Apocryphal books added to the Bible by the Council of Trent — AD 1546.

39. Immaculate Conception of the Virgin Mary, proclaimed by Pope Pius IX — AD 1854.

40. Infallibility of the Pope in matters of faith and morals, proclaimed by the Vatican Council — AD 1870.

41. Public schools condemned by Pope Pius XI — AD 1930. Assumption of the Virgin Mary by Pope Pius XII — 1950.

42. Mary proclaimed Mother of God by Pope Paul VI in 1965.

THE STRUCTURE OF DANIEL

FOUR VISIONS REVEAL GOD'S PLAN TO SAVE HIS PEOPLE

One Major Line of Prophecy From 606 BC — to the Establishment of Christ's Kingdom

VISION 1 - DAN 2	VISION 2 - DAN 7	VISION 3 - DAN 8	VISION 4 - DAN 10-12
HEAVENLY SCENE **DAN 2:1, 19** **GOLD HEAD** **SILVER BREAST & ARMS** **BRASS BELLY & THIGHS** **IRON LEGS** **IRON & CLAY —** **FEET & TOES**	**HEAVENLY SCENE** **DAN 7:2-14** **LION** **BEAR** **LEOPARD** **DREADFUL BEAST** **LITTLE HORN**	**HEAVENLY SCENE** **DAN 8:2-14** **RAM** **HE GOAT** **"OUT OF ONE OF THEM"** **LITTLE HORN** **"WAXED EXCEEDING GREAT"**	
INTERLUDE QUESTION **DAN 2:26** **WHAT IS THE** **SECRET OF** **THE DREAM?**	**INTERLUDE QUESTION** **DAN 7:16** **WHAT IS THE** **TRUTH OF** **ALL THIS?**	**INTERLUDE QUESTION** **DAN 8:15** **WHAT IS THE** **MEANING OF** **THIS VISION?**	
HISTORIC-PROPHETIC **OUTLINE** **DAN 2:36-43** **BABYLON** **MEDO-PERSIA** **GREECE** **ROME (PAGAN IMPERIAL)** **OUTLINE EXTENDS TO:** **AD 476**	**HISTORIC-PROPHETIC** **OUTLINE** **DAN 7:17-25** **BABYLON** **MEDO-PERSIA** **GREECE** **ROME (PAGAN IMPERIAL)** **ROME (PAPAL NO. 1)** **OUTLINE EXTENDS TO:** **AD 1798**	**HISTORIC-PROPHETIC** **OUTLINE** **DAN 8:20-25** **(BABYLON IS REIGNING)** **MEDO-PERSIA** **GREECE** **ROME (PAGAN IMPERIAL)** **ROME (PAPAL NO. 1)** **ROME (PAPAL NO. 2)** **OUTLINE EXTENDS TO:** **AD 1844**	
ANSWER TO QUESTION **DAN 2:44** **GOD OF HEAVEN** **CONSUMES ALL THESE** **KINGDOMS!** **ENDTIME EVENT** **DAN 2:45** **"STONE KINGDOM"** **SECOND COMING OF JESUS**	**ANSWER TO QUESTION** **DAN 7:26** **JUDGMENT SITS** **WITH THE** **"ANCIENT OF DAYS!"** **ENDTIME EVENT** **DAN 7:27** **"KINGDOM GIVEN** **TO THE SAINTS"**	**ANSWER TO QUESTION** **DAN 8:25** **HE [PERSECUTOR]** **SHALL STAND UP** **AGAINST** <u>THE</u> **"PRINCE!"** **ENDTIME EVENT** **DAN 8:25** **"PERSECUTOR BROKEN** **WITHOUT HAND"**	

Note: Only God pulls back the curtain of time in each vision to reveal future events.

Looking Ahead: History and Introduction to Daniel 9

History:

- Jerusalem was laying in ruins, the walls of the city were broken down and the gates burned. The temple had been destroyed long ago and the Jews no longer had a sanctuary or place to worship. It seemed their Hebrew social and religious economy lay in ruins.

- The promise of a coming Messiah to a nation which seemed no longer to exist, appeared, at this point, an impossibility. After 68 years of exile, the Jews had become comfortable in Babylon and had lost their desire to return.

- According to the Scriptural prophecies of Jeremiah, Daniel understood there were only two more years to complete the prophecy of Babylonian captivity. He was desperate that God should move to deliver His people and prepare the nation for the coming Messiah.

- Daniel wanted to see this time prophecy fulfilled so that the Jews would be permitted to return to Jerusalem to rebuild the streets, the walls, and replace the gates. He was waiting and hoping for a decree from the king of Medo-Persia to give the Jews permission to return. However, Darius the Mede had no interest in permitting the Jews to return to rebuild their city.

- In Daniel 8:27, Daniel assumed his regular duties in the king's court, when Gabriel finally returns years later with the explanation of the Daniel 8:14 timeline.

Note: Daniel 6:28 explains that Daniel "prospered in the reign of Darius, and in the reign of Cyrus the Persian." Previously, Daniel had been spared execution in the lion's den. Because of his abilities, his integrity, and his steadfast relationship with the living God, Daniel was appointed to be a high official in the government of the new conqueror. As Joseph prospered in Pharaoh's court (GEN 39-50), Daniel prospered in the courts of the kings of Babylon and the kings of Medo-Persia.

Introduction:

- Daniel 9 consists mainly of timelines and will not be found on the Daniel Structure Chart. The chart addresses Historic-Prophetic Outlines only.

- Daniel 9:24-27 is a detailed explanation of a portion of the 2300 day prophecy of Daniel 8:14. Both chapters form one vision even though separated by many years. This chapter shows that we are currently living in the "hour of judgment" [or the great Day of Atonement in the Heavenly Sanctuary].

- At the close of chapter 8, Daniel did not fully understand the vision. Daniel understood the "cleansing of the sanctuary," [that was connected with the Day of Atonement], but he didn't understand the significance of the 2300 days of Daniel 8:14.

- While Daniel was alive, there was no earthly sanctuary that could be cleansed, because Nebuchadnezzar had destroyed that place of worship in Jerusalem. A period of 2300 literal days extends a little over six years, and nothing happened in an earthly sanctuary during the lifetime of Daniel. In fact, at the time of the vision in chapter 8, Daniel was still living in the third year of the reign of Belshazzar in Babylon. (Medo-Persia, Greece, Rome, and the Little Horn Papacy did not yet exist!) Therefore it was self evident that the 2300 day timeline must surely refer to a far-future event. Daniel could not count out those days, because he did not know when to begin counting to ascertain when the Investigative Judgment would begin and ultimately bring that evil Little Horn, which was to "wax exceeding great," to its end. (DAN 7:10-11) He needed greater understanding from Gabriel.

- Daniel's lingering question: Was Daniel 8:14 talking about 2300 "days" or 2300 "years?" According to Ezekiel 4:6, (with its Year-day Computation Principle of interpretation), the prophecy meant 2300 years before the "cleansing of the sanctuary." None of this seemed to fit with Jeremiah's prophecy of 70 years. Daniel's greatest concern was about the calculation of time and how it was to come together. Gabriel was sent in Daniel 9 to complete what he had started in Daniel 8:16; "... make this man to understand the vision."

Note: Throughout Daniel 9, the "2300 days" will be referred to as "2300 years."

DANIEL
The Story of the Rise and Fall of Earthly Kingdoms

CHAPTER 9

VISION THREE
(Part Two)

First Year of Darius the Mede
(538 BC)

1 In the first year of Darius the son of Ahasuerus, of the seed of the Medes, which was made king over the realm of the Chaldeans;

Daniel Studies Jeremiah

2 In the first year of his reign I Daniel understood by books the number of the years, whereof the word of the LORD came to Jeremiah the prophet, that he would accomplish seventy years in the desolations of Jerusalem.

Daniel's Prayer of Confession and Repentance

3 And I set my face unto the Lord God, to seek by prayer and supplication, with fasting, and sackcloth, and ashes:

4 And I prayed unto the LORD my God, and made my confession, and said, O Lord, the great and dreadful God, keeping the covenant and mercy to them that love him, and to them that keep his commandments;

This chapter begins with **Daniel** considering the time of Jewish captivity in Babylon. In two years, the 70 year captivity would be complete. Daniel's prayer, (verses 3-19), utters confession of the sins of the Jewish nation, and requests restoration of Jerusalem and the temple. In verses 20-27, Gabriel arrives to comfort Daniel, and explain the rest of the prophecy from Daniel 8:14. Additional "mini" timelines, within the 2300 year timeline of Daniel 8:14, give specific information about the appointed time for the first advent of the Messiah.

Verse 1

DAN 6:28 Daniel prospered in the reign of Darius, and in the reign of Cyrus the Persian.

Verse 2

2 CHRON 36:21 To fulfil the word of the LORD by the mouth of Jeremiah, until the land had enjoyed her sabbaths: for as long as she lay desolate she kept sabbath, to fulfil threescore and ten years.

JER 25:11-12 And this whole land shall ... serve the king of Babylon seventy years. 12 when seventy years are accomplished, that I will punish the king of Babylon ... for their iniquity, and the land of the Chaldeans, and will make it perpetual desolations.

**Daniel's Prayer for
Deliverance from Captivity**

Note:
- Daniel didn't understand how Jeremiah's prophecy connected with the 2300 years. Then he read Jeremiah 29:13, "And ye shall seek me, and find me, when ye shall search for me with all your heart."
- Daniel began to pray. Most of this chapter consists of Daniel's prayer. While Daniel was praying, Gabriel arrives at the time of the evening sacrifice to offer the explanation of the sanctuary prophecy presented in Daniel 8:14, about fourteen years earlier.

Verse 4

"And I prayed unto the LORD" — In Daniel's prayer:
1. He prayed in a serious, sincere and solemn manner; (vs 3)
2. God's righteousness was priority over his own; (vs 16)
3. It was evident that he had a knowledge of the Scriptures; (vs 5)
4. He confessed his own sins and the sins of his people; (vs 16)
5. He wanted to see the glory of God and His sanctuary; (vs 17)
6. God's promises were claimed. (vs 18)

"to them that keep his commandments" — Daniel understood that the Lord's promise for deliverance at the appointed time was of a conditional nature. If the promise failed, man was to blame, not the Lord. Love for God, through a surrendered heart, will result in the keeping of His Commandments. (JOHN 14:15) The exile of the Jewish people was due to willful disobedience. Daniel begins to petition the Lord for forgiveness; for deliverance of His promises given in Jeremiah's writings.

Daniel's Prayer Continues

5 We have sinned, and have committed iniquity, and have done wickedly, and have rebelled, even by departing from thy precepts and from thy judgments:

6 Neither have we hearkened unto thy servants the prophets, which spake in thy name to our kings, our princes, and our fathers, and to all the people of the land.

7 O Lord, righteousness belongeth unto thee, but unto us confusion of faces, as at this day; to the men of Judah, and to the inhabitants of Jerusalem, and unto all Israel, that are near, and that are far off, through all the countries whither thou hast driven them, because of their trespass that they have trespassed against thee.

8 O Lord, to us belongeth confusion of face, to our kings, to our princes, and to our fathers, because we have sinned against thee.

9 To the Lord our God belong mercies and forgivenesses, though we have rebelled against him;

10 Neither have we obeyed the voice of the LORD our God, to walk in his laws, which he set before us by his servants the prophets.

Verse 5

Daniel's reading of the Scriptures called attention to God's exiles in different time periods. i.e.

1. Moses' counsel to future exiles; (LEV 26)
2. Solomon's prayer for future exiles; (1 KINGS 8:46-53)
3. Jeremiah's letter to the Babylonian exiles. (JER 29:15-20)

These Scripture passages indicated that sin was the cause of God's people experiencing exile. Upon confession and repentance, the exiles would be extended forgiveness and restoration to their homeland once more. Daniel based his prayer on the following verses and pleaded for the Jewish people to return as a nation to Jerusalem.

LEV 26:40-42 If they shall confess their iniquity, and the iniquity of their fathers, with their trespass which they trespassed against me, and that also they have walked contrary unto me. 41 and they then accept of the punishment of their iniquity: 42 <u>Then will I remember my covenant</u> with Jacob … and I will remember the land.

> Conditional Promise of Blessing

JER 18:7-10 At what instant I shall speak concerning a nation, and concerning a kingdom, to pluck up, and to pull down, and to destroy it; 8 If that nation … turn from their evil, I will repent of the evil that I thought to do unto them. 9 And at what instant I shall speak concerning a nation, and concerning a kingdom, to build and to plant it; 10 If it do evil in my sight, that it obey not my voice, <u>then I will repent of the good</u>, wherewith I said I would benefit them.

> Conditional Promise of Constant Tribulation

NEH 9:33 Howbeit thou art just in all that is brought upon us; for thou hast done right, but we have done wickedly.

JER 14:7 O LORD, though our iniquities testify against us, do thou it for thy name's sake: for our backslidings are many; we have sinned against thee.

Verse 6

2 CHRON 36:15-16 And the LORD God of their fathers sent to them by his messengers … because he had compassion on his people. 16 But they mocked the messengers of God, and despised his words, and misused his prophets, until the wrath of the LORD arose against his people, till there was no remedy.

Daniel's Prayer Continues

11 Yea, all Israel have transgressed thy law, even by departing, that they might not obey thy voice; therefore <u>the curse is poured upon us</u>, and the oath that is written in the law of Moses the servant of God, because we have sinned against him.

12 And <u>he hath confirmed his words</u>, which he spake against us, and against our judges that judged us, by bringing upon us a great evil: for under the whole heaven hath not been done as hath been done upon Jerusalem.

13 As it is written in the law of Moses, all this evil is come upon us: yet made we not our prayer before the LORD our God, that we might turn from our iniquities, and understand thy truth.

14 Therefore hath the LORD watched upon the evil, and brought it upon us: for the LORD our God is righteous in all his works which he doeth: for we obeyed not his voice.

15 And now, O Lord our God, that hast brought thy people forth out of the land of Egypt with a mighty hand, and hast gotten thee renown, as at this day; we have sinned, we have done wickedly.

16 O Lord, according to all thy righteousness, I beseech thee, let thine anger and thy fury be turned away from thy city Jerusalem, thy holy mountain: because for our sins, and for the iniquities of our fathers, Jerusalem and thy people are become a reproach to all that are about us.

Verse 11

"the curse is poured upon us" — DEUT 27:15-26 (curses to avoid):

15 Cursed be the man that maketh any graven or molten image ...
16 Cursed be he that setteth light by his father or his mother ...
17 Cursed be he that removeth his neighbour's landmark ...
18 Cursed be he that maketh the blind to wander out of the way ...
19 Cursed be he that perverteth the judgment of the stranger, fatherless, and widow ...
20 Cursed be he that lieth with his father's wife; because he uncovereth his father's skirt ...
21 Cursed be he that lieth with any manner of beast ...
22 Cursed be he that lieth with his sister, the daughter of his father, or the daughter of his mother ...
23 Cursed be he that lieth with his mother in law ...
24 Cursed be he that smiteth his neighbour secretly ...
25 Cursed be he that taketh reward to slay an innocent person ...
26 Cursed be he that confirmeth not all the words of this law to do them. And all the people shall say, Amen.

Verse 12

LAM 2:17 The LORD hath done that which he had devised; <u>he hath fulfilled his word</u> that he had commanded in the days of old ... and <u>he hath caused thine enemy to rejoice over thee</u>.

Verse 14 *(Today's English Version)*

DAN 9:14 Thou, O LORD our God, were prepared to punish us, and you did, because you always do what is right, and we did not listen to you.

Note: God's lessons are intended for our instruction and learning.

Verse 15

Daniel recalls God's great deliverance of His people from Egyptian bondage at the time of the Exodus. He bases his plea upon that great act of God's mercy.

Verse 16

Daniel's plea is not based on the goodness of the people, but on the Lord's deeds of righteousness and gracious dealings with the Jewish nation in the past.

Daniel's Prayer Closes

17 Now therefore, O our God, hear the prayer of thy servant, and his supplications, and cause thy face to shine upon thy sanctuary that is desolate, for the Lord's sake.

18 O my God, incline thine ear, and hear; open thine eyes, and behold our desolations, and the city which is called by thy name: for we do not present our supplications before thee for our righteousnesses, but for thy great mercies.

19 O Lord, hear; O Lord, forgive; O Lord, hearken and do; defer not, for thine own sake, O my God: for thy city and thy people are called by thy name.

Note: In Daniel's prayer, a full account of sin is followed by a full confession of sin. In all aspects, God is vindicated. Recognizing that the sins of the people had brought on many calamities, Daniel acknowledges that these lessons of afflictions were designed to teach the people in the way they should go.

Hos 13:9   O Israel, thou hast destroyed thyself; but in me is thine help.

Verse 19

Daniel is anxious that this promise of deliverance at the end of 70 years is not delayed. He pleads with the Lord to hasten His reply.

James 5:16   The effectual fervent prayer of a righteous man availeth much.

Gabriel, the Master Teacher

20 And whiles I was speaking, and praying, and confessing my sin and the sin of my people Israel, and presenting my supplication before the LORD my God for the holy mountain of my God;

21 Yea, whiles I was speaking in prayer, even the man Gabriel, whom I had seen in the vision at the beginning [Daniel 8:19], being caused to fly swiftly, touched me about the time of the evening oblation [sacrificial offering].

22 And he informed me, and talked with me, and said, O Daniel, I am now come forth to give thee skill and understanding.

23 At the beginning of thy supplications the commandment came forth, and I am come to shew thee; for thou art greatly beloved: therefore understand the matter, and consider the vision [of Daniel 8 and 9].

Verses 20-23

Note: In Daniel 8:15-16, Daniel saw and heard Michael command, "Gabriel, make this man understand the vision." But in Daniel 8:27, Daniel "fainted and was sick certain days." Daniel was not in any condition to receive the information from Gabriel. About fourteen years later Gabriel returned, in response to the command "to make this man understand the vision."

Gabriel Lays Out His Lesson Plans

Gabriel's focus was to point out the major objectives of the lesson. The grand theme of all prophecy has to do with the plan of salvation — God's eternal purpose to: 1) restore in man the image of His Maker; 2) overcome and obliterate sin; 3) establish His kingdom. The 2300 year prophecy was to extend to the beginning of the Investigative Judgment. By the time the judgment would be completed, *sin* would be eradicated from God's people (the living and the dead). Only then, could God bring in "everlasting righteousness" (the Stone Kingdom of Daniel 2). This was to be the work of the Messiah, who would be named "Jesus." He would *save His people from their sins. Sin* is the great separator between God and man. It was Jesus who was to become, after His resurrection, the great High Priest Mediator between God and man. His purpose was to give man power to overcome **sin**.

Gabriel came to help Daniel "to understand and consider," that the information in Daniel 9:24-27 would:

1. Enable Daniel to count out the 2300 year timeline;
2. Reassure Daniel that the city of Jerusalem and the temple would be rebuilt;
3. State what would happen to the Jewish nation and to their holy city, Jerusalem;
4. Determine the exact dates for the Messiah's ministry and His sacrificial death;
5. Explain the Mt. Sinai covenant and its termination;
6. Predict the fall of Jerusalem in AD 70;
7. Explain the Everlasting Covenant's final fulfillment.

Prophetic Key #24 The rest of the chapter will be explaining the timelines in this vision of:

- Seven weeks to the restoration of Jerusalem;
- Seventy weeks to the stoning of Stephen;
- Sixty-nine weeks to the anointing of the Messiah;
- One-half week from the anointing to crucifixion of the Messiah;
- Another, one-half week from the crucifixion to the stoning of Stephen;
- 2300 year timeline (given within the Heavenly Scene of Daniel chapter 8). As noted on page 141, this 2300 symbolic day timeline equals 2300 literal years and reaches to AD 1844 and the cleansing of the Heavenly Sanctuary (that had been cast down in Daniel 8:11). (See Appendix 9B, Parts 1-5 on pages 250-255, for extra help and explanations of individual timelines.)

Looking Ahead: Gabriel came to Daniel, giving him instruction concerning the 2300 year timeline. Although this chapter does not mention this long timeline, the entire passage of verses 24-27 is an explanation, and instruction, as to how to date the beginning and ending of this long prophetic timeline. Gabriel divides this timeline into smaller parts, with explanations.

DANIEL

The Story of the Rise and Fall of Earthly Kingdoms

*The Biblical Interpretation for
the 2300 Year Prophecy
of Daniel 8:14 and
the Seventy Weeks Prophecy*
(Explained with Hebrew Poetry*)

**24 <u>Seventy weeks</u> are determined
upon thy people …**

*(*See Note for Hebrew Poetry on page 245 and
Appendix 9A on page 249.)*

<u>Verse 24</u>

The vision of Daniel 8 is given in the symbolic language of *horns* of the Ram, the He Goat and the Little Horn. The following timelines contained in the last verses of this chapter are all part of the 2300 year timeline that was given in Daniel 8:14 and spoken in symbolic language. The first symbolic timeline to be addressed is the 70 weeks, contained within the 2300 year timeline. The following page explains how voices begin and end the first two timelines of 2300 years and 70 weeks.

 Prophetic Key #24a/b Each prophetic <u>symbolic</u> timeline must be converted to prophetic literal time using the Year-day Computation Principle.

Prophetic Key #24c Timelines that cross from BC to AD must follow the rule of adjustment.

Prophetic Key #26 Timelines begin and end with voices or legislative decrees. Note: The timelines in this vision have historical dates.

Timelines Begin With Three Decrees Spoken of as One Commandment

1. **Cyrus the Great** issued a decree in 537 BC which gave the Jews permission to return to Jerusalem, authorizing them to rebuild the temple (but <u>not the city</u>). (See EZRA 1:2-4; 7:11-13.) The first exiles returned to Jerusalem in 536 BC at the end of the 70 years captivity in Babylon. Many times the Samaritans stopped their work. (See ISA 44:28.)

2. **Darius I** issued a second decree in approximately 520-519 BC for completion of rebuilding the temple. This task was accomplished in 516 BC with the temple being dedicated in 515 BC. This decree did not designate the <u>rebuilding of the city</u>.

3. **Artaxerxes** issued a third decree (EZRA 7:12-26) which was carried out by Ezra in **<u>457 BC</u>.** This decree was the <u>effective one which actually started the work on the city</u>. Again their enemies tried to stop the work causing a thirteen year delay. Eventually, Artaxerxes issued a letter of authorization to resume the work. However, it was the 457 BC decree that initiated the return to Jerusalem to rebuild the streets and the walls. This gave Jerusalem its legal rebirth. Jerusalem was restored to capital city status.

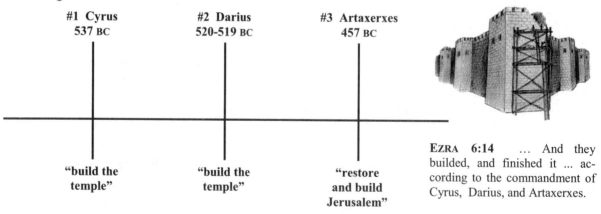

**Three Decrees were Issued for the Rebuilding
of the Temple and the City of Jerusalem**

#1 Cyrus	#2 Darius	#3 Artaxerxes
537 BC	520-519 BC	457 BC
"build the temple"	"build the temple"	"restore and build Jerusalem"

EZRA 6:14 … And they builded, and finished it … according to the commandment of Cyrus, Darius, and Artaxerxes.

VOICES that begin and end the SYMBOLIC TIMELINE of the 2300 YEARS

SYMBOLIC TIMELINE: 2300 Years

DECODING the BEGINNING VOICE by Scripture:
- **DAN 9:25** from the going forth of the commandment [decree] to restore and to build Jerusalem.

APPLICATION for the BEGINNING VOICE of 2300 years:
- The 2300 years (of DAN 8:14) began in the year 457 BC when Artaxerses issued a third decree (by legislative voice) to rebuild and restore Jerusalem. Ezra carried out this decree. (See EZRA 7:11-26.)

BEGINNING VOICE for 2300 Years —

**Artaxerxes' Voice or Decree
in
457 BC**

DECODING the ENDING VOICE by Scripture:
- **DAN 8:14** he said ... Unto two thousand and three hundred days; then shall the sanctuary be cleansed.
- **DAN 7:10** the judgment [voice of court] was set, and the books were opened.

APPLICATION for the ENDING VOICE of 2300 years:
- 2300 years after 457 BC, the legislative voice in the Heavenly Sanctuary ended the 2300 years timeline, and began the time of Investigative Judgment with the house of God on Earth. It's purpose was to restore the Sanctuary which had been cast down in Daniel 8:11. (Also see Appendix 9B, (Part 5), on page 254-255.)

ENDING VOICE for 2300 Years —

**Heavenly Legislative Voice
in
AD 1844**

VOICES that begin and end the SYMBOLIC TIMELINE of the 70 WEEKS

SYMBOLIC TIMELINE: 70 weeks

DECODING the BEGINNING VOICE by Scripture:
- **DAN 9:25** from the going forth of the commandment [decree] to restore and to build Jerusalem.

APPLICATION for the BEGINNING VOICE of 70 weeks:
- In the year 457 BC, Artaxerses issued a third decree (a legislative voice), to rebuild Jerusalem. This was carried out by Ezra. (See EZRA 7:11-26.) Note: The 70 weeks is part of the 2300 year timeline.

BEGINNING VOICE for 70 Weeks —

**Artaxerxes' Voice or Decree
in
457 BC**

DECODING the ENDING VOICE by Scripture:
- **ACTS 7:54, 57, 59** When they heard these things, they were cut to the heart. 57 Then they cried out with a loud voice, and stopped their ears, and ran upon him with one accord. 59 And they stoned Stephen.

APPLICATION for the ENDING VOICE of 70 weeks:
- In the year AD 34 the nation of Israel spoke through their official legal body, the Sanhedrin council, (the nation's political voice), taking legal action to stone Stephen, a missionary of the New Testament church. (Also see Appendix 9B, (Part 2), on page 251.)

ENDING VOICE for 70 Weeks —

**Nation of Israel Spoke
to Stone Stephen
in
AD 34**

241

*The End of the Mt. Sinai
Covenant with the
Hebrew Nation
(in Hebrew Poetry)*

**24 Seventy weeks are <u>determined</u>
upon thy people** ["<u>to put an end
to</u>" the Mt. Sinai Covenant with
Hebrew Israel] **and upon thy holy
city** [Jerusalem] ...

*The Final Fulfillment
of the Everlasting Covenant*

... to ¹**finish the transgression,
and** ²**to make an end of sins, and**
³**to make reconciliation for iniquity, and** ⁴**to bring in everlasting
righteousness, and** ⁵**to seal up the
vision** ⁶**and prophecy, and** ⁷**to
anoint the most Holy.**

<u>**Verse 24**</u> (Concluded)

"determined"— *Strong's* OT#2852 <u>to cut off</u>, i.e. (figuratively) to decree:
KJV - determine.

Definition: *"<u>determined</u>"* — to put an end to ... to come to an end:
"<u>expire</u>." *The Winston Dictionary, College Edition 1946.*

Since Mt. Sinai, the Hebrew nation had been under contract or "covenant"
with God. At the end of 70 weeks (or 490 literal years) that covenant
would be terminated or cut off. With this vision, the Jews had only a certain amount of time left for them to continue in that covenant relationship.
(See page 248 for timeline table and Appendix 9C, pages 256-257.)

Note: The Messiah, through the Everlasting Covenant, was to accomplish
the following:

1.   To finish the transgression [the time frame needed for the Jews to fill
     their "cup of iniquity"];
2.   To make an end of sins [ending the <u>sacrificial sin offerings</u>];
3.   To make reconciliation for iniquity [accepting Christ's sacrifice for
     our sins];
4.   To bring in everlasting righteousness [complete reconciliation of man
     to God];
5.   To seal up the vision [fulfilling the predictions of the first coming of
     the Messiah];
6.   To seal up the prophecy [to fulfill the prophecies of Daniel 8-9];
7.   To anoint the most Holy [anointing the Most Holy place in the Heav-
     enly Sanctuary as Christ enters His final ministry in AD 1844].

In the earthly sanctuary there was a <u>***Day of Judgment***</u> once a year for the
purpose of blotting out the records of the sins deposited in the sanctuary,
and cleansing the people. At the end of this 2300 year timeline, the Court
in Heaven would begin the ***<u>Investigative Judgment</u>*** — a "blotting out of
sin" in the final intercession of the great High Priest, Jesus Christ.

The Jewish leaders crucified their Messiah in AD 31.
Why did the Mt. Sinai Covenant to the Jewish nation
extend to AD 34? Because, God is not vindictive and
does not retaliate. Even though the leaders crucified
Jesus, He still gave the whole nation every opportunity to repent and accept the Messiah. Jesus' ministry
lasted for three and a half years. After His ascension
to heaven, God still sent the disciples to the Jews, to
teach the nation of Israel that Christ was the fulfillment of all the Messianic prophecies. His purpose
was to draw them back to Him.

In AD 34 the Sanhedrin (legal voice of the nation)
took action to stone Stephen. The Mt. Sinai Covenant had contracted the nation to be a witness, a
missionary, and to bring the world the knowledge of
the coming Messiah. They could not be His witnesses if they were stoning His followers. Therefore, the nation cut themselves off from the Mt.
Sinai Covenant by their own legal action. Jesus
thereby confirmed that the Jews were His chosen
nation. After AD 34 the Gentiles were given full
opportunity to be grafted into the Everlasting Covenant. (Stephen followed the teaching in Romans
1:16 that the gospel was to go to the Jews first.)

The Decree of 457 BC
(in Hebrew Poetry)

25 Know therefore and understand, that from the going forth of the commandment [decree] **to restore and to build Jerusalem ...**

*The Messiah Began
His Ministry in AD 27
(in Hebrew Poetry)*

25 ... unto the Messiah the Prince shall be seven weeks, and threescore and two weeks [AD 27]: **the street shall be built again, and the wall, even in troublous times.**

Verse 25

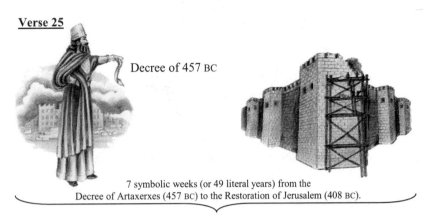

Decree of 457 BC

7 symbolic weeks (or 49 literal years) from the
Decree of Artaxerxes (457 BC) to the Restoration of Jerusalem (408 BC).

EZRA 7:11-13 Now this is the copy of the letter that the king Artaxerxes gave unto Ezra the priest, the scribe even a scribe of the words of the commandments of the Lord, and of his statutes to Israel. 12 Artaxerxes, kings of kings, unto Ezra the priest ... 13 I make a **decree** that all they of the people of Israel, and of his priests and Levites, in my realm, which are minded of their own free will to go up to Jerusalem, go with thee.

The decree of Artaxerxes in 457 BC is the beginning voice for:

1. 2300 years (See Appendix 9B, Part 5, pages 254-255.)
2. 70 weeks (See Appendix 9B, Part 2, on page 251.)
3. 7 weeks (See Appendix 9B, Part 1, on page 250.)
4. 69 weeks (7 + 62) (See Appendix 9B, Part 3, page 252.)

"The date is now firmly established as 457 BC by four independent sources:

- Greek Olympiad dates
- Ptolemy's Canon
- Elephantine Papyri
- Babylonian Cuneiform tablets

"All four lines of chronological evidence point unanimously and harmoniously to the fact that the seventh regional year of Artaxerxes I extended from Nisan (month 1) in the spring of 458 BC to Adar (month 12) in the spring of 457 BC. From the extensive amount of evidence available, these dates can be considered as firmly and irrevocably fixed.

"After Ezra arrived in Palestine in the fifth month of the seventh year of Artaxerxes's reign (EZRA 7:8), he implemented the decree. In older Jerusalem, the Jewish months were numbered from spring to spring. Therefore, the fifth month fell between mid-July and mid-September on our calendar (depending on the timing of the Jewish New Year's day in a given year). The fifth month of the seventh year of Artaxerxes fell in late summer or early autumn of 457 BC. The decree was implemented soon afterward." Jonathan Gray, *Ark of the Covenant*, pp. 145, 570.

SYMBOLIC TIMELINE: 7 Weeks

DECODING the BEGINNING VOICE by Scripture:

- **DAN 9:25** from the going forth of the commandment [decree] to restore and to build Jerusalem.

APPLICATION for the BEGINNING VOICE of 7 weeks:

- In the year 457 BC Artaxerses issued a third decree (by legislative voice) to rebuild Jerusalem. This was carried out by Ezra. (See EZRA 7:11-26.) Note: The 7 weeks was part of the 69 weeks. Both started with the same event.

BEGINNING VOICE for 7 Weeks —

Artaxerxes' Voice or Decree in 457 BC

DECODING the ENDING VOICE by Scripture:

- **NEH 6:15** So the wall was finished.
- **NEH 12:27** And at the dedication of the wall of Jerusalem they sought the Levites … to keep the dedication with gladness, both <u>with thanksgivings</u>, and <u>with singing</u>.
- **NEH 13:3** Now it came to pass, when they had heard the [speaking of the] <u>law</u> …

APPLICATION for the ENDING VOICE of 7 weeks:

- When the temple, streets, and wall were finished and dedicated, there was singing. Nehemiah 13 records the reinstitution of Jewish laws from the book of Moses. (Also see Appendix 9B, (Part 1), on page 250.)

ENDING VOICE for 7 Weeks —

Singing and Thanksgiving in 408 BC

SYMBOLIC TIMELINE: 69 Weeks

DECODING the BEGINNING VOICE by Scripture:

- **DAN 9:25** from the going forth of the commandment [decree] to restore and to build Jerusalem.

APPLICATION for the BEGINNING VOICE of 69 weeks:

- In the year 457 BC Artaxerses issued a third decree (by legislative voice) to rebuild Jerusalem. This was carried out by Ezra. (See EZRA 7:11-26.) Note: The 69 weeks began with the same event as the 7 weeks.

BEGINNING VOICE for 69 Weeks —

Artaxerxes' Voice or Decree in 457 BC

DECODING the ENDING VOICE by Scripture:

- **ACTS 10:38** <u>God anointed Jesus</u> of Nazareth with the Holy Ghost and with power.
- **MATT 3:16-17** And Jesus, when he was baptized … the heavens were opened unto him … 17 And lo <u>a voice from heaven</u>, saying, This is my beloved Son, in whom I am well pleased.

APPLICATION for the ENDING VOICE of 69 weeks:

- In the year AD 27 Jesus was anointed with baptism. God's voice was a proclamation of this event. (Also see Appendix 9B, (Part 3), on page 252.)

ENDING VOICE for 69 Weeks —

God's Voice from Heaven in AD 27

DANIEL

The Story of the Rise and Fall of Earthly Kingdoms

*The Messiah Crucified
in AD 31
(in Hebrew Poetry)*

26 And after threescore and two weeks shall Messiah be <u>cut off</u>, but not for himself ...

*The Fall of Jerusalem
in AD 70
(in Hebrew Poetry)*

26 ... and the <u>people of the prince</u> that shall come shall destroy the city and the sanctuary; and the end thereof shall be with a flood, and unto the end of the war desolations are <u>determined.</u>

<u>Verse 26</u>

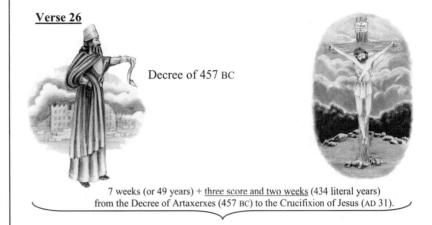

Decree of 457 BC

7 weeks (or 49 years) + <u>three score and two weeks</u> (434 literal years) from the Decree of Artaxerxes (457 BC) to the Crucifixion of Jesus (AD 31).

Note: The Messiah was "<u>cut off</u>" or crucified, "but not for himself" — that is, He was crucified for us (our sins).

"<u>people of the prince</u>" — refers to the army of Rome. The prince refers to the Caesar, or Roman Emperor, Titus. In AD 70 the Romans destroyed the city and the temple therein. Half a million Jews are said to have perished. This would have almost depopulated Palestine. The fate of Jerusalem was <u>determined</u> (by the vision) long before it happened. Rome was to be the desolating power.

Jerusalem Destroyed in AD 70

A Note About Hebrew Poetry

It is necessary to understand that Daniel 9:24-27 is referring to ***two*** separate items:
1. The rebuilding of the city of Jerusalem, and
2. The coming of the Messiah.

These verses are written in a style of Hebrew poetry. Only as this fact is understood, does the language of that passage become clear. In the English language, poetry rhymes and has certain rhythms. Hebrew poetry is different. It is composed of parallel statements which balanced each other, reinforcing the concepts within. Gabriel's instruction was given in the form of Hebrew poetry. Daniel had two concerns:
1. He wanted to know what was going to happen to the Jewish Nation and to their holy city, Jerusalem;
2. He wanted to know when the Messiah would come.

Gabriel answered both these questions in poetic form which is demonstrated in Appendix 9A on page 249.

The Seven Year Ministry of
Christ and His Disciples
AD 27-34
(in Hebrew Poetry)

27a And he [Jesus with His disciples] **shall confirm** [carry out] **the** [Mt. Sinai] **covenant with many** [Israelites] **for one week** [or seven literal years from AD 27-34] **...**

In the "midst of the week" —
The Crucifixion in AD 31
(in Hebrew Poetry)

27b ... and in the midst of the week [AD 31] **he shall cause the sacrifice** [sanctuary sacrificial services] **and the oblation** [sanctuary cereal offerings] **to cease ...**

Dating the Year of AD 27

In Mark 1:15 Jesus began His public ministry by declaring "The time is fulfilled, and the kingdom of God is at hand." Luke 3:1-2 gives us seven historical facts to pinpoint this date as AD 27:

1. 15th year of Tiberius Caesar, can be easily identified as AD 27;
2. Pontius Pilate;
3. Herod, tetrarch of Ituraea;
4. Lysanius, tetrarch of Abilene;
5. Annas, high priest;
6. Caiaphas, high priest;
7. John the Baptist's ministry.

Verse 27a

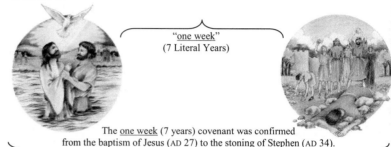

"one week"
(7 Literal Years)

The one week (7 years) covenant was confirmed
from the baptism of Jesus (AD 27) to the stoning of Stephen (AD 34).

"confirm the covenant with many" — The Mt. Sinai covenant was promised to the Jewish nation until the end of the 70th week, which ended in AD 34. Jesus, through His ministry, carried out the covenant promise for the first 3½ years to AD 31. (MATT 15:24) After the crucifixion, the disciples were commissioned to keep the covenant promise to the Jews for the last 3½ years to AD 34.

ACTS 13:46 Then Paul and Barnabas waxed bold, and said, It was necessary that the word of God [Mt. Sinai Covenant] should first have been spoken to you [the Israelite Jews]: but seeing ye put it from you, and judge yourselves unworthy of everlasting life, lo, we turn to the Gentiles [in AD 34].

Verse 27b

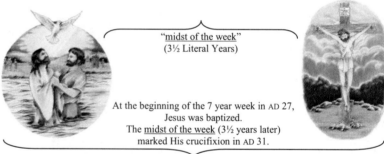

"midst of the week"
(3½ Literal Years)

At the beginning of the 7 year week in AD 27,
Jesus was baptized.
The midst of the week (3½ years later)
marked His crucifixion in AD 31.

"shall cause the sacrifice and the oblation to cease" — The animal sacrifices pointed to the death of Christ. The oblations were voluntary offerings connected to the blood sacrifices. All this (and more) came to an end at the cross. This was also verified when the veil of the temple was rent in two, indicating there was no further purpose for the sacrifices. Yet, the Jews continued the sacrificial system until the destruction of Jerusalem in AD 70. (See page 248 — "What Was Abolished at the Cross?")

MATT 27:50-51 Jesus, when he had cried again with a loud voice, yielded up the ghost. 51 And, behold, the veil of the temple was rent in twain from the top to the bottom; and the earth did quake, and the rocks rent.

SYMBOLIC TIMELINE: 1 Week

DECODING the BEGINNING VOICE by Scripture:
- **MATT 3:16-17** And Jesus … was baptized … he saw the Spirit of God descending like a dove. 17 And lo a voice … saying, This is my beloved Son, in whom I am well pleased.

BEGINNING VOICE for 1 Week —

God's Voice from Heaven
in
AD 27

APPLICATION for the BEGINNING VOICE of 1 week:
- When Jesus was baptized (anointed) in the year AD 27, God's voice proclaimed the beginning of His Son's ministry. (Also see MARK 1:15.)

DECODING the ENDING VOICE by Scripture:
- **ACTS 7:54, 57, 59** When they heard these things 57 they cried out with a loud voice 59 And they stoned Stephen.

ENDING VOICE for 1 Week —

Nation of Israel Spoke
to Stone Stephen
in
AD 34

APPLICATION for the ENDING VOICE of 1 week:
- In the year AD 34 the voice of the nation of Israel spoke through their official legal body, taking legal action to stone Stephen. (Also see Appendix 9B, (Part 4), on page 253.)

SYMBOLIC TIMELINE: Midst of the Week

DECODING the BEGINNING VOICE by Scripture:
- **JOHN 19:30** When Jesus therefore had received the vinegar, he said, It is finished: and he bowed his head, and gave up the ghost.

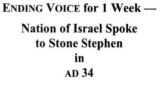

BEGINNING VOICE for
Midst of the Week —

Jesus' Voice
in
AD 31

APPLICATION for the BEGINNING VOICE of Midst of the Week from Autumn AD 27 to Spring of AD 31:
- Jesus' own voice began the timeline for the Midst of the Week when He laid down His life.

DECODING the ENDING VOICE by Scripture:
- **ACTS 7:54, 57, 59** When they heard these things 57 they cried out with a loud voice 59 And they stoned Stephen.

ENDING VOICE for
Midst of the Week —

Nation of Israel Spoke
to Stone Stephen
in
AD 34

APPLICATION for ENDING VOICE of Midst of the Week:
- In the year AD 34 the voice of the nation of Israel spoke through their official legal body, taking legal action to stone Stephen. (Also see Appendix 9B, (Part 4), on page 253.)

The Final Destruction of Jerusalem
(in Hebrew Poetry)

27c ... and for the overspreading of abominations he shall make it desolate, even until the consummation [utter end at the Second Coming], **and that determined** [utter destruction] **shall be poured upon the desolate** [the kingdom that devastates].

Verse 27c

Note: The prophecy of Daniel 9:27 continues to predict the fate of Jerusalem, but brings the timing "even until the consummation" or the Second Coming of Christ. The final destruction of old Jerusalem is described.

"he" — the pronoun "he" is set in the description of "abominations" and refers to "desolations" or destructive work of the anti-Christ. (See DAN 12:11.) The "overspreading of abominations" refers to his influence and world-wide activity when "all the world" shall wonder after the beast and receive his mark of authority. (See REV 13.)

"consummation" — *Strong's* OT#3617 a completion; adverb, completely; also destruction: KJV - altogether, (be, utterly) consume, consummation, was determined, (full, utter) end, riddance.

"determined" — *Strong's* OT#2782 to point sharply, i.e. (literally) to wound: KJV - decide, decree, determine, maim, move.

Note: The last part of this verse simply says "that" — the prophecy regarding Jerusalem — has predicted its termination, and destruction "shall be poured [out] upon the desolate" [city].

Prophetic Timeline #4: Details and Specifics

Timeline #4 (Length of Timeline)	Subject (of Timeline)	Prophetic Scripture For Timeline	Timeline Begins (with)	Speaking VOICE (Decree)	Timeline Ends (with)	Legislative & Judicial Action (Date)
490 years (70 weeks)	Nation of Israel	DAN 9:24 EZRA 7:11-26 and ACTS 7:57, 59	Return of God's People from Babylon to Jerusalem 457 BC	Artaxerxes' Decree of 457 BC	Stoning of Stephen — Israel "cut off" from the Mt. Sinai Covenant	Voice of Sanhedrin Decree AD 34

"What Was Abolished at the Cross?"

The Bible is clear as to what was abolished at the cross.

1. The sacrificial system and the oblations: "... in the midst of the week he shall cause the sacrifice and the oblation to cease." (DAN 9:27) *Oblations* means *offerings* according to *Strong's Concordance*. These offerings were the wine and grain offerings offered along with the lamb sacrifices. See Numbers 28.

2. The civil penalties for violation of the law: Since Israel was a Theocracy, they had to have punishments written for breaking the law much like any country does. However, since we are no longer under a Theocracy, we are to obey the laws of the land we live in, provided these laws do not break the Laws of God. Jesus demonstrated this when they brought the adulterous woman to Him and He did not advocate stoning her. Elsewhere Jesus said to give Caesar what is due Caesar. (JOHN 8:3-11, MATT 22:21, and ACTS 5:29) At the Second Coming, however, God Himself will punish the wicked according to His Civil Law. For instance, under the Civil Law, Sabbath breakers were to be stoned. Under the Seventh Plague, (which is the Second Coming), God will stone the wicked, who refuse to observe His Holy Days, with hail weighing seventy pounds. (REV 16:21)

3. The Levite Priesthood: The New Testament says that we are now all kings and priests. (See REV 1:6.)

4. Circumcision: Circumcision of the "flesh," has been replaced with circumcision of the "heart." (ACTS 15)

5. The temple services: God demonstrated that the temple services came to an end at the cross when the curtain in the temple was rent from top to bottom exposing the Most Holy Place, which only the High Priest was permitted to see. (MATT 27:51) The temple services do not include God's special rest days such as the Seventh-day Sabbath and the Feast days. We know this because Jesus and Paul kept the Seventh-day Sabbath and the Feast Holy Days, inviting others to do the same. (Review Appendix 7D, pages 128-134.)

The Mt. Sinai Covenant
Old or First Covenant
With the Nation of Israel
and their Capital City, Jerusalem

The Everlasting Covenant
New or Second Covenant
With the Redeemed of All Ages
Through the Promised Messiah

Note: The literary structure of the prophetic verses (Daniel 9:25-27), displays a back-and-forth movement between two themes: 1) The Messiah, and 2) The City of Jerusalem. **The anti-Christ is not part of the main theme in these passages**.

DAN 9:24a Seventy weeks are determined [cut off] upon *thy people* [Israel] and upon thy holy *city* to ...

DAN 9:24b [The **Messiah**] ... finish the transgression, [rebellion against God] and to make an end of sins, [of "missing the mark"] and to make reconciliation for iniquity, and to bring in everlasting righteousness, and to seal up the vision and prophecy, and to anoint the most Holy.

Construction of Jerusalem

DAN 9:25a Know therefore and understand, [begin counting the 70 weeks and the 2300 year timeline] that from the going forth of the commandment [decree] to restore and to build *Jerusalem* ... [in **475 BC**] shall be seven weeks ...

Coming of the Messiah

DAN 9:25b ... unto the **Messiah** the Prince shall be seven weeks, [until Jerusalem is fully restored in 49 years] ... [then, adding the previous seven weeks] and threescore [60 weeks] and two weeks [= 69 weeks to His anointing or baptism in **AD 27**] ...

DAN 9:25c ... the street shall be built again, and the wall, even in troublous times [by **408 BC**].

Death of the Messiah

DAN 9:26a And after threescore and two weeks shall *Messiah* be cut off, [crucified] but not for himself [but for our sins]: ...

Destruction of Jerusalem

DAN 9:26b ... and the people [army] of the prince [of Rome] that shall come shall destroy the *city* [in **AD 70**] and the sanctuary; [temple] and the end thereof shall be with a flood, [terrible destruction] and unto the end of the war desolations [destructions] are determined.

Covenant of the Messiah

DAN 9:27a And *he* [the **Messiah**] [and the everlasting covenant] shall confirm the [Mt. Sinai] covenant with many [Israelites] for one week: [**AD 27 to AD 34**] and in the midst of the week [**AD 31**] he shall cause the sacrifice and the oblation to cease ...

Desolation of Jerusalem

DAN 9:27b ... and for the overspreading of abominations [evil] he shall make it [the city of Jerusalem] desolate, [miserable] even until the consummation [the very end of time], and that [which is] determined [or prophesied] shall be poured upon the desolate [desolator or anti-christ].

*See page 245 for note on Hebrew Poetry.

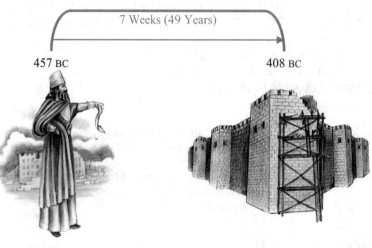

7 Weeks (49 Years)

457 BC   408 BC

The Decree to   Restoration of
Restore   Jerusalem
Jerusalem   Complete

Daniel 9:25   Daniel 9:25
Ezra 7:11-26   Nehemiah 12, 13

DAN 9:25 Know therefore and understand, that from the going forth of the commandment [decree] to restore and to build Jerusalem … <u>shall be seven weeks</u> … the street shall be built again, and the wall, even in troublous times.

SYMBOL: "shall be <u>seven weeks</u>"

DECODING by Scripture:
- EZE 4:6; NUM 14:34 "<u>each day for a year</u>"

APPLICATION:
1. 7 symbolic weeks = 49 symbolic days.
2. **Prophetic Key #24a** Each symbolic day = one literal year.
3. 49 symbolic days = 49 literal years.
4. **EZRA 7:6-7** This Ezra went up from Babylon … and the king granted him all his request. 7 And there went up some of the children of Israel … in the seventh year of Artaxerxes the king.
5. According to secular history, the seventh year of Artaxerxes was 457 BC. (One can also calculate backwards from the established historical date of the crucifixion to confirm the date of 457 BC.)
6. 457 BC + 49 years = 408 BC.
7. Jerusalem was restored 49 years later in 408 BC. This included the temple, street, walls and the Jewish government system.

Important Note: The year of 457 BC is one of the most easily established dates of history through the discovery of a double-dated papyrus known as "Kraeling 6." This discovery was on the island of Elephantine in the River Nile. The Canon of Ptolemy, which lists kings, astronomical observations, Greek Olympiads, along with indirect reference in Greek history to Persian affairs, easily establishes the seventh year of Artaxerxes as 457 BC. Review the quote by Jonathan Gray on page 243.

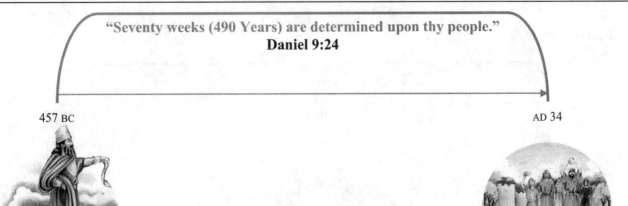

"Seventy weeks (490 Years) are determined upon thy people."
Daniel 9:24

457 BC

AD 34

The Decree to
Restore
Jerusalem

Daniel 9:25
Ezra 7:11-26

Stoning of Stephen
and Gospel Goes
to the Gentiles

Acts 7:57, 59

DAN 9:24-25 Seventy weeks are determined upon thy people [Jewish nation] … 25 from the going forth of the commandment [decree] to restore and to build Jerusalem.

SYMBOL: "seventy weeks"

DECODING by Scripture:
- EZE 4:6; NUM 14:34 "each day for a year"

APPLICATION:
1. 70 symbolic weeks = 490 symbolic days.
2. **Prophetic Key #24a** Each symbolic day = one literal year.
3. 490 symbolic days = 490 literal years.
4. The timeline of 70 symbolic weeks, or 490 literal years, contains the first ministry of Jesus Christ that began on this earth in AD 27. The timeline ended in AD 34 with the stoning of Stephen.
5. From the time that Artaxerxes issued the command to restore Jerusalem, until the completion of the 70th week, was to be 490 years.
6. **The Rule of Adjustment:** When a date calculation is made from a BC date to an AD date, or from an AD date to a BC date, the addition or subtraction of one year is required to complete the calculation. There is no zero year when going from BC to AD. Therefore —
7. 457 BC + 483 years = AD 33 $\pm\underline{1}$ = AD 34.

8. To fulfill the Mt. Sinai Covenant, the Jewish nation had another 490 years to remain the special people of God. During this time they were under covenant to keep God's laws, statutes, and judgments. They were to be his witnesses, giving the truths of salvation to all the world. (See Appendix 9C, pages 256-257, for information on Covenants of God and the Mt. Sinai Covenant.)

MATT 18:21-22 Then came Peter to him, and said, Lord, how oft shall my brother sin against me, and I forgive him? till seven times? 22 Jesus saith unto him, I say not unto thee, Until seven times: but, Until seventy times seven.

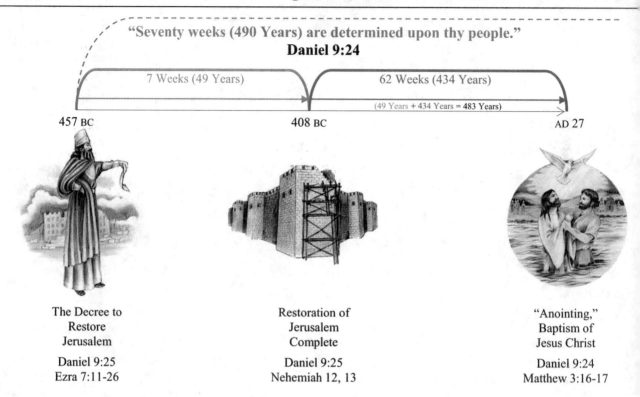

"Seventy weeks (490 Years) are determined upon thy people."
Daniel 9:24

7 Weeks (49 Years)	62 Weeks (434 Years)

(49 Years + 434 Years = 483 Years)

457 BC   408 BC   AD 27

The Decree to Restore Jerusalem	Restoration of Jerusalem Complete	"Anointing," Baptism of Jesus Christ
Daniel 9:25 Ezra 7:11-26	Daniel 9:25 Nehemiah 12, 13	Daniel 9:24 Matthew 3:16-17

DAN 9:25 Know therefore and understand, that from the going forth of the commandment [decree] to restore and to build Jerusalem unto the Messiah the Prince shall be <u>seven weeks</u>, <u>and threescore and two weeks</u>.

SYMBOL: "shall be <u>seven weeks</u>, <u>three score and two weeks</u>"

DECODING by Scripture:
- **EZE 4:6; NUM 14:34** "<u>each day for a year</u>"

APPLICATION: (7 + 60 + 2 = 69 weeks)
1. <u>7</u> symbolic weeks = 49 symbolic days.
2. <u>60</u> (three score) and <u>two</u> weeks = 62 symbolic weeks or 434 symbolic days.
3. 49 symbolic days + 434 symbolic days = 483 symbolic days (from the decree).
4. **Prophetic Key #24a** Each symbolic day = one literal year.
5. 483 symbolic days = 483 literal years.
6. From the time that Artaxerxes issued the command to restore Jerusalem, until the anointing of the Messiah the Prince was 483 years.
7. **The Rule of Adjustment:** When a date calculation is made from a BC date to an AD date, or from an AD date to a BC date, the addition or subtraction of <u>one year</u> is required to complete the calculation. There is no zero year when going from BC to AD. Therefore —
8. 457 BC + 483 years = AD 26 <u>+ 1</u> = AD 27.

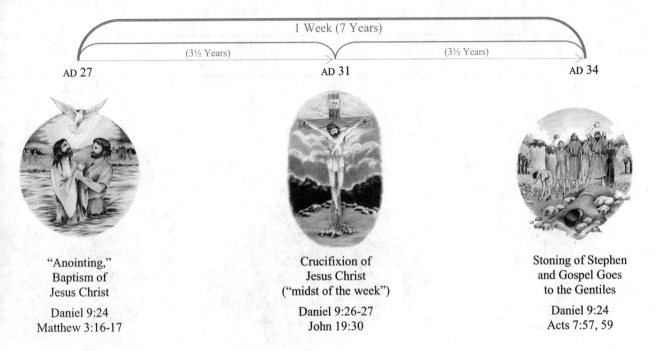

1 Week (7 Years)

(3½ Years)   (3½ Years)

AD 27   AD 31   AD 34

"Anointing,"
Baptism of
Jesus Christ

Daniel 9:24
Matthew 3:16-17

Crucifixion of
Jesus Christ
("midst of the week")

Daniel 9:26-27
John 19:30

Stoning of Stephen
and Gospel Goes
to the Gentiles

Daniel 9:24
Acts 7:57, 59

DAN 9:25, 27 Know therefore and understand, that from the going forth of the commandment [decree] ... unto the Messiah the Prince shall be seven weeks, and threescore and two weeks. 27 And he shall confirm the covenant with many for <u>one week</u> ...

SYMBOL: "<u>one week</u>"

🔑 **DECODING by Scripture:**
- **EZE 4:6; NUM 14:34** "<u>each day for a year</u>"

APPLICATION:
1. 1 symbolic week = 7 symbolic days.
2. **Prophetic Key #24a** Each symbolic day = one literal year.
3. 7 symbolic days = 7 literal years.
4. From the anointing of Jesus in AD 27, the Jewish nation was to be given seven more years to be heralds of the gospel until AD 34. At the end of that *one prophetic week,* the Jewish nation "spoke" through the Sanhedrin and stoned Stephen, the great missionary. This marked the end of the Mt. Sinai Covenant that God had promised to the Jewish people.
5. AD 27 + 7 years = AD 34.

DAN 9:27 ... in the <u>midst of the week</u> he shall cause the sacrifice and the oblation to cease.

SYMBOL: "<u>midst of the week</u>"

🔑 **DECODING by Scripture:**
- **EZE 4:6; NUM 14:34** "<u>each day for a year</u>"

APPLICATION:
1. 1 symbolic week = 7 symbolic days
2. **Prophetic Key #24a** Each symbolic day = one literal year.
3. 7 symbolic days = 7 literal years.
4. "midst" of 7 years = 3½ years.
5. The autumn of AD 27 marked the beginning of the ministry of Jesus the Messiah. Three and one half years later [Spring of AD 31], He was "cut off" and caused the "sacrifice and the oblation to cease." (DAN 9:27) The sacrificial services of the sanctuary were no longer necessary once Jesus, the Lamb, spilled His blood for the ultimate sacrifice of sin.
6. For an additional three and one half years from AD 31 to AD 34, the disciples continued to preach the gospel to the Jewish nation before going to the Gentiles.
7. Autumn AD 27 + 3½ years = Spring AD 31.

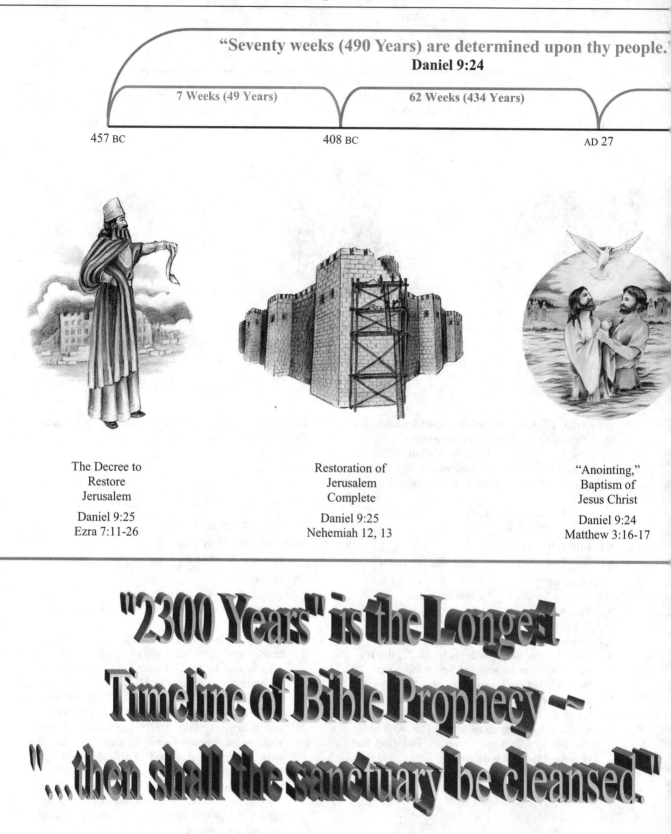

"Seventy weeks (490 Years) are determined upon thy people."
Daniel 9:24

7 Weeks (49 Years)   62 Weeks (434 Years)

457 BC   408 BC   AD 27

The Decree to
Restore
Jerusalem

Daniel 9:25
Ezra 7:11-26

Restoration of
Jerusalem
Complete

Daniel 9:25
Nehemiah 12, 13

"Anointing,"
Baptism of
Jesus Christ

Daniel 9:24
Matthew 3:16-17

"2300 Years" is the Longest Timeline of Bible Prophecy – "...then shall the sanctuary be cleansed."

Note: This chart is not done to scale.

1 Week (7 Years)

1810 Years to Sanctuary Cleansing

(Daniel 8:14: 457 BC + 2300 Years = AD 1844)

AD 31   AD 34   AD 1844

Crucifixion of
Jesus Christ
("midst of the week")

Daniel 9:26-27
John 19:30

Stoning of Stephen
and Gospel Goes
to the Gentiles

Daniel 9:26-27
Acts 7:57, 59

Cleansing of the
Heavenly Sanctuary
Commenced

Daniel 8:14; 7:10
1 Peter 4:17

DAN 9:25; 8:14   25 from the going forth of the commandment [decree] to restore and to build Jerusalem ... 14 Unto <u>two thousand and three hundred days</u> [years]; then shall the sanctuary be cleansed.

SYMBOL: <u>"two thousand and three hundred days [years]"</u>

DECODING by Scripture:

- **EZE 4:6; NUM 14:34**   "<u>each day for a year</u>"

APPLICATION:

1. 2300 symbolic days.
2. **Prophetic Key #24a**   Each symbolic day = one literal year.
3. 2300 symbolic days = 2300 literal years.
4. The 2300 year timeline reveals the <u>second ministry of Jesus Christ</u> that began in the Heavenly Sanctuary in AD 1844.

5. **The Rule of Adjustment:** When a date calculation is made (passing through the "zero" year) from a BC date to an AD date, or from an AD date to a BC date, the addition or subtraction of <u>one year</u> is required to complete the calculation. Therefore —
6. 457 BC + 2300 years = AD 1843 <u>± **1**</u> = AD 1844.
7. In 1844, the 2300 year timeline **ended**, but Christ's ministry of Investigative Judgment for the dead **began** at that date. (1 PETER 4:17) The Investigative Judgment is still in process and will continue for all the living on this earth up to the Close of Probation.
8. This Investigative Judgment scene was introduced in Daniel 7:9-14, brought to view in Daniel 8:14 and explained in Daniel 9:24-27. The Investigative Judgment is described more fully in Revelation 20.

Note: There is often confusion regarding the <u>Covenants of God</u>. We hear about the "old" covenant and the "new" covenant and wonder what the difference is and why there were two covenants. Well, actually, there's a little more to it than that. This page will present the beginning of a study on the covenants. Remember: God cannot change, and His covenants will never be changed or altered.

TWO COVENANTS? THREE COVENANTS? OR MORE?

There were three covenants, vital to understanding:

1. The First, Old, or Creation Covenant made with all created beings;
2. The Second, New, or Everlasting Covenant made with all <u>fallen</u> mankind, (beginning with Adam) and,
3. The Mt. Sinai Covenant made with the Hebrew Nation.

The first two listed above established fundamental relationships between God and His created beings. The Mt. Sinai Covenant was simply a reiteration and amplification of the first two. Notice the diagram of the covenants. The covenants made with Noah and Abraham and others, generation after generation, were simply reiterations of the Creation Covenant and the New Covenant.

THE MT. SINAI COVENANT

Israel was called to be the depositories of God's Truth, His Laws, and His covenants. They were to be the keepers of truth which was revealed in the sacrificial system as it pointed to the coming Savior. They were to explain the plan of salvation to all who would listen. They were contracted, or covenanted, to be a nation of *missionaries* to the world. By precept and example, they were to be a revelation of the character and love of God in saving man from eternal ruin. God did not select them out of arbitrary favoritism, but to do a special work for Him. They were to build His Kingdom.

Two factors must be considered in this Mt. Sinai Covenant: First, God's stated obligation to them, and secondly, Israel's stated obligation to Him. There are always at least two parties involved in a contract or covenant.

---

1. THE CREATION COVENANT
<u>Obey and Live: Disobey and Die</u>
(Relationship to the Laws of God)

From the Foundation   For Eternity

of the World

2. THE NEW OR EVERLASTING COVENANT
The Plan of Salvation
(Before the Foundation of the World)
(Reconciliation to the Laws of God)

The Lamb Slain   Eternal Benefit →

3. THE MT. SINAI COVENANT

1437 BC   to   AD 34

God stated His part as follows:

5 Now therefore, <u>if</u> ye will obey my voice [The Laws of God] **indeed, and keep my covenant,** [contract] **then ye shall be a peculiar treasure unto me above all people: for all the earth is mine:**
6 And ye shall be unto me a kingdom [a whole nation] **of priests, and an holy nation** [as representatives or missionaries]. **Ex 19:5-6**

Israel responded on their part, by saying:

"All that the Lord hath spoken we will do."
Ex 19:8

The prophet Daniel saw, in prophetic vision, that the nation would fill their missionary purpose <u>only until the end</u> of the *seventy weeks,* or until AD 34. He wrote:

- **DAN 9:24** Seventy weeks are determined [cut off] upon thy people.

The *seventy weeks* was a symbolic timeline. Symbolic time is interpreted and changed into literal time by the use of the Year-day Computation Principle stated in Scripture as follows:

- **EZE 4:6** I have appointed thee each day for a year.

- **NUM 14:34** Each day for a year, shall ye bear your iniquities.

The symbolic *seventy weeks* timeline represented 490 literal years. (Seventy weeks of seven days each = 490 symbolic days.) According to the Year-day Computation Principle, the 490 symbolic days represented 490 literal years.

The instructing angel informed Daniel that the counting of those 490 years should begin at the specific date when a decree would be issued to permit the Jews to return home to rebuild Jerusalem after their Babylonian captivity. That decree was issued by Artaxerxes in 457 BC. This is what the angel said to Daniel:

- **DAN 9:25** Know therefore and understand, that [**begin counting out the 490 years**] <u>from</u> the going forth of the commandment [decree] to restore and to build Jerusalem ... the streets shall be built again, and the wall, even in troublous times.

In the year AD 34 the nation of Israel spoke through their official legal body, the Sanhedrin council, (which was the voice of the nation) taking legal action to stone Stephen.

- **ACTS 6:8, 7:59** And Stephen, full of faith and power, [a great witness and *missionary*] did great wonders and miracles among the people. And they stoned Stephen.

Instead of the Israelites being missionaries and witnesses of their promised Messiah, as they had promised to be according to the Mt. Sinai Covenant-contract, they determined to take legal action to put God's missionaries to death. Therefore, ***they cut themselves off from that Mt. Sinai Covenant*** relationship. It was they who finally ***ended*** the Mt. Sinai Covenant. The Mt. Sinai Covenant came to its end in AD 34 at the death of Stephen.

Originally, the Israelites had broken their part of the Mt. Sinai Covenant in less than forty days! Within that time, they apostatized by worshipping the golden calf. *The people broke their part of the covenant almost at once.* But, God kept His part of the Mt. Sinai Covenant until AD 34. The Jewish leaders crucified their Messiah in AD 31, but God did not reject the Jewish Nation even then. He sent the apostles to them for an additional three and an half years until, by their own legal action, they ended their Mr. Sinai covenant relationship.

A Sample Legal Contract for the Mt. Sinai Covenant

TERMS

I, <u>God</u>, Party of the First Part, do promise that ye shall be unto me: (See EX 19:45)

An Holy nation	*(A Theocracy)*
A kingdom of priests	*(A missionary nation to educate the world of the plan of salvation)*
A peculiar treasure	*(Above all people)*

You shall live in the land of Canaan.

We, <u>Israel</u>, Party of the Second Part, do promise to:
Obey the Ten Commandments Moral Law;
    (EX 24:7)
Obey the statutes, judgments, and laws of worship;
    (DEUT 11:1)
Build a sanctuary to educate the plan of salvation;
    (EX 25:2-8)
Practice the sacrificial system; (LEV 1-27)
Proclaim the gospel by sanctuary typology
to the world; (DEUT 15:6; EX 25:8)
Obey the civil laws of the nation; (EX 24:21-23)
Obey the laws of health and welfare.
    (EX 24:12; LEV 11)

Be it known to all present, that this solemn covenant-contract was established at Mt. Sinai on the date of (<u>Pentecost</u>) <u> the third month in the fourteenth day of the month in the year of</u> (approximately) <u>1437 BC</u>.

Appendix 9D — The "Truth" and the "Counterfeit" of Daniel 9:24-25

True Prophetic Interpretation

False Prophetic Interpretation

THE NATION OF LITERAL ISRAEL IS ALLOTTED 70 SYMBOLIC WEEKS TO WITNESS TO OTHER NATIONS OF THE PLAN OF SALVATION AND THE COMING MESSIAH

DAN 9:24 Seventy weeks are determined upon thy people ...

Teaching of Truth to Study the 70th Week:

- *Seventy weeks* is a very important timeline of *symbolic* time. This prophecy pinpoints the first arrival of the Messiah.

Calculation:

- 70 *symbolic* weeks (7 days in a week) = 490 days.
- 490 *symbolic* days = 490 *literal* years.

Seventy weeks [490 years of the Mt. Sinai Covenant relationship with ancient Israel] are <u>determined</u> [or will be cut off] upon thy people [The Nation of *literal* Israel].

Teaching of Truth on Literal Israel:

- Literal Israel was intended to be a *missionary nation* to teach the world the truths of a coming Messiah. God ordained them as a <u>covenanted people</u>.
- From Daniel's prophecy, they were allotted 490 years to give the message of the coming Messiah.
- Should they fail that mission and reject their Messiah, their covenant with God would be terminated!
- At the end of the 70 weeks, *Spiritual Israel* [those that accept Jesus Christ as the Messiah] would then be covenanted as *missionaries* to the world.

Counterfeit Teachings to Disregard the 70th Week:

1. "70th Week" is a nebulous term that does not require serious study — a thought that aligns with the 1656 Rabbinic curse announced in Poland: "May his bones and his memory rot who shall attempt to number the seventy weeks." This curse attempts to discourage the study of the 70 week prophecy.
2. The 70th Week is not that important as it only refers to endtime events just before the Second Coming of Jesus. (Daniel 8:17 is misapplied here.)
- **These teachings are Satan's counterfeit!**

Counterfeit Teachings on Modern Israel:

1. Many devout Christians believe that the nation of Israel today is "still" God's covenanted people and that modern Israel has **_not_** been cut off as the covenant people.
2. They also believe that modern Israel is still the focus of prophecy in the New Testament and do not realize that the "vineyard has transitioned" over to the New Covenant Christians — Spiritual Israel.
- **Modern Israel as God's covenant people is a counterfeit teaching of Satan!**

THE MESSIAH WILL BEGIN HIS MINISTRY AT THE BEGINNING OF THE 70TH WEEK

DAN 9:25 ... unto the Messiah the Prince shall be seven weeks, and threescore and two weeks ...

Teaching of Truth: — The Messiah Has Come!

- The *seventy weeks* [or 490 years] of Israel's probationary time began in 457 BC with a decree.
- The Messiah was anointed to His ministry in AD 27 at the end of the 69th week or the beginning of the 70th week.
- Literal Israel rejected Jesus Christ as the Messiah in the midst of the 70th week in AD 31.

Know therefore and understand, [that you will begin counting out the "2300 year" timeline of Dan. 8:14 and the *seventy weeks,* or 490 years] that from the going forth of the commandment [Decree issued by Artaxerxes in 457 BC] to restore and to build Jerusalem unto the Messiah the Prince [Jesus' baptism and anointing] shall be seven weeks, and threescore and two weeks.

Counterfeit Teachings: — Messiah Has Not Come!

1. Today, the Orthodox Jews believe that the Messiah has not yet come. They are still looking for His coming to begin His ministry!
2. They believe that He will walk through the east gate of Jerusalem. Plans are in place to rebuild their temple and re-establish the sacrificial system in preparation for His arrival.
- **These teachings are Satan's counterfeit!**

Appendix 9D — The "Truth" and the "Counterfeit" of Daniel 9:27

True Prophetic Interpretation

False Prophetic Interpretation

THE 70TH WEEK OF SYMBOLIC TIME = AUTUMN AD 27 — AUTUMN AD 34

DAN 9:27 And he shall confirm the covenant with many for one week ...

Teaching of Truth for the 70th Week:
- 70 weeks is the original timeline.
- 69 weeks = threescore + two weeks + seven weeks.
- 70 weeks - 69 weeks = 1 week, the last week of the prophecy when the Messiah will appear.
- This is <u>one</u> *symbolic* week or 7 *literal* years.
- <u>This last week is connected to the 69 weeks in one continuous timeline</u>.
- The ministry of Jesus began at the beginning of the 70th week in the Autumn of AD 27.
- After the cross in AD 31, His work was continued by the apostles.
- The prophetic week ended in the Autumn of AD 34, with the stoning of Stephen. There was no *severe tribulation* for God's people at this time.

Note:
- **DAN 12:7** refers to a <u>three and a half year</u> tribulation of God's people just before "all these things shall be finished." It does not predict a seven year timeline of tribulation for anyone!

Counterfeit Teachings for the 70th Week:
1. Theologians today <u>extract</u> the 70th week (or seven years) from the 70 week timeline and place it down at the end of time just before Jesus comes.
2. Many theologians today who expound on prophecy declare that the *70th week*, or *one week*, is still in the future and refers to a time of "seven years tribulation" and the "Rapture Theory." This "Rapture Theory" at the end of time is totally unbiblical.

 Prophetic Key #22 Timelines are <u>never severed</u>. Once a timeline begins, it runs the full length and ends!

- **This is another counterfeit teaching of Satan — to split up a timeline! It is <u>not</u> Biblical!**

THE MIDST OF THE 70TH WEEK = SPRING AD 31

DAN 9:27 ... and in the midst of the week he shall cause the sacrifice and the oblation to cease.

Teaching of Truth for the "midst of the week:"
- The *midst of one [symbolic] week* = the *midst of 7 symbolic* days = 3½ *symbolic* days .
- 3½ *symbolic* days = 3½ *literal* years.
- After 3½ *literal* years, Jesus' sacrifice ended the sanctuary services, including all blood sacrifices and offerings forever!

And he [the Messiah — Jesus of Nazareth] shall confirm the [Mt. Sinai] covenant with many [Jews] for one week [seven literal years] and in the midst of the week [three and a half years] he [Jesus] shall cause the sacrifice [of the sanctuary services] and the oblation [offerings] to cease.

Counterfeit Teaching for the "midst of the week:"
1. Many theologians today who expound on prophecy declare that the Jews will commence all the earthly Sanctuary services at the beginning of the future *70th week.*
2. Many believe: In the *midst of the week,* (3½ years later), the anti-christ will *cut off* their Sanctuary services. Anti-Christ is given as the theme of verse 27 instead of the Messiah!
- **This is Satan's counterfeit teaching!**

Note:
- The only Sanctuary services that the Bible speaks about after the cross, are in Heaven, where Jesus Christ is ministering on behalf of His children.

RECAPPING STRUCTURE CHART
Four Historic-Prophetic Outlines of Earthly Kingdoms in the Book of Daniel

The "Symbols" of Daniel 2, 7, and 8 (Image, Beasts, and Horns) and the "Literal" Kings of Daniel 11
Consistently Refer to the Succession of Persecuting Kingdoms Surrounding God's People.

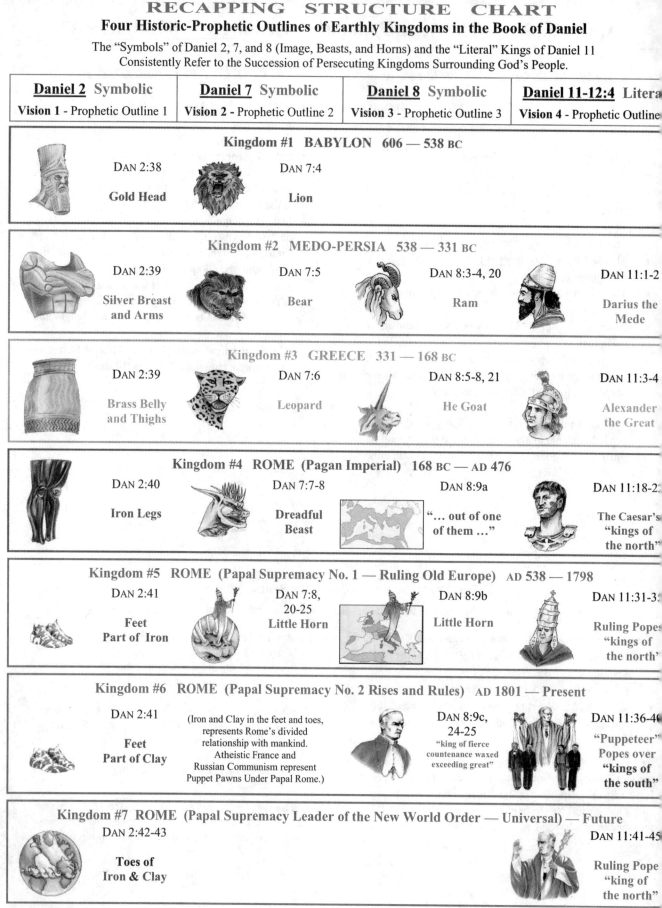

Daniel 2 Symbolic	**Daniel 7** Symbolic	**Daniel 8** Symbolic	**Daniel 11-12:4** Litera
Vision 1 - Prophetic Outline 1	Vision 2 - Prophetic Outline 2	Vision 3 - Prophetic Outline 3	Vision 4 - Prophetic Outline

Kingdom #1   BABYLON   606 — 538 BC

DAN 2:38 — Gold Head
DAN 7:4 — Lion

Kingdom #2   MEDO-PERSIA   538 — 331 BC

DAN 2:39 — Silver Breast and Arms
DAN 7:5 — Bear
DAN 8:3-4, 20 — Ram
DAN 11:1-2 — Darius the Mede

Kingdom #3   GREECE   331 — 168 BC

DAN 2:39 — Brass Belly and Thighs
DAN 7:6 — Leopard
DAN 8:5-8, 21 — He Goat
DAN 11:3-4 — Alexander the Great

Kingdom #4   ROME   (Pagan Imperial)   168 BC — AD 476

DAN 2:40 — Iron Legs
DAN 7:7-8 — Dreadful Beast
DAN 8:9a — "… out of one of them …"
DAN 11:18-2: — The Caesar's "kings of the north"

Kingdom #5   ROME   (Papal Supremacy No. 1 — Ruling Old Europe)   AD 538 — 1798

DAN 2:41 — Feet Part of Iron
DAN 7:8, 20-25 — Little Horn
DAN 8:9b — Little Horn
DAN 11:31-3: — Ruling Pope "kings of the north"

Kingdom #6   ROME   (Papal Supremacy No. 2 Rises and Rules)   AD 1801 — Present

DAN 2:41 — Feet Part of Clay
(Iron and Clay in the feet and toes, represents Rome's divided relationship with mankind. Atheistic France and Russian Communism represent Puppet Pawns Under Papal Rome.)
DAN 8:9c, 24-25 — "king of fierce countenance waxed exceeding great"
DAN 11:36-4(— "Puppeteer" Popes over "kings of the south"

Kingdom #7 ROME (Papal Supremacy Leader of the New World Order — Universal) — Future

DAN 2:42-43 — Toes of Iron & Clay
DAN 11:41-45 — Ruling Pope "king of the north"

This chart shows the <u>recapping</u> of kingdoms in a "vertical" format.

DANIEL
The Story of the Rise and Fall of Earthly Kingdoms

CHAPTER 10

HEAVENLY SCENE
VISION FOUR
(Literal "kings")

**An Introduction to
Daniel's Fourth Vision**

(535 BC)

**1 In the third year of <u>Cyrus king
of Persia</u> a thing*** [vision of the
Fourth Historic-Prophetic Outline]
**was revealed unto Daniel, whose
name was called Belteshazzar;
and the thing** [prophetic vision]
**was true, but the time appointed
was long** [extended from 538 BC to
the "eve" of Christ's Stone King-
dom]**: and he understood the
<u>thing</u>** [the <u>vision</u> given in literal
language]**, and had understand-
ing of the vision.** [In the previous
three symbolic visions, Daniel had
been given understanding, either
from God or the angel Gabriel.]

*Note: *Strong's* definition OT#4406
for *"<u>thing</u>"* is a command, or in this
case the prophecy itself. (See DAN
2:5.)

Introduction: See **The Structure of Daniel** Chart on page 367. The
Fourth Vi sion includes Daniel chapters 10-12. The **Heavenly Scene** of
literal "kings of the north and kings of the south" is presented in Daniel
10:1 — along with a visit from "Michael" [Son of God] in verses 7 and 8.
The presence of Michael at the beginning and end of the vision is unique
to this vision — indicating that Michael is fully in charge of each event.
Vision Four presents the **Historic-Prophetic Outline** of these literal
"kings" in Daniel 11:1-45 revealing in order the **LAST SIX KINGDOMS**
around the people of God after Babylon fell. Michael appears again at the
end of the Outline in Daniel 12:1-4. Note: The Historic-Prophetic Outline
in Vision Four extends *time* from 538 BC to the *eve* of Christ's Stone
Kingdom.

Verse 1

**Daniel Receives a Vision
of the Fourth
Historic-Prophetic Outline**

**HEAVENLY SCENE
DAN 10:1
KINGS OF THE NORTH
AND
KINGS OF THE SOUTH
OF
EARTHLY KINGDOMS**

Note: Only God pulls back the curtain of
time to reveal future *events*.

Historical Background Information

606-538 BC: Babylon ruled for 68 years before falling captive to the
Medo-Persian Kingdom.
538-536 BC: During the last two years of the 70 years of captivity, God's
people are still in Babylon, under Darius the Mede who is now the
"king." (See DAN 11:1.) The following prophecies convinced Daniel the
time had come for God's people to return and restore Jerusalem.

2 CHRON 36:20-21 And them that
had escaped from the sword carried he
away to Babylon; where they were
servants to him and his sons <u>until the
reign of the kingdom of Persia</u>: To
fulfil the word of the LORD by the
mouth of Jeremiah, until the land had
enjoyed her sabbaths: for as long as
she lay desolate she kept sabbath, to
fulfil threescore and ten years.

JER 25:11-12 and these nations shall
serve the king of Babylon seventy
years … and when seventy years are
accomplished, that I will punish the
king of Babylon.

Prophetic Key #6 This
vision follows the same
literary structure as the visions of Daniel 2, 7, and 8.

Prophetic Key #8 Understanding secular history will
unfold the interpretation of
this prophetic vision.

Review **Prophetic Keys #10-
13, #18-21** All of these keys
apply to this vision which
supplies the most information
of all visions.

The Story of the Rise and Fall of Earthly Kingdoms

Historical Background Information (Continued)

538 BC: Cyrus is chosen by God to overthrow Babylon and free His people. (Daniel is approximately 88 years old.)

ISA 44:28 That saith of Cyrus, He is my shepherd, and shall perform all my pleasure: even saying to Jerusalem, Thou shalt be built; and to the temple, Thy foundation shall be laid.

537 BC: In the first year of Cyrus, a decree is issued to fulfill the prophecy in Jeremiah 25:1-2 to rebuild the temple at Jerusalem.

EZRA 1:1-3 Now in the first year of Cyrus king of Persia, that the word of the LORD by the mouth of Jeremiah might be fulfilled, the LORD stirred up the spirit of Cyrus king of Persia, that he made a proclamation throughout all his kingdom, and put it also in writing, saying, 2 Thus saith Cyrus king of Persia, The LORD God of heaven hath given me all the kingdoms of the earth; and he hath charged me to build him an house at Jerusalem, which is in Judah. 3 Who is there among you of all his people? his God be with him, and let him go up to Jerusalem, which is in Judah, and build the house of the LORD God of Israel, (he is the God,) which is in Jerusalem. (Also see ISA 45:13.)

Daniel's Three Weeks of Fasting and Prayer (535 BC)

2 In those days I Daniel was mourning three full weeks.

3 I ate no pleasant bread, neither came flesh nor wine in my mouth, neither did I anoint myself at all, till three whole weeks were fulfilled.

4 And in the four and twentieth day of the first month, as I was by the side of the great river, which is Hiddekel [Tigris];

Verses 2-4

536 BC: The 70 years of captivity of God's people completed.
535 BC: Daniel receives the Fourth Vision during the third year of Cyrus. However, Daniel is *mourning* due to the reports that the work on the temple at Jerusalem had ceased, owing to the strong opposition from the Samaritans who refused to acknowledge the decree of Cyrus in 537 BC. These Samaritans, tried to convince King Cyrus to rescind his decree. Daniel was aware of this conflict and began to *fast and pray* for three weeks.

*Michael (Son of God) Comes
to Encourage Daniel*

5 Then I lifted up mine eyes, and looked, and behold a certain man [Michael the Archangel] **clothed in linen, whose loins were girded** [at the waist] **with fine gold of Uphaz:**

*A Theophany:
Daniel Sees
Michael the Archangel
as the
"Man Clothed in Linen"*

6 His body also was like the beryl, and his face as the appearance of lightning, and his eyes as lamps of fire, and his arms and his feet like in colour to polished brass, and the voice of his words like the voice of a multitude.

*Daniel's Vision by the
River Hiddekel*

7 And I Daniel alone saw the vision: for the men that were with me saw not the vision; but a great quaking fell upon them, so that they fled to hide themselves.

Verses 5-7

Note: Later in verse 13, Gabriel explains to Daniel that the Heavenly Visitor (of verse 5) was "Michael" - also known as "Michael the Archangel," "chief prince," or the "Son of God," (known as Jesus Christ in the New Testament). Michael, was on His way to help Gabriel in the dispute with Satan in Persia. But first, He stopped to encourage Daniel. Whenever Michael becomes engaged in a dispute with Satan, He takes the "title" of "Michael the Archangel." (See JUDE 9.) The clothing of Michael and Jesus Christ (in REV 1:13-16) is very similar. The slight differences in the clothing give information about the Son of God; whether He is "ministering as our High Priest" or, "as a warrior" contending with Satan. When Jesus is ministering as our High Priest in the Heavenly Sanctuary, He is girded with a golden girdle around the paps [chest]. In Daniel 10:5 Michael is girded with fine gold at the waist. Review Daniel 8:15-16 and note again the following definition:

"Michael" — *Strong's* OT#4317 Miyka'e; from OT#410; who (is) like God?; Mikael, KJV - Michael.

*King Nebuchadnezzar Recognized
the "Son of God"*

DAN 3:25 He answered and said, Lo, I see four men loose, walking in the midst of the fire … and the form of the fourth is like the Son of God.

"loins" — *Strong's* OT#4975 to be slender; properly, the waist or small of the back; only in plural the loins: KJV - greyhound, loins, side.

"girded" — *Strong's* OT#2296 to gird on (as a belt).

Definition: *"theophany"* — An appearance of God to a man; a divine manifestation. *The Heritage Illustrated Dictionary.*

DAN 12:7 And I heard the man clothed in linen, which was upon the waters of the river.

REV 1:13-15 And … one like unto the Son of man, clothed with a garment down to the foot, and girt about the paps with a golden girdle. 14 His head and his hairs were white like wool, as white as snow; and his eyes were as a flame of fire; 15 And his feet like unto fine brass, as if they burned in a furnace.

REV 2:18 who hath his eyes like unto a flame of fire, and his feet are like fine brass;

REV 19:12 His eyes were as a flame of fire, and on his head were many crowns; and he had a name written, that no man knew, but he himself.

Also see: EZE 9:2-3, 11; 10:2, 6-7.

**While Daniel is in Vision,
Michael the Archangel
Appears With
Encouragement**

DANIEL

CHAPTER 10   The Story of the Rise and Fall of Earthly Kingdoms

*The Condition of a
True Prophet While in Vision*

8 Therefore I was left alone, and saw this great vision [of Michael the Archangel], **and there remained no strength in me: for my comeliness** [vigor] **was turned in me into corruption, and I retained no strength.**

9 Yet heard I the voice of his [Gabriel's] **words: and when I heard the voice of his words, then was I in a deep sleep on my face, and my face toward the ground.**

10 And, behold, an hand [of Gabriel] **touched me, which set me upon my knees and upon the palms of my hands.**

11 And he [Gabriel] **said unto me, O Daniel, a man greatly beloved, understand the words that I speak unto thee, and stand upright: for unto thee am I now sent. And when he had spoken this word unto me, I stood trembling.**

*Angel Gabriel Explains
the Unseen Struggle*

12 Then said he unto me, Fear not, Daniel: for from the first day that thou didst set thine heart to understand, and to chasten thyself before thy God, thy words were heard, and I [Gabriel] **am come for thy words.**

13 But the prince of the kingdom of Persia [Satan] **withstood me one and twenty days: but, lo, Michael, one of the chief princes, came to help me; and I remained there with the kings of Persia** [Cyrus and the other kings of Persia].

Verses 8-11

After Daniel received the vision of the Fourth Historic-Prophetic Outline and Michael the Archangel, he is interrupted by a visit from the angel Gabriel. Gabriel gives Daniel understanding about his visit with Michael. Verse one mentions that Daniel understood the "thing" — the "vision" of the Historic-Prophetic Outline.

"And behold, an hand touched me."

"O Daniel, understand the words that I speak unto thee, and stand upright."

Verses 12-13

Note: Gabriel comes to strengthen Daniel when Michael has released him from his "twenty-one day" post of contending with Satan — the prince of Persia. Once Satan is defeated by Michael, Cyrus is free to execute the right decision and reinforce the temple reconstruction in Jerusalem.

*Scripture Identifies
Satan as the Prince*

EPH 6:12   For we wrestle not against flesh and blood, but against principalities, against powers, against the rulers of the darkness of this world, against spiritual wickedness in high places.

JOHN 12:31   Now is the judgment of this world: now shall the prince of this world be.

JOHN 14:30   Hereafter I will not talk much with you: for the prince of this world cometh, and hath nothing in me.

Also see: JUDE 9; DAN 12:1; REV 12:7-8.

INTERLUDE QUESTION VISION FOUR

"What shall befall thy people in the latter days?"

The Vision Concludes With an Endtime Application

14 Now I am come to make thee understand what shall befall thy people in the latter days: for yet **the vision is for many days** [a long time into the future].

15 And when he had spoken such words unto me, I set my face toward the ground, and I became dumb.

True Prophets Do Not Breathe During a Vision

16 And, behold, one like the similitude of the sons of men touched my lips: then I opened my mouth, and spake, and said unto him that stood before me, O my lord, by the vision my sorrows are turned upon me, and I have retained no strength.

17 For how can the servant of this my lord talk with this my lord? for as for me, straightway there remained no strength in me, neither is there breath left in me.

18 Then there came again and touched me one like the appearance of a man, and he strengthened me,

19 And said, O man greatly beloved, fear not: peace be unto thee, be strong, yea, be strong. And when he had spoken unto me, **I was strengthened**, and said, Let my lord speak; for thou hast strengthened me.

Reminder: See **The Structure of Daniel** Chart on page 367. Vision Four is now moving from the **Heavenly Scene** to the **Interlude Question**. The **Interlude** is an interruption between the **Heavenly Scene** and the **Historic-Prophetic Outline**. This **Interlude Question** is addressed in Daniel 10:14. The Historic-Prophetic Outline will give the answer of what is going to happen to God's people in the latter days.

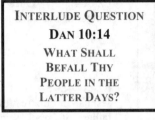

> **INTERLUDE QUESTION**
> **DAN 10:14**
> **WHAT SHALL BEFALL THY PEOPLE IN THE LATTER DAYS?**

> **HEAVENLY SCENE**
> **DAN 10:1**
> **KINGS OF THE NORTH AND KINGS OF THE SOUTH OF EARTHLY KINGDOMS**

> **INTERLUDE QUESTION**
> **DAN 10:14**
> **WHAT SHALL BEFALL THY PEOPLE IN THE LATTER DAYS?**

Verses 14-15

Gabriel gives Daniel understanding to the "vision" question, "What shall befall thy people in the latter days?" The answer will be found in Daniel 11 and concludes in Daniel 12:1 at the end of the Historic-Prophetic Outline.

DAN 8:26 And the vision of the evening and the morning which was told is true: wherefore shut thou up <u>the vision; for it shall be for many days</u>.

ISA 41:10 Fear thou not; for I am with thee: be not dismayed; for I am thy God: <u>I will strengthen thee</u>; yea, I will help thee; yea, I will uphold thee with the right hand of my righteousness.

*The Fourth Vision Will
Reveal More Truth*

20 Then said he, Knowest thou wherefore I come unto thee? and now will I return to fight with the prince of Persia [Satan]**: and when I am gone forth, lo, the prince of Grecia** [Alexander the Great] **shall come.**

21 But I will shew thee that which is noted in the scripture of truth: and there is none that holdeth with me in these things, but Michael your prince.

Introduction to Chapter 11

Verses 20-21

Note: The angel Gabriel returns to fight Satan (prince of Persia) and assures Daniel that all the enemy forces are being held back during the reign of Cyrus and his son Cambyses — a total of seven and a half years. (See EZRA 4:3-5.) Once the protection of Gabriel was withdrawn, the Persian Kingdom was quickly taken by Alexander the Great from Greece.

EZRA 4:3-5 But Zerubbabel, and Jeshua, and the rest of the chief of the fathers of Israel, said unto them, Ye have nothing to do with us to build an house unto our God; but we ourselves together will build unto the LORD God of Israel, as king Cyrus the king of Persia hath commanded us. 4 Then the people of the land weakened the hands of the people of Judah, and troubled them in building, 5 And hired counsellers against them, to frustrate their purpose, all the days of Cyrus king of Persia, even until the reign of Darius king of Persia.

**Alexander the Great
is the
"prince of Grecia"**

**The Story of the Rise and Fall
of "kings" and their Kingdoms
is Given in "Literal" Language**

Note: The Fourth Historic-Prophetic Outline <u>recaps</u> the three Historic-Prophetic Outlines in Daniel 2, 7, and 8. These previous Outlines revealed the rise and fall of kingdoms. The Fourth Outline in Daniel 11 does not name the kingdoms.

The kings are not named but are described by outstanding accomplishments or given titles, such as a "raiser of taxes," or "king of the north," or "the abomination of desolation." These titles are not symbols. There is no symbolism in Daniel chapters 10-12. The settings (contexts) are all given in <u>literal language</u> and therefore all timelines in this vision must be interpreted as "literal time." (Review Prophetic Key #18.)

The only logical method of application of an Historic-Prophetic Outline is to keep every verse <u>in sequence</u> and align it to sequential historical events. Therefore, the notes in the right column list those historical events which fulfill the verses in the left column. (The colors of the crowns will match with the colors of the kingdoms in the first three visions.)

DANIEL
The Story of the Rise and Fall of Earthly Kingdoms

Reminder: See **The Structure Daniel** Chart on page 367. Daniel 11 begins the **Historic-Prophetic Outline** of the Fourth Vision. This Prophetic Outline names all six kingdoms that followed fallen Babylon and closes when Michael stands up to deliver His people. The Recapping Structure Chart (page 260) reviews the information of the kingdoms in the first three visions. Daniel 11 recaps the information for the entire Book. **Prophetic Key #18** There are no symbols in this vision.

CHAPTER 11

HISTORIC-PROPHETIC OUTLINE
VISION FOUR

Daniel Received the Fourth Vision in Approximately 535 BC

The Historic-Prophetic Outline of Earthly "kings" is Contained in Daniel 11:1-45 Beginning in 538 BC

First Year of Darius the Mede
(538 BC)

1 Also I [angel Gabriel from Daniel 10] **in the first year of Darius the Mede, even I,** [Gabriel] **stood to confirm and to strengthen him** [Daniel].

2nd Kingdom
538 — 331 BC

HISTORIC-PROPHETIC OUTLINE DAN 11:1-45 (BABYLON HAS FALLEN) MEDO-PERSIA

(BABYLON HAS FALLEN)

The Kingdom of Babylon is not included in this vision because it had already fallen to Medo-Persia. Darius the Mede was the first "king" to be placed on the throne in 538 BC by Cyrus the Great. Cyrus took the throne two years later when Darius [his uncle] died. Note: When there is a Prophetic <u>Outline</u> of kingdoms in the Bible, the Bible always gives the information of where to start the Outline.

Darius the Mede is the first "king" in this chapter.

HEAVENLY SCENE DAN 10:1 KINGS OF THE NORTH AND KINGS OF THE SOUTH OF EARTHLY KINGDOMS
INTERLUDE QUESTION DAN 10:14 WHAT SHALL BEFALL THY PEOPLE IN THE LATTER DAYS?
HISTORIC-PROPHETIC OUTLINE DAN 11:1-45 (BABYLON HAS FALLEN) MEDO-PERSIA

"Babylon" has fallen and is not included in this vision. It is in brackets because it holds the position of the First Kingdom.

Verse 1

- The Historic-Prophetic Outline in Daniel's Fourth Vision began in the first year of Darius the Mede.
- Back in the Prophetic Outline of the Second Vision, (DAN 7:5) the Medes and the Persians were represented by a symbolic bear which "<u>raised up itself on one side</u>" and in the Third Vision of DAN 8:3-4 where the Ram had "<u>one horn higher</u>."
- This indicated that the Medes and Persians were not equal in strength.
- Although this verse begins with a reference to the Medes, in the next verse it begins to describe the stronger kings of Persia and their doings which brought about the fall of Medo-Persia and the rise of the Grecian Kingdom.

The Four Remaining
Kings of Persia
(530-465 BC)

2 And now will I shew thee the truth. Behold, there shall stand up yet three kings [Cambyses, Smyrdis, Darius I] **in Persia; and the fourth** [Xerxes] **shall be far richer than they all: and by his strength through his riches he shall stir up all against the realm of Grecia** [Final defeat of Xerxes was at the battle of Salamis in 480 BC].

Xerxes I

The Four Remaining
Kings of Persia

1. Cambyses: 530-522 BC
2. Smyrdis: 522 BC
3. Darius I Hystaspes: 522-486 BC
4. Xerxes I (or Ahasuerus): 486-465 BC

Verse 2

Prophetic Key #12 The Historic-Prophetic <u>Outline</u> begins to move forward.

The names of the first three Persian kings were:
1. Cambyses,
2. Bardiyya, (an imposter who ruled claiming to be Smyrdis), and
3. Darius I Hystaspes.

- History books give a long list of the kings who sat on the thrones of the Medes and the Persians. In Daniel 11, not every king who ruled down through the ages is mentioned.
- The objective of an Historic-Prophetic Outline is not intended to be just an historical record.

Prophetic Key #10 The Daniel 11 Historic-Prophetic Outline offers only the information sufficient to recognize context, sequence, continuity, and historical alignment; and refers only to those kings who brought about the <u>rise and fall of the kingdoms</u>.

- It mentions kings who had to do with events critical to the people of God, to the life of Christ, and to the antichrist.

- The Bible is a Judeo-Christian book and its prophecies are directed to the people of God — to the Jews in the Old Testament and the Christians in the New Testament.
- The Prophetic Outlines of Daniel <u>do not</u> trace the rise and fall of empires and great civilizations such as those of South and Central America, China, Japan, and others <u>which did not affect the people of God</u>.

- The name of the 4th king was Xerxes, the Persian king Ahasuerus described in the Book of Esther. (The drama of the Book of Esther adds interest to Daniel 11.)
- Xerxes was actually the second king to stir up trouble with Greece.
- If he had read the prophecies of Daniel, he would have known that Greece was to become the Third Kingdom. Perhaps he would not have been so foolish as to stir up war against them!
- But when a king is rich, he is tempted to build up his military strength. Then what?
- He must stir up trouble so the military will have something to do.
- Xerxes I [Ahasuerus] was the last Persian king to invade Greece; and now the prophecy passes over nine minor rulers to introduce the "mighty king," Alexander the Great.
- Thus, Medo-Persia eventually fell. Greece came to power in 331 BC.

DANIEL

The Story of the Rise and Fall of Earthly Kingdoms

Reminder: See **The Structure of Daniel** Chart on page 367. In just a few verses the Historic-Prophetic Outline has moved from Medo-Persia to Greece following the Outlines given in the previous three visions.

Prophetic Key #12 Outlines must always move forward in time.

HISTORIC-PROPHETIC
OUTLINE
(CONTINUED)
VISION FOUR

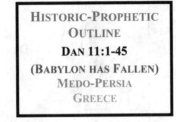

HISTORIC-PROPHETIC
OUTLINE
DAN 11:1-45
(BABYLON HAS FALLEN)
MEDO-PERSIA
GREECE

HEAVENLY SCENE
DAN 10:1
KINGS OF THE NORTH
AND
KINGS OF THE SOUTH
OF
EARTHLY KINGDOMS

INTERLUDE QUESTION
DAN 10:14
WHAT SHALL
BEFALL THY
PEOPLE IN THE
LATTER DAYS?

HISTORIC-PROPHETIC
OUTLINE
DAN 11:1-45
(BABYLON HAS FALLEN)
MEDO-PERSIA
GREECE

The Fall of Medo-Persia,
the Second Kingdom —
The Rise of Greece,
the Third Kingdom
(331BC)

3 And a mighty king [Alexander the Great] **shall stand up,** [come to the throne] **that shall rule with great dominion,** [clear to India] **and do according to his will** [as a great conqueror].

Alexander the Great
Defeated Xerxes
in the
Battle of Arbela
in 331 BC

Verse 3

- Alexander the Great was described in the Historic-Prophetic Outline of the Third Vision of Daniel 8:5 as a "notable horn."
- (Symbolic "horns" represent "kings" as they reign over a great kingdom. See Daniel 8:20.)
- Alexander, while still young, was famous for his military conquests which extended from Macedonia and Greece to northwest India, from Egypt to the Jaxartes River east of the Caspian Sea — the largest kingdom the world had yet known.

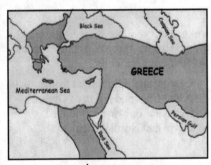

3rd Kingdom
331 — 168 BC

DAN 8:5 And as I was considering, behold, an he goat [Grecian kingdom] came from the west on the face of the whole earth, and touched not the ground: and the goat had a notable horn between his eyes [Alexander the Great].

DANIEL

*The Break-up of Greece —
the Third Kingdom
(323-280 BC)*

4 And when he [Alexander the Great] **shall stand up, his kingdom shall be broken,** [in 323 BC] **and shall be divided** [in 301 BC] **toward the four winds** [directions] **of heaven;** [like the four heads of the Leopard in DAN 7:6] **and not to his posterity,** [his feeble son was not able to take charge] **nor according to his dominion which he ruled: for his kingdom shall be plucked up, even for others** [his four generals] **beside those.**

Alexander the Great
Dies Suddenly in 323 BC

Verse 4

• Alexander had scarcely reached the pinnacle of his power when he was cut down by sudden illness. He died in 323 BC.

• Alexander's kingdom was not to go to his "posterity." His son was feeble, and not able to take the throne, so it was divided up between his four army generals.

DAN 8:8 Therefore the he goat waxed very great: and when he was strong, the great horn was broken; and for it came up four notable ones <u>toward the four winds of heaven</u>.

**The Death of
Alexander the Great**

Note: "... his kingdom shall be broken, and shall be divided <u>toward the four winds</u> [four directions] <u>of heaven</u>. History records that Alexander's kingdom became divided between his four army generals:

1.	**Cassander**	West	Greece, and influence at Rome
2.	**Lysimachus**	Northwest	Asia Minor and North of Greece
3.	**Seleucus**	North and East	Syria and Babylon to the East
4.	**Ptolemy**	The South	Egypt and North Africa

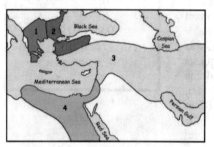

Divisions of Greece by 301 BC

1. **Cassander**
2. **Lysimachus**
3. **Seleucus**
4. **Ptolemy**

• These four kingdoms of Greece were reduced down to three kingdoms in 280 BC (see maps on page 271) and then into two major divisions.

• The successors of Cassander were very soon conquered by Lysimachus, and his kingdom; Greece and Macedon, were annexed to Thrace.

• Lysimachus was in turn conquered by Seleucus, and Macedon and Thrace were annexed to Syria.

• These facts prepare the way for an application of verse 5.

• From here on, prophecy speaks of only two divisions because the whole of Alexander's kingdom finally resolved itself into these two kingdoms — Egypt and Syria — known as "king of the north" and "king of the south" respectively.

The Divisions of the Kingdom of Greece

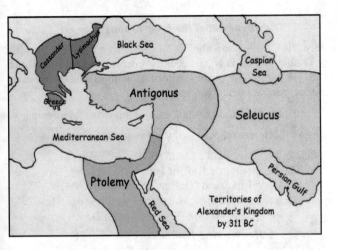

Territories of
Alexander's Kingdom
by 311 BC

- Immediately after Alexander's death in 323 BC, his generals distributed among themselves the provinces of the Kingdom of Greece.
- **316 BC**: Antigonus drove Seleucus out of Babylon. The main struggle was then between Antigonus and the united efforts of Cassander, Lysimachus, and Ptolemy along with Seleucus. Conflicts continued in Greece, the islands, and surrounding areas. Boundaries were constantly shifting.
- **312 BC**: Seleucus regained Babylon and united the eastern provinces.
- **311 BC**: Antigonus stood as the strongest of the five principal leaders of Alexander's broken kingdom before further division.

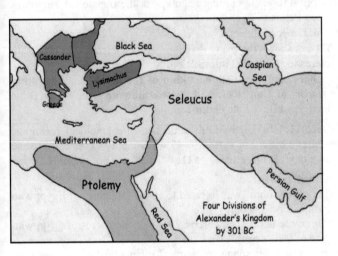

Four Divisions of
Alexander's Kingdom
by 301 BC

- **306 BC**: Antigonus declared himself king of the whole Grecian Kingdom.
- Next, Cassander, Lysimachus, Seleucus, and Ptolemy usurped the royal title in their respective territories.
- **301 BC**: Antigonus was killed and his territory was divided between Lysimachus and Seleucus.
- At this point, there was no hope of a unified kingdom, and the four main kingdoms emerged.
- By 301 BC the four divisions of Alexander's kingdom was settled.

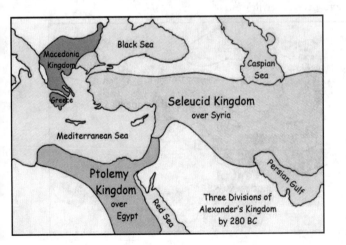

Three Divisions of
Alexander's Kingdom
by 280 BC

- **281 BC**: Seleucus killed Lysimachus leaving three great Hellenistic kingdoms to dominate the near east, known as: Macedonia, the Seleucid Kingdom of Syria, and the Ptolemy Kingdom of Egypt.
- **280 BC**: Seleucus is killed; his son, Antigonus, began to rule. For some years, a long line of Seleucid kings ruled large parts of Asia Minor.
- Before the time of Christ, these three Hellenistic kingdoms each successively became a province under Pagan Imperial Rome.
- *"Hellenist"* — a Grecian Jew; a Jew who used the Greek language.
- *"Hellenistic"* — pertaining to the *Hellenists*. The *Hellenistic* language was the Greek spoken or used by the Jews who lived in Egypt and other countries, where the Greek language prevailed. The Greek language and culture had a very large influence on the Jewish nation.

The Alignment of the Four Visions

Prophetic Key #10 Notice how the vision in Daniel 11 is aligning with the first three Outlines. This is NOT needless repetition because the Bible student must begin in the right place and proceed with careful attention to context, sequence, continuity, and alignment.

- Biblical Principles and Hermeneutics must involve careful research.

Prophetic Key #4 Scripture unlocks Scripture as stated below:

> **The Hermeneutic Rule of Isaiah 28:9-13**
> "Line Upon Line" and "Outline Upon Outline"
> "Whom shall he teach knowledge? … Line upon line, line upon line …"

Establishing Foundations

- The Historic-Prophetic Outline begins with the transfer of kingdoms from Medo-Persia to Greece.
- The fall of Greece follows.
- Page 271 has shown the many divisions of the Grecian Kingdom with extra interesting historical information.
- The prophecy continues with the **"king of the north"** and the **"king of the south" of Daniel 11:5-14.** These titles are given by the Bible itself throughout the whole Outline.

Note: Daniel 11:5-14 begins with addressing geographical locations. These same titles are used in verses 36-45 which apply to the end of time and to our own day. **Prophetic Key #21c** "Titles" are <u>not</u> symbols.

The map below illustrates:
1. The "king of the south" was referred to as the Ptolemies of <u>Egypt</u> who were south of God's people (Israel);
2. The "king of the north" was referred to as the Seleucids of <u>Syria</u> who were north of God's people (in Israel).

In later verses these titles change identity as other kingdoms gained control of the respective territories.

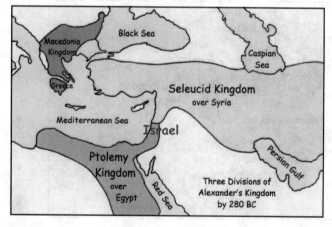

Note: Prophecy always centers around God's people. In the Old Testament, Israel was the center of Biblical prophecy. After Christ's time, Christianity (God's people) had spread throughout the world.

Who Would Become the Fourth Great Kingdom?

KINGS OF THE SOUTH AND KINGS OF THE NORTH

THE PTOLEMIES		THE SELEUCIDS	
Ptolemy I Soter	304-283	Seleucus I Nicator	305-280
Ptolemy II Philadelphus	285-246	Antiochus I Soter	280-261
		Antiochus II Theos	261-246
Ptolemy III Euergetes	246-221	Seleucus II Callinicos	246-225
		Seleucus III Ceraunos	225-223
Ptolemy IV Epiphanes	221-203	Antiochus III the Great	223-187
Pagan Imperial Rome Appears on the Scene Around 200 BC			
Ptolemy V Epiphanes	203-181	Seleucus IV Philopater	187-175
Ptolemy VI Eupator	181	Antiochus IV Epiphanes	175-164
Ptolemy VII Philometer	181-145	Antiochus V Eupator	164-150
Etc. to 51 BC		Etc. to 65 BC	
Cleopatra VI	51-30		

Note: Names and dates will vary slightly between different historical records.

Egypt (The Ptolemy's) ("king of the south") Aspire to Become the Fourth Kingdom but the "king of the north" is Stronger

5 And the king of the south [Ptolemy I Soter] **shall be strong, and one of his** [Alexander the Great's] **princes** [Seleucus I Nicator of Syria]; **and he** [Seleucus I] **shall be strong above him** [Ptolemy I], **and have dominion; his** [Seleucus I] **dominion shall be a great dominion** [Seleucus I Nicator of Syria had ¾'s of Alexander's dominion so it was considered "stronger" or "greater."]

Verse 5

- From the time that Alexander died, it was many years until Rome appeared on the horizon.
- In the meantime, Syria and Egypt both had the same aspirations — to become a fourth great kingdom. Both of them, especially Egypt, built up their military strength.

Prophetic Key #13 This INTERLUDE between the fall of Greece and the rise of the Pagan Imperial Roman Kingdom is NOT brought to view in the first three Historic-Prophetic Outlines of Daniel, but this Fourth Outline adds extra details in a most fascinating way.

The Rising Military Might of Egypt — "king of the south"

- The military strength of Egypt is described as being "strong."

"king of the north" is Stronger

- As noted on the former map, Seleucus I Nicator became possessor of ¾'s of Alexander's dominion, and established a more powerful kingdom than that of Egypt.

Orientation:

> ## Prophecy Centers Around the People of God

- In the days of Medo-Persia, Greece, and Pagan Imperial Rome, most of God's people lived in the Holy Land of Palestine. All prophecy revolved around them. They were the geographical center of prophetic utterance in the Old Testament times.

Prophetic Key #7 Prophecy is history written before it happens.

- History is better understood with maps!
- The following map notes the location of God's people, (the Jews at that time) in **Israel** and those nations which were to the north and to the south of them.

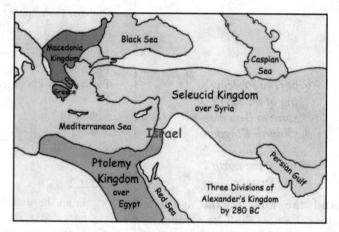

- From the standpoint of the Israelites living in Judah, Syria's ruler (including the province of Babylon) was **north** of them, and referred to as the **"king of the north."**
- Egypt was to the **south** of Israel, and the Jews referred to the ruler of Egypt as the **"king of the south."**
- When Alexander the Great (of Greece) died, his kingdom was divided into four parts. Eventually, the four kingdoms were reduced to the two main kingdoms of Egypt and Syria.
- There were no threats to God's people from the Mediterranean Sea on the west or the desert to the east.
- But the "king of the north" and the "king of the south" gave them much difficulty!

Prophetic Key #7 Prophecy is given to enable God's people to know where they are in the stream of time. By the study in verses 5-13, Israel was able to discern the progress of prophetic application.

- Each time that Egypt marched up across Israel to attack Syria, God's people could trace that prophetic fulfillment.
- In the same way, as Syria marched back down to counter-attack, God's people could also watch that fulfillment.
- The same applies to those who possess an understanding of the **endtime prophecies.** In like manner, Daniel 11:40-45 and 12:1-3 apply to endtime events.

DANIEL
CHAPTER 11 — The Story of the Rise and Fall of Earthly Kingdoms

Egypt's Aspiration to Become the Fourth Great Kingdom

- **Review:** Previously, the Medes and the Persians had successfully joined themselves together to build a great kingdom.
- Perhaps the Syrians and the Egyptians could do the same.
- In those days, alliances (or agreements) were made by marriages between the ruling families.
- Verse 6 gives the information of what happens next.

Verse 6

The Story of Berenice Ptolemy and Laodice, the Seleucid

- **250 BC:** King Ptolemy II Philadelphus of Egypt and King Antiochus II Theos of Syria attempted to guarantee peace between their countries by having King Antiochus II marry King Ptolemy's daughter, Berenice.
- Therefore, Berenice, princess of Egypt, came into an agreement to marry the king of Syria to develop the fourth great kingdom.
- To get there she would have to pass through Israel.
- She came in a great procession of horses and chariots, decorated to the hilt, in all the glory and riches Egypt had to offer.
- With her came friends, servants, slaves, and all that it took to travel in those times.

Prophetic Key #12 Prophecy is usually understood at the time of fulfillment. The Jews must have been very impressed with this display. If they were reading the Book of Daniel, they could have looked at Daniel 11:6 and said, "Oh, here she comes!"

- According to the marriage contract, intended to unite the two nations, she was to sit beside Antiochus II Theo of Syria on his throne.
- But, Antiochus II already had a wife, Laodice, who had borne him a son [Seleucus II Callinicos] to be heir to the throne. What was he to do with Laodice?
- He divorced Laodice and put her, and their son [Seleucus II Callinicos], off the throne, out of the court, and into the background.
- Many of the Syrian people were offended by this and they schemed to get Laodice back on the throne.

- When Berenice had a son, Laodice became extremely upset!
- As well, Antiochus II realized he didn't care for Berenice very much.
- He divorced Berenice when her father, king of Egypt died, and took Laodice back again.
- Laodice had become bitter. She was afraid of what her husband would do next. What was she to do?
- Using her royal powers, Laodice managed to poison the king, and as soon as he died, Laodice's friends and loyal supporters placed her and her son [Seleucus II Callinicos] back on the throne.
- They murdered Berenice, her son, and all the Egyptians in her court fulfilling the prophecy in the last part of verse 6.
- The efforts to create a fourth great kingdom by marriage fell apart.
- (**Note:** This was all foretold by God almost 300 years before it happened.)

Egypt and Syria Aspire to be the Fourth Kingdom by Marriage and a Ruling Heir
(250 BC)

6 And in the end of years [about 35 years after the death of Seleucus I Nicator] **they** [Antiochus II and Ptolemy II] **shall join themselves together** [make an alliance through marriage to be the fourth world kingdom]; **for the king's daughter of the south** [Berenice Ptolemy] **shall come to the king of the north** [Antiochus II] **to make an agreement ...**

Berenice Murdered
(246 BC)

6 ... but she [Berenice] **shall not retain the power of the arm** [protection was removed from her]; **neither shall he** [the Seleucid king, Antiochus II] **stand, nor his arm** [he died and all protection was removed from both of them]: **but she shall be given up** [murdered], **and they that brought her** [Berenice's Egyptian court], **and he that** [was] **begat** [of] **her,** [Berenice's son] **and he** [Antiochus II] **that strengthened her in these times.**

*Berenice's Brother
("king of the south")
Takes Revenge*

7 But out of a branch of her [Berenice's] **<u>roots</u> shall one** [her brother, Ptolemy III Euergetes] **stand up in his estate** [raised an Egyptian army], **which shall come with an army, and shall <u>enter into the fortress</u>** [Seleucis, Syria] **of the king of the north,** [Seleucus II Callinicos and mother Laodice] **and shall deal against them, and shall prevail** [become victorious]:

**Ptolemy III Euergetes
"king of the south"**

Verse 7   *Retaliation*

- The events of verse 6 were not to go unnoticed.
- The *"roots"* of Berenice Ptolemy were her brother, Ptolemy III Euergetes, who heard of the murder of his sister, and all the Egyptians who had come from Egypt.
- Ptolemy III took revenge for these murders, invaded Syria, and slew Laodice.
- Ptolemy took the city of Seleucia, which was kept for some years afterward by the garrisons of the kings of Egypt. Thus did he *"<u>enter into the fortress of the king of the north</u>."*

8 And [he, Ptolemy III] **shall also carry captives into Egypt their gods, with their princes, and with their precious vessels of silver and of gold; and he shall continue more years than the king of the north** [Ptolemy III died in 221 BC and survived Seleucus II by 4-5 years].

Verse 8

- Before returning home, Ptolemy III plundered 40,000 talents of silver and precious vessels and 2,500 images of the gods which Cambyses [530-522 BC] had formerly taken from Egypt and carried into Persia.
- After the retaliation for Berenice's death, Ptolemy III returned to Egypt instead of ruling in the north. Why? He had heard of a rebellion within, and against, the state of Egypt.
- The Egyptians, who were totally given to idolatry, honored Ptolemy with the title "Euergetes" for restoring their gods and hailed him as their benefactor.
- (In Greek *"benefactor"* is *"euergetes"* — hence Ptolemy III *Euergetes*.)
- Ptolemy III was now content with himself and did not attack the Syrians again as long as he lived.

9 So the king of the south [Egyptian Ptolemy III] **shall come into his** [Seleucus II] **kingdom, and shall return into his own land** [Egypt].

Verse 9

- This verse just reviews the story of how Ptolemy came into Seleucus' kingdom (possessing nearly all of it as far as India), but he returned to his own land of Egypt due to a raised sedition (conduct or language inciting to rebellion against the authority of the state.)
- If Ptolemy would not have been recalled by this domestic sedition, he would have possessed the whole kingdom of Seleucus without war or battle.

The Story of the Rise and Fall of Earthly Kingdoms

The Continuing Feud Between Egypt and Syria — Neither Can Become the Fourth Kingdom
(219 BC)

10 But his [Seleucus II Callinicos] **sons** [Seleucus III Ceraunos and Antiochus III the Great] **shall be stirred up, and shall assemble a multitude of great forces: and one** [Antiochus III] **shall certainly come, and overflow, and pass through** [219 BC]**: then shall he return,** [to conquer Palestine] **and be stirred up, even to his fortress.**

Verse 10   *The Feud*

- When families begin to hate each other, it often continues down through generations.
- This feud continued between Egypt and Syria with both kingdoms always marching through Israel.

> **Note:** Sometimes God's people would be under Syrian rule and then under Egyptian rule as these battles were fought. They needed to know these things to understand there would be an end to their troubles one day. These prophecies gave encouragement to them — just as the endtime prophecies are intended to give encouragement to God's people today.

- <u>Seleucus II Callinicos</u>, who was in exile, fell from a horse and died.
- His two sons began to avenge the work of their father.
- Seleucus III Ceraunos (the eldest) took the throne first, and after a short reign from 225-223 BC he was poisoned by his generals.
- Antiochus III the Great [the youngest] was proclaimed king and actually was the more capable one to be king.
- Antiochus III recovered Seleucia and Syria from Egypt by overcoming Egyptian general Nicolas.
- Antiochus III had thoughts of invading Egypt, but didn't, and returned home.
- Thereafter Antiochus III set out upon a systematic campaign to conquer Palestine from his rival, Ptolemy IV, during which he penetrated Transjordan.
- Both sides bargained for peace and yet prepared for war.
- Antiochus III was the *"one"* who would certainly *"overflow and pass through."*

"kings of the north and south in conflict"

Kings of the North and South in Conflict
(217 BC)

11 And the king of the south [Ptolemy IV Epiphanes] **shall be moved** [in 217 BC] **with choler** [a bad temper]**, and** [he] **shall come forth and fight** [the Battle of Raphia] **with him** [Antiochus III]**, even with the king of the north** [Antiochus III]**: and he** [Antiochus III] **shall set forth a great multitude** [great army]**; but the multitude** [army of Antiochus III] **shall be given into his** [Ptolemy IV] **hand.**

Verse 11

- Ptolemy IV Epiphanes succeeded his father Ptolemy III Euergetes of Egypt shortly AFTER Antiochus III the Great became King of Syria.

Ptolemy IV (king of the south) was:
- An ease-loving prince;
- Aroused at prospect of Antiochus III invading Egypt;
- Moved with *"choler"* due to past losses and future danger;
- Sent a large army to check on Syria <u>but</u> Syria was doing the same checking on Egypt.

Antiochus III (king of the north) was:
- Also called "Magnus the Great" and he conducted several campaigns;
- Defeated at the Battle of Raphia (217 BC) by Ptolemy IV Epiphanes of Egypt.

Antiochus III of Syria <u>was defeated</u> even though he had:
- 62,000 footman, 6000 horsemen and 102 elephants.
- 14,000 were slain and 4000 taken as prisoners.
- His army went into the hands of Ptolemy IV.

After the Battle of Raphia he conducted more campaigns to regain former territory — then he turned his fury on Egypt again.

The Continuing Feud . . .

12 And when he [Ptolemy IV Epiphanes] **hath taken away the multitude** [army of Antiochus III], **his** [Ptolemy's] <u>**heart shall be lifted up; and he**</u> [Ptolemy IV] **shall cast down many ten thousands** [Jews]**: but he** [Ptolemy IV] <u>**shall not be strengthened by it.**</u>

Ptolemy IV Epiphanes
"king of the south"

Verse 12

Ptolemy IV Epiphanes did not make good use of his victory:

- Gave himself up to uncontrolled indulgence of feasting and passions;
- His heart was lifted up by his success which caused his own subjects to rebel against him;
- "<u>Lifting up his heart</u>" — by having transactions with the Jews;
- He went to Jerusalem and tried to forcefully enter the Holy Place of the Temple;
- The Jews restrained him and he left very angry with the Jews;
- In Alexandria (capital in Northern Egypt) he killed 40,000 — 60,000 Jews (even though the Jews were most favored at that time);
- This <u>did NOT strengthen his kingdom</u>, but almost totally ruined it.

> Between verses 12 and 13, peace lasted about 14 years after the Battle of Raphia between Syria and Egypt. During this time:
> - **Antiochus III** suppresses rebellion in his kingdom (212-204 BC) and recovers the eastern and western territories from India to the Aegean, becoming "king of the north" again over most of Alexander's former kingdom.
> - About **203 BC** Ptolemy IV Ephiphanes (king of the south) and his wife died. Their five year old son, Ptolemy V Epiphanes, ascended to the throne.

Ptolemy V Epiphanes
"king of the south"

A Five Year Old, (Ptolemy V Epiphanes) ["king of the south"] Becomes Pharaoh in Egypt (203 BC) "king of the north" Invades "king of the south's" Territory in Palestine (201 BC)

13 For the king of the north [Antiochus III] **shall return,** [after 14 years of peace] **and shall set forth a multitude** [an army] **greater than the former** [army— an immense army]**, and shall certainly come after certain years** [to invade the Egyptian territory of Palestine] **with a great army and with much riches.**

Verse 13

- The accession of the boy child Ptolemy V Epiphanes presented Antiochus III with the opportunity of avenging himself upon the Egyptians.
- He now prepared for a second attack on Egypt.

Antiochus III the Great:

- Thought he could overcome the young (vulnerable) Ptolemy V Ephiphanes, so he raised an immense army against Egypt;
- Others wished to join them to split up Egypt, thinking a five year old didn't have a chance. An easy victory over the king was expected.
- **201 BC:** On the way to Egypt, he invaded Egyptian territory in Palestine.

> **Pagan Imperial Rome Emerges Approximately 200 BC**

- **Pagan Imperial Rome** was the mistress of the "then known" Mediterranean world and had begun to enter into contracts with the east.
- The **Romans** interfered on behalf of the young king of Egypt and determined that Ptolemy V Epiphanes should be protected from the ruin devised by Antiochus III (of Syria) and Philip of Macedonia.
- **Rome** saw an opportunity to control Egypt without war!
- The declaration was made. ***"We, Rome, will protect the boy-king!"***
- Thus, **Rome** began to take Egypt under its dominion.

Enemies Seek to Destroy Egypt
(201 BC)

14 And in those times there shall many [rebellious Egyptians; Antiochus III; Philip of Macedon] **stand up against the king of the south:** [5 year old Ptolemy V Epiphanes] ...

(The last portion of this verse follows on the next page.)

<u>Verse 14</u>

"many" — Those that rose up against Infant Ptolemy were *"many."*

1. Antiochus III the Great from Syria;
2. Agathocles (Prime Minister of Egypt) and provinces rebelled against the boy child Ptolemy V Epiphanes;
3. Alexandrians rose against their Prime Minister Agathocles (putting him and his family to death);
4. Philip of Macedonia teamed with Antiochus III to divide the dominions between them.

- This was the "rising up against the king of the south" to fulfill the prophecy.
- <u>NOTE</u>: **This verse is describing Ptolemy V Epiphanes in Egypt — NOT — Antiochus IV Epiphanes from Syria.**

Pagan Imperial Rome Emerges Approximately 200 BC

- **200 BC:** Rome was the mistress of the western Mediterranean and had begun to enter into contracts with the east.

- **197 BC:** Rome defeats Macedonia and set up the Greek states under her protection. Antiochus III takes Palestine.

- **190 BC:** Rome defeated Antiochus III the Great.

- **168 BC:** Battle of Pydna — Rome ended the monarchy of Macedonia and divided it into four confederacies.

- **168 BC:** Rome's power and mastery over the East is reasoned by the removal of the monarchs from the three Hellenistic kingdoms. Rome exercised complete control.

Reminder: See **The Structure of Daniel** Chart on page 367. The His-toric-Prophetic Outline is now moving forward to introduce the Fourth Kingdom around God's people. **Prophetic Key #11** The Fourth Kingdom in this Outline aligns with the Fourth Kingdom in first three visions.

HISTORIC-PROPHETIC
OUTLINE
(CONTINUED)
VISION FOUR

HISTORIC-PROPHETIC
OUTLINE
DAN 11:1-45
(BABYLON HAS FALLEN)
MEDO-PERSIA
GREECE
ROME (PAGAN IMPERIAL)

*Pagan Imperial Rome
Conquers Macedonia
at the Battle of Pydna
(168 BC)*

Verse 14 (Continued)

Pagan Imperial Rome
Rising to Become
the **"king of the north"**
Through the **"Caesars"**

HEAVENLY SCENE
DAN 10:1
KINGS OF THE NORTH
AND
KINGS OF THE SOUTH
OF
EARTHLY KINGDOMS

14 ... also the robbers of thy peo-ple [introducing the new power of Rome] **shall exalt themselves to establish the vision** [of Daniel] **but they shall fall.** [Macedonia fell in 168 BC and later, Syria fell in 65 BC.]

(This portion of the verse is repeated on the next page.)

*Ptolemy V's Guardian
Appointed by
Roman Senate to Aristomenes*

- The first act of Aristomenes was to offer protection against the threatened invasion of Antiochus III and Philip of Macedon.
- **Providence** raised up the Romans to interfere and reduce these ene-mies. Thus ended the Kingdom of Greece. This establishes the previous visions of Daniel.

INTERLUDE QUESTION
DAN 10:14
WHAT SHALL
BEFALL THY
PEOPLE IN THE
LATTER DAYS?

HISTORIC-PROPHETIC
OUTLINE
DAN 11:1-45
(BABYLON HAS FALLEN)
MEDO-PERSIA
GREECE
ROME (PAGAN IMPERIAL)

4th Kingdom
168 BC — AD 476

Rule of Antiochus IV Epiphanes (175-164 BC)

- During his brief reign of 12 years, Antiochus IV nearly exterminated the religion and culture of the Jews.
- Eventually the Jews rose in revolt and drove his forces from Judea.
- In **168 BC, Rome had conquered Macedonia** and made that country a part of its kingdom. Then Pagan Imperial Rome became the **"king of the north"** because of their connection with the people of God and being an earthly government ruling around Palestine.
- (Earthly governments are not introduced into prophecy until they be-come connected with the people of God in some way.)
- Seven years later, in 161 BC, Pagan Rome became connected with the Jews, the people of God at that time, by the famous Jewish League. Here the Jews were under Rome as a "protectorate."

The Story of the Rise and Fall of Earthly Kingdoms

The Robber Romans

14 ... also <u>the robbers of thy people</u> [introducing the new power of Rome] **shall exalt themselves to <u>establish the vision</u>** [of Daniel 7] **but they** [Macedonia and Syria] **shall fall.**

Pagan Imperial Rome —
"The Robber Romans"
Rising to Become
"king of the north"
Through the **"Caesars"**

Verse 14 (Concluded)

"robbers" — *Strong's* OT:6530; from OT:6555; violent, i.e. a tyrant: KJV - <u>destroyer</u>, <u>ravenous</u>, robber.

DAN 7:7 ... a fourth beast, dreadful and terrible, and strong exceedingly; and it had great iron teeth: it <u>devoured</u> and <u>brake in pieces</u>, and <u>stamped the residue with the feet of it</u> ...

- This new power is now introduced as *"the robbers of thy people."*
- How? The Romans were known as *robbers* or *breakers* of the people because they taxed the people heavily. The people were forced into slave labor to build roads, aqueducts, and walls with heavy rock foundations. These old roads may be seen in many parts of the old world yet today. Many were chained in the bottom of ships to become oarsmen in the Roman navy. They also built the great road of London with slave labor. <u>Rome was known as a *grinding force* or an *iron kingdom*</u>.

Rome emerged and was destined by prophecy to:
1. Control the "then known" world;
2. Exert a mighty influence — to the end of time.
3. The Romans first made themselves felt in the affairs of Syria and Egypt. Later, the Romans robbed the Jews of their independence in 63 BC. In AD 70 they destroyed the temple and the city of Jerusalem.
4. Rome "speaks" and shatters the dreams of Syria and Macedonia.
5. Rome was determined to protect the boy child Ptolemy V Epiphanes.
6. While Syria and Macedonia were meditating to "piecemeal" Ptolemy V Epiphanes' kingdom, God raised up the Romans against them (even though their crimes were most horrible) and reduced Syria and Macedonia under Roman rule.
7. Pagan Imperial Rome was a nation ruled by harsh laws which punished by crucifixion, the pointed stake, and other forms of torture.
8. Subjugated nations felt this *iron* oppression. Israel also came under the iron fist of Roman rule.

This verse explains that the coming of Rome would *"establish the vision."* What vision? The vision(s) concerning the Fourth Kingdom.
1. Daniel 2, the vision of the *iron legs* is established as well as —
2. Daniel 7, the vision of the *dreadful beast* with *iron teeth*.
- The last phrase of Daniel 11:14 says, "but they shall fall."
- The enemies of the boy Pharaoh all fell under Roman rule.

~ This completes the first 14 verses of the Fourth Historic-Prophetic Outline. Already the action has aligned with the first four kingdoms of the previous visions. The prophetic expositor is now on solid ground of alignment of all four visions, and is ready to move forward.

> ### Historical Review of Events Between Rome and Syria
>
> (The following is the <u>only application</u> that could be found in secular history. There were no dates given to establish this time frame. Comments are made as the verse continues the narrative begun in verse 13, concerning Antiochus III's second campaign in Palestine. <u>Remember</u>: if the proper application cannot be found, then it is better to leave the verse alone. The following information is given as an example of what may have happened.)

While Syria and Egypt Feud, Rome's Influence Increases — Israel Cannot Influence the Outcomes

15 So the king of the north [Antiochus IV] **shall come, and cast up a mount** ["a mound" that is siege works] **and take the most fenced cities** [Sidon, one of the strongest]: **and the arms** [armies] **of the south** [Scopas of Egypt] **shall not withstand, neither his chosen people,** [his choicest generals] **neither shall there be any strength to withstand.**

Verse 15

Historical Review:

- (203-181 BC: Reign of boy child Ptolemy V Epiphanes.)
- (223-187 BC: Reign of Antiochus III the Great.)
- Education of Ptolemy V Epiphanes was entrusted to Roman Lepidus.
- Aristomenes was appointed as guardian of Ptolemy V for protection from:
    — Philip (of Macedonia) and
    — Antiochus (of Syria).
- <u>Through the Romans</u>: Egyptian General Scopus was then dispatched to raise reinforcements for the Egyptian army.
- The army of Scopas marched into Palestine and Syria and reduced all Judea to the authority of Egypt — this was through the <u>power of Rome</u>.
- Antiochus III (of Syria) tried to recover Palestine and Syria from Egypt, but Scopas of Egypt opposed him.
- The armies met at the Jordan and Scopas was defeated and pursued to Sidon and surrendered there.
- Three generals of Egypt were sent to free Scopas with no success.
- Scopas surrendered. He and 10,000 of his men were permitted to depart stripped and destitute.
- Here was the "taking of the most fenced cities" by the "king of the north." (Sidon was one of the strongest cities of that time.)
- Here was the failure of the arms of the south to withstand, and the failure also of the people, which the "king of the south" had chosen; namely, Scopas.
- Basically: Egypt did not stand against Antiochus III.

The KEY for Understanding the Term —
"king of the north"

1. Syria was <u>geographically</u> the "king of the north."
2. When **Pagan Imperial Rome** conquered Syria, its armies came down from the north into Israel. As a result, **Pagan Imperial Rome** secured the title **"king of the north,"** even though there is no specific mention in Scripture until verse 40.
3. Later, when **Pagan Imperial Rome** gave the sceptre of "power, seat, and authority" over to the Bishops of Rome (and the Popes), the <u>Papacy</u> then secured the title "king of the north" as in Daniel 11:31-45.

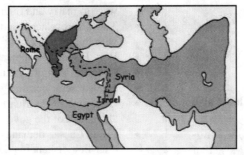

Map Illustration

Roman armies left Rome and had to march over Syria; come down through Syria to enter Israel from the North. Thus, Rome became known as the "king of the north."

**Syria, the Former "king of the north," is
Conquered by Rome (65 BC) —
Pagan Imperial Rome now Becomes
<u>"king of the north"</u>**

*Pagan Imperial Rome
Has Uncontested Control
Over Syria and Egypt,
Along With Roman
Occupation of Israel
(65 BC)*

16 But he that cometh against him shall do according to his own will, and none shall stand before him [Rome]**: and he shall stand** [enter] **in the <u>glorious land</u>** [Palestine and Jerusalem, a holy mountain] **which by his hand shall be consumed** [conquered].

<u>Verse 16</u> (Brief Review)

- Egypt had not been able to stand against Antiochus III — "king of the north" and Antiochus Asiaticus could not stand before ROME in 65 BC. No kingdom could resist the rising [iron] power of Rome.
- (Reminder: the Romans became connected with the Jews by alliance in 161 BC — a date that holds a prominent place in the prophetic calendar. The Jews were now under Rome in a protectorate relationship.)
- Syria was conquered in 65 BC and added to the Roman Kingdom when Pompey defeated Antiochus Asiaticus.

"glorious land"— *Strong's* OT#6643 and OT#6638 in the sense of prominence; splendor; <u>beautiful</u>: KJV - glorious, <u>goodly</u>, <u>pleasant</u>.

Note: Palestine was a land of *milk and honey* for ancient Israel. Favored by the shield of Omnipotence, and providing many spiritual and secular advantages, Israel was put in a geographical position to accomplish a work for God. Palestine's location was at the crossroads of the ancient world which encouraged Israel's interaction with mankind. God purposed to raise up a favored nation, that would be the depository of His ways. Pagan Rome literally invaded and conquered this ancient glorious land — beautiful Jerusalem.

- Rome stood in the *glorious land* in 63 BC when Pompey intervened in a dispute between two Jewish brothers (Hyrcanus and Aristobulus) — rivals to the throne of Judea. <u>Pompey</u> demolished the walls of Jerusalem and <u>imposed tribute on the Jews</u>. At this time Palestine was invaded and incorporated into the Roman Kingdom.
- For the first time Jerusalem was placed in the hands of Rome by conquest. The Roman power was to hold the *glorious land* in its iron grasp till it had utterly consumed it.

*Pagan Imperial Rome —
"king of the north"*
Under
Julius Caesar

*Egypt Aspires to Merge
With Rome (47 BC) —
Cleopatra, Queen of Egypt,
Has a son by
Julius Caesar*

17 He [Julius Caesar] **shall also set his face to enter** [Egypt] **with the strength of his whole kingdom, and upright ones** [those that gave their word to enter into alliance with Rome] **with him; thus shall he do: and he** [Egypt] **shall give him the daughter of women** [Cleopatra]**, corrupting her: but she shall not stand** [with Julius] **on his side, neither be for him** [for she had her own political interests].

Verses 17-19

Review of History: Julius Caesar and Cleopatra of Egypt

- Rome conquered Macedon (Greece), Thrace, Syria, and Judea.
- EGYPT was all that remained of the whole kingdom of Alexander the Great. Rome pursued Egypt.

~ In 51 BC Ptolemy Auletes dies and:

- Left the crown to: Cleopatra and Ptolemy XII (9 and 10 years old.) This was through a former agreement with Rome.
- Ptolemy Auletes' final wishes stated that Cleopatra and Ptolemy XII were to marry and reign jointly in Egypt.
- They were placed under the guardianship of the Romans in 51 BC with Pompey in charge.
- But: Roman Pompey and Roman Julius Caesar quarreled and fought.
- Pompey fled to Egypt and was murdered by Ptolemy's orders.
- Julius Caesar became guardian of Cleopatra and Ptolemy.
- Cleopatra began quarreling with Ptolemy when he deprived her of "her share of the government."
- Julius Caesar demands they come before him to settle this question after first disbanding their armies.
- Cleopatra and Ptolemy were not happy about Julius' orders.
- Julius Caesar reminded them he was acting in agreement with the will of their father.
- Advocates were to appear to plead the case of both Cleopatra and Ptolemy.
- Cleopatra decided she would be there in person. She was wrapped in a carpet and rolled out before Julius. He was 50 and she was 22.
- Julius Caesar decreed the siblings would rule jointly on the throne.
- Pothinus (Chief minister of the state) was the one who was principally instrumental in expelling Cleopatra from the throne. He spread a rumor among the people that Julius Caesar's plan was to put Cleopatra on the throne.
- There was open rebellion and Egypt tried to destroy Rome's fleets.
- Julius won the battle at the Nile. Brother Ptolemy tried to escape, but drowned.
- **47 BC: All of Egypt submitted to Julius Caesar in Rome.** Alexander's Hellenistic Kingdom was now totally absorbed by Rome.
- Julius Caesar stayed in Egypt much longer than intended. Cleopatra became his mistress and bore him a son. (However, Julius' adopted son, Octavius, was legal heir to the Roman throne.) As a result, Egypt and Rome did not merge.
- **44 BC:** Julius was assassinated and Cleopatra joined herself to Mark Antony, an enemy of Julius' adopted son, Octavius.
- **31 BC:** Octavius defeated the combined forces of Cleopatra and Antony.
- **30 BC:** Antony's suicide opened the way for Octavius to rule.
- Cleopatra committed suicide rather than join herself to Octavius.
- **30 BC:** This was the end of Egypt's dynasty. Egypt became a province of the Pagan Imperial Roman Kingdom.

> 🔑 **Prophetic Key #13** Verses 5-17 have given extra information **not** contained in the first three visions. Neither Egypt nor Syria became the fourth great kingdom. It was Rome, rising from the west which fulfilled the prophecy of Daniel 8:9a. So far, Daniel 11 has described various methods by which Egypt and Syria fought, made alliances, entered into leagues, intermarried, and through intrigue, sought to become the fourth great kingdom. King after king "stood up" or took the place of the one before him, so that the account is *continuous and in perfect sequence.*

Further Conquests by
Julius Caesar
"king of the north"

18 After this shall he [Julius Caesar] **turn his face unto <u>the isles</u>** [a new enemy], **and shall take many** [gain many victories]: **but a <u>prince</u> for his own behalf** [a prince from his own court] **shall cause the reproach offered by him to cease** [see notes on death of Julius]; **without his own reproach he shall cause it to turn upon him** [Julius' words about death came true for him].

Julius Caesar
Betrayed by Brutus
(44 BC)

19 Then he [Julius Caesar] **shall turn his face toward <u>the fort of his own land</u>** [Rome]: **but he shall stumble and <u>fall</u>** [Julius dies], **and <u>not be found</u>** [ceases to exist].

Verse 18

More Review of History:

- War in other parts of the kingdom, (Syria and Asia Minor), drew Julius away from Egypt.
- *"the isles"* — The Bosphorus, North Africa, and Spain.
- *"prince"* — refers to a military commander under Julius Caesar who asked Julius what was the best way to die (or cease).
- Julius Caesar said the best death is a "sudden one." That is exactly what he got — the very next day.

Death of Julius Caesar

Verse 19

History Continues:

- After Julius Caesar had conquered Syria and Asia Minor, he defeated the last fragments of Pompey's party in Africa and Spain.
- He then returned to Rome — *"the fort of his own land."*
- Surrounded by his own men, Julius Caesar *"fell and was not found"* — OR "shall not come forth." (*Strong's* OT#4672 for the word *"found.")*
- **44 BC:** Julius Caesar was assassinated in Rome at the hands of 60 fellow Romans, led by Commander Longinus who "put an end to the insolence of Julius Caesar."
- Julius Caesar had practiced military butchery for his own personal ambitions.
- Julius Caesar had attempted to replace the Roman republican form of government with a personal dictatorship. <u>This led to his death.</u> (Predicted in verses 18 and 19 for emphasis.)
- Julius died suddenly, surrounded by men he had cared for, had promoted, or had spared. He was struck down, struggling, till he fell dead at the foot of Pompey's statue. Thus he suddenly "stumbled and fell, and was not found," in 44 BC.

Note: Most individuals who have studied the history of Rome are well acquainted with the story of Julius Caesar's death. His trusted friend, Brutus, turned traitor, and put a dagger in Caesar's heart.

DANIEL

The Story of the Rise and Fall of Earthly Kingdoms

Jesus is Born
During the Reign of
Augustus Caesar —
"Raiser of Taxes"
(4 BC)

20 Then shall stand up in his estate [estate of Julius Caesar] **a raiser of taxes** [Octavius, who is later called Augustus Caesar] **in the glory of the kingdom** [Rome — now the pinnacle of greatness]: **but within few days** [after a rule of 40 years] **he shall be destroyed,** [Augustus dies at age 76] **neither in anger, nor in battle** [dies in his sleep at Nola in AD 14].

(This verse repeated on the next page.)

Pagan Imperial Rome —
"king of the north"
Under
Augustus Caesar

Augustus Caesar was
Rome's "Raiser of Taxes"
at the time of Jesus' birth.
He died in AD 14 at age 76.

<u>Verse 20</u>

- Julius Caesar had adopted <u>Octavius</u>.
- Octavius joined Mark Antony and Lepidus to avenge the death of Julius Caesar.
- Once Octavius was firmly established he was given the title of <u>Augustus Caesar</u>. (Caesar Augustus, in Luke 2:1.)
- He became supreme ruler once Antony and Lepidus were dead.
- He was emphatically *"a raiser of taxes"* as Luke 2:1 speaks about.
     Taxes: = 1/4 of annual income of ALL CITIZENS.
            = 1/8 capital levy on all freed men.
- *"glory of the kingdom"* — Rome reached its pinnacle of greatness under Augustus Caesar and never saw a brighter hour. There was peace, justice, discipline, learning, and a curbing of luxury.
- **At this hour, Jesus Christ was born — 4 BC.**
- 18 years after the taxes were brought in (which seemed like only a *few days* to Daniel), Augustus died in his sleep after a reign of 40 years.

Of Interest:

1. Augustus founded the Roman Kingdom AND the position of <u>Roman Emperor</u>. Therefore, the word "Augustus" quickly became a synonym for "Emperor" and every Emperor was known as an "Augustus."
2. In the 5th and 6th centuries after Christ, the head of the Roman state **was succeeded by the HEAD of the ROMAN CHURCH.** Until that time, the men who acted as **Bishops,** or the **Bishop of Rome,** were laying the foundation for the Pope to become the "head of the church" and "corrector of heretics."

Other Notes:

1. Augustus Caesar was known for taking census and registering the people for the purpose of taxation.
2. These tax collectors were called the "publicans" in the New Testament.

Verse 20 establishes the time of Christ in this
Historic-Prophetic Outline, by naming a
"raiser of taxes." LUKE 2:1-5

*Jesus is Born
During the Reign of
Augustus Caesar —
"Raiser of Taxes"*
(4 BC)

20 Then shall stand up in his estate a raiser of taxes in the glory of the kingdom but within few days he shall be destroyed, neither in anger, nor in battle.

The fact that the Messiah was born in Bethlehem, that his parents went there to register (and pay the taxes), gives the correct timing and place for the fulfillment of verse 20 of the Historic-Prophetic Outline of Daniel 11. Prophecy points to events which revolve around the coming of Jesus Christ — the Messiah.

4 BC — Birth of Jesus

LUKE 2:1-5 And it came to pass in those days, that there went out a decree from Caesar Augustus, that all the world should be taxed.

2 (And this taxing was first made when Cyrenius was governor of Syria.)

3 And all went to be taxed, every one into his own city.

4 And Joseph also went up from Galilee, out of the city of Nazareth, into Judaea, unto the city of David, which is called Bethlehem; (because he was of the house and lineage of David:)

5 To be taxed with Mary his espoused wife, being great with child.

Tiberius Caesar
(AD 12)

21 And in his [Augustus Caesar's] **estate shall stand up <u>a vile person</u>** [Tiberius Caesar], **to whom they** [Roman citizens] **shall not give the honour of the kingdom: but he** [Tiberius Caesar] **shall come in peaceably, and obtain the kingdom by <u>flatteries</u>.**

Pagan Imperial Rome —
"**king of the north**"
Under
Tiberius Caesar

Tiberius Caesar
reigned with his father,
Augustus Caesar,
from AD 12-14.

<u>Verse 21</u>

Some History:

- Livia, the wife of Caesar Augustus, wanted him to nominate Tiberius to the throne. He was her son from another husband. But, Augustus said: "Your son is too vile to wear the purple of Rome."
- Instead, Augustus nominated Agrippa — but he died.
- Augustus was pressured again by Livia to appoint Tiberius.
- Finally Augustus consented.
- However the citizens of Rome never gave Tiberius love, respect, and honor.
- During the life of Augustus, Tiberius "behaved himself."
- Tiberius reigned together with Augustus from about AD 12-14 and thus "came into the kingdom peaceably," without opposition," and under false appearances with a "servile senate" that "flattered him."
- **AD 14:** Tiberius Caesar followed Augustus to the throne at age 29.

"*flatteries*" — *Strong's* OT#2519; from OT#2505; properly, <u>something very smooth</u>; i.e. a treacherous spot; figuratively, blandishment: KJV - flattery, slippery.

The following circumstances attended his accession to the throne — fulfilling the words of prophecy:
1. False appearances of his past;
2. Flattery on the part of the servile senate;
3. Possession of the kingdom without opposition.

"*a vile person*" — The traits and practices of Tiberius included:
1. Tyranny — (absolute power was used unjustly and cruelly — he conducted savage campaigns with much bloodshed);
2. Hypocrisy (false appearance of feelings and beliefs that he did not possess);
3. Debauchery (moral corruption);
4. Constant Intoxication!

CHAPTER 11   The Story of the Rise and Fall of Earthly Kingdoms

The Crucifixion of *Jesus*
(AD 27)

22 And with the arms of a flood shall they [the Jews] **be overflown** [conquered] **from before** [suffer death]; **yea, also the** <u>prince of the covenant</u> [Jesus Christ].

<u>Verse 22</u>

- Luke 3:1 confirms it was the 15th year of Tiberius Caesar when John the Baptist was preaching.
- AD 12: Tiberius Caesar began reigning with his step-father Augustus. This is when his reign began. He took the throne in **AD 14**.
- AD 12 + 15 years = AD 27 for the timeframe of Luke 3:1.

Note: The <u>**Prince of the Covenant**</u> (in verse 22) was none other than Jesus Christ, the Messiah. He was "broken" or conquered and crucified in AD 31. The reason that He was broken was to fulfill the <u>covenant promises</u> that a Savior would come to die for the sins of the people.

<u>**Prince of the Covenant**</u> is also referred to in Daniel 9:24-27.

DAN 9:24-27

24 Seventy weeks are determined upon thy people and upon thy holy city, to finish the transgression, and to make an end of sins, and to make reconciliation for iniquity, and to bring in everlasting righteousness, and to seal up the vision and prophecy, and to anoint the most Holy.

25 Know therefore and understand, that from the going forth of the commandment to restore and to build Jerusalem unto the <u>Messiah the Prince</u> shall be seven weeks, and threescore and two weeks: the street shall be built again, and the wall, even in troublous times.

26 And after threescore and two weeks shall <u>Messiah be cut off, but not for himself</u>: and the people of the prince that shall come shall destroy the city and the sanctuary; and the end thereof shall be with a flood, and unto the end of the war desolations are determined.

27 And he shall confirm the covenant with many for one week: and in the midst of the week he shall cause the sacrifice and the oblation to cease ...

AD 31 — Death of Jesus (Prince of the Covenant)
AD 34 — Fulfillment of the Mt. Sinai Covenant

Note: In AD 34, (three and one-half years after the death of Jesus), the Mt. Sinai Covenant with God's chosen people of Israel ended with the stoning of Stephen. Because Israel rejected the Savior, prophecy no longer centered around (<u>literal</u>) Israel, but around the followers of Christ (<u>Spiritual</u> Israel). Many of God's "New Covenant People" were centered in Rome and began to move into the whole world. See Daniel 9:24-27 in the left column and review the Daniel 9 timelines along with Appendix 9C (Covenants of God) on pages 256-257.

An Alignment of Daniel 11:20-22 with Daniel 9:24-27

DAN 9	69 Weeks to Jesus' Baptism (AD 27)	Midst of the week "cut off" (AD 31)	Confirms Covenant (to AD 34)
DAN 11 (4 BC)	Birth of Jesus	"Broken" — Crucified	Prince of the Covenant

The Challenges of Prophetic Exposition of Daniel 11:23-31

Orientation

- The events outlined in Daniel 11:23-31 are challenging because the persons referred to are not named but referred to only as "he" and "him."
- The events also happened so long ago that the average person is not familiar with the historical records.
- Some historical records from the death of Christ to the rise of the Papal Kingdom are available but difficult to link with these verses (as has been noted.)
- Early church history is NOT always reliable, having rested in the hands of monks/kings and others who did not mind changing records to suit their needs.
- There are at least five different possible interpretations for these verses, that can present difficulty when studying this passage. The events must center around the people of God; not necessarily historical events in other places of the world.

The Variant Views of Prophetic Expositors

- Many prophetic expositors do not treat this passage of Scripture (verses 23-31) in a unified manner.
- In many cases they simply admit that they do not understand these verses, but make "tentative" suggestions.
- In other cases they have ignored important hermeneutic principles. Therefore, their conjectures are far removed from the nature and purpose of the Prophetic Outlines of the Book of Daniel.

Failure to Observe Hermeneutic Principles

- In the work of some famous prophetic expositors, the very _logic_ of prophetic exposition is lacking.
- They fail to observe **context, sequence, continuity, and alignment in the Historic-Prophetic Outline!**
- For example: One expositor came to verse 23 and then moved _backward_ in the stream of time more than 170 years!
- Another contemporary expositor, at verse 24 _jumped forward a whole millennium to the crusades! Then he moved_ backward _in verse 30 to AD 538!_
- **Daniel 11:22 describes the crucifixion.**
- It is imperative that ALL verses before and after Daniel 11:22 be kept in sequence to follow the AD 31 crucifixion, in an orderly, chronological manner.

Mistaking Parts of the Outline Itself, to be an Explanation of Other Verses

- A common error is to take certain verses out of sequence and continuity in the Prophetic Outline of Daniel 11, in an effort to force private interpretations of preceding verses!
- The Bible is very plain that the angel Gabriel came to Daniel to give an explanation of the Prophetic Outline in the vision of Daniel 8. There is no mention of an angel instructor in Daniel 11. All verses make up one sequential unit, forming one steady, forward movement.

The Loss of Focus

- One important factor in the prophetic exposition of Daniel is to remember that every Prophetic Outline focuses on the **rise and fall of kingdoms**.
- Within each Outline, there is marvelous sequencing and continuity, as one kingdom falls and another rises.

Failure to Recognize the Fifth Kingdom

- Prophetic expositors generally do not understand that the Book of Daniel reveals the rise and fall of _seven kingdoms_.
- They do not recognize the fact that as **Pagan Imperial Rome** (the Fourth Kingdom) fell, the Fifth Kingdom, **Papal Rome No. 1,** rose to power and continued to rule from AD 538-1798. A transfer of power, seat, and authority from one kingdom to another is vividly depicted.

Reiteration of Unrelated Trivia

- Daniel's prophecies are not given as a reiteration of mere historical data. All specifics are given to explain **_major_** events which bring about the rise and fall of kingdoms.
- They are not just a reiteration of battles, dates, names, and places, but give the reasons or call attention to the actions which brought about the rise and fall of kings (rulers) and their kingdoms.

Prophecy Centers Around the People of God — His Church

- All these events are vitally connected to the situations which surround the people of God in all ages; first, Old Testament Israel, and then New Testament Christians.
- They are not simply historical accounts — but explain the powerful rise of persecutors, the progress of the plan of salvation, the great controversy between Christ and antichrist, and God's great deliverances.

A Correct Method of Study for Daniel 11:22-35

- Verses 22-35 describe the time span from AD 31 to AD 1798, and keeps all the verses in an orderly sequence.
- These verses are also understood to focus on the weakening of **Pagan Imperial Rome** and the rising power of the Roman Bishops in establishing **Papal Supremacy No. 1.**

> Daniel 11:23 — is the transition from "Literal" Israel to "Spiritual" Israel (or Christianity).

- **In prophecy, if there is an obscure phrase, it is better to leave it open for more information than to project a personal opinion, which is absolutely forbidden in valid prophetic exposition.**

Daniel 11:23-35 Aligns with the Prophetic Outlines of Daniel 7 and 8 — Giving Added Details

- The Historic-Prophetic Outline of Daniel 7 pictures a direct transition from the ten <u>horns</u> on the *beast* to the *Little Horn*. The Outline in Daniel 8 also pictures a direct transition from the *higher horn* of the Ram, to the *notable <u>horn</u>* of the He Goat, on to the *Little <u>Horn</u>* of the Papacy before focusing on the "king of fierce countenance."

- The Fourth Historic-Prophetic Outline of Daniel 11, adds details and explains <u>how these transitions were made</u>, and how they link with the *"daily"* of Daniel 8.

Hermeneutic Guidelines to Remember with Regard to Daniel 11:23-35

- **Prophetic Key #10** An Historic-Prophetic Outline is arranged with each verse in chronological order, moving <u>forward in context, sequence, alignment, and continuity</u>, with no insertions or explanation, unless specifically called for in the Scripture itself.

- **Prophetic Key #11** The sequence of verses must link with the sequence of historical events. Then, one Historic-Prophetic Outline will align with other Outlines. The application of the Outline always relates to the rise and fall of kingdoms.

- **Prophetic Key #12** A Prophetic Outline continues verse after verse without interruption unless the Bible specifically introduces an interpretation or explanation.

- **Prophetic Key #13** Each succeeding Outline <u>gives increasing details</u> to enlarge the picture of the great controversy between Christ and Satan.

Keeping these introductory thoughts in mind, it is now time to move forward from Daniel 11:22 (AD 31), and view the gradual fall of Pagan Imperial Rome. The rising power of the Bishops of Rome, who eventually formed Papal Supremacy No. 1 (AD 538), follows in quick succession.

Introduction for Daniel 11:23-30

Verses 23-30 are very difficult to understand because of a lack of historical records for the time frame of AD 190 — 538. There may be as many as five different historical applications to these verses, **but, the correct application must align with Daniel's previous visions**.
- Daniel 7 prophesized three [Arian] horns would be uprooted by the Little Horn.
- Daniel 8 prophesized Truth would be cast to the ground and the "daily taken away."

Prophetic Key #12 "Time" in an Outline always moves forward — never backwards. Prophecy is usually understood at the time of fulfillment. Daniel 11 must align with these principles. (Many have suggested that these verses describe the Crusades from the 11th to the 13th centuries. This cannot be, as this application is out of harmony with the timeframe established by the verses.)

The theme of these verses present an intense struggle between the Bishops of Rome and the Roman Emperors. Constantine was the first "so called" Christian Emperor. During his rule, the Roman church was wracked with controversy over the nature of the Trinity. This ultimately involved the theology of the three Arian tribes — the Heruli, the Vandals, and the Ostrogoths. Constantine feared his Roman Kingdom would crumble if the church was divided on religious issues. In response, he turned to the Roman Bishops for a solution. This led to the Council of Nicea in AD 325 which eventually settled the disputes of the:
1) Easter controversy, <u>and</u> the
2) Arian controversy.

Only one more challenge remained for the Church of Rome — and that was to establish its own:
3) "power, seat, and authority" [the "daily"].

By verse 31, the Roman Emperors lost their influence over the Roman Kingdom. Papal Rome easily, and progressively, seized the sceptre of power, as prophesized in the previous two visions. (Daniel 11:41-42 prophesizes "three foes" that the next Roman Kingdom will uproot. This aligns with the "three unclean spirits like frogs" recorded in Revelation 16:13.)

Pagan Imperial Rome —
"king of the north"
Under
Roman Caesars

The Bishops of Rome Supplant the Roman Caesars — The Bishops Gain Prestige (2nd Century)

23 And after the league [agreement] **made** [by the Roman Emperor] **with him** [the Bishops of Rome] **he** [Roman Bishop] **shall work deceitfully: for he shall come up, and <u>shall become strong with a small people.</u>**

The Growing Power of the Bishops of Rome

<u>Verse 23</u>

- After the crucifixion, Christ's followers were described as *"<u>a small people.</u>"*
- They suffered terrible persecutions.
- Christianity was now centered in Rome, the capital city of the entire Pagan Imperial Roman Kingdom.
- Paul knew that once the gospel would reach Rome, it would spread light to all parts of the world.
- Both Paul and Peter died in Rome; the church prospered in Rome.
- The Bishops of the church of Rome became very important persons, eventually gaining the favor of the Emperors of Rome through craft and deceit.
- **Note:** In order to gain power, the Bishops of the church at Rome needed the favor of the (sun worshipping) Emperors of Rome.
- The Bishops of the Roman church worked *"<u>deceitfully</u>"* to bring in apostasy, denying the pure doctrine of Jesus taught by the apostles. (Note the following quote.)

An Historical Record *"<u>shall become strong with a small people.</u>"*

"In the second century the aims of the sun worshipping emperors and those of the theologians [Bishops of Rome] ran parallel. There was an ambitious scheme on foot to blend all religions into one of which the 'sun [son] was to become the central object of adoration.' The bishops of Rome decided to eclipse any public attraction which pagan festivals could offer ... they determined to bring together Easter, a yearly festival, and Sunday, a weekly holiday sacred to the sun, to make the greatest church festival of the year." B. G. Wilkinson, *Truth Triumphant,* pp. 123-125. (Emphasis supplied.)

- This action was extremely important because it laid the foundation for the sacredness of Sunday, not only as a yearly Easter service, but as a weekly day of worship. This was in direct opposition to the Fourth Commandment of the sacred and Holy Law of God. This action also violated the proper celebration of the Passover Jewish Festival. Other yearly Festivals were replaced with Pagan customs. This accomplishment, exalted the position of the Bishops of Rome. Note: Easter is the Pagan celebration substituted for the Passover ceremony. See Daniel 7:25 on page 107 and Appendix 7D on pages 126-134.

DANIEL

*The Roman Bishops Attain
Supreme Ecclesiastical Power
Over All Others
(Victor 1 Forces the Easter Issue)
(AD 190)*

24 He shall enter peaceably even upon the fattest places of the province; and <u>he</u> [Bishop of Rome] **<u>shall do that which his fathers have not done</u>, nor his fathers' fathers** [excommunicate defiant churches and rule over the state]; **he shall scatter among them the prey, and spoil, and riches: yea, and he shall forecast his devices against the strong holds, even for a time.**

Verse 24

The Easter Controversy

- In the early Christian Church the resurrection had been celebrated at the time of the Passover each year.
- The lunar phases caused the celebration of the Messiah's death and/or resurrection to fall on <u>any day of the week</u>.
- But the Pagan Romans introduced a new calendar. The Bishops of Rome determined to bring Paganism and Christianity together and set a new rule for the date of the resurrection. The resurrection celebration was to fall on the "first **<u>Sunday</u>** after the first full moon after the vernal equinox."
- They called this celebration "Easter" after the goddess of fertility. (The female hormone, Estrogen, is named from Ishtar, Astarte, or Estra.)

> "Victor I [the Bishop of Rome, AD 189-198] ... issued a *decree* [AD 190] ordering the clergy everywhere to observe *<u>Easter on the first Sunday following the first full moon after the spring equinox</u>*. They had observed Passover according to the moon calendar. *<u>Never before Victor I, had any bishop dared to ... command the clergy to obey his decrees</u>* ... *("doing what his fathers have not done")*. [The Churches of the east resisted Rome, which caused the great schism formation of the Eastern Orthodox Church. They were <u>anathematized</u>, or excommunicated]. This was the first assay of Papal usurpation *[the Bishop of Rome taking supreme power as "Head" over Christian churches]."*
> B. G. Wilkinson, *Truth Triumphant,* pp. 124-125. (Emphasis supplied.)

- **Note:** The western churches around Rome went along with the idea of Easter, but the churches in Asia resisted this union with sun worship, by refusing to be a part of it. They are known today as the Eastern Orthodox Church. They <u>do not celebrate Easter on Sunday unless it falls on Sunday</u> according to the lunar phases.
- A great controversy was created by those that refused to enter into this new Easter Sunday mindset. These Christians were "scattered" and/or persecuted. (Review "God's Festivals Through History" on page 130.)
- e.g. A Bishop from Asia, named Polycarp, came to Rome in an attempt to reason with the Roman Bishop about the Easter Issue. It did no good. He was murdered on his return home.
- *"he shall do that which his fathers have not done"* — Victor I, through the Easter controversy, exalted himself and the Roman office over all Christian churches. <u>This was an important first step toward Papal, self proclaimed, power, seat, and authority.</u>
- In AD 325, Emperor Constantine put an end to the Easter controversy at the Council of Nicea. His letter decreed that all Christians should follow the guidelines of the Church of Rome, in their observance of Easter on the first Sunday after the first full moon of Spring.

Note: The word, "time," as used in the literal text of verse 24 should be understood according to its Hebrew connotation (OT#6256) meaning "when, now, after, season, so long." <u>It is NOT symbolic time!</u>

The Arian Controversy

*The Bishop of Rome Uses
State Force to Fight Arius,
[Bishop of Egypt]
(Constantine works together with
Roman Bishops in hopes the
Kingdom will hold together)
(AD 318-325)*

25   And he shall stir up his power and his courage against the king of the south with a great army; and the king of the south shall be stirred up to battle with a very great and mighty army; but he shall not stand: for they shall forecast devices against him.

*(Please note: Verses 25-30 have many
pronouns referring to a variety of
different individuals, in the same verse.
For these verses, each verse will be
given again with a description
in brackets of who the pronoun
may be addressing.
These are very difficult verses.
Extra study would be helpful.)*

(25 And he [Bishop of Rome] **shall stir up his** [the Emperor's] **power and his courage** [OT#3824 heart] **against the king of the south** [Bishop Arius of Egypt in AD 318] **with a great army** [in response to Arian persecution of Bishops in Rome]**; and the king of the south shall be stirred up to battle with a very great and mighty army; but he** [Arianism] **shall not stand: for they** [Bishops and Emperor of Rome] **shall forecast** devices [a "plan" that no one would be allowed to interpret the Scriptures except the Bishop/Pope of Rome] **against him** [Arian and his followers ⸺ 300 Bishops were anathematized and their doctrine torn to pieces at the Council of Nicea in AD 325]**.)**

**"Arius" — "king of the south" in Egypt
is in conflict with the Bishops of Rome
who used the armies of Rome
to fight his cause.**

Verse 25

- **Note:** The **"king of the south"** is a title (not a symbol) and it refers to a powerful ruler in Egypt, as it did geographically in DAN 11:5-14.
- **But:** the focus of this passage is on the rising power of the Bishop of Rome and those who opposed his power to rule over religious issues.
- Verse 25 is referring to a "king" or Bishop over the <u>theological realm</u>. Arius, a Bishop in Egypt, (AD 250-336) originated what is known as the doctrine of Arianism.

"Arianism" — The doctrines of Arius, deny that Jesus was the same substance as God and holding instead that He was only the highest of created beings. *The Heritage Illustrated Dictionary*

Arius was the troublesome "king of the south" in Alexandria, Egypt. His doctrines on the Trinity were contradictory to those of the Bishop of Rome. This problem stirred up political and physical conflict in the Roman Kingdom beginning in AD 318. Three other tribes, (Heruli, Vandals and Ostrogoths), embraced the heretical teachings declaring Christ had a beginning and was a created being. Arianian theology demonstrated that the Bible could be misused. The Bishops of Rome had decided that the Scriptures would be dangerous if the laity and priests had permission to interpret the Bible. The Roman church had been instituting positions of tradition where passages of Scripture were doctrinally contrary to its desires for status, authority, and control over spiritual and social issues. Any others that presented Truth from the Scriptures would threaten their position on tradition. On page 54 of *Truth Triumphant*, B. G. Wilkinson states:

> The Council of Trent, 1545, whose decisions are supreme authority on doctrine in the Roman Catholic Church, speaks as follows on written and unwritten tradition: "The sacred and holy, aecumenical and general Synod of Trent ... following the examples of the orthodox fathers, receives and venerates with equal affection of piety, and reverence, all the books both of the Old and of the New Testament,—seeing that one God is the author of both, *as also the said traditions,* as well those appertaining to faith as to morals, as having been dictated, either by Christ's own word of mouth, or by the Holy Ghost, and preserved by a continuous succession in the Catholic Church." Cardinal Gibbons, *The Faith of Our Fathers,* p. 86, 76th ed. (Emphasis supplied.)

"forecast devices against him" — the Bishops of Rome would not allow Arius (or anyone else) the authority to interpret Scripture. This right was to be held by the Bishop/Pope of Rome exclusively. At the Council of Nicea, 300 Bishops were anathematized and their doctrine "torn to pieces."

"courage" — *Strong's* OT#3824 from OT:3823; the heart.

"devices" — *Strong's* OT#4284 from OT:2803; <u>an intention</u>, <u>plan</u> (whether good or bad, a plot): KJV - cunning (work), curious work, purpose, thought.

Arianism Defeated by Council of Nicea
(AD 325)

26 Yea, they that feed of the portion of his meat shall destroy him, and his army shall overflow: and many shall fall down slain.

(26 Yea, they [the army of Rome] **that feed of the portion of his meat** [supported by the king's treasury in Rome] **shall destroy him,** [those that follow Arianism] **and his army shall overflow: and many shall fall down slain.** [Arianism defeated in AD 381 at the Council of Nicea].**)**

Arianism Outlawed
(AD 381)

27 And both these kings' hearts shall be to do mischief, and they shall speak lies at one table; but it shall not prosper: for yet the end shall be at the time appointed.

(27 And both these kings' [the Emperor of Rome and the Arian Bishops] **hearts shall be to do mischief** [plot against each other—the Arian conflict lasted for 56 years to AD 381], **and they shall speak lies at one table;** [Arian Bishops said they would follow the Nicene Creed, but they would not admit that Arius taught error] **but it shall not prosper:** [Arianism was outlawed in AD 381] **for yet the end shall be** [regardless of what the Emperors did, Rome was going to fall anyway] **at the time appointed** [in AD 476 — ending the Fourth Kingdom].**)**

Roman Bishops Save Tradition

28 Then shall he return into his land with great riches; and his heart shall be against the holy covenant; and he shall do ~~exploits~~, and return to his own land.

(28 Then shall he [Bishop of Rome] **return into his land with great riches** [his right to interpret the Scriptures along with Pagan traditions]; **and his heart shall be against the holy covenant;** [or against the Holy Scriptures by placing tradition above the Scriptures] **and he shall do ~~exploits~~, and return to his own land.)**

Verse 26

- The Bishops of Rome had no army to literally fight against the theological onslaught from the Arian tribes. The Emperor supplied his army to the Bishops for this purpose.
- Emperor Constantine called the Council of Nicea in AD 325 to settle the dispute over Arianism. He declared the Roman Kingdom would hold to the beliefs of the Bishops in Rome. Not everyone agreed!

Verse 27

- After Constantine, every new Emperor that ruled, waivered on whether Arianism was to be accepted or not. This controversy of 56 years (AD 325-381), whether a literal or verbal battle, came to an end when Arianism was outlawed in AD 381. However, many religions still embrace this belief today.
- For the Arian Bishops that wished to avoid exile, they must agree with the Nicene Creed and denounce Arianism. Many would never admit that Arius actually taught error. Numerous lies were "spoken at one table" to avoid excommunication and exile.
- This verse predicts that: 1) Arianism will not prosper; 2) The Pagan Imperial Roman Kingdom will end at the appointed time given in Daniel 7:20. (See pages 101-102.)

Verse 28

- In AD 381, Emperor Theodosius called the Bishops to a Council in Constantinople. This Council finalized the Nicene Creed and outlawed Arianism. The Bishops of Rome are finally satisfied and return to their own land.
- "_great riches_" — Perhaps these "riches" were the Roman Bishops "right to control" and "right to interpret" the Scriptures. As a result of this position, the Bishops would always maintain the right to interpret Scripture in light of church tradition. The conflict with Arian Theology had clearly demonstrated to the established church leadership that "uncontrolled" interpretations of the Scriptures could severely conflict with the stability of the established Church. This was not to be tolerated.
- "_against the holy covenant_" — The Roman Bishops placed "tradition" above (or against) the Holy Scriptures.
- "_the holy covenant_" — provided a crucified Savior, a High Priest in the heavens, and a simple plan of salvation.
- A counterfeit system of salvation by works, a human priesthood, and confessional had been fully instituted. The doctrines, rituals, and practices of sun worship were brought into the church, supplanting the simplicity of the Gospel.

"_exploits_" — Strong's OT#9999 This word was added by the translators.

29 At the time appointed he shall return, and come toward the south; but it shall not be as the former, or as the latter.

(**29 At the time appointed he** [Pagan Imperial Rome] **shall return, and come toward the south;** [making sure all Arian tribes were totally rooted out by AD 538] **but it shall not be as the former,** [of entering Egypt] **or as the latter** [of entering Judea].**)**

Barbarian Tribes Attack Rome —
Pagan Rome Falls AD 476

30 For the ships of Chittim shall come against him: therefore he shall be grieved, and return, and have indignation against the holy covenant: so shall he do; he shall even return, and have intelligence with them that forsake the holy covenant.

(**30 For the ships of Chittim** [the Vandals to the South] **shall come against him** [Emperor of Rome]: **therefore he shall be grieved** [defeated], **and return** [retreat], **and have indignation** [fury] **against the holy covenant: so shall he do; he** [Emperor of Rome] **shall even return** [to work with the Bishop of Rome against invaders], **and have intelligence** [make distinguishing perceptions] **with them** [Bishops] **that forsake the holy covenant** [Holy Scriptures].**)**

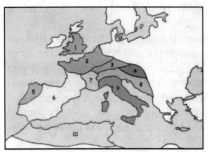

Barbarian Divisions of
Pagan Imperial Rome
(Arian Tribes Listed in Red)

1. Anglo-Saxons
2. Franks
3. Alamanni
4. Lombards
5. Seuvi
6. Visigoths
7. Burgundians
8. Heruli
9. Ostrogoths
10. Vandals

Verse 29

- The focus on this verse describes the progressive decline and fall of the Pagan Roman Kingdom.
- The Arian adversaries were a much more potent foe than at the beginning of the religious conflict. Maintaining control over the Arian revolt became more difficult for the Emperor(s) than at the first.
- The Bishops of Rome used the armies of the state to increase their power to establish theological control over western Christendom. Pagan Imperial Rome itself was crumbling by AD 400. The ten horns of the fourth beast (of Daniel 7:7-8) were appearing on the scene. These ten Barbarian tribes were forming the states of modern Europe. The capital city of Rome was being attacked and was near collapse.

Verse 30

- *"ships of Chittim"* — These Vandal ships attacked Rome from Cyprus. The Emperor negotiated with the Roman Bishops who outwardly claimed to possess the Scriptures, and yet did "forsake the holy covenant" through their acceptance of Pagan traditions.
- *"holy covenant"* — Expositors in the past understood this to refer to the Holy Scriptures (Book of the Covenant). The Arian faith was embraced by the Heruli, the Ostrogoths, and Vandals. These three Arian tribes had conquered Rome and became bitter enemies of the Roman Catholic church.
- The internal religious tension had caused unending problems for the Emperor of Rome. <u>The Bible soon came to be regarded as a dangerously divisive book</u> that should not be read by the common people. All questions of interpretations <u>were to be submitted to the Bishop (Pope) of Rome, to be settled by him.</u> Therefore, Emperor Justinian, established the Bishop of Rome with the power (seat and authority) necessary to be the head of the church and the <u>corrector of heretics</u>.
- Thus **Pagan Imperial Rome** was fading off the scene by AD 476 and being replaced by the great Fifth Kingdom of **Papal Rome No. 1**. This Fifth Kingdom is represented by the *iron* that extends into the feet of the statue in Daniel 2.
- By controlling both secular and religious affairs, Papal Rome became a religio-political power that was diverse from the other powers that proceeded it. (DAN 7:23; 8:9) The Arian tribes were still a formidable rival and had to be defeated before Papal Rome could assume complete power.
1. **AD 493:** Heruli Arian Tribe rooted out by Ostrogoth leader.
2. **AD 534:** Vandal Arian Tribe vanquished by Emperor Justinian.
3. **AD 538:** Ostrogoth Arian Tribe withdrew from Rome which marked the end of their power.

(Note: After AD 538 the Bishops had so much power they became the Popes.)

Reminder: See **The Structure of Daniel** Chart on page 367. The Historic-Prophetic Outline has addressed Medo-Persia, Greece, and Pagan Imperial Rome in the first 30 verses of Daniel 11. Papal Supremacy No. 1 enters the Historic-Prophetic Outline in Daniel 11:31 and continues to Daniel 11:35. The reign of this kingdom continued for 1260 years from AD 538-1798 (see Daniel 7:25 timeline), ruling in place of the fallen kingdom of Pagan Imperial Rome. This kingdom continues to expand to many parts of the world, eventually evolving into Papal Supremacy No. 2.

HISTORIC-PROPHETIC OUTLINE
(CONTINUED)
VISION FOUR

*The **Roman Emperor** Justinian Unites Church and State*
(AD 533-538)

31 And arms shall stand on his part ...

Pagan Imperial Rome has Fallen and is No Longer "king of the north"

The Fall of the
Fourth Kingdom
AD 476

31 ... and they shall pollute the sanctuary of strength, and shall take away the daily ~~sacrifice~~ **...**

The New "king of the north" Arrives —

The Rise of the
Fifth Kingdom
(Papal Supremacy No. 1)
(AD 476-538)

31 ... and they shall place the abomination that maketh desolate.

(This verse will be repeated several times on the following pages.)

HISTORIC-PROPHETIC OUTLINE
DAN 11:1-45
(BABYLON HAS FALLEN)
MEDO-PERSIA
GREECE
ROME (PAGAN IMPERIAL)
ROME (PAPAL NO. 1)

Verse 31

The Emergence of the 5th Kingdom: Papal Supremacy No. 1

- As Rome was falling, the Emperor turned over what was left of his armed forces to the Bishop of Rome.

- *"sanctuary"* — A place of worship; the union of church and state enabled the church to use the state to enforce dogma. False religions of Pagan origin and worldly enterprises desecrated worship, and thereby "polluted the sanctuary" of the true God. Pagan error and church tradition were displacing truth.

- Spiritually, it was polluted. Politically, the Roman church and Bishop were "set up" or established in place of Pagan Imperial Rome.

- AD 533: Emperor Justinian issued a decretal letter which was to constitute the Pope as the "head" of all the churches and to be the "corrector of heretics."

- AD 538: When the three Arian tribes were "rooted up," the Papacy was able to enforce Justinian's decree and increase it's ecclesiastical power, seat, and authority. At this point, the Popes were more and more established as men of state as well as of the church. Often, they became political rulers of the state.

HEAVENLY SCENE
DAN 10:1
KINGS OF THE NORTH
AND
KINGS OF THE SOUTH
OF
EARTHLY KINGDOMS

INTERLUDE QUESTION
DAN 10:14
WHAT SHALL BEFALL THY PEOPLE IN THE LATTER DAYS?

HISTORIC-PROPHETIC OUTLINE
DAN 11:1-45
(BABYLON HAS FALLEN)
MEDO-PERSIA
GREECE
ROME (PAGAN IMPERIAL)
ROME (PAPAL NO. 1)

*The Roman Emperor Unites
Church and State*

**31 And <u>arms</u> shall stand on his
part ...**

> **Pagan Imperial Rome has Fallen
> and is No Longer
> "king of the north"**

*The Fall of the
Fourth Kingdom
(AD 476)*

**31 ... and they shall pollute the
sanctuary of strength, and shall
take away the daily** ~~sacrifice~~ ...

**Papal
Supremacy
No. 1**

*The New "king of the north"
Arrives —*

*The <u>Rise</u> of the
Fifth Kingdom
(Papal Supremacy No. 1)
(AD 476-538)*

**31 ... and they shall place the
<u>abomination that maketh deso-
late.</u>**

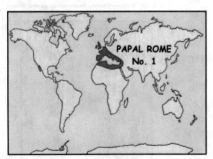

**Papal Roman Kingdom in AD 538
Illustrated in Red**

Verse 31 (Continued)

*The Establishment of Papal Supremacy No. 1 —
Identification of the "Abomination that Maketh Desolate"*

"<u>arms(s)</u>" **1:** weapons of offence or defense. [from: use of the arm for fighting and combat]. *The Winston Dictionary.*

- Jesus introduced the term *<u>abomination that maketh desolate</u>* in Matthew 24:15.
- The disciples proudly showed Him their great temple in Jerusalem, but to their great surprise, He told them that not one stone would stand upon another. (MATT 24:2)
- When He told them the temple would be destroyed, that also included the destruction of the city of Jerusalem in AD 70.
- Jesus warned them of the sign of immediate destruction of Jerusalem by stating that *the abomination of desolation* would be set up.
- **MATT 24:15-16** When ye therefore shall see the <u>abomination of desolation</u>, spoken of by Daniel the prophet, stand in the holy place, (whoso readeth, let him understand:) 16 Then let them which be in Judaea flee into the mountains:

"abomination of desolation" — The Bible is its own interpreter. Matthew 24 does not define this term, but Luke 21:20-21 does.

- **LUKE 21:20-21** And when ye shall see Jerusalem compassed with armies, [of Rome] then know that <u>the desolation</u> thereof is nigh. 21 Then let them which are in Judaea flee to the mountains; and let them which are in the midst of it depart out; and let not them that are in the countries enter thereinto.
- **Note:** In Luke, only the word "desolation" is written but the content of the two verses are in agreement.
- Jesus said they were to watch for the <u>Roman</u> armies to surround Jerusalem. The Christians who believed and acted on the prophecy, fled from the city to the small town called Pella. They escaped the three and one-half year siege which destroyed the city and the temple.
- (The importance of this prophecy will be understood later. It links with the last generation with regards to the three timeline prophecies in Daniel 12.)
- **So, who is the "abomination that maketh desolate?"**
- **Note:** The word, "desolate" is also spoken of as "desolation," or that which has to do with destruction and the scattering, or persecution, of the people of God. It was **Pagan Imperial Rome** which surrounded and destroyed the city of Jerusalem. But the prophet, Daniel, saw Rome in <u>two phases</u> — political and religious.
1. He first saw it as **Pagan Imperial Rome,** that surrounded Jerusalem in AD 70. (This kingdom fell in AD 476.)
2. In verse 31, Daniel saw **Rome again as a Fifth Kingdom in its Papal phase** referring to it as "the abomination that maketh desolate" — **the Papacy or Papal Rome** — a persecutor!

> ## Definition:
> ## "The Abomination of Desolation"
> ## is Papal Rome!

> ### The "Abomination of Desolation"
>
> As time moves forward to the final consummation of prophecy, the Papal Supremacy expands to include all religious systems that are antichrist in nature. These systems have held the "Cain" mindset of "righteousness by works" (GEN 4:1-16) throughout all the ages of the Great Controversy between Christ and Satan. See **Ephesians 2:8-9** — "For by grace are ye saved through faith; and that not of yourselves: it is the gift of God: 9 Not of works, lest any man should boast."

The Roman Emperor Unites Church and State

31 And arms shall stand on his part ... [the Bishop of Rome had the Roman army at his disposal]

The Fall of the Fourth Kingdom (AD 476)

31 ... and they shall pollute the sanctuary of strength, and shall take away the daily ~~sacrifice~~ **...**

The Rise of the Fifth Kingdom (Papal Supremacy No. 1) (AD 476-538)

31 ... and they shall place [or establish] **the abomination that maketh desolate.**

Verse 31 (Continued)

> ### Names of the Papacy
>
> DAN 7:8; DAN 8:9 .. "the little horn"
> DAN 8:13 .... "transgression of desolation"
> DAN 8:23 .... "a king of fierce countenance"
> DAN 11:40 .... "king of the north"
> DAN 11:31; 12:11 ... "abomination that maketh desolate" [persecutes]
> 1 JOHN 2:18, 22 ..... "antichrist"
> 2 THESS 2:8 .... "that wicked"
> 2 THESS 2:3 .... "man of sin," "son of perdition,"
> "opposeth and exalted himself above God,"
> "he is _as_ God," "he _is_ God."
> REV 13-20 .... "beast" [kingdom]

"The Westminster Confession of Faith (1647), ratified and established by an act of the British Parliament, declares: 'There is no other head of the Church but the Lord Jesus Christ: nor can the Pope of Rome, in any sense be head thereof; but is that Antichrist, that man of sin and son of perdition, that exalteth himself in the church against Christ, and all that is called God.' " Phillip Schaff, *The Creeds of Christendom, With a History and Critical Notes.* Vol. III, Chap. 25, Sec. 6, pp. 658, 659.

> ### Comparison of Names and Titles of the Papacy
>
> 1. "little horn" .... a religious-political **power**
> 2. "king" .... administrative **"head of the church"**
> 3. "abomination that desolates" . **unclean thing** that **persecutes**
> 4. "antichrist" .... **usurper** of Christ's offices and titles
> 5. "that Wicked" .... **evil person**
> 6. "son of perdition" .... **son of Satan** to be burned
> 7. "man of sin" .... man **against the laws of God**
> 8. "beast" .... *7th kingdom with Papal head*

- The establishment of the **Papal Roman Kingdom** was brought about by the use of the Imperial Roman army.
- **Note:** Whenever there is a change in governmental administration, it is necessary to control the standing army.
- As Pagan Rome fell, the military was controlled more and more by the **Bishop of Rome.** The Bishop of Rome used their new found strength to enforce their dogmas.

*The Roman Emperor Unites
Church and State*

31 And arms shall stand on his part ... [the Bishop of Rome had the Roman army at his disposal]

*The Fall of the
Fourth Kingdom
(AD 476)*

31 ... and they shall pollute the sanctuary of strength, and shall take away the <u>daily</u> ~~sacrifice~~ **...**

*The <u>Rise</u> of the
Fifth Kingdom
(Papal Supremacy No. 1)
(AD 476-538)*

31 ... and they shall place [establish] **the abomination that maketh desolate.**

<u>Verse 31</u> (Continued)

Note:

- For a review on the supplied word of *sacrifice* see Daniel 8:11 on page 155.
- For a review on the word *daily* see Daniel 8:11 on pages 156-159.

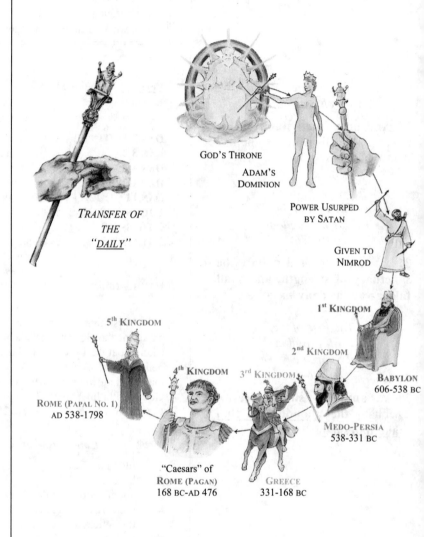

TRANSFER OF THE *"DAILY"*

GOD'S THRONE

ADAM'S DOMINION

POWER USURPED BY SATAN

GIVEN TO NIMROD

1st KINGDOM

2nd KINGDOM

BABYLON
606-538 BC

MEDO-PERSIA
538-331 BC

3rd KINGDOM

GREECE
331-168 BC

4th KINGDOM

"Caesars" of
ROME (PAGAN)
168 BC-AD 476

5th KINGDOM

ROME (PAPAL NO. 1)
AD 538-1798

An Alignment of Daniel 8:9-13 with Daniel 11:31

DAN 8 "the daily taken away"	"Christ's sanctuary [church] cast down/truth trodden under foot by transgression."	
DAN 11 "take away the daily"	"sanctuary [Christ's church] polluted"	"maketh desolate"

The Roman Emperor Unites
Church and State

31 And arms shall stand on his part ... [the Bishop of Rome had the Roman army at his disposal]

The Fall of the
Fourth Kingdom
(AD 476)

31 ... and they shall pollute the sanctuary of strength, and shall take away the daily ~~sacrifice~~ **...**

Pagan Imperial Rome
Passes the Sceptre of Power to
Papal Rome No. 1

The Rise of the
Fifth Kingdom
(Papal Supremacy No. 1)
(AD 476-538)

31 ... and they shall place [establish] **the abomination that maketh desolate.**

Verse 31 (Concluded)

Conclusion on the "Daily"

When **Pagan Imperial Rome** fell in AD 476, the *"daily"* sceptre of power was *"taken away"* by the **Papal Kingdom**. This new kingdom had the power to grasp the *"daily"* (power, seat, and authority) and hold it for 1260 years (AD 538-1798).

"The Daily — taken away" is the
Continuum of power, seat, and authority
which is taken away from one kingdom
and given to the next.
This is the central theme of the entire Book of Daniel.

Daniel 11:31 Paraphrased

And arms [the armies of Pagan Imperial Rome]
shall stand on his part [shall defend the Papacy],
and they [the Roman Bishops]
shall pollute the sanctuary of strength [shall bring in forms of sun worship (paganism) into God's Church].

And they [— the Papacy]
shall take away the daily [shall take away (or usurp) the power, seat, and authority from Pagan Imperial Rome]

and they [the Roman Bishops]
shall place [shall establish the power, seat, and authority that was set up by the Popes]

the abomination that maketh desolate [the corrupted Papal system that shall desolate or persecute the true believers in God].

In plain language the text simply says:

- The Papacy will use the armies of Pagan Imperial Rome to enforce Roman Catholic dogma. The Bishops of Rome shall bring pagan apostasy into the Christian Church. Then the Bishops of Rome will grasp power, seat, and authority, transferred from the Emperors of Rome and establish Papal Supremacy No. 1. Papal Supremacy No. 1 is the Fifth Kingdom which will persecute the people of God for 1260 years (AD 538-1798).

- **Note:** In AD 538 the Bishops had so much power they became the *Popes* — a figure considered to have unquestioned authority. The inquisitions were a formal tribunal in the Roman church directed at the suppression of heresy. *(Summary from: The Heritage Illustrated Dictionary on "Popes" and "Inquisition.")*

*The Waldensian Resistance
to Rome
(Papal Supremacy No. 1)
(AD 1300s)*

"king of the north" —
Papal Supremacy
No. 1

32 And such as do wickedly against the covenant shall he corrupt by <u>flatteries</u> [smoothness]: but the people that do know their God shall be strong and do exploits.

Verse 32

Justinian's Decretal Letter

- **Note:** Justinian, the Emperor of Pagan Imperial Rome, was known as "the codifier of law." He wrote a **"decretal letter"** [making a decree] in AD 533 that the Bishop of Rome was to become "Head" of all Christian churches, and to have the power of state to enforce the dogma of the church.

- This meant that the Bishop of Rome could determine who was a heretic and use the power of state to punish or cause such persons to perish.

- However, the Bishop of Rome was not able to subdue his "Arian" enemies [the Heruli, Vandals, and Ostrogoths] until AD 538 at which time he gained military power. From then on, the Bishop of Rome was known as the **Pope** — or — **"Head of the Church."**

- As time went on, those who opposed the Roman Bishop were tried in the courts of the Inquisition.

- **AD 538-1798:** Over the 1260 year reign of the Papal power, millions were tortured and put to death.

- *"flatteries"* — Comes from the Hebrew words OT#2514 and OT#2505 in the *Strong's Concordance* and has the meaning of "smoothness." The great power of Rome has been displayed throughout time in its beauty of pageantry, ceremonies, art, wealth, rituals, special holidays, sainthood, indulgences, confessional forgiveness, penances, crusades, missions, and "mysteries."

Typical Waldensian Stone Building

*Resistance to Rome,
(Papal Supremacy No. 1)
and
Persecutions Through the
Dark Ages in Europe*

33 And they that understand among the people shall instruct many: yet they shall fall by <u>the sword, and by flame, by captivity,</u> and <u>by spoil, many days</u>.

Verse 33

The Waldensians

- God has always had a people on the earth in every age who worshipped Him, and willingly followed His ways. The Waldensians (and other people of God) rejected and resisted, unto death, the forms of false worship.

- From the time that the Little Horn, or "abomination that maketh desolate," was officially established in AD 538, the Waldensians were hidden away in the mountains of Europe. They retained the Bible in their own language.

- During the centuries they sent out missionaries all over Europe to bring copies of the Bible to the people. In Italy, they lived simply and kept the truth alive by instructing many.

- *"the sword"* — The Waldensians were persecuted by the swords of Rome. For a time, the great mountains were their refuge.

- *"by flame"* — The Waldensians were brought before the courts of the Inquisition, condemned as *heretics,* and burned at the stake.

- *"by captivity"* — Many languished in prisons and dungeons, in chains and under torture until they died.

- *"by spoil"* — Their homes and properties were confiscated.

- These persecutions continued *many days* which extended into many centuries.

Resistance of the Waldensians

*The Protestant Reformation
and Fanaticism
(AD 1300-1700)*

34 Now when they [God's people] **shall fall** [by various forms of persecution], **they shall be <u>holpen with a little help</u>** [God will help them and prosper the work of the Reformation]: **but many shall cleave to them with flatteries.**

*Reformers Who Follow
Bible Truth
Shall be Tested and Killed*

35a And some of them [Protestant Reformers] **of understanding shall fall,** [such as Huss and Jerome who were burned at the stake, but this is meant], **to try them, and to purge** [them and their movement], **and to make them white** [purify their characters and establish the movement of Protestantism through martyrdom]
...

*(Last part of this verse is given
on the next page.)*

<u>Verses 34-35a</u>

Events of the European Protest-ant Reformation

- During this time Roman Catholicism was basically the only religion of Europe. This church was very rich and powerful, holding absolute control over the nations of Europe until about the 1300s when protests began to arise against the doctrines and practices of the Papal System.
- From within the church, churchmen began to criticize the administration of the church and <u>doubt</u> some of its teachings.
- <u>This protest began to **inflict a wound** on the Papacy</u>.
- In the 1300s John Wycliffe declared that the people had the right to read and interpret the Bible for themselves. He translated the Latin version of the Bible to English in 1382. His ideas were also preached by John Huss and influenced the life and teachings of Martin Luther.
- In the early 1500s Luther became the great leader of the Reformation in Germany. Some of his protests were against:
  a. The clergy for selling indulgences;
  b. The authority of the pope;
  c. Binding vows taken by monks and nuns;
  d. Celibacy of the clergy.
- After Luther, many reformers took their stand and challenged the old religious doctrines and traditions of the Papal Church. Thousands began to break ties with the church and move away from the Kingdom of Papal Roman.

Ways in Which God "<u>sent a little help</u>"

- 1100s: Waldensian ministers
- 1300s: John Wycliffe
- 1400s: John Huss and Jerome of Prague
- 1500s: Martin Luther strengthens the Protestant Reformation

AD 1300 — 1700

Note: In the providence of God, various factors helped the European Reformation.
1. The invention of the printing press;
2. The German princes who issued "safe conduct;"
3. The mountain chains that kept the persecutors away;
4. The rise of sympathetic kings and queens;
5. The unusual circumstances that permitted the defeat of the Spanish Armada against Protestant England;
6. The expertise in scholarly translation of the Bible;
7. The setting up of schools to educate the common people giving them opportunity to read the Bible for themselves.

Important Note: Daniel has used repetition of information in his four visions to ensure the reader has a good understanding. The next several pages will also be repeating various portions of information, to lock in an awareness for the broader content of the verses in Daniel 11:35b-39. Not all the information can be given, as this is a very extensive study. For additional research, (aside from Daniel 8), a wide selection of material is available through books, DVD presentations, and websites on the internet. See Appendix 12C on page 388 for reference suggestions.

"king of the north"
Looses its position
but, _NOT_ its title.

Pope Pius VI
falls and ends
Papal Supremacy
No. 1

The Fifth Kingdom Falls —
Papal Supremacy No. 1
Over Europe Ends
(AD 1798)

35b ... even to the <u>time of the end</u> [AD 1798]: **because it is yet for a <u>time appointed</u>.**

"Berthier [through Napoleon] entered Rome on the tenth of February, 1798, and proclaimed a republic ... Half of Europe thought Napoleon's veto would be obeyed, and that with the Pope the Papacy was DEAD." Rev. Joseph Rickaby, *The Modern Papacy,* p. 1.

<u>Verse 35b</u> (Concluded)

The End of the *Fifth Kingdom* in AD 1798

- *"the time of the end"* — refers to the <u>end</u> of the 1260 year prophecy of Daniel 7:25 that began in AD 538 with Justinian's decree.
- *"time appointed"* — was <u>appointed</u> or <u>specified</u> by a Biblical time-line. All the Biblical timelines of Scripture have an appointed **"time to begin"** and a **"time to end."** See Daniel 7:25, pages 108 and 109.

The Historical Fulfillment of Daniel 7:25 and 11:35

- **Reminder:** Prophecy is simply history written in advance. It is necessary for history to give the detailed facts as to what happened in the year AD 1798 that brought the Papal power to its end.
- **History:** Napoleon ruled over an Atheistic French government and aspired to bring all Europe under his control.
- The Pope of Rome <u>did not approve of his plans</u> and worked in various ways to prevent it.
- Finally Napoleon, being an Atheist, wrote a letter to the Pope, threatening to take him off his throne.
- When the Pope continued to interfere, Napoleon sent his general, Berthier, to Rome; captured the Pope on February 10, 1798 and took him back to France. Pope Pius VI died August 29, 1799 in Valence, France. The new Pope no longer held "the daily" (power, seat, and authority), even though he still held ruling powers. At this time most of the Protestants relaxed and thought the Papacy was no longer a threat.

An Alignment of Daniel 7:25 with Daniel 11:35

DAN 7:25	"they shall be given into his hands until a time, times, and the dividing of time"	1260 years
DAN 11:35	"even to the time of the end [of the timeline] because it is yet for a time appointed"	AD 1798

In **Revelation 13:3** John saw the same things in vision — and extended the prophecies of Daniel with more details pertaining to the endtime. John saw the Fifth Head as though it were wounded to death.

- Question: Is the Papacy still wounded today? YES! However, the wound is ALMOST totally healed.
- When the wound is totally healed, **ALL** the world will wonder [be amazed; be held in "awe"] after the beast.
- People are so awed and amazed at the <u>healing</u> of the Papal "head" since AD 1798 that they come from all over the world to give "honour and worship" to the present day Pope. Religious leaders greatly respect his efforts to bring the churches together. During the Pontifical Reign of John Paul II, church relations improved with the Protestants, Muslims, Hindus, the Orthodox church, and with the Jews. At his death, dignitaries, leaders, and presidents from over 80 countries were present at the Vatican to extend their respects.

- Once the "wound" is healed, the Papacy will have total and absolute control of *"power, seat, and authority"* over <u>all</u> mankind through the New World Order. *It will then have power to <u>persecute and attempt to destroy God's people</u>.* (REV 13:7)

Reminder: See **The Structure of Daniel** Chart on page 367. The Historic-Prophetic Outline has followed the three previous Outlines and addressed the first five kingdoms. Verses 36-39 give a detailed description of the erroneous teachings of the "king" of the next Papal system. Immediately after the 1798 wound, Papal Rome No. 2 began to rise, with the intent to recover its past status of world leadership and control. In the next 200 years, many encyclicals were written to re-establish Rome's reputation. This work forms the foundation for the rule of the last Roman Kingdom on this earth. (See Appendix 11A on page 352.)

HISTORIC-PROPHETIC OUTLINE
(CONTINUED)
VISION FOUR

Note: From AD 1798 onward, it seemed that Atheism and Communism were set to dominate and rule the world. (A review of the secular history is given in Appendices 8D and 8E.) Daniel 8 brings forward the Sixth Kingdom with the head titled as a Roman "king of fierce countenance." Even though the Papal System received a wound, the system was "alive and well," and working underground. Puppet systems such as Atheism and Communism, were used to further her goals of being a world leader once again. The verses of Daniel 11:36-39 speak of a "king." This is a direct reference to the Papal System of the previous verses. However, this is <u>not</u> the "king of the north" connected to the time frame of 538-1798, but rather the "king of fierce countenance" that arose thereafter. This title is an excellent description for the Scripture verses. Indeed, many Christians have been persecuted during the reign of the "king of fierce countenance" and its Popes since 1798. These Popes were very dedicated in earning back their lost status through the writing of encyclicals, papal bulls, and apostolic letters. (Appendix 11A on page 352, gives a very brief review of what was happening from 1801 onward.) The phrases of verses 36-39 give added information while lining up with the phrases in Daniel 8:23-25 describing the "king of fierce countenance."

HISTORIC-PROPHETIC OUTLINE

DAN 11:1-45

(BABYLON HAS FALLEN)
MEDO-PERSIA
GREECE
ROME (PAGAN IMPERIAL)
ROME (PAPAL NO. 1)
ROME (PAPAL NO. 2)

The king controls the sceptre of "Power, Seat, and Authority" behind the first godless "puppet" systems of Atheism in AD 1798 through to Communism in AD 1929-1989

Napoleon represents Atheism

"Stalin" Generals represent Communism

6th Kingdom — Phase 1
Papal Rome No. 2
Over Atheistic-Communism
AD 1801 — Present
(Refer back to page 197.)

HEAVENLY SCENE

DAN 10:1

**KINGS OF THE NORTH
AND
KINGS OF THE SOUTH
OF
EARTHLY KINGDOMS**

INTERLUDE QUESTION

DAN 10:14

**WHAT SHALL
BEFALL THY
PEOPLE IN THE
LATTER DAYS?**

HISTORIC-PROPHETIC OUTLINE

DAN 11:1-45

(BABYLON HAS FALLEN)
MEDO-PERSIA
GREECE
ROME (PAGAN IMPERIAL)
ROME (PAPAL NO. 1)
ROME (PAPAL NO. 2)

*The "king"
[of fierce countenance]
(Papal Supremacy No. 2)
Slowly Begins to Rise
(After AD 1798)*

36 ¹**And the king shall do according to his will;** ²**and he shall exalt himself, and magnify himself above every god,** ³**and shall speak marvellous things against the God of gods,** ⁴**and shall prosper till the indignation be accomplished:** ⁵**for that that is determined shall be done.**

(This verse repeated on the next page.)

"The church has the right to require that the Catholic religion shall be the only religion of the state, to the exclusion of all others." *Pope Pius IV.*

Note: The verses of Daniel 3 keep repeating the image, the self-exaltation of the king and the system he set up; the demands to worship and serve the image and himself. The oft repeated concepts given in Daniel 3 set the stage for the future actions of Papal Supremacy No. 2.

Vs 1: king set up the image

Vs 2: gathered all the rulers to the image the king set up

Vs 3: all the rulers were gathered to the image the king set up

Vs 5: when you hear the musick, fall down and worship the image the king set up

Vs 7: people fell down and worshipped the image the king set up

Vs 12: certain Jews did not worship the image which the king set up

---

Verse 36

Note: It is important to remember that the major goal of the Papacy is to achieve domination of the New World Order. Whatever needs to be done to achieve this goal, will be done. Verse 36 gives a good summary of Papal characteristics and related events. Further emphasis in verses 37-39 of his erroneous teachings have been added by Scripture, to firmly establish his character.

The "king" — Papal Supremacy No. 2

¹*"And the king shall do according to his will"* —

- Describes the "king" from the previous verses, namely Papacy No. 1 evolving into Papacy No. 2. His *will* is to have full control of ALL.
- Nothing comes in his way to stop his plans. In Daniel 2, King Nebuchadnezzar was given the interpretation of the image in his dream. However, in Daniel 3, he went ahead and *"set up"* a golden image with his own plans in mind.
- The Papal "king" takes away the "daily" of Daniel 8:11. How? He fosters and promotes the self-glorification of man, while at the same time, attacking the deity/daily (power, seat, and authority) of Christ. Jesus Christ becomes just "another man."

²*"and he shall exalt himself and magnify himself above every god"* —

- References back to Daniel 8:11, 25, and 2 Thessalonians 2:4, where he magnifies himself above every god, and proclaims himself "king of kings and lord of lords," a title reserved only for Deity.
- If "he" is above God, then "he" also demands worship as God.
- Through magnifying self, "he" sets up an image for worship, commands ALL to obey his word, and commands ALL to worship and serve the image. Compare to the notes in the left column for Daniel 3 where "ALL the rulers of the provinces were gathered together" and commanded to fall down and worship the image with the orchestration of the six musical instruments. The Babylonian king announced that only those who *worship and serve* would retain their lives.
- The Papal Church has set up guidelines that *only those obedient to the traditions of the church* will obtain eternal salvation.

³*"and shall speak marvelous things against the God of gods"* —

- This phrase references to the "king of fierce countenance" in Daniel 8:23 and 25 that has retained the blasphemous characteristics of Papal No. 1 given in the Scripture of Daniel 7:25.

⁴*"and shall prosper till the indignation be accomplished"* —

"indignation" — *Strong's* OT#2195 from OT#2194; **strictly froth at the mouth**, i.e. **fury**: KJV - angry, indignation, **rage**.

Definitions: Webster's 1939 National Dictionary

"indignation" — Anger at what is unworthy, unjust, dishonourable, or anger mingled with contempt or disgust.

"indignity" — An action intended to lower the dignity of another; insult.

"dignity" — Elevation or rank; degree of excellence; moral worth; qualities suited to inspire or command respect and reverence.

- With fury and rage, this Papal "king" fills his cup of iniquity as in Daniel 8:23-25 and 3:13. In this process, the "age of the gentiles" is fulfilled in the mind, character, and personality of the unbeliever.

Prophetic Key #11 Historic-Prophetic Outlines **MUST** align with the chronological order of secular historical events and they **MUST** align with each other. Each succeeding vision recaps the kingdoms of the previous vision in a forward progressive movement. The vision of Daniel 8 stated Papal No. 1 (Little Horn) was followed by Papal No. 2 (king of fierce countenance).

Prophetic Key #8 Extra information is being added in this part of the vision.

4 *"and shall prosper till the indignation be accomplished"* — (Continued)
At the same time there are other events taking place:
1. The "cleansing of the Heavenly Sanctuary" is being completed;
2. Judgment for ALL mankind on this earth is completed;
3. The sheep are separated from the goats as the chaff is separated from the wheat (MATT 3:12);
4. Probation has closed for ALL mankind;
5. "Day of Atonement" in the Heavenly Sanctuary is completed.

- Those that disobey the word of the Papal "king" see a display of his fierce anger towards them and the administration of the death penalty. See DEUT 28:49-50 and DAN 3:6.
- When this is accomplished, then God's wrath is displayed through the outpouring of the Seven Last Plagues given in Revelation 16.

5 *"for that that is determined shall be done"*

- This will fulfill the prophecy of Daniel 2:45, "the dream is certain, and the interpretation of it sure."
- DAN 11:45 … yet he shall come to his end, and none shall help him.
- **Note:** The ancient Babylonian King Nebuchadnezzar of Daniel 3 is a model for the ruling kingdom in Daniel 8:23-25; 11:36-45 and Revelation 13-18.

36 [1]And the king shall do according to his will; and he shall exalt himself, and magnify himself [2]above every god, and shall speak marvellous things against the God of gods, and [3]shall prosper [4]till the indignation be accomplished: for that that is determined shall be done.

(See Appendices 11A and 11B on pages 352-353.)

The Rise of the Jesuit Order

Note: "… the Jesuit Order at last reached the pinnacle of its power and prestige in the early eighteenth century. It had become more influential and wealthier than any other organization in the world. It held a position in world affairs that no oath-bound group of men has ever held before or since … nearly all the Kings and Sovereigns of Europe had only Jesuits as directors of their consciences, so that the whole of Europe appeared to be governed by Jesuits only." Boyd Barrett, *The Jesuit Enigma*, p. 209.

Verse Linkage and Comparisons to "king of fierce countenance" in Daniel 8

[1] *"And the king shall do according to his will; and he shall exalt himself, and magnify himself"* — compare with:
- DAN 8:9 *"waxed exceeding great"*
- DAN 8:10 *"waxed great"*
- DAN 8:11 *"he magnified himself"*
- DAN 8:23 *"a king of fierce countenance … shall stand up"*
- DAN 8:24 *"his power shall be mighty"*
- DAN 8:25 *"he shall magnify himself in his heart"*

[2] *"above every god, and shall speak marvellous things against the God of gods"* — compare with:
- DAN 8:10 *"waxed great even to the host of heaven"*
- DAN 8:11 *"magnify himself even to the prince of the host"*
- DAN 8:25 *"he shall also stand up against the Prince of princes"*

[3] *"shall prosper"* — compare with:
- DAN 8:12 *"it practiced, and prospered"*
- DAN 8:24 *"shall prosper, and practice"*
- DAN 8:25 *"shall cause craft to prosper in his hand"*

[4] *"till the indignation be accomplished"* — compare with:
- DAN 8:10 *"cast down some of the host and of the stars to the ground, and stamped upon them"*
- DAN 8:11 *"daily was taken away … sanctuary was cast down"*
- DAN 8:12 *"against the daily … cast down the truth to the ground"*
- DAN 8:13 *"sanctuary and the host to be trodden under foot"*
- DAN 8:19 *"in the last end of the indignation: for at the time appointed the end shall be."*
- DAN 8:24 *"shall destroy wonderfully … shall destroy the mighty and the holy people"*
- DAN 8:25 *"by peace shall destroy many"*

The "king"
[of fierce countenance]
(Papal Supremacy No. 2)
Establishes New Changes

37 [1]**Neither shall he regard the God of his** [fore] **fathers,** [the true God of heaven] [2]**nor the desire of women,** [strong family units] [3]**nor regard any god** [pagan or Christian]: [4]**for he shall magnify** [exalt] **himself above all.**

(This verse repeated on the next page.)

Verses 37

The "king" — Papal Supremacy No. 2

Verse 37 emphasizes many of the concepts given in the previous verse including the continuation of erroneous teachings. This king will not continually regard the true Creator God, or the Pagan gods of the previous kingdoms, but rather, at the end of time, he regards Lucifer as his god of worship. The "king" allows Satan himself to be the fulfillment of the following text.

ISA 14:12-14 How art thou fallen from heaven, O Lucifer, son of the morning! ... 13 For thou hast said in thine heart, **I** will ascend into heaven, **I** will exalt my throne above the stars of God: **I** will sit also upon the mount of the congregation, in the sides of the north: 14 **I** will ascend above the heights of the clouds; **I** will be like the most High.

[1]*"neither shall he regard the God of his fathers"*

- The apostolic Church had a pure faith and unswerving interest to uphold the God of truth. As Rome gradually became the center of administrative Christian power, Pagan influences compromised the truth. They no longer worshipped the God that sent the apostles and evangelists into the world to preach the pure doctrine.
- Bishops and Popes were elevated as "God." Finally they ruled against the very Being they claimed to represent. Instead of regarding the true God — councils, traditions, and apocryphal writings were strictly observed.
- Salvation and forgiveness was through the priests and the church rather than through Jesus Christ. Priests were also gatekeepers of heaven, hell, and purgatory magnifying themselves above the "power, seat, and divine authority" of the God of heaven.

[2]*"nor the desire of women"*

- The Papal system denied women's role in the priesthood.
- Marriage was denied to nuns who served the church. As a result, nuns became sex slaves to the priests.
- Celibacy was instituted in the early Roman Church to preserve the property for the church. Therefore, on the death of the Bishops, the church was the heir, not the women.
- For the Jesuit, his allegiance is never given to a wife, but to his Superior General only!

GEN 3:16 Unto the woman he said ... thy desire shall be to thy husband, and he shall rule over thee.

Verses 37 (Continued)

[3] *"nor regard any god"*

- This system does not appear to regard the true Creator God of his forefathers, nor any Pagan god. Bishops and Popes are set up as "God."
- For the initiates in the Secret Societies, Lucifer is "god;" also, man was told that "ye shall be as gods." (GEN 3:5)

> "The true name of Satan, the Kabalists say, is Yahweh [God] reversed; for Satan is not a black god, but a negation of God. For Initiates [of Secret Societies], this is not a Person, but a **Force** ..." Albert Pike, *Morals and Dogma*, p. 102.

[4] *"for he shall magnify himself above all"*

- Bishops and Popes control and manipulate lives, acting as God but representing the character of Satan until it totally consumes the mind, character, and personality of the leaders and the people. This links to:

2 THESS 2:3-4 for that day shall not come, except ... that man of sin be revealed ... 4 Who opposeth and exalteth himself above all that is called God, or that is worshipped; so that he as God sitteth in the temple of God, shewing himself that he is God.

Verse Linkage and Comparisons to
"king of fierce countenance" in Daniel 8

[1] *"neither shall he regard the God of his fathers ... nor regard any god"* — compare with:

- DAN 8:10 *"waxed great even to the host of heaven"*
- DAN 8:11 *"he magnified himself even to the prince of the host"*
- DAN 8:25 *"he shall also stand up against the Prince of princes"*
- DAN 11:36 *"magnify himself above every god ... shall speak marvelous things against the God of gods"*

[2] *"he shall magnify himself above all"* — compare with:

- DAN 8:9 *"waxed exceeding great"*
- DAN 8:10 *"waxed great"*
- DAN 8:11 *"he magnified himself"*
- DAN 8:23 *"a king of fierce countenance ... shall stand up"*
- DAN 8:24 *"his power shall be mighty"*
- DAN 8:25 *"magnify himself in his heart"*
- DAN 11:36 *"he shall exalt himself, and magnify himself"*

---

37 [1]**Neither shall he regard the God of his fathers, nor the desire of women, nor regard any god::** **for** [2]he shall magnify himself above all.

DANIEL

The "king"
(Papal Supremacy No. 2)
Establishes his Power

38 But in his estate [1]**shall he honour the God of forces** [Satan/Lucifer]**: and** [2]**a god whom his fathers knew not** [3]**shall he honour with gold, and silver, and with precious stones, and pleasant things.**

(This verse repeated on the next page.)

Definition of: "God of forces"

"The **devil** is the personification of Atheism or Idolatry. For the Initiates, this is not a Person, but a **Force**, created for good, but which may serve for evil. It is the instrument of Liberty or Free Will. They represent this **Force**, which presides over the physical generation; under the mythological and horned form of the God Pan; thence came the he-goat of the Sabbat, brother of the Ancient Serpent, and the Light-bearer or Phosphor, of which the poets have made the false Lucifer of the legend." Albert Pike, *Morals and Dogma*, p. 102.

Thought Questions

1. Do people still thoughtlessly serve, worship, and bow down to the dictates of religious leadership as in Daniel 3?
2. Are people's minds turned over to leadership because they have been trained that way as in Daniel 3?
3. Are the majority that follow the dictates of religious leadership following the counsel in MATT 7:14 ... strait is the gate, and narrow is the way, which leadeth unto life, and few there be that find it?
4. How serious was the Lord when He said we are hopeless, unless we turn our lives and minds totally over to Christ?

Verses 38

The "king" — Papal Supremacy No. 2

[1]*"shall he honor the God of forces"* —

- The Inquisition was run by the Roman military army of the Jesuits and later by the Dominicans. This system had the mind, character, and personality of Satan. It was man powered and Satan driven.

1 TIM 4:1 in the latter times some shall depart from the faith, giving heed to seducing spirits, and doctrines of devils.

- This system worships Saints; the Virgin Mary as protector, mediator, and redeemer; and angels as guardians. This leaves out worship of the true God, and the only Mediator, Jesus Christ.
- As the "antithesis" to Christianity, this system will encourage Atheistic-Communism and all godless nations to worship Lucifer (not the God of his fathers).
- Through arrogance, honor and power, the Papacy assumed it was its own fortress — impervious to any opposition or powers that might seek to curtail its authority. Who could come against an institution with such wealth?

Papal King has the Mindset of God

DAN 4:30 Is not this great Babylon, that **I** have built for the house of the kingdom by the might of **my** power, and for the honour of **my** majesty?

ISA 47:8 ... thou that art given to pleasures, that dwellest carelessly, that sayest in thine heart, **I am, and none else beside me**; **I shall not sit as a widow, neither shall I know the loss of children** …

REV 18:7 for she saith in her heart, **I sit a queen, and am no widow**, and shall see no sorrow.

[2]*"a god whom his fathers knew not"* — *(Continuing theme from verse 37)*

- The Papal power has deviated from the God of heaven and paid loyalty to a god the early Christian church fathers did not know. They transferred the worship from the God of heaven to man himself — the Pope. The Pope is not only worshipped, but declared to be "god on earth." This is blasphemy of the highest order. **"We hold upon this earth the place of Almighty God."** Pope Leo XIII in an encyclical letter dated June 20, 1894.
- The Papacy has introduced gods from Paganism and mysticism. As a result idols and icons have entered the church. Much of the worship style has been borrowed from Pagan traditions. (See Appendices 8F, 8G, 8H, on Paganism in the Church, pages 226-231.)
- Worship of the Virgin Mary increases. She is also proclaimed as "Mediatrix" (Mediator) and "Co-redemptrix" (Our Redeemer).

[3]*"shall he honor with gold, and silver, and with precious stones, and pleasant things"* —

- Priceless gifts and costly ornaments have been bestowed upon images of the Virgin and of the saints. (REV 17:4; 18:16)

DAN 11:43 ... he shall have power over all the treasure of gold and silver and over all the precious things of Egypt ...

REV 18:12-13, 16 The merchandise of gold, and silver, and precious stones, and of pearls, and fine linen, and purple, and silk, and scarlet, and all thyine wood, and all manner vessels of ivory, and all manner vessels of most precious wood, and of brass, and iron, and marble, 13 And cinnamon, and odours, and ointments, and frankincense, and wine, and oil, and fine flour, and wheat, and beasts, and sheep, and horses, and chariots, and slaves, and souls of men. 16 Alas, alas, that great city, that was clothed in fine linen, and purple, and scarlet, and decked with gold, and precious stones, and pearls!

The "holy body" of St. Maximin decked in costly array.

38 But in his estate [1]**shall he honour the God of forces: and** [2]**a god whom his fathers knew not** [3]**shall he honour with gold, and silver, and with precious stones, and pleasant things.**

Verse Linkage and Comparisons to "king of fierce countenance" in Daniel 8

[1]*"shall he honour the God of forces"* — compare with:

- DAN 8:10 *"cast down some of the host and of the stars to the ground"*
- DAN 8:11 *"daily was taken away ... sanctuary was cast down"*
- DAN 8:12 *"against the daily ... cast down the truth to the ground"*
- DAN 8:13 *"sanctuary and the host trodden under foot"*
- DAN 8:24 *"shall destroy wonderfully ... shall destroy the mighty and the holy people"*
- DAN 8:25 *"by peace shall destroy many"*
- DAN 11:36 *"till the indignation be accomplished"*

[2]*"a god whom his fathers knew not"* — compare with:

- DAN 11:39 *"with a strange god"* — worship of the Virgin Mary is set up as "Mediator" and "Redeemer" in place of Jesus Christ.

[3]*"shall he honour with gold, and ... pleasant things"* — compare with:

- DAN 8:12 *"it practiced, and prospered"*
- DAN 8:24 *"shall prosper, and practice"*
- DAN 8:25 *"shall cause craft to prosper in his hand"*
- DAN 11:36 *"shall prosper"*

The "king"
[of fierce countenance]
(Papal Supremacy No. 2)
Gains World Recognition

39 Thus [1]**shall he do in the most strong holds** [of Secret Societies] [2]**with a strange god** [Lucifer], [3]**whom he shall acknowledge and increase with glory** [through worship]: [4]**and he shall cause them** [the rulers] **to rule over many,** [5]**and shall divide the land** [of the Earth into ten regions] **for gain.**

(This verse repeated on the next page.)

Verses 39

The "king" — Papal Supremacy No. 2

[1]*"shall he do in the most strong holds"* —
- The strong holds of the Papacy include all the Secret Societies.
- There are increasingly stronger ties with the Protestant countries, all political and all religious leaders, and the New Age Movement.
- The Western World is another puppet of the Papacy.

[2]*"with a strange god"* —
- Describes the god of Lucifer that gives the Papacy its power.

> "Lucifer, the Light Bearer! Strange and mysterious name to give to the Spirit of Darkness! Lucifer, the Son of the Morning! Is it he who bears the light, and with its splendors intolerable blinds feeble, sensual or selfish Souls? Doubt it not!" Albert Pike, *Morals and Dogma,* p. 321.

> "It is Satan who is God of our planet and the only God." Helena Petrovna Blavatsky, *The Secret Doctrine,* pp. 215, 216, 220, 245, 255, 533. (Vol. VI)

REV 13:4   And they worshipped the dragon [Lucifer/Satan] which gave power unto the beast ...

[3]*"whom he shall acknowledge and increase with glory"* —
- Lucifer is honored through the worship of the sun god on the venerable day of the sun — Sunday.

[4]*"and he shall cause them [kings of the earth] to rule over many"* —
- Soon, the Papacy will rule over of ALL the world community. The exceptions are those whose names are written in the Book of Life.

REV 13:8   And <u>all</u> that dwell upon the earth shall worship him, whose names are not written in the book of life.

[5]*"shall divide the land for gain"* —
- The Earth's entire land mass has been divided into ten regions by the Club of Rome.
- Each of these ten divisions will have a "puppet king" which will be ruled by the New World Order.
- The earth's land mass will be divided and ruled under this Fascist New World Order, for the glorification of mankind. (REV 18:12-16)

> ### This "king" Will Rule Over Many by Dividing the Earth's Land Mass
>
> "In 1975, the Club of Rome had produced a blueprint for a World Government, in which the whole world was to be divided into ten economic zones, with one person as a ruler of each region. The emerging united Europe had been described by Enoch Powell, retired British statesman, as a reappearance of the old 'Holy Roman Empire.' This was seen as a move toward a New World Order." Jonathan Gray, *Ark of the Covenant,* p. 504.

DAN 11:43 This "king" shall "... have power over all the treasure of gold and silver and over all the precious things of Egypt ..."

The World Divided into Ten Economic Zones

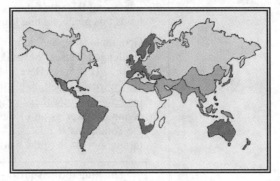

DAN 2:44 And in the days of these [ten] kings shall the God of heaven set up a kingdom ...

DAN 8:23, 25 ... a king of fierce countenance, and understanding dark sentences ... shall cause craft to prosper in his hand ... "only that the Church [system] might be the gainer in the end ... and that the end justifies the means."
(Part of the Jesuit Oath.)

CNN News: Thursday, January 1, 2004 Posted 14:21 GMT (10:21 pm HKT) **Pope calls for a new world order — VATICAN CITY (AP)** — "Pope John Paul II rang in the new year on Thursday with a renewed call for peace in the Middle East and Africa and the creation of a New World Order based on respect for the dignity of man and equality among nations."

39 Thus shall he do in the most strong holds [1]**with a strange god, whom he shall acknowledge and** [2]**increase with glory:** [3]**and he shall cause them to rule over many, and** [4]**shall divide the land for gain.**

(Review Appendices 11A and 11B on pages 352-353.)

Verse Linkage and Comparisons to "king of fierce countenance" in Daniel 8

[1]*"with a strange god"* — compare with:
* DAN 11:38 *"a god whom his fathers knew not"*

[2]*"increase with glory"* — compare with:
* DAN 8:9 *"waxed exceeding great"*
* DAN 8:10 *"waxed great"*
* DAN 8:11 *"he magnified himself"*
* DAN 8:23 *"shall stand up"*
* DAN 8:24 *"his power shall be mighty"*
* DAN 8:25 *"magnify himself in his heart"*
* DAN 11:36 *"shall exalt himself, and magnify himself"*
* DAN 11:37 *"shall magnify himself above all"*

[3]*"and he shall cause them to rule over many"* — compare with:
* DAN 8:10 *"cast down some of the host and of the stars to the ground"*
* DAN 8:11 *"daily was taken away ... sanctuary was cast down"*
* DAN 8:12 *"against the daily ... cast down the truth to the ground"*
* DAN 8:13 *"sanctuary and the host trodden under foot"*
* DAN 8:24 *"shall destroy wonderfully ... shall destroy the mighty and the holy people"*
* DAN 8:25 *"by peace shall destroy many"*
* DAN 11:36 *"till the indignation be accomplished"*
* DAN 11:38 *"shall he honour the God of forces"*

[4]*"shall divide the land for gain"* — compare with:
* DAN 8:12 *"it practiced, and prospered"*
* DAN 8:24 *"shall prosper, and practice"*
* DAN 8:25 *"shall cause craft to prosper in his hand"*
* DAN 11:36 *"shall prosper"*
* DAN 11:38 *"shall he honour with gold, and silver, and with precious stones, and pleasant things"*

The "king of the south"
Represents Godlessness
(Atheistic-Communism)
(AD 1798)

40 And at the time of the end shall the king of the south [Atheistic France in 1798] **push at him** [Papal No. 2, "king of the north"] …

(This last part of this verse will be given on the next several pages.)

(See Appendix 11C on pages 354-356.)

History of Russia's Conquests

Many countries came under the control of this puppet kingdom through revolution. Communism's design was to infiltrate, indoctrinate, and bring about a revolution. Most of the countries which were brought into Russia had previously been Catholic-dominated nations. As a result, Catholicism began to loose its power base.

As communist revolutions spread over the world, the Papacy was pro-vided with a tool in Russia. As a common enemy to themselves and an (USA) ally in the Western Hemisphere, the way was prepared for strong alliances, described in later verses. The way has now been opened for the "king of the north" to sweep the "king of the south" away.

Verse 40

The Struggle Between Atheism and the Papacy

Review: The "king of the north" originally represented Syria. Syria was conquered by **Pagan Imperial Rome,** which, in turn, relinquished control to **Papal Rome.** The prophetic reference, "king of the north," made an interesting transition through these kingdoms. Today, **Papal Rome** still holds this prophetic title <u>king of the north</u>.

Geographically, the "king of the south" was Egypt. At the time Pharaoh challenged Moses, he said, "Who is the LORD that I should obey his voice?" (Ex 5:2) Here Pharaoh did <u>not</u> acknowledge the Creator God. <u>The spirit of rebellion against the Creator God is also manifested in the governments of Atheistic-Communism.</u> Humanism, or self-glorification, is another expression of this rebellion. The prophetic reference "king of the south," as it relates to this rebellion, has made interesting progress throughout much of the world.

> The king of the south — **pushed at** — the king of the north.

Napoleon Signs a Concordat with the Papacy in 1801

"Many of the men in those days [of 1798] imagined that the dominion of the Pope had come to an end, and that the knell of the temporal power was then sounding among the nations. This supposition, however, proved to be erroneous. The French republicans were very anxious that Rome should not have another Pope. But as the reverses of the revolutionary armies had left Southern Italy to its ancient masters, the cardinals were able to proceed to an election at Venice. They elected, on March 14th, 1800, Barnabas Chiaromonti, who assumed the name of Pius VII.

"The first transaction of this Pope was a negotiation with the government of France, of which Napoleon Buonaparte, was the First Consul …

"He [Napoleon] felt that, as the large majority of the inhabitants of France knew no other form of faith than Romanism, it must become the established religion of the country. Accordingly we find that he now began negotiations with the Pope, which issued in a Concordat in July, 1801, whereby the Roman Catholic religion was once more established in France. He also left Pius in possession of his Italian principality." Arthur Robert Pennington, *Epochs of the Papacy,* pp. 450-452.

While the government of France moved away from Atheism, the fundamental Atheistic philosophy moved towards the USSR where it would find voice in revolution. The "king of the south" surfaced in the 1917 Bolshevik Revolution by seizing the crown from the Russian Czar. The crown remained under the control of Atheistic-Communism until its collapse in 1989.

<table>
<tr><td>

Endtime Conflict Between
Papal Supremacy
and
Atheistic-Communism

</td></tr>
</table>

*The "king of the north"
Rising as a Strong
Sixth Kingdom
(AD 1989)*

40 ... and the <u>king of the north</u> [Papal Rome No. 2] **shall come against him** [USSR Communism in 1989] ...

President Reagan and Pope John Paul II took the spotlight on the cover of Time Magazine with the headline, "Holy Alliance." These two men stood against the inhumanities and dangers of Communism, and together with Gorbachev brought about the collapse of the Soviet Union.

"Time" — February 24, 1992

Time magazine reported that Papal Rome secretly worked with the United States to bring down Communism. On June 7, 1982, the two leaders "agreed to undertake a clandestine campaign to hasten the dissolution of the communist empire." This agreement was described as "one of the great secret alliances of all time."

<u>Verse 40</u>   (Continued)

The Struggle Between the Papacy and Atheism

- The French Revolution began in 1789. The Papacy was wounded by the "king of the south" in 1798, fulfilling the 1260 year timeline.
- Pope John Paul II visited Poland in 1979. Atheistic-Communism fell in 1989 with the collapse of the Berlin Wall.
- History records that Atheism gained a stronger foothold in Catholic countries than Protestant countries. In countries where Atheism has fallen, that country has returned to Catholicism. **"No [European] Christian nation which did not adopt the principles of the Reformation before the end of the sixteenth century [has ever] adopted them. Catholic communities since that time have become infidel [and we could add, Communist] and become Catholic again, but none has become Protestant."** Karl Rudolf Hagenback, *History of the Church in the Eighteenth and Nineteenth Century,* Vol. 2, p. 91.
- Atheistic attacks on Catholicism have indeed caused concern within the Papacy.

Characteristics of Papal Rome

a) Daniel 7: Papal Rome overcame three horns representing the Heruli, Vandals, and Ostrogoths.
b) Daniel 8: Papal Rome overcame three directions including the south, the east, and the pleasant land of Palestine.
c) Daniel 11: Papal Rome will overcome three foes. <u>The first foe is Atheistic-Communist ideology</u>.

<table>
<tr><td>

Papal Supremacy — **<u>pushed at</u>** — **Atheistic-Communism.**

</td></tr>
</table>

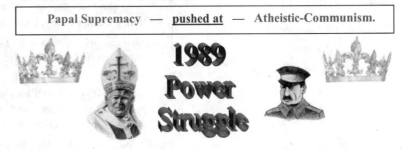

Review: History documents that the Papacy (through her Secret Societies), set up Atheism and Communism to seize control in many of the nations of the world. This evil system of Communism was used as a tool in the hands of the Papacy to bring part of the world under its control. The Papacy fostered the Atheistic French Revolution. Then through Napoleon, it moved the Atheistic paradigm across Europe to Russia. Communist Russia was developed as antithesis to the West (the thesis). Out of this thesis (West), antithesis (East) struggle, emerges a synthesis — one step closer to a New World Order. Remember:

- Adam Weishaupt, founder of the Illuminati, planned the French Revolution many years in advance.
- Napoleon was a high degree Freemason that carried out these plans of the Revolution; declared France a republic; intended to remove the Popes from their seat forever; then, in 1801 signed a concordat with the newly elected Pope to reinstate the Catholic religion in France.
- The Jesuits set up the Russian Revolution. It is recorded that the Roman Catholic Church is responsible for the hellish wars in Russia.
- Then, after managing all these Atheistic-Communistic countries for years, the Pope/Papacy brought down Communism in Russia and the Eastern European Bloc.

40 **And at the time of the end shall the king of the south** [Atheistic France in 1798 and Communistic USSR in 1917] **push at him** [Papal king of the north] **and the king of the north** [Papal No. 2] **shall** [ascend and] **come against him** [ascend upon USSR Communism in 1989] ...

Collapse of the Communistic Kingdom! Through Political Powers, the Papacy Used the Might of Nations to Bring Down the "king of the south"
(AD 1989-1991)

40 ... like a whirlwind [take away fearfully like a storm] ... **with chariots, and with horsemen** [military power], **and with many ships** [economic strength] ...

(This last part of this verse will be given on the next page.)

Verse 40 (Continued)

Note: Verse 40 teaches that the "king of the north" would sweep away the "king of the south" in a very powerful fashion, while also strengthening its own power base.

"push" — *Strong's* OT#5055 to but with the horns; figuratively, to war against: KJV - gore, push down, pushing.

Note: The USSR was pushing all over the world to absorb Roman Catholic churches, properties, and enterprises. *"Push"* is a perfect description of the action of the USSR. Not only did it push all over the world, but in 1953, just behind the Vatican, a large billboard sign said in huge letters, "JOIN THE COMMUNIST PARTY." That year, Italy nearly fell to Communism. Ever since AD 1798, there has been an enmity between Roman Catholicism and this Atheistic political advancement.

"against" — *Strong's* OT#5921 properly, the same as **OT#5920**; above, over, upon, or against.

OT#5920: from OT#5927 to ascend, intransitively (be high) or actively (mount).

"whirlwind" — *Strong's* OT#8175 to storm; by implication, to shiver, i.e. fear: KJV - be (horribly) afraid, fear, hurl as a storm, be tempestuous, come like (take away as with) a whirlwind.

Papal Tactics "Sweep Over Communism" and "Ascend to Power"

Chariots and Horsemen are related to **military power** in Bible prophecy.

"chariots" — *Strong's* OT#7393 from OT#7392; a vehicle; by implication, a team; cavalry; by analogy a rider.

"horsemen" — *Strong's* OT#6571 from OT#6567; a steed (as stretched out to a vehicle); a driver (in a chariot).

1 KINGS 1:5 Adonijah ... exalted himself, saying, I will be king: and he prepared him **chariots and horsemen**, and fifty men to run before him.

1 KINGS 20:1 And Ben-hadad the king of Syria gathered all his host together: and there were thirty and two kings with him, and **horses**, and **chariots**: and he went up and besieged Samaria, and warred against it.

Ships are often associated with **economic strength** in Bible prophecy.

Ps 107:23 They that go down to the sea in **ships**, that do business in great waters.

REV 18:17, 19 And every **shipmaster**, and all the company in **ships**, and **sailors**, and as many as trade by sea ... 19 ... were made rich all that had ships in the sea.

Note: It is clear from Bible prophecy and current history that the cold war was mainly lost on the economic front. Russia could not keep up its heavy military expenditures to the neglect of the basic needs of its people.

*The First Foe Falls —
Atheistic Ideology*

*The Push of the Sixth Kingdom
Papal Rome No. 2
("king of the north")*

40 ... and he shall enter into the [communist] countries, and shall overflow and pass over.

Verse 40 (Concluded)

Note: The Papacy allied itself with the USA, using economic, social, religious, political, and military pressure to bring about the collapse of Communism. Once the Polish Communist Party collapsed politically, there was no way to prevent the collapse of the other Communist <u>countries</u> in the Eastern European Bloc. Atheism no longer had a government voice.

"countries" — *Strong's* OT#776 <u>the earth at large</u>.

"overflow" — *Strong's* OT#7857 <u>to gush</u>; by implication, to inundate, cleanse; by analogy, to gallop, <u>conquer</u>: KJV - drown, (over-) flow, rinse, run, rush, wash (away).

"pass over" — *Strong's* OT#5674 <u>to cross over</u>; used very widely of any transition (literal or figurative); specifically, <u>to cover</u>.

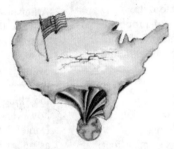

The Significant Ally of the Papacy

The events related to the fall of Communism and the political involvement of the USA, indicates that the USA had formed an alliance with an enemy which was also preparing to bring her under its control. The USA claims to be a Protestant country. However, *the USA surrendered its Protestant beliefs when it came to the aid of the Papacy.* To meet the definition of Protestant, one must oppose Popery, and maintain a firm rejection of any type of alliance with her. The next area of conquest for the Papacy is the *glorious land.* (See DAN 8:9c. **Note:** *Glorious land* and *pleasant land* are both *Strong's* OT#6638. Also see Appendix 11C, pages 354-356, on how prophetic terms are used in the secular press.)

Additional Notes for the "Time of the End" and Endtime Events

Keeping the important principles in mind, that *each verse of a Prophetic Outline must move forward in time*, consider the following:

- What was the date in history when the "time of the end" in Daniel 11:35 was fulfilled?
- To what event did the "time of the end" refer in Daniel 11:35?
- Does each additional verse in the Prophetic Outline of Daniel move forward in time?
- Does the "time of the end" in Daniel 11:40 refer to the <u>same</u> date in Daniel 11:35?

Note:

1. Daniel 11:35 — refers to the end of the 1260 year timeline and to the specific date of AD 1798.
2. That phrase, "time of the end," also refers to the span of time <u>from</u> AD 1798 <u>to</u> the end of earth's history. It includes all that has happened since AD 1798.
3. It can mean, *endtimes,* or *latter days,* as in Daniel 11:40 or, in Daniel 12, to the last generation.

4. A common error in prophetic exposition is that of ignoring the <u>forward movement of an Historic-Prophetic Outline</u>.
5. Just because "the time of the end" referred to AD 1798 (verse 35), many Bible students have *assumed* that the phrase "time of the end," as used in other verses, in Daniel 11 and 12, must <u>always</u> refer to that same date. **This has caused unending confusion**.

Questions:

- What was the reason that so many prophetic expositors a century ago did not understand Daniel 11 much beyond verse 35?
- Is it <u>reasonable</u> to expect Bible students of the past century to do the study for the ENDTIME GENERATION, and also be able to recognize events contemporaneous to our own day?
- What are the obligations of earth's last generation?

Important Note: The last part of this vision brings the action of the Fourth Historic-Prophetic Outline right up to current events, and beyond, to the end of time.

Orientation Review

In a study of Historic-Prophetic Outlines, there are several principles which the Bible student must continually keep in mind. This is <u>absolutely true</u> in regard to the verses of Daniel 11:41-45.

The Forward Movement

1. Our God is a God of <u>order</u>. (1 COR 14:40)
2. Prophecy is history written in advance.
3. History happens on a line of time in which events occur in a sequence that always <u>moves forward in time</u>.
4. Historic-Prophetic Outlines are a series of Bible verses which are also written in an orderly manner in which each verse follows the one before it.
5. If there is to be any logical matching of prophetic verses to the orderly sequence of historical (and future) events, then each progressive verse of the Outline must also move forward in time.

Sequence and Continuity

1. The Historic-Prophetic Outlines in the Book of Daniel reveal the rise and fall of kingdoms.
2. In Historic-Prophetic Outlines, a cause and effect relationship must be recognized.
3. In ALL cases, the rising kingdom caused the fall of the one which preceded it.
4. This <u>sequence and continuity</u> follows historical patterns.

Consistency of Application

1. The Bible student must be <u>consistent</u> in the treatment of each verse in an Historic-Prophetic Outline: <u>to move forward in each verse</u>, seeking for the historical or future application in <u>sequence and continuity</u>.
2. One must refrain from leaping forward or moving backward in time.

The Historic-Prophetic Outline of Daniel 11 is no exception. The Bible student must not back up, (i.e. must not consider certain verses to be explanations of other verses), or think of them as reiterations of the same events previously brought to view.

Daniel 11:41-45 **must follow the events of verses 35 to 40**. Verse 35 brought to view the *appointed time,* or end of the 1260 day-year period that occurred in AD 1798. Verse 40 brings to view the year 1989 as the collapse of Communism. (Reminder: The verses of Daniel 11:36-39 are deeper explanations of erroneous teachings of the Papal System from 1801 onward.)

Note: Secular history provides the information of what happened between the verses of 35 and 36 in Daniel 11. As the <u>first</u> Papal "king of the north" was taken off the scene in AD 1798; the <u>next</u> Papal "king of the north" <u>begins to slowly rise to power retaining the characteristics of the former Papal king</u>. This follows the pattern of the Little Horn in Daniel 7. By AD 476 Pagan Imperial Rome was broken up into ten divisions. At that time the Little Horn began to rise to power, rooting out three Arian tribes in the process. By AD 538 the Little Horn was established as a ruling Papal power, seizing the scepter of "power, seat, and authority" from Pagan Imperial Rome.

Atheistic-Communism found a strong governmental voice in Russia. However, this kingdom was a pawn (or puppet) in the hands of the Papacy, as previously documented. Before moving forward to the next set of events, the verses in Daniel 11:36-39 described in detail the erroneous teachings of the Papacy before it removes the "king of the south" in verse 40. Daniel has shown how verses 36-39 closely resemble several verses in Daniel 8 that describe the "king of fierce countenance" as ruler of the Sixth Kingdom. Compare these verses to 2 Thessalonians 2:3-12 describing "that Wicked one," at the very end of time. Secular history demonstrates how the Russian system was ruled by the Papal system, entangling Atheism and Communism in its web of deception. (Review Appendix 11B on page 353.)

Review of Terms from Daniel 8

- "ram" =
  Medo-Persia (vs 3, 20)

- "he goat" =
  Greece (vs 5, 8, 21)

- "four notable ones" =
  four divisions of Greece (vs 8)

- "out of one of them" (one of the four divisions) =
  Pagan Imperial Rome (vs 9a)

- "came forth a <u>little horn</u>" =
  Papal Supremacy No. 1 (vs 9b)

- "which waxed exceeding great" =
  Papal Supremacy No. 2 (vs 9c)

- "king of fierce countenance" =
  Title for Papal Supremacy No. 2 (vs 23)

Prophetic Keys # 10-13 <u>Sequence and Continuity</u>
The Principle of Historic-Prophetic Exposition: All verses following Daniel 11:40 <u>must move forward to events which occurred after 1989!</u>

At the time of writing, the fulfillment of prophecy in Daniel 11 pivots between verses 40 and 41. The following verses begin a section of partially unfulfilled prophecy. Although some future unfulfilled prophecy can be discerned from past historical events and fulfilled prophecy, it is nonetheless wise to tread carefully through these verses. The Scriptures give this assurance:

- **JOHN 14:29** I have told you before it come to pass, that, when it is come to pass, ye might believe.

- **LUKE 8:17** For there is nothing hidden that will not be disclosed, and nothing concealed that will not be known or brought out into the open. NIV

These promises give assurance that future events will clarify prophecy perfectly. God's people must be patient and watch with eagerness.

Only a brief review of some historical events has been given in the previous pages. For more information of past history, each reader is encouraged to search the internet, read books, or review available video and DVD material relating to the prophecies of Daniel. (Some suggestions are given in Appendix 12C on page 388. Other brief reviews of information are included in Appendix 8D on pages 185-209, and 8E on pages 210-225.)

What follows is a presentation of "possible application" of prophecy. Certainly, the reader is encouraged to study and search with a prayerful heart, ever mindful of daily current events that lead to greater fulfillment of prophecy in God's Word. The purpose of prophecy is not only to outline the details of world events for the future, but as the Savior said, "that, when it is come to pass, ye might believe."

The overall theme in the last verses of Daniel 11 speak of intense conflict over the whole earth. Daniel 8:23-25 also provided a vivid description of this conflict. One thing is sure: the final movements in these verses will be rapid.

Fulfilled prophecy will be understood by the earnest Bible student. Prophecy is history written in advance of its fulfillment. The Bible student can compare history and prophecy and find the perfect fit.

Promises From Scripture

1 THESS 5:1-6 But of the times and the seasons, brethren, ye have no need that I write unto you.

2 For yourselves know perfectly that the day of the Lord so cometh as a thief in the night [to those that believe not].

3 For when they shall say, Peace and safety; then sudden destruction cometh upon them, as travail upon a woman with child; and they shall not escape.

4 But ye, brethren, are not in darkness, that that day should overtake you as a thief.

5 Ye are all the children of light, and the children of the day: we are not of the night, nor of darkness.

6 Therefore let us not sleep, as do others; but let us watch and be sober.

ROM 13:11 And that, knowing the time, that now it is high time to awake out of sleep: for now is our salvation nearer than when we believed.

Prophetic Key #7 Prophecy is given to enable God's people to know where they are in the stream of time.

Prophetic Key #12 Prophecy is usually understood at the time of fulfillment.

DANIEL

The Story of the Rise and Fall of Earthly Kingdoms

*The Second Foe Falls —
USA and Other
Protestant Nations Meet the
Specifications of Prophecy
(Future)*

41 He [Papal No. 2, "king of the north"] **shall enter also into the glorious*** [OT#6638: goodly] **land** [USA and other Protestant Nations], **and many** ~~countries~~ [people] **shall be overthrown ...**

(This last part of this verse will be given on the following pages.)

***Note:** glorious land is the same Strong's word number as pleasant land in Daniel 8:9c.*

Prophetic Key #5 For the words *glorious land* and *pleasant land,* a Strong's Concordance is helpful to clarify meaning.

Prophetic Key #7 As prophecy is fulfilled, God's people will know where they are in the stream of time.

Prophetic Kay #13 More information is given in this part of the vision.

"We will rule the United States, and lay them at the feet of the vicar of Jesus Christ [the Pope], that he may put an end to their Godless system of education, and *impious laws of liberty of conscience which are an insult to God and man.*" Charles Chiniquy, *Fifty Years in the Church of Rome,* p. 282. (Emphasis supplied.)

Verse 41

"countries" — *Strong's* OT#9999 NOTE: inserted word (x); This word was added by the translators ... it is not in the original text.

Note: The word *countries* is found in verses 40, 41, and 42. This is the only verse were the word has been added by the translators. This addition creates confusion regarding the proper understanding of this verse.

When defining the terms in this verse, it must be remembered that the experiences of ancient (literal) Israel provide important lessons for modern (Spiritual) Israel to consider.

"glorious" — *Strong's* OT#6643 from OT:6638 in the sense of prominence; splendor; also a gazelle (as beautiful): KJV - beautiful, goodly.

DEUT 3:25 I pray thee, let me go over, and see the good land [Palestine] that is beyond Jordan, that goodly mountain, and Lebanon.

Note: *Glorious land* is sometimes defined as a *goodly land.* The goodly land of Palestine was a *promised inheritance,* prepared by God and designed to fulfill a specific purpose for ancient Israel. The Israelites entered the goodly land so that the surrounding heathen nations might be constrained to glorify the God of Israel. This land was located at the crossroads of the ancient world which facilitated Israel's ease of interaction with mankind. God purposed to raise up a favored nation, that would be the depository of His law and His witnesses in the land.

DAN 11:16 ... and he shall stand in the glorious land, [Jerusalem] which by his hand shall be consumed.

Note: Daniel 11:16 speaks of Pagan Rome's conquest of Jerusalem as the *glorious land.* It was "literally" invaded. Verse 41 speaks of Papal Rome "spiritually" conquering the modern *glorious land,* as entering the land, not standing in it. For Spiritual Israel, the USA and other Protestant nations, such as Canada and Australia, are favored lands which God provided as an asylum for His people at the time of the end. These lands were set aside by God to accomplish the same purpose for Spiritual Israel as did Palestine for ancient Israel. (Both references to the *glorious land* in Daniel 11 identify the entrance of Rome into the land that serves as a haven, or refuge, for Israel.) In the future, the Papal "king of the north" will enter into the glorious land through political craft and deceit and set up an image that reflects the fascist, mind, character, and personality of the Papal System. This will culminate in the passage of a religious National Sunday Law, legislated by a government. Countries founded upon the strict principles of separation of church and state should never tolerate this kind of legislative action that infringes upon "God given rights and freedoms." Other Protestant Nations will imitate this Sunday legislation.

United States Constitution Verses the Church of Rome

"The most sacred principle of the United States Constitution is the equality of every citizen before the law. The fundamental principle of the Church of Rome is the denial of that equality. Liberty of conscience is proclaimed by the United States, a most sacred principle which every citizen must uphold ... But liberty of conscience is declared by all the popes and councils of Rome, a most godless, unholy, and diabolical thing, which every good Catholic must abhor and destroy at any cost." Charles Chiniquy, *Fifty Years in the Church of Rome,* p. 284.

Some Historical Facts of the Protestant "Glorious Land"

1776: The United States of America was founded on Biblical principles as declared in the Constitution and Bill of Rights. This new land was to be forever free from any involvement with an earthly monarch or pope.

1951: President Harry Truman <u>failed</u> in his effort to have the United States Senate affirm his appointment of General Mark Clark to become the Ambassador to the Vatican! (By 1984 this appointment was a reality.)

1960: Kennedy allayed these fears [of the people] in 1960 when he spoke before the Greater Houston Ministerial Association. In his address he said, "I believe in an America where the separation of church and state is absolute — where no Catholic prelate would tell the President (should he be Catholic) how to act … where no church or church school is granted any public funds or political preference … where no public official either requests or accepts instructions on public policy from the Pope … where no religious body seeks to impose its will directly or indirectly upon the general populace or the public acts of its officials." He went on to ask that he be judged not on the basis of propaganda, but on his behavior in Congress, giving as an example his "declared stands against an Ambassador to the Vatican."

See: http://www.americanrhetoric.com/speeches/johnfkennedyhoustonministerialspeech.html

"In 1960, John Kennedy went from Washington to Texas to assure Protestant preachers that he would not obey the pope." *Washington Times,* April 16, 2001.

1962-1965: Vatican II Council. Result: The Ecumenical Movement. This movement has lulled Protestants into a sense of amnesia. They seem to have lost all memory of Papal history even when John Paul II in 1998 threatened "whoever," — not just the Roman Catholic faithful — but whoever did not abide by Roman Catholic dogma would be "punished as a heretic." (Apostolic Letter, *Ad tuendum fidem).*

1984: President Reagan <u>was successful</u> in appointing William Wilson as the first Ambassador to the Holy See to establish full diplomatic relations. This was a catalyst towards the collapse of Communism in Poland and other countries. Thomas P. Melady was the second Vatican Ambassador that assisted in bringing down the Iron Curtain in 1989.

2006: Francis Rooney is the seventh Ambassador of the United States to the Holy See ever since full diplomatic relations were established in 1984.

"In 2001, George Bush came from Texas up to Washington to assure a group of Catholic bishops that he would obey the pope." *Washington Times,* April 16, 2001.

"The best way to honor Pope John Paul II, truly one of the great men, is to take his teachings seriously, to listen to his words and put his words and his teachings into action here in America!" Patricia Zapoa, *Catholic News Service,* March 24, 2001.

"protestant" — Any Christian belonging to a sect descending from those that seceded from the Church of Rome at the time of the Reformation.
American Heritage Dictionary

Thought Questions:
To meet the definition of Protestant, one must protest Popery, and maintain a firm denial of any type of alliance with the Papal See. How does this align with the historical facts that have been mentioned?

What would be some of the historical facts of other Protestant Nations such as: Canada, Great Britain, Australia, New Zealand, South Africa, etc.?

Papal Rome will overcome three "foes" in the endtimes.
1. The first foe taken down was the Atheistic ideology.
2. The Papacy's <u>second foe will be</u> the *glorious land* of the United States and other Protestant nations. These nations over the years have been conditioned through political craft and religious deceit, to fall into line with its dogma.

2004: CNN News: Thursday, January 1, 2004   Posted 14:21 GMT (10:21 pm HKT) **Pope calls for a new world order — VATICAN CITY (AP)** — "Pope John Paul II rang in the new year on Thursday with a renewed call for peace in the Middle East and Africa and the creation of a New World Order based on respect for the dignity of man and equality among nations."

Thesis + Antithesis = Synthesis

Thesis: Terrorism

+

Antithesis: Fear of the People

=

Synthesis: Enforcement of Sunday Laws in the USA and other Protestant Countries

Present to Future

The king of the north by Peace Accords Destroys Many

DAN 8:25 And through his policy also he shall cause craft to prosper ... and by peace shall destroy many.

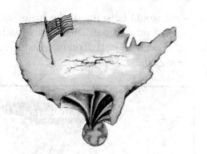

Papal No. 2 as the "king of the north" Spiritually Enters the United States of America and Other Protestant Nations (Future)

41 He [king of the north] **shall enter also into the glorious land** [USA and Protestant nations], **and many** ~~countries~~ [people] **shall be overthrown ...**

Some Escape From the "king of the north"

41 ... but these shall escape out of his [Papal] **hand ...**

(This last part of this verse will be given on the following pages.)

Verse 41 (Continued)

Description of Papal No. 2

DAN 8:23 a <u>king of fierce countenance</u>, [Papal No. 2] <u>and understanding dark sentences</u>, shall stand up.

Action of Papal No. 2

DAN 8:24 he shall <u>destroy wonderfully</u>, and shall <u>prosper, and practise</u>, and shall destroy the mighty and the holy people.

Mandate of Papal No. 2

DAN 8:25 through his policy also he shall cause <u>craft to prosper</u> in his hand; and he shall <u>magnify himself</u> in his heart, and <u>by peace shall destroy many</u> ...

"overthrown" — *Strong's* — OT#3782 to totter or waver (<u>through weakness</u> of the legs, especially the ankle); to falter, stumble, faint or fall.

"many ... shall be overthrown" — represents the *spiritually weak people* that will be overcome through submitting to the mandate of the church/state power. The Papacy spiritually takes control of the *glorious land* at the passage of a religious National Sunday Law. Those who *escape out of his hand* are contrasted by those who are *overthrown*.

"but these shall escape out of his hand" — The word *hand* is used to represent the power and authority exercised by the Papacy when it enters the Protestant countries and overthrows many. (See Appendices 11D and 11E on pages 357-365.) The authority of the Papacy is stated thus:

Thought Question

The USA is a very powerful nation in the world today. If they are the first to enforce a religious National Sunday Law, how soon would the remaining Protestant nations follow suit? Why?

Prophetic Key #12
Prophecy is usually understood at the time of fulfillment.

> "By the very act of changing the Sabbath into *Sunday*, which Protestants allow of; and therefore they fondly contradict themselves, by keeping *Sunday* strictly, and *breaking most other feasts* commanded by the same Church." Henry Tuberville, *An Abridgment of the Christian Doctrine*, p. 58.

There are two groups that escape the *hand* of the "king of the north."
- First Group: consists of those from God's flock on this earth.
- Second Group: consists of those that have been trapped in Babylon; a system laced with doctrinal error and deceitfulness.

*God's People Escape
From Papal Rome No. 2
"king of the north"*

41 ... but these [God's people] **shall escape out of his** [Papal] **hand, even Edom, and Moab, and the chief of the children of Ammon.**

(This part of the verse is repeated on the next four pages.)

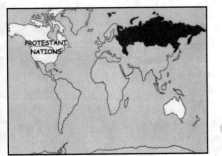

**6ᵗʰ Kingdom — Phase 2
Papal Rome No. 2
Over Protestant Nations (Future)**

Verse 41 (Continued)

First Group: The Escape of God's Flock — the "144,000"

Note: The first group that escapes from the hand of the papacy are from the *house of God*. They are named the *"144,000."*

1 PETER 4:17 For the time is come that <u>judgment must begin at the house of God</u>: and if it first begin at us, what shall the end be of them that obey not the gospel of God?

REV 14:1 And I looked, and, lo, a Lamb stood on the mount Sion, and with him <u>an hundred forty and four thousand</u> ...

<u>*"Edom, Moab, chief of the children of Ammon"*</u> — These names represent three divisions within the *house of God*. The original meaning of these names in Hebrew gives additional insight into each group.

"Edom" — *Strong's* OT#128 taken from **Adam** or **Adamah** — meaning *redness*.

Red is the color of blood. The 144,000 will overcome because they will be covered by the blood of the Lamb. This *blood* is their escape from the king of the north. They will be alive to see Jesus come. (See REV 7:4; 14:1-3.)

REV 12:11 And they <u>overcame him by the blood of the Lamb</u>, and by the word of their testimony.

"Moab" — *Strong's* OT#4124 **Mow'ab** ... means *father*.

Note: From the word, *Ab*, comes the word *Abba* meaning *father*. In the following texts, *Abba* is used in connection with the 144,000.

REV 14:1 And I looked, and, lo, a Lamb stood on the mount Sion, and with him an hundred forty and four thousand, having his <u>Father's name written in their foreheads</u>.

MARK 14:36 And he said, <u>Abba, Father</u>, all things are possible unto thee.

ROM 8:15 but ye have received the Spirit of adoption, whereby we cry, <u>Abba, Father</u>.

The Father's mind, character, and personality, is written in the foreheads (or minds and actions) of the 144,000. This is the Seal of God. These will escape from the king of the north. They will **NEVER ACCEPT** the *mark of the beast*. (REV 13:16)

REV 7:2-3 I saw another angel ... having the seal of the living God: and he cried with a loud voice ... 3 Saying, Hurt not the earth ... the sea, nor the trees, till we have <u>sealed the servants of our God in their foreheads</u>.

**God's People Escape
From Papal Rome No. 2
*"king of the north"***

41 ... but these [God's people] **shall escape out of his** [Papal] **hand, even Edom, and Moab, and the <u>chief of the children of Ammon</u>.**

<u>Verse 41</u> (Continued)

First Group: Escape of the 144,000 — Concluded

"Ammon" — Strong's OT#5983 means ***tribal***.

Twelve **tribes** receive the seal of God. *Twelve* represents God's church.

REV 7:4-8 And I heard the number of them which were sealed: and there were sealed <u>an hundred and forty and four thousand</u> of all the [twelve] tribes of the children of Israel. 5 Of the tribe of Juda ... of Reuben ... of Gad ... 6 of Aser … of Nepthalim … of Manasses … 7 of Simeon … of Levi … of Issachar … 8 of Zabulon … of Joseph … of Benjamin, [all] were sealed twelve thousand [each].

"chief" — Strong's OT#7225 means ***firstfruit***.

The following text describes the 144,000 as *firstfruits* because they are the *first company* of God's people to receive the Seal of the Living God. The Seal of God is the <u>character *of God*</u> written in the foreheads [minds] preparing the 144,000 to live through the Seven Last Plagues without a Mediator. They will **NEVER ACCEPT** the mark of the king of the north (the beast).

REV 14:4-5 These are they which were not defiled with women; for they are virgins. These are they which follow the Lamb whithersoever he goeth. <u>These were redeemed from among men, being the firstfruits unto God</u> and to the Lamb. 5 And in their mouth was found no guile: for <u>they are without fault before the throne of God</u>.

Note: The Seal of God protects the 144,000 from the king of the north.

Conclusion: The word meanings of Edom, Moab, and Ammon describe the character of the 144,000 who will live through the final crisis, (the Seven Last Plagues), and will see Jesus come in the clouds of heaven.

REV 14:1, 3 And I looked, and, lo, a Lamb stood on the mount Sion, and with him an hundred forty and four thousand, having his Father's name written in their foreheads. 3 And they sung as it were a new song ... and no man could learn that song but the hundred and forty and four thousand, which were redeemed from the earth.

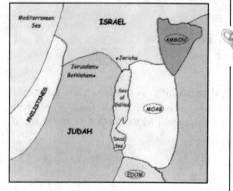

**Edom, Moab,
and Ammon Were Tribes
Situated in the Land of Palestine
Close to God's People**

God's People Escape
From Papal Rome No. 2
"king of the north"

41 ... but these [God's people] **shall** escape **out of his** [Papal] **hand, even** Edom, **and Moab, and the chief of the children of Ammon.**

Verse 41 (Continued)

Second Group: Escape of the Great Multitude from Babylon

Review: The Sunday Law is the catalyst that begins the process of separation of God's people from the world. The first group to escape are the 144,000. They give the Loud Cry to the world to "come out of Babylon."

"escape" — *Strong's* OT#4422 to be smooth, to escape (as if by slipperiness); causatively, to release or rescue; specifically.

Note: The word here translated *escape,* means to escape "as if by slipperiness," as well as "to release or rescue." The definition implies that prior to their escape, the three tribes were in the hands of the Papacy. The Loud Cry message is a call for Christ's *other sheep* to flee out of Babylon.

The second group that escapes have heeded the Master's Loud Cry. In Revelation 7:9, this group is referred to as a *great multitude*. They do not give heed to seducing spirits and doctrines of devils. (1 TIM 4:1-2)

"Other Sheep" are Called Out

JOHN 10:16 And other sheep I have, which are not of this fold: them also I must bring, and they shall hear my voice; and there shall be one fold, and one shepherd.

Edom, Moab, and Ammon represent those *other sheep,* who respond to the final Loud Cry message of Revelation 18:4. Edom, Moab, and Ammon represent the tribes that are found in the *great multitude* of those who escape the mark of the Beast.

A Great Multitude Escape

REV 7:9 After this I beheld, and, lo, a great multitude, which no man could number, of all nations, and kindreds, and people, and tongues, stood before the throne, and before the Lamb, clothed with white robes, and palms in their hands.

"Edom" was another name for Esau, meaning *"red."* Esau was the brother of Jacob (also known as "Israel"). Therefore, the tribe of Edom and the tribe of Israel are related. Esau was a profane fornicator who had rejected his birthright for the pleasures of this world. God's people from this group will escape the king of the north.

HEB 12:16 Lest there be any fornicator, or profane person, as Esau, who for one morsel of meat sold his birthright.

*God's People Escape
From Papal Rome No. 2
"king of the north"*

41 ... but these [God's people] **shall escape out of his** [Papal] **hand, even Edom, and <u>Moab</u>, and the chief of the children of <u>Ammon</u>.**

<u>Verse 41</u> (Concluded)

Second Group: Escape of the Great Multitude — Concluded

Note: Christ referred to Sodom, and Lot's *escape,* as an illustration of the end of the world. Lot represents those who are removed, (by the commencing Loud Cry), from *the false religious systems.* Daniel uses the tribes of Moab and Ammon as they identify with Lot's experience in leaving Sodom. (Reminder: The angels grabbed hold of Lot and physically removed him, and his family, from Sodom. They did not "leave" on their own. This is an example of man's inclination toward self-dependency.)

LUKE 17:29-30 But the same day that Lot went out of Sodom it rained fire and brimstone from heaven, and destroyed them all. 30 Even thus shall it be in the day when the Son of man is revealed.

Note: Christ's illustration of "the day when the Son of man is revealed," contains a reference to the following tribes of Moab and Ammon.

"Moab" means *father;* a tribe that descended from the incestuous relationship between Lot and his oldest daughter. Some of those that have committed spiritual adultery against God, will choose to honor Him and escape the king of the north.

GEN 19:36-37 Thus were both the daughters of Lot with child by their father. 37 And the firstborn [daughter of Lot] bare a son, and called his name Moab: the same is the father of the Moabites.

"Ammon" means *kinsmen,* or possibly *paternal uncle;* a tribe that descended from the second incestuous relationship between Lot and his youngest daughter. These will also escape the king of the north.

GEN 19:38 And the younger [daughter of Lot], she also bare a son, and called his name Benammi: the same is the father of the children of Ammon unto this day.

Note: These three tribes are close spiritual relatives of Spiritual Israel. They are characterized by fornication or incest, thereby identifying their involvement with unlawful relationships — a prime characteristic of modern/symbolic Babylon. The history of these ancient tribes demonstrates the hatred and resistance to the work of God and His people. These modern spiritual tribes will oppose the work of God's modern-day people until the Loud Cry drives home its message. Then, they will come out of Babylon. (See EZE 25:12; ZEPH 2:8-10.)

In the reference to Zephaniah it was prophesied that God's remnant people would not only spoil them but also possess them. In ancient times these three tribes opposed God's people. Their false worship was a continual snare to the nation of Israel. These three tribes were involved in the Pagan religions of the day which were in direct opposition to the true worship of God. Edom, Moab, and Ammon will not only escape the hand of the Papacy, but respond to the love of God and His people.

DANIEL

The Story of the Rise and Fall of Earthly Kingdoms

God's People Escape
From Papal Rome No. 2
"king of the north"

41 He [king of the north] **shall enter also into the glorious** [goodly] **land,** [United States] **and many** ~~countries~~ [people] **shall be overthrown: but these** [God's people] **shall escape out of his** [Papal] **hand, even Edom, and Moab, and the chief of the children of Ammon** [two groups of people: the 144,000 and the mixed multitude from Babylon].

Verse 41 (Review)

First Group Called
From the House of God

1 PETER 4:17 For the time is come that judgment must begin at the house of God: and if it first begin at us, what shall the end be of them that obey not the gospel of God?

The Loud Cry to Escape Babylon
Given by the 144,000

REV 18:4 And I heard another voice from heaven, saying, Come out of her, my people, that ye be not partakers of her sins, and that ye receive not of her plagues.

A Great Multitude Escape
(Christ's "Other Sheep")

REV 7:9 After this I beheld, and, lo, a great multitude, which no man could number, of all nations, and kindreds, and people, and tongues, stood before the throne, and before the Lamb, clothed with white robes, and palms in their hands;

The Wicked Do Not Escape

1 TIM 4:1-2 Now the Spirit speaketh expressly, that in the latter times some shall depart from the faith, giving heed to seducing spirits, and doctrines of devils; 2 Speaking lies in hypocrisy; having their conscience seared with a hot iron.

REV 22:15 For without [the New Jerusalem] are dogs, and sorcerers, and whoremongers, and murderers, and idolaters, and whosoever loveth and maketh a lie.

How does this Scripture
apply to future events?

ZECH 8:22-23 Yea, many people [great multitude] and strong nations shall come to seek the LORD of hosts ... 23 ... even shall take hold of the skirt of him that is a [Spiritual] Jew, saying, We will go with you: for we have heard that God is with you.

For Extra Study, Read Jeremiah 48 and 49

Curses were pronounced on the following tribes:
- Philistines; Ammonites; Damascus; Kedar; Hazor; Elam; Babylon.

The following three tribes were linked to Abraham and received a blessing.
- Edom (JER 49:11); MOAB (JER 48:47); AMMON (JER 49:6).
- **GEN 25:30:** Esau's name was changed to Edom when he sold his birthright. Esau was a grandson of Abraham.
- **GEN 19:37-38:** The tribes of Moab and Ammon came through the daughters of Lot, a nephew of Abraham.

The Third Foe Falls —
"Egypt Shall Not Escape"
From *Papal Rome No. 2*
"king of the north"
(Future)

42 He shall stretch forth his hand [of power] **also upon the countries: and the land of Egypt shall not escape.**

(This verse will be repeated on the following page.)

Verse 42

Review: When the "king of the north" enters the *glorious land* of the Protestant countries, there are some who escape his *hand* and some who are overthrown. The word *hand* is used to represent power and authority. Note the comment by Henry Tuberville on page 322 — the authority of the Papacy is Sunday observance.

"hand" — Strong's OT#3027 a hand; the open one; indicating power, means, direction, etc.

Note: The use of the word *hand* in this verse points to a power which brings another power under its dominion, influence, and control. Verse 41 indicated that the USA and other Protestant nations will be brought under the spiritual control of the Papacy. (Review page 323 for Daniel 11:41, of how this action will complete Phase 2 of the Sixth Kingdom.)

(The king of the north swept away the king of the south in 1989. Verse 40 did not indicate a *hand,* but shows that the southern king does come under the control of the northern king. The northern king *enters,* but does not stretch forth his hand. Recent historical events do not demonstrate that Russia and the Eastern European Bloc countries came under the spiritual control of the Papacy in 1989.)

"Egypt shall not escape" — The land of Egypt represents the remainder of the entire world. Many countries will not escape the iron fist of Papal Rome! (Note the maps on page 329.) The word translated as *escape* in this verse is different from the word translated as *escape* in verse 41.

"escape" — Strong's OT#6413 feminine of **OT#6412**; deliverance; concretely, an escaped portion.

OT#6412 from OT#6403; a refugee:-- (that have) escaped, fugitive.

Note: Verse 41 conveyed an idea of being saved by "slipping out of a hand" which had previously been clasped. (See page 325 for *Strong's* definition of *"escape"* OT#4422.) Verse 42 introduces the Papal leader in the process of bringing the world into harmony with the Papacy. The "third foe" will be overcome, allowing the Papacy to ascend to the throne of the world. At this point, the king of the north ceases to be simply a church. It grasps the position of the ruling geopolitical/religious power in total control of a New World Order. This position was taken away in verse 40 by the pushing action of the king of the south in 1798. The deadly wound will be fully healed when the Papacy stretches forth his hand upon the world (all countries), and seizes complete *control* of their economies [silver and gold]!

A look into the future: As ancient Egypt was decimated by plagues, before Pharaoh would consent to the great I AM, so will the stubborn, spiritually rebellious, modern *symbolic* Egypt be devastated by the Seven Last Plagues explained in Revelation 16.

Thesis + Antithesis = Synthesis

Future "king of the north" — Papal Rome's New World Order is Next!

"The church has the right to require that the Catholic religion shall be the only religion of the state, to the exclusion of all others." *Pope Pius IV.*

Thesis: World Religions
+
Antithesis: World Politics
=
Synthesis: Establish the One World Government
(A Religious, Political, New World Order
Enforcing the Universal Sunday Law)

---

42 He shall stretch forth his hand [of power] **also upon the countries: and the land of Egypt** [godless nations] **shall not escape.**

Verse 42 (Continued)

Verse 42 includes control over the remainder of godless nations in the world referred to as *Egypt*.

"Egypt" — After the fall of Communism and Protestant nations, the remainder of the world is referred to as *Egypt* — or godless nations. See the map below for: "6th Kingdom — Phase 3." In verse 43, these godless nations are further divided into two classes — Libya and Ethiopia.

Comparison of Three Conquering Situations of Rome

a) **DAN 7:24: Papal Rome No. 1** conquered three horns with the armies of its allies between AD 476-538 — a literal historical event. These three horns represented the Heruli, the Vandals, and the Ostrogoths. Then Papal Rome began to rule with power in the Dark Ages!

b) **DAN 8:9c: Papal Rome No. 2** will conquer three geographical areas: the south, the east, and the pleasant land.

c) **DAN 11:40-42: Papal Rome No. 2** will be complete when it has overcome the world's last three "foes" in the endtimes. They are indicated on the map of the "6th Kingdom — Complete." These are three spiritual battles, with literal consequences.

1. The first foe was overcome between 1989-1991: the ideology of Atheistic-Communism.
2. The Papacy's second foe to conquer will be the *glorious land* of all the Protestant nations.
3. The Papacy's third and final foe to conquer will be the remaining godless nations of the world, represented as *Egypt*.
- **Then** the Kingdom of Papal Rome No. 2 is complete. It will then transition to the 7th Kingdom — the Papal Rome New World Order. This will be the final kingdom as shown in verse 43.

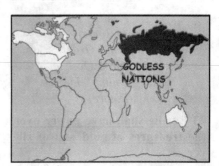

**6th Kingdom — Phase 3
Papal Rome No. 2
Over Godless Nations — Future**

**Once the 6th Kingdom is Complete,
it Transitions to the 7th Kingdom —
Papal Rome's New World Order
Over All Nations (Future)**

Reminder: See **The Structure of Daniel** Chart on page 367. This **Historic-Prophetic Outline** now introduces the last kingdom as **Papal Rome's New World Order** (N.W.O.), along with a detailed description of activities that will be carried out by this future kingdom. A knowledge of these seven kingdoms gives identification to the seven heads on the Composite Beast of Revelation 13:1-3. The Book of Revelation gives much greater detail with regards to the Seventh Kingdom at the end of time.

HISTORIC-PROPHETIC OUTLINE (CONCLUDED)
VISION FOUR

"king of the north" has the Whole World in his Hands

Future Papal Rome's New World Order Has Control Over a "Buying-Selling" Decree (Future)

43 But he shall have power over the treasures of gold and of silver ...

(The last portion of the verse is given on the next page.)

7th Kingdom — Papal Rome's New World Order Over the Whole World (Future)

HISTORIC-PROPHETIC OUTLINE
DAN 11:1-45
(BABYLON HAS FALLEN)
MEDO-PERSIA
GREECE
ROME (PAGAN IMPERIAL)
ROME (PAPAL NO. 1)
ROME (PAPAL NO. 2)
ROME (PAPAL N.W.O.)
OUTLINE EXTENDS TO: THE END OF TIME

Verse 43

"But he" — The Papacy (as part of Babylon) will control world finance.

REV 13:17 that <u>no man might buy or sell</u>, save he that had the mark, or the name of the beast, or the number of his name.

"shall have power over the treasures of gold and of silver" — Babylon represents all false religions and aspects of modern-day society that uphold self-exaltation in place of the worship of the true God. The Papacy, as part of Babylon, holds a vast amount of wealth in her possessions. She holds the *purse strings* in many financial enterprises throughout the world. The Papacy will again enforce religious dogma on all of mankind. "He who has the gold, makes the rules."

REV 17:4 And the woman [church] was <u>arrayed in purple and scarlet colour, and decked with gold and precious stones and pearls</u>.

HEAVENLY SCENE
DAN 10:1
KINGS OF THE NORTH AND KINGS OF THE SOUTH OF EARTHLY KINGDOMS

INTERLUDE QUESTION
DAN 10:14
WHAT SHALL BEFALL THY PEOPLE IN THE LATTER DAYS?

HISTORIC-PROPHETIC OUTLINE
DAN 11:1-45
(BABYLON HAS FALLEN)
MEDO-PERSIA
GREECE
ROME (PAGAN IMPERIAL)
ROME (PAPAL NO. 1)
ROME (PAPAL NO. 2)
ROME (PAPAL N.W.O.)
OUTLINE EXTENDS TO: THE END OF TIME

Reminder: The **Papal System** has held the title **king of the north** since AD 538. This title has been retained even though their "sceptre of power" <u>appeared to be dominated</u> by the rise and rule of Atheistic-Communism in Russia. In the near future when the deadly wound is completely healed, the **king of the north** will then fully regain the "sceptre of power" and become leader of the Seventh Kingdom over the **New World Order**. (Continued on the next page ...)

*Future
Papal Rome
Has Control Over the
Poor and Rich*

*Egypt Marches
in "Step" With the
New World Order*

43 ... and over all the precious things of Egypt [godless nations]: **and the <u>Libyans</u>** [the poor countries] **and the <u>Ethiopians</u>** [the rich countries] ... **shall be at his steps.**

Prophetic Key #5   For verses 43-45, a Strong's Concordance is helpful to clarify meanings.

Prophetic Key #12   Prophecy is usually understood at the time of fulfillment.

BBC 1 April 2004: "The Pope was the only one to be a world evangelist; he could visit all faiths — Islam and Judaism. He prepared the way for a religious new world order."

(Reminder continued from page 330.)
As a kingdom, formed of church and state, it will have total control and power for a short period of time. The enforcement of the Universal Sunday Law is its mark of authority. This kingdom is the last vestige of the iron legs (in Daniel 2) as it moves down through the feet and into the toes of iron and clay. (See Appendix 11D, page 359, Caption: *"Dies Domini Encyclical, May 1998."*)

<u>**Verse 43**</u>   (Continued)

Daniel Divides the World into Two Groups — Poor and Rich

"<u>Libyans</u>"— *Strong's* OT#3864 a dry region.

The *Libyans,* lived on the fringe of the desert, west of Egypt. Their location prevented them from attaining any measure of prosperity. Throughout their history they had cast a longing eye toward Egypt and the fertile Nile valley. They attempted to invade Egypt several times, but were always defeated. *Egypt* represents the entire world, while Libya represents what is labeled today as the <u>Third World</u> — the poor, underprivileged, and downtrodden countries which long to move up to the prosperity of the affluent, western world.

"<u>Ethiopians / Ethiopia</u>"— This ancient area included part of western Arabia, bordering the Red Sea. The Egyptians coveted Ethiopia because of the gold mines in its mountains and its wealth in cattle, ivory, hides, and ebony. Products from Central Africa entered Egypt through Ethiopian traders. The wealth of Egypt first passed through the hands of the shrewd Ethiopian traders. Ethiopia represents the most affluent countries of the world — the rich!

Note: Daniel links up with John's testimony in Revelation that identifies the Papacy as controlling the two world classes of *Libyans* and *Ethiopians.*

John Divides <u>ALL</u> the World

REV 13:16   And he causeth all, both small and great, **rich and poor,** free and bond, to receive a mark in their right hand, or in their foreheads.

"<u>shall be at his steps</u>" —

"<u>steps</u>" — *Strong's* OT#4703 from **<u>OT#6805</u>**; a step; companionship.

<u>OT#6805</u> to pace, i.e. step regularly; to march.

Note: To be at the steps of the **king of the north** is to march with him as he runs over the whole world. In his book, *Keys of This Blood,* Malachi Martin (a Vatican insider), reflected John Paul II's view of the structure of the countries of the world. The following quote, clearly demonstrates how a *contemporary map* of the world would have been drawn by John Paul.

"In short, that contemporary map of shame would be the graphic expression of the atrocity we have come to describe so blandly as the division of the world into **North and South,** which is to say, in plainer terms, the division of nations, and of populations within nations, into **rich and poor** ...

"It is just such a map of shame that Pope John Paul does hold up to the world in his moral assessment of the geopolitical arrangements that are setting up our future for us ...

"On the modern map of world shame that is the subject of so much of John Paul's attention, North and South do not figure as precise geographical terms. Instead, they are global frontiers where **wealth and poverty** divide not only nations, but societies within nations.

"Whether it is applied in the confines of the United States, or in the world at large, John Paul's moral assessment of **North and South** is simple and clear. In a morally adjusted economy, he insists, the rich should not get richer if the poor get poorer." Malachi Martin, *Keys of This Blood,* pp. 163-164, 171. (Emphasis supplied.)

"king of the north"
is Troubled by
Messages from the
East and North

"Tidings out of the east"
are the
Loud Cry Message of
Christ's Second Coming
(Future)

44 But tidings out of the east
[message of Christ's Second Coming] ... **shall trouble him ...**

(This part of the verse is given
again on the next page.)

Verse 44

"shall trouble him" — This phrase will be addressed before the *"tidings from the east and the north."* The word translated as *trouble* is also used in Daniel 5:6, 9.

"trouble" — *Strong's* OT#926 to tremble inwardly, be suddenly alarmed, agitated, afraid, or dismayed.

Note: The **king of the north** recognizes a message which brings forth a reaction within himself. This parallels Belshazzar's reaction in Daniel 5:6, where the mysterious hand writing appeared upon the palace wall.

"tidings" — represent a message which will greatly disturb the **king of the north.** The key to this alarming message is identified with the directions of the east and the north — both associated with Jesus Christ.

"tidings out of the east" — represent Christ's coming. These messages (fully explained in REV 14 and 18:1-4 as the Loud Cry/Latter Rain) will infuriate [trouble] the **Papacy.** God's people will again identify him as they had during the Reformation as the antichrist, **"king of fierce countenance,"** or the **"abomination that maketh desolate."** These tidings from the east identify the sealing message — sealed for God's eternal kingdom.

REV 7:2-3 And I saw another angel ascending **from the east**, having the seal of the living God: and he cried with a loud voice to the four angels, to whom it was given to hurt the earth and the sea, 3 Saying, Hurt not the earth, neither the sea, nor the trees, till we have sealed the servants of our God in their foreheads.

The sealing message from the east is part of the Third Angel'sMmessage in:

REV 14:9-10 And the third angel followed them, saying with a loud voice [Loud Cry], If any man worship the beast [political/religious Papal System] and his image [Protestant Nations and Fascist New World Order], and receive his mark in his forehead, or in his hand, 10 The same shall drink of the wine of the wrath of God [Seven Last Plagues].

The Third Angel's Message goes out to ALL the world, and will be a test for everyone on earth. This message enrages the **king of the north.** God's people are overcome by affliction and distress, described in the Bible as the time of Jacob's trouble.

JER 30:5-7 For thus saith the LORD; We have heard a voice of trembling, of fear, and not of peace. 6 ... I see every man with his hands on his loins ... all faces are turned into paleness? 7 Alas! for that day is great ... none is like it: it is even the time of Jacob's trouble; but he shall be saved out of it.

"Tidings out of the north"
are the
Loud Cry Message of
God's Final Judgment
(Future)

44 But <u>tidings</u> out of the east and <u>out of the north</u> [God's judgment message] **shall trouble him ...**

Verse 44 (Concluded)

"<u>tidings ... out of the north</u>" — represent judgment messages. In the days of ancient Israel, the enemies of God's people [Assyria and Babylon] launched their attacks against Israel's apostasy from the north. (JER 25:1-2, 9; EZE 9:2-10) In like manner, God will execute His final judgment message, from the north, against the enemy of His people. God the Father has always been the ***true King of the North***. (LEV 1:11; EZE 8:3-4)

PS 48:1-2 Great is the LORD, and greatly to be praised in the city of our God ... 2 ... the joy of the whole earth, is mount Zion, <u>on the sides of the north</u>, the city of the great King.

Note: Satan has always coveted the position in the north. He worked through earthly leaders to have control of the earth as king of the north, trying to mimic God's position in the heavenly courts.

ISA 14:13 For thou hast said in thine heart, <u>I will ascend into heaven</u>, I will exalt my throne above the stars of God: <u>I will sit</u> also upon the mount of the congregation, <u>in the sides of the north</u>.

Note: Not only do east and north represent messages of the return of Christ, but they identify the judgment as well. Isaiah 41:2, 25-27, identifies Christ as the One who would be raised up from the east and the north. It is a message of Christ's righteousness; the last message of mercy to a dying world — the message of Christ's character.

ISA 41:2, 25-27 Who raised up the righteous man <u>from the east</u> ... and made him rule over kings? 25 <u>I have raised up one from the north</u>, and he shall come ... upon princes as upon morter, and as the potter treadeth clay. 26 Who hath declared from the beginning that ... <u>He is righteous</u> ... 27 The first shall say to Zion, Behold, behold them: and I will give to Jerusalem <u>one that bringeth good tidings</u>.

The Final Death Decree
is Legislated

44 ... therefore he [Papacy] **shall go forth with great fury to destroy, and utterly <u>to make away many</u>** [issue a death decree].

(See Appendix 11D, page 362,
under the Caption of:
THE POPE: Leader of World Religious Leaders.)

Death Decree in Daniel 3

DAN 3:12-13, 19 certain Jews ... have not regarded thee ... nor worship the golden image which thou hast set up. 13 Then Nebuchadnezzar in his rage and fury commanded to bring these men before the king. 19 ... and the form of his visage was changed therefore he spake, and commanded that they should heat the furnace one seven times more ...

Note: This death decree <u>was</u> carried out! God's children were delivered.

Death Decree in Daniel 11:44

"<u>to make away many</u>" — is to carry on a purge, or legislate and enforce a <u>Death Decree</u> against God's people. A response to the Loud Cry (Latter Rain) is given to the world to "come out of Babylon." (This is explained more fully in REV 13:15 and 18:1-4.)

Note: This death decree <u>**will not**</u> be carried out. God's people will be delivered from it as the three Hebrews were delivered from the fiery furnace in Daniel 3.

"king of the north"
Will Divide the
People on this Earth

Papal Rome's
New World Order
Plants His Palace Between
Two Groups of People
(#1 "Spiritual" Application)
(Future)

45 And he shall <u>plant</u> the <u>taber-</u>
<u>nacles</u> of his <u>palace</u> <u>between the</u>
<u>seas</u> in the glorious holy moun-
tain ...

(This part of the verse given again
on the next two pages.)

Review (Verses 40-44)

1. A deadly wound was inflicted upon the Papacy in 1798.
2. In a three-step program, the Papacy returns to its former position of power.
   a. The Papacy retaliates against the forces of the **king of the south:** Communistic Russia and Eastern European Bloc countries fall.
   b. The Papacy enters the *glorious land* of the United States and other Protestant nations around the world. The entrance into these countries is through National Sunday Laws — a law that patronizes the Papal System. Years of political and religious craft and deceptions have laid the ground work for these National Sunday Laws.
   c. All the world, represented by Egypt, is brought under the command of the Papal System.
3. The Papal **king of the north** has gained control of the finances of the world. This restores the Papacy to the exalted position she held during the 1260 years of the Dark Ages.
4. Tidings out of the east and north infuriate the Papacy. A Universal Death Decree against God's people is legislated to silence God's world-wide message, "... come out of her my people." God's people are delivered from this death decree.

Verse 45

Note: The last verse in this chapter brings forth two applications: 1) the "Spiritual," and 2) the "Literal."

1. The "Spiritual" Application

Note: The action of placing oneself between a message of God and its intended recipients is used in this verse. The **king of the north** will establish himself as the only spiritual head and political ruler of the last earthly kingdom (a Fascist One World Government).

"plant" — *Strong's* OT#5193 properly, **to strike in**, i.e. **fix**; specifically, to plant (literally or figuratively): KJV - fastened, plant.

"tabernacles" — *Strong's* OT#168 from **OT#166**; a tent (as clearly **con-spicuous from a distance**): KJV - covering, (dwelling) place), home, tabernacle, tent.

OT#166 to be clear: KJV - **shine**.

"palace" — *Strong's* OT#643 apparently of foreign derivation; a pavilion or palace-tent: KJV - palace.

"between the seas in the glorious holy mountain"

"between the seas" — represents the *seas of peoples* aligned with the enemy of God.

REV 17:15 The <u>waters</u> which thou sawest, where the whore [Papacy] sitteth, <u>are peoples, and multitudes, and nations, and tongues</u>.

45 And he shall plant the tabernacles of his palace between the seas in the <u>glorious holy mountain</u> ...

(This part of the verse given again on the next page.)

<u>Verse 45</u> (Continued — "Spiritual" Application)

"glorious holy mountain" — represents God's church. The Protestant Lands of verse 41 are where God's people and truth were placed to facilitate the proclamation of the Loud Cry. God's church that is raised up to proclaim this message is the *holy mountain*. Both the *land* and the *church* are *glorious*. They are two different entities, though they are closely related. Note the following Scripture:

ISA 2:2-3   And it shall come to pass <u>in the last days</u>, that the mountain of <u>the LORD'S house</u> shall be established in the top of the mountains, and shall be exalted above the hills; and all nations shall flow unto it. 3 And many people shall go and say, Come ye, and let us go up to <u>the mountain of the LORD</u>, to <u>the house of the God</u> of Jacob; and he will teach us of his ways, and we will walk in his paths: for out of Zion shall go forth the law, and the word of the LORD from Jerusalem.

Note: Daniel 11:45 describes the dividing line for humanity, illustrated by the palatial tents of the man of sin.
1. On one side are those who reflect the man of sin's character, of self-exaltation. This group lives in violation of God's Law (truths).
2. Those on the other side reflect the self-sacrificing love of Jesus, their King — those that find delight in obedience to His Law and all truth.

PS 1:2   But his <u>delight</u> is in the law of the LORD; and <u>in his law doth he meditate day and night</u>.

PS 40:8   I <u>delight</u> to do thy will, O my God: yea, <u>thy law is within my heart</u>.

PS 119:174   I have <u>longed</u> for thy salvation, O LORD; and <u>thy law is my delight</u>.

Note: The enemy has always desired to plant his Satanic throne between the worshippers of God and the Heavenly Father — *"between the seas in the glorious holy mountain."* On behalf of Satan, the Papal System is portrayed as being in the <u>middle ground between these two groups of people</u>. The Papal System has been the primary object used by Satan to prevent the people of the world from hearing the message of the Loud Cry. With the Papacy's position in the middle, the people who reject the last message of warning are on one side, while God's people stand on the other side. Probation (Judgment) closes when the world has been completely divided into these two camps.

Prophetic Key #12   Prophecy is usually understood at the time of fulfillment. (e.g. When the Seven Last Plagues are poured out, God's people will know Judgment has closed.)

Papal Rome's
New World Order
Plants His Palace Between
Two Groups of People
(#2 "Literal" Application)
(Future)

45 And he shall <u>plant</u> the <u>tabernacles</u> of his <u>palace</u> <u>between the seas</u> in the <u>glorious holy mountain</u> ...

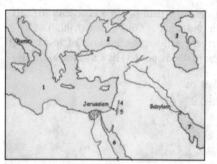

Seven Seas Surrounding Jerusalem

1. Mediterranean Sea
2. Black Sea
3. Caspian Sea
4. Sea of Galilee
5. Dead Sea
6. Red Sea
7. Persian Gulf

"A Jesuit cardinal named Augustine Bea showed us how desperately the Roman Catholics wanted Jerusalem at the end of the third century. Because of its religious history and its strategic location, the Holy City was considered a priceless treasure. A scheme had to be developed to make Jerusalem a Roman Catholic city." Jack Chick, *The Prophet Part 6*, p. 5.

<u>Verse 45</u> (Continued — "Literal" Application)

Reminder: The last verse in this chapter can bring forward two applications: 1) the "Spiritual" and 2) the "Literal."

The Capital of the New World Order With Papal Head
2. A Possible "Literal" Application

Reminder: The **king of the north** may establish himself as the spiritual head and political ruler of the last kingdom (One World Government) in the city of Jerusalem.

- *"plant"* — means to establish or *set up.*
- *"tabernacles"* — has to do with a *place of worship.*
- *"palace"* — represents a *seat of government.*

Therefore:

- The **Papacy** may set up a special place of worship and government.
- Pope John Paul II declared that Jerusalem, the *holy city,* is not subject to the political disputes of the Middle East, but that Jerusalem shall be a **place of worship for all religions and all nations**.
- The Holy See is the seat of government for the Papacy which is now situated in the city of Rome.
- When the New World Order is established with a Papal head, (known in Revelation as the **beast**, with its religious and political components), the capital city of Jerusalem could be set up as the future world government headquarters.

"between the seas" — Jerusalem is surrounded by *seven seas* as noted on the map.

In prophecy, could God give a view of the capital city of the New World Order to:

1. Reveal His foreknowledge;
2. Give an understanding of the significance of current events;
3. Give recognition of the complete picture of the rise and fall of kingdoms, their kings/rulers and capital cities, from the city of Babylon to the last earthly kingdom?

"glorious, holy mountain" — refers to the old city, Jerusalem, situated on Mt. Sion (Zion). (See DAN 9:16, 20 and MATT 5:34.)

God's People Get Inside Information

- God's people who study and understand prophecy are called **WISE**. (DAN 12:10)
- Question: Daniel 11:45 indicates that Jerusalem could be the religeo-political capital for the whole world. Does this agree with Revelation 16:14-16, where "the kings of the earth and the whole world" will finally be gathered together?

Note: The Battle of Armageddon (under the Sixth Plague) is NOT that of a conflict with nations fighting against nations.

- By the time of the Sixth Plague, the *kings* or *nations* are all <u>*unified and gathered together*</u> to accomplish the legislation which is intended by Satan to exterminate God's true Commandment keeping people. (REV 12:17)
- <u>*This legislation will gather the "kings of the earth" to enforce a Universal* **Death Decree** *upon those who will NOT bow down and worship the image of the beast*</u>. (Parallel typology is found in Daniel 3.)

The Fall of the
Last Iron Kingdom
Future Papal Rome's
New World Order

THE END!

45 ... yet he shall come to his end, and none shall help him.

Review (Verses 44-45)

1. There is a severe reaction of the Papal **king of the north** to the Loud Cry message of Christ's righteousness. Represented by the *tidings* from the *east and north,* is fear and anger.
2. Once the whole world has been divided into two classes — judgment and probation close.
3. The Papacy then launches forth with a plan to *destroy and take away many* of God's people in retaliation for the Seven Last Plagues being poured out.
4. God's people are protected from the Universal Death Decree.
5. Verse 45 concludes: The Papacy and all of Babylon falls — *he shall come to his end, and none shall help him.*

Verse 45 (Conclusion)

The Fall of the *Last Kingdom*

- *"yet he [the king of the north] shall come to his end and none shall help him"* — is a phrase that clearly demonstrates that the Historic-Prophetic Outline in Daniel 11 is in complete harmony with the previous three Prophetic Outlines found in Daniel 2, 7, and 8. Christ's kingdom is established once the Papal System is ended!

DAN 8:25 he shall also stand up against the Prince of princes; but he shall be broken without hand.

ISA 47:11 desolation shall come upon thee suddenly, which thou shalt not know.

Connecting Structure

The **king of fierce countenance** in Vision Three
— connects to —
the **king of the north** in Vision Four.

DAN 8:25 but he shall be broken without hand.

BROKEN!

DAN 11:45 he shall come to his end and none shall help him.

THE END!

1 THESS 5:3
For when they shall say, Peace and safety; then sudden destruction cometh upon them.

Prophetic Key #11 The structure of Daniel's Book has been written by *recapping*.

The Alignment of the Four Historic-Prophetic Outlines and the Fall of the Seventh Kingdom

DAN 2:45 "the stone ... brake in pieces, the iron, the brass, the clay, the silver, and the gold."
DAN 7:26 "But the judgment shall sit, and they shall take away his dominion."
DAN 8:25 "he shall be broken without hand."
DAN 11:45 "he shall come to his end, and none shall help him."

Note: The "Chapter numbers" were added by the translators. They are not inspired! The Fourth Vision does not end at Daniel 11:45, but includes Daniel 12:1-4 for the Answer and Endtime Event.

CHAPTER 12

Reminder: See **The Structure of Daniel** Chart on page 367. Following the **Historic-Prophetic Outline** of the Fourth Vision is the **Answer** given in Daniel 12:1 to the **Interlude Question** of Daniel 10:26. At the beginning of the vision in Daniel 10, Michael was seen. Now He appears again to deliver His people from the last persecutor! The **Endtime Event** affirms God's deliverance of His people.

> **ANSWER TO QUESTION**
> **DAN 12:1**
> **MICHAEL STANDS UP AGAINST THE PERSECUTOR!**
>
> **ENDTIME EVENT**
> **DAN 12:1-3**
> **"GOD'S PEOPLE ARE DELIVERED"**

> **HEAVENLY SCENE**
> **DAN 10:1**
> **KINGS OF THE NORTH AND KINGS OF THE SOUTH OF EARTHLY KINGDOMS**

> **INTERLUDE QUESTION**
> **DAN 10:14**
> **WHAT SHALL BEFALL THY PEOPLE IN THE LATTER DAYS?**

> **HISTORIC-PROPHETIC OUTLINE**
> **DAN 11:1-45**
> **(BABYLON HAS FALLEN)**
> **MEDO-PERSIA**
> **GREECE**
> **ROME (PAGAN IMPERIAL)**
> **ROME (PAPAL NO. 1)**
> **ROME (PAPAL NO. 2)**
> **ROME (PAPAL N.W.O.)**
> **OUTLINE EXTENDS TO: THE END OF TIME**

> **ANSWER TO QUESTION**
> **DAN 12:1**
> **MICHAEL STANDS UP AGAINST THE PERSECUTOR!**
>
> **ENDTIME EVENT**
> **DAN 12:1-3**
> **"GOD'S PEOPLE ARE DELIVERED"**

The "Connector" Word
— "And" —

1 And at that time shall Michael stand up ...

The Extension of the Daniel's Fourth Vision Into Daniel 12:1-4

<u>Verse 1</u>

- *"And"* — is the "connector" word which binds the Daniel 12:1-4 passage to the previous Prophetic Outline.

- *"at that time"* — refers back to the time when "he shall come to his end, and none shall help him."

- The Fourth Historic-Prophetic Outline found in Daniel 11 extends from verse 1 in *sequence and continuity* to verse 45 and ends in Daniel 12:3 with a glorious reward for the righteous.

- Daniel 12:4 is the "tidy-up" verse that ends the Fourth Historic-Prophetic Outline.

ANSWER TO QUESTION

*("What shall befall thy people
in the latter days?")*

VISION FOUR

*Michael Stands Up to
Deliver His People
From the Death Decree
of Revelation 13:15*

1 And at that time <u>shall Michael</u> [Son of God] **<u>stand up</u>, the great prince which standeth for the children of thy people: and there shall be <u>a time of trouble</u>,** [after Close of Probation when the Seven Last Plagues/Trumpets trouble the wicked] **such as never was since there was a nation even to that same time: ...**

ENDTIME EVENT
VISION FOUR

God's People Delivered

... and at that time <u>thy people shall be delivered</u>, [from enemies, sin, and the grave] **every one that shall be found written in the book** [of life].

**Time Runs Out
For This Earth**

Verse 1

Note: This verse has often been linked to the Close of Probation (or Close of Judgment) when Jesus Christ finishes His legal work in the Most Holy Place of the Heavenly Sanctuary, but the words *"And at that time,"* referring to the end of the Seventh Kingdom, give the verse a specific endtime application.

ENDTIME EVENT
DAN 12:1-3
"GOD'S PEOPLE
DELIVERED"

Michael of the Old Testament is Jesus Christ of the New Testament

"shall Michael stand up ... thy people shall be delivered" — Yes, Jesus Christ finishes His work in the Most Holy Place of the Heavenly Sanctuary. He then proceeds with three deliverances for His people. First, He —

1. Delivers them from <u>sin</u> before the Close of Probation. (1 PETER 4:17) Then later, He —
2. Delivers His people from the evil <u>enemies</u> who legislate a Universal Death Decree. (REV 13:15) And at last, He —
3. Delivers His people from the <u>grave</u> and the <u>second death</u>. (REV 2:11)

- Once Michael has finished delivering His people from their sins, their enemies, and the grave — then He returns to this earth with all the angels of heaven, to claim His children for eternity. This is the great Second Coming of Jesus, as King of kings, and Lord of lords.

- *"a time of trouble"* — The primary meaning of Daniel 12:1-3 when connected to the Daniel 11 Historic-Prophetic Outline, is dealing with a <u>final</u> time of trouble, "such as never was since there was a nation, even to the same time," which includes the Seven Last Plagues of Revelation 16. This brings the action down to the <u>very end of time</u>.

*Two Special Groups are
Resurrected
at the Voice of God
Before the
Second Coming of Jesus*

**2 And <u>many of them that sleep in
the dust of the earth shall awake</u>,
<u>some to everlasting life</u>, and
some to shame and everlasting
contempt.**

(This verse repeated on the next page.)

**At God's Voice,
There is "A"
Special Resurrection of
<u>Some</u> of the Righteous**

Verse 2

First Special Group Resurrected at the Voice of God

1. A Special Resurrection of <u>SOME</u> of the Righteous

- *"<u>many of them that sleep in the dust of the earth shall awake, SOME</u>"* — of them awake to everlasting life by a "great voice." Not **all** of the righteous dead awake to receive their reward at this event. This is a "small, special, resurrection" of <u>some</u> of the righteous dead that are risen <u>before</u> the Second Coming of Jesus. The rest of the righteous dead are raised with the last trump **at** the Second Coming of Jesus.

> *A. At **Jesus'** death, His <u>loud voice</u>
> raised some of the saints.*

MATT 27:50-53 Jesus, when he had cried again with **<u>a loud voice</u>**, yielded up the ghost. 51 … and the earth did quake, and the rocks rent; 52 And the graves were opened; and many bodies of the saints which slept arose, 53 And came out of the graves after his resurrection … and appeared unto many.

> *B. The <u>great voice</u> of God
> calls <u>some</u> of the righteous dead
> from the grave to receive the reward
> of everlasting life before Jesus comes.*

REV 16:17 And the seventh angel poured out his vial into the air; and there came **<u>a great voice</u>** out of the temple of heaven, from the throne, saying, It is done.

> *C. The <u>Voice</u> of the Archangel
> at the last trump calls the rest
> of the saints from the grave.*

1 THESS 4:15-17 By the word of the Lord, that we ... shall not prevent them which are asleep. 16 For the Lord himself shall descend from heaven with a shout, with **<u>the voice of the archangel</u>**, and <u>with the trump of God: and the dead in Christ shall rise first</u>: 17 Then we which are alive and remain shall be caught up together with them in the clouds, to meet the Lord in the air: and so shall we ever be with the Lord.

*Two Special Groups are
Resurrected
at the Voice of God
Before the
Second Coming of Jesus*

2 And <u>many of them that sleep in the dust of the earth shall awake,</u> some to everlasting life, and some to shame and everlasting contempt.

**At God's Voice,
There is "Another"
Special Resurrection of
<u>Some</u> of the Wicked
Which Includes the:
High Priest, Chief Priests,
Elders, Scribes,
and those who
Crucified Him**

*Note: In **MARK 8:34** Jesus was addressing a group of people that also included His disciples. A few verses later in chapter 9:1, He mentions that <u>some standing there</u> would not taste death until they saw the kingdom of God. It is very likely that "some" of those standing there were the very ones that had a part in the crucifixion. These very people will be raised <u>before</u> the Second Coming, to see God's kingdom come. Then, they will be smitten with the brightness of His coming, only to be resurrected again [1000 years later] to receive the second and final death.

<u>Verse 2</u> (Concluded)

Second Special Group Resurrected at the Voice of God

2. A Special Resurrection of <u>SOME</u> of the Wicked

- *"<u>many of them that sleep in the dust of the earth shall awake, SOME</u>"* — of them are the wicked dead which are risen to "shame and everlasting contempt." This is the special resurrection of Revelation 1:7, before the rest of the wicked dead are resurrected at the end of the millennium [1000 years later] described in Revelation 20.

A. Before the Second Coming of Jesus

REV 1:7 Behold, he cometh with clouds; and every eye shall see him, and <u>they also which pierced him.</u>

MATT 26:64 Jesus saith unto him ... Hereafter shall ye see the Son of man sitting on the right hand of power, and coming in the clouds of heaven.

- As noted in the Scriptures above, *"they also which pierced him"* will *behold* Jesus when He comes. Therefore, these wicked individuals are resurrected some time <u>before</u> the Second Coming of Jesus. See the following texts as to who these wicked ones will be.

Identification of "special" Wicked for the "special" Resurrection

MARK 14:53, 56 And they led Jesus away to the high priest [Caiaphas]: and with him were assembled all the chief priests and the elders and the scribes ... 56 And the chief priests and all the council sought for witness against Jesus to put him to death. (See **MATT 26:57**.)

MARK 8:34;* 9:1 34 And when he had called the people unto him with his disciples also ... 1 ... he said unto them, Verily I say unto you, That there be <u>some</u> of them <u>that stand here,</u> which <u>shall not taste of</u> [the second] <u>death, till they have seen the kingdom of God come with power</u> [at the end of time].

MATT 27:35 And they crucified him, and parted his garments, casting lots.

MARK 14:61-62 Again the high priest asked him, and said unto him, Art thou the Christ, the Son of the Blessed? 62 And Jesus said, I am: and ye shall see the Son of man sitting on the right hand of power, and coming in the clouds of heaven.

PS 22:18 They part my garments among them, and cast lots upon my vesture.

B. State of the "living" Wicked <u>at</u> the Second Coming of Jesus

REV 19:11, 21 And I saw heaven opened, and behold a white horse; and he that sat upon him was called Faithful and True. 21 And the remnant [of the wicked] <u>were slain with the sword of him that sat upon the horse.</u>

2 THESS. 2:8 And then shall that Wicked be revealed, whom the Lord shall consume with the spirit of his mouth, and <u>shall destroy with the brightness of his coming.</u>

The Wise Will Understand the Entire Book of Daniel

3 And they that be <u>wise</u> [understanding the Scriptures correctly] **shall shine as the brightness of the firmament; and they that turn many to righteousness as the stars for ever and ever.**

*The **End** of the Fourth Historic-Prophetic Outline*

Verse 3

"<u>wise</u>" — *Strong's* OT#7919; to be intelligent: KJV - consider, expert, <u>instruct</u> ... (give) <u>skill</u> ... <u>teach</u>, <u>make to understand</u>, <u>wisdom</u>.

Prophetic Key #29 The Historic-Prophetic Outline ends with a statement of the *wise* during the reign of the Seventh Kingdom. They understand the prophecies and teach others. No day or hour is known, as verified in Matthew 24:36.

The Closure of the Four Historic-Prophetic Outlines

- **Note:** Over the centuries, the meaning of the Book of Daniel has gradually unfolded.

- The people of God recognized and understood the identity of each kingdom as it rose and fell.

- The European Reformers comprehended much in Daniel 7, regarding the Fifth Kingdom — the Papacy of Old Europe.

- Between 1798 and 1845, the prophetic expositors of the Great Christian Awakening recognized that in Daniel 8, the 2300 year timeline was being unsealed and fulfilled in 1844. They had prophetic insight and began to <u>teach</u>.

- As the Berlin wall, and the puppet Kingdom of Atheistic-Communism, fell many Bible prophetic expositors recognized that Daniel 11:40 had been fulfilled. As a result they began to <u>teach</u>.

- Now, at the end of time, the students of prophecy recognize that the Seventh Kingdom is forming in what is known as the New World Order with a Papal Head. It is the Seventh Kingdom described in Revelation 13 and warned against in Revelation 14. Only those who love to read, study, and believe the Word of God will be given this understanding. The <u>wise</u> understand and are instructed to <u>teach</u> this wisdom to others. (See DAN 12:10.)

- This Book, which was once sealed shut to understanding, has been opening like a rose. **It is the last generation and the 144,000 who will see it fully revealed**.

Prophetic Key #11 The Historic-Prophetic Outline in this vision has aligned perfectly with the first three visions. See the fully illustrated chart on page 260 which reveals the <u>recapping</u> of the four Outlines and their alignment with each other. The overall structure reveals the <u>forward progressive movement</u> of the Book, with each Outline <u>adding more detail</u> right up until the last great resurrection of the dead.

An Invitation from Jesus

JOHN 5:39 Search the scriptures; for in them ye think ye have eternal life: and they are they which testify of me.

Promises from Jesus

JOHN 8:32: And ye shall know the truth, and the truth shall make you free.

MARK 4:22, 25 For there is nothing hidden <u>which will not be revealed</u>, **nor has anything been kept secret** but that it should come to light. 25 For whoever has, to him <u>more will be given</u>; but whoever does not have, even what he has will be taken away from him.

"Tidy-Up" Verse for
Vision Four

4 But thou, O Daniel, <u>shut up the words</u>, and seal the book, even to the time of the end: many shall <u>run to and fro</u>, and <u>knowledge shall be increased</u>.

Prophetic Key #30 Daniel 12:4 is the "tidy-up" verse for the Fourth Historic-Prophetic Outline which has revealed all seven earthly persecuting kingdoms around God's people. Vision Four follows the same structural pattern as Vision Three. The Outline is given in the first part of the vision, with timelines following in the second part of the vision.* The last nine verses in Daniel contain three timelines that throw a flood of light on events that will transpire right up to the very eve of the Second Coming of Jesus. These verses also give additional information about the rule of the Seventh Kingdom, and God's Holy People.

*Comparison of Visions 3 and 4

Vision 3: Daniel 8 contains the first part of the vision that gives all the necessary information for the Outline. In the second part of the vision, (Daniel 9:24-27), several timelines are addressed.

Vision 4: Daniel 11—12:4 contains the first part of the vision that gives all the necessary information for the Outline. In the second part of the vision, (Daniel 12:5-13), three timelines are addressed.

Verse 4

- All four Historic-Prophetic Outlines have come to an end. Daniel is instructed to "shut up the words and seal the book."

- *"shut up the words"* — These *sealed words* were not to be understood until the *end of time*. This timeframe will begin with the rule of the Seventh Kingdom.

Prophetic Key #4 Scripture unlocks Scripture through the principle of Isaiah 28:9-13. Prophecy is fully understood at the time of fulfillment.

- *"run to and fro"* — is referring to the time-honored searching of the Bible, "here a little and there a little." (ISA 28:9-13)

- *"knowledge shall be increased"* — is the understanding of the entire Book of Daniel from <u>chapter 1 all the way through chapter 12 with application to the proper timeframes</u>.

- In Vision Four, the following three timelines are connected to events that bring history to its close during the reign of the Seventh Kingdom. <u>The last nine verses are known as an EPILOGUE in the Fourth Vision and are the focus of the entire Book of Daniel</u>.

Prophetic Key #10 The timeframe of the seventh earthly kingdom is still in the future. In every vision, <u>time must move forward</u>. Therefore, the following timelines cannot move backward and be interpreted in the timeframe of the Dark Ages. They can only move forward to events in the future. These timelines are NOT hung on *time* like the **past events of other timelines in Daniel**. These three timelines are hung on future EVENTS which are described in the Book of Revelation.

Prophetic Key #18 No symbols are used in the only literal vision of Daniel 10-12. Therefore, the following timelines will be correctly interpreted as literal time. Once the correct events transpire, the *beginnings* of the timelines will be understood <u>and dated</u>. These timelines reveal the final events at the close of this world's history which brings the controversy to a climax, define the length of the persecution of God's people, and promise a great deliverance from the final death decree of Revelation 13:15.

Further Note: God had not permitted previous generations to see the entire picture provided in the Epilogue of Daniel 12:5-13. It is very appropriate that the last generation should have the most understanding and insight into <u>all</u> prophecy. Prophecy is intended to give security and orientation and to let God's people know of a certainty where they are in the stream of time. These last few verses of Daniel are of incredible importance to everyone.

Michael Asks Daniel to
Seal the Words
of Daniel 12:5-13
Till the End of Time

Daniel 10-12:4 — Review of the Historic-Prophetic Outline in Vision 4

1. Vision 4 uses literal language to introduce the literal "kings of the north" and "kings of the south." (This vision is given in a full literal style for very good reason.)
2. Vision 4 describes and reveals the **Seven earthly kingdoms** surrounding God's people.
3. Vision 4 extends from 538 BC to the very "eve" of Christ's Second Coming in One Major Line of Prophecy.
4. Vision 4 <u>repeats</u> the former information. The Outline adds the last missing necessary information to complete the historical drama. (Note: Vision 4 provides the full interpretation of the seven heads on the beast of Revelation 13:1-3.)
5. Vision 4 is completely written with literal language and interpreted with the aid of secular history. There are NO symbols whatsoever — "king of the north" and "king of the south" are **titles, — not symbols.** These titles begin with "geographic locations," but then expand to global proportions. The action still surrounds God's people.
6. The Outline of Vision 4 applies the "king of the north" and "king of the south" according to secular history, and continues to <u>recap and review</u> the sequence of kingdoms in Visions 1, 2, and 3.

   (**1ˢᵗ Kingdom** = Fallen BABYLON was the first kingdom even though not mentioned here.) (606 — 538 BC)

   2ⁿᵈ Kingdom = Darius the Mede = MEDO-PERSIA (538 — 331 BC)

   3ʳᵈ Kingdom = Mighty King (Alexander the Great) = GREECE (331 — 168 BC)

   - **New Information:** The Outline of Vision 4 gives additional information of the struggle between Syria (in the north) and Egypt (in the south). Both were striving for world domination. Vision 1 prophesized the Fourth Kingdom would be Rome. Secular history establishes the validity of the prophecy.

   4ᵗʰ Kingdom = ROME, specifically the Caesars of PAGAN IMPERIAL ROME. (168 BC — AD 476). The Caesars, through political scheming, obtained the title "king of the north" by conquest of Syria. **New Information includes:**
   a) Daniel 11:20 dates the birth of Jesus Christ as 4 BC.
   b) Daniel 11:22 dates the death of Jesus Christ as AD 31. (Note how time continues to move forward with each verse.)

   5ᵗʰ Kingdom = <u>Popes</u> as [the former] "kings of the north" = PAPAL SUPREMACY NO. 1 (AD 538 — 1798) The timeline of 1260 years was prophesized in Daniel 7:25. Daniel 11:35 dates 1798 as the apparent end of this kingdom.

   - **Note:** Papal Supremacy No. 1 is addressed in Daniel 11:31-35. There is NO 1260 year timeline repeated in these verses since the timeline had been given in Daniel 7:25. There is no need to repeat the "timeline" information. God gives the timelines ONCE and only ONCE. He does it right the first time.

   6ᵗʰ Kingdom = "king [of fierce countenance]" = the "rising" PAPAL SUPREMACY NO. 2 in Daniel 11:36-42 (AD 1801 — Present). These verses emphasize the erroneous teachings of the wounded Papal System, seeking world domination. During this timeframe the Papacy is the puppeteer of the "king of the south," — the Atheistic-Communistic kingdom of Russia. The information for this piece of secular history was provided in Daniel 8. When the Papacy had no further need for the ways of this puppet kingdom, it was dismantled (1989) with the fall of the Iron Curtain. Communism is no longer a world threatening power today. It had been <u>potter's clay</u> (part of the feet in the Daniel 2 image) molded in the hands of the <u>iron Papal System</u>.

   - **New Information:** Daniel 11:40 dates the year 1989 as the fall of the powerful puppet nation known as Atheistic-Communist Russia. Vision 4 then adds information of the three foes that the 6ᵗʰ Kingdom has to conquer.
     1. Atheistic-Communism: crumbled between the years 1989-1991. It is no longer a world threatening power.
     2. Protestant Nations of the world: Kingdom #6 will gain entrance into these nations with the legislation of National Sunday laws in the future.
     3. Godless Nations of the world: Known as "Egypt," these nations will march in step with Kingdom #6. In the future, once this foe is conquered, Kingdom #6 will transition to Kingdom #7.

   - <u>New Information:</u> 7ᵗʰ Kingdom = [the latter] "king of the north" = PAPAL ROME'S NEW WORLD ORDER which will be the last kingdom on this earth — ruling for a very short time. Daniel 11:43-45 still has future application.

7. **Datable Time:** Vision 4 extends time **to the <u>eve</u> of the great Second Coming.**
   - **VISION 4** reveals information for the "gap" of time between AD 1844 — and the <u>eve of the great Second Coming</u>. **IN THIS VISION** all the events for the "gaps of time" from the former visions have been addressed and accounted for. **Note: This vision has MOVED FORWARD IN TIME as far as it can go**.
8. **Emphasis in Vision 4** is on the Seventh Kingdom — the PAPAL ROMAN NEW WORLD ORDER ("king of the north") which is the last dominant king in the three timelines given in the Epilogue of Daniel 12.
9. **Vision 4 Tidy-up Verse:** Daniel 12:4 is the verse that **ends** the Historic-Prophetic Outline of Vision 4. Following the structure of Vision 3, the following nine verses in Daniel 12:5-13 introduce three timelines that have to do with the events of the last kingdom in the Fourth Outline and how the drama of the end of this world comes to its conclusion.
10. **Endtime Event:** Vision 4 ends with Michael standing up to deliver His people from a Death Decree, sin and the grave. There are two special resurrections before Christ returns: one for *some* of the righteous and one for *some* of the wicked.

HE STRUCTURE OF DANIEL'S FOURTH OUTLINE

The Rise and Fall of Earthly Kingdoms Surrounding God's People

One Major Line of Prophecy From 606 BC — to the Very Eve of Christ's Kingdom

DANIEL 10-12 (Vision 4 uses **Literal** language for the following Historic-Prophetic Outline.)
The **LITERAL KINGS** represent Literal Kingdoms in the Outline.

(#1 BABYLON HAS FALLEN)

DARIUS THE MEDE
DAN 11:1-2

#2 MEDO-PERSIA
538 — 331 BC

ALEXANDER THE GREAT
DAN 11:3-4

#3 GREECE
331 — 168 BC

Beginning in 323 BC — The "Ptolemy's of Egypt" and "Seleucids of Syria" fail in their lengthy struggle against each other to be the next earthly kingdom. DAN 11:5-17

JULIUS CAESAR
44 BC DAN 11:18-19

#4 ROME
168 BC — AD 476

Pagan Imperial Rome

(Ruled by Roman Caesars)

AUGUSTUS CAESAR
4 BC DAN 11:20

Birth of Jesus
4 BC
DAN 11:20

"kings of the north"

TIBERIUS CAESAR
AD 12 DAN 11:21

Death of Jesus
AD 27
DAN 11:22

Struggle and Fall of Arianism
AD 270 — 538 DAN 11:23-29

PAGAN IMPERIAL ROME FALLS
DAN 11:30

RULING POPES
DAN 11:31-35

#5 ROME
AD 538 — 1798

Papal Rome No. 1
"kings of the north"

DAN 11:40-42

POPES AS PUPPETEERS
DAN 11:36-42

#6 ROME
AD 1801 — Present
(Future*)

Papal Rome No. 2
1 Puppets "kings of the south"
(Atheistic-Communism)
*2 Enters the Glorious Lands of Protestantism (Future)
*3 Power Over Godless Nations

RULING POPE
DAN 11:43-45

#7 ROME
(Future)

Papal Rome N.W.O.
"king of the north"
"he" comes to his end.

The END of ALL 4 Historic-Prophetic Outlines in Daniel

VISION #

4

Vision Four
Time extends from 538 BC — Future

Connecting Structure

DANIEL'S THIRD OUTLINE

The "king of fierce countenance" of Vision 3 (Papal Rome No. 2) connects with ...

PAGAN IMPERIAL ROME

Black Sea

Mediterranean Sea

"WAXES EXCEEDING GREAT"
(Future) DAN 8:9c

#6 ROME
(Papal Supremacy No. 2)
Rises (AD 1801) and
Rules (Present)

"he" [king of fierce countenance]
is broken "without hand"
at Jesus' Second Coming
DAN 8:25

VISION #

3

Between Visions 3 & 4

DANIEL'S FOURTH OUTLINE

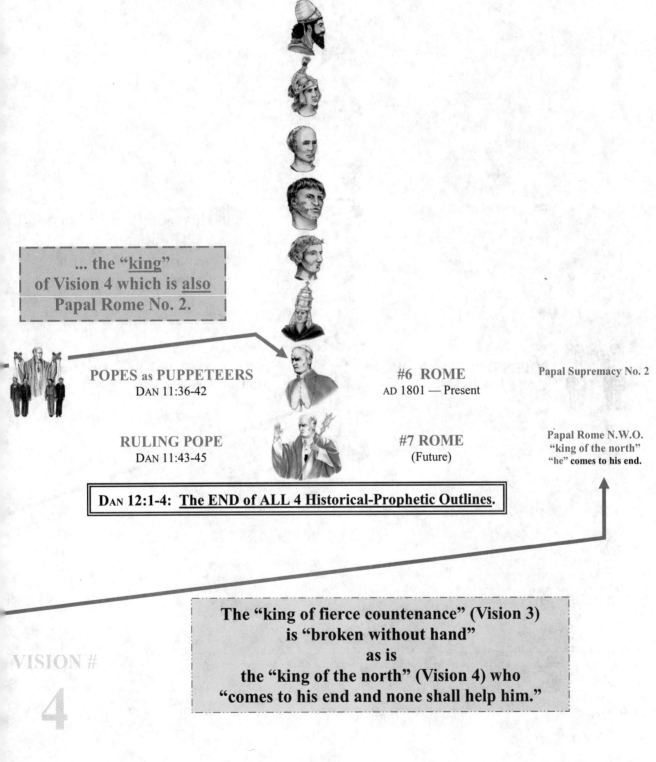

... the "king"
of Vision 4 which is also
Papal Rome No. 2.

POPES as PUPPETEERS
DAN 11:36-42

#6 ROME
AD 1801 — Present

Papal Supremacy No. 2

RULING POPE
DAN 11:43-45

#7 ROME
(Future)

Papal Rome N.W.O.
"king of the north"
"he" comes to his end.

DAN 12:1-4: The END of ALL 4 Historical-Prophetic Outlines.

The "king of fierce countenance" (Vision 3)
is "broken without hand"
as is
the "king of the north" (Vision 4) who
"comes to his end and none shall help him."

VISION #
4

Connecting Structure

DANIEL'S <u>FOURTH</u> OUTLINE

This "king" in Vision 4 is
Puppeteer over
"kings of the south"
(Atheistic-Communism)
which connects with ...

 POPES as PUPPETEERS
Dan 11:36-42

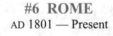

#6 ROME
AD 1801 — Present

Papal Supremacy No.

VISION #

4

Between Visions 4 & 1

The iron Roman Kingdom of the legs continues down into the feet and toes culminating with the Papal Rome New World Order at the end of time.

... the "CLAY" in the Image of Vision 1
which represents *mankind*.
The Roman Papacy will be able to manipulate
ALL of mankind that do not have
their names written in the Book of Life.
The "Clay" also includes a *remnant* of mankind that
do not bow down
to the dictates of the false religious leader(s).

CLAY
n the Feet

VISION #

1

Connecting Structure

DANIEL'S FOURTH OUTLINE

#2 MEDO-PERSIA
538 — 331 BC

(#1 BABYLON HAS FALLEN)

#3 GREECE
331 — 168 BC

#4 ROME
(Pagan Imperial)
168 BC — AD 476
(Ruled by Roman Caesars)

#5 ROME (Papal No. 1)
AD 538 — 1798

#6 ROME (Papal No. 2)
AD 1801 — Present

#7 ROME (Papal N.W.O.)
(Future)

 DAN 2:44   And <u>in the days of these kings</u> shall the God of heaven set up a kingdom, which shall never be destroyed.

"ten kings of the earth"
give their sovereignty (or *daily*)
to the 7th Kingdom
(Future)

At the end of the world just before the Stone Kingdom is set up, the Papal New World Order will reign with the "<u>ten kings</u>" of REV 17:12, over <u>ALL</u> mankind that do not have their names written in the Book of Life (REV 3:8). These "kings" connect with ...

Between Visions 4 & 1

DANIEL'S <u>FIRST</u> OUTLINE

The first four earthly kingdoms are <u>revealed</u> in the first Outline as:

    #1 Babylon
    #2 Medo-Persia
    #3 Greece
    #4 Rome

The last four divisions all belong to Rome.

IRON in the FEET
DAN 2:41

CLAY in the FEET
DAN 2:41

> The iron of the legs continues down into the feet and toes as the Roman Kingdom in its Papal form. The last form of the Roman Kingdom is found at the end of the toes — a New World Order.

**IRON & CLAY
in the TOES**
DAN 2:42-43

... the "<u>toes</u>" in the image.

VISION #

1

Appendix 11A — Papal Encyclicals from 1801-2000

Note: The 1260 year reign of the Roman Papacy ended in AD 1798 when Pope Pius VI was removed from his seat in the Vatican under Napoleon's orders. Jesuit historian Joseph Rickaby recalls — "… half Europe thought … that [along] with the Pope the Papacy was dead." *The Modern Papacy,* in *Lectures on the History of Religions,* Vol. 3, Lecture 24, 1910, page 1. Step by step, through the next fourteen pontificates, the Papacy needed to discover ways to gain back their lost recognition. Some of these ways were through the writing of encyclicals, signing concordats, and issuing apostolic letters, and papal bulls. A <u>very brief review</u> is given of the reigning Popes and their aim for supreme ascendancy over <u>all</u> world leaders, governments, and religions. (See the website Papal Encyclicals Online for more information.)

Pope Pius VII 1800-1823

- **1801** Signed a Concordat with Atheistic France restoring Catholicism as the state religion. Later, Concordats were also signed with Prussia and Russia.
- **1814** Restored the Jesuit Order throughout the world.
- **1816** Condemned the 1804 British Bible Society for making the Word of God available to the people.

Pope Leo XII 1823-1829

- Appointed Bishops in the liberated nations of Latin America, which extended Papal control.
- **1825** Enforced the "index and the Holy Office" [of the Inquisition], favouring Jesuits; the territory was infested with spies intent on stamping out anything close to another revolution.

Pope Pius VIII 1829-1830

- **Encyclical** *Traditi humilitati nostrae* protested that the Bible Societies were contributing to the breakdown of religious, social, and political order.

Pope Gregory XVI 1831-1846

- **1832 Encyclical** *Mirari vos* denounced freedom of conscience and the press; and opposed the separation of church and state.
- **1844 Encyclical** *Inter praecipuas* denounced the London Bible Society.

Pope Pius IX 1846-1878

- **1854 Papal Bull** *Ineffabilis Deus* approved the new doctrine of the *Immaculate Conception of Mary.*
- **1869-1870 Vatican Council I** approved Papal Infallibility, even to the dismay of Catholics.
- Found faithful allies in Anglican priests, Hort and Westcott, to publish an adulterated version of the Scriptures — in place of trying to ban the Bible.
- **1864 Encyclical** *Quanta cura* [Syllabus of Errors] stated:
  a) All religious liberty of conscience to be removed;
  b) Catholicism to be the only religion of the state, to the exclusion of all other forms of worship;
  c) Papal Church has temporal power to use force, directly or indirectly, as she wishes.
- Reestablished the Roman Catholic hierarchy in England (1850), and in the Netherlands (1853).

Pope Leo XIII 1878-1903

- **1888 Encyclical** *Libertas humana* [Human Liberty] — Liberty of worship is NO liberty, but is a degradation, and the abject submission of the soul to sin.
- *Summa Theologica:* Heretics need to be separated from the church by excommunication, and also severed from the world by death through the secular tribunal, or the local government.
- **Encyclical** *Libertas humana* — No freedom of thought, speech, writing, or worship.
- **Encyclical** *Rerum Novarum* — The State to legislate Sunday as the day of worship for everyone.

Pope Pius X 1903-1914

- **Greatest Achievement** was the setting in motion of the systematization of canon law. He also instituted a form of secret mind police, spying on his own members, encouraging Freemasonry in the Church.

Pope Benedict XV 1914-1922 (Vatican Prisoner)

Pope Pius XI 1922-1939

- **1929 Lateran Treaty** signed between the Holy See and Mussolini which guaranteed the Vatican City absolute independence and Papal State sovereignty.
- **1930 Encyclical** *Casti connubial* condemned the use of contraceptives as a means of birth control.

Pope Pius XII 1939-1958

- **1933 Concordat** with Germany, signing a treaty with Hitler, guaranteeing the loyalty of the German Roman Catholics to the Hitler regime.

Pope John XXIII 1958-1963

- **Encyclical** *Pacem in Terris* [Peace on Earth] — see DAN 8:25 "by peace shall destroy many."
- **1962-1965 Vatican Council II** focused on Ecumenism to increase Papal influence and restore relations with Protestantism under a façade of a friendly, amicable Pope. In four short years the Protestants dropped their guard — again!

Pope Paul VI 1963-1978

- **1964** Proclaimed Mary to be Mother of the church.
- **Vatican Council II** set up four situation rooms to bring all religions back into the Roman system including Islam, Christian groups, Eastern Orthodox/Anglican churches, and the non-Christian religions of the world.

Pope John Paul I 1978 — Reign of 34 days

Pope John Paul II 1978-2005

- **1998 Apostolic Letter** *Ad Tuendom Fidem* — Dissenters condemned from the Roman Catholic faith are to be punished as heretics.
- **1998 Encyclical** *Dies Domini* [Day of the Lord] — Civil legislation for Sunday worship is a worker's right which the State must guarantee.
- **2000 Encyclical** *Dominus Iesus* — Salvation is obtained only through the Roman Catholic church.

Appendix 11B — Alignment of Scripture Phrases for the Sixth Kingdom

Note: Each new vision in Daniel must align with the previous visions. There are Scripture verses in Daniel 8 describing the Sixth Kingdom as "waxed exceeding great" in verses 9c-12; a "king of fierce countenance" as the king of Papal Supremacy No. 2 in verses 23-25. Phrases in Daniel 11:36-39 align with Daniel 8:10-13 and 23-25 using very similar wording to describe the same king and kingdom known as the "king." Compare these phrases with 2 THESS 2:3-9.

Daniel 8:10-13

These verses are part of the Heavenly Scene in Vision 3 describing the Sixth Kingdom which **"waxed exceeding great."**

9 ... which waxed exceeding great,
toward the south,
and toward the east,
and toward the pleasant land.

10 And it
waxed great,
even to the host of heaven;
and it
cast down some of the host and of
the stars to the ground,
and stamped upon them.

11 Yea,
he magnified himself
even to the
prince of the host,
and by him the
daily sacrifice **was taken away,**
and the place of his
sanctuary was cast down.

12 And an host was given him
against the daily sacrifice
by reason of transgression,
and it
cast down the truth to the ground;
and
it practised, and prospered.

13 Then I heard one saint speaking,
and another saint said unto that
certain saint which spake,
How long shall be the vision
concerning the daily
sacrifice, and the
transgression of desolation,
to give both the
sanctuary and the host to be
trodden under foot?

Daniel 8:23-25

These verses are part of the Historic-Prophetic Outline in Vision 3 describing the Sixth Kingdom ruled by the **"king of fierce countenance."**

23 And in the latter time of their
kingdom, when the
transgressors are come to the full,
a king of fierce countenance,
and
understanding dark sentences,
shall stand up.

24 And
his power shall be mighty,
but not by his own power:
and
he shall destroy wonderfully,
and
shall prosper, and practise,
and
shall destroy the mighty and the
holy people.

25 And through his policy also he
shall cause craft to prosper
in his hand;
and
he shall magnify himself in his
heart,
and
by peace shall destroy many:
he shall also stand up against the
Prince of princes;
but he shall be broken without hand.

Daniel 11:36-39

These verses are part of the Historic-Prophetic Outline in Vision 4 describing the power of the sixth **"king"** that rules the Sixth Kingdom.

36 And the king shall do according
to his will; and he shall exalt himself, and magnify himself
above every god,
and
shall speak marvellous things
against the God of gods,
and
shall prosper
till the indignation
be accomplished:
for that that is determined
shall be done.

37 Neither shall he regard the God
of his fathers,
nor the desire of women,
nor regard any god:
for
he shall magnify himself above all.

38 But in his estate
shall he honour the God of forces:
and
a god whom his fathers knew not
shall he honour with gold, and sil-
ver, and with precious stones,
and pleasant things.

39 Thus shall he do in the most
strong holds
with a strange god,
whom he shall acknowledge and
increase with glory:
and
he shall cause them to rule over
many,
and
shall divide the land for gain.

Appendix 11c — Daniel 11:40 Prophecy Confirmed in the Secular Press

Note: The alliance between the USA and the Papacy is addressed in these press articles, including the military and economic role played by the USA. Incredibly, we find the authors of these secular articles were frequently led to choose words in illustrating their stories which are the same words found in the Biblical description of Daniel 11:40. God intends for His people to see that these historical events are a direct fulfillment of prophecy.

An incredible part of this history is that God, through Daniel, concisely described these events in just one verse, containing only fifty words.

- "Gorby's Bow To The Roman Legions" — Title in the *U.S. News & World Report.*

- "The Soviet president's session Friday with Pope John Paul II is the latest development of a revolution in the Communist world that the pope helped spark and Gorbachev has allowed to happen." *U.S.A. Today,* cover story, 1989.

- "Until recently, the battalions of Marxism seemed to have the upper hand over the soldiers of the Cross. In the wake of the Bolshevik Revolution of 1917, Lenin had pledged toleration but delivered terror. 'Russia turned crimson with the blood of martyrs,' says Father Gleb Yakunin, Russian Orthodoxy's bravest agitator for religious freedom. In the Bolsheviks' first five years in power, 28 bishops and 1,200 priests were cut down by the red sickle. Stalin greatly accelerated the terror, and by the end of Khrushchev's rule, liquidation of the clergy reached an estimated 50,000. After World War II, fierce but generally less bloody persecution spread into the Ukraine and the new Soviet bloc, affecting millions of Roman Catholics and Protestants as well as Orthodox." *Time,* December 4, 1989.

- "In private meetings with heads of state, back room consultations with dissident groups and persistent propagandizing for his crusade against tyranny, he [Pope John Paul II] has helped bring about the greatest policy change since the Russian Revolution." *Life,* December 1989.

- "His [Pope John Paul II] triumphant tour of Poland in 1979, says Polish bishop, altered the 'mentality of fear, the fear of police and tanks, of losing your job, of not getting promoted, of being thrown out of school, of failing to get a passport. People learned that if they ceased to fear the system, the system was helpless.' Thus was born Solidarity, backed by the church and led by such friends of the pope as Lech Walesa and Tateusz Mazowieke, who subsequently became the Soviet bloc's first Christian Prime Minister." *Time,* December 4, 1989.

- "In 1935 Josef Stalin, absolute ruler of the Soviet Union, was given some unsolicited advice. Make a propitiatory gesture to the Vatican, he was told. Pushed too far, his country's Catholics might become counter-revolutionary. Stalin's great mustache amplified his sneer. "The Pope. And how many divisions has he?" The answer then was that he has none. The answer now is that he *needs* none. The structures of Communism are crumbling to the touch." *Life,* December 1989.

- "Of all the events that have shaken the Soviet bloc in 1989, none is more fraught with history — or more implausible — than the polite encounter to take place this week in Vatican City. There, in the spacious ceremonial library of the 16th century Apostolic Palace, the czar of world atheism, Mikhail Gorbachev, will visit the Vicar of Christ, Pope John Paul II ... The moment will be electric, not only because John Paul helped inflame the fervor for freedom in his Polish homeland that swept like brush fire across Eastern Europe. Beyond that, the meeting of the two men symbolizes the end of the 20th century's most dramatic spiritual war, a conflict in which the seemingly irresistible force of Communism battered against the immovable object of Christianity ... While Gorbachev's hands-off policy was the immediate cause of the chain reaction of liberty that has swept through Eastern Europe in the past few months, John Paul deserves much of the longer-range credit." *Time,* December 4, 1989.

Note: Here the word "swept" is used, and to sweep away is the definition for "come against like a whirlwind." This event is described as the twentieth century's most dramatic spiritual war, while identifying Gorbachev as the czar of world Atheism as synonymous with being the czar of world Communism. Secular authors recognize Communism as — Atheism.

- "The Triumph Of John Paul II—The tide of freedom washing over Eastern Europe answers his most fervent prayer." *Life,* December, 1989.

Note: The word "overflow" means to "wash away," as with water. Who was choosing the words for these secular reporters?

Appendix 11c — Daniel 11:40 Prophecy Confirmed in the Secular Press

Chariots and Horsemen

- "In 1981, the Communist bloc got another shock. A new American President, Ronald Reagan, began fulfilling his promise to challenge the Soviets, not placate them. Over the next few years, he accelerated the military buildup and announced the Strategic Defense Initiative (SDI), a space-based system for protecting against missile attack. He backed anti-Communist rebels in Nicaragua, Angola, Cambodia, and Afghanistan. And with American troops, he liberated the island of Grenada from Communist thugs … The Soviets' confidence was shaken … The Western Europeans also pressured the Soviets. NATO forged ahead with military modernization. German voters spurned Soviet 'peace overtures' and elected a government that voted to deploy new intermediate-range missiles … Military pressure from America and its Western allies had caused the Soviets to flinch." *Reader's Digest,* March 1990.

With Many Ships

- "Gorbachev has also grasped the fact that political and economic survival depends upon the goodwill of the Soviet people, among whom Christians have always outnumbered Communists. Gorbachev, moreover, needs the cooperation of the West, observes Father Mark, a reform-minded Orthodox priest in Moscow, who considers Gorbachev's program within the U.S.S.R. 'a result of foreign policy necessity.' " *Time,* December 4, 1989.

- "In the 1980s communist economies, always inefficient, went belly up. Before, they had laced consumer and luxury goods. Now perennial shortages of staples worsened as well. When Soviet miners went on strike in 1989, their demands included soap, toilet paper, and sugar." *Reader's Digest,* March 1990.

- "For Gorbachev, the ferment in the Baltics is shaking not just a small corner of the empire built by Lenin and Stalin, but the foundations of the empire itself. The nationalities question is a potent distillation of many other signs, from a crumbling economy to violent ethnic clashes, that the breathtaking disintegration of the Soviet empire in Eastern Europe may not stop at the Soviet border. As the economy deteriorates and shortages grow, public disillusionment with Communism and with Gorbachev himself is rising, and hostile republics, nationalities and interests groups are competing more fiercely for political power and for shares in the shrinking economy. Corruption and crime are rampant; miners and railway workers threaten to cut off fuel supplies during the bitter winter; Azerbaijanis cut the rail line to an Armenian enclave in their midst; farmers hoard food, leaving city shelves bare." *U.S. News and World Report,* January 15, 1990.

The Whirlwind Begins

- "In Poland the freedom movement was born almost three decades ago when the bishop of Krakow sought approval to build a new church. When Communist authorities denied his application, the bishop had a giant cross erected and celebrated open-air masses. The Communists tore it down. The church members replaced it over and over until finally the Communists gave up." *Jubilee,* April 1990.

Note: Who was that bishop of Krakow? None other than Pope John Paul II.

- "With the Pope's support, Solidarity (Polish Labor Union) was formed, and John Paul II sent word to Moscow that if Soviet forces crushed Solidarity, he would go to Poland and stand with his people." *Reader's Digest,* March 1990.

Note: There was an assassination attempt on Pope John Paul II in 1981 apparently ordered by the prophetic "king of the south" — the Soviet Union.

- "In May 1981, before a vast audience in St. Peter's Square, Pope John Paul was shot and severely wounded by Mehmet Ali Agea. There was immediate speculation that the Turkish gunman had been sent by East bloc plotters from Bulgaria, sponsored by the Soviet secret police. Their aim: to silence the one man capable of shaking the foundations of international Communism." *Life,* December 1989.

- "With the Pope's support, Solidarity (Polish Labor Union) was formed, and John Paul II sent word to Moscow that if Soviet forces crushed Solidarity, he would go to Poland and stand with his people. The Soviets were so alarmed that they hatched a plot to kill him … The Pope cautioned Solidarity leaders, particularly his friend Lech Walesa, to proceed slowly. They did. In 1988 General Wojciech Jaruzelski, the Polish Communist leader, went to them offering a deal. Solidarity insisted on an election which it carried with some 80 percent of the vote. When the Communist government fell, the impact on Eastern Europe was electrifying." *Reader's Digest,* March 1990.

- "When Tadeusz Mazowiecki took over in August 1989 as Poland's first non-Communist prime minister in forty-five years, he was asked if he was a socialist. 'I am a Catholic,' he answered tersely." *U.S. News and World Report,* May 21, 1990.

- "Last year Lithuania's two leading bishops were returned to head dioceses after a combined 53 years of internal exile, and the cathedral in Vilnius, previously used as an art museum, was restored for worship. This year the Belorussian republic got its first bishop in 63 years. That paved the way for Archbishop Angelo Sodano, who oversees the Vatican's foreign relations, to make the arrangements for Gorbachev's historic visit to the Holy See.

  "These concessions to Catholicism are only part of Gorbachev's religious liberalization." *Time,* December 4, 1989.

Note: World news presents that Catholicism allied itself with the United States, using economic, social, religious, political, and military pressure to bring about the collapse of Communism. In spite of the wonderful stories of evangelistic triumphs in Eastern Europe, rest assured that the Papacy is rapidly moving to reclaim its former stranglehold upon those countries. Daniel 11:40 teaches that Catholicism will overrun and cross over these countries as she "overflows and passes through."

- *Time magazine, February 24, 1992, chose the title,* **"Holy Alliance,"** to discuss this coming together of the United States and the Vatican as they sought to bring down Communism. According to this magazine, President Reagan and Pope John Paul II agreed, "to undertake a clandestine campaign to hasten the dissolution of the communist empire … The operation was focused on Poland … Both the pope and the president were convinced that Poland could be broken out of the Soviet orbit if the Vatican and the United States committed their resources to destabilizing the Polish government and keeping the outlawed Solidarity movement alive after the declaration of martial law in 1981."

The magazine elaborated on the secret nature of this alliance, and the closeness of the Vatican and the leadership of the United States. It draws the connection between the Vatican and the labor unions, identifying Solidarity as one of the main players in this intrigue. It also labels the use of the USA military, the CIA, labor unions, and finance, as key tools in this collaboration.

Appendix 11D — Catholic Acknowledgements Confirm the Sabbath

The Beginning of Sunday Keeping

If Saturday has always been the Bible Sabbath, **Where did Sunday observance come from?** Protestant secular history records that Sabbath observance was changed from Saturday to Sunday long before there was a Protestant religion, and long before any reformers such as Huss, Jerome, Wycliffe, and Luther.

Constantine's Sunday Law of AD 321

- "On the venerable Day of the Sun let the magistrates and people residing in cities rest, and let all workshops be closed. In the country, however, persons engaged in agriculture may freely and lawfully continue their pursuits; because it often happens that another day is not so suitable for grain-sowing or for vine-planting; lest by neglecting the proper moment for such operations the bounty of heaven should be lost. (Given in the 7th day of March, Crispus and Constantine being consuls each of them for the second time.)" *Codex Justinianus,* lib. 3, tit. 12, 3; translated by Philip Schaff, *History of the Christian Church,* Vol. 3, (1902), p. 380.

- "The festival of Sunday, like all other festivals, was always only a human ordinance, and it was far from the intentions of the apostles to establish a divine command in this respect; far from them and from the early apostolic church, to transfer the laws of the Sabbath to Sunday. Perhaps, at the end of the second century a false application of this kind had begun to take place; for men appear by that time to have considered laboring on Sunday as a sin." Johann Neander, *Neander's Church History,* as translated by Henry John Rose, p. 186.

The Catholic Church claims to have made this change, according to the following quote:

- "The Catholic Church for over one thousand years before the existence of a Protestant, by virtue of her divine mission, changed the day from Saturday to Sunday ... The Protestant world at its birth found the Christian Sabbath too strongly entrenched to run counter to its existence ... The Christian Sabbath is therefore *to this day*, the acknowledged offspring of the Catholic Church as spouse of the Holy Ghost, *without a word or remonstrance from the Protestant World."* *Rome's Challenge, The Catholic Mirror,* September 23, 1893. (Emphasis supplied.)

Protestantism Lost the Reformation at The Council of Trent Because of the Sabbath

- "Many Roman Catholic members at the Council of Trent were ready to accept the Bible and the Bible only when the Archbishop of Reggio came into the council with the following argument to the party who held for Scripture alone: 'The Protestants claim to stand upon the written word only. They profess to hold the Scripture alone as the standard of faith. They justify their revolt by the plea that the church has apostatized from the written word and follows tradition. Now the Protestants claim, that they stand upon the written word only, is not true. Their profession of holding the Scripture alone as the standard of faith, is false. PROOF: The written word explicitly enjoins the observance of the seventh day as the Sabbath. They do not observe the seventh day, but reject it. If they do truly hold the Scripture alone as their standard, they would be observing the seventh day as is enjoined in the Scripture throughout. Yet they not only reject the observance of the Sabbath enjoined in the written word but they have adopted and do practice the observance of Sunday, for which they have only the tradition of the Church. Consequently the claim of Scripture alone as the standard, falls, and the doctrine of 'Scripture and tradition' as essential, is fully established, the Protestants themselves being judges.' " Archbishop Reggio made his speech at the last opening session of Trent, on the 18th of January, 1562. J. H. Holtzman, *Canon and Tradition,* published in Ludwigsburg, Germany, in 1859, p. 263.

Note: There was no getting around this, for the Protestant's own statement of faith — the Augsburg Confession, of 1530 — had clearly admitted that the observation of the Lord's day had been appointed by the church only.

- "They [the Catholics] allege the change of the Sabbath into the Lord's day, contrary, as it seemeth, to the Decalogue; and they have no example more in their mouths than the change of the Sabbath. They will needs have the Church's power to be very great, because it hath dispensed with a precept of the Decalogue." The Augsburg Confession (Lutheran), Part 2, art. 7, in Philip Schaff, *The Creeds of Christendom,* Vol. 3, p. 64.

- "Pope Pius 1566 commanded by council of Trent. 'It pleased the church of God that the religious celebration of the Sabbath day should be transferred to the Lord's day (Sunday).' " *Chatechismus Romanus,* 1867, Chap. 3.

- "The Sunday ... is purely a creation of the Catholic Church." *American Catholic Quarterly Review,* January 1883.

- "Protestants in discarding the authority of the Roman [Catholic] Church, has no good reasons for its Sunday theory, and ought logically to keep Saturday as the Sabbath." John Gilmary Shea, in the *American Catholic Quarterly Review,* January 1883.

- "Sunday ... It is a law of the Catholic . Church alone..." *American Sentinel (Catholic),* June 1893.

- "… the observance of Sunday by Protestants is an homage they pay, in spite of themselves, to the authority of the Catholic Church." Monsignor Louis Segar, *Plain Talk About Protestantism of Today,* p. 213.

The additional following quotes are acknowledgements from Roman Catholic authors about the change of the Sabbath.

- "**Question:** How prove you that the church hath power to command feasts and holy days?
  Answer: By the very act of changing the Sabbath into Sunday, which Protestants allow of; and therefore they fondly contradict themselves, by keeping Sunday strictly and breaking most other feasts commanded by the same Church." H. Tuberville, *An Abridgement of Christian Doctrine,* p. 58.

- "**Question:** Is the observance of Sunday as the day of rest a matter clearly laid down in Scripture?
  Answer: It certainly is not; and yet all Protestants consider the observance of this particular day as essentially necessary to salvation. To say we observe the Sunday because Christ rose from the dead on that day, is to say we act without warrant of Scripture; and we might as well say that we should rest on Thursday, because Christ ascended to heaven on that day, and rested in reality from the work of redemption." Dr. Stephen Keenan, *The Controversial Catechism,* p. 160.

- "**Question:** Have you any other way of proving that the Church has power to institute festivals of precept?
  Answer: Had she not such power, she could not have done that in which all modern religionists agree with her — she could not have substituted the observance of Sunday, the first day of the week, for the observance of Saturday, the seventh day — *a change for which there is no Scriptural authority*." Dr. Stephen Keenan, *A Doctrinal Catechism,* 3rd Edition, p. 174. (Emphasis supplied.)

- "This was the inconsistency of the Protestant practice with the Protestant profession that gave to the Catholic Church her long-sought and anxiously desired ground upon which to condemn Protestantism and the whole Reformation movement as only a selfishly ambitious rebellion against the Church authority. And in this vital controversy the key, the chiefest and culminative expression, of the Protestant inconsistency was in the rejection of the Sabbath of the Lord, the seventh day, enjoined in the Scriptures, and the adoption and observance of the Sunday as enjoined by the Catholic Church.

"And this is today the position of the respective parties to this controversy. Today, as this document shows, this is the vital issue upon which the Catholic Church arraigns Protestantism, and upon which she condemns the course of popular Protestantism as being 'Indefensible,' self-contradictory, and suicidal. What will these Protestants, what will this Protestantism, do?

- "But the Protestant says: How can I receive the teachings of an apostate Church? How, we ask, have you managed to receive her teachings all your life, in direct opposition to your recognized teacher, the Bible, on the Sabbath question." *The Christian Sabbath* 2nd. Ed.; Baltimore; *The Catholic Mirror,* 1893, pp. 29, 30.

- "*Reason and sense demand the acceptance of one or the other of these alternatives; either Protestantism and the keeping holy of Saturday, or Catholicity and the keeping holy of Sunday. Compromise is impossible.*" *The Catholic Mirror,* December 23, 1893. (Emphasis supplied.)

- "You may read the Bible from Genesis to Revelation, and you will not find a single line authorizing the sanctification of Sunday. *The Scriptures enforce the religious observance of Saturday, a day which we never sanctify.*" Cardinal Gibbons, *The Faith Of Our Fathers,* 92nd Edition, p 89. (Emphasis supplied.)

The Roman "Decretalia"

- "He [the pope] can pronounce sentences and judgments in contradiction to the rights of nations, to the law of God and man … He can free himself from the commands of the apostles, he being their superior, and from the rules of the old testament … The Pope has the power to change times, to abrogate laws, and to dispense with all things, over the precepts of Christ." *Decretal, de Translat. Episcop. Cap.*

- "The Pope's will stand for reason. He can dispense above the law; and of wrong make right, by correcting and changing laws." Pope Nicholas, Dist. 96, Quoted in *Facts for the Times,* 1893, pp. 55, 56.

- "Of course the Catholic church claims that the change was her act, and the act is a MARK of her ecclesiastical power." Cardinal Gibbons, *Faith Of Our Fathers.*

- "The Bible says remember that thou keep holy the Sabbath day. The Catholic church says No! By my divine power I abolish the Sabbath day and command you to keep holy the first day of the week. And lo the entire civilized world bows down in reverent obedience to the command of the holy Catholic church. Father Enright, *American Sentinal,* June 1893.

- "She took the pagan Sunday and made it the Christian Sunday … and thus the pagan Sunday, dedicated to Balder, became the Christian Sunday sacred to Jesus." *Catholic World,* March 1894, p. 809.

- "Sunday is a Catholic institution, and its claims to observance can be defended only on Catholic principles ... *From the beginning to the end of Scripture there is not a single passage which warrants the transfer of weekly public worship from the last day of the week to the first.*" *Catholic Press (Sydney),* August 25, 1900. (Emphasis supplied.)

- "If Protestants would follow the Bible, they should worship God on the Sabbath Day. **In keeping the Sunday they are following a law of the Catholic Church.**" Albert Smith, *Chancellor of the Archdiocese of Baltimore,* replying for the Cardinal in a letter dated February 10, 1920. (Emphasis supplied.)

- "Sunday is our mark of authority ... The Church is above the Bible, and this transference of Sabbath observance is proof of that fact." *Catholic Record,* September 1, 1923. (Emphasis supplied.)

- "**Question:** Which is the Sabbath day?
  Answer: Saturday is the Sabbath.
  Question: Why do we observe Sunday instead of Saturday?
  Answer: We observe Sunday instead of Saturday because the Catholic Church in the council of Laodicea [AD 336] transferred the solemnity from Saturday to Sunday." Peter Geiermann, *The Convert's Catechism of Catholic Doctrine,* 1934, p. 50.

- "Nothing in the comportment of Jesus gave the slightest hint that he would have considered it preferable to transfer the Sabbath observance to any other day." *The New Catholic Encyclopedia,* Vol. 12, p. 781.

- "The New Testament makes no explicit mention that the apostles changed the day of worship, but we know it from tradition." *The New Revised Baltimore Catechism (1949),* p. 139. (Emphasis supplied.)

Note: As can be seen, the Sabbath was not changed by God, or by Jesus Christ. Sunday observance is based on tradition!

MATT 15: 3, 6, 9 But He answered and said to them, Why do you also transgress the commandment of God by your tradition? ... ye have made the commandment of God of none effect by your tradition ... But in vain do they worship Me, teaching for doctrines the commandments of men.

"vain" — *Strong's* NT#3155 (through the idea of tentative manipulation, i.e. unsuccessful search, or else of punishment); folly, i.e. (adverbially) to no purpose.

Note: Jesus is saying, "There's no purpose to your worship if you teach man's commandments in place of My Commandments."

- "Sunday is founded not on Scripture, but on tradition, and is a distinctly Catholic institution." *Catholic Record,* September 17, 1893. (Emphasis supplied.)

MARK 7:6, 7, 9 These people honor me with their lips, but their hearts are far from me. 7 They worship me in vain; their teachings are but rules taught by men ... 9 And he said to them, You have a fine way of setting aside the commands of God in order to observe your own traditions. NIV

- "The authority of the church could therefore not be bound to the authority of the Scriptures, because the Church had changed ... the Sabbath into Sunday, not by command of Christ, but by its own authority." *Canon and Tradition,* p. 263. (Emphasis supplied.)

ACTS 20:29, 30 For I know this, that after my departure grievous wolves will come in among you, not sparing the flock; and out of you yourselves will rise up men speaking perverted things, in order to draw away the disciples after themselves.

Vatican II and Sunday

- ANY EFFORT IS TO BE MADE TO MAKE SUNDAY A REST DAY "Moreover, any endeavor that seems to make Sunday a genuine 'day of joy and rest from work' should be encouraged." *Documents of Vatican II,* p. 117.

- "Not the Creator of the Universe, in Genesis 2:1-3, but the Catholic Church 'can claim the honor of having granted man a pause to his work every seven days.' " S. C. Mosna, *'Storia della Dominica,'* 1969, pp. 366-367. (Emphasis supplied.)

From the Jesuit Catechism

- "**Question:** What if the Holy Scriptures command one thing, and the Pope another contrary to it?
  Answer: *The Holy Scriptures must be thrown aside.*"

- "**Question:** What is the Pope?
  Answer: He is the Vicar of Christ, King of Kings, and Lord of Lords, and there is but one Judgment-Seat belonging to God and the Pope." Roy Livesey, 1998, *Understanding the New Age, World Government and World Religion,* p. 104. (Emphasis supplied.)

Dies Domini Encyclical, May 1998

- THE DAY OF REST "64 ... Only in the fourth century did the civil law of the Roman Empire recognize the weekly recurrence, determining that on "the day of the sun" the judges, the people of the cities and the various trade corporation would not work. (107) Christians rejoiced to see thus removed the obstacles which until then had sometimes made observance of the

Lord's day heroic. They could not devote themselves to prayer in common without hindrance. (108) It would therefore be wrong to see in this legislation of the rhythm of the week a mere historical circumstance with no special significance for the Church and which she could simply set aside. Even after the fall of the Empire, the Councils did not cease to insist upon the arrangements regarding Sunday rest. When, through the centuries, she has made laws concerning Sunday rest (109) the Church has had in mind above all the work of servants and workers, certainly not because this work was any less worthy when compared to the spiritual requirements of Sunday observance, but rather because it needed greater regulation to lighten its burden and thus enable everyone to keep the Lord's Day holy. In this matter, my predecessor Pope Leo XIII in his Encyclical Rerum Novarum spoke of Sunday rest as a worker's right which the State must guarantee ... Therefore, also in the particular circumstances of our own time, Christians will naturally strive to ensure that civil legislation respects their duty to keep Sunday holy." *Dies Domini,* May 1998.

- "AD TUENDAM RIDEM, by which certain norms are inserted into the Code of Canon Law and into the Code of Canons of the Eastern Churches." *Catholic World News.*
  Can. 1436 1. Whoever denies or places in doubt any truth that must be believed with divine and Catholic faith, or repudiates the Christian faith as a whole, and does not come to his senses after having been legitimately warned, is to be punished as a heretic or as an apostate by major excommunication; a member of the clergy, furthermore, can be punished by other penalties, not excluding deposition." (Note: the chief Catholic theologian at the time of this encyclical, was Ratzinger, who must have given his approval for this document that all canon law be subjected on everyone.)
  "2. Aside from such cases, whosoever rejects a doctrine proposed, as definitely to be held, by the Roman Pontiff or the College of Bishops exercising their authentic Magisterium, or else accepts a doctrine condemned by them as erroneous, and does not come to his senses after having been legitimately warned, is to be punished by an appropriate penalty.
  "5. We order that everything decreed by Us in this Apostolic Letter motu proprio be firm and valid and we command that it be inserted into the universal law of the Catholic Church that is, into the Code of Canon Law and into the Code of Canons of the Eastern Churches, respectively exactly as set forth above, anything to the contrary notwithstanding." Given at Rome, St. Peter's, 18 May 1998, in the twentieth year of Our Pontificate.

Question: Which law requires that heretics be punished? Pope John Paul II responds:

- Pope John Paul II said: "A person who violates the sanctity of Sunday is to be punished as a heretic." *Detroit News,* July 7, 1998, p. 1.

News Article
POPE LAUNCHES CRUSADE TO SAVE SUNDAY
Sunday Times, May 7, 1998
(in) Apostolic Letter *Dies Domini*
of the Holy Father John Paul II
to Bishops, Clergy and faithful of the Catholic Church
on keeping the Lord's day holy:

- Dies Dierum: Sunday: the Primordial Feast, Revealing the Meaning of Time, "The spiritual and pastoral riches of Sunday, as it has been handed on to us by tradition, are truly great. Significantly, the Catechism of the Catholic Church teaches that 'the Sunday celebration of the Lord's Day and his Eucharist is at the heart of the Church's life.' " *Dies Domini.*

- "As they listen to the word proclaimed in the Sunday assembly, the faithful look to the Virgin Mary, learning from her to keep it and ponder it in their hearts (cf. Luke 2:19). With Mary they learn to stand at the foot of the Cross, offering to the Father the sacrifice of Christ and joining to it the offering of their own lives. With Mary, they experience the joy of the Resurrection, making their own the words of the Magnificat which extol the inexhaustible gift of divine mercy in the inexorable flow of time: 'His mercy is from age to age upon those who fear him:' (Luke 1:50). From Sunday to Sunday, the pilgrim people follow in the footsteps of Mary, and her maternal intercession gives special power and fervour to the prayer which rises from the Church to the Most Holy Trinity." *Dies Domini.*

- "Most Christians assume that Sunday is the biblically approved day of worship. The Roman Catholic Church protests that it transferred Christian worship from the biblical Sabbath (Saturday) to Sunday, and that to try to argue that the change was made in the Bible is both dishonest and a denial of Catholic authority. *If Protestantism wants to base its teachings only on the Bible, it should worship on Saturday.*" *Rome's Challenge,* December 2003, See website: www.Immaculateheart.com/maryonline. (Emphasis supplied.)

Appendix 11D — Catholic Acknowledgements Confirm the Sabbath

Most All of the World Supports Papal Rome

- *"Nowhere in the Bible do we find that Christ or the apostles ordered that the Sabbath be changed from Saturday to Sunday.* We have the commandment of God given to Moses to keep holy the Sabbath day, that is the seventh day of the week, Saturday. Today most Christians keep Sunday because it has been revealed to us by the Church outside the Bible." *The Catholic Virginian,* October 3, 1947. (Emphasis supplied.)

- "In all their official books of instruction Protestants claim that their religion is based on the Bible and the Bible only, and they reject tradition as even a part of their rule of faith … *There is no place in the New Testament where it is distinctly stated that Christ changed the day of worship from Saturday to Sunday. Yet, all Protestants follow tradition in observing Sunday."* *Our Sunday Visitor,* June 11, 1950. (Emphasis supplied.)

- "The observance of Sunday by the Protestants is an homage they pay, in spite of themselves, to the authority of the Catholic Church." Father Segur, *Plain Talk About Protestantism,* p. 213. (Emphasis supplied.)

What Does it Mean to be Ecumenical?

- "The word 'ecumenical' is derived from the Greek term oikoumene, which may be translated as 'the whole inhabited world.' It is in seeing this world as God's that we see ourselves as one. It is in seeing all the world's people as made in God's image that we are called to protect the welfare of every one." (World Council of Churches web page.)

- "The world's major religions in the end all want the same thing, even though they were born in different places and circumstances on this planet. What the world needs today is a convergence of the different religions in the search for and definition of the cosmic or divine laws which ought to regulate our behavior on this planet. World-wide spiritual ecumenism, expressed in new forms of religious cooperation and institutions, would probably be closest to the heart of the resurrected Christ." Muller, R., 1982. *New Genesis: Shaping & Global Spirituality,* Anacortes, WA, *World Happiness and Cooperation,* p. 120.

- "My great personal dream is to get a tremendous alliance between all the major religions and the UN." Muller, R. 1982, *New Genesis: Shaping & Global Spirituality,* Anacortes, WA., *World Happiness and Cooperation,* p. xiii.

- "The final object of ecumenism, as Catholics conceive it, is unity in faith, worship, and the acknowledgement of supreme spiritual authority of the Bishop of Rome." Priest J. Cornell.

- LUTHERAN LEADER SAYS POPE MIGHT BE GLOBAL SPOKESPERSON FOR ALL CHRISTIANS, Friday Church News Notes, July 6, 2001 (David W. Cloud, Fundamental Baptist Information Service, P.O. Box 610368, Port Huron, MI 48061-0368, fbns@wayoflife.org) — "Ishmael Noko, general secretary of the Lutheran World Fellowship, said in March that Lutherans 'can certainly look to the Pope' as 'one of the spiritual leaders in the world today.' He went on to say that the ecumenical movement requires Christians to look into the possibility that the Pope should become the 'global spokesperson for all Christians.' "

- BBC 1 April 2004: "The Pope was the only one to be a world evangelist; he could visit all faiths — Islam and Judaism. He prepared the way for a religious new world order."

On Larry King Live
After the Death of Pope John Paul II, *April 2, 2005:*

- Billy Graham declared the Pope: "The moral leader of the world."

- April 24, 2005 Interviewed on NBC's "Meet the Press," Jesuit priest and *Ignatius Press* founder Jeseph Fessio said: "Those who rebel against the Church's authentic teachings are rebelling against God."

- According to U.S. News & World Report in 1997, Ratzinger warned: "… that the use of Scripture to evaluate Church teaching 'was one of the most dangerous currents to flow out of the Vatican.' " *Defender of the Faith, U.S. News & World Report,* May 2, 2005, p. 38. (Emphasis supplied.)

- Cardinal J. Ratzinger wrote: "Other churches are no sisters of ours, the Vatican insists." *The Independent,* September 5, 2000.

Note: The Roman Catholic Church is not a "sister church" to any other churches, since she is the "mother church" (or the MOTHER OF HARLOTS) that the Protestant churches broke away from.

 REV 17:4-5 And the woman was arrayed in purple and scarlet colour, and decked with gold and precious stones and pearls, having a golden cup in her hand full of abominations and filthiness of her fornication: 5 And upon her forehead was a name written, MYSTERY, BABYLON THE GREAT, THE MOTHER OF HARLOTS AND ABOMINATIONS OF THE EARTH.

Appendix 11D — Catholic Acknowledgements Confirm the Sabbath

The POPE: Leader of World Religious Leaders

- 1999 Interfaith Meeting: "As reported in the Associated Press, with the Dalai Lama, sitting by his right side, this October [1999] in Rome the Pope presided at a special council of some 2000 religious leaders of various faiths, sects, and cults." Dr. Cathy Barns, 2001, *Billy Graham and His Friends,* p. 420.

- "The Pontiff told the assembled Buddhist monks, Zoroastrian priests, Catholic cardinals, Hindu gurus, American Indian shamen, Jewish rabbis, and ecumenical clergy that all must join in condemning the Christian fundamentalists who abuse speech and whose efforts at converting others incite hatred and violence.

  "All present were in accord on two key points: (1) Pope John Paul II was endorsed by consensus as the planet's chief spiritual guide and overseer; and (2) Religious fundamentalists who refuse to go along with the global ecumenical movement are to be silenced. *They must be denounced as 'dangerous extremists' full of hate."* True Bible believers denounced at Papal Conference Power of Prophecy (March 2000, Vol., 2000-03, p. 3.) (Emphasis supplied.)

How does George Bush Feel About Pope Benedict XVI?

- *Time,* May 2, 2005, p. 44: George Bush called Pope Benedict XVI: "A man that serves the Lord."

- President and Mrs. Bush Congratulate Pope Benedict XVI at The South Lawn of The White House. THE PRESIDENT: "Laura and I offer our congratulations to Pope Benedict XVI. He's a man of great wisdom and knowledge. He's a man who serves the Lord. We remember well his sermon at the Pope's funeral in Rome, how his words touched our hearts and the hearts of millions. We join with our fellow citizens and millions around the world who pray for continued strength and wisdom as His Holiness leads the Catholic Church. Thank you all." (This statement is direct from the White House in 2005.)

- "The wall of separation between church and state that was erected by secular humanists, and other enemies of religious freedom, has to come down. *Those opposing our views are the new facists."* Keith Tournier, *Time,* January 1995. (Emphasis supplied.)

Pope Benedict XVI and the Sunday Issue

- SUNDAY MASS SHOULD BE SEEN AS A JOY, SAYS POPE *Catholic Online,* June 12, 2005. VATICAN CITY, JUNE 13, 2005 (Zenit) - "We Can't Live Without It," He Tells Crowd at Angelus. "Sunday Mass is not an imposition but a joy and a need for Catholics," says Benedict XVI.

Events of Pope Benedict's Speech at Bari on May 29, 2005

- Bari (AsiaNews) - "Benedict XVI has once again reaffirmed his priority for a commitment to ecumenism which, he has repeated once again, calls for 'not only words but concrete gestures.' In Bari, celebrating Mass to close the 24th Eucharistic Congress before 200,000 faithful, *the Pope defined Sunday as a necessary instrument* to leave the desert of 'frenetic consumerism, religious indifference and secularism which is closed to transcendence.' ... This Eucharistic congress, which comes to a close today, intended to present Sunday again as a 'weekly Easter,' expression of the identity of the Christian community and center of its life and mission. The theme chosen, *'We Cannot Live Without Sunday.' "* (Emphasis supplied.)

"The Pope Trumpets Sunday" Philadelphia Trumpet November 2005, pp. 1-3

- "In front of 200,000 in the Italian city of Bari, Benedict declared that the *reinforcement of Sunday worship is fundamental to his mission.*"

"Pope Benedict is committed to reinstating the active observance of the Roman Catholic Church's chief icon: SUNDAY. He knows that to popularize religion in Europe, he has to reintroduce a means of promoting what marketers call *brand loyalty. The most historic brand the pope can offer to bond the people together is the ancient day of worship, fashionable since Babylon, the old day of the sun — Sunday.* Hence his promotion of that old Roman brand is his recent addresses."

"Note the terms Pope Benedict used in his May 29 mass to motivate the people to return to this ancient Roman practice: 'Sunday, day of the Lord, is the propitious occasion to draw strength from him, who is the Lord of life. The Sunday precept, therefore, is not a simple duty imposed from outside. To participate in the Sunday celebration and to be nourished with the **Eucharistic bread** *is a need of a Christian,* who in this way can find the necessary energy for the journey [of life] to be undertaken. ... We must rediscover the joy of the Christian Sunday."

"The intensity of the papal commitment to enforcing Sunday worship in Europe was underlined in the pope's statements as reported by one of Italy's most popular conservative newspapers. It reported his words as follows: *'We cannot live without Sunday. ...* The religious *holiday of obligation is not a task imposed from the outside, but a* duty of the Christian.' " *Corriere Dalla Sera,* May 29, 2005. (Emphasis supplied.)

Appendix 11E — Protestant Acknowledgements Confirm the Sabbath

As noted in Appendix 11D, Catholic authors have admitted that their Papal church changed the Sabbath to Sunday.

- "The Catholic Church, for over one thousand years before the existence of a Protestant, by virtue of her divine mission, changed the day from Saturday to Sunday ... The Protestant world, at its birth, found the Christian Sabbath [Sunday] too strongly entrenched to run counter to its existence ... The Christian Sabbath is therefore, to this day, the acknowledged offspring of the Catholic church." *The Catholic Mirror,* September 23, 1893.

Notice: A thousand years before a Protestant even existed this change was made! Yet, scores of Protestant churches are standing guard over a Pagan holiday. They are believing, defending, and guarding a false doctrine that has found its way into the church through tradition, not through Scripture. Most Protestant churches are guarding this doctrine while most of their members know *nothing of its origin.* In the following quotes, Protestant authors from the past have written similar acknowledgements that the Scriptures do not support the doctrine of the Sabbath being changed to Sunday. These statements also portray the shaky foundation on which Sunday observance rests.

Baptist

- "There was and is a commandment to keep holy the Sabbath day, but that Sabbath day was not Sunday ... There is no scriptural evidence of the change of the Sabbath institution from the seventh day to the first day of the week." Dr. Edward T. Hiscox, (author of the *Baptist Manual) New York Ministers Conference,* November 13, 1893.

- "There was never any formal or authoritative change from the Jewish seventh-day Sabbath to the Christian first day observance." William Owen Carver, *The Lord's Day In Our Day,* p. 49.

- "Of course, I quite well know that Sunday did come into use in early Christian history as a religious day, as we learn from the Christian Fathers and other sources. But what a pity that it comes branded with the mark of paganism, and christened with the name of the sun god, when adopted and sanctioned by the papal apostasy, and bequeathed as a sacred legacy to Protestantism!" Dr. Edward T. Hiscox, author of *The Baptist Manual,* in a paper read before a New York Minister's conference held November 16, 1890.

- "The Early Church celebrated the first day of the week as the Lord's day, but to many people the Sabbath is Saturday, which is in the Old Testament Scriptures." Dr. Billy Graham, *Decision,* April 1989, p. 2.

Congregationalist

- "It must be confessed that there is no law in the New Testament concerning the first day." *Buck's Theological Dictionary,* p. 403.

- "There is no command in the Bible requiring us to observe the first day of the week as the Christian Sabbath." Orin Fowler, A.M., *Mode and Subjects of Baptism.*

- "The current notion that Christ and His apostles authoritatively substituted the first day for the seventh, is absolutely without any authority in the New Testament." Dr. Lyman Abbott, *Christian Union,* January 19, 1882.

- "The Christian Sabbath [Sunday] is not in the Scriptures, and was not by the primitive church called the Sabbath." *Dwight's Theology,* Vol. 4, p. 401.

- "It is quite clear that, however rigidly or devoutly we may spend Sunday, we are not keeping the Sabbath ... The Sabbath was founded on a specific, divine command. We can plead no such command for the obligation to observe Sunday ... There is not a single sentence in the New Testament to suggest that we incur any penalty by violating the supposed sanctity of Sunday." R. W. Dale, D.D., *The Ten Commandments,* pp. 106, 107.

Lutheran

- "The observance of the Lord's day [Sunday] is founded not on any command of God, but on the authority of the Church." Augsburg Confession Of Faith, quoted in *The Catholic Sabbath Manual,* Part 2, Chapter 1, Section 10.

- "The seventh day He [God] did sanctify for Himself. This had the special purpose of making us understand that the seventh day in particular should be devoted to divine worship. Although man lost his knowledge of God, nevertheless God wanted this commandment about sanctifying the Sabbath to remain in force." Martin Luther, Comments on Genesis 2:3, *Luther's Works.*

- "They [the popes] allege the change of the Sabbath into the Lord's day, contrary as it seemeth, to the Decalogue; and they have no example more in their mouths than the change of the Sabbath. They will needs have the church's power to be very great, because it hath dispensed with a precept of the Decalogue." Philip Schaff quoting Martin Luther, *The Creeds of Christendom,* Vol. 3, p. 64.

Appendix 11E — Protestant Acknowledgements Confirm the Sabbath

Episcopal

- "Is there any command in the New Testament to change the day of weekly rest from Saturday to Sunday? None." *Manual of Christian Doctrine*, p. 28.

- "We have made a change from the seventh day to the first day, from Saturday to Sunday, on the authority of the one holy Catholic and apostolic church of Christ." *Why We Keep Sunday*, p. 28.

- "Not any ecclesiastical writer of the first three centuries attributed the origin of Sunday observance either to Christ or to His apostles." Sir William Domville, *Examination Of The Six Texts*, pp. 6, 7 (Supplement).

- "Where are we told in Scripture that we are to keep the first day at all? We are commanded to keep the seventh; but we are nowhere commanded to keep the first day … The reason why we keep the first day of the week holy instead of the seventh is for the same reason that we observe many other things, not because the Bible, but because the church has enjoined it." Isaac Williams, D.D., *Plain Sermons On The Catechism*, Vol. 1, pp. 334-336.

- "The Bible commandment says on the seventh day thou shalt rest. That is Saturday. Nowhere in the Bible is it laid down that worship should be done on Sunday." Phillip Carrington, *Toronto Daily Star*, October 26, 1949.

Church of England

- "The seventh day of the week has been deposed from its title to obligatory religious observance, and its prerogative has been carried over to the first, under no direct precept of Scripture." William E. Gladstone, *Later Gleanings*, p. 342.

- "There is no word, no hint, in the New Testament about abstaining from work on Sunday … Into the rest of Sunday no divine law enters … The observance of Ash Wednesday or Lent stands on exactly the same footing as the observance of Sunday." Canon Eyton, *Ten Commandments*, pp, 62, 63, 65.

- "The Saturday is called amongst them by no other name than that which formerly it had, the Sabbath. So that whenever, for a thousand years and upwards, we meet with *Sabbatum* in any writer of what name so ever, it must be understood of no day but Saturday." Peter Heylyn, *History of the Sabbath*, Part 2, Chapter 2, Section 12.

Methodist

- "Take the matter of Sunday … there is no passage telling Christians to keep that day, or to transfer the Jewish Sabbath to that day." H. F. Rall, *Christian Advocate*, July 2, 1942.

- "The reason we observe the first day instead of the seventh is based on no positive command. One will search the Scriptures in vain for authority for changing from the seventh day to the first." Clovis G. Chappell, *Ten Rules for Living*, p. 61.

- "It is true there is no positive command for infant baptism … nor is there any for keeping holy the first day of the week." Dr. Binney, M. W., *Theological Compendium*, p. 103.

- "There is no intimation here that the Sabbath was done away with or that its moral use was superseded, by the introduction of Christianity." Adam Clarke, *The New Testament of Our Lord and Savior Jesus Christ*, New York, Vol. 2, p. 524.

Anglican

- "Reverend Philip Carrington, Anglican Archbishop of Quebec, sent local clergymen into a huddle today by saying outright that there was nothing to support Sunday being kept holy. Carrington definitely told a church meeting in this city of straight laced Protestantism that tradition, not the Bible, had made Sunday the day of worship." *Toronto Daily Star*, October 26, 1949.

- "Almost all churches throughout the world celebrate the sacred mysteries (the Lord's supper) on the Sabbath of every week … yet the Christians of Alexandria and at Rome, on account of some ancient tradition, have ceased to do this." *Ecclesiastical History*, Bk. 5, Ch. 22, NPNF 2nd Series, Vs., p. 132.

- "Many people think that Sunday is the Sabbath, but neither in the New Testament nor in the early church, is there anything to suggest that we have any right to transfer the observance of the seventh day of the week to the first. The Sabbath was and is Saturday and not Sunday …" Rev. Lionel Beere, *Church and People*, September 1, 1947.

Moody Bible Institute

- "The Sabbath was binding in Eden and it has been in force ever since. This fourth commandment begins with the word, 'Remember,' showing that the Sabbath already existed when God wrote the law on the tables of stone at Sinai. How can men claim that this one commandment has been done away with when they will admit that the other nine are still binding?" Dwight L. Moody, *Weighed and Wanting*, p. 47.

- "We have abundant evidence both in the New Testament and in the early history of the church to prove that gradually Sunday came to be observed instead of the Jewish Sabbath, apart from any specific commandment." Norman C. Deck, *Moody Bible Institute Monthly*, November 1936, p. 138.

Appendix 11E — Protestant Acknowledgements Confirm the Sabbath

Presbyterian

- "A change of the day to be observed from the last day of the week to the first. There is no record, no express command authorizing this change." N. L. Rice, *The Christian Sabbath,* p. 60.

- "The Sabbath is a part of the Decalogue, the Ten Commandments. This alone forever settles the question as to the perpetuity of the institution … Until, therefore, it can be shown that the whole Moral Law has been repealed, the Sabbath will stand … The teaching of Christ confirms the perpetuity of the Sabbath." T. C. Black D.D., *Theology Condensed,* pp. 474-475.

- "God instituted the Sabbath at the creation of man, setting apart the seventh day for that purpose, and imposed its observance, as a universal and perpetual moral obligation upon the race." Dr. Archibald Hodges, Tract No. 175 of the Presbyterian Board of Publication.

Waldensian Observance of the Sabbath

- "The Reformers held that the Waldensian Church was formed about 120 A.D., from which date on, they passed down from father to son the teachings they received from the apostles." B. G. Wilkinson, *Our Authorized Bible Vindicated,* p. 35.

Note: Down through the ages God has always had His people who observe His Holy Days. God preserved the true Christian faith through the Waldenses who were probably converts of the apostles and maintained their faith for centuries.

- "That the heresy of those he calls Waudois, or poor people of Lyons, was of great antiquity. Mongst all sects, saith he, cap. 4. that either are or have been, there is none more dangerous to the Church than that of the Leonists, and that for three reasons: the first is, because it is the sect that is of the longest standing of any; for some say it hath been continued down ever since the time of Pope Sylvester, and others, ever since that of the Apostles. The second is, because it is the most general of all sects; for scarcely is there any country to be found, where this sect hath not spread itself." Peter Allix D.D., *The Ecclesiastical History of the Ancient Churches of the Piedmont and the Albigenses,* p. 185.

- "… it can be seen that Sunday in the early Christian centuries was not a holy day of divine appointment, but was rather, appointed by man, and physical labor was carried on. From the quotations of church historians which follow, it will be seen that in the churches of the East as well as in all the churches of the West, except Rome, the Sabbath was publicly observed by those who were courageous enough to withstand the rising tide of those endeavoring to appease a sun-worshiping heathen world which gave special prominence to Sunday. In Contrast to the questionable beginnings of Sunday, consider the seventh-day Sabbath at the same time. The following two quotations have been given before, but are worthy of repetition. Socrates, a church historian of the fourth century, wrote thus: 'For although almost all the churches throughout the world celebrate the sacred mysteries on the Sabbath of every week, yet the Christians of Alexandria and at Rome, on account of some ancient tradition, have ceased to do this.' " (Socrates, *Ecclesiastical History,* b. 5, ch. 22, found in Nicene and Post-Nicene Fathers, 2nd Series, Vol. 2.)" B. G. Wilkinson, *Truth Triumphant,* p. 256.

- "Another quotation from the church historian, Sozomen, who was a contemporary of Socrates, declares: 'The people of Constantinople, and almost everywhere, assemble together on the Sabbath, as well as on the first day of the week, which custom is never observed at Rome or at Alexandria.' " (Sozomen, *Ecclesiastical History*, b. 7, ch. 19, found in Nicene and Post-Nicene Fathers, 2nd Series, Vol. 2.)" B. G. Wilkinson, *Truth Triumphant,* p. 256.

- "The Waldenses were so thoroughly a Bible people that they kept the seventh-day Sabbath as the sacred rest day for centuries. Two centuries after Pope Gregory I (A.D. 602) had issued the bull against the community of Sabbathkeepers in the city of Rome, a church council which disclosed the extent of Sabbathkeeping in that peninsula was held at Friaul, northern Italy (c. A.D. 791). Friaul was one of the three large duchies into which the Lombard kingdom had been originally organized. This council, in its command to all Christians to observe the Lord's Day, testified to the wide observance of Saturday as follows: 'Further when speaking of that Sabbath which the Jews observe, the last day of the week, which also all peasants observe.' (Mansi, Sacrorum Conciliorum Nova et Amplissima Collectio, Vol. 13, p. 852.) About one hundred years later (A.D. 865-867), when the sharp contest between the Church of Rome and the Greek Church over the newly converted Bulgarians and their observance of the Sabbath came to the front, the question again entered into the controversy, as can be seen in the reply of Pope Nicolas I to the one hundred six questions propounded to him by the Bulgarian king." (Peter Allix, *The Ancient Churches of Piedmont,* p. 154 as on CD paging from Ages Software.)

THE STRUCTURE OF DANIEL

FOUR VISIONS REVEAL GOD'S PLAN TO SAVE HIS PEOPLE

One Major Line of Prophecy From 606 BC — to the Establishment of Christ's Kingdom

VISION 1 - DAN 2	VISION 2 - DAN 7	VISION 3 - DAN 8	VISION 4 - DAN 10-12
HEAVENLY SCENE	**HEAVENLY SCENE**	**HEAVENLY SCENE**	**HEAVENLY SCENE**
DAN 2:1, 19 GOLD HEAD SILVER BREAST & ARMS BRASS BELLY & THIGHS **IRON LEGS** IRON & CLAY — FEET & TOES	**DAN 7:2-14** LION BEAR LEOPARD **DREADFUL BEAST** **LITTLE HORN**	**DAN 8:2-14** RAM HE GOAT "OUT OF ONE OF THEM" LITTLE HORN "WAXED EXCEEDING GREAT"	**DAN 10:1** **KINGS OF THE NORTH** AND **KINGS OF THE SOUTH** OF **EARTHLY KINGDOMS**
INTERLUDE QUESTION	**INTERLUDE QUESTION**	**INTERLUDE QUESTION**	**INTERLUDE QUESTION**
DAN 2:26 WHAT IS THE SECRET OF THE DREAM?	**DAN 7:16** WHAT IS THE TRUTH OF ALL THIS?	**DAN 8:15** WHAT IS THE MEANING OF THIS VISION?	**DAN 10:14** WHAT SHALL BEFALL THY PEOPLE IN THE LATTER DAYS?
HISTORIC-PROPHETIC OUTLINE	**HISTORIC-PROPHETIC OUTLINE**	**HISTORIC-PROPHETIC OUTLINE**	**HISTORIC-PROPHETIC OUTLINE**
DAN 2:36-43 BABYLON MEDO-PERSIA GREECE ROME (PAGAN IMPERIAL)	**DAN 7:17-25** BABYLON MEDO-PERSIA GREECE ROME (PAGAN IMPERIAL) ROME (PAPAL NO. 1)	**DAN 8:20-25** (BABYLON IS REIGNING) MEDO-PERSIA GREECE ROME (PAGAN IMPERIAL) ROME (PAPAL NO. 1) ROME (PAPAL NO. 2)	**DAN 11:1-45** (BABYLON HAS FALLEN) MEDO-PERSIA GREECE ROME (PAGAN IMPERIAL) ROME (PAPAL NO. 1) ROME (PAPAL NO. 2) ROME (PAPAL N.W.O.)
OUTLINE EXTENDS TO: AD 476	**OUTLINE EXTENDS TO:** AD 1798	**OUTLINE EXTENDS TO:** AD 1844	**OUTLINE EXTENDS TO:** THE END OF TIME
ANSWER TO QUESTION	**ANSWER TO QUESTION**	**ANSWER TO QUESTION**	**ANSWER TO QUESTION**
DAN 2:44 GOD OF HEAVEN CONSUMES ALL THESE KINGDOMS!	**DAN 7:26** JUDGMENT SITS WITH THE "ANCIENT OF DAYS!"	**DAN 8:25** HE [PERSECUTOR] SHALL STAND UP AGAINST <u>THE</u> "PRINCE!"	**DAN 12:1** MICHAEL STANDS UP AGAINST THE PERSECUTOR!
ENDTIME EVENT	**ENDTIME EVENT**	**ENDTIME EVENT**	**ENDTIME EVENT**
DAN 2:45 "STONE KINGDOM" SECOND COMING OF JESUS	**DAN 7:27** "KINGDOM GIVEN TO THE SAINTS"	**DAN 8:25** "PERSECUTOR BROKEN WITHOUT HAND"	**DAN 12:1-3** "GOD'S PEOPLE ARE DELIVERED"

Note: Only God pulls back the curtain of time in each vision to reveal future events.

Understanding the Chart: Daniel's Epilogue (Daniel 12:5-13)

Epilogue Given by Jesus

Introduction

The Chart for Daniel's Epilogue is found on page 369. The last nine verses in the Book of Daniel are known as the Epilogue and are the most controversial, and misunderstood verses in the whole Book. **When** the **structure** of the first three visions is understood, **then** the Fourth Vision will also be correctly understood. The Epilogue is the last part of the Fourth Vision that ushers in the Second Coming. Daniel understood the first four Historic-Prophetic Outlines, **but** he did not understand the three timelines in the Epilogue. **He had NOT seen this part of the prophecy given in this kind of word picture before.** Daniel asked ONE question (12:6) and he received three very brief answers (in the form of three timelines). This still did not give him understanding. He was told the words were closed up and sealed till the end of time. Daniel wrote down the Epilogue at the end of his Book, even though he did not understand it. The complete answers to Daniel's question on the three timelines are NOT found in Daniel's Book, but rather in Revelation, where John reveals all the information about endtime events just before Jesus returns to this earth. Understanding the **structure** and correct use of the **Prophetic Keys** is necessary to comprehend Daniel's Book.

Definition: *"Epilogue"* — How the work is finished.
Webster's Dictionary

Note: **The Epilogue is the most important part of Daniel's Book** and presents a general question of, "How long shall it be to the end of these wonders?" The answer follows in three timelines that throw a flood of light on events that will transpire right up to the very "eve" of the Second Coming of Jesus. In Daniel's Epilogue, Jesus is the main character. Jesus Christ gives a detailed explanation of how He will finish the work and overcome all the earthly persecutors of His people. This theme is carried forward and elaborated upon in Revelation.

EPILOGUE [GENERAL] QUESTION:

DAN 12:6 How long shall it be to the end of these wonders?

EPILOGUE ANSWER GIVEN IN THREE TIMELINES:

1. DAN 12:7 Persecution of God's people will last 1260 days.
2. DAN 12:11 Persecutor will reign for 1290 days.
3. DAN 12:12 God's people must wait 1335 days for the blessing.

DANIEL'S EPILOGUE
THE EPILOGUE FOR ALL FOUR VISIONS
Endtime Events Fulfilled in Three Timelines of "Literal Days"

Jesus as the **Main Character**
Gives the **Epilogue**

- An **Epilogue** is given at the end of a historical opera or play. After the play is finished and the curtain closes, the main character comes out and explains the historical significance to the audience.
- **Daniel's Epilogue** (or summary) is explained by Jesus Christ as the "closing up period" that begins with the rule of the Seventh Kingdom. This includes all the events of the three timelines in Daniel 12:5-13 to the very "eve" of Christ's Second Coming.

EPILOGUE [GENERAL] QUESTION:

Daniel 12:6 How long shall it be to the <u>end</u> of these wonders?

EPILOGUE ANSWER GIVEN IN THE FOLLOWING THREE TIMELINES

QUESTION: How long will God's people be persecuted?
ANSWER: Daniel 12:7
Persecution of God's people will last 1260 days.

QUESTION: How long will the persecutor reign?
ANSWER: Daniel 12:11
The persecutor will be crushed after 1290 days and none shall help him.

QUESTION: How long must God's people wait for the Blessing?
ANSWER: Daniel 12:12
Wait 1335 days for the Blessing.

Note: The **Epilogue** includes the last three timelines that begin and end *during the reign* of the seventh earthly kingdom.

Papal Rome's leader of the New World Order is the **KEY** player of the Seventh Kingdom of the Fourth Historic-Prophetic Outline <u>and</u> in the Epilogue verses of Daniel 12:7, 11, and 12. The Epilogue is given full interpretation in the second prophetic Book of Revelation.

THE EPILOGUE ENDS AT THE VERY "EVE" OF CHRIST'S SECOND COMING

Daniel's Four Visions are "almost" totally fulfilled.
Upon complete fulfillment of the Epilogue timelines,
the Stone Kingdom of Jesus will be set up.

CHAPTER 12

The Fourth Vision
Extends Through
<u>The Epilogue</u>
of Daniel 12:5-13

DANIEL'S EPILOGUE
VISION FOUR

(CONCLUSION OF
ALL FOUR VISIONS)

*Daniel Overhears an
Intended Conversation*

5 Then I Daniel looked, and, behold, there stood other two, the one on this side of the bank of the river [Hiddekel]**, and the other on that side of the bank of the river.**

6 And one said to the man clothed in linen, [Michael/Jesus] **which was** <u>upon the waters of the river</u> ...

*The Epilogue's
General Question*

6 ... How long shall it be to the <u>end</u> **of these wonders?**

Prophetic Key #7 As prophecy is fulfilled, God's people will know where they are in the stream of time.

Prophetic Kay #13 More information is given in this part of the vision.

Reminder: See **The Structure of Daniel** Chart on page 367. Note that all Four Historic-Prophetic Outlines have been fully explained in the visions of Daniel. The EPILOGUE chart on page 369, along with the verses in Daniel 12:5-13 (and Revelation), explain how each of these visions will end in the last part of the Fourth Vision. All of Daniel's Fourth Vision is written in <u>literal language</u>. Daniel hears the Epilogue questions being directed to Michael [Son of God], and three short answers are given in return. (The charts on pages 384-385 will be helpful for the study of this Epilogue.)

Prophetic Keys #18 and 19 There are no symbols used in the last part of this vision. The timelines are to be interpreted as prophetic literal time.

<u>DANIEL'S EPILOGUE</u>

Definition
How the work is finished.

**EPILOGUE
[GENERAL] QUESTION**

How long shall it be to the
<u>end</u> of these wonders?
DAN 12:6

**Jesus, the Main Character,
Gives the Epilogue**

Verses 5-6

DAN 8:13 Then I heard one saint speaking, and another saint which spake, said unto the certain *saint* Palmone [margin reference for Palmone: Jesus the wonderful Numberer, Revealer of Secrets].

DAN 10:5 Then I lifted up mine eyes, and looked, and behold a certain man <u>clothed in linen</u>.

Note: Verse 6 describes Jesus as the High Priest in the typical garment that was worn on the Day of Atonement. This event began in heaven in the year AD 1844. This is also a "Theophany" or vision of God. (Review Daniel 8:13, 15-16 on pages 140 and 142.)

The answer to the General Epilogue Question is given in another three short questions and answers in verses 7, 11, and 12.

**Jesus in Dialogue
With Two Others**

"end" — *Strong's* OT# 7093 "getes," pronounced *kates*. Means: <u>utmost end</u>, termination point, <u>Border edge</u> [of time]. **Note:** The timeframe of the 1260 years of the Dark Ages, is NOT the *utmost end of time*.

The Forward Progressive Movement of the Book of Daniel

Daniel 2	Babylon	Medo-Persia	Greece	Rome (Pagan)				"Stone Kingdom"
				AD 476				
Daniel 7	Babylon	Medo-Persia	Greece	Rome (Pagan)	Rome (Papal 1)			"Kingdom Given to the Saints"
					AD 1798			
Daniel 8	Babylon	Medo-Persia	Greece	Rome (Pagan)	Rome (Papal 1)	(Judgment of Man)		"Rome (Papal 2) is Broken"
						AD 1844		
Daniel 11-12:4		Medo-Persia	Greece	Rome (Pagan)	Rome (Papal 1)	Rome (Papal 2)	Rome (Papal NWO) (Endtime)	"Comes to his End"
Daniel 12:5-13	EPILOGUE					Timeframe of the Dark Ages		THREE TIMELINES 1260 Literal Days 1290 Literal Days 1335 Literal Days

THE STRUCTURE OF THE BOOK OF DANIEL

Reveals the Recapping Structure of the Four Historic-Prophetic Outlines and

THE FORWARD, PROGRESSIVE MOVEMENT OF THE BOOK IN DATABLE TIME FROM: 606 BC — TO THE END OF TIME

The "Truth" of Daniel's Structure

1. The Daniel 2 Outline reveals the rise and fall of the first Four Kingdoms. The red dotted line indicates the large *gap of time* with no information between AD 476 and the establishment of the Stone Kingdom.
2. The Daniel 7 Outline reveals the rise and fall of a Fifth Kingdom, which was larger and lasted longer than any before it. The *gap of time* has now been shortened considerably from AD 1798 to when the "saints receive the kingdom."
3. The Daniel 8 Outline recaps and enlarges the explanation of Daniel 7 and reveals the Sixth Kingdom. The *gap of time* is shortened a bit more from AD 1844 to the end of the world.
4. The Fourth Outline of Daniel 11 brings the action to the end of time, revealing all seven persecuting kingdoms. The last Roman Kingdom, will be a One World Order with a Papal head.

The recapping of the four Outlines assures the prophetic expositor that he is headed in the right direction. Each additional Outline adds more details, filling in the gap between the fall of Rome and the endtime. Each additional Outline brings the actions forward in time, and ends with divine events related to the Second Coming of Jesus. The **green diagonal line** extends from AD 476 **forward** to the Epilogue timelines. These future timelines explain how the work of salvation is finished at the very end of time, just before the Second Coming of Christ.

The "*Dismantling*" of Daniel's Structure

Unfortunately, there are many misinterpretations of the three timelines in Daniel 12. Instead of allowing these timelines to have their proper *future fulfillment,* they have been tampered with. Sometimes, all three timelines are forced backwards into the era of the Dark Ages (AD 538-1798). The result is indicated by the orange arrow and box. In the Structure of Daniel, the Outlines always move forward in time. Therefore, the timelines in Daniel 12 must follow this pattern and move forward from the last kingdom in the Daniel 11 Outline, to the *end of this world.*

Prophetic exposition that *dismantles* the future application of the timelines, creates confusion. This misrepresentation:

1. Does not permit Daniel 12:5-13 to answer the question of "How long shall it be to the ***end*** of all these wonders?"
2. Takes the three timelines out of their Epilogue setting and places them back many centuries, thereby violating the structure of the "Forward, Progressive Movement" of Daniel's Book; (See Appendix 12B.)
3. Wrests the timelines out of their literal language context, of *literal days* and assigns them the prophetic symbolic meaning of *literal years*. This is a misapplication of the literal context of the Fourth Vision;
4. Obscures the focus of the final controversy;
5. Destroys the linkage between DAN 12 and REV 13;
6. Denies prophetic insight into current events.

Jesus Takes an Oath and Gives Answers

DANIEL'S EPILOGUE

FIRST QUESTION

HOW LONG WILL GOD'S PEOPLE BE PERSECUTED?

ANSWER

DAN 12:7

PERSECUTION WILL LAST 1260 DAYS!

*Daniel Sees **Jesus** Take an Oath to Tell the Truth in Answering the Question*

7 And I heard the man clothed in <u>linen</u>, [Michael/Jesus] **which was <u>upon the waters</u> of the river, when he held up his <u>right hand</u> and his <u>left hand</u> unto heaven, and <u>sware</u> by him that liveth for ever ...**

(The last part of this verse is given on the next page.)

 Prophetic Key #7 As prophecy is fulfilled, God's people will know where they are in the stream of time.

Prophetic Kay #13 More information is given in this part of the vision on the last three timelines of Daniel.

HEB 6:13 For when God made promise to Abraham, because he could <u>swear</u> by no greater, he <u>sware</u> by himself.

REV 10:5-6 And the angel which I saw stand upon the sea and upon the earth lifted up his hand to heaven, 6 And <u>sware</u> by him that liveth for ever and ever, who created heaven ... and the earth ... and the sea.

Verse 7

"linen" — *Strong's* OT#906 <u>bad</u>; perhaps from OT#909 (in the sense of divided fibres); flaxen thread or yarn; hence, a linen garment: KJV - linen.

Note: *"bad"* (pronounced *"bod"*) is the description of the linen garment that was worn by the High Priest on the typical Day of Atonement. (See LEV 16:4.) The rest of the year, the *glorious garments,* (including blue, purple, scarlet, and gold), were worn, over the white linen. *The glorious garments were taken off on the Day of Atonement.* In this verse, Daniel notices only a white linen garment which is a description of the garment of Jesus our High Priest in the Most Holy Place of the Heavenly Sanctuary, during the heavenly *Day of Atonement* that began in AD 1844. (See DAN 8:14.)

Prophetic Key #12 The verse sequencing is moving time forward, beginning with AD 1844. Therefore, to maintain continuity, the following verses must also move forward in time.

"man ... upon the waters" — No man, but Jesus was capable of walking on the water.

MATT 14:25 And in the fourth watch of the night Jesus went unto them, <u>walking on the sea.</u>

"right hand" — *Strong's* OT#3225 the right hand or side of a person or other object (as the stronger and more dexterous); <u>locally, the south.</u>

"left hand" — *Strong's* OT#8040 [through the idea of wrapping up]; properly, dark (as enveloped), i.e. <u>the north;</u> hence (by orientation), the left hand.

"sware" — *Strong's* OT#7650 to seven oneself, i.e. swear (<u>as if by repeating a declaration seven times</u>): KJV - adjure, charge (by an oath, with an oath), feed to the full.

Note: No greater oath than this could ever be sworn.

Jesus Takes an Oath and Gives Answers

Jesus held up both hands as a <u>double promise</u> to His people that all things will be finished in the prophetic time.

Jesus Answers the Question of "How Long?" With a Timeline of 1260 Literal Days

7 ... that it shall be for a time,* times, and an half ...

**"time"* — Strong's OT#4150 moed`, an appointed time.

Daniel Sees an Endtime Persecutor

7 ... and when he [Papal "king of the north"] **shall have accomplished to scatter** [shatter and disperse] **the power** [and Loud Cry] **of the holy people, all these things** [1260 literal days] **shall be finished.**

Verse 7 (Concluded)

Prophetic Keys #24 a/d and #25 These keys gives the correct way to calculate the term *time* in the literal context of the Fourth Vision. Because of the literal context of Daniel 11 and 12, *"a time, times, and an half"* — must be counted as prophetic *literal* time (i.e. 1260 literal days).

Note: The last *Loud Cry* is also dispersed during the 1260 literal days.

"accomplished" and *"finished"* — Strong's OT#3615 to end, whether intransitive (to cease, be finished, perish) or transitive (to complete, prepare, consume): -accomplish, cease ... destroy (utterly), make clean riddance.

DAN 8:24 And his power shall be mighty ... and shall destroy the mighty and the holy people.

"scatter" — Strong's OT#5310 to dash to pieces, or scatter: KJV - be beaten in sunder, break (in pieces), broken, dash (in pieces), cause to be discharged, dispersed, be overspread, scatter.

Note: Persecution of God's people (during the reign of the last persecutor) will last no longer than 1260 literal days. *Timelines* are not shortened, but the days of persecution can be shortened.

MATT 24:21-22 For then shall be great tribulation, such as was not since the beginning of the world to this time 22 but for the elect's sake those days [of persecution] shall be shortened.

Prophetic Keys #26 and #27 All timelines "begin and end" with *voices* or *legislative decrees.*

Prophetic Key #12 Prophecy is usually understood at the time of fulfillment.

Thunder No. 3
(Beginning Voice)
REV 13:5-7
Voice of the Beast "Universal Sunday Law" (USL)

Thunder No. 5
(Ending Voice)
REV 13:15
Beast's Voice for "Universal Death Decree"

1260 Days of Persecution on God's People
"... he [persecutor] shall ... scatter the holy people." DAN 12:7

(Note: "Thunders" are assigned a random number. See Appendix 12A, pages 384-385.)

Prophetic Timeline #5: Details and Specifics

Timeline #5 (Length of Timeline)	Subject (of Timeline)	Prophetic Scripture For Timeline	Timeline Begins (with)	Speaking VOICE (Thunder No. 3)	Timeline Ends (with)	Legislative & Judicial Action (Thunder No. 5)
1260 Literal Days (Future)	Persecution of God's "Holy People"	DAN 12:7 and REV 13:5-7, 15	Persecution of God's People - ALL the Wicked Worship the Beast (Future)	Legislation of Universal Sunday Law by Papal Rome New World Order (Future)	Legislated Universal Death Decree for God's People (Future)	Legislative Voice for Universal Death Decree REV 13:15 (Future)

*The Timeline Will Not Be
Understood Until the Endtime*

8 And I heard, but I understood not: then said I, O my Lord, what shall be the <u>end</u> of these things?

9 And he said, Go thy way, Daniel: for the <u>words</u> [the matter] **are closed up and sealed till the time of the <u>end</u>** ["border end" when time for this earth ends].

*Only the Wise Will Understand
the "Three Timelines"
in Daniel 12:7, 11, and 12*

10 Many <u>shall be purified</u>, and made white, and tried; but <u>the wicked shall do wickedly</u>: and none of the wicked shall understand; but <u>the wise</u> [those that seek with all their heart] **<u>shall understand</u>.**

<u>Verses 8-9</u>

Jesus gave Daniel the answer to his question raised in verse 6 in the *words* of the Epilogue of Daniel 12:7-12. Daniel 10:1 records he understood the Fourth Historic-Prophetic Outline. Daniel also understood the 1260 year timeline of Daniel 7:25; but **he did not understand** this 1260 literal day timeline because he had not seen it before. *The meaning of the words were to be sealed till the endtime or the time just before the Second Coming of Jesus.* Daniel was told that the endtime generation would understand. (DAN 12:10)

Daniel is told the "words" of the three timelines are closed up and sealed till the "endtime" generation.

"<u>words</u>" — Strong's OT#1697 a word; by implication, <u>a matter</u> (as spoken of) or thing.

"<u>end</u>" — Strong's OT#7093 qets (kates); contracted from **OT#7112**: an extremity ... KJV - after, (<u>utmost</u>) <u>border, end</u>. (**Note:** AD 1798 or 1844 are <u>not</u> the utmost, border end of time.)

OT#7112 qatsats (kaw-tsats'); <u>to chop off</u> (literally or figuratively): KJV - cut (asunder, in pieces, in sunder, off), utmost.

<u>Verse 10</u>

God's People "shall be purified"

ZECH 13:9 And <u>I will</u> bring the third part through the fire, and will <u>refine them as silver is refined, and will try them as gold is tried</u>: they shall call on my name, and I will hear them: I will say, It is my people: and they shall say, The LORD is my God.

*The Wicked Will Not
Understand the Truths
of Prophetic Scripture and
"shall do wickedly"*

JOHN 8:47 He that is of God heareth God's words: <u>ye therefore hear them not, because ye are not of God</u>.

*"the wise shall understand"
the Prophetic Truths
of God's Word*

JOHN 14:29 And now I have told you before it come to pass, that, when it is come to pass, ye might believe.

Note: Review DAN 12:3 — "wise." (See: MARK 13:29; LUKE 21:28, 31.)

DANIEL

The Story of the Rise and Fall of Earthly Kingdoms

DANIEL'S EPILOGUE

SECOND QUESTION

HOW LONG WILL
THE PERSECUTOR REIGN?

ANSWER

DAN 12:11

THE PERSECUTOR WILL
BE CRUSHED AFTER
1290 DAYS!

The Persecutor Will Reign For
1290 Literal Days,
Before he is Crushed

The Sovereignty of the Nations
(the "Daily")
Will be Taken Away

11 And from the time that the daily ~~sacrifice~~ **shall be taken away ...**

Verse 11

Reminder: *"sacrifice"* is a supplied word.

Note: The last persecutor will begin his reign with the persecution of God's people as prophecy states in Revelation 13:5-7. Before this can be accomplished, the persecutor must seize the *"daily,"* or the *"power to rule."* This involves controlling the *sovereignty* of ALL the nations. This sovereignty must be *"taken away"* from all nations in order to set up a New World Order or One World Government, possibly with headquarters in Jerusalem. (Review Daniel 11:45.)

DAN 11:45 And he shall plant [set up] the tabernacles of his palace between the seas in the glorious holy mountain.

Note: See pages 298-299 for definition of "abomination that maketh desolate" and pages 334-336 for how and where the "desolation" is set up.

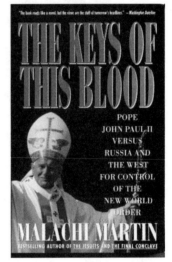

Pope John Paul II has already established that future **Papal Rome** will be instrumental in setting up the New World Order with all the kings of the earth.

(See REV 17:12)

Future
Papal "king of the north"
Will Take Control of the
New World Order

11 ... and the abomination that maketh desolate set up [between God and His people in literal Jerusalem, the glorious holy mountain] ...

1290 Literal Days of
Future Reign of
Papal "king of the north"

11 ... there shall be a thousand two hundred and ninety [literal] **days.**

(This verse repeated on page 377.)

DAN 11:45 but he shall come to his end, and none shall help him [after 1290 days he will be "broken without hand"].

DAN 8:25 And through his policy also he shall cause craft to prosper in his hand; and he shall magnify himself in his heart, and by peace shall destroy many: he shall also stand up against the Prince of princes; but he shall be broken without hand.

THE END!

After 1290 Days "he shall
come to his end,
and none shall help him."

"The Daily" Completes the Full Cycle of "Transfer of Power"

An Illustration of the *"Daily"* Continuum of Power, Seat, and Authority —
(Crown, Throne, and Sceptre)
— "That Which Stretches Indefinitely, From Everlasting to Everlasting"

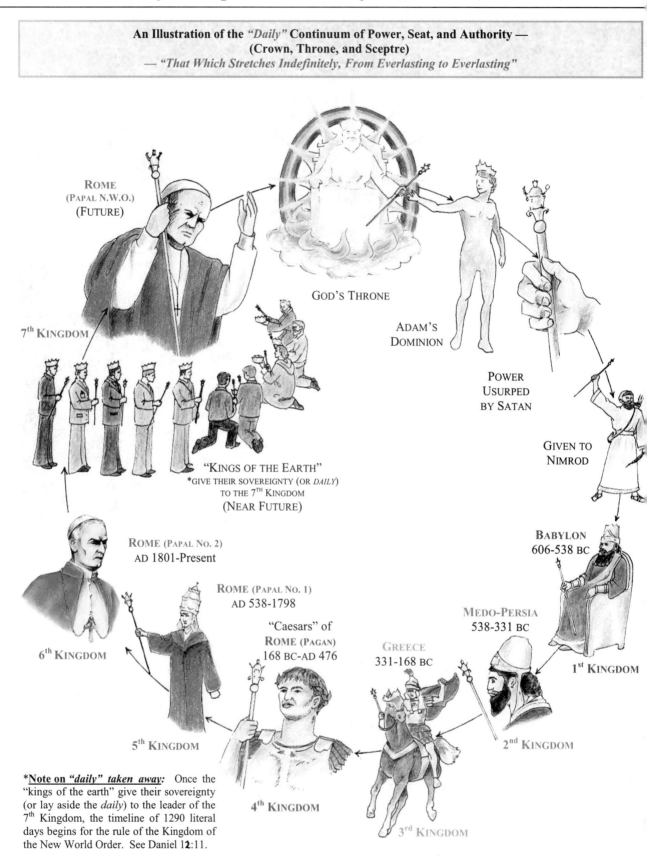

ROME
(PAPAL N.W.O.)
(FUTURE)

7ᵗʰ KINGDOM

GOD'S THRONE

ADAM'S
DOMINION

POWER
USURPED
BY SATAN

GIVEN TO
NIMROD

"KINGS OF THE EARTH"
*GIVE THEIR SOVEREIGNTY (OR *DAILY*)
TO THE 7ᵗʰ KINGDOM
(NEAR FUTURE)

BABYLON
606-538 BC

ROME (PAPAL NO. 2)
AD 1801-Present

ROME (PAPAL NO. 1)
AD 538-1798

"Caesars" of
ROME (PAGAN)
168 BC-AD 476

MEDO-PERSIA
538-331 BC

GREECE
331-168 BC

6ᵗʰ KINGDOM

1ˢᵗ KINGDOM

5ᵗʰ KINGDOM

2ⁿᵈ KINGDOM

***Note on *"daily" taken away:* ** Once the
"kings of the earth" give their sovereignty
(or lay aside the *daily*) to the leader of the
7ᵗʰ Kingdom, the timeline of 1290 literal
days begins for the rule of the Kingdom of
the New World Order. See Daniel 12:11.

4ᵗʰ KINGDOM

3ʳᵈ KINGDOM

*Earthly Nations Give Their
Sovereignty to
Papal "king of the north"*

11 And from the time that the daily [power, seat, and authority, of all nations] ~~sacrifice~~ **shall be taken away** and [their sovereignty laid aside in order that], **the abomination that maketh desolate** [Papal Rome New World Order can be] **set up, there shall be a thousand two hundred and ninety days.**

Verse 11 (Concluded)

Note: The Papacy's literal reign in the future 1290 days, begins when he receives the sovereignty over <u>ALL</u> the nations of the earth. At present, the *kings of the earth* are already surrendering their sovereignty through political, economic, and religious manipulation. Once the Papacy grasps the *"sceptre of power,"* the timeline of 1290 days begins. Also note that the 1260 and 1290 day timelines begin at the <u>same</u> time. *God's people cannot be "persecuted" unless a "persecutor" is reigning.* As a result, the 30 days of the persecutor's reign extends <u>beyond</u> the 1260 days. Revelation 13-18 adds further information on all three timelines.

"taken away" — *Strong's* OT#5493 cuwr (soor) to turn off: KJV - to lay away or lay aside. (See page 376 for the note on the *"daily"* taken away.) Note: Compare with Daniel 8:11 on page 159 where the meaning of *taken away* is one of *absorption* rather than *laying aside* in a willing manner.

Thunder No. 3
(Beginning Voice)
REV 13:5-7
**Voice of the Beast
"Universal Sunday Law"
(USL)**

Thunder No. 5
(Ending Voice)
REV 13:15
**Beast's Voice
for "Universal
Death Decree"**

1260 Days of Persecution on God's People "... he [persecutor] shall ... scatter the holy people." DAN 12:7	
Thunder No. 4 (Beginning Voice) REV 13:5-7 **USL Begins the Reign of the Persecutor**	**Thunder No. 7** (Ending Voice) REV 16:17-19 **Voices of Doom End the Persecutor**
1290 Days of Reign of the Persecutor "... the abomination that maketh desolate ..." DAN 12:11	—— 30 Days ——
(Note: "Thunders" are assigned a random number. See Appendix 12A, pages 384-385.)	Reign of Kings / Fall of Babylon REV 16:19
	REV 17:12 "one hour" or 15 Days / REV 18:10 "one hour" or

Prophetic Keys #12 and #26 Prophecy is usually understood at the time of fulfillment. The 'speaking' of a nation is the action of its legislative and judicial authorities.

Prophetic Timeline #6: Details and Specifics

Timeline #6 (Length of Timeline)	Subject (of Timeline)	Prophetic Scripture For Timeline	Timeline Begins (with)	Speaking VOICE (Thunder No. 4)	Timeline Ends (with)	Legislative & Judicial Action (Thunder No. 7)
1290 Literal Days (Future)	Reign of Persecutor - Papal Rome New World Order	DAN 12:11 REV 13:5-7* (*These verses speak of a 1260 day timeline, which are also the start of the 1290 day timeline.)	Reign of the Persecutor - Papal Rome New World Order (Future) REV 13:5-7	Legislation of Universal Sunday Law by Papal Rome New World Order (Future) REV 13:16-17	"Fall of Babylon" including: - Papacy - Apostate Protestantism - Dragon REV 16:17-19 REV 18:19, 21	Heavenly "Voices of Doom" End the Persecutor's Reign (Future) REV 16:17-19

DANIEL'S EPILOGUE
THIRD QUESTION
HOW LONG MUST GOD'S PEOPLE WAIT FOR THE BLESSING?
ANSWER
DAN 12:12
WAIT 1335 DAYS FOR THE BLESSING!

God's Voice Announces:
Blessing of Deliverance
From the Death Decree
and the
Day and Hour of
Jesus' Coming

The Saints Will Wait
1335 Literal Days
To Be Delivered

12 Blessed is he that waiteth, and cometh to the thousand three hundred and five and thirty days.

Verse 12

Note: God's people will wait 1335 literal days for their deliverance when the Revelation 13:11 prophecy of the beast from the "earth" is fulfilled. When the voice of Thunder No. 2 speaks, God's people will know where they are in the stream of *prophetic time;* that they must wait 1335 days for God's blessing of deliverance.

ISA 25:9 And it shall be said in that day, Lo, this is our God, we have <u>waited</u> for him, and he will save us.

Sceptre Returned Back to God

ISA 14:3, 5 And it shall come to pass in the day that the LORD shall give thee rest from thy sorrow, and from thy fear, and from the hard bondage wherein thou wast made to serve, 5 <u>The LORD hath broken the staff of the wicked, and the sceptre of the rulers.</u>

ISA 30:30 And the LORD shall cause <u>his glorious voice to be heard</u>, and shall shew the lighting down of his arm, with the indignation of his anger, and with the flame of a devouring fire, with scattering, and tempest, and hailstones.

Prophetic Timeline #7: Details and Specifics

Timeline #7 (Length of Timeline)	Subject (of Timeline)	Prophetic Scripture For Timeline	Timeline Begins (with)	Speaking VOICE (Thunder No. 2)	Timeline Ends (with)	Legislative & Judicial Action (Thunder No. 6)
1335 Literal Days (Future)	God's Holy People are to "Wait" for the Blessing of Deliverance	DAN 12:12 REV 13:11 and REV 16:17	Power of USA & Protestant Nations Join Papal Rome Through Church/State Sunday Laws (Future) DAN 11:41	Legislated Date of the National Sunday Law by the United States & Protestant Nations (Future) REV 13:12	God's Voice of Deliverance from Universal Death Decree and "Time of Jacob's Trouble" (Future) REV 9:13; 16:17	Effective Date for the Universal Death Decree & God's Voice of Deliverance (Future) REV 13:15; 16:17

The Three Timelines of Daniel 12

Important Note: Out of the three timelines, the 1335 day timeline is the last one to be mentioned, even though it is the <u>first</u> timeline to begin. A *National Sunday Law* will be legislated in the United States before a ***Universal*** *Sunday Law* is legislated in the world. The details of this study are in Revelation 13. When Daniel received the Epilogue timelines in his vision, he did not understand them, and repeatedly asked "how long would it be till the end of these things." Daniel was given only three short answers — hardly enough to be satisfactory. There are no full explanations of these timelines in Daniel's Book. John the Revelator was given visions with complete details and full explanations to understand how these three timelines run concurrently. A major part of the study in Revelation includes Daniel's three timelines. (See Appendix 12A, pages 384-385 for more details and study helps.)

Thunder No. 2
(Beginning Voice)
REV 13:11-12
Voice of Lamb-like Beast
"National Sunday Laws"
(NSL)

Thunder No. 6
(Ending Voice)
REV 16:17
Voice of God*
Deliverance
from the "wait."

> **1335 Days to "Wait for the Blessing"**
> "Blessed is he that waiteth ..." DAN 12:12

Thunder No. 3
(Beginning Voice)
REV 13:5-7
Voice of the Beast
"Universal Sunday Law"
(USL)

Thunder No. 5
(Ending Voice)
REV 13:15
Beast's Voice
for "Universal
Death Decree"

> **1260 Days of Persecution on God's People**
> "... he [persecutor] shall ... scatter the holy people." DAN 12:7

Time of Jacob's Trouble
JER 30:7

Thunder No. 4
(Beginning Voice)
REV 13:5-7
USL Begins the
Reign of the
Persecutor

Thunder No. 7
(Ending Voice)
REV 16:17-19
Voices of Doom
End the
Persecutor

> **1290 Days of Reign of the Persecutor**
> "... the abomination that maketh desolate ..." DAN 12:11P

— 30 Days —

(Note: "Thunders" are assigned a random number. See Appendix 12A, pages 384-385.)

Reign of Kings

REV 17:12
"one hour"
or
15 Days

Fall of Babylon
REV 16:19
REV 18:10
"one hour"
or
15 Days

Prophetic Keys #12 and #26
Prophecy is usually understood at the time of fulfillment. The 'speaking' of a nation is the action of its legislative and judicial authorities.

*Note: The "Voice of God" is the <u>**kingpin**</u> that locks all three timelines together — a paragon or model of excellence!
1. The 1335 literal day "Wait" of God's people;
2. The "Time of Jacob's Trouble" (ends with effective date for the Death Decree);
3. The reign of all worldly kings along with the beast.

*The Entire Book of Daniel
Will be Understood at the
"End of the Days"*

**13 But go thou thy way till the
end be: for thou <u>shalt rest</u>, and
<u>stand in thy lot at the end of the
days.</u>**

*The **End** of Daniel's
Fourth Vision and the Book*

The Last Generation Will See These Prophecies Fulfilled

Today, <u>all the words</u> of Daniel's prophecies are almost completely fulfilled. Very soon, the last three timelines in Daniel 12:7-13 will begin to usher in the greatest moment of earth's history where Jesus comes to take His children home.

"Almost Fulfilled"

Verse 13

ISA 57:2   He shall enter into peace: they <u>shall rest</u> in their beds, each one walking in his uprightness.

REV 14:13   Blessed are the dead which die in the Lord … that they <u>may rest</u> from their labours; and their works do follow them.

"<u>stand in thy lot at the end of the days</u>" — The prophecies of Daniel's three timelines in chapter 12 have been resting for a long time. Near the close of the *end of time,* Daniel's prophecies will rise and stand with great significance for the last generation.

Note: Answers to the "How long?" questions, (numbers 2, 3, and 4) asked in Daniel 8:13, can now be answered in Daniel 12.

2. How long shall be the vision? It shall be 1290 literal days from the beginning to the end of the future reign of Papal Rome's New World Order. (DAN 12:11)

3. How long shall the transgression of desolation reign? Until the end of the 1290 days when the "daily" [power, seat, and authority] returns to God. (DAN 12:11)

4. How long shall this power transgress in its persecution of God's people? After 1260 literal days, all these things shall be finished. (DAN 12:7)

Thoughts to Consider:

1. Assess the reasons why the Epilogue was given only once in four visions!

2. On the complete Structure Chart of Daniel (page 367) where would the proper placement of the Epilogue timelines be — in the first three visions?

3. How does the complete "Structure" of Daniel confirm that the Epilogue's literal timelines will be in the future? (Part of this structure is explained on page 371.)

General Review and Theme of Vision Four: "Christ the Victor!"

- The last vision reviewed the political kingdoms of history with substantial detail of the Grecian Kingdom. Babylon was not included because it had passed off the world scene.

- The reader is given a full history lesson on the seven earthly persecuting kings and kingdoms, with focused prophecies pertaining to the last kingdom. Christ is Victor as "King of kings" and "Lord of lords."

- Daniel 12 is the <u>only</u> chapter in the Bible that contains three timelines running concurrently just before the Second Coming. These timelines are the climax of the Fourth Vision as well as the whole Book of Daniel. It is of utmost importance in the unfolding of Revelation.

- These timelines give God's people assurance that their deliverance from sin and death is imminent.

Daniel 12:5-13 — Review of the "Epilogue" for ALL Four Visions

1. The Epilogue is found in the last nine verses of Daniel 12. (**Note:** All the information contained in the Epilogue is New Information. None of it has been given in any of the previous visions.) The Epilogue follows the same "Forward, Progressive Movement" given in the first four Outlines of Daniel. The Forward, Progressive Movement can be summarized as:
   a) The Historic-Prophetic Outline in Vision 1 of Daniel 2 moves datable time forward from **606 BC to AD 476**.
   b) The Historic-Prophetic Outline in Vision 2 of Daniel 7 moves datable time forward from **606 BC to AD 1798**.
   c) The Historic-Prophetic Outline in Vision 3 of Daniel 8 moves datable time forward from **538 BC to AD 1844**.
   d) The Historic-Prophetic Outline in Vision 4 of Daniel 11-12:4 moves time forward from **538 BC to the very eve of the Second Coming of Jesus**.
   e) Daniel 11 closes "gaps of time" that were evident in the previous three visions. e.g. The vision of Daniel 2 had a "gap" of time (with missing information) from AD 476 to the Second Coming.
   f) The Epilogue introduces the events surrounding the key player, Papal Rome, and its New World Order. The three timelines in the Epilogue become effective once this New World Order receives sovereignty over all the world. The three timelines provide detailed information of the last day events just prior to the Second Coming of Jesus. (Revelation expounds on these three timelines.)
2. The Epilogue is given in full literal style (no use of symbols), continuing in the same literal language of Daniel 10-12:4. As a result, it is not necessary to convert the three prophetic timelines from "days into years."
3. The Epilogue contains three prophetic literal timelines of 1260 days, 1290 days, and 1335 days that are given Future Application. (Note: These timelines are not classified as "Futurism." They are simply to be fulfilled in the future. For an explanation of the difference between "Future Application" and "Futurism" see Appendix 12B on pages 386-387.)
4. The Epilogue deals primarily with the events surrounding God's Holy People and the end of the *iron* Roman Kingdom.
5. The Epilogue timeframe reveals information for the "gap" of time between the rise of the Roman Papal New World Order and the eve of Christ's Second Coming.
6. The Epilogue information is not a repeat of information in any other vision. The Epilogue contains a brief summary of the final events that will occur just before:
   a) The arrival of the Stone Kingdom in Vision 1 of Daniel 2:45;
   b) The "saints receive the kingdom" in Vision 2 of Daniel 7:27;
   c) The "king of fierce countenance is broken without hand" in Vision 3 of Daniel 8:25; and
   d) The "king of the north comes to his end, and none shall help him" in Vision 4 of Daniel 11:45.
7. The Epilogue adds the last missing information needed to complete the historical drama right up to the Second Coming of Jesus.
8. The Epilogue timelines of 1260 days, 1290 days, and 1335 days begin and end with "speaking voices" or legislative and judicial decrees. No dates are given in prophecy for the commencement of these timelines. The Epilogue does not give dates for the Second Coming of Jesus.
9. The Epilogue timelines are not "hung on time" that can be dated. The Epilogue timelines are "hung on future events" that will be initiated with "speaking voices" during the reign of the last Roman Kingdom. Secular history offers insight into the events and interpretation of Papal Supremacy No.1, its transition and continuation to Papal Supremacy No. 2, and finally, its culmination in Papal Rome's New World Order.
10. The Epilogue timelines cannot apply to the events surrounding the Kingdom of Papal Rome found in Daniel 7:8, 20, Daniel 8:9b, and Daniel 11:32-35 representing Papal Supremacy No. 1 during the 1260 years of persecution in the Dark Ages. To throw these timelines backward in time, would violate the "Forward, Progressive Movement" structure in Daniel's Book. If Daniel had intended these timelines to be understood in the timeframe of the Dark Ages, he would have had to write these 1260, 1290, and 1335 day timelines in the verses of Daniel 7:8, 20 and Daniel 11:32-35.
11. The Epilogue timeline of 1260 days is **NOT** the same as the Daniel 7:25 timeline of 1260 years.
12. The Epilogue timeline of 1260 days (of Daniel 12:7) was **NOT** understood by Daniel because he had not seen it in any previous visions. Daniel was acquainted with the long timeline of 1260 years in Daniel 7:25. The 1260 days timeline of Daniel 12:7 was outside his understanding. Therefore, regarding the 1260 days, Daniel 12:8 records, "I heard, but I understood not."
13. The Epilogue timeline of 1260 days in Daniel 12:7 declares "all these thing shall be **finished**." The 1260 year timeline of Daniel 7:25 did **NOT** "finish all these things."
14. The Epilogue timelines are given only **ONCE** (in Daniel) and are **NOT** a repeat of any former timelines in Daniel's prophecies.
15. The Epilogue timelines are meant to give encouragement, hope, and joy of the soon coming of Jesus Christ our Lord. No other timeline in Daniel had this mandate for endtimes.

THE STRUCTURE OF DANIEL'S EPILOGUE
THE FALL OF THE LAST ROMAN KINGDOM SURROUNDING GOD'S PEOPLE
meframe: Future Last Roman Earthly Kingdom to — the Very Eve of Christ's Kingdom

DANIEL 12:5-13 Vision 4 uses **Literal** language for the Epilogue.
The **Days** represent **LITERAL DAYS** in Daniel's Epilogue.

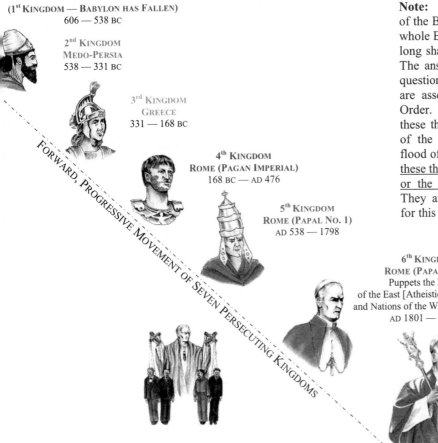

(1ˢᵗ KINGDOM — BABYLON HAS FALLEN)
606 — 538 BC

2ⁿᵈ KINGDOM
MEDO-PERSIA
538 — 331 BC

3ʳᵈ KINGDOM
GREECE
331 — 168 BC

4ᵗʰ KINGDOM
ROME (PAGAN IMPERIAL)
168 BC — AD 476

5ᵗʰ KINGDOM
ROME (PAPAL NO. 1)
AD 538 — 1798

6ᵗʰ KINGDOM
ROME (PAPAL NO. 2)
Puppets the Nations
of the East [Atheistic-Communism]
and Nations of the West [Democracy]
AD 1801 — Present

7ᵗʰ KINGDOM
ROMAN PAPAL
NEW WORLD ORDER
Future

FORWARD, PROGRESSIVE MOVEMENT OF SEVEN PERSECUTING KINGDOMS

Note: Daniel 12:5-13 presents the Epilogue of the Book of Daniel where the climax of the whole Book is given. Daniel 12:6 asks, "How long shall it be to the end of these wonders?" The answer to that question (and three other questions) is found in the three timelines that are associated with the Roman New World Order. It is evident, from the context, that these three timelines extend to the "very eve of the great Second Coming" and throw a flood of light on events then to transpire. <u>It is these three timelines that are the "coup 'd etat" or the **focus** of the whole Book of Daniel.</u> They are the encouraging, endtime message for this hour in earth's history.

Daniel 12:1-4: <u>The END of ALL Four Historic-Prophetic Outlines</u>

Daniel 12:5-13 — THE EPILOGUE: Uses Literal Language. **ALL** timelines are in <u>Literal Days</u>.

Reminder: *"Epilogue"* —
Defines how the work is finished during the reign of the Papal New World Order.

Future 1335 <u>Days</u> — **"Wait for the Blessing"** DAN 12:12

Future 1260 <u>Days</u> — **"Persecution of God's People"** DAN 12:7

Future 1290 <u>Days</u> — **"Reign and Fall"** of Papal Rome N.W.O. DAN 12:11

Persecution Ends —
The Stone Kingdom of
Jesus Strikes!
DAN 12:7

Vision Four Time extends from
538 BC — to the very Eve of
Christ's Second Coming.

The End of ALL Four Visions!

VISION #
4

Appendix 12A — The Seven Thunder "VOICES"

Thunder No. 1
Ended the 2300 Year Prophecy in AD 1844 — the beginning of:
a) Heavenly Day of Atonement
b) Investigative Judgment for the Dead

DAN 8:14

The Seven Thunder "VOICES"
of Revelation 10 are Identified by:
1. The "Voice" that Ended the 2300 Year Timeline of DAN 8:14;
2. The "Voices" which will Begin and End the Timelines of Daniel 12:7, 11, and 12.*

Thunder No. 2
(Beginning Voice)
REV 13:11-12
Voice of Lamb-like Beast
"National Sunday Laws"
(NSL)

Thunder No. 6
(Ending Voice)
REV 16:17
Voice of God**
Deliverance from the "wait"

1335 Days to "Wait for the Blessing"
"Blessed is he that waiteth ..." DAN 12:12

Thunder No. 3
(Beginning Voice)
REV 13:5-7
Voice of the Beast
"Universal Sunday Law"
(USL)

Thunder No. 5
(Ending Voice)
REV 13:15
Beast's Voice for "Universal Death Decree"

1260 Days of Persecution on God's People
"... he [persecutor] shall ... scatter the holy people." DAN 12:7

Time of Jacob's Trouble
JER 30:7

Thunder No. 4
(Beginning Voice)
REV 13:5-7
USL Begins the Reign of the Persecutor

Thunder No.
(Ending Voice)
REV 16:17-19
Voices of Doo
End the Persecutor

1290 Days of Reign of the Persecutor
"... the abomination that maketh desolate ..." DAN 12:11

— 30 Days —

(Note: "Thunders" are assigned a random number.)

Reign of Kings	Fall of Babylon
REV 17:12	REV 16:19
	REV 18:10
"one hour"	"one hour"
or	or
15 Days	15 Days

*The 'speaking' of a nation is the action of its legislative and judicial authorities.
** The **"Voice of God"** is the <u>kingpin</u> that locks all three timelines together.
Note: The complete answers to the Epilogue Questions are found in Revelation.

Appendix 12A — Thunder Sequence, Timeline Definitions, and Events

THUNDER SEQUENCE	DEFINED BY A TIMELINE	EVENT	SCRIPTURE
Thunder 1	2300 Day-Years Ended	**Investigative Judgment Began for the Dead**	DAN 8:14 REV 4 and 5
Thunder 2	1335 Days Begin	**National Sunday Laws in Protestant Countries**	DAN 11:41; 12:12 REV 13:11-12
Thunder 3	1260 Days Begin	**Universal Sunday Law in the World** Persecution Begins	DAN 11:42; 12:7 REV 13:5-7, 15
Thunder 4	1290 Days Begin (Note: the 1260 and 1290 Literal Days Begin at the Same Time)	Papal New World Order (NWO) Begins Its Sign of Authority is "The Mark of the Beast" (The Seal of God) The Final Test — Investigative Judgment Begins for the Living	DAN 11:42; 12:11 REV 13:5-7 REV 13:16-18 REV 14:1-5 REV 14:15-19
Thunder 5	1260 Days End	**Universal Death Decree Legislation Date** Reign of Kings for "one hour" Begins — [15 Literal Days] Time of Jacob's Trouble	DAN 11:44; 12:7 REV 13:15 REV 17:12-13 JER 30:7
Thunder 6	1335 Days End	**Voice of God** Effective Date for the Universal Death Decree	DAN 12:12 ISA 30:30 REV 13:15 REV 16:17
Thunder 7	1290 Days End	Voices of Doom Fall of Babylon in "one hour" Ends — [15 Literal Days] Papal New World Order Ends	DAN 11:45; 12:11 REV 16:17-18 REV 18:10, 17, 19 REV 16:19

Note: The Seven Thunders are found in Revelation 10:3-4.

Appendix 12ʙ — Definitions for Futurism, Preterism, and Future Applicatic

A Jesuit Technique

As the Jesuits in the Middle Ages used the technique of interchanging the literal and symbolic language of Daniel 7 *to protect Papal Rome,* so today, many theologians of all denominations use the same technique of ***interchanging literal and symbolic language*** of the three timelines of Daniel 12:7-12 *to again avert the accusing finger away from Papal Rome.*

The Historicist "School" of Prophetic Exposition

In the Middle Ages, Martin Luther and other reformers used the methods of study called the "Historicist 'School' of Prophetic Exposition." They applied the prophecy of the Little Horn of Daniel 7, with its timeline of *"time, times and a dividing of time"* in Daniel 7:25, to Papal Rome. Prophetic expositors, down through the centuries, have understood that the word *time* is Biblical terminology referring to a *year* of 360 days (or twelve months of 30 days each). This is made clear in Genesis 7:24 and 8:3 where "one hundred and fifty days" are equated to "five months."

When the Biblical term, *time* was understood by the Reformers to refer to a *year* of 360 days, the *"time, times and a dividing of time"* of Daniel 7:25 became clear. (See page 109 with reference to Daniel 7:25.)

The Symbolic Language and Context of Daniel 7

Prophetic expositors had long understood that the *"time, times and dividing of time"* of Daniel 7:25 was equal to 1260 days. The reformers also recognized that the timeline of Daniel 7:25 was ***couched in the symbolic context of symbolic "beasts."*** Therefore, they understood that the 1260 *days* was ***symbolic time.*** To determine the amount of literal time spoken of in Daniel 7:25, they used the Year-day Computation Principle as specified in Ezekiel 4:6 and Numbers 14:34, where the Lord said, "I have appointed thee each [symbolic] day for a [literal] year."

The European Reformers, as well as the prophetic expositors of all Protestant denominations in the 1800s, understood that the Daniel 7:25 timeline was ***symbolic*** time and that the 1260 ***symbolic*** days refer to 1260 years of Papal Supremacy No. 1 which occurred from AD 538-1798.

It was understood that the Roman Papacy had been given "power, seat, and authority" by the decretal letter written by Emperor Justinian in AD 533 and implemented in 538. This decree gave the Bishop of Rome legal title to become the "Head of the Church" and temporal power to use the state to enforce its religious dogma. Exactly 1260 years later, (in 1798), General Berthier, under the direction of Napoleon of France, *appeared* to have ended the Papal Supremacy in 1798 by arresting the Pope and tak-

ing him back to France where he was imprisoned and died. (Review pages 190-192 on Napoleon.)

The prophetic exposition of the Daniel 7:25 *"time, times and the dividing of time"* was a powerful force to effect the separation of Protestantism from Rome. Most of northern Europe broke away from Romanism in the sixteenth and seventeenth centuries. This was a major set back to the ecclesiastical and political authority of the Roman Church. The Popes needed to find a defense against the prophetic exposition of the Daniel 7:25 timeline!

What is FUTURISM?

Papal Rome used the Jesuit Order to deny the Protestant prophetic exposition of the timeline of Daniel 7:25. Francisco Ribera, a Jesuit priest ignored the symbolic language and symbolic context of Daniel 7 with its symbolic "beasts," "heads," and "horns." Ribera took the *"time, times and the dividing of time"* of the timeline of Daniel 7:25 **OUT** of its symbolic context and treated it as **LITERAL TIME.** He declared the "1260" to be literal days or a literal three and a half years. Ribera then placed the literal three and a half years far into the **future** declaring that it referred to the Little Horn as an ***unidentified antichrist*** yet to rise up in the end time. Protestants slowly bought into the misinterpretation. This took the accusing finger off Papal Rome! This Jesuit technique, taking a timeline OUT of CONTEXT, ***interchanging symbolic and literal language,*** throwing the application far into the future, is known as **FUTURISM.**

"FUTURISM" VERSUS "FUTURE APPLICATIONS"

"Futurism" is often confused with **"Future Application."** A "Future Application" is a valid and correct application of a prophecy to a future event. For example, the prophecies which deal with the 1000 year timeline of Revelation 20 are legitimately applied to the future, and are a "Future Application," not "Futurism." All the prophecies which point to a future Second Coming of Jesus are not "Futurism" but "Future Application." The Seven Last Plagues, and many events predicted in Revelation, also apply to the future. Prophetic exposition which simply applies a prophecy to future events, using the correct context, is not using the Jesuit technique of "Futurism," but a valid "Future Application." When the timelines of Daniel 12 are *applied* to future events, that is simply a "Future Application," ***not futurism!*** When critics of a future application of Daniel 12, label it as "Futurism," they are presenting misinformation.

What is PRETERISM?

Louis d'Alcazar, another Jesuit Priest, used the same Jesuit technique of *interchanging symbolic and literal language*, ignoring the **symbolic language**, and treating the *"time, times and the dividing of time,"* or "1260" of Daniel 7:25 as *literal time*. He then placed the three and half literal years in the distant past, as having been fulfilled in the persecution of the Jews. This technique is called **PRETERISM**.

Definitions of "Prophetic" and "Symbolic"

The words, "prophetic," and "symbolic" are often confused. They do NOT mean the same thing! The word, *prophetic* comes from the word, *prophecy*. All prophecy, whether written in literal or symbolic language is *prophetic*. Any timeline that is mentioned in prophecy is *prophetic*. Only when a prophecy uses symbols, placing a timeline in a *symbolic context*, is it *symbolic*. When there is no symbolism, the literal context makes the prophecy *prophetic*, but not *symbolic*. Misuse of these terms brings about much confusion.

When to Use the Year-day Computation Principle

When a prophetic timeline is couched in **symbolic language** and **symbolic context**, it is necessary to determine the literal time involved by using the Year-day Computation Principle. If there is no symbolic context, then there is no need to use the Year-day Principle. *This is an hermeneutic principle of prophetic exposition.* There is nothing in the Scriptures which declares that the Year-day Principle has ever been done away with, or ended, in 1844 with the longest timeline in the Bible of 2300 years! That is an erroneous assumption.

Both Francisco Ribera and his Jesuit technique of "Futurism," and Louis d' Alcazar with "Preterism," were successful in removing the accusing finger from Papal Rome. These Jesuit techniques were later accepted into Protestantism and gave rise to the false Rapture Theory prevalent at this time. It is imperative to understand that whenever Jesuit techniques of *interchanging symbolic and literal language* are used, there follows a train of evil circumstances, heresy, and error.

How Do We Apply This Information to Daniel 12?

Today, many theologians use the satanic Jesuit technique of *interchanging literal and symbolic language* on the three timelines of Daniel 12. (There are thousands who do not yet understand the issue, thousands who don't care, and thousands who have investigated these matters carefully and correctly discern truth from error!)

There is NO symbolic language in Daniel 12. It is written in *literal language*. Daniel 12 contains none of the symbolism found in Daniel 7. In Daniel 12 there are no symbolic "images," "toes," "beasts," "horns," "wings," "eyes," "mouth," or "winds." Daniel 12 is a prophecy and therefore is "prophetic," but it is **not "symbolic."** There is a descriptive name mentioned in Daniel 12:11, "the abomination that maketh desolate," but that is merely a title and not symbolism. The fact that a prophecy was given in vision, does not make it symbolic. It is the literal language that defines a **literal context**.

Neither does the Biblical terminology of *"time, times, and an half,"* of Daniel 12:7 make the context symbolic. Just as the seven *"times"* of Daniel 4:16 referred to seven **literal years,** so, according to the "Rule of First Mention," the *"time, times, and an half"* of Daniel 12:7 refers to three and an half **literal years or 1260 literal days.** The "1290 days," and the "1335 days" also refer to **literal time.**

The timelines of Daniel 12 are written in literal language, and are couched in *literal context.* Therefore, the "days" and "times" are literal time. **That is: "days" = literal days; and the** *"time, times, and an half"* **are counted out as 1260 literal days. The 1290 and 1335 are also literal days.**

In spite of this, many modern theologians arbitrarily declare the three timelines of Daniel 12 to be *symbolic time!* Then, these theologians apply the Year-day Principle (which may NEVER be used on literal time prophecies), to declare that the three timelines of Daniel 12 have been fulfilled in the *past*, starting in AD 508 and, ending in 1843! They ignore the fact that seven times in Daniel 12, the text plainly declares that these timelines are dealing with the **"end"** of time, when **"all these things shall be finished."** (DAN 12:7) The Hebrew meaning of the word, "end" as used in Daniel 12 is **"utmost end," "border edge,"** and **"termination point"** of time! The Hebrew root word has the meaning of the "cutting off," or "chopping off," (of time) according to *Strong's Analytical Concordance*. We have not yet reached the "border edge" of time. These facts designate the Daniel 12 timelines as future events.

Modern or Endtime "Preterism"

Those that use this technique of interchanging literal and symbolic language are placing the fulfillment of these three timelines in the distant past. This is **Preterism.** It diverts the accusing finger from Papal Rome, in its current and future Supremacy.

The Secret Terrorists
(Book One)

The United States is in more danger today than she has ever been. A secret terrorist organization has been working within to destroy America, its Constitution, and everything for which she stands. This book gives all the details, and shows how far this terrorist organization has been able to progress in the destruction of America.

The 'secret' of the 'Secret Terrorists' isn't so secret anymore. In the last few years, an abundance of information has come forward through books, videos, and internet service to alert God's people as to what is happening with the 'Inner Circle' (or the Jesuit Order) within the Roman Papal system. Only a small portion of information can be given in this manuscript to alert the reader of the unseen dangers.

These two books, written by Bill Hughes, are small, compact, paperbacks that will give the reader a good overview as to what the Jesuit plan is. The books are well documented for personal research and follow-up.

Order from:

Truth Triumphant
PO Box 1417
Eustis, Florida
USA 32727

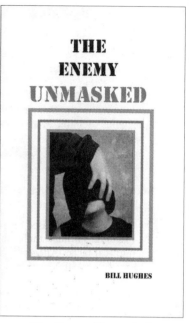

The Enemy Unmasked
(Book Two)

An enemy has been stalking America for over 200 years. She is about to apply the death grip from which America will never recover. This book will tell who the enemy is, who they have used in history, who is aiding them today, and how the final scenes will unfold. This book is very valuable for understanding the prophecies in Revelation.

Total Onslaught DVD Series by
Dr. Walter J. Veith of
Amazing Discoveries

Dr. Walter Veith has done intensive study on Biblical prophecy and current world events. His findings are documented with many excellent quotes.

With this DVD seminar, the Bible Student will obtain the complete concept behind current endtime deceptions. The series will expose Satan's final attack on Jesus Christ and the lies that are being told to keep us as pawns in Satan's endtime plans.

Order Phone: 1-866-572-9457

Amazing Discoveries	Amazing Discoveries
PO Box 189	PO Box 4480
7101C — 120th Street	Blaine, WA
Delta, BC Canada	USA
V4E 1P4	98231-4480

Glossary

~ A ~

Alignment — In the Book of Daniel each vision aligns with the previous vision in an orderly fashion. The latter vision always adds extra information. Throughout Scripture, word pictures align with other word pictures. For example:
  a) Noah coming out of the pre-flood days;
  b) The Hebrews coming out of Egypt;
  c) Abraham coming out of Ur;
  d) Lot coming out of Sodom;
  e) God's people coming out of *spiritual* Babylon.
Alignment helps the Bible student determine if he is on the right track when studying prophecy and other parts of Scripture.

Allegory — A short story based on an historical outline or incident, teaching spiritual truths through the figurative description of real facts. Allegories can be found in literal prophecy that do not contain symbolism. In the Bible, the Books of Song of Solomon and Esther are allegories. (Also see Galatians 4:24.)

Angel — a created being that acts as a messenger for God. Also see: *Archangel, Michael.*

Angel, Gabriel — an heavenly messenger angel for God that was sent to give Daniel understanding. Gabriel also delivered special messages to others, such as Mary and Joseph, regarding the birth and life of Jesus.

Antithesis — The direct opposite of sharply contrasting ideas.

Antitype — is that which fulfills the "type." e.g. Jesus the "Lamb of God" and His sacrifice on Calvary is the antitype (the Lamb) fulfillment of the sacrificial lamb in the Old Testament Sanctuary service.

Apostate — an individual or religious body that has forsaken the true teachings of Jesus Christ as presented in the Bible.

Apostate System — a religious body or kingdom that has forsaken the principles and teachings of Jesus Christ. Many traditional beliefs in this system are founded in Paganism and covered in the garb of Christianity. It is a counterfeit system of worship with many of the characteristics of the anti-christ.

Appendix — the collection of supplementary material, found at the end of the chapter/vision.

Application — If a prophecy is written using symbols, the first step toward understanding the prophecy is decoding or interpreting the symbol. Then an application is made to the correct persons or circumstances.

Application, Dual — Some prophecies contain a twofold meaning or a dual application. This two-fold meaning contains another fulfillment some time after the first fulfillment. e.g. Matthew 24:3. The disciples asked a **dual** question and Jesus gave them a **dual** answer in Matthew 24:15. It included the destruction of Jerusalem in AD 70 by the Romans, and the Roman Papal persecuting system at the end of time.

Application, Primary — In dual applications, primary means first in **importance** and not necessarily in time or sequence. Any prophecy that is rightly interpreted into an endtime application, is of primary importance over all other applications.

Application, Secondary — In dual applications, secondary refers to that of lesser importance. Many prophecies have been interpreted with an historical application. When these prophecies also contain an endtime application, the historical application becomes secondary in importance.

Archangel, Michael — Archangel refers to the top commander over (as an arc) all the angels. Michael (interpretation: "He who is as God is") refers to the Son of God. Therefore, the Son of God is the top Commander of all the created angels. Michael the Archangel is not a created being. He is the Son of God, the Creator.

Arianism — Doctrines of the Bishop Arius denying that Jesus Christ was the same substance as God and holding instead that He was only the highest of created beings.

Atheism — The denial or disbelief in the existence of any God.

~ B ~

Babylon, literal — This term represents the first of four kingdoms (in Daniel's visions) that ruled from 606–538 BC.

Babylon, spiritual — This is a term often used to describe the "symbolic Babylon" of today which manifests all the characteristics of literal (ancient) Babylon. Spiritual Babylon is a component of the "Beast" (or Antichrist) in the Book of Revelation. It is the same system that Noah, Abram, Lot, Daniel and his three friends, were instructed to "come out" of. It is a system founded on the character of Satan; a system that is Satan inspired and "self" driven. It is not just a religious system. It is a system where everything from religion to status, money, university degrees, cars, clothes, houses, etc., work together to train up people in the exaltation of a selfish character.

~ C ~

Capitalism — is the possession of capital, especially its concentration in the hands of a few: the power of combined capital.

Ceremonial Law — The word *ceremonial* is not in the King James Bible. This term is used to designate the sacrificial system and offerings connected with the earthly Sanctuary up until the time of the cross. The sacrifices could be either "blood" or "bloodless" depending on the requirement. The offerings [oblations] were the wine and grain offerings that accompanied the sacrifices. Daniel 9:27 is clear that at the cross [the midst of the week] the sacrifices and oblations ceased. Jesus Christ's sacrifice fulfilled these requirements. (Also see: *Sanctuary, Earthly.*)

Glossary

Chart: Structure of Daniel — The completed chart (on page 367) is the roadmap, giving guidance and understanding to the structure of the four Heavenly Visions and Outlines in Daniel. (This chart builds with each new vision. See the end of each vision/chapter.)

Chart: Structure of Revelation — This chart has the same attributes as the Daniel Chart. It contains eight Heavenly Visions as given to John the Revelator. (See pages 398-399.)

Charts — All charts are given as a review and summary of the most important information contained in a chapter or vision.

Christianity — This religion is founded on the teachings and deity of Jesus Christ.

Close of Probation — This event occurs first in the Heavenly Sanctuary. Once Jesus, the High Priest, leaves the Most Holy Place of the Heavenly Sanctuary, He is no longer mediating on the behalf of mankind for the forgiveness of sin. Every living person is either "sealed for eternal life" or "marked for eternal death." (See REV 22:11.)

Communism — A system characterized by the absence of social classes and by common ownership of productive means.

Concordat — A written arrangement with the Vatican, which officially recognized only Catholicism as the national religion; the state was in accord, or agreement, with the Vatican. All other religions were banned, and severely persecuted by the power of the state which signed the Concordat. To a citizen in such a Catholic nation, their ultimate authority was the Pope, not the leader of the nation. The Pope wielded both "temporal and spiritual" authority over the citizens. Germany and Italy had Concordats with the Vatican.

Context — The verbal or written environment in which a word, or group of words, occurs. Often the grammatical content (whether symbolic or literal) determines the context of a verse, or verses, of Scripture. Context may also determine the "tense" whether past, present, or future.

Continuity — An uninterrupted succession of verses. Within the Historic-Prophetic Outlines in Daniel's visions, each verse of the Outline must continue forward in the progression of time. Once a prophetic verse establishes an "historical date" the Outline follows events from that date forward. e.g. Daniel 11:20 establishes the date of Jesus' birth as 4 BC. The following verses must continue forward from that date.

~ D ~

Datable Time — This is the last date of historical time in each of Daniel's visions. Each vision has events that attach to an historical date. e.g. The first vision in Daniel 2 takes the reader as far as AD 476 in datable time. The next piece of information that is given speaks of the future Stone Kingdom at the end of the world. (This time has not yet been established because it is still in the future. Datable time always relates to historical events.) Each vision moves forward in datable time thus enlarging the overall structure of Daniel's Book.

- Daniel 7 moves datable time forward to AD 1798.
- Daniel 8 moves datable time forward to AD 1844.
- Daniel 11-12 moves datable time forward to the current day and includs the endtime events which are to follow.

Dialectic Thinking — From *Merriam-Webster:* **Dialectic** … the Hegelian process of change in which a concept or its realization passes over into and is preserved and fulfilled by its opposite … development through the stages of thesis, antithesis, and synthesis in accordance with the laws of dialectical materialism … any systematic reasoning, exposition, or argument that juxtaposes opposed or contradictory ideas and usually seeks to resolve their conflict … the dialectical tension or opposition between two interacting forces or elements. **Dialectical Materialism** 1: the Marxist theory that maintains the material basis of a reality constantly changing in a dialectical process and the priority of matter over mind.

~ E ~

Ecclesiastical — This term pertains to a church, especially an organized institution. An **ecclesiastic** is a clergyman or priest.

Eisogesis — imposing one's own fantasy and interpretation upon the Scriptures. This occurs when the student does not apply the four principles of Bible study: Context, Continuity, Sequencing, and Word Picture Alignment. (Also see: *Exegesis.*)

Empire/Empires (as in world empires) — A political unit, usually larger than a kingdom and often comprising a number of territories or nations, ruled by a single authority. The term kingdom is used in the Book of Daniel. The Four Kingdoms of Daniel are not to be equated with "world empires."

Encyclicals — as pertains to the Papal System: a document or papal letter on a serious and/or timely subject matter intended to inform many, whether, in the church or the world.

Endtime Events — are the last events just before the Second Coming of Jesus. This is the ending to every vision given in the Historic-Prophetic Outline charts. For a quick review see:

1. Vision 1 (Daniel 2) on pages 44-45;
2. Vision 2 (Daniel 7) on pages 112-113;
3. Vision 3 (Daniel 8-9) on pages 172-173;
4. Vision 4 (Daniel 10-12) on pages 344-345.

Epilogue — This term explains how the work is finished as it applies to the historical opera or play. After a play is finished and the curtain closes, the Main Character comes out and explains the historical significance to the audience. Michael/Jesus is the main Character of Daniel's Epilogue found in Daniel 12:5-13. He gives a detailed explanation of

Glossary

how He will finish the work and overcome all earthly persecutors of His people. The Epilogue summary begins with the rule of the Seventh Kingdom and includes all the events in the future three timelines found in the Epilogue verses. This theme is carried forward and elaborated upon in the Book of Revelation.

Europe, Old — refers to the territory under the rule of Papal Rome No. 1 from AD 476 through the Dark Ages to 1798.

Europe, New — refers to the continent of Europe as is known today.

Exegesis — an exercise of permitting the Bible to be its own interpreter. Following and applying all the rules of "Hermeneutic Principles" is crucial.

Exposition — explanation of Scripture which exposes the true meaning of the text.

Exposition vs. Interpretation vs. Application — When the Bible is allowed to be its own interpreter, exposition brings forth the true meaning of Scripture. In some cases historical data is needed to give fuller meaning. Proper application of this historical data must be made to Scripture. The Bible student must take into consideration: the time frame, context, sequence, and continuity of the verses under review.

~ F ~

Fascism — A system of government that exercises a dictatorship of the extreme right, typically through the merging of the state and business leadership, together with a belligerent nationalism. *American Heritage Dictionary.* "*Fascism* is the regime that corresponds most closely to the concepts of the Church of Rome." Pierre van Paassen, *Days of Our Years,* p. 265.

Figures of Speech — are a list of various devices that are used to advance ideas. Also see: *metaphor, similes, type, antitype, allegories, parable.*

Freemasons — Members of the Free and Accepted Masons, an international secret fraternity that is also closely connected to the Secret Society of the Jesuits. Also known as Masons. (For more information see Appendix 8E on pages 210-225.)

~ G ~

Glorification — divine perfection or excellence that fits God's children for eternal life.

Gnostic — The Gnostics were a sect of philosophers that arose in the first stages of Christianity, who pretended they were the only men who had a true knowledge of the Christian religion. They formed for themselves a system of theology, agreeable to the philosophy of Pythagoras and Plato, to which they accommodated their interpretations of Scripture. They held that all natures, intelligible, intellectual, and material, are derived by successive emanations from the infinite fountain of deity. *Noah Webster 1828.*

~ H ~

Heavenly Scene — Each of the visions in the Book of Daniel begin with an Heavenly Scene. Sometimes they are given in the form of a dream (as with king Nebuchadnezzar in Daniel 2) or in the form of a vision. Heavenly Scenes that were given using symbolic typology require Biblical interpretation.

Hegelian Principle — Pertaining to the philosophy of Georg Wilhelm Friedrich Hegel (1770-1831). The planned conflict is between a thesis and an antithesis with intent to bring about a planned synthesis. Often this synthesis then becomes the new "thesis" whereby the process begins all over again. The ultimate synthesis of the Papal System is to be in control of the coming New World Order. The Masonic Motto used to describe this Hegelian Philosophy is "Ordo Ab Chao" or "order out of chaos." (See page 196 for an example of the Hegelian Principle designed by Karl Marx.)

Hermeneutics — The science of discovering, stating, and applying the rules which govern Bible study to determine the meaning that God intends for us to have.

Historic-Prophetic Outline — In the Book of Daniel this Outline always follows the Interlude Question. The Outline follows the same sequence of kingdoms in each vision. At the end of the Outline, information is given to provide an answer to the Interlude Question.

History — The is the branch of knowledge that records past events. Secular history is very important for the correct understanding and application of prophecy. History is prophecy fulfilled.

Humanism — A system of thought that asserts the importance of man over God. This system (of worship) began with Cain who had the mindset to worship "his own way" rather than "God's way."

~ I ~

Illuminati — Persons regarded as atheists or radical republicans during the 18th century (such as the Freemason, or the freethinkers). Also see: *Freemasons* and *Jesuits.*

Interlude Question — is an interruption in the flow of action between the Heavenly Scene and the Historic-Prophetic Outline. In the Book of Daniel each vision begins with an Heavenly Scene. Before the Historic-Prophetic Outline interpretation is given to Daniel, there is an interruption in the form of a question. This question receives the answer after the Historic-Prophetic Outline is completed.

Interpretation — is the process in which one language is changed into another.

~ J ~

Jesuits — These are members of the Society of Jesus, a Roman Catholic order founded by Ignatius Loyola in 1534. (See Appendix 8D, page 186, for more information.)

Judgment, Executive — This is the final execution of God's judgment. It is the destruction of the wicked. After the wicked receive their just reward, (or wages of sin), the earth is cleansed and re-created.

Judgment, Investigative — The Investigative Judgment for this earth began in AD 1844 when Jesus, our High Priest, moved from the Holy Place to the Most Holy Place in the Heavenly Sanctuary. (See Appendix 8C, on pages 182-183, for more information. Daniel 9:24 gives information on how to calculate the 2300 day-year timeline from 457 BC to AD 1844.) This event coincides with the Heavenly Day of Atonement in which all the dead and living (that have ever professed Christ) are judged in an investigative process to determine whether they are believers or unbelievers. Scripture gives several examples such as:
a) Sheep or goats (MATT 25:33);
b) Wise or foolish (MATT 25:1-13);
c) Wheat or tares (MATT 13:30).
The result is eternal life or eternal death.

Justification — In *theology*, remission of sin and absolution from guilt and punishment; or an act of free grace by which God pardons the sinner and accepts him as righteous, on account of the atonement of Christ. *Noah Webster 1828.*

~ K ~

Kingdom/kingdoms — In the Book of Daniel, this is a dominion or territory ruled by a king, a ruler, a Caesar, an Emperor, a Bishop, or a general that surrounded the people of God. The seven kingdoms addressed in Daniel are all persecutors of God's people. Kingdoms in Prophetic Outlines, follow the same sequence of recapping in all four visions of Daniel.

~ L ~

Line of Prophecy, Major — The Book of Daniel has one major line of prophecy from 606 BC to the establishment of Christ's kingdom. All four visions work within this timeframe.

Line of Prophecy, Minor — Within the individual Historic-Prophetic Outlines there may be shorter timelines. These are minor lines of prophecy. e.g. Daniel 7:25 mentions a 1260 year "line of prophecy" (AD 538-1798) contained within the vision's major line of prophecy that extends from 606 BC to the "saints receiving the kingdom."

Literal — This is the exact meaning of words or the text. In the literal vision of Daniel 11, proper application from secular history must be applied to the pronouns to determine the exact meaning of a verse, or sequence of verses. Uniting of secular history with Bible verses bring clarity and understanding.

Little Book — The Book of Daniel is known as the "Little Book" in Revelation 10:2.

Loud Cry — another term for the "Latter Rain." The Loud Cry will grow in intensity and reach its climax as the legislation and enforcement of National and Universal Sunday Laws come onto the stage. The message is the same as it has always been: "come out of Babylon." This includes rejecting man-made laws regarding worship.

Lunar Time — This is the time it takes for the moon to revolve around the earth in one complete cycle of moon phases. The lunar phases also mark out the seasons. (See Ps 104:19.)

~ M ~

Masons — see Freemasons.

Metaphor — The substitution of one word by the use of another word with characteristics that fit the situation more aggressively. e.g. For a grumpy spouse: "he was a *bear* this morning at the breakfast table!" e.g. REV 9:1 "a star fell from heaven." "Star" can be another word for Lucifer.

Moral Law — The Ten Commandments as spoken and written by God and given to Moses; found in Exodus 20.

~ N ~

National Sunday Laws — are current laws in many states and countries. Once legislated, individuals will have to sacrifice "liberty of choice," to live within the guidelines of the man-made law, or choose to worship the true Creator God by honoring the Biblical Sabbath enacted in the Garden of Eden. National Sunday Laws will be legislated first by the Protestant nations of the world.

New Europe — refers to the continent of Europe as is known today.

New World — refers to the new lands, such as the United States and Canada, that were opened up by the Pilgrims in their search for a land of political and religious freedom, without a reigning king or Pope.

New World Order (One World Government) — This is the ultimate political and religious synthesis of the Papal System. To be ruler of the whole world, enforcing one religion for all, is its goal.

~ O ~

Old Europe — refers to the territory under the rule of Papal Supremacy No. 1 up until the time of AD 1798 when the Papal Little Horn was "wounded" (exposed) by the Protestant Reformation.

Outline — An Outline is an organized framework which flows from verse to verse in order or sequence, providing a thumbnail sketch of what can be expected to unfold.

Outline, Historic-Prophetic — The Book of Daniel addresses events during the reign of persecuting kingdoms which surround God's people. If the Outline is written containing symbols, the Bible must give the interpretation

Glossary

of the symbol. The Bible expositor can then determine the literal interpretation. Application of secular historical facts provide clarity. When the Outline is written using literal language, the proper application of secular history gives the interpretation. All the events in an Outline have a "Forward, Progressive Movement" in time.

~ P ~

Pagan — This is a person who is considered a heathen, a Gentile, an idolater, or one who worships false gods. They refuse to receive Christianity, and deny the true Creator God.

Papal (apostate) System — This system (lead by the Papal See) has combined Pagan and Christian beliefs, under the pretence of a Christian denomination. This system also manifests the characteristics of the anti-christ and demands worship that belongs only to the true Creator God. The Scriptures equate this system with ancient Babylon of the past and symbolic Babylon of the future. (See Appendices 8F, 8G, and 8H on pages 226-231.)

Parable — is a short story based on a true or fictitious incident that teaches a spiritual truth. See Matthew 25 for the "Parable of the Ten Virgins."

Prologue — An introduction to a book or play as it pertains to background events. In *Daniel* this would include some events that happened prior to 606 BC, as given on pages 7-10.

Prophecy — an inspired prediction of what is to take place in the future. Prophecy is unfulfilled history.

Prophetic — Parts of Scripture that are prophetic, foretell future events. Many of the prophetic events have now been fulfilled thereby supporting historical data. All the prophecies in Scripture are 100% accurate.

Prophetic Keys — are the principles and guidelines of Hermeneutics used to understand prophecy. Thirty general principles are given on pages 16-21.

Prophetic Literal Time — Timelines within prophecy are always prophetic. Any timeline that is encased within a vision where there are no symbols present, is interpreted as "literal time" only.

Prophetic Symbolic Time — When "time" is encased within a vision using symbolism, it is called prophetic symbolic time. *Symbolic time* must be calculated with the Year-day Computation Principle to prophetic literal time. (See page 14 for principles on "time and timelines.")

Prophetic Time — Any "time element" in prophecy is prophetic time which determines what is to occur whether the time element is literal or symbolic. The terms "prophetic" and "symbolic" are **NOT** interchangeable terms in the prophecies of Scripture. All symbolic timelines are prophetic. All literal timelines are prophetic. Review Prophetic Keys #14-25, on pages 18-21.

~ R ~

Recapitulation — is another way of saying "recapping" or reviewing.

Recapping — is to summarize, or use repetition, intentionally. Daniel's Four Visions are built on the structure of recapping.

Reformation — A 16th century movement to reconstitute the life and teaching of Western Christendom, resulting in the separation of the Protestant churches from the Roman Catholic Church.

~ S ~

Sanctification — The act of consecration of an individual by God. It is based on God's grace and the individual's desire to respond.

Sanctuary, Earthly — In Exodus 25:8 God instructs Moses to build a sanctuary in the wilderness so He could dwell among His people. This was to be an exact pattern of the Heavenly Sanctuary. (EX 25:40) The Old Testament Sanctuary services were designed to teach God's people the plan of salvation through the services of the sacrifices, ordinances and God's Holy Feast days. The sacrificial Lamb represented Jesus Christ, Who was the Lamb slain from the foundation of the world. Once Jesus died on the cross, the earthly sanctuary services, sacrifices, and offerings of the Old Testament were fulfilled. Jesus ascended to continue the sanctuary ministry of High Priest in the first apartment (Holy Place) of the Heavenly Sanctuary. Since the cross, God's Feasts and Festivals including the seven annual Holy Days (as found in Leviticus 23) have transitioned from the earthly sanctuary to the Heavenly sanctuary. Appendix 7c (pages 126-134) explains the history of the Feasts from before Creation, all the way to the New Earth. The Bible is clear as to what was abolished at the cross.

1. The sacrificial system and the oblations: "… in the midst of the week he shall cause the sacrifice and the oblation [offerings] to cease." (DAN 9:27) The oblations, or offerings, were wine and grain offerings offered along with the lamb sacrifices. See Numbers 28.

2. The civil penalties for violation of the law: Since Israel was a Theocracy, it had to have punishments written for breaking the law much like any country. Since we are no longer under a Theocracy, we are to obey the laws of the land we live in, provided these laws do not contradict the Laws of God. At the Second Coming, when God's people will once again come under the divine Theocracy, God Himself will reinstate the original civil penalties and punish the wicked according to His Civil Law. For instance, under the Civil Law, Sabbath breakers were to be stoned. Under the Seventh Plague, which is the Second Coming, God will stone (with hail) the wicked who refuse to observe His Holy Days . (REV 16:21)

3. The Levite Priesthood: The New Testament says that we are now all kings and priests. (REV 1:6)

4. Circumcision of the flesh: See ACTS 15 for the transition to circumcision of the "heart" instead of the "flesh."

5. The temple services: God demonstrated that the temple services came to an end at the cross when the curtain in the temple was rent from top to bottom exposing the Most Holy Place, which only the High Priest was permitted to see. (MATT 27:51) The temple services do not include God's special rest days, like the Seventh-day Sabbath and the Feast Days. We know this because Jesus and Paul kept the Seventh-day Sabbath and the Feasts and invited others to do the same. (See Appendix 7D, pages 126-134.)

Sanctuary, Heavenly — At the ascension of Jesus in AD 31, He began His High Priest Ministry in the Holy Place of the Heavenly Sanctuary. At the end of the 2300 day-year prophecy of Daniel 8:14, Christ moved to the Most Holy Place to begin His work of Judgment (in AD 1844). This brings to focus the beginning of the Heavenly Day of Atonement. Once He leaves the Most Holy Place, Probation will be forever closed for mediation and forgiveness of sins. Shortly afterward, Jesus returns to this earth to receive His Kingdom. This ends the need for a Heavenly Sanctuary dealing with the sin problem.

Sanctuary, High Priest — This person had special authorization to minister in the sacred things of the earthly sanctuary. He also acted as the mediator between God and man, offering sacrifices for the sins of men. (HEB 5:1; 8:1-3) The High Priest wore a very distinctive garment from the common priests. Although the High Priest could perform any of the duties of the common priest, the right to enter the Most Holy Place, on Day of Atonement, was exclusively his.

Sanctuary, Holy Place — The first apartment of the sanctuary, whether it is the earthly or heavenly. On Earth, the Holy Place was fully functioning every day.

Sanctuary, Most Holy Place — This is the second apartment of the earthly or heavenly sanctuary. The High Priest entered here only once a year on the Day of Atonement, to cleanse the sanctuary from all the confessed sins of the people. Right now, Jesus is our High Priest carrying out this work of "cleansing the sanctuary" from past sins. Once this work is complete, He will be able to return for His people.

Secret Societies — These are societies that work behind the scenes using the Hegelian Principle. The ultimate goal is to birth the final synthesis of a combined world religious-political order known as the New World Order or One World Government. Some Secret Societies are: Jesuits, Illuminati, Freemasons, Knights of Columbus, Skull and Bones, Dominicans, Franciscans, Opus Dei; Knights Templar, etc.

Simile — is simply a comparison using the words "like" or "as." e.g. REV 9: faces as the faces of men; tails like unto scorpions.

Solar Year — the time that it takes for the earth to make one complete cycle around the sun. In Genesis 7 and 8, a *time* (or one year), contained 360 days. Since the days of the flood, this *time* has been altered. All *time* in prophecy is based on 360 days in a year. Various adjustments in the yearly calendar had to be made to allow for the discrepancy between the 360 day year and the 365¼ day year.

Spiritual Israel — Up until AD 34, God's people were represented by the literal nation of Israel. (See Appendix 9C on pages 256-257.) From that time on, the gospel of Jesus Christ and salvation was to be given to all the world. Those that accept this gospel are known as Spiritual Israel. (See the end of page 13 for more detail and Scripture verses.)

Spiritual Babylon — see Babylon, spiritual.

Structure, Connecting — Each vision has a strong connecting link to each succeeding vision. This ties the visions together. When any of the visions are misinterpreted, this connecting link is broken and Daniel's structure is dismantled. An example of some of the structure is:

1. Ten divisions of Rome connect to the ten horns on the dreadful beast that represents Pagan Imperial Rome in Daniel 7.

2. The Little Horn in Daniel 7 connects to the Little Horn in Daniel 8. (There is also a connecting link with judgment.)

3. The "king of fierce countenance" in Daniel 8 connects to the "king" in Daniel 11:36-40.

4. The "king of the north" in Daniel 11:41 connects to the "feet and toes of iron and clay" of Daniel 2:44.

5. In the study of Revelation 17 the "ten kings" connect to the [ten] "toes" of the image in Daniel 2.

6. The "seven kings" brought forward in the Book of Daniel connect to the "seven heads" of the Composite Beast in Revelation 13. (These seven kings are spread over seven kingdoms.)

• Not only is there connecting structure within the individual visions of Daniel and Revelation — there are also strong connecting structure links between the two Prophetic Books. These connecting links ensure the correct interpretation for endtime events.

Structure of Prophetic Visions — An orderly arrangement of each vision that follows a distinct pattern. Daniel's visions follow this orderly pattern:

1. Heavenly Vision;

2. Interlude Question;

3. Historic-Prophetic Outline;

4. Answer to Interlude Question and information pertaining to Endtime Events.

See Prophetic Key #6 on page 16; also see page 367 for the complete chart of the Structure of Daniel; page 383, for the Structure of Daniel's Epilogue.

Symbol — an unreal picture or design that stands for something else. e.g. a "flag" stands for a country; the lion with eagle's wings stood for the Kingdom of Babylon.

Glossary

Symbolic — is the use of symbols whether it be for people, places, things, language, kingdoms, or timelines. Once a symbol is used, (giving a picture of something that is not real), the Bible expositor then knows what rules must be followed to arrive at the correct interpretation. Note the following examples:

- **Symbolic "beasts"** — represent literal kingdoms. (DAN 7:17)

- **Symbolic "crowns"** — also represent literal kingdoms. A king that rules a kingdom usually has a crown. (2 CHRON 23:11)

- **Symbolic "day"** — represents a literal day using the Year-day Computation Principle of Ezekiel 4:6 and Numbers 14:34.

- **Symbolic "earth"** — represents a sparsely populated territory. (Compare with Symbolic "sea.")

- **Symbolic "heads"** — represents a literal kingdom. In Daniel 2:38 the "head of gold" represented king Nebuchadnezzar and the Kingdom of Babylon.

- **Symbolic "horns"** — represent literal kingdoms. In Daniel 8:20 the angel Gabriel interpreted the two horns of the Ram as the kings of Media and Persia. In verse 21, the great horn of the He Goat is identified as the first king of Greece.

- **Symbolic "metals"** — represented individual, literal kingdoms. In the image of Daniel 2, the gold, silver, brass, and iron each represented a distinct literal kingdom.

- **Symbolic "sea"** — or "waters," represents peoples, nations, tongues, and multitudes in very populated territories. (See REV 17:15) The "sea" represents populated areas, and the "earth" represents sparsely populated areas.

- **Symbolic "time"** — is a timeline encased in a symbolic context. For interpretation, prophetic symbolic "time" must be converted to prophetic literal "time" using the Year-day Computation Principle. (See Prophetic Keys 22-25 on pages 20-21.) The term "symbolic time" is <u>never</u> to be interchanged with the term "prophetic time." See: *Prophetic Symbolic Time.*

- **Symbolic "winds"** — The "four winds of heaven" resemble a region of the sky, depicting a "north, east, south, or west" direction. For example: all four directions of the wind.

- **Symbolic "wings"** — of an eagle or fowl designate great strength and swiftness of movement from birds of prey. In Daniel this represents the swiftness of one kingdom overtaking another kingdom. (HAB 1:8)

Symbols — in the Historic-Prophetic Outlines direct how the interpretation is to proceed. When symbols are used, the Bible must give the interpretation. The Prophetic Keys show how to decode these symbols.

Synthesis — The combining of separate ideas (thesis and antithesis) to form a coherent whole.

System, Apostate — see Apostate System.

~ T ~

Tables — are an orderly display of data arranged with rows and columns for the purpose of an overall picture or review. Many of the timelines are given in "table form" to show how these timelines begin, end, and work together.

Theophany — An appearance of God to a man; a divine manifestation.

Thesis — A proposition maintained by argument.

Time of Trouble — For the righteous, it will be a time of death penalties, persecution, fines, and imprisonments. For the wicked, it will be a time for the pouring out of the Seven Last Plagues of Revelation 16.

Timelines — All timelines in a prophecy are prophetic time. If a timeline is encased in a symbolic context, the time is considered to be prophetic <u>symbolic</u> time. For correct interpretation of the timeline, the Year-day Computation Principle is used to convert the timeline to prophetic literal time. Timelines encased in a literal context do not need any conversion.

Type — A real animal or a type that stands for something else — such as the lamb in the Sanctuary services in the Old Testament stood for Jesus, the Sacrifice in the New Testament. Also, the real lion was a type that stood for Jesus, King of kings, and the priest of the Old Testament stood for Jesus in His priestly ministry. The real laver stood for the baptismal cleansing of sin.

~ U ~

Universal Death Decree — Those that refuse to relinquish their religious freedoms and come into line with the Universal Sunday Law will come under a Universal Death Decree. They will not be tolerated. As in the Dark Ages, religious dogma will be the rule. Those that do not respond, will be classified as "heretics" and dealt with accordingly.

Universal Sunday Law — This worldwide law will be legislated and enforced shortly after the implementation of the National Sunday Law in the United States and other Protestant countries. The decree will be made for ALL to worship on Sunday over any other day. This law will severely restrict individual religious freedom and liberty of conscience, guaranteed by constitutions of many nations.

Glossary

~ V ~

Verse Sequencing — The interpretation of an Historic-Prophetic Outline must follow the orderly arrangement of the sequence of verses in that Outline. Some verses may appear to have several interpretations that attach to different historical dates. The proper application must be selected to keep the verses in sequence, thereby following the flow of datable, historical events. One cannot come to a verse and move backward, or skip forward in time, taking the verse out its of sequence. The Historic-Prophetic Outline in Daniel 11—12:4 of the Fourth Vision is an excellent example. (Also see Prophetic Key #11 on page 17.)

Vision, Literal — Daniel received the fourth and last vision in a literal form. He understood the vision since the Outline of kingdoms was merely recapping on the first three visions. At the end of the last vision, in the Epilogue of Daniel 12:5-13, three literal timelines were given that Daniel did not understand. The reason he did not understand these timelines was because he had not seen them in any of the previous three visions. He understood the 1260 year timeline of Daniel 7:25, but he could not understand the 1260 day timeline of Daniel 12:7. They are not the same time period. The Daniel 12:7 timeline is fully explained in the chapters of Revelation 13-18.

Vision, Symbolic — These visions contained symbols which represented something that was not real in the unfolding Historic-Prophetic Outline. These symbols require Biblical interpretation.

Visions/Dreams — are given through supernatural means as a vehicle to predict future events surrounding God's people. Daniel 1:17 records *"Daniel had understanding in all visions and dreams."* Daniel's understanding in each vision was the *Historic-Prophetic Outline* of the various reign of kingdoms, not necessarily the *Timelines*. Daniel did not understand the 2300 day timeline in Daniel 8:14 until Gabriel explained it to him many years later (DAN 9:24-27). In the Epilogue of the Fourth Vision, Daniel did not understand the placement of the three timelines as given in Daniel 12:7-12. He did understand the *Outline* of kingdoms, but not these three *Timelines*. This time he was instructed to "seal up the words" till the end of time — when — the three timelines would be understood, and Daniel would stand in his lot again.

Voices — Either the voice of God, man, or national legislative assemblies are needed to begin and end prophetic timelines.

~ W ~

Words (scroll) — The *words* in Daniel speak of a certain *matter* that was to happen. At the end of the Fourth Vision, these *words* were sealed up, and were not meant for Daniel's understanding. These *words* are unsealed in the Book of Revelation, and spoken of as a "little book." (REV 10:9)

World, New — refers to the new land of the United States, Canada, etc. opened up by the Pilgrims in their search for a land of political and religious freedom without a reigning king or Pope.

~ X ~

~ Y ~

Year, Creation Solar — From the time of Creation down to the Flood, it is likely the solar year consisted of 360 days for the earth to complete one cycle. The prophets used this original 360 *time* or *year* in prophecy.

Year, Modern Solar — consists of 365¼ days for the earth to revolve around the sun in one cycle.

~ Z ~

Looking Ahead to the Study of Revelation

The study of Daniel gives the Bible student a good foundation for understanding prophecy through application of Prophetic Keys. *REVELATION* is the prophetic companion Book to Daniel. Both of these Books should always be studied together to see the complete prophetic picture. Keep in mind that Daniel is mostly an historical Book. The last few verses in Daniel 8, 11, and 12 are still future events that must transpire on this earth. When studying Revelation, according to the proper application of Prophetic Keys, the prophecies reveal the endtime events.

In the past, many have studied Revelation the same way they have studied Daniel. This brought forth an historical interpretation very close to what the Book of Daniel presents. Keep in mind there is no need for God to repeat any historical application twice. When He gave the first historical application it was right the first time. The strong emphasis in Revelation is on the future endtime application — for God's last generation people just before the Second Coming of Jesus. Revelation expounds on the Epilogue of Daniel 12:5-13.

Revelation is a very exciting Book. Some of the new things to be found in Revelation are:

1. The meanings of the Seven Churches, Seven Seals, Seven Trumpets, Seven Thunders, Seven Angels, Seven Last Plagues, "ten kings," the "eighth," the Seal of God, Mark of the Beast, and much more;
2. The full explanation of the three timelines from Daniel 12;
3. Detailed explanation of the Composite Beast of Revelation 13, which links to the Seven Kingdoms in Daniel's Book;
4. Detailed explanation of "another beast" in Revelation 13 that rose out of the earth;
5. Complete explanations on the Judgment Hour message and the reaping of the three harvests of the earth;
6. Fuller explanations on the fall of Babylon, and how these events relate to the three timelines in Daniel 12;
7. Events that happen <u>after</u> the Second Coming, and how the sin problem is dealt with for eternity.

Those that have enjoyed the study of Daniel will not want to miss the exciting companion study in the next book, *REVELATION Understanding the Visions of John.* This new book will have the same format as *DANIEL.* Each verse will be dealt with in an orderly manner. The following two pages give a preview of the chart on the "Structure of Revelation." The next prophetic Book of *REVELATION* will follow this chart which serves as the roadmap to guide the reader through each vision, verse by verse. Each of the eight visions will be addressed in the same manner as Daniel's four visions.

Published by: Prophecy Song
ISBN: 0-9738632-2-6

	FIRST MAJOR LINE OF PROPHECY		
	REVELATION 1-11 (TIMEFRAME: AD 31 TO THE SECOND COMING)		
VISION 1	**VISION 2**	**VISION 3**	**VISION 4**
HEAVENLY SCENE	**HEAVENLY SCENE**	**HEAVENLY SCENE**	**HEAVENLY SCENE**
REV 1	REV 4, 5	REV 8:2-5	REV 11:1-2
THE HOLY PLACE	MOST HOLY PLACE	GOLDEN CENSER THROWN DOWN	MEASURING ASSESSMENT
CHRIST'S HIGH PRIESTLY MINISTRY BEGAN	THE INVESTIGATIVE JUDGMENT BEGAN	INVESTIGATIVE JUDGMENT ENDS	"IS THE TEMPLE, (OR KINGDOM), SACRIFICE, AND WORSHIPPERS, COMPLETE?"
AD 31—100	AD 1844	CLOSE OF PROBATION	
PROPHETIC OUTLINE (HISTORIC)	**PROPHETIC OUTLINE** (HISTORIC & FUTURE)	**PROPHETIC OUTLINE** (FUTURE)	**PROPHETIC OUTLINE** (FUTURE)
REV 2, 3	REV 6	REV 8:6—9:21	REV 11:3-11
7 LETTERS TO THE 7 CHURCHES	7 LAST SEALS BEGIN SEALS 1-6	7 LAST TRUMPETS BEGIN TRUMPETS 1-6	1260 DAYS TWO WITNESSES
	INTERLUDE	**INTERLUDE**	**INTERLUDE**
	REV 7	REV 10	REV 11:12-13
	144,000 SEALED	144,000 WITNESS "TIME NO LONGER"	144,000 AND THE LAW VINDICATED
	ENDTIME EVENT	**ENDTIME EVENT**	**ENDTIME EVENT**
	REV 8:1	REV 10:3-11	REV 11:14-19
	SEAL 7	7 THUNDER EVENTS FULFILLED	TRUMPET 7

SECOND MAJOR LINE OF PROPHECY			
REVELATION 12-22 (TIMEFRAME: WAR IN HEAVEN TO ETERNITY)			
VISION 5	**VISION 6**	**VISION 7**	**VISION 8**
HEAVENLY SCENE	**HEAVENLY SCENE**	**HEAVENLY SCENE**	**HEAVENLY SCENE**
REV 12 THE WOMAN THE DRAGON THE MANCHILD **REV 13** COMPOSITE BEAST LAMB-LIKE BEAST	**REV 15:1-8** SMOKE FILLS THE TEMPLE NO MAN CAN ENTER NO MEDIATOR CLOSE OF PROBATION	**REV 19** THE SECOND COMING OF JESUS EXECUTIVE JUDGMENT	**REV 21** NEW JERUSALEM NEW HEAVEN AND NEW EARTH
PROPHETIC OUTLINE (HISTORIC AND FUTURE) **REV 12:6** PERSECUTION FOR 1260 YEARS **REV 12:10-14** PERSECUTION FOR 1260 DAYS **REV 13** PERSECUTOR!	**PROPHETIC OUTLINE** (FUTURE) **REV 16, 17** 7 LAST PLAGUES BEGIN PLAGUES 1-6	**PROPHETIC OUTLINE** (FUTURE) **REV 20:1-3** 1000 YEARS BEGIN	**PROPHETIC PROMISE** (FUTURE) **REV 22** "I COME QUICKLY"
INTERLUDE **REV 14:1-5** 144,000 SEALED	**INTERLUDE** **REV 18:1-4** 144,000 WITNESS POWER ANGEL GIVES THE LOUD CRY	**INTERLUDE** **REV 20:4-6** 144,000 REIGN 1000 YEARS	
ENDTIME EVENT **REV 14:6-11** 3 WARNING ANGELS **REV 14:15-20** 3 HARVESTING ANGELS	**ENDTIME EVENT** **REV 18:5-24** PLAGUE 7 FALL OF BABYLON	**ENDTIME EVENT** **REV 20:7-15** 1000 YEARS END THIRD COMING OF JESUS	

Thoughts to Ponder: Who has our Allegiance? ...

Introduction

Every being on this planet has an innate tendency to worship "something" or "someone." Even though there are many different belief systems in this world, our "worship" will be given over to one of two systems — either a "System of Selflessness" or a "System of Selfishness." In the beginning, all the created beings were faced with this decision. Revelation 12:4 states that one-third chose to follow the "System of Self Exhaltation." It is no different on this planet today. Right now, all people are being sifted and separated into one system or the other. The "System of Selflessness" is governed by the Creator God. The "System of Selfishness" is governed by Satan and his followers on this planet. As a result, the followers on either side will "do something" to pay homage to the system they uphold and adore. The following is a short comparison between these two systems. The "System of Selflessness" is based on "freedom of choice." The "System of Selfishness" is ultimately based on a "demand" from a system that does not allow personal freedom and choice. The Book of Revelation will elaborate on these two systems.

Before sin ever entered the universe, God had a plan to save His created beings from the eternal penalty of death. Sin cannot abide in the presence of a Holy God. The first sin in heaven introduced a malignant cancer to God's perfect universe. These first "sinners" refused to acknowledge their sin. As a result, sin and sinners were cast out of heaven, and forced to dwell here on this planet.

This spiritually infected the progress of mankind on this planet. Immediately, God's plan to save the sinner from eternal separation was put into action. This plan of salvation was based on the purest form of Love there could ever be. The plan was sealed when Christ, the Lord and Creator, gave His life on the cross to pay the price. The sacrifice was all inclusive. It was made for everyone on this planet. Each individual is given the *choice* of either accepting, or rejecting, the Gift.

Those that accept this Gift, respond in heartfelt appreciation to what Jesus Christ has done for them. They are willing to follow His example in word and deed. This is not "works" in order to obtain salvation. This is "willing compliance" *because they have salvation.* When one ponders the willing sacrifice given on the Roman cross, it is impossible to imagine that a mere man could add any of his corrupt "works" to produce a better Love Gift. It's not possible! Salvation is by the Lord's grace through faith, not through a program of "prescribed works." (See EPH 2:8-9.)

Group A — God's "System of Love"

1. **Who is worshipped?** The true Creator God.
2. **Mandate of the Creator:** Provide a sacrifice for the sinner to remove the death penalty.
3. **Mandate of the worshipper:** "Believe on the Lord Jesus Christ and be saved!!" (ACTS 16:31)
4. **Response of the worshipper:** More Love to God and mankind through willing compliance.
5. **Works done by:** the Creator God and the Holy Spirit.
6. **Result:** Eternal Relationship.

The Whole Plan of Salvation is the Work of God

The Holy Bible is God's Word of Love to His creation. The following is a small sample of these truths.

JOHN 6:29 Jesus answered and said unto them, This is the work of God, that ye believe on him whom he hath sent.

ISA 45:22 Look unto me, and be ye saved, all the ends of the earth: for I am God, and there is none else.

ACTS 16:31 And they said, Believe on the Lord Jesus Christ, and thou shalt be saved, and thy house.

ACTS 4:12 Neither is there salvation in any other: for there is none other name under heaven given among men, whereby we must be saved.

MARK 16:16 He that believeth and is baptized shall be saved; but he that believeth not shall be damned.

JOHN 6:47 Verily, verily, I say unto you, He that believeth on me hath everlasting life.

JOHN 3:15 For God so loved the world, that he gave his only begotten Son, that whosoever believeth in him should not perish, but have everlasting life.

1 JOHN 3:23-24 And this is his commandment, That we should believe on the name of his Son Jesus Christ, and love one another, as he gave us commandment. 24 And he that keepeth his commandments dwelleth in him, and he in him. And hereby we know that he abideth in us, by the Spirit which he hath given us.

JOHN 14:15 If ye love me, keep my commandments.

1 JOHN 5:3 For this is the love of God, that we keep his commandments: and his commandments are not grievous [or burdensome].

1 JOHN 2:4 He that saith, I know him, and keepeth not his commandments, is a liar, and the truth is not in him.

EPH 2:8-9 <u>For by grace are ye saved through faith</u>; and that not of yourselves: <u>it is the gift of God</u>: 9 Not of [burdened] works, lest any man should boast.

HAB 2:4 the just shall live by his faith.

GAL 2:16 Knowing that a man is not justified by the works of the law, but by the faith of Jesus Christ, even we have believed in Jesus Christ, that we might be justified by the faith of Christ, and not by the works of the law: for by the works of the law shall no flesh be justified.

GAL 3:28-29 There is neither Jew nor Greek, there is neither bond nor free, there is neither male nor female: for ye are all one in Christ Jesus. 29 And if ye be Christ's, then are ye Abraham's seed, and heirs according to the promise.

REV 14:12 Here is the patience of the saints: here are they that <u>keep the commandments of God, and the faith of Jesus</u>.

JOHN 6:40 And this is the will of him that sent me, that every one which seeth the Son, and believeth on him, may have everlasting life: and <u>I will raise him up at the last day</u>.

MATT 7:21 Not every one that saith unto me, Lord, Lord, shall enter into the kingdom of heaven; but he that doeth the will of my Father which is in heaven.

REV 20:12 And I saw the dead, small and great, stand before God; and the books were opened: and another book was opened, which is the book of life: and <u>the dead were judged</u> out of those things which were written in the books, <u>according to their works</u>.

Conclusion

There is absolutely nothing that man can do to add to gift of salvation. Look at the cross! What "works" in your life do you think you can do to add to that? There is nothing! The Creator has done everything, and given everything. His followers must learn to rest in Him. This is an ongoing realization of the hopelessness of man's situation, outside of God's provision for him. Those that choose to follow God's plan, will apply the Bible principles in their life. This is the key to developing the mind, character, and personality of the Saviour. As this takes place, the "doing," that one undertakes, becomes sanctified in the Lord. As the character is changed within, selfishness is progressively destroyed. This is the mystery of God in the life of the believer. He works. We respond. As we are willing, He is able to finish this perfect work in us.

> **Group B — Satan/Man's "System of Selfishness"**
> 1. **Who is worshipped?** Other 'gods' or the 'god of self' — ultimately the worship of Satan.
> 2. **Mandate of other 'gods:'** Appeasement!
> 3. **Mandate of the worshipper:** "Works!"
> 4. **Response of the worshipper:** "More self-driven works!" A fuller manifestation of selfishness in the heart, mind, character, and personality!
> 5. **Works done by:** man's ways.
> 6. **Result:** Eternal Separation.

Allegiance to Satan's System is Ultimate Destruction

There are many mysteries in this world. The "mystery of iniquity (sin)," is one of these mysteries that cannot be explained. It's here and has to be dealt with! The Bible says:

2 THESS 2:7-10 For the <u>mystery of iniquity</u> doth already work: only he who now letteth will let, until he [who is filled with unconfessed sin] be taken out of the way.

8 And <u>then shall that Wicked be revealed</u>, <u>whom the Lord</u> shall consume with the spirit of his mouth, and <u>shall destroy with the brightness of his coming</u>:

9 Even him, <u>whose coming is after the working of Satan</u> with all power and signs and lying wonders,

10 And with all deceivableness of unrighteousness in them that perish; because they received not the love of the truth, that they might be saved.

The Book of Daniel has shown how Satan has always coveted the worship of mankind. His attempt to gain worship in heaven failed. His attempt on this planet is meeting with greater success. He cares not if mankind worships "this god or that god," (such as Allah or Buddha), material items, money, luxury, etc. As long as mankind does not give his allegiance and worship to the Creator, Satan has won.

Many still worship gods of gold, silver, wood, stone, ivory or self. These gods do nothing for the worshipper except demand more food, more flowers, more incense, more "things," etc. These gods "take" — they cannot give. The worshippers of these gods believe that life now, and in the hereafter, will be better IF they just do more. This is  a program of "works" that leads nowhere! The consequence of this worship is eternal separation. (Review Appendices 3A and 3B on pages 54-57.)

Conclusion

PSALM 2:1-3

1 Why do the nations conspire
and the peoples plot in vain?
2 The kings of the earth take their stand
and the rulers gather together
against the LORD
and against his Anointed One.
3 "Let us break their chains," they say,
"and throw off their fetters." NIV

EPHESIANS 5:8-14

8 For though once your heart was full of darkness, now it is full of light from the Lord ...

9 Because of this light within you, you should do only what is good and right and true.

11 Take no part in the worthless pleasures of evil and darkness, but instead, rebuke and expose them.

12 It would be shameful even to mention here those pleasures of darkness that the ungodly do.

13 But when you expose them, the light shines in upon their sin and shows it up, and when they see how wrong they really are, some of them may even become children of light! TLB

Winston Churchill, the famous English Prime Minister during World War II, once said,

*"Most men
occasionally stumble over the truth,
but they pick themselves up
and continue on
as if nothing had happened."*

Daniel's Book has focused
on the story of
the rise and fall of earthly kingdoms
from 606 BC up until
the Second Coming of Jesus.
Any earthly king that wore a crown,
also ruled with a scepter
that acknowledged his
"power, seat, and authority."

Romanism and all godless nations
that uphold and promote Luciferian worship
are exposed in the prophecies of Daniel.
This is not meant
to launch a campaign
of hate and discrimination (bigotry)
against the individuals
in these religious systems.

However . . .
These systems should be
thoroughly studied by all citizens
and their doctrines and aims
widely exposed.
This is a very important and crucial obligation.

We now understand some of the facts concerning prophecy and history. Will you stumble over the truth here and go on as if nothing has happened or will you begin to analyze history and current events in the light of prophecy and search for the Truth of the Bible?

HOSEA 4:6

*My people are destroyed for lack of knowledge:
because thou hast rejected knowledge,
I will also reject thee,
that thou shalt be no priest to me:
seeing thou hast forgotten the law of thy God,
I will also forget thy children.*

Notes

Notes

Notes

Notes